William Burges
AND THE HIGH VICTORIAN DREAM

William Burges

AND THE HIGH VICTORIAN DREAM

J. Mordaunt Crook

JOHN MURRAY

© J. Mordaunt Crook 1981

First published 1981
by John Murray (Publishers) Ltd
50 Albemarle Street, London WIX 4BD

Printed in Great Britain by
The Camelot Press, Southampton

British Library Cataloguing in Publication Data
Crook, Joseph Mordaunt
William Burges and the High Victorian dream.
1. Burges, William
2. Architects – Wales – Biography
I. Title
720'.92'4   NA997.B/
ISBN 0–7195–3822–X

IN MEM. C.H.-R.

CONTENTS

ACKNOWLEDGEMENTS

This book had a tragic pre-history and a hazardous gestation. Without the help and expertise of a whole circle of Burges enthusiasts it could never have been written. My thanks go, first to the Marquess of Bute whose generosity and hospitality maintain the tradition established by Burges's greatest patron; secondly to the Goldsmiths' Company for timely – and patient – financial assistance; and thirdly to Mr John Harris and Dr Michael Darby who allowed my book to take precedence over their own cherished projects: the long-awaited catalogues of Burges drawings in the R.I.B.A. and V. and A. collections. Sotheby's Belgravia generously re-photographed Charles Handley-Read's unique collection of contemporary Burges illustrations. At Mount Stuart, Miss Catherine Armet proved an invaluable guide among the Bute family archives. At the V. and A., Mr Clive Wainwright, Mr Simon Jervis and Mrs Shirley Bury instructed me in the mysteries of Burges's furniture and metalwork. At Cardiff Castle Mr J. T. Ineson and Mrs Pauline Sargent gave me access to the drawings in their care. At Worcester College, Oxford, at Harrow School, at St Paul's Cathedral and at Trinity College, Hartford, Conn., Miss Lesley Montgomery, Mr S. Patterson, Mr A. R. B. Fuller, Mr R. Crayford and Mr R. S. Emerick were especially helpful. At Trinity and King's Colleges, Cambridge, Dr R. Robson and Dr K. Polack allowed me scrutiny of collegiate manuscripts. Elsewhere Mr Martin Harrison checked my findings in the field of stained glass, and Miss Dorothy Bosomworth did the same for mosaic decoration. In Welsh and Scottish topography my guides have been Mr Peter Howell, Miss Catherine Cruft and Mr David Walker. In things theological I have relied on Mr Derek Jennings. And in more commercial matters, in sale room and gallery, I have been helped by Mr Peyton Skipwith and Mr Michael Whiteway. Several owners of Burgesiana allowed me access to their treasures, notably Mr Auberon Waugh, Mr R. B. Weller, Mrs B. E. Mallock, Mrs E. Gunn and Mr Wentworth Watson. Dr Mark Girouard read the bulk of the book in typescript and made a number of useful suggestions. The typescript itself was meticulously prepared by Miss Sheelagh Taylor. Two of my pupils – Dr Penelope Hunting and the Hon. Laura Grenfell – helped willingly with preliminary research. Another pupil, Lady Cecil Kerr, travelled extensively with me, hunting manuscripts and photographs, in England, Wales and Scotland. Miss Jean Crego looked after me in America. Travel in Europe was made possible by the enthusiasm and energy of my wife – Susan Mayor of Christie's – and the Hon. Christopher Lennox-Boyd, chauffeur, topographer and genealogist extraordinary. Together we covered thousands of miles – in Ireland, France, Italy and Sicily – in happy pursuit of Billy Burges. Last but not least, over the past ten years, my publisher has displayed kindness beyond the call of duty, and patience beyond the limits of commercial prudence.

St John's Lodge
Regent's Park

EXPLANATION

Like William Burges, I returned to Gothic by way of reaction: a reaction in his case to the austerity of Neo-Classicism; in mine to the aridity of Neo-Classical scholarship. In England, and even in Scotland, the mid-Victorian period saw the break-up of the Classical tradition under the impact of accelerating Romanticism. From Belgravia to South Kensington is still not more than a stroll. But in architectural terms that short distance represents nothing less than an architectural revolution. Similarly, in the later 1960s, a new generation of British and American critics began to reject the certainties of the Modern Movement – that rationalised megalomania which looked back to Ledoux and forward with Le Corbusier. A wave of revulsion against tower blocks, against bureaucratic building, against all the high-rise horrors of multinationalism, swung popular taste away from Modern Architecture – 'plain ... huge and hateful ... the Modern Age in Arms'.[1] The pundits went back to their books. They began to seek again an architecture of humanism: human in scale, intelligible in detail, expressive in design, humble in philosophy; an architecture which communicates rather than alienates; an architecture of colour and wit; an architecture to be enjoyed rather than endured.[2] They went back to the Victorians. The result was an upswing of Romanticism, a new phase in the endless dialogue of Classic and Romantic impulses.[3]

This flight from Modernism has been part of a wider process: a flight from reason. A new generation has grown up distrustful of rationality, at least in its grosser forms. It thinks small. It pins its faith on feeling, imagination, intuition. It hungers for visions rather than propositions, magic rather than machinery. The eager voices of the Pre-Raphaelites call again, fresh and clear. So, without apology, here is a book about a peripheral Pre-Raphaelite, a Victorian architect of genius named William Burges.

A biography of Burges poses peculiar problems. He was not just an architect, ranking in any Victorian short-list with Pugin, Butterfield, Street and Shaw. He was also a wide-ranging scholar, an intrepid traveller, a pungent critic, a coruscating lecturer, a brilliant decorative designer and an hilarious companion. His range of friends runs the whole gamut of Pre-Raphaelite London. His list of patrons reads like a roster of vintage eccentrics. A strictly architectural study would therefore be quite inappropriate. What I have tried to do is to set his life and work in the context of Victorian Romanticism. Hence the title, *William Burges and the High Victorian Dream*.

The first chapter – The Dream – deals with the Victorian vision of the Middle Ages. The second – The Dreamer – introduces us to Billy Burges and his friends. The

third – In Search of Style – is in some ways the heart of the book; it explains the
obsession which haunted Victorian architects: the search for a new style. Then follow
four chapters dealing with Burges's own work, his answers to the stylistic
conundrum: Renaissance, Gothic, Feudal and Fantastic. These chapters combine
description, analysis and anecdote in an attempt to reveal the whole process of design
from commission to completion. Their structure is episodic rather than chronological,
and for very good reasons. Burges's career was astonishingly diverse but unhappily
brief: he won his first major commission at thirty-five, and died at fifty-three. His
style, therefore, does not 'develop' from commission to commission. Once
established, after twenty years' preparation, his 'design language' had merely to be
applied, and he applied and re-applied the same vocabulary with increasing subtlety
and gusto. Like Tennyson, he re-used and refashioned his favourite 'dodges' again
and again. But the circumstances of each commission, or group of commissions, are
separate and distinct, often dramatically so. His career is a mosaic rather than a
tapestry. And the material is formidably diverse. Not only architecture, but stained
glass, metalwork, ceramics, mosaic, sculpture, textiles, jewellery and furniture:
Burges rivals Pugin as the greatest art-architect of the Gothic Revival. All these aspects
demand documentation – and there is documentation here in plenty. Burges was, after
all, a master of detail. But explanation is the overriding aim: to explain the making of
some bizarre and beautiful objects; to explain the gestation of some of the most
extraordinary buildings ever built.

Illustrations, of course, form part of the explanatory process. These have been
arranged under five broad headings: Architecture, Sculpture, Painted Decoration
(including stained glass and mosaic), Furniture and Metalwork. Such divisions
purposely cut across chronological and typological boundaries. So, to redress the
balance, two appendices – listing all Burges's designs and publications – have been
compiled on strictly chronological lines.

Explanations out of context are usually meaningless – and the context of mid-
Victorian art and architecture is only beginning to be explored. In preparing this book
I found, again and again, that a reliable background of research – especially in
decorative arts and the theory of design – was simply non-existent. Nothing could be
taken for granted. Explaining each facet of Burges's mind became a multiple process
of discovery. I had somehow to communicate the excitement of that exploration. I
had also to broaden the basis of the book, to switch from biography to contextual
analysis and back again, from topography to the technicalities of design, without
breaking the spell of narrative. Perhaps intelligibility has been sacrificed to detail: the
burden of fact is just too great. But the effort of comprehension is worth making. 'No
one ever forgets Burges's work.'[4] And scholars at least will know where to look: to the
section on Waltham Abbey for the design and manufacture of stained glass; to the
section on Cork Cathedral for architectural sculpture; to the sections on London and
Brighton churches for ecclesiastical metalwork; to the section on drawing for

architectural draughtsmanship; to the section on Tower House for painted furniture and secular metalwork; to the sections on Worcester College Chapel and St Paul's Cathedral for marble and mosaic; to the section on Cardiff Castle for ceramic tiles and painted decoration; to the sections labelled 'talking' and 'laughing' for the Pre-Raphaelites at play.

So many dreams, so few of them built. Cathedrals from Lille to Brisbane, from Edinburgh to Truro; a multi-quadrangled university in Connecticut; a multi-domed art school in Bombay; Law Courts apparently designed to turn London into Camelot; a scheme to make St Paul's Cathedral out-dazzle St Peter's, Rome. These remained fantasies. But at Cardiff Castle and Castell Coch – Wagnerian creations for the richest man in the world; in his own Tennysonian retreat at Tower House, Kensington; at Cork Cathedral and Waltham Abbey; in two exquisite Yorkshire churches, Skelton and Studley Royal; in painted furniture, in tombs and monuments; in stained glass; in mosaic and bronze, silver and gold; in jewels and treasures without number, Burges turned the Middle Ages into magic, draining the exuberance – and the torment – of his own strange genius in pursuit of the High Victorian Dream.

[The figures in square brackets in the text refer to the illustrations.]

COLOUR PLATES

I Cardiff Castle: the Arab Room (*c.* 1879–82).

II Cardiff Castle: the Summer Smoking Room (*c.* 1869–73).

III Cardiff Castle: Chaucer Room Ceiling (*c.* 1877–90).

IV Castel Coch: Lady Bute's Bedroom (1879–91).

V Lord Bute's Water Bottle (1880). Makers: Barkentin and Krall.

VI Claret Decanter (1866) designed by Burges for James Nicholson. Maker: R. A. Green.

VII The Yatman Cabinet (1858). Painted by E. J. Poynter.

VIII Burges's Great Bookcase (1859–62; 1870).
Artists: E. J. Poynter, H. Holiday, F. Smallfield, S. Solomon, D. G. Rossetti, A. Moore, T. Morten, C. Rossiter, W. F. Yeames, J. A. Fitzgerald, F. Weekes, H. Stacy Marks, N. J. N. Westlake and E. Burne-Jones.

IX Knightshayes, Devon: Burges's design for the Drawing-Room Chimneypiece:
  'The Assault on the Castle of Love'.

X Cardiff Castle: the Study: Dragon Window (1884). Cartoonist: C. Campbell.

XI St Mary, Studley Royal: Revelation Window (c. 1873). Cartoonist: F. Weekes.

PRELUDE

'Others after us will show the light where we have only seen darkness.'

When T. L. Donaldson – that stout Victorian classicist – set out a chart of the world's architectural history, he experienced some difficulty in describing the architecture of his own age. In the end he plumped for a single label: CHAOS.[1] Between the two World Wars, Donaldson's verdict was warmly endorsed – for very different reasons – by both the leading critical camps: the Neo-Georgians and the pundits of the Modern Movement. Victorian architecture, which both worried and delighted the Victorians, had by the 1920s become merely embarrassing: at best an unhappy interlude between Neo-Classicism and Modernism; at worst a period of grotesque bad taste, associated with religious cranks like Pugin and Socialist crackpots like Ruskin and Morris.

Slowly the pendulum began to swing. A few rogue critics started to drift away from the herd. Victorian architecture was emerging from the shadows of its own excess. In the 1920s, Kenneth Clark found it intriguing,[2] and Goodhart-Rendel found it fascinating.[3] In the 1930s Dudley Harbron found it curious,[4] and John Betjeman found it fun.[5] Evelyn Waugh's generation, a generation which had previously made that fatally 'easy leap . . . from the puritanism of Ruskin to the puritanism of Roger Fry',[6] began at last to enjoy itself. As Sir John Summerson put it, Victorian architecture was rescued by those twin deodorants, charm and wit.[7] In the 1940s, a German immigrant, Nikolaus Pevsner, began to nudge the English into taking their Victorian buildings seriously – albeit as pioneers of modernism rather than works of art in their own right.[8] In the 1950s an East Coast American art history professor, Henry-Russell Hitchcock, even started to make the subject academically respectable.[9] The drift became a stampede. During the 1960s the environmental bandwaggon began to roll, and a new generation jumped gleefully aboard. Victorian studies assumed the proportions of a growth industry; architectural history revelled in a new professionalism; and membership of the Victorian Society topped two thousand. One man linked these two generations – the older dilettanti and the younger professionals – Charles Handley-Read.

'Who was Charles Handley-Read?' That was the title he chose for an autobiographical sketch prepared only a couple of years before his death. Its introspection began with a description of his parents' bourgeois lifestyle, and ended with a denial of his own gentility. His father, Edward Harry Read, had been a successful magazine illustrator whose First War diagrams on gunnery technique won him an M.B.E. and a Captaincy in the Machine Gun Corps. His mother, Eva Mary Handley, was a militant suffragette and one of the first women to qualify professionally in both medicine and dental surgery. On marriage their surnames were amalgamated by deed poll, and it was as Capt. E. H. Handley-Read that Charles's father became the first artist to exhibit war pictures – at the Crystal Palace – under the title of 'The British Firing Line'. Later on he was able to indulge his hobbies: country walks, collecting old books, sketching abroad, visits to the Chelsea Arts Club.[10] Dr Handley-Read's Harley Street practice was substantial. Young Charles – born in 1916 – was cared for by nannies, fed with cream teas in Marylebone High Street, and sent off to Bryanston and Cambridge.

> If any old-fashioned persons survive to read these pages, [Charles recalled] the paragraphs about my parents will have aroused their suspicions. An M.B.E. won't quite do, it is not a gentleman's decoration, while as for my mother's career, even E. M. Forster remarked that careful people were dubious about knowing their dentist. . . . No one played the class-game more searchingly than my friend Yorick Smithies who used to say of me, as of other Cambridge friends: 'Handley-Read is not a gentleman. This is not a criticism. . . .' At least I knew better than to argue. So in my case, with a great show of trying to get at the truth, Yorick sometimes adjusted his verdict: 'Handley-Read's best claim to being considered a gentleman is that he doesn't seem to care whether he is one or not.' But Yorick was not really fooled, for on questions of class and accent his judgements were unerring. My accent was alright, but I was no gentleman. Behind the touches of worldly success achieved by my parents there lay the working-class origins of my father and the lower middle-class origins of my mother.

At St Catherine's College, Cambridge, Handley-Read read architecture.[11] He had a natural gift for draughtsmanship and composition. At that date his design vocabulary was inevitably International Modern, in the manner of Oliver Hill. But already – partly through the influence of Geoffrey Webb, then Slade Professor – he was starting to show a keen interest in the historic styles. And outside the architecture tripos he cast his net wide: travel, drama, music, literature and philosophy – especially the linguistic philosophy of Wittgenstein. There was only one serious dent in his intellectual armour. At his Finals viva one examiner is said to have asked another: 'how can a man who draws like that possibly write like this?'

As a child, Handley-Read had been educated in a Quaker preparatory school. As an undergraduate in the late 1930s, his response to the coming international maelstrom was a private retreat into pacifism. At the outbreak of war he was directed into hospital service. He spent several years at the Lingfield Epileptic Colony, a home for epileptic children. There he pioneered a course of art therapy, and pictures painted by children under his direction were exhibited in London, Paris and elsewhere. An admiring Picasso is said to have remarked that perhaps he 'needed a few fits'.

After the war Handley-Read went back to Bryanston as art master. There, in Norman Shaw's Neo-Georgian mansion, he wore a navy blue velvet smoking jacket and floppy bow tie. After hours, he served his pupils vodka and Wyndham Lewis. The effect was 'electric'.[12] His room can be easily imagined:

> There were expensive continental editions of works on architecture, there were deep armchairs, an object like an ostrich egg sculptured by Brancusi, a gramophone with a prodigious horn and a library of records. . . . It is true that the bath was served only by a gas-burning apparatus which at the best gave a niggardly trickle of warm water and, at the worst, exploded in a cloud of poisonous vapours, but apparatus of that kind is the hall mark of the higher intellectuals all the world over.[13]

Charles's long-horned gramophone – painted blue and gold – is still remembered by ex-Bryanston boys.[14] And – later on – nobody who stayed any time at his house in Ladbroke Road will ever forget its decayed and spartan plumbing.

Bryanston was comfortable and secure. But Charles hankered after the London world, and he wanted to write. He took a job at Dagenham Technical College – where he stayed until 1962 – and began to force his long-standing interest in Vorticism into a book on Wyndham Lewis. That slim study appeared – after agonies of preparation – in 1951.[15] In the year of the Festival of Britain he had at last got the Modern Movement out of his system. The way was clear for a new obsession. At first he dallied with European Mannerism.[16] Then in 1952 came the turning point in his life: the Exhibition of Victorian and Edwardian Decorative Arts organised by Peter Floud and mounted at the Victoria and Albert Museum.[17]

Among his companions at that mouth-watering show was a young art-historian from the Courtauld Institute, Lavinia Stainton. She was the daughter of one of Lutyens's patrons, Evelyn Stainton of Barham Court, near Canterbury.[18] In 1953 they married. Thus began one of the great partnerships in the history of collecting. There were no children: Charles used to say that children were very 'overrated'. Lavinia's speciality was Victorian sculpture, particularly the work of Alfred Stevens and Sir Alfred Gilbert. From the start, Charles was more eclectic. But by the early 1960s he had pinned all his hopes and dreams on one central, all-consuming passion: the work of William Burges.

Burges became the presiding deity at 82 Ladbroke Road: his bed, his washstand, his decanters, his inkstand, his cutlery, his books, his drawings. But there was so much more besides. Charles and Lavinia moved in during 1958. During the next twelve years their trickle of acquisitions became first a flood and then an avalanche. Charles's mother, her brother Osborne, and her sister 'Lylie' died within a year of each other in 1964–5. Charles inherited nearly £100,000.[19] He was rich now, and eager to buy. The telephone never stopped ringing. His collection became legendary. 'I am not frightened,' he once wrote – with dry understatement – 'by large or outrageous examples.'[20] In fact he drew up an illustrated mock-advertisement for distribution to friendly dealers: '"Knock-out" or "Thunderbolt" High Victorian Gothic urgently required! . . . inlaid, painted, carved or any other finish. The mostest the better.'

Take a typical evening visit. Charles would greet us, slim and dapper, in smoking jacket and velvet slippers. We would be ushered first into the front drawing-room, crowded with fringe Pre-Raphaelites and Renaissance Revival furniture piled high with lustrous vases. He hated what he called 'the tasteful gap'. 'The prevailing Victorian gloom,' Bevis Hillier remembered, 'was relieved by splashes of exotic colour, when the mystic light from an enamelled wall-shrine caught the lustre of a De Morgan plate or the iridescence of Art Nouveau glass.'[21] Before we had time to take in more than a fraction of these treasures, Charles would be motioning us towards the dinner table. The accumulation of objects had driven the dining-room and kitchen – quite literally – into a corner. And what a kitchen: tucked away in two cupboards, one for the cooker, one for the sink. These small receptacles served a tiny dining-room dominated by three pieces of Gothic furniture: an octagonal table and two buffets, ebony inlaid with ivory, designed by Sir John Soane for the Gothic Library at Stowe and discovered by Charles in the Portobello Road. After dinner came the dénouement: black coffee in the back drawing-room, heavy with tapestry, marble and bronze; glittering with glass by Tiffany and Gallé. Through the cigar smoke and brandy fumes, a midnight litany of Victorian names rose like an incantation: Gimson and Godwin; De Morgan and Devey; Minton, Martin and Mortimer Menpes; Eastlake, Gillow, Liberty and Stevens; Christopher Dresser and Charles Rennie Mackintosh; Albert Moore and Stacy Marks; Pugin, Butterfield, Street, Scott, and Burges, Burges, Burges. . . .

Those ground-floor rooms were as much Lavinia's territory as Charles's. The real fun began upstairs. There we would munch bread and cheese for lunch, perched precariously on Liberty chairs, hemmed in by De Morgan tiles and volumes of *The Builder*. In those upstairs rooms, Charles's bedroom, library, kitchen and bathroom, enthusiasm hovered on the brink of kleptomania. Some days the floor resembled the basement of some lunatic museum. Mixed up with *objets d'art* were the fragments of books unwritten, pathetic monuments to 'writer's block'. Pencils, blotters and ink-bottles; foolscap sheets scored with sentences felt too fiercely to be formed; paragraphs written, crossed out, rewritten, then rubbed out in despair; random index cards crammed with crabbed script; tables set up for writing and then abandoned; pills, tablets and alarm-clocks; yellowing xerox-sheets, carcasses of forgotten catalogues, off-prints gathering dust. And what dust! Lavinia had retreated years before to her basement quarters, to her Gilbert statuettes and her beloved Alfred Stevens.

I can hear him now, coughing nervously as he puffed away at a miniature cigar. He smoked cigars continuously. He left the butts, stubbed out with slow precision, in ashtrays placed strategically in every room. His voice was reedy and syllabic; his conversation low-keyed, self-effacing, fastidious; a matter of pauses, questions, careful phrasing and exquisite diction. In speech he was without hesitation. On paper he was paralysed. 'I write,' he told John Betjeman, 'in the constipated style: every word is weighed in the balance and found wanting. How to charge words with more meaning than they normally hold is something I shall never discover, but you have the secret. Change the medium and Burges shared it too.'[22] Handley-Read never found the secret. A lifetime spent struggling to write produced just seventeen articles.[23]

Sometimes he did break through. Here is a nugget of criticism chipped painfully from a page of pencil-scribbled notes.

> The paintings and studies of Cayley Robinson[24] will appeal, I think, to anyone like myself who can accept as a legitimate artistic ideal the attempt to capture no more than a mood, an effect of light, an intimate family scene charged with a hint of resignation shared by the sadness of the earth; poignant, not chic like the French intimists. The range is limited, the demands on technical skill not particularly searching; the effects demand no major gift of the imagination nor any difficult response from the observer, for there is nothing new, nothing challenging or disagreeable to grapple with, little but wistful pleasure. A little of this kind of thing is enough, but then only a handful of painters attempted it – Atkinson Grimshaw, for example, Lavery in his youth, Edward Stott, George Clausen, Will Rothenstein in a few early works, and Cayley himself – not many more. Some of Cayley's scenes could have been described by Forrest Reid, a master of delicately charged emotional relationships; an event in Forrest Reid's youth, for instance, the scene in an upstairs room when he shows a boy, perhaps of his own age, his early attempts to write.[25] One of those hushed interiors, glowing in lamplight or firelight, the figures sitting or standing round a table, still and silent . . . a timeless moment caught by the painter and thus indefinitely sustained.

Handley-Read's dilemma was the High Victorian dilemma in microcosm – 'Criticism or Creation,' as the *Building News* put it in 1868: 'the present is an age of picking to pieces . . . the critical faculty is . . . developed at the expense of the creative;' perhaps 'the critical faculty is incompatible with the faculty of creation. Either the propensity to find fault becomes in time so strong that the man begins to criticise his own work, and fails to produce anything capable of surviving the ordeal; or else the energy of the brain is so concentrated on the business of fault-finding that there is none to spare for any other enterprise.'[26] Perceptive High Victorians feared this triumph of

learning over creativity. Theirs was the dilemma of historicism. Handley-Read's was
the dilemma of the scholar appalled at his own erudition, floundering for those simple
truths which would alone make sense of his own learning. Alas, he would have agreed
with William Blake's dictum: 'to generalise is to be an Idiot. To particularise is the
alone distinction of merit.'[27] Characteristically, one of his abortive projects was a book
to be called *Anatomies of High Victorian Design*. The fundamental problem of Victorian
studies has always been the vast mass of material. 'The history of the Victorian age,'
wrote Lytton Strachey, 'will never be written: we know too much about it. For
ignorance is the first requisite of the historian.'[28] Huge quantities of evidence cloud the
eye and numb the brain. The short way out, chosen by Goodhart-Rendel and
Betjeman – essays, sketches, *belles-lettres* – was closed for Handley-Read. 'Phrase-
making' he once called it.[29] And the long-haul approach of Pevsner or Hitchcock was
quite beyond him. His own intellectual predicament was typical of the state of
Victorian architectural studies in general: eager to catalogue, but terrified of
explanation. In Handley-Read's case excessive caution was reinforced by a dangerous
dose of the Wittgenstein syndrome. At Cambridge he had been drawn into the orbit
of that great philosopher. Whatever the merits of linguistic analysis in clarifying
philosophical terms, it proved fatal to an art-historian of Handley-Read's
temperament: he became incapable of synthesis. Hence his embarrassing admiration
for what he called my own 'synoptic talent'.

In the summer of 1970 I completed an essay on William Burges's extraordinary
patron, the 3rd Marquess of Bute.[30] At that time I was just starting a sabbatical at the
Warburg Institute, immersed in Neo-Classicism[31] and *The King's Works*.[32] Bute was
almost an aberration, stemming from the accident of my lecturing at Bedford College,
London University, in what had once been the 3rd Marquess's town house, St John's
Lodge, Regent's Park.[33] Charles leapt at the chance.

82, Ladbroke Road, London, W.11.   August 13, 1970.
Dear Joe,
    Congratulations on your Bute essay. I am now reading it compulsively, for
pleasure, and for the third time.... Now look. You have just edited Eastlake's
Gothic Revival,[34] obviously with complete success. You are already pretty well
soaked in the 3rd Marquess of Bute. You know all about Smirke,[35] and will soon
make some pretty definitive utterances on Classicism. All this ... is the perfect
corrective for anyone tackling a major Victorian Goth. And now you know what
is coming. When you have done your year on Classicism, why not do Burges?...
partnership is less than I am now looking for. I want to hand the job over, and you
would do it to perfection. You would have a completely free hand; the book
would be your book. All my source material would be at your disposal, no strings
attached; also all my cards (for what they are worth), all my notes.... If you were
to ask me to sit in the back row and contribute squeaky noises, I would do that. If

you wanted a 'chronological outline', I would prepare it (on that I have made a fair start). . . . And I could help over furniture and metalwork. But . . . I repeat. It would be your book . . . not many High Victorian architects could stand up to an architectural historian with a sense of humour. . . . How about it? Think it over.

That will do for the moment,

Yours,

Charles.

Handley-Read's Burges notes were aptly described by Simon Jervis as really 'an anthology of false starts'.[36] Writing was slow and painful for him, a form of self-inflicted torture. Among his papers I found one pencilled page, representing a full morning's work: each paragraph time-checked in the margin. The scribbled notes start at 10 a.m., then diverge into *apologia*:

. . . (12.30 p.m.) a nervous breakdown, after my effort for the Burlington,[37] but far worse than this, . . . there came from one of Lavinia's literary friends (Marion Rawson) the dismissive conclusion I had heard once before: 'of course he can't write'. It was Maurice Bicknell at Cambridge who in the late thirties had made the same remark, which I have remembered ever since as a challenge. And there lies the hurt. Working on William Burges, I had spent myself to the utmost, in an attempt to write well, to think clearly and carefully, to prune out the conjunctive ands and howevers, to avoid the jingles, the assonances and dissonances which sometimes flaw even the best paragraphs of experienced authors. It was nothing to me to re-type a paragraph fifteen or twenty times after a pencil draft like this one, trying out trifling changes of words and punctuation, for I could never hear the effect in my mind's eye, had always to see it on paper. What is more, I was always terribly slow to see an improvement, even when it stared me in the face. (1 p.m.: three hours' work). . . .

'Confessions of a Second-Rate Sensitive Mind.' Charles might almost have adopted Wordsworth's poem as his banner: 'O damned vacillating state!' An undergraduate diet of diluted Wittgenstein destroyed the certainties of all belief and hobbled the momentum of his thinking. He read restlessly, first one book, then another; quickly into a subject, and quickly out again. Of course he was a perfectionist: writing, lecturing, collecting; mixing cocktails or skating in Vienna. But beneath the polished surface there was always a withering sense of *ennui*: the price he paid for that quicksilver mind and eagle eye. Philosophy he tried; then Politics. Both proved hollow and empty of truth. 'I've tried Tory, Liberal, Labour and Communist,' he told me about the time of the 1970 election; 'and I want to tell them all – "you're wrong".' Only Art remained. The years, he used to tell me, last no longer than the flicker of a match. So he worked with an intensity which was positively feral. 'A morning,' he used to quote Berenson, 'is a very precious thing.' He squeezed every ounce out of his perceptions, and stockpiled memories like a miser. But after years of searching, grubbing away among the recesses of Tennyson's *Palace of Art*, he found just dust. There was a terrifying bleakness about his last few months. Egged on by dealers, he surrounded himself with treasures he could not catalogue, planning exhibitions he knew he would never see. His last, unfinished work was a catalogue of his own collection.

Handley-Read was a museum man *manqué*. The museum mind thinks in terms of catalogues, acquisitions, attributions, identifications, descriptions. The historian must grapple with *explanations*: the 'how' at least, even if he leaves the 'why' to metaphysicians. Frightened of attempting anything approaching explanation, Charles took refuge in LISTS: lists of architects, lists of artists, lists of dates, lists of designers, lists of manufacturers, lists of books to read and people to write to, lists of places to visit and people to see. The lists were endless and always unfinished; each one postponing the awful moment of composition. He was at his best among a small group of *cognoscenti*, or at a seminar of young students. Then his enthusiasm flared, his wit began to flicker, and his encyclopaedic knowledge – diffidently revealed – became positively spell-binding. In formal lectures, however, he swamped his audience with a tidal wave of detail. And as a writer he invariably baulked at argument, panicked, and fell back on chronology. He lacked perspective. He lacked system. His genius – like that of Burges – was for detail. But most of the details – the sources, the comparisons, even the references – died with him. When the time came for me to pick up the threads I had to begin all over again.

Part of the trouble stemmed from his use of assistants. He 'wrought too long with delegated hands'.[38] Much of their work was mechanical, staking out the ground, making appointments, ordering photographs. 'I am prepared,' he wrote to a friend in 1965, 'to do any amount of searching among piles of drawings and piles of letters – I have several times had to strip to the waist in dark cellars for days at a time.'[39] Such spasms, however, were seldom followed by bouts of composition. The root of the matter was simple enough: he suffered from a paralysing sense of intellectual inferiority. Lectures, for him, were traumas made bearable by tranquillisers.[40] His notes became a labyrinth of indecision:

> And every margin scribbled, crost, and cramm'd
> With comment, densest condensation, hard
> To mind and eye.[41]

The eye stayed firm, but not the mind.

I saw him – for the last time as it happened – in September 1971, drinking coffee at the V. and A. He looked hunched and strangely shabby. Silence for several weeks. Then the crash. I remember that Sunday very clearly. The telephone ringing;

Lavinia's voice tense and brittle as spun-glass: 'No joke ... Charles killed himself last night.'

His exit was cold and deliberate, in the Stoic manner. Just a scatter of pencilled notes; directions to his family, apologies to his friends. They held a memorial service at Holy Trinity, Sloane Street. It was a bitterly cold evening in November. Inside, art nouveau metalwork by Henry Wilson gleamed dully in the candlelight. A soprano with long fair hair sang Mozart's 'Laudate Dominum' from 'Vesperae solemnes de confessore'. Its cadences floated uncannily in the air. Brian Reade delivered the address. Lavinia wore purple. A few days later she came to dinner and we unloaded Burges from her car: mounds of dusty blue files, racks of unmarked slides, letters written and rewritten, off-prints, photographs, lecture notes, indexes – the debris of a decade. And four pieces of treasure-trove: Burges's diary, his Dante, his ink stand, and his illuminated copy of Tennyson. On top of the pile Charles had scribbled a message: 'All this is precious Burges material'. Lower down he had inserted a slip of paper containing an extract from a contemporary commentary on Ruskin: 'others after us will show the light where we have only seen darkness.'[42]

Did he know the obituary of the Victorian architect Raphael Brandon? Commenting on Brandon's suicide in 1877, the *Building News* observed: 'Some time ago we noticed a change in this gentleman's appearance – an anxious and careworn expression, betraying the yielding of an overwrought constitution to a highly sensitive temperament.'[43] Like the legendary female suicide from Dorchester, Handley-Read's nerves were 'too finely spun' to stand the shock and battering of existence. He too suffered, and suffered fatally, from 'an excess of sensibility'.

But there was worse to follow. Charles killed himself on 15 October 1971. Lavinia did the same on 9 December, like Oenone at the death of Paris. That house held too many memories. A year or so later almost the only other scholar to write creatively on Burges – Professor W. G. Howell of Cambridge[44] – was killed outright in a car smash. The dream was becoming a nightmare.

The legal and financial complications of the Handley-Reads' double suicide were formidable. Their joint estate was worth a quarter of a million pounds.[45] Despite appeals in the press[46] and pleas to national museums, their great collection was broken up. Charles worried fearfully about the ethics of inheritance. He had hoped to clear his conscience by forming a collection and bequeathing it to a museum, Cambridge perhaps, or Leicester. In the scramble that followed, some of the choicest pieces went to the Victoria and Albert Museum, the Fitzwilliam, and the Cecil Higgins Art Gallery at Bedford. But much of the rest was simply sold. The cream of the collection was exhibited in the Diploma Galleries of the Royal Academy in Spring 1972. The catalogue of that exhibition, *Victorian and Edwardian Decorative Art*, edited by Simon Jervis, has become a classic.

Charles Handley-Read will be remembered as a great collector, 'an archaeologist of the arts',[47] the man who 'discovered' William Burges. His instincts as a connoisseur had nothing to do with fashion. He rejoiced in possession, arrangement and sheer accumulation. He was born with an eye for a bargain and an appetite for the chase. Towards the end these obsessions made him solitary, almost cenobitic. He was terrified of burglars. He saw fewer and fewer friends. Our last lunch together was at the R.I.B.A. Drawings Collection, next to the Courtauld Institute in Portman Square. John Harris served trout and Scarlatti. Charles dismembered his fish with a skill which was positively surgical. Afterwards we strolled over to the Fine Art Society Gallery in New Bond Street. I left him there, plotting some secret purchase: how he loved secrets; how he revelled in the furtive thrills of detection and acquisition. When his collection was at last put on show at Burlington House in March 1972, Charles was indeed revealed as 'Magpie to an Age'.[48] But in some ways the essence of that age remained for him a half-closed book.

PART ONE

Chapter One

THE DREAM

'The more materialistic Science becomes, the more angels shall I paint.'
EDWARD BURNE-JONES

Joy, mirth, music, madness: those were the meanings of 'dream' in early medieval literature. From the thirteenth century onwards – Burges's adopted age – these images of minstrelsy and revelry give way to the fancies and illusions of sleep, and thence to the objects and artistic visions of creative fantasy.[1] Dream, drama, drug: the etymology is confused, but the alliteration is compelling. Close to, the Pre-Raphaelite castle shines bright and vivid, its detail precise to the point of hallucination. Far off, its battlements are grey and misty, filtered through the fumes of opium.

The High Victorian Dream took several shapes. A flight from reality, perhaps. Eclectic scholarship, certainly; plus a dash of cultural imperialism, which plundered in order to absorb. But its essence was Romanticism, that *mal romantique* which revels in the remote and feeds off the fantastic. Romanticism is the language of sophisticates, of complex societies that cultivate simplicity, of civilisations that have lost their innocence and replaced it with neurosis. It is a language of vicarious experience, of blind enthusiasms and inverted values. Such was the mid-Victorian obsession with the medieval world, its excesses, its crudities, its certainties. Theirs was a longing – far stronger than mere nostalgia – for a world of magic and fixed values; a yearning for stability in an age of change.[2] Theirs was a dream fundamentally historicist and profoundly unhistorical. In Chesterton's phrase, they saw the Middle Ages 'by moonlight'. One man who drank deep of this Romantic potion was the architect William Burges.[1–2]

Burges felt the tug of distant places: the ancient world, the dark ages, the Far East. His fantasies were born of curiosity and fuelled by an appetite for the exotic. They took him beyond France, Germany and Italy, to Sicily, to Greece, to Constantinople. They led him to smoke opium; to cultivate the arts of Norway and Japan; to eat off cloisonné and to drink from rock crystal. With a few like-minded patrons he conjured up a closed Gothic existence, a private Palace of Art, an architecture of dreams, a world of jewels and gems and painted furniture, of laughter and bright colours.

His dream was the dream of a generation which thought it could redeem the evils of industrialism by re-living the art of the Middle Ages. It was a dream born in the aftermath of the Napoleonic Wars, in the hopelessness of the Hungry Forties. It died, sated with indulgence, during the 1870s and 1880s.

High Victorian art and architecture lasted little more than twenty years: the customary dates are 1851 to 1870. But the ideas which sparked off that extraordinary phase were conceived during the troubled decades of the 1830s and 1840s. Pugin's *Contrasts* (1836) was an explosive political document. The Pre-Raphaelite Brotherhood was born in the year of revolutions, 1848. The *Ecclesiologist* (1842–68) had its roots in a whole spectrum of socio-religious attitudes. It is, therefore, in the realm of political rather than artistic theory that we must first look for the origins of High Victorian aesthetics.

'Fluent Benthamites and muddled Coleridgeans.'[3] Those are the categories into which we can divide the bulk of Victorian thinkers. On one side the intellectual establishment: the Utilitarians – the apostolic trio Bentham, James Mill and John Stuart Mill – with their hedonistic calculus and gospel of *laissez-faire*. Macaulay was their mouthpiece. Facts were their forte. Samuel Smiles and Gradgrind became their folk heroes, machinery their magic. Competition was the air they breathed. Ruskin called them 'the steam-whistle party'.[4] They learnt their economics in Manchester and their ethics in Gower Street. Their view of society was atomistic, individualistic, libertarian. They looked to the future. On the other side were the critics of orthodox liberalism: the radicals, the rebels, the visionaries, the reactionaries, the utopians. Their view of society was organic, interdependent, communistic, socialistic or paternal – anything but liberal. They looked to the past. Myths were their mainstay. They dealt in dreams.

That division runs like a giant geological fissure through the whole of nineteenth-century thought. In politics it divides Gladstone from Disraeli; in religion Samuel Wilberforce from Pusey; in economics Ricardo and his school from the followers of Friedrich List; in philosophy J. S. Mill and the Utilitarians from T. H. Green and the Idealists. If Liberalism was the dominant creed of Victorian England, it was a creed with many critics, both inside and outside the Liberal establishment. As a working ethic it was above all concrete, practical, pragmatic. Its vice was materialism. And, in return, its critics proffered mystical alternatives: Ruskin the philosophy of beauty; Carlyle the philosophy of power; Matthew Arnold the philosophy of true culture; and Newman – the ultimate critic of materialism – transcendental truth. As Burne-Jones put it, 'in an age of sofas and cushions', Newman 'taught me to be indifferent to comfort; and in an age of materialism he taught me to venture all on the unseen'.[5] Indeed it was Burne-Jones who put the whole debate in a nutshell: 'the more materialistic Science becomes, the more angels shall I paint'.[6]

Who were these dreamers, these backward-looking visionaries? Broadly speaking, they were those who preferred a medieval vision – an inspirational mythology – to the materialism, the ugliness, the injustice of industrial society. Many were Tories. Some were Socialists. What they had in common was a conviction that the industrial revolution had alienated man from nature and smothered his inmost being; that capitalism was death. We call them Romantics. They looked to the Middle Ages. Some found Socialism, some found Toryism. Some just found the Middle Ages.

ROMANTIC TORIES

First, the Romantic Tories. Mainstream Toryism rests ultimately on a view of society that is organic rather than atomistic, interdependent rather than competitive, hierarchical rather than egalitarian. Duties rather than rights are its chief concern. Its focus is the community rather than the individual; order and authority are its foundation; it counters reason with imagination; and it answers the myth of the Noble Savage with the myth of Original Sin. At the crucial period of its development – the late eighteenth and early nineteenth centuries – its philosophers are Burke and Coleridge, its novelists Scott and Disraeli, its pundits Cobbett and Southey. Their trump card is a recurrent Romantic illusion: the dream of a Golden Age.

Goethe was one of those who placed that Golden Age firmly in the Middle Ages. His *Götz von Berlichingen* (published in 1771; translated by Scott in 1799) glorifies the chivalric ideal. Its values – echoed for instance in Scott's *Quentin Durward* (1823) – are aristocratic, feudal and paternal. Scott's novels add up to an heroic apologia for the Middle Ages. Each chapter is an explicit lament for a vanished world, and an implicit attack on the materialism of the Modern Age. 'But the age of chivalry is gone': Burke's *Reflections on the Revolution in France* (1790) echo down the years. 'The age of chivalry is gone. That of sophisters, oeconomists, and calculators, has succeeded; and the glory of Europe is extinguished for ever.'[7]

William Cobbett put the Tory Radical viewpoint in its simplest form: a yearning for 'old England'; a pre-Reformation, pre-industrial England; a vanished world of noble lords and stout yeomen; 'a world in which rich and poor were symbiotically, rather than parasitically related';[8] a stable, pastoral world of true values, unsullied by paper money or machinery; a world of bread, and beef, and beer. The corruption of that world began with the Reformation: a 'thing ... engendered in beastly lust brought forth in hypocrisy and perfidy, and cherished and fed by plunder, devastation, and by rivers of English and Irish blood'.[9] Corruption became destruction with the advent of the Industrial Revolution: the connection between Protestantism and Capitalism – individual salvation in this world and in the next – seemed clear to Cobbett beyond all doubt.[10] Whatever the hardships of a medieval peasant, the torments of a proletarianised wage-slave were far worse: 'Talk of *vassals*! Talk of *villains*! Talk of *cerfs*! ... did feudal times ever see any of them, so debased, so absolutely slaves, as the poor creatures who, in the "*enlightened*" North, are *compelled* to work fourteen hours in a day, in a heat of *eighty-four degrees*; and who are liable to punishment *for looking out at a window of the factory*!'[11] Oh for 'the days of the Veres and Percies, and Cliffords, and Nevilles',[12] the days of 'long-tried principles ... ancient families ... ancient establishments ... king ... laws ... magistracy ... church ... and country'.[13] In their place he found only 'money and manufactures'; 'the nasal twang of a methodistical nose';[14] 'masters and slaves, a very few enjoying the extreme of luxury, and millions doomed to the extreme of misery'.[15]

For Coleridge feudalism was a solution to the eternal problem of government: the reconciliation of order and liberty. He called it a 'chain of independent interdependents'.[16] Its basis was a spiritual cohesion, a harmony based on a community of faith. And it was the collapse of that faith – cotton mills instead of cathedrals – which Southey lamented so eloquently in his *Colloquies*.[17] Southey's edition of Malory's *Morte d'Arthur* (1817) was for the Pre-Raphaelites a 'precious book'; 'we feasted on it', Burne-Jones recalled.[18] For Coleridge – addicted to laudanum and opium – his dream of a medieval Golden Age was indeed delirious. For Southey – a natural conservative – it was a settled state of mind: the Reformation meant worldliness, industrialism meant exploitation, democracy meant mediocrity.[19]

Such ideas became the mental furniture of Young England. The Young England group of the 1840s took medievalism into politics. By the time he became Prime Minister in 1841, Sir Robert Peel's working alliance with the progressives – reformers, free-traders, dissenters – was unmistakable. Young England called in the Middle Ages to redress this imbalance in the philosophy of the Conservative Party. Lord John Manners, later Duke of Rutland and lord of Belvoir Castle, was their chief dreamer;[20] George Smythe, later Lord Strangford, their ablest spokesman;[21] Alexander Baillie-Cochrane, later Lord Lamington, their historian.[22] All three were up at Cambridge in the later 1830s, together with A. J. Beresford-Hope, Augustus Stafford O'Brien, Frank Courtenay and Lord Lyttelton. There they embraced Anglo-Catholicism and ecclesiology, the Cambridge Movement of the liturgists. The Cambridge Camden Society – soon to be the Ecclesiological Society – was based in Trinity College. Its stalwarts, John Mason Neale (of *Hymns Ancient & Modern*), Benjamin Webb and Beresford-Hope, were all Trinity men. Its President, Archdeacon Thorp, was a Fellow and Tutor at the same college.[23] Unlike the Oxford Movement, the Cambridge Movement concentrated on aesthetics rather than theology, and stayed firmly within the Anglican fold.[24] But both movements shared the omnipresent medievalism of Young England. In 1838, a fortnight after first hearing Faber during a lakeside holiday near Windermere, Manners noted in his diary that he and Smythe had 'virtually pledged [themselves] to attempt to restore what? I hardly know – but still it is a glorious attempt ... and all, or nearly all the enthusiasm of the young spirits of Britain is with us.'[25]

Such naïvety undermined Young England from the start. In a sonnet addressed to

Faber, Manners begins:

> I cannot live in dreams my whole life long . . .[26]

But his whole life was indeed spent in medieval reverie. Faber replied, accurately enough:

> Thou art entranced, young dreamer! in the past.[27]

Inside Parliament these Cambridge dreamers linked up with neo-feudalists like Peter Borthwick[28] and W. B. Ferrard. Outside Parliament, supporters of Young England temporarily included John Walter of *The Times* and Richard Monckton Milnes, later Lord Houghton. But the party's existence was brief. It disintegrated in 1846 over the Repeal of the Corn Laws. Young England lives on, in fact, only in the pages of *Coningsby* (1844).[29] For Disraeli was its novelist and leader combined.

Manners first met Disraeli at dinner in 1841: 'D'Israeli talked well, but a little too well'.[30] That initial doubt was soon overcome. Disraeli became Manners's political prophet. And under his leadership Manners became three times First Commissioner of Works: in 1852, 1858 and 1866. In that office, however, he struck only two blows for Art. He successfully defended Alfred Stevens's Wellington Monument in St Paul's; and he fought Palmerston in vain for Gilbert Scott's Gothic Foreign Office. Such petty battles are a measure of Young England's failure. Only Disraeli came anywhere near to translating the paternalist dreams of Young England into state action. Perhaps accidentally, perhaps intuitively, his 'leap in the dark' with the Reform Act of 1867 enfranchised the Tory working man; his social legislation of the 1870s went some way towards eradicating a few of the evils exposed in *Sybil* (1845); and – temporarily at least – his imperialist ethic turned a dream of the past into a vision of the future.

The Oxford Movement and the Cambridge Movement – High Anglicanism at Oxford and Romantic Tory ecclesiology at Cambridge – shared the same philosophical roots. Late in 1838 one of his tutors at Trinity College, Cambridge, wrote to Lyttelton as follows: 'It is extremely curious . . . to observe what a very great influence the Oxford School is beginning to exert in Cambridge. It is quite obvious, however, in all cases that are most conspicuous (viz. Smythe, John Manners, and Hope, the two former of whom were bitten by one Faber at the Lakes during the rainy weather last summer), that the religious views have grown out of the political, and that if we strip off the hide of Newman we shall find Filmer underneath.'[31] From politics to religion, and from religion to economics were two short steps. 'This is clear,' sighed Manners in 1841; 'nothing but monastic institutions can christianise Manchester.'[32]

One book above all was the 'breviary'[33] of Young England: Kenelm Digby's five volumes of learned and unreadable romance, *The Broad Stone of Honour*, at first subtitled *Rules for the Gentlemen of England*, and later *The True Sense and Practice of*

Chivalry (several editions, 1822 onwards). Burne-Jones kept it by his bedside all his life, along with Digby's eleven cyclopean volumes entitled *Mores Catholici, or Ages of Faith* (1831–40): 'sillyish books both, but I can't help it, I like them.'[34] Digby was a convert to Roman Catholicism. He was one of a whole generation of Romantic medievalists who found their Holy Grail in Rome. At Trinity College, Cambridge, he became friendly with Ambrose Phillipps de Lisle, a fellow Leicestershire squire and a fellow convert.[35] At that date – the late 1820s – they were probably the only Catholics at Cambridge. But there were soon to be many more.[36] It was Phillipps who became Pugin's first great patron, employing him to design the first monastery built in England since the Reformation. One of those who contributed generously to its construction was John Talbot, 16th Earl of Shrewsbury, 'good Earl John', a hero beyond even the heros of Charlotte Yonge's novel *The Heir of Redclyffe* (1853).

Outside this charmed circle – but spiritually very close – were two lesser Pre-Raphaelite poets: Coventry Patmore and Aubrey de Vere. Patmore became a Catholic in 1864, but remained on close terms with London's literary and artistic circles all his life. His house at Herron's Ghyll, Sussex – rebuilt by J. F. Bentley in 1866–7 – became a veritable microcosm of medievalism.[37] By contrast, Aubrey de Vere was an outsider by temperament and situation. A sensitive critic, a sub-Tennysonian bachelor poet, a convert (1851) to Catholicism and a romantic paternalist, he never forgot the Irish tragedies of the 1840s. A friend of Manning and Newman, he lived into old age at Curragh Chase, near Adare, in a plain classical house near the ruins of a Franciscan monastery on the banks of the River Maigue. For Ruskin 'the Middle Ages had their wars and agonies, but also their intense delights';[38] for de Vere they 'constituted the devout, joyous though often incoherent childhood of Europe'.[39] The world of Coventry Patmore and Aubrey de Vere – still more the world of Kenelm Digby – was a world more serious and sympathetic than the world of the Eglinton Tournament (1839).[40] But it was a dream-world none the less.

'Chivalry,' Kenelm Digby defined as 'only a name for that general spirit or state of mind which disposes men to heroic and generous actions and keeps them conversant with all that is beautiful and sublime in the intellectual and moral world. It will be found that . . . this spirit more generally prevails in youth than in the later periods of men's lives.'[41] Chivalry had little to do with learning: 'We have now that principle, the curse of a reading age, which leads men to idolize the acuteness of intellect and to despise the virtues of the heart. In a word we have in this age the dispositions and the principles which have been substituted for those of Chivalry and for all those generous thoughts and feelings which bound men to their religion and their country.'[42] As for titles, 'Gentleman' was the noblest of all: 'The degrees of nobility were not to interfere with its fundamental principle that one gentleman cannot be more gentle than another.'[43] 'Look at those poor dead figures on the tombs of knights, with the Cross on their breast and their armed hands raised in prayer. Where shall we find so much religion and honour and dignity among the living as beams from that cold stone?'[44]

Digby it was, says Ruskin, 'from whom I . . . first learnt to love nobleness'.[45] And despite the influence of Carlyle's Calvinism, despite what he called 'my own pert little Protestant mind', Ruskin too came to feel that after the Reformation, 'it was no longer possible to attain entire peace of mind, to live calmly and die hopefully'.[46] Phillipps called *Mores Catholici* that 'Golden Book . . . it has many times overpowered me as with a torrent of celestial delight . . . I could fancy myself listening to the melodies of the Angels'.[47] Appropriately, Kenelm Digby's family rest today close to Pugin, in the little chapel of St John, built in 1859 next to Pugin's own church of St Augustine's, Ramsgate, to the designs of Pugin's son.[48]

More than any of these men, it was Ambrose Phillipps de Lisle who believed in Gothic. 'I have no more doubt,' he wrote, 'of its ultimate and universal triumph than I have of that of Christianity itself.' The sanctity of Counter-Reformation saints, he believed, was attained 'in *spite* of the Renaissance', with all its 'classical sensualism' and 'dangerous elegance'. In building Baroque churches the Jesuits were only turning 'Satan's own weapons against himself'. The nadir of Renaissance impulses was reached in the French Revolution: the mob set up 'a naked Prostitute on the Altar of Notre Dame at Paris. . . . Thank heaven a brighter day has at length dawned . . . the revival of Christian art is a thing decreed by all the greatest geniuses of Europe. It must prevail, nothing can stop it . . . its ultimate triumph is certain'.[49] No wonder Montalembert called him 'a perfect MEDIAEVAL man'.[50]

> Phillipps, deep-read in medieval books,
> Had Heav'n around him, Heav'n in his looks.[51]

As a boy he was the first since the Reformation to erect an altar cross in an Anglican church; as a young man the first to construct a Catholic rood screen, the first to build an open-air Calvary, the first to hold public processions of the Blessed Sacrament, the first to found a monastery.[52] His most learned writings were all on one theme: Mahomet as Antichrist. With Montalembert he visited the ruins of every Cistercian abbey founded in England during the time of St Bernard.[53] He was the perfect patron for Augustus Welby Pugin.

It was the prophets of Romantic Toryism – particularly Cobbett, Southey and Kenelm Digby – who helped to mould Pugin's most influential work: *Contrasts* (1836), one of the sacred texts of medievalism, and a key document in the history of the Gothic Revival.[54] *Contrasts* was a full-blooded diatribe not only against Neo-Classicism but against the whole ethos of bourgeois Liberalism. Pugin's starting point was simple: 'the Roman Catholic Church was the only true one, and the only one in which the grand and sublime style of architecture can ever be restored.'[55] With graphic text, and plates more graphic still, he contrasted the nineteenth century with the fourteenth, the old world and the new. Gower Street was the Enemy: University College, London, a building designed by Wilkins, decorated by Flaxman, and the very citadel of Benthamite thinking.[56] Gothic was the Dream, the only dream of all 'who have prayed, and hoped, and loved' through the dark night of Protestant Taste; its revival will be 'truly ravishing, the realisation of all their longing desires. . . . Oh! then, what delight! what joy unspeakable! when one of the solemn piles is presented to them in all its pristine life and glory! the stoups are filled to the brim; the rood is raised on high; the screen glows with sacred imagery and rich device; the niches are filled; the altar is replaced sustained by sculptured shafts, the relics of the saints repose beneath, the body of our Lord is enshrined in its consecrated stone; the lamps of the sanctuary burn bright; the saintly portraitures in the glass windows shine all gloriously; and the albs hang in the oaken aumbries, and the cope chests are filled with orphreyed baudekins; and pix, and pax, and chrismatory are there, and thurible and cross'.[57]

In 1833–4 Phillipps had employed William Railton, architect of Nelson's Column, to add a Tudor Gothic manor house to

The ivied ruins of forlorn Grace-Dieu.[58]

But it was Pugin whom he commissioned to design the Abbey of Mount St Bernard in Charnwood Forest nearby, England's first monastery since the Reformation.[59] It was a project conceived as the first step towards Phillipps's lifelong dream: the reconversion of England to Catholicism. For this purpose the Cistercian order was re-established in the form of a Trappist community, three centuries after its suppression by Henry VIII. Thanks to Phillipps, the Charnwood Hills echoed to the sound of Gregorian chant.

Pugin never fulfilled his greatest ambition. 'I have passed my life,' he once remarked, 'in thinking of fine things, studying fine things, designing fine things, and realising very poor ones.' Only St Giles, Cheadle, satisfied him: '*Perfect Cheadle*, Cheadle my consolation in all my afflictions.'[60] But it is impossible to overestimate the influence of Pugin's writings – particularly *True Principles* (1841) – on English architects. 'That wonderful man,' as Burges called him,[61] was the lodestar of a generation of Goths. 'Acknowledged or unacknowledged,' announced *The Builder* in 1843, 'Pugin is Pope in Gothic.'[62] 'I was awakened from my slumbers,' Gilbert Scott recalled, 'by the thunder of Pugin's writings . . . his image in my imagination was like my guardian angel, and I often dreamed that I knew him.'[63] Thanks to Pugin, the Gothic Revival seemed almost to become 'a preternatural heaven-born impulse'.[64] But within his chosen religious community Pugin felt trapped.

In any battle for the re-conversion of England, the old Catholic families naturally formed a base; the Howards, the Cliffords, the Talbots, the Stonors, the Stourtons, the Throckmortons . . . educated at Stonyhurst, or Oscott, or Ushaw, or Prior Park. But by the 1840s congregations in many areas were mostly composed of Irish immigrants. And leadership, inevitably, came from Rome. As the nineteenth century progressed – Catholic Relief Act (1791), Catholic Emancipation (1829), Restoration of the Catholic Hierarchy (1850) – English Catholicism moved further away from its older, recusant base.[65] Conflicts within the community – at least over the externals of Faith – were inevitable. And Pugin's identification of Gothicism with Catholicism predictably ran into trouble.

'Protestants,' he complained in 1839, 'in many cases are far better inclined to Catholicism than half the soi-disant Catholics in our days ... the Catholics will cut their own throats.'[66] He found the hierarchy chary of full-blown medievalism. Cardinal Wiseman even attempted to remove Pugin's screen at St Chad's, Birmingham. This act of threatened 'ambonoclasm' wounded him 'like a stab'. 'I am resolved to live or die, stand or fall, for the *real thing*. ... My dear Phillipps we nearly *stand alone* if we except the [High Anglican] Oxford men [e.g. J. R. Bloxam of Magdalen, 'the Father of Ritualism']. ... Every building I effect is profaned ... were it not for the Oxford men I should quite despair.'[67] Alas! those 'Oxford men' who returned to Rome, like Faber and Newman, turned out to be 'the most disappointing people in the world. They were three times as Catholic in their ideas before they were reconciled to the Church. It is really quite lamentable. ... A man may be judged by his feelings on Plain Chaunt. If he likes Mozart he is no chancel and screen man. By their music you shall know them, and I lost all faith in the Oratorians when I found they were opposed to the old song'.[68] Phillipps agreed: Gregorian chant was Heaven; operatic and orchestral church music was Hell. The temporary Oratory in King William Street, London, drove Pugin to distraction: the Lowther Concert Rooms had been hired for services. 'Has your Lordship heard,' Pugin thundered to Shrewsbury, 'that the Oratorians have opened the Lowther Rooms as a chapel!! – a place of the vilest debauchery, masquerades, etc. – one night a MASQUE BALL, next BENEDICTION ... perfectly monstrous. ... What a degradation for religion! Why, it is worse than the Socialists.'[69] When in 1839 the College of Propaganda in Rome refused to countenance any revival of the ancient form of chasuble, Phillipps described the event as 'a death-blow to the Catholic cause in England'.[70] Aesthetic heresy was everywhere. But Pugin was adamant: 'Down with the Pagan Monster.'[71]

Pugin never converted Newman to Gothic. And Phillipps never converted England to Catholicism.[72] But between them they scored at least one triumph: Mount St Bernard was built. Burne-Jones went there as a youth, and cherished its memory to the end: 'and more and more,' he wrote in 1896, 'my heart is pining for that monastery in Charnwood Forest. ... I saw it when I was little and have hankered after it ever since.'[73] In a way it was an attempt to atone for that great symbolic crime of the Reformation: the destruction of the monasteries. 'The ghost of medieval monasticism,' writes Dom David Knowles, 'remained and remains to haunt this island. The grey walls and broken cloisters, the

bare ruin'd choirs, where late the sweet birds sang,

speak more eloquently for the past than any historian would dare.'[74] The Gothic Revival was in part an act of atonement for the vandalism of long ago.

None atoned more lavishly than Pugin's other great patron, the 16th Earl of Shrewsbury. Shrewsbury was not a millionaire. But he was immensely generous. Parish churches at Cheadle and Uttoxeter; the monastery of Mount St Bernard;[75] the chapel at Oscott College; the chapel at Alton Towers; the church, hospital and school at Alton Castle; an Oratorian church at Cotton; a convent at Handsworth; and the cathedrals of St Chad's, Birmingham, and St George's, Southwark – all these were built wholly or partly from his benefactions.[76] It was Shrewsbury who first employed the young Pugin at Alton Towers; Shrewsbury who made him Professor of Ecclesiastical Art at Oscott. It was Shrewsbury who installed the learned ecclesiologist Dr Rock as his chaplain at Alton. And after the 14th Duke of Norfolk's secession in 1851, he was – nominally at least – England's leading Catholic layman. But he was not a political figure. Even the Gothic Dream was for him a matter of inclination rather than conviction. There is something curiously aloof about his whole career. 'The Universe,' Phillipps wrote to him in January 1848, at the start of that year of turmoil, 'is in a state of Revolution, moral and physical too: what we shall come to at last, I cannot guess. . . . Meanwhile you must watch it from the Gothick loop-holes of your venerable Towers . . . amid the noble valleys of Alton, with Religion and peace and plenty around you.'[77]

In the same year Pugin was writing to John Hardman in Birmingham, ordering muskets for each member of his Ramsgate household: 'Don't forget the muskets. We shall want them before long. What a horrible state of things in France. . . . What a government. What liberty. What scurrility. I would shoot any Chartist as I would a rat or a mad dog. Send me muskets.'[78]

ROMANTIC SOCIALISTS

So much for Romantic Toryism. Romantic Socialism began with premises which were similarly medieval, and ended with conclusions which were equally authoritarian. Both traditions of thought denied the validity of libertarian principles. The 'Feudal Socialism' of Carlyle, the Christian Socialism of Kingsley and Maurice, the 'Aesthetic Socialism' of Ruskin, the Revolutionary Socialism of Marx and Morris – all these repudiated the individualist assumptions of bourgeois democracy and looked back to the Middle Ages for inspiration or explanation.

Carlyle's political philosophy defies neat categorisation. In a sense he is the link between Romantic Toryism and Romantic Socialism. His sources of inspiration were German and French as much as English. He was fired initially by the Romantic medievalism of Herder, Wackenroder, Novalis and the Schlegels. From German Idealist philosophers like Fichte he borrowed the framework of a God-centred universe and the idea of the Hero. From Saint-Simon he derived the notion of a civilisation both cyclic and progressive.[79] But it was the coincidence of two visits in September 1842 – to the workhouse of St Ives and to the ruins of St Edmund's Abbey – which sparked off that masterpiece of medievalism, *Past and Present* (1843). In 1840 the Camden Society had published the *Chronicle of Jocelyn of Brakelond*. That document supplied Carlyle with material for a devastating comparison between England in the twelfth century and England in the nineteenth.

> Gurth, born thrall of Cedric the Saxon, has been greatly pitied by Dryasdust and others. Gurth, with the brass collar round his neck, tending Cedric's pigs in the glades of the wood, is not what I would call an exemplar of human felicity: but Gurth, with the sky above him, with the free air and tinted boscage and umbrage round him, and in him at least the certainty of supper and social lodging when he came home; Gurth to me seems happy, in comparison with many a Lancashire and Buckinghamshire man of these days, not born thrall of anybody! Gurth's brass collar did not gall him: Cedric *deserved* to be his master. The pigs were Cedric's, but Gurth too would get his parings of them. Gurth had the inexpressible satisfaction of feeling himself related indissolubly, though in a rude brass-collar way, to his fellow mortals on this Earth. He had superiors, inferiors, equals – Gurth is now 'emancipated' long since; has what we call 'Liberty'. Liberty, I am told, is a divine thing. Liberty when it becomes the 'Liberty to die by starvation' is not so divine.[80]

Carlyle's remedy was a call for the application of medieval virtues to the vices of modern society: a veritable 'chivalry of labour'; an escape from the mechanistic universe, the grinding 'Logic Mill' of *laissez faire*. In essence, it was a call for the feudalisation of society under the eye of a paternal state. Captains of Industry must take on the mantles of Arthurian heroes. 'Hero Kings, and a whole world not unheroic';[81] that was the dream, but a dream moulded by the mechanisms of the Modern Age: 'Legislative interference, and interferences not a few, are indispensable.'[82] Carlyle defies most party tags: he is Tory, Socialist and Fascist. Only one negative label is clear: he is certainly not a Liberal.

Like Carlyle, Ruskin never doubted the superiority of the Middle Ages over the modern world in all but inessentials. 'The Middle Ages,' he told Charles Eliot Norton in 1876, 'are to me the only ages. . . . All modern science and philosophy produces abortion. That miracle-believing faith produced good fruit – the best yet in the world.'[83] And even in inessentials – the vain apparatus of living – medieval man was rich: 'the medieval centuries . . . were . . . the bright ages; ours are the dark ones. I do not mean metaphysically, but literally. They were the ages of gold; ours are the ages of umber . . . we build brown brick walls, and wear brown coats. . . . Their gold was dashed with blood; but ours is sprinkled with dust. . . . The profoundest reason of this darkness of heart is, I believe, our want of faith.'[84]

To the young Burne-Jones, Ruskin's writings were the authentic voice of truth: 'in prose what Tennyson is in poetry, and what the Pre-Raphaelites are in painting'.[85] His books were 'the best books in the world';[86] 'his noble words used to make me shake and tremble'.[87] At Oxford Morris read Ruskin aloud, chanting rather than reading 'those weltering oceans of eloquence'.[88]

Ruskin based much of his aesthetic on a single proposition: the interconnexion of art and morality.[89] This connexion – the Morality of Art – was a two-way process: society made art, and art made society. 'Art for Art's sake' was a corrupting heresy.[90] 'The sensation of beauty,' he wrote, 'is not sensual on the one hand, nor is it intellectual on the other, but is dependent on a pure, right and open state of the heart.'[91] In a perfect world – medieval Venice, as he envisioned it – the separation of art and morality could never occur. 'Examine once more,' he urges, 'those ugly goblins, and formless monsters, and stern statues, anatomiless and rigid; *but do not mock at them*, for they are the signs of the life and liberty of every workman who struck the stone; a freedom of thought, and rank in scale of being, such as no laws, no charter, no charities can secure; but which it must be the first aim of all Europe at this day to regain for her children.'[92] Alas! the eighteenth century had invented the industrial process, the nineteenth century the democratic process. Pleasure-in-work had been replaced by pleasure-in-profit. Representational democracy – the bogus freedom of the ballot box – had replaced true freedom:[93] a communal freedom based on trust; freedom in the heart of man. And the pursuit of wealth had been substituted for the pursuit of beauty. 'There is slavery in our England.'[94] Society had lost its soul.

Like Carlyle, Ruskin looked to a new moral government to lead humanity out of this aesthetic desert. The Parable of the Prodigal Son became for him a paradigm of the anti-democratic process: 'The lost son began by claiming his rights. He is found when he resigns them. He is lost by flying from his father, when his father's authority was only paternal. He is found by returning to his father, and desiring that his authority may be absolute, as over a hired stranger.'[95] Like Morris, Ruskin also looked to a form of Utopian Socialism as the likeliest agent for the generation of virtue. In his later years – tortured by dreams and hallucinations[96] – he spent much of his time and energy in an abortive Socialist organisation, the Guild of St George. One of the young Oxford men who broke stones with him on the road to Hinksey was a member of Magdalen College named Oscar Wilde. The trappings were more than symbolically medieval. It represented a coherent – if possible – attempt to revive the medieval guild system in a world which had replaced the humane values of feudalism by the crude cash-nexus of capitalism.[97] For Ruskin 'the real science of political economy' was not a system for maximising wealth, but 'that which teaches nations to desire and labour for the things that lead to life'.[98]

Ruskin's Romantic Socialism was almost as hierarchic and paternal as Disraeli's Romantic Toryism. 'My continual aim,' he wrote, 'has been to show the eternal superiority of some men to others, sometimes even of one man to all others.'[99] *Fors*

Clavigera (1871–84) adds up to a metaphysical justification of the chivalric principle: the social order as a reflection of the natural order, but designed by God to secure the protection of the weak by the strong. Medieval trappings are attractive but ultimately irrelevant. Their value is symbolic: the medieval ideal is only 'an ideal, a myth, a mental construct'.[1] 'The things that actually happened,' Ruskin explains, 'were of small consequence; the thoughts that were developed are of infinite consequence.'[2]

Morris too employed the medieval ideal as an instrument of regeneration. With Burne-Jones at Oxford in 1853 he dreamt of founding a monastic community to lead a 'crusade and holy warfare against the age'.[3] Beneath the surface of his early romantic verse there is a violence closer to nightmare than to dream.[4] But this suppressed anger only belatedly took on political form. With Burne-Jones and Rossetti in London in 1856, Morris formed what was in effect the second Pre-Raphaelite Brotherhood. 'Apart from the desire to produce beautiful things,' he recalled in 1894, 'the leading passion of my life has been and is hatred of modern civilisation.'[5] 'My work,' he had admitted in 1856, 'is the embodiment of dreams.'[6] But in Morris's case the Dream took on an overtly didactic form. He was not just a 'Dreamer of dreams,' still less 'the idle singer of an empty day.'[7] He was a 'Communist Utopian'[8] who summoned up the Middle Ages to redress the iniquities of contemporary capitalism. By 1881 he had in fact lost faith in orthodox Pre-Raphaelitism: 'feverish and dreamy', out of tune with 'the general sympathy of simple peoples'.[9] Pre-Raphaelitism had served its purpose as an intellectual staging-post in Morris's emergence as 'our greatest diagnostician of alienation'.[10]

Like Pugin and Ruskin, however, Morris always cherished Gothic art and architecture, not just for its own sake, but as an agent of moral revolution. In a famous passage he called Ruskin's chapter from *The Stones of Venice* (1851–3) – 'On the Nature of Gothic and the Role of the Workmen Therein' – 'one of the very few necessary and inevitable utterances of the century. To some of us when we first read it, it seemed to point out a new road on which the world should travel . . . [the only] way out of the folly and degradation of Civilisation.'[11] 'For [Morris],' writes Mackail, 'the word architecture bore an immense, and . . . almost . . . transcendental, meaning. Connected at a thousand points with all the other specific arts which ministered to it out of a thousand sources, it was itself the tangible expression of all the order, the comeliness, the sweetness, nay, even the mystery and the law, which sustain man's world and make human life what it is.'[12] That might almost have been written of Pugin or Ruskin. All three saw architecture as an emanation of society: man builds his habitation in his own image. But unlike Pugin and Ruskin, Morris seized upon medieval values – artistic and social – as a spur to political action, in effect as the basis of revolution. A new architecture meant a new society. Pugin had tried to reform society by reforming art. Morris set out to reform art by reforming society.[13] Aesthetic regeneration was 'not basically a question of art at all'.[14] It was a matter of politics and economics.

For there are two sides to William Morris: the medievalist and the Marxist, the

Romantic and the Revolutionary, each reinforcing the other. Marx himself was no medievalist. But he did identify the collapse of feudalism as the first link in a chain of events leading directly to the creation of capitalism and ultimately to revolution and the dictatorship of the proletariat.

> The bourgeoisie, [states the *Communist Manifesto*, 1848] wherever it has got the upper hand, has put an end to all feudal, patriarchal, idyllic relations. It has pitilessly torn asunder the motley feudal ties that bound man to his *natural superiors*, and has left remaining no other nexus between man and man than naked self-interest, than callous *cash-payment*. It has drowned the most heavenly ecstasies of religious fervour, of chivalrous enthusiasm, of philistine sentimentalism, in the icy water of egotistical calculation. It has resolved personal worth into exchange value, and in place of the numerous indefensible chartered freedoms, has set up that single unconscionable freedom – Free Trade. In one word, for exploitation, veiled by religious and political illusions, it has substituted naked, shameless, direct, brutal exploitation.[15]

Now Morris was no political economist. Once, at a meeting in Glasgow, a troublesome heckler asked: 'Does comrade Morris accept Marx's theory of value?' Morris replied angrily: 'I do not know what Marx's theory of value is, and I'm damned if I want to know ... political economy is not my line, and much of it appears to me to be dreary rubbish. But I am, I hope, a Socialist none the less.'[16] Still, Morris absorbed Marx more easily than Marxism could absorb Morris.[17] Marxist history probably lay behind Morris's change of interest: from the age of the troubadours to the age following the Black Death. He studied the watershed between declining feudalism and emergent capitalism, the struggle between guild and artisan in the fourteenth and fifteenth centuries. And there he found that false turning, that pivot of Marxist thinking, when craftsmen became wage-slaves; when the enclosure movement expropriated peasants and made possible 'the breeding of money'; when artisans sloughed off the protective fetters of their guilds and embraced instead the chains of capitalism.[18] The next stage – the emergence of bourgeois democracy – Marx regarded as a sham. And Morris held much the same view of 'the wearisome shilly-shally of parliamentary politics'.[19] Marxist teaching certainly formed the basis of Morris's two visionary novels, *A Dream of John Ball* (1888) and *News from Nowhere* (1891).[20] There we see the society of which Morris dreamed, pre-industrial, communal, and content.

> Not seldom, [he told an audience in 1885,] I please myself with trying to realize the face of medieval England; the many chases and great woods, the stretches of common tillage and common pasture quite unenclosed; the rough husbandry of the tilled parts, the unimproved breeds of cattle, sheep, and swine ... the strings of

packhorses along the bridle-roads ... the little towns, well bechurched, often walled; the villages just where they are now ... but better and more populous; their churches, some big and handsome, some small and curious, but all crowded with altars and furniture and gay with pictures and ornament; the many religious houses, with their glorious architecture; the beautiful manor-houses, some of them castles once, and survivals from an earlier period; some new and elegant; some out of all proportion small for the importance of their lords. How strange it would be to us if we were landed in fourteenth-century England! ... that rigidly ordered caste society ... with its rough plenty, its sauntering life, its cool acceptance of rudeness and violence ... [that] old feudal hierarchy, with its many-linked chain of personal responsibilities.[21]

There was of course a paradox at the heart of Morris's career. Pre-Raphaelite art was made possible by capitalist patrons like Millar and MacCracken, Rae and Leyland, Leathart, Graham and Plint. As a young man Morris himself lived on a private income derived from mining shares; and in middle age he became famous as the head of a firm (Morris & Co.) 'ministering', as he bitterly remarked in 1876, 'to the swinish luxury of the rich'.[22] Between 'Mad Morris' the visionary and 'Millionaire Morris' decorator of Balmoral and St James's Palace, there could be no easy rapport. Hence the unreality of his dream. Engels in fact dismissed him as 'a settled sentimental Socialist,' adding 'Morris is all very well as far as he goes, but it is not very far'.[23]

In *A Dream of John Ball* Morris actually portrays himself as 'The Dreamer'. And it was as 'the dreamer of the Middle Ages' that Yeats remembered him staring out of the portrait by G. F. Watts, with eyes 'like the eyes of some dreaming beast'. 'The dream-world of Morris,' Yeats concluded, 'was as much the antithesis of daily life as with other men of genius, but he was never conscious of the antithesis and so knew nothing of intellectual suffering.'[24] He never wrestled, for example, with the incompatibility of liberty and equality, or with the awkward fact that equality and justice are not necessarily the same thing. If Yeats's judgement holds true for Morris, it holds truer still for Burne-Jones and Rossetti. For with the Pre-Raphaelites we come to our third category of dreamer: the apolitical artist.

ROMANTIC ARTISTS

Like others of his generation, young Burne-Jones was spellbound by Ruskin and bewitched by Dante Gabriel Rossetti. 'Rossetti,' Val Prinsep recalled, 'was the planet round which we revolved. We copied his very way of speaking. All beautiful women were "stunners" with us. Wombats were the most delightful of God's creatures. Medievalism was our *beau idéal* and we sank our own individuality in the strong personality of our adored Gabriel.'[25] 'He was to me as Pope and Emperor,' Burne-Jones admitted, 'my glorious Gabriel,' a 'man who could lead armies and destroy

empires.'[26] Theirs was a hilarious dream world, of 'laughter, and songs, and jokes, and
... volleys of ... soda-water corks',[27] a veritable Round Table of undergraduates and
artists – 'Morris and his glorious company of martyrs'[28] – with Rossetti at their head,
and lovely, raven-haired Jane Burdon already set for the part of a doomed Queen
Guenevere. Arguing late into the night with Swinburne; splashing paint about the
Oxford Union. ... 'What fun we had in that Union!,' Val Prinsep recalled; 'What
Jokes! What roars of laughter! ... O tempera, O Morris. ...'[29] Through it all, as Max
Beerbohm suggested, ran 'a silver thread of lunacy'.[30] And on it Ruskin set the seal of
his approval: 'Jones you are gigantic!'[31] No wonder, looking back on the
phenomenon of Pre-Raphaelitism, Georgiana Burne-Jones confessed: 'I felt in the
presence of a new religion.'[32]

As a religion, Pre-Raphaelitism was salvationist rather than evangelistic. Rossetti's
father had interpreted Dante in terms of a giant masonic cryptogram, an allegory of
political revolution. But when Rossetti applied his own introspective vision to the
problem of Dante's imagery, he managed to reduce *La Vita Nuova* to a reflection of his
own Romantic ego.[33] Politics meant little to him, and economics less. His comment
on Ruskin's *Unto this Last* was brutish: 'Who could read it, or anything about such
bosh?'[34] Even more than his followers, Rossetti was – as Walter Pater pointed out – 'a
solitary prisoner' in his 'own dream world ... Dreamland ... is to him ... a real
country, a veritable expansion of, or addition to, our waking life'.[35] His favourite
picture of Janey Morris was inevitably entitled 'The Day Dream'.[36] More than most
Pre-Raphaelites, he relied on narcotics for his visions, on regular doses of laudanum
and chloral. His paintings – like those of Holman Hunt and the young Millais – suggest
a vividness of detail and colour which is closer to hallucination than to nature.

> ... in my dream I could see even very far off things much closer than we see real
> material things on the earth ... the trumpets sang in long solemn peals as they all
> rode on together, with the glimmer of arms and the fluttering of banners, and the
> clinking of the rings of the mail, that sounded like the falling of many drops of
> water deep into the deep still waters of some pool that the rocks nearly meet over;
> and the gleam and flash of the swords, and the glimmer of the lance-heads and the
> flutter of the rippled banners, that streamed out from them, swept past me, and
> were gone, and they seemed like a pageant in a dream, whose meaning we knew
> not; and those sounds too, the trumpets, and the clink of the mail, and the thunder
> of the horse-hoofs, they seemed dream-like too – and it was all a dream.[37]

With Burne-Jones the Dream is so intense as to be almost tangible. Here he is in
1854, still at Oxford, wandering on 'pilgrimage to Godstow ruins and the burial place
of Fair Rosamund':

> I came back in a delirium of joy the land was so enchanted with bright colours,
> blue and purple in the sky, shot over with a dust of golden shower, and in the

water a mirror'd counterpart, ruffled by a light west wind – and in my mind pictures of the old days, the abbey, and long processions of the faithful, banners of the cross, copes and croziers, gay knights and ladies by the river bank, hawking parties and all the pageantry of the golden age – it made me feel so wild and mad that I had to throw stones into the water to break the dream. I never remember having such unutterable ecstasy, it was quite painful in intensity, as if my forehead would burst. I get frightened of indulging now in dreams, so vivid that they seem recollections rather than imaginations, but they seldom last more than half-an-hour; and the sound of earthly bells in the distance, and presently the wreathing of steam upon the trees where the railway runs, called me back to the years I cannot convince myself I am living in.[38]

Next summer Burne-Jones visited Beauvais with Morris, reading Keats along the way.[39] Years later he found the memory still fresh:

I saw it and remember it all – and the processions – and the trombones – and the ancient singing – more beautiful than anything I had ever heard and I think I have never heard the like since. And the great organ that made the air tremble – and the greater that pealed out suddenly, and I thought the Day of Judgement had come – and the roof and the long lights that are among the most graceful things man has ever made. . . . What a day it was, and how alive I was, and young – and a blue dragon-fly stood still in the air so long that I could have painted him. Oh me, what fun it was to be young. Yes, if I took account of my life and the days in it that most went to make me, the Sunday at Beauvais would be the first day of creation.[40]

'Sighing after the infinite with the Schlegels. . . .'[41] Late in life he visited Exeter Cathedral, and felt the same powerful but indefinite emotions:

The big church made me happy – and the fierce kings carved in the West front – fierce persons like Gunnar and Hogni – truculent, terrific tyrants. . . . Then we went [in] to hear the music, and little boy-demons sang so it was as if heaven opened for a bit – and I wished I had been good, or ever could be good, and wished it was all true about what they say or that I could see it, and wished and wished and WHISHT.[42]

No wonder Rossetti called him 'one of the nicest young fellows in *Dreamland*'.[43]

Burne-Jones shared Morris's dream of a lost Utopia. He felt that burning regret for a vanished past, the 'cosmic homesickness' of all Pre-Raphaelites.[44] But he was not a political animal; he kept faith with that vision in his own studio. As early as 1856 he vowed to 'work hard and paint visions and dreams and symbols for the understanding of people'.[45] More consciously than Rossetti, more subtly than Morris, he spent his life seeking the numinous in an alien world, groping for a symbolic language to express the invisible, pursuing those 'richly coloured images of a historical or legendary past' which might 'serve also as metaphors for the life of the human spirit'.[46] In middle age he once felt tempted to activism. But by 1879 he had made his decision: 'I shall never try again to leave . . . the little world that has the walls of my workroom for its furthest horizon; – and I want Morris back to it, and want him to write divine books and leave the rest. Some day it will all change violently, and I hate and dread it but say beforehand it will thoroughly serve everybody right – but I don't want to see or foresee it, or dwell upon it.'[47]

Back, therefore, to the world of 'The Sleeping Beauty', 'The Briar Rose', 'The Sleeping Knights'. He refused even to read Zola or Tolstoy because they were 'just like life'.[48] By 1897 the doors of that private dream-world were indeed sealed fast. Georgiana Burne-Jones tells the story. 'A pity it is I was not born in the Middle Ages,' mused the Grand Old P.R.B. 'People would then have known how to use me – now they don't know what on earth to do with me. The time is out of joint . . . Rossetti could not set it right and Morris could not set it right – and who the devil am I, who the devil am I? . . . [Still] what does it matter . . .? I have learned to know Beauty when I see it, and that's the best thing.'[49] Towards the end of his life Burne-Jones entered totally into the spirit of his greatest painting, 'The Sleep of Arthur in Avalon', heading his letters 'Avalon' and even sleeping in the pasture of the dying King.[50]

In poetry and music the tension between Art and Life was no easier to resolve. Tennyson and Wagner walked the same tightrope between symbol and sensation. Wagner's territory was the Gothic North. Tennyson was less cosmic and rather more precise. Whereas Coleridge escaped to Xanadu, and Morris to Iceland, Tennyson's chosen dreamland was Arthurian Wessex. Now historians[51] tell us that Arthur was a fifth-century warrior, probably of Roman extraction, who temporarily delayed the disintegration of Romano-British society with a series of spectacular victories over the barbarian English invader, notably the Battle of Badon in 495. The legendary Arthur, however, symbol of a golden age, led a much more varied existence. He first appears in the sixth century in the writings of Gildas. In the twelfth century he develops a double persona: the chivalrous paragon of Norman poets, and the belligerent Plantagenet hero of Geoffrey of Monmouth's *Historia*. In the fifteenth century Malory's *Morte d'Arthur* gave the legend definitive form: an armoured dream of peaceful governance in an age afflicted by the Wars of the Roses. Faced with the sum of these accretions, Tennyson added a final ingredient: the code of a muscular Christian gentleman. In essence, his *Idylls of the King* represented the ultimate literary expression of the High Victorian Dream: a rebellion against industrialism and its attendant capitalist ethic, an appeal from commerce to chivalry, from Birmingham to Avalon.

Dreams are the very stuff of Tennyson's poetry. The whole corpus of his work includes some 270 dream-images.[52] *The Dreamer* was the last poem he completed.

'Dreams are true while they last, and do we not live in dreams?'[53] As Oxford freshmen in 1853 Morris and Burne-Jones were entranced: Tennyson was 'the only guide worth following far into dreamland'.[54] Keats and Coleridge, Chaucer and Froissart, Malory and Tennyson: those were the writers enshrined in the Pre-Raphaelite pantheon. But throughout Tennyson's poetry runs a conscious attempt to relate real and ideal, image and meaning, past and present – 'to consolidate,' as he put it, 'our gossamer dreams into reality.'[55] Life in Tennyson may be drugged with *The Lotos Eaters*, or paralysed by beauty in *The Palace of Art*; it may be glimpsed through a world of mirrored shadows as in *The Lady of Shalott*, or lost like *The Kraken* in murky sleep. But Beyond the languorous images, behind the Arthurian scenery of *The Idylls*, duty points an accusing finger. 'Tennyson,' a Cambridge friend warned him right at the start of his career, 'we cannot live in Art.'[56] That warning went home. When another friend used opium to escape the responsibilities of existence, Tennyson was stern: 'What are you about – musing, and brooding and dreaming and opium-eating yourself out of this life and into the next. . . . I can see nothing for you but stupefaction, aneurism, confusion, horror and death.'[57] The theme of *The Palace of Art* was central to his thinking. In fact its tensions lay at the heart of the Pre-Raphaelite dilemma. 'I send you a sort of allegory,' Tennyson explained, of a soul 'That did love Beauty only,' a soul that did not see the interrelationship of Beauty, Good and Knowledge.[58] Towards the end Morris came to despise the Poet Laureate as a tired, Establishment figure. But then Tennyson had no pretensions as a political theorist. He was a dreamer, not an activist. His reaction to Morris's conversion to Socialism was predictable: 'He's gone crazy!'[59]

Wagner is a world on his own. But he has much to tell us about the Pre-Raphaelite Dream. Wagner's *Ring* was written as a battle-cry against the politics, morals and social system created by the Industrial Revolution. At least that was Bernard Shaw's interpretation in 1898.[60] Evil was the post-industrial ethos; Good the natural order of the pre-industrial world. Surely, therefore, *The Ring* must have electrified William Morris, revolutionary Socialist and master of the Icelandic saga? Alas! Morris – like Ruskin – was, by his own admission, 'a non-musical man'. He considered the theatre an unsuitable medium, anyway, for the production of elemental art: 'I wish to see Wagner uprooted.'[61] Not so Burne-Jones. For him Wagner's music was indeed the embodiment of the Dream. In 1884 he visited the Albert Hall and listened, enthralled, to Wagner's *Parsifal*: 'He made sounds that are really and truly (I assure you, and I ought to know) the very sounds that were to be heard in the Sangrael Chapel. I recognised them in a moment and knew that he had done it accurately.'[62] The autonomy – and the impossibility – of the High Victorian Dream could hardly be better expressed.

★   ★   ★   ★

In the words of William Morris, these dreamers – these Regency radicals, these Victorian visionaries – were all 'crying out "Look Back! Look Back!"'[63] John Stuart

Mill said they had 'eyes in the back of their heads'.[64] But when they did look back, peering dimly through the mists of the Middle Ages, they found very largely what they wanted to find. Some found Toryism: Burke, Cobbett, Coleridge, Southey, Disraeli, Pugin. Some found Socialism: Carlyle (in his own strange way), Ruskin, Morris, Marx. Some – like Rossetti and Burne-Jones – simply found the Middle Ages, and were content to fall in love with what they found. It is easy to mock them: bucolic Tories; Socialists in stained glass attitudes. But let no one dismiss them too lightly. We measure their dream by the humanity of its ideals, by the genius of its prophets, by the brilliance of its artefacts – lamps of beauty in a darkening world.

After 1870, the High Victorian Dream – that is, medievalism as an instrument of salvation – had begun to dwindle. By the end of the century it had become an embarrassment. The artist as saviour sinks into the artist as sybarite, the artist as entertainer. The critic is no longer a moralist. He is a magician. 'The proper aim of Art,' wrote Macmurdo's friend Selwyn Image in 1882, 'is aesthetic. It is not come among us to teach us how to be good, but to teach us how to be happy.'[65] The Goths give way to the Aesthetes. Tennyson and the Pre-Raphaelites are replaced by Oscar Wilde and Aubrey Beardsley. For Carlyle read Pater. 'This recognition,' wrote Oscar Wilde in 1882, 'of the primary importance of the sensuous element in art, this love of art for art's sake, is the point in which we of the younger school have made a departure from the teaching of Mr Ruskin – a departure definite, different and decisive.'[66] Art had become a means of personal fulfilment rather than an instrument of social salvation. By the 1870s even Burne-Jones had abandoned undiluted medievalism. 'When I think of the conceit and blindness of ten years ago,' he told G. F. Watts, 'I don't know whether most to lament that I was ever like that or that I ever woke out of such a baseless dream.'[67] By 1871 he had broken with Ruskin and Rossetti, those twin idols of his youth.[68] He still believed in art as 'the power of bringing God into the world'.[69] But he no longer felt the Middle Ages to be unique in their manifestation of that process. He had already travelled from the Middle Ages to the Renaissance. And his artistic pilgrimage was soon to move him on – and, still more, others after him – first from transcription to idealisation, and then from eclecticism to abstraction. Even the Arts and Crafts movement diluted its Puritan premises, dabbled with the philosophy of the Aesthetes and ended up as *Art Nouveau*. Aestheticism was an indulgent, autocentric aesthetic which denied the whole ethical thrust of the Gothic Revival. By separating Art and Society it paved the way – paradoxically – for the dehumanised art and architecture of today. Instead of looking backwards, art had begun to look forwards, forwards to all that Morris feared: an architectural revolution without a social revolution; forward in fact to the nightmare of the Modern Movement: an admass society housed in mass concrete.

One night in 1900, a well-known artist was sitting alone in his studio. There was a crash of footsteps on the stairs, and another artist burst in, dancing and frantically waving an evening paper. 'Ruskin's dead,' he gasped; and again, in triumph: 'Ruskin's dead! Thank God Ruskin's dead! ... Give me a cigarette.'[70] There was more to that outburst than the ordinary impatience of youth. Art – and architecture too – had turned its back on the High Victorian Dream.

Now it is time to narrow our focus a little. This book deals with many architects and many patrons. But it concentrates on four particular dreamers: A. J. B. Beresford-Hope, M.P.[3]; George Frederick Robinson, 1st Marquess of Ripon[4]; John Patrick Crichton-Stuart, 3rd Marquess of Bute[11]; and the man for whom all three acted as patron – William Burges, architect. Each was idiosyncratic to the point of eccentricity. But each falls neatly into one of our three categories of dreamer. Ripon was a Romantic Socialist. Hope and Bute were Romantic Tories. Burges was just a Romantic. It is to Burges that we must look first. For Burges is the hero of this book, the most dazzling exponent of the High Victorian Dream. Pugin conceived that dream, but never lived to see it; Rossetti and Burne-Jones painted it; Tennyson sang its glories; Ruskin and Morris formulated its philosophy; but only Burges built it.

Chapter Two

THE DREAMER

'I was brought up in the 13th century belief, and in that belief I intend to die.'
WILLIAM BURGES, 1876

Enter Georgius Oldhousen. . . . A small, bustling bachelor, plump, short-sighted and shabby; he twitches nervously as he talks, gabbling a little, with his head on one side, his tongue lolling, his eyes popping, his eye-glass swinging as he waves his arms. Georgius is a comic character in a rambling, three-decker novel, *The Ambassador Extraordinary*, published in 1879 by Professor Robert Kerr, architect, journalist and pundit. The plot of the novel is absurd, its characterisation lamentable. Still, as one reviewer noticed, 'take the story out . . . and there is really some amusement to be got out of the rest of it.'[1] In particular, there is Georgius Oldhousen. Georgius is an architect, in love with the Middle Ages. Georgius is an artist, in love with his own image. Georgius is a fool, and Georgius is a genius. Georgius is William Burges.[2]

> His profession is architecture, but architecture of a very advanced order . . . muscular . . . 13th century . . . with a *soupçon* of Transitional. . . . He is not exactly young in years, being five-and-thirty; but he is in an odd way youthful in appearance, and in manners Georgius can never grow old. His egotism is unbounded; but . . . seldom gives offence, because of the guileless exaggeration and perfect good nature which deprives it of all force. If anybody ever thinks of contending with Georgius in argument, the hopelessness of the endeavour becomes apparent in a moment, when a glance at his countenance shows how childlike are his convictions . . . [His] strong point . . . is a disdain for Common Sense. . . . His vocation is Art . . . [a] matter of Uncommon Sense.[3]

Georgius has an office decorated in the medieval style. It has painted ceilings, stained glass windows 'representing King Arthur and the Knights of the Round Table', and allegorical tapestries 'of no great pictorial merit and of doubtful delicacy, but of indisputable authenticity'.[4] Outside, in his quarter-acre of garden, Georgius dreams of building a miniature castle, complete with moat, drawbridge and bartizans:

1 William Burges as a young man: a painting
   by E.J. Poynter inside the Yatman Cabinet
   (1858).

3 Alexander J. B. Beresford-Hope, M.P.
   (1820–87): Romantic Tory. Photograph
   (1874).

2 William Burges in middle age: sketched
   from a photograph.

4 George Frederick Robinson, 1st Marquess
   of Ripon (1827–1909): Romantic Socialist.

5 Extracts from the thirteenth-century sketch-book of Wilars De Honecort, redrawn by William Burges.

'Don't I wish I had been born in the 13th century. . . . I look to the past . . . you know.'[5]

Georgius's brother, the Rev. Theophilus Oldhousen, 'is one of those excellent young men who doubt whether the Reformation was not a mistake'.

'Of all things in the world I hate things that are modern, you know'. . . .
 'Just so', says Theo. . . . 'And do you think the 16th century is ancient enough?'
 'No', says Georgius, 'I don't.'[6]

For Georgius has no fear of Popery in art.

'Ain't we all Romish? . . . Via-Median fiddlestick! There's no such thing old fellow. There are Pagan architects and Christian architects; and I'm a Christian architect.'[7]

And Georgius is never short of precedents.

'What's the use of being an archaeologist if you can't suppose this and can't believe that?'
 'But what authority, my dear boy –'
 'I can always', says Master Georgius, quietly dropping his glass, 'find an authority. . . . I hate what they call plain evidence; you might as well be a lawyer, or a policeman.'[8]

One night Georgius dines with the Ambassador, Viscount Malign, at His Excellency's Renaissance palazzo, Mount Medusa, overlooking the River Thames. As they go down to dinner, 'Master Georgius and His Excellency . . . bring up the rear; and His Excellency politely apologises to Master Georgius for having no lady to give him. Master Georgius says, with his usual frankness, it doesn't matter. . . .'[9] Our Georgius is not exactly a ladies' man. As he munches his way through the menu, he dreams of Gothicising the embassy, and obliterating all the Ambassador's 'commonplace classical things'.

'Even his footmen; by Jove! If I had four niggers like those – or Mongols, or Caffres, or whatever they are – devils if you like –'
 'Pray hush, George', says Mariana.
 'Well I will; but . . . if I had those four fellows, you know, I should dress them in something like a better costume . . . in turbans . . . and parti-coloured surcoats. . . .'
 'Why not simply as beefeaters?', says Mr Gay.
 'Too late a period', replies the architect; 'for my part I would have made that house altogether of the beginning of the 14th century. The four Africans I should look upon as captive Saracens . . . [their] legs . . . being of different colours – one

black, probably, and the other yellow, you know. Then I should have another fellow at the hall door, and I should make him a soldier, I think, with beaver, gorget, and camail, and jambières, two-handed sword, shield, and axe. . . .'

As for the house itself, that 'is easily managed', says Georgius, dropping his eyeglass; 'if the Viscount will give me the commission, I'll have it all licked into shape in six months so that no one could recognise it. At present every part of it is more disgustingly classic than another. That long gallery – of course smashing all the mirrors the very first thing – I should make the Hall, with a good piece of it cut off at one end for the Screens, and a Porch there for entrance.'

'But that would be on the lawn', says Mr Gay.

'So much the better; there ought not to be any lawn. Then I would go in for three jolly big bay windows; and the Dais would be at the further end – the dining-room end – and the Reredos for the fire in the middle of the floor, you know . . . with a louvre somehow or other over it to let out the smoke. . . . Then I should go in for a Minstrels' Gallery – there's plenty of light – over the Screens. Then the present drawing room would be the kitchen . . . and the dining room the Chamber, where the owner and his particular friends the ladies and gentlemen would sleep – of course on the floor – leaving the hall, you know, for the commoner guests and servants. By Jove! what a fine thing I should make it! Magnificent! And then I should go in for doing away with all that rubbish of a cortile, you know, and staircase, and throw the place open to the sky, with very likely the well in the middle – no pumps, you know, and water laid on, and that nonsense.'

'It would be a radical change', says Mr Gay, 'to say the least of it.'

'That's what we want, if any rich man would have the spirit to do such a thing. Then the upper storey I should very likely do away with altogether, and go in for new roofs of different heights. . . . The basement I should simply fill up.'

'The occupants of such a house', says Mariana, 'ought to be costumed *en suite*, George.'

'Of course', says Georgius, refixing his glass, 'I take that for granted. Have a wardrobe and dressing-rooms at the gate. People drive up; go into the lodge; take off their modern things and put on ancient; and then drive on to the house; and change again on leaving. . . . I'll try it [at home] with my clerks. I know my clients would like it immensely, or they wouldn't be coming to me. . . .'[10]

TRAINING

William Burges was born in London on 2 December 1827, the eldest son of Alfred Burges, a marine engineer. He grew up in a world of plans and projects, cross-sections, calculations and specifications: the son of an engineer in the heroic age of British engineering. The family as a whole were much involved in building. William's younger brother, Alfred Edward, trained briefly as an architect.[11] His sister Mary married one of the better architects of the Gothic Revival, Richard Popplewell Pullan. His niece Elizabeth married George Ormiston, Chief Engineer to the Bombay Harbour Authority. And Mary's godfather, John Leschallas – a close family friend and benefactor – was also one of the biggest building contractors in London.[12]

With James Walker (1781–1862), second President of the Institution of Civil Engineers, Alfred Burges formed one of the most successful engineering partnerships of the nineteenth century. Harbours, dockyards, fortifications, canals, embankments, bridges, breakwaters, lighthouses – these were the stock-in-trade of Messrs. Walker and Burges, government engineers. They were works which employed thousands and cost millions. The Smalls Lighthouse, the Ayre Point Lighthouse;[13] work at Westminster Bridge[14] and Blackfriars Bridge;[15] the approaches at Yarmouth[16] and Maplin;[17] harbours at Belfast,[18] Dover,[19] Harwich,[20] Alderney,[21] Jersey,[22] and Portland[23] – these were among their best-known commissions. But the work for which they became most famous was the Westminster Embankment, the foundation in effect for no less a building than the new Houses of Parliament.[24] It was there, perhaps, in the mid-1840s, that young Billy Burges fell under the spell of the ultimate Goth, A. W. N. Pugin. Alfred Burges presented his son with a copy of Pugin's *Contrasts* on his fourteenth birthday.[25] Father and son seem always to have been fairly close: Burges stayed mostly in the family house until his late twenties, first in York Road, Lambeth and then in Dartmouth Row, Blackheath. Alfred Burges was a rich man: he died worth £113,000, mostly in railway stock.[26] It was he who made possible his son's aesthetic lifestyle. And in 1865 it was probably Alfred Burges who determined the whole course of his son's later career. As engineer to the Bute Docks at Cardiff, he was in a position to introduce his son to the greatest patron in the history of the Gothic Revival, the 3rd Marquess of Bute.[27]

Alfred Burges sent his eldest son to school at King's College, London, in 1839.[28] In those days King's College School occupied the basement storeys of Sir Robert Smirke's bleak Neo-Classical building next to Somerset House in the Strand. It turned out to be a good choice. One of young Burges's contemporaries was Dante Gabriel Rossetti; another was William Michael Rossetti; and all three boys may have been taught to draw by no less an art-master than John Sell Cotman. As a schoolboy Burges was already 'excessively short-sighted' with 'a chubby face like a cherub on a tombstone'.[29] In 1843 he moved upstairs to the College proper.[30] So far he had studied Latin, Greek, German and French – though his favourite reading as a child was of a lighter kind, *Pickwick Papers* or *Nicholas Nickleby*.[31] Now he worked at General Literature and Science, and for the first time tackled the science of construction on an academic basis. But after less than one year, studying for a King's College Associateship, he left university to take up articles in the office of Edward Blore.[32] Later on he was to become an Honorary Fellow of his college.[33] But he never executed that reconstruction of the College Chapel of which he once had high hopes.[34] Behind him he left instead the customary schoolboy legacy: a carving of his own name. In Burges's case, however, we are assured that the letters were powerfully cut, and unusually bold.[35]

Burges was articled to Blore late in 1844 at the age of sixteen. By that date Blore had been 'Special Architect' to both William IV and Queen Victoria, and there was scarcely a more prestigious name in the profession.[36] Within months Burges was a member of the Ecclesiological Society.[37] At the age of seventeen he was already mixing with the vanguard of the Gothic Revival. At Blore's he was given responsibility for several minor jobs: lodges in Windsor Great Park (1845);[38] fittings at Moreton Hall, Cheshire (1845)[39] and Thicket Priory, Yorkshire (1846);[40] details in Glasgow Cathedral (1846)[41] and – *mirabile dictu* – some decorative work in Buckingham Palace (1848).[42] These were all fragmentary commissions, sweepings from the great man's drawing board. At the same time young Burges was also involved in one building of rather more importance: Lambeth Palace; and one structure of transcendent significance for any budding Goth: Westminster Abbey. At Lambeth he took part in work on the Archbishop's private chapel (1846).[43] Thirty years later he was to return to Lambeth as architect of a major restoration. But in 1846 he was still practically unknown. At Westminster, however, he was rather more in the public eye. Blore had been Surveyor of Westminster Abbey since 1827, and was now on the brink of retirement. As his assistant, Burges was in a strong position. No young medievalist could have chosen a better apprenticeship: seventeen years old, and working at Westminster Abbey – 'that divine citadel', as Burne-Jones called it; 'that beautiful heaven'.[44] With Blore, Burges shared the excitement of – and the credit for – one of the most important Gothic discoveries of the century: the uncovering of the famous thirteenth-century retable.[45] Years later, recalling that discovery in a book about the Abbey edited by Blore's successor, Gilbert Scott, Burges reminded the next generation that – for those who cared to look – the Abbey constituted a veritable architectural Bible.

Throughout his life he respected Blore as a good scholar and a beautiful draughtsman. But he also reacted against Blore's essentially pictorial approach. And he came to scorn Blore's limited archaeology.[46]

As an articled pupil, Burges pored over books by John Carter and A. W. Pugin. Carter's crude, hand-tinted copper engravings of late medieval antiquities would later make him squirm. And even then the dedication to Horace Walpole must have conjured up the ghost of Batty Langley. But no adolescent Goth could possibly resist those fevered frontispieces: cavernous cathedrals thronged with shadowy figures, praying in the Age of Faith; brawling in the Age of Reformation. And any budding archaeologist would thrill to vignettes of sculpture and carving, and folio plates of painted glass.[47] Pugin was a more serious matter. At least one of the master's works –

Timber Houses of the 15th and 16th centuries – was illuminated in gold by the young Burges and indexed in Gothic script.[48] In 1852 he served on the Pugin Memorial Committee. And as late as 1867–8 we find him presenting copies of Pugin's *Gothic Furniture* (1810; 1825–7) to the R.I.B.A. Library.[49]

Blore retired from general practice in 1849, and Burges entered the office of Matthew Digby Wyatt as an 'improver'.[50] At that time Wyatt was best known as an authority on geometrical mosaic.[51] And it was probably this interest in the decorative arts of the Middle Ages which drew Burges to him in the first place. In that year, however, Wyatt began a second career which catapulted him into government circles: he became an expert in the application of fine art to industry. With Owen Jones and Henry Cole he set out to encourage the production of good manufactured art for public use; to capitalise aesthetics and – unlike Pugin, Ruskin and Morris – to tame the machine in pursuit of art.[52] Under Prince Albert's aegis, Wyatt was responsible first for a report on the Paris Exhibition of 1849,[53] then for an exploratory enquiry into the willingness of British manufacturers to support similar exhibitions in this country,[54] and finally for the vast secretarial and administrative burdens of the 1851 Exhibition.[55] That was the turning point in his career. A gold medal from Prince Albert and a £1,000 prize; collaboration with Brunel at Paddington Station, with Owen Jones at the Crystal Palace, Sydenham, and with Gilbert Scott at the India Office, Whitehall; the Secretaryship of the R.I.B.A.; the first Slade Professorship at Cambridge; a Knighthood and the R.I.B.A. Gold Medal. With the triumph of the Crystal Palace show, Wyatt became the knighted laureate of industrial art. Burdened with honours and broken by overwork, he died at the age of fifty-seven in 1877.[56]

Burges's part in Wyatt's apotheosis was limited to supplementary design and historical research. There were, no doubt, minor works to do: a memorial window to William Huskisson in Chichester Cathedral, for instance.[57] But the big job was the 1851 Exhibition. Burges probably helped Wyatt assess competition entries for the exhibition buildings, and to prepare alternative schemes prior to the production of 'Paxton's Palace'.[58] He certainly acted as Wyatt's research assistant in the production of *Metal Work and its Artistic Design* (1852)[59] and *The Industrial Arts of the Nineteenth Century* (2 vols. 1853–4).[60] The first of these books contains explanatory articles on the technology of metal as well as an historical survey of the subject, copiously illustrated with meticulous drawings. Burges was responsible for the article on Damascening as well as for more than forty vignettes of medieval ironwork ranging from door-handles in Nuremburg, Brussels and Brescia to jewelled treasures in the cathedrals of Cologne and Mayence. The second book was rather more lavish and much more popular in its appeal. In effect, it constituted a pictorial record of the Great Exhibition. Lavish chromolithographs and an expansive text hymned the dubious beauties of scores of exhibits. Burges contributed fourteen articles ranging over furniture, stained-glass, enamels, damascening and metalwork. He does not hesitate to criticise the debased state of the applied arts in many fields. Even today it is difficult to turn the pages of Wyatt's volumes – and of the mammoth official 1851 Catalogue – without an occasional frisson: by any reasonable standard, many of the objects exhibited are aesthetically indefensible. A comparison, for instance, between Wyatt's 1851 volumes and J. B. Waring's parallel text for 1862[61] suggests major improvements in several fields – fields in which Burges had by then become something of a leader.

Burges's training with Matthew Digby Wyatt brought him painfully into contact with some of the grosser productions of early Victorian industrial art: the Birmingham Exhibition of 1849, for example;[62] or parts of the 1854 rooms at the Sydenham Crystal Palace.[63] Reform of the industrial arts became one of the principal aims of Burges's aesthetic career. His Royal Society of Arts Cantor Lectures, *Art and Industry* (1865), carried Wyatt's campaign to a new generation.

In the long run, therefore, Digby Wyatt's influence set Burges on a path which shaped much of his career: he was to play a key role in the High Victorian renaissance of the applied arts. His contact with Wyatt had broadened his eclectic range and – to a lesser extent – fortified his confidence in the machine. Wyatt had attacked Ruskin for his reactionary aesthetics:

> Instead of boldly recognising the tendencies of the age, which are inevitable . . . instead of considering the means of improving those tendencies, [he takes refuge in the Middle Ages]. Our course in this 19th century may be hateful . . . but as it *is* our course, wise men should recognise the fact.

According to Wyatt, Ruskin's refusal to do so prevented his arriving at any 'consistent theory of mechanical repetition as applied to art', and doomed him to a 'very lop-sided view of railways and railway-architecture'. Maybe. But for all his optimism, Wyatt himself had only the haziest vision of the future:

> What future glories may be in reserve, when England has systematised a scale of form and proportion, and a vocabulary of its own in which to speak to the world the language of its power . . . we may trust ourselves to dream, but we dare not predict.[64]

Burges was to prove equally vague. But for the time being his dreams were concentrated not on the problems of industrial design in the future, but on the artistic glories of the past.

In the early 1850s Burges was known less as an architect than as an archaeologist. The work of his which caused most stir in 1852 was a reconstruction of the Shrine of St Edward the Confessor, complete with all the apparatus of medieval Catholicism.[65] At this stage he was also less well known as a designer of decorative art than as a fantasist of untapped talent, an architect in embryo.

Some of these private fantasies have been recorded by George Aitchison:

He would first be an architect, and build himself a specimen of every ordinary human construction except a cathedral; he would amass enormous wealth, and spend some of it in realising his views in his own house; he would marry; he would ... become a Member of Parliament, and correct some of the abuses of society; he would then go into the church, become a bishop, and, with his wealth, build a perfect cathedral of the most costly materials, adorned with the most perfect specimens of all the subsidary arts; and, when this was done, he would end his days as a monk or a hermit.[66]

Predictable enough, in a generation nourished on Pugin and Walter Scott. What distinguished Burges's visions was their richness and completeness. 'No Arab,' Aitchison records, 'ever had more gorgeous visions than Burges.' The house of his dreams

was to be of perfect Medieval pattern, full of quaint carvings, and blazing with colour, hung with costly stuffs embroidered in gold, and lighted by silver lattices whose storied panes were of cut gems. He was to have jewelled chalices to drink from, and aloe and sandal wood to burn.[67]

Again, predictable enough. But in Burges's case most of those dreams came true, in the astonishing house he eventually built for himself in Kensington. Meanwhile, Digby Wyatt had christened him 'Troy'.[68] And it was on visions of 'Troy Town' – the fantastic medieval city of dreams – that Billy Burges first cut his teeth as a budding Corbusier of Gothicism.[69]

While working with Wyatt, Burges had also formed an informal partnership with a rather more congenial spirit: Henry Clutton. Clutton had joined Blore's office in 1834. By 1851 he was an established architect, with an expanding reputation for progressive Gothic. It was in that year that Burges joined him,[70] first as an assistant and then as a partner. And in that shifting relationship lay the seeds of trouble. Initially Burges seems to have been employed on research, decoration and typography. With Clutton he travelled in France in the year of the Great Exhibition, making sketches for Clutton's book on *The Domestic Architecture of France*.[71] Burges continued work on these drawings in 1852, and the volume appeared in 1853.[72] More interestingly, Burges joined Clutton in restoring the Chapter House at Salisbury Cathedral (1854–6), in designing churches at Dunstall, Staffs. (1851–3)[73] and Hatherop, Glos. (1853–5),[74] and in fitting up Ruthin Castle, Denbighshire (1851–6) and Breamore House, Hants. (1855–6).[75] He may also have worked on Clutton's St John, Limehouse (1853). These joint exercises set precedents for a full-scale partnership: the competition for Lille Cathedral in 1855. Together they visited Lille;[76] together they prepared a set of plans of amazing elaboration; together they fooled the judges by submitting their English drawings in French packing-cases. The result was a triumph. But they never worked together again. In Burges's diary for 1856 appears a short entry, enigmatic but final: 'Row with Clutton. May 13.'[77]

Now Clutton was a nephew of Cardinal Manning. Manning became a Roman Catholic in 1851, and Clutton followed suit in 1857.[78] Henceforward he worked exclusively for Catholic patrons. Was the argument with Burges about religion? Or – more likely – did Burges simply feel that he had now outgrown a dependent relationship? Perhaps the partnership with Clutton was beginning to prove unequal, more unequal – and less stable – than those of Pugin and Barry or Nesfield and Norman Shaw. Either way, the time had come to set up on his own. Within weeks of his break with Clutton, Burges moved into his own office at 15 Buckingham St, Strand.[79] Thanks to his father, he had sufficient income to risk independent practice.[80] He had means, he had talent. He had learnt his trade, and he had travelled.

TRAVELLING

Burges regarded travel as essential for any young architect. 'All architects should travel,' he believed, 'but more especially the art-architect; to him it is absolutely necessary to see how various art problems have been resolved in different ages by different men.' Hence the value of the R.I.B.A.'s Soane Medallion and Pugin Studentship: poor young architects must travel too. 'I should recommend staying long in one place, and mastering thoroughly one or two things; anybody with money can rush from town to town. ...'[81] Burges had money, and no need to rush.

For Pugin's generation, architectural travel had mostly meant the medieval churches of England. Pugin had dreamt of 'Durham the destination of some; Lincolnshire's steepled fens for others; Northamptonshire's and Yorkshire's venerable piles; Suffolk and Norfolk coasts; Oxford, Devon, and Warwick – each county should indeed be a school, for each is a school where those who run may read, and where volumes of art lie open to all enquirers.'[82] The next generation looked further afield; and Burges looked further than any: to France and Belgium, to Germany, Austria and Switzerland, to Spain and Portugal, to Italy, Sicily and Greece, to Turkey, to Egypt, to Scandinavia, to Japan.

Burges had been sketching in Sussex in 1845, in Lincolnshire in 1846, in Norfolk in 1847.[83] In 1848 he spent three months in Ely – that was where he first met Gilbert Scott[84] – and he returned in 1852 to measure Prior Crauden's Chapel with C. Bruce Allen.[85] In 1849 he went abroad for the first time at the age of twenty-one. Appropriately, his first trip was to Normandy and Paris.[86] Next year he went a little further, to Belgium and Germany.[87] By 1851 he was working with Clutton in Paris, Beaune and Troyes.[88] In 1852 he made only a brief trip to Paris.[89] But early in 1853 he was back in France, visiting Bourges, Nevers, Blois, Amboise, Orleans, Paris and Lille.[90] These expeditions were no more than an *hors d'oeuvre*, however, for what Burges rightly called his 'Long Journey'. After all, he had only scratched the surface of French Gothic, and he had yet to visit Italy.

Burges set out on his Long Journey on 13 April 1853,[91] having first taken a crash course in Italian.[92] He travelled by way of Dieppe and Rouen to Paris, stopping *en route* at Malines, Ecouis, Les Andelys and Mantes. Then came one of the turning points in his life. In quick succession he visited Beauvais, Amiens, Noyon and Châlons-sur-Marne. He had discovered the glories of Early French. His companion on this part of the journey was Frederick Warren, and together – perched precariously on scaffolds – they measured and drew the mighty apse of Beauvais. Over the years Burges returned again and again to Beauvais, generally staying there with his friend Delaherche. He visited this particular shrine on no less than eleven occasions, as against four each for Rouen and Amiens, and two each for Châlons, Tours and Chartres.[93] Other triumphs of Early French he visited in years to come, and admired: Laon, Soissons, Etampes, Coutances, Bayeux, Nesle, Narbonne, Caen, Rheims, St Quentin, Saumur. And he was to travel in Southern France too, notably to Avignon, Bordeaux, Carcassonne, Perigueux, Cannes, Arles and Nîmes. But there was never anything to match Beauvais, and nothing like that first visit at the age of twenty-five.[94]

From Paris Burges moved South in the Autumn of 1853, to Lyons, Avignon and Marseilles, where he took ship for Italy. After stopping at Genoa and Leghorn, he reached Rome on 10 November. To a young Goth like Burges, Rome was an ordeal rather than a pleasure. He disliked the High Renaissance, and he loathed Baroque. His notebook for 1854 is endorsed:

> This book belongs to an architect
> Who after a sojourn in Rome
> Finding nought to improve his mind
> Determined on going home
> Thinking St Peter's quite a sell
> And Apollo Belvedere as well.[95]

Rome may not have been all that Burges hoped for – though he did design to visit it again, in 1873, 1877 and 1879.[96] In 1853–4 it was at least a useful place to meet other artists – E. J. Poynter for instance[97] – or to see Overbeck's studio.[98] And it made a good Winter base, a stepping off point for explorations further South. In the spring of 1854, therefore, Burges set out for Naples and thence set sail for Sicily. Sicily made a powerful impression on him, with its burning sun and blinding light, its hillsides shrouded in blue-grey mist. There he saw for the first time the shimmering vaults of Palermo, and the glittering mosaics of Monreale. The rest of his life would be devoted to colour. Then back he went to Naples, where he 'went in costume to the Cervara';[99] to Capri and Salerno; to the frescoes of Pompeii and the primeval grandeur of Paestum. Then Rome again: time for trips to Frascati and Ostia, Fusano and Tivoli, before deciding to head North.

It was in Rome, in the Winter of 1853, that Burges first met Aitchison: they were competitors for the same horse on a trip from the Porta del Popolo to the walls of ancient Veii and the rock-cut tomb of the Lucumo. At that time Burges was helping Leighton with the details of his 'Procession of Cimabue's Madonna'.[1] And it was at Leighton's suggestion that the two young architects travelled together to Assisi. There, staying in a private house at 1/6d. per day, in the Summer of 1854, Burges suffered agonies of indigestion from 'a continued diet of pigeons stuffed with rosemary'.[2] Undeterred, he continued to read Dante[3] and Sacchetti, and to study the painted decorations in the chapels of St Francis. Then on they went, taking in Foligno, Cortona, Arezzo, Perugia and Florence, Siena, Pisa and Pistoia. Their plan was first to work out an itinerary from Murray's Handbook, then to take a bird's-eye view of each town from its highest point, and finally to note and measure its buildings, monuments and decorations.

Burges had come to Italy not to see Gothic church architecture – English and French ecclesiastical Gothic were infinitely preferable – but to study secular buildings and medieval decorative work: mosaic, painting and metalwork. At Perugia he worked on the Sala del Cambio; at Siena on the Palazzo Tolomei – with visits to San Gimignano della bella Torre and Boccaccio's house at Certaldo; at Pisa he took in the Campo Santo; at Pistoia the Palazzo della Communità and that wondrous altar frontal of enamel and silver known as the Paliotto; at Florence, among many other things, the battlements of the Palazzo Vecchio and the staircase of the Bargello. In Florence Burges was taken ill again: he spent his convalescence designing the binding studded with marble butterflies which later adorned his illuminated copy of Tennyson.[4] Worse sickness threatened: Tuscany was riddled with cholera. So the two young architects thought it wise not to go to Venice, and wiser still to quit Italy altogether. From Leghorn they took ship to Marseilles.

Back in France, Burges's prohibition on ecclesiastical Gothic was lifted. Besides the timber hospital roof at Beaune and the Hôtel Chambellan in Dijon, he measured the sculptured porches at Sens and at Notre Dame in Dijon, as well as part of the cathedral at Troyes, before going on to Châlons-sur-Marne, and thence returning to London in November 1854. He had been abroad nearly twenty months. Years later Aitchison recalled how, on tour, they had planned to 'do no work on fête days, but always take a stroll in the country'. Alas, 'I do not think we ever did; for, before we even reached the suburbs, Burges always espied a by-street that promised to contain some archaeological treasure'.[5]

On his return Burges moved into lodgings at York Buildings in the artistic quarter of the Adelphi.[6] But he was soon away again: 1855–6 was the hectic year in which he entered the Lille competition. During this period Burges spent a good deal of time with Clutton, studying Early French prototypes in Paris, Beauvais, Senlis, Chartres and Rouen.[7] Equally hectic was 1856–7, the year of the competition for a Crimean Memorial Church in Constantinople. This time Burges went to North Italy with

Poynter, gathering materials for a different sort of style: a progressive development of Southern Gothic. His itinerary took him to Turin, Vercelli, Novaro, Milan, Monza, Como, Brescia, Verona, Venice, Padua and Genoa. These were places he would visit again in 1860–61,[8] 1873[9] and 1879.[10] Florence too: he stayed there six weeks with Barber and Smallfield in 1861;[11] and Mantua, Parma, Bologna and Pavia. On these later visits he also had particular reasons for going: the Florence Exhibition of 1862; the Naples town-planning scheme (1865);[12] the Florence Cathedral competition (1863); the commission to redecorate St Paul's Cathedral (1873). Burges's travels were not the random peregrinations of a dilettante enthusiast. They were calculated raids on the architectural treasures of a whole sub-continent. That was certainly the case in 1856–7. He needed precedents for the Crimea Memorial Church, and he found them[13] And then, having won that competition, he celebrated by visiting Constantinople itself.

So far Burges's travels had been part of his own education. In Padua and Venice, however, he felt stirred to publish. His visit to Padua resulted in a detailed article on the Ragione. His visit to Venice produced a similar piece on the capitals of the Ducal Palace. On his return in 1856 Burges found that Didron, the greatest of French iconographers, had already prepared memoranda on the Ducal Palace. The two authors resolved, therefore, on joint publication. The result, which appeared in French in 1857, was not entirely happy: they disagreed about chronology.[14] Controversy began to simmer. By then, however, Burges was far away, in Turkey and Greece.

Turkish art and architecture proved to be crucial in the formation of Burges's personal style. Its position as a link between the Eastern and Western traditions made it irresistible to his eclectic appetites. He arrived in Constantinople in 1857 expecting the dreaming minarets of Grelot's engravings,[15] and the fierce warriors portrayed by Vercellio.[16] In that he was disappointed. Fire had destroyed many buildings. Western fashions – 'the Lady Wortley Montagu style', for instance, or 'that indescribable rendering of the Renaissance, so popular in France under the régime of Louis Philippe' – had corrupted native traditions. Even so, the debased architecture of 16th–18th century Constantinople seemed 'infinitely better than any either in Paris or in London'.[17] And individual mosques were still magnificent. Particular houses were still occasionally decked out in characteristic gold and red. Public fountains – that at Tophana, for instance, or the formidable fountain of Ahmet II, outside the Seraglio – still dispensed water from coloured stone and gilded marble. And nearby, in Pera and Galata, were medieval suburbs, still intact.

Galata turned out to be 'an almost perfect city of the middle ages. . . . What Oxford is to England, Nuremberg to Germany, or Assisi to Italy, Galata is to the East'. From ancient stone walls to pierced iron doorknockers, Galata delighted his medieval eye. So did the plain merchants' houses, and the Palazzo del Podesta, begun in 1316. Burges was indeed fortunate: much of Pera was destroyed by fire, soon after his visit, in 1871. But in 1857 – despite an earlier fire in 1831 – he was still able to examine Turkish medieval vernacular architecture *in situ*. 'Nothing can be more effective, but at the same time more severe', he noted; for 'with the exception of the corbels ... many of which are simply rounded ... not ... a single yard of moulding could be found in the whole of them'. And as for the great mosques, in the ancient centre of the city, their architectural lessons were obvious. Firstly, 'the importance of massing ornament in certain places ... such as caps and cornices [instead of distributing it] over the whole surface ... covering the whole with reedy mouldings and fizzy crochets, and still more fizzy pinnacles ... thereby [cutting] ... up all breadth of effect'. And secondly, 'that where a column is wanted to do real work it should be massive, and not like a tobacco-pipe, and that this column will not look worse if it be diminished [in the classical way], or if its capital be connected with that of its neighbour with a tie rod'. 'Very thick walls to keep out the heat, and tie rods to bind them together in case of earthquake [rather than buttresses – 'very often fatal to all breadth of effect'], are the just requisites of building well in a very hot climate.'[18] Such factors Burges certainly bore in mind when designing the Crimea Memorial Church, Brisbane Cathedral, and the Bombay School of Art.

Burges found Santa Sophia spoilt by the low trajectory of its mighty dome. He preferred the mosque of Suleiman the Magnificent, its soaring dome positively 'eating up the space' at its centre. But there was no denying the splendour of marble at Santa Sophia, or its great pavement of *opus alexandrinum*, or the mosaics, once four acres of them, glittering dully on a ground of gold. Burges would have preferred those mosaics to spread downwards, from the vaulting to the walls, as at Monreale and Palermo. Still, he had no objection to the walls as they were, opulently faced with marble sheeting. Uncooperative Turks prevented him from making measured drawings in the Summer of 1857. So he was forced to rely for details on Fossati[19] and Saltzenberg.[20] But here and elsewhere in Constantinople he saw more than enough to confirm his admiration for Byzantine and Turkish art. The Iznik tiles of the tomb of Sultan Selim II, for instance; the glittering stained glass of the Suleimanyeh; or the mosque of Bayazid II. Of this latter group of buildings, he wrote:

> The court or harem, with its porphyry and verd antique columns, its incrustations of marble, its fountain, its trees supported by lattices covered by vines and, above all, the large flocks of pigeons fed by the alms of the faithful (for the Mohammedans are extremely humane to all animals except man), make one of the most delightful scenes I have ever witnessed. The only thing at all approaching it is the West front of St Mark's, at Venice: but there we are painfully impressed by the want of verdure; here, on the contrary, we have all – the architecture, the coloured marble, the murmur of the fountain, the trees and pigeons, besides the bright costume of the women.[21]

Did Burges manage to gain access to the labyrinthine corridors of the Harem in

Topkapi Saray? Did he peer through the shimmering sub-aqueous light in the tiled Salon of Murat II? Presumably not. Even so, the great mosques were surely enough: the Blue Mosque, with its multiple domes and semi-domes, a cascade of grey and gold; the rich carving and richer inlay, mosaics and tiles – richest of all – around the glorious Sehzade; the woodwork inside the Suleimanyeh, inlaid with ivory and mother of pearl; the exquisite mosaics and frescoes of St Saviour in Chora, or Kariye Camii to give it its vernacular name. It was the economy, 'breadth' and 'massiveness' of these great mosques which Burges admired above all. Even the complexity of the stained glass windows in the mosque of Suleiman the Magnificent – masterpieces by that incomparable glazier Ibrahim the Drunkard – could be explained in geometrical terms.[22] 'Those who have seen these windows', he added, 'will confess that Aladdin's windows of jewels are no fable, but simply an exaggeration.'

Burges found the lighting of the mosques in Constantinople ingenious and beautiful: in the words of the Koran, 'God is the light of the heavens and of the earth'. 'Innumerable small gas lamps' were hung from iron bars arranged in geometrical shapes and suspended from wire chains. 'They are very numerous and hung very low indeed', he noted; so 'the whole effect must be that of walking under a sea of light. I am afraid in our modern buildings we do not light up quite enough, and when we do, it is with flaring masses of gas which blind the spectator.'[23]

Perhaps Burges enjoyed a Turkish bath, sweating silently on the belly-stone of the eighteenth-century Cagaloglu Hamami; gazing domewards through the misty vapours, like some dream sultan in an undersea palace.[24] Later on he certainly took Turkish baths in London. And was it, perhaps, in Constantinople that Burges first tasted opium?

On the way to Constantinople, and again on the way back, Burges visited Athens.[25] Such a visit was not only rare for a High Victorian Goth, it was almost unique. But then his aesthetic sympathies were so much broader than those of his contemporaries. Burges had no objection at all to Greek art. It was Neo-Classicism he despised: 'If . . . "Classic" . . . means Greek, or even Roman . . . I would take off my hat to it – although even the best Roman is bad enough. But what is ordinarily meant by "Classic" is the vilest Renaissance of George III's time.'[26] Burges regarded the whole Neo-Classic movement as an aesthetic aberration, a compound of mandarin archaeology and misdirected romance. But Greek art he never despised. He admired its coins, its jewellery and its sculpture intensely. 'The Parthenon', he thought, 'must have been superior to the West end of any Medieval cathedral.'[27] Years later he would recommend all students to 'go to Athens, and see Greek art *in situ*, for a knowledge of Greek art will be [an architect's] sheet anchor during his artistic life. He will be saved many an error in composition if he only asks himself, "What would a Greek have said to this?"'[28] A knowledge of Greek art, he believed, would have prevented several of his contemporaries from degenerating into the illiteracy of the Queen Anne Revival.[29] Unlike many Goths – Gilbert Scott for one[30] – Burges had actually seen the wonders of the Acropolis. And, like his friends Godwin and Seddon, he saw in Greek art and in Early French Gothic a fundamental identity of spirit.[31] The point to remember was that the Middle Ages had absorbed the antique. The nineteenth century must assimilate both: 'Let us do what they did in the Middle Ages, and not neglect antiquity, but press it into our service.'[32]

Such catholicity was too much for most Victorian Goths. They found his later interest in Switzerland and Spain easier to swallow. When Burges visited Switzerland with Frederick Smallfield in 1861,[33] and Somers Clarke in 1869,[34] he was following a path pursued by others, notably Street and Pullan.[35] When he visited Spain with Lord Bute in 1874,[36] he had no need to take up its archaeology: Street had been there twenty years before.[37] To a certain extent this was also true of Burges's enthusiasm for Eastern art.

The magic of the Orient was certainly part of the High Victorian Dream. Lethaby summed it up in a memorable passage:

> Caliphs and Emirs, Mahomet, Arabs, Turks and Saracens 'who had nothing white but their teeth'; Spain, Africa, Egypt, Persia; Cordova, Toledo, Seville, Palermo, Babylon, and Alexandria with its harbour and ships; silk from Alexandria, gold of Arabia, embroideries, 'olifants' and ivory chairs, helmets and swords ornamented with carbuncles, saddles covered with gold and gems, painted shields, bright gonfalons, camels and lions.[38]

It was a land vicariously familiar to Victorian Romantics, the troubadour territory of the *Chanson de Roland*. And unlike the ancient world or the dark ages, it still existed, if only in reflected form. Classicists could walk the streets of Herculaneum or Pompeii. But for the medievalist that concrete experience, that actualised 'dream was far more difficult to attain. It is true', Burges admitted, 'that we have the literature, the costume, and to a certain extent the buildings; but there is no Pompeii to give us an insight into the domestic life; . . . our only resource [therefore] is to study Eastern nations who, less changeable than those of the West, still keep up the manners and costumes of the time of the Crusades'.[39] Hence his interest in Constantinople, and also in Japan.

Byzantine and Turkish influences in West European Gothic always intrigued him. In 1856 he presented the Archaeological Institute with drawings of a thirteenth-century mitre preserved in the public museum at Beauvais. This rare object, made of linen damask with orphreys embroidered with fleurs de lys, had survived the holocaust of 1793 by sheer accident: it had been nailed to the top of a wooden press in the cathedral sacristy. Its background pattern – formalised birds and foliage – was believed by Burges to be founded upon the traditions of Byzantine art, popularised throughout Europe by Mahometan weavers who had been transported from Greece to Sicily by the Norman Kings.[40] Such decorative survivals corresponded, he found, to the formalised Arabic inscriptions on vestments found in a twelfth-century Bishop's tomb opened at Bayonne in 1853 and later placed in the Hôtel de Cluny at Paris.[41] Europe at that date had been supplied with 'Saracenic' fabrics of gold and silk from the East, via Jerusalem and Constantinople. Thus the twelfth-century vestments found in the tomb of Henry VI of Sicily, in Palermo Cathedral, were strikingly oriental – imitations, perhaps, of Damascus or Baghdad. And the designs of the animals in particular – perhaps the lions, antelopes and peacocks referred to in the inventory of the Capella Reale for 1309 – resembled an even more bizarre example: the ivory hunting horn preserved in the Treasury at Aix-la-Chapelle, said to have been given by Haroun-al-Raschid to the Emperor Charlemagne.[42] Again, there were Imperial Coronation robes, once in Nuremburg and later in Vienna, which had an entirely Eastern flavour: the cope even boasted a Cufic inscription announcing its date (1133) and place of manufacture (Palermo).[43]

Such abstruse discoveries emphasise not only the breadth of young Burges's interests, but also the depth of his research. And it was scholarship with a purpose.

Burges never visited Egypt. But the applied art of Islamic Cairo, derived at second hand from archaeological books, became a key ingredient in his own decorative style. Similarly he never visited the Holy Land or Japan. But the arts of Tokyo and Jerusalem exercised a powerful if vicarious influence on his work. It was the same, incidentally, with Norway. Unlike Morris, Burges never visited Scandinavia. But he was certainly intrigued by Norwegian vernacular timberwork.

Burges thought the Church of the Holy Sepulchre in Jerusalem peculiarly fascinating. There he discovered mosaics which rivalled those of the Capella Reale at Palermo or the Cathedral at Monreale. More important, he also found there a model of twelfth and thirteenth-century art by imported French workmen, showing the modern architect 'how to adapt the most severe architecture to the necessities of a burning climate, and to a country where the almost total want of wood entailed the necessity of flat roofs. Had we followed their example of sound good sense,' Burges noted, 'in the works required in our Colonies and in India, we should never have seen such a monstrosity as [R.C. Carpenter's] Calcutta Cathedral, to say nothing of sundry Lincolnshire churches with their large windows and high roofs transplanted to the burning climate of India.'[44] Such lessons were not lost on him when he had himself to design buildings for tropical zones.

Two of Burges's Cambridge friends – the Rev. George Williams and Professor Robert Willis – had already tackled the architectural problems of the Church of the Holy Sepulchre.[45] So had the redoubtable James Fergusson. So had a French archaeologist, the Comte de Vogué. Burges, therefore, had little original comment to make. What he could do was to protest at the building's present state: 'encased' by a Greek architect in 1808 'in his own abominable architecture'; and to put about the idea that some sort of a replica might be created in England: 'Why should we not – instead of doing the regulation long choir and narrow nave, timber roofs, with the consequent pinnacles, panels, and tracery – for once make a copy, or rather a restoration (for it comes to this) of that edifice for which our ancestors were content to leave all, and often to die on the sands of Palestine?'[46] Of course it remained a dream, like the round chapel of the Holy Grail in German mythology. Burges had to rest content with a miniature replica, placed in the pious hands of C. E. Lefroy at Fleet church, Hampshire.[98]

Burges's feeling for oriental art was based partly on its obvious exoticism, partly on its retention of medieval techniques. In 1862 he visited the Japanese Court at the International Exhibition, and was amazed:

> If the visitor wishes to realize the real Middle Ages, he must visit the Japanese Court, for at the present day the arts of the Middle Ages have deserted Europe, and are only to be found in the East. Here in England we can get medieval objects manufactured for us with pain and difficulty, but in Egypt, Syria, and in Japan you can buy them in the bazaars. Even at Constantinople we have seen damascened work, translucid champlevé, and painted enamels all placed side by side in the shop, and all modern. But in the Japanese Court we see still rarer articles; there are cases filled with the most wonderful little groups of men and animals carved in ivory ... [and] bronzes, most marvellously cast and of different colours.

And then there was India. In the same show India boasted intricate mail and exquisite gold filigree:

> Egypt and India also exhibit the most beautiful stuffs woven with gold thread, some of the *kinkhab* of the latter country strongly reminding us, by the fineness of the work and the comparative smallness of the pattern, of those few tissues of the twelfth and thirteenth centuries which have been rescued from the shrines of the saints or the sepulchres of the rich. Turkey has some few ornaments in silver filigree, but her Oriental civilisation is evidently dying out. It is much to be regretted, however, that there is no Persian department, for, with the exception of the Japanese, they of all nations have most preserved the medieval feeling.

But 1862 was Japan's moment. Japanese mail, Japanese egg-shell china, Japanese lacquer cabinets. ... 'Truly the Japanese Court is the real medieval court of the Exhibition.'[47]

So many Japanese tricks of design appealed to him. Portrait-buttons, asymmetrically or diagonally composed; a piece of copper stamped with a sitting deer, coloured and gilt; a bronze 'vase, or rather tazza, supported by rock-work, which is evidently supposed to be below the surface of the deep, for there are sundry gilded fishes attached to it'; another vase with lions-head handles recalling details on the doors of Augsburg Cathedral lacquered cabinets, some inlaid with 'complex geometrical patterns', others with clasps and hinges of tinned metal; suits of armour; ivory ornaments, carved,

6 'The Sabrina Fountain, Gloucester', from a drawing (1856) by William Burges.

SAINT:SIMEON:STYLITES: BY W. BURGES.

7 'St Simeon Stylites', from a drawing (1860) by William Burges.

stained, coloured and inlaid; 'a fish-dish . . . elaborately gilt'; pocket-handkerchiefs of mulberry-bark paper; egg-shell china saucers 'where the side of the boat lifts up and shows a pleasure-party inside'; 'shells cut in two, with lacquered fishes painted in the recesses' – these and many others fascinated Burges and supplied him with a ready source of ideas.[48] And he was not alone.[49] Japanese art was a shot-in-the-arm for Gothic revivalists: for 'the student of our reviving arts of the thirteenth century . . . an hour, or even a day or two, spent in the Japanese department will by no means be lost time, for these hitherto unknown barbarians appear not only to know all that the Middle Ages knew, but in some respects are beyond them and us as well'.[50] In textiles, for instance. 'The best thing anybody wanting cloth of gold, brocade-silks and carpets, could possibly do, would be to seek them in India, China, Turkey, or Japan. In fact, the eastern nations are as much in advance of us in artistic textile fabrics and enamels, as we are of them in railways and machinery.'[51]

Others joined in the cult of Japan, notably of course his close friend E. W. Godwin. But Burges must have been one of the first to collect Japanese prints.[52] And it fell to Burges not only to assimilate in his designs the Eastern and Western medieval traditions, but to propagate this aesthetic reciprocity in his own office, by taking a Japanese as his assistant and by sending out an ex-pupil to transform the architecture of Japan.

But in his early thirties all that lay in the future. In the mid-1850s he had won two international competitions, for Lille Cathedral and for the Crimea Memorial Church at Constantinople. Lille had established him as an international figure; Constantinople had confirmed that position. In 1857 he was even called in to advise on an iconographical scheme for the clerestory of Cologne Cathedral.[53] To win two international competitions in successive years was unprecedented. Success had come to him within months of setting up independent practice. But both projects remained still-born. He had to wait several more years before he was in a position to execute a major work. Happily, as Ewan Christian put it, Burges 'knew how to wait for success'.[54] He waited, and he drew.

DRAWING

Most of Burges's letters have vanished. So has the original text of his diary. But his drawings survive in abundance: hundreds of impulsive sketches, scores of compressed vignettes; images of an intense and wayward mind.[55] His handwriting could be appalling. When absence abroad prevented him from correcting proofs, his written manuscript was likely to produce a host of errors.[56] When he came to summarise his career in an 'Abstract of Diaries', inspired perhaps by his friend Didron's 'succinct and . . . lucid' autobiography,[57] he wisely delegated the task to an amanuensis. Had correspondence survived in bulk, any student of Burges would surely have ended up as short-sighted as the master himself. But his letters have gone: we only have

Godwin's word that they were crammed with 'merry quips, quaint conceits, good advice to students, and kindly chaff'.[58] Still, we do have his printed papers – an amazing list, some two hundred items or more – rambling, repetitious and unindexed, scattered liberally among the back numbers of mid-Victorian periodicals. From these, from his notebooks and from his sketches and working drawings, it is possible to piece together a portrait of a particular type of Victorian: the Pre-Raphaelite architect.

Burges accepted Pre-Raphaelite principles implicitly. These he defined – rather naïvely – as 'to copy nature carefully, to use pleasant bright colours, and to give sentiment to the figures'.[59] If pressed, he might have fallen back on a *Building News* leader of 1874:

> In certain aspects the Gothic Revival may be aptly compared with the Pre-Raphaelite movement in painting. Both were profoundly in earnest, and in both the rejection of certain qualities of artistic attractiveness ultimately led to a protest from within their own body. The dominant motive in the Gothic Revival was constructive. It sought eagerly for the rudimentary impulses in building, and devoted its energies to carrying into view the structural facts which are actually important. The Pre-Raphaelite movement in painting showed an equal worship of Naturalism. Everything was to be true and natural, and nothing was to be composed.[60]

In other words, the Pre-Raphaelite reaction against academicism, and the reaction of Puginian Gothic against the Picturesque, stemmed from a similar – if dog-eared – aesthetic impulse: the pursuit of Truth.

The relationship between the Gothic Revival and Pre-Raphaelitism was in fact the subject chosen for debate at the twenty-first anniversary meeting of the Ecclesiological Society in 1860.[61] Beresford-Hope took the chair. Burges, Street, Bodley, Digby Wyatt, Teulon, Seddon, Pullan, Truefitt, Ferrey, Slater, Clayton, Skidmore, Barraud, Clarke, St Aubyn, Gambier Parry, Prichard and Benjamin Webb were all there. And discussion hinged upon the connection between the principles of the Pre-Raphaelites and the principles of the Gothic Revival. Waving a copy of *The Germ*, Beresford-Hope began by defining the double basis of Pre-Raphaelitism: firstly, 'a sort of mysticism, half-hieratic, half-theological, and withal chivalrous'; secondly, 'a most strong and determined realism – a determination to paint nature absolutely, as naturally, or more naturally, than nature itself'. Having said as much, he then went on to provoke his audience – perhaps for the purposes of debate – by denying the connection between Pre-Raphaelitism and the Gothic Revival: 'Surely the very essence of Gothic architecture was the imaginative scale which it created – the production of the idea of infinity within limited space, while in Classical architecture finite and measured dimensions were the artist's aim. How then could the minute realism of Pre-

Raphaelitism accord with that architecture which was essentially imaginative and spiritual?' Similarly, Pre-Raphaelite naturalism accorded ill with the Gothic Revival's increasing tendency towards conventionalised ornament.

From the floor, Burges was first to jump up and disagree:

> The Pre-Raphaelites had tried to do in painting all that the Cambridge Camden Society did in architecture. They went back to the first elements . . . [of nature] in the same manner that architects were referred to the old churches . . . [But] the Pre-Raphaelites began much later than . . . the Gothicists. Architects had by that time learned to design, but painters were yet in their tutelage . . . [However] Rossetti, Hunt and Millais, still adhered to nature, and were improving: he expected that the world would be delivered by their labours from the [classical] conventionalism under which it had been bound.

Millais's 'Huguenot' gave Burges grounds for hope;[62] Browning's 'St Praxed' confirmed his optimism.[63] The Pre-Raphaelite ethic had destroyed the last elements of Neo-Classicism.

J. P. Seddon agreed. He reminded ecclesiologists that the Pre-Raphaelites had indeed begun by protesting against 'slop' – the diluted academic conventions once associated with Reynolds. Gambier Parry went further. He reiterated the notion of a pre-Reynoldsian return to pure colouring, and on it based both the link between the Pre-Raphaelites and the Gothic Revival and the hope of a future style.[64] Then Street spoke, backing Burges to the hilt. He had previously explained that 'the Pre-Raphaelite movement is identical with our own. What the Pre-Raphaelites are doing for painting must be done for architecture – if at all – by the thirteenth-century men. . . . We *are* medievalists and rejoice in the name. . . . We are medievalists in the sense of wishing to do our work in the same simple but strong spirit which made the man of the thirteenth century so noble a creature, in the same way exactly . . . as the Pre-Raphaelites have taken their name, not because they wish for an instant to copy what other men have done . . . but because they, as we, see in the name a pledge of resistance to false and modern systems of thought and practice in art'.[65] Street concluded by repeating Burges's view that decorative abstraction did not place the Gothic Revival outside the Pre-Raphaelite pale. Each movement was the 'natural accompaniment' of the other.[66] Both shared as their basis the Puginian quest for Truth. And part of that quest was the cult of colour.

Burges looked about Victoria's London, and looked in vain for colour. Exterior polychromy seemed almost a lost art.[67] The tinted marble of the Acropolis, the glazed mosaic of Giotto's campanile at Florence, the painted statuary of Amiens, the gorgeous polychromy of St Mark's, Venice, the terra-cotta of the Ospedale in Milan, the tiled roofs of St Andrea, Vercelli – where were their nineteenth-century equivalents?

> Let anyone go into Harley St, Baker St, or any other respectable thoroughfare, and look at the houses, and then ask himself whether they are either beautiful objects or things to study. Carefully looked into, they resolve themselves into very dirty brick walls, pierced with a certain number of square holes, one house exactly resembling its next neighbour. I protest, in spite of modern opinion, I like the painted stucco of Belgravia better than what is called the honest brick of Baker Street.[68]

Mosaics by Salviati or Fisher, Minton's majolica – whose colours Burges preferred to those of Lucca della Robbia – these were the only chinks of light on an otherwise gloomy scene. But these and other industrial processes might still transform the exteriors of British buildings. The leading industrial country in the world might surely harness its technological might to the chariot wheels of art. 'With these advantages I really see no reason why we should not have buildings in smoky London glowing with imperishable colour.'[69] Meanwhile, he told architectural students, 'paint the walls of your studios . . . illustrate your Tennyson'.[70] An architect must indeed be a veritable master of arts: painting and sculpture, as well as mere structure, must be his domain.[71]

This lust for colour, which Burges shared with so many of his mid-Victorian contemporaries, coincided with – and indeed may well have been stimulated by – two related meteorological factors: the coincidence in the 1860s and 1870s of abnormally heavy cloud and high rainfall, and the pollution of the atmosphere by unprecedented levels of industrial smoke.[72] Ruskinian polychromy was as much an answer to Dickensian smog as a reaction against Neo-Classical purity. From his window in Buckingham St, overlooking the Thames, Burges must have cursed the foggy air of London as he dreamt of the clear morning light of Florence, or the blinding glare of Sicily.

Colour certainly mattered enormously to Burges. His imagination thrived on heraldic polychromy. He experimented with pigments himself, playing with ingredients for the preparation of burnished gold, or dyeing ivory and vellum with madder tints out of a recipe in Theophilus.[73] He loved the swirling hues of oriental dress. But all around him he saw monotony in the age of Gradgrind, the subfusc suit and the stove-pipe hat.

> Since the great French Revolution all colour has been gradually dying out of the male costume, until we have got reduced to our present gamut of brown, black and neutral tint . . . the chimney-pot hat and the swallow-tailed coat.[74]

Londoners in search of colour were reduced to the nightly charade of West End theatres, or the daily ritual of Horse Guards Parade. Away on the Bosphorus Turkish ladies outshone the damsels of the reign of Edward I. But – in Hyde Park in the 1860s – Englishwomen wore dresses which destroyed in form what little they gained in colour. Like Godwin, he hoped for a reformation in dress. Both men put their principles into practice by occasionally dressing up in medieval garb. Burges's architectural sketches often show ladies in wimples, men in gaudy doublets and parti-coloured hose. In sartorial revolution he sensed the seeds of aesthetic renaissance. Of course there was no prospect of such a revolution outside the limits of his own dream world. He knew it, and he didn't care.

Burges regarded the study of costume as integral to the study of architecture. He made a point of including illustrations of medieval costume in his own volume of *Architectural Drawings* (1870). In 1869 he presented a rare book on costume to the Architectural Association, for consultation by students.[75]

> If you understand by architecture only a knowledge of the anatomy of houses, or the supervision of their erection, the study of costume can be of no advantage to you unless in your lighter moments you may want to dress for that most ridiculous of institutions, a fancy ball. If, on the other hand, you view Architecture as the Great Art, entailing a knowledge, more or less, of most of all the other arts, costume may be very useful indeed. It will often enable you to fix dates for buildings or pictures; it will enable you to realise past scenes and past times; it will add a colouring to your reading, and finally will do something toward making you what a good architect should always aim at being – viz. an accomplished gentleman.[76]

Illuminated MSS. supplied the bulk of evidence for medieval dress.[77] But there were also secondary authorities. For armour and military costume he recommended the works of Hewitt[78] and Demmin,[79] and Sir Samuel Rush Meyrick's account of his own famous collection at Blore's Goodrich Court, Herefordshire.[80] For monumental brasses he suggested the handsome publications of Stothard,[81] Hollis[82] and Waller,[83] plus the less costly works of Boutell[84] and Haines.[85] Among general works on costume he admired those of Hefner,[86] Shaw,[87] Bonnard,[88] Willemin,[89] Fairholt[90] and Quicherat.[91] But in one book he had a particular interest: Lonsdale and Tarver's *Medieval Costume* (1874).[92] Both authors were his protégés, and the whole volume bears the impress of his influence. But Burges willingly admitted that there were only two masters in this field: J. R. Planché, playwright and herald, whose *Encyclopaedia of Costume* (1876–9) was the fruit of half a century of research;[93] and Viollet-le-Duc, whose *Mobilier Français* (1858–75) Burges described as beyond the reach of 'any other architect'. He had, of course, great respect for E. W. Godwin's expertise in matters of costume. And when a production of Henry V at the Queen's Theatre committed sartorial and heraldic howlers, yet dared to credit them to Godwin's advice, Burges protested vehemently.[94] His comments on the costume used in productions of 'Jane Shore' at The Princess's Theatre and 'Richard III' at Drury Lane were caustic.[95]

The fact that Burges considered such matters not only relevant to architecture but integral to it, tells us much about his attitude to the profession in general. He deplored the fragmentation of art. 'An artist [and] an architect', he believed, 'are one and the same thing.'[96] 'The decorations of a building', he maintained, 'should be under the absolute control of the architect.' The new Palace of Westminster had fatally compromised that principle. Hence the unsuitability – in Burges's eyes – of the majority of its wall paintings. Any architect, therefore, must himself master the principles of all the decorative arts – 'those, Arts which are almost as essential as Architecture itself to produce a perfect building'.[97] An artistic Renaissance would only flow from a broader practice and a still broader training. 'In fine, it ought to be as disgraceful for an architect not to know the figure, as it would be not to be able to design a piece of tracery'.[98]

One of the encouraging signs at the 1862 Exhibition had been a novel breaking-down of artistic subdivisions.

> Junior architects are following the example of the great men of the Middle Ages, and are gradually becoming artists as well as architects. ... When we see one architect designing stained glass windows, another secular and domestic plate, a third furniture combined with colour, and a fourth sculpture, we feel that this is surely a right good beginning and that there is no occasion to despair of the result. Most certainly the present generation will not see men like Donatello, and so many others of his age, who were equally good in all the fine arts; but if the present [Gothic Revival] movement goes on, it will surely be no unreasonable expectation that such men may appear some two generations hence.[99]

Well, Burges may have underestimated the centrifugal pressures of industrialism, but at least he anticipated some of the ideals of the Arts and Crafts movement. And in the 1860s, at any rate, he still hoped that the Ecclesiological Society would act as an agent of aesthetic reformation: that it would enter upon a 'second phase' of activity, condemning bad design in the applied arts as vigorously as it had once condemned bad architecture.[1] That hope was not fulfilled. In 1868 the Ecclesiological Society was dissolved. The Gothic Revival began to lose momentum. And that longed-for Renaissance of the applied arts was postponed.

Burges regarded himself, therefore, first and foremost as an artist: an art-architect, in the jargon of the day. In many ways he was a Pre-Raphaelite in all but name. For him the battle between architects and surveyors was more important than the Battle of the Styles.[2] 'The greater number of buildings in the City', he complained, 'are utterly abominable, and the cause is that they have been designed by surveyors and not by architects.'[3] One way out, he thought, would be to encourage the profession to adopt the principle of the division of labour, leaving art-work where it belonged: in the hands of the art-architect. Significantly, he chose the occasion of Ruskin's refusal of the

R.I.B.A. Gold Medal in 1874 to state defiantly: 'a man could not be a good surveyor and a good artist at the same time, and he would be sure to fail if he attempted it'.4 He had no time for surveyors – whom he considered only peripherally professional – still less for sub-professional profiteers who mixed the production of designs with the supply of materials.5 He considered advertisement incompatible with professional status.6 In 1879 he stirred the Royal Institute of the Architects of Ireland into polling its members on the subject of professional charges. And only a year before his death he was still trying to clarify and regularise the R.I.B.A.'s code of professional conduct.7 But for Burges's professional credo we must turn to a letter written at the end of his life, to a young architect, and published posthumously in an American journal:8

> There are various sorts of practice, all of which are open to you ... you might become simply a house doctor, or a warehouse architect, or a light-and-air man, or an architectural policeman (i.e. a district surveyor), or a general practitioner: and it is quite possible to make *money* by any of these, the amount depending on the extent of the practice, and that again upon the number of friends, besides the amount of the importunity and impudence by which the work may be solicited.
>
> But reflect; are any of these men artists? It is true that when they die they may have made money, but what else will they leave to the world beside that? Their names are simply written in water ... [But] there is another course open to you by which you may perhaps be the means of leaving some beautiful things to posterity, and by which your name may possibly survive after you have quitted this life ... why not try to be an artist ... a creator of works of art? ...
>
> You know something of modern construction, enough to enable you to practise without letting your building fall. You can draw well, and in an architectural and geometrical manner; but I know nothing of your perspectives, and your free-hand drawing is woolly, and wants precision. Above all, you are very defective in the human figure. (You have, I presume, a fair knowledge of the history of architecture.)
>
> Now I recommend you to employ your next two years in three principal things:
>
> 1. The drawing of the human figure: this is really the foundation of all good taste. I don't mean that you should spend weeks frizzling up a figure in chalk, for you are not going to be a painter, but that you should learn to draw correctly and know the bones and muscles which go to make up the outline, and, in fact, to be able to account for everything you see.
>
> 2. A serious course of reading. ... Philosophy and science will not help you so much as works of the imagination. ... Homer, Aristophanes, Aeschylus, Herodotus, Xenophon, Virgil, Horace, Apuleius ... Dante, Chaucer, Shakespeare, 'Faust', 'Robinson Crusoe', 'Undine' and Lane's translation of the 'Arabian Nights'. ...

3. To carefully study and draw various beautiful things; and whether the said thing be a piece of jewelry or a piece of iron-work, or a building or portion of a building – to do it thoroughly, to find out its construction and why this and that is done, the basis of the ornamentation, the particular form of the curves, and never leave it until you know all about it. . . . Do everything by common sense; don't make a drawing when you can make a rubbing, and regard all your drawing in the light of evidence which is worth nothing if it is not authentic.

In a sense, this posthumous advice almost takes the form of a fragmentary autobiography. Nearly twenty years before, he had summed up his prescription for architectural excellence as follows: 'The truth is, that design in architecture depends upon a man's mind and a man's eye, and the only way to educate them . . . is by a proper course of *belles lettres* for the one, and a constant study of the figure for the other.'[9] Burges became an architect by instinct as well as by design: he trained himself to master the requisite techniques of both architecture and the fine and applied arts. But that mastery was conditioned by, and subordinate to, the appetites of a romantic imagination. He was indeed the Pre-Raphaelite architect.

He was not interested in academic rules. Rulebooks led only to automatic architecture: design by numbers. 'Rules', he wrote, 'are made only for incapables.'[10] 'No rule can be deduced except the golden one – "Whatever looks best *is* best."' Sticklers for rules and proportions appear to forget that no two Classic buildings are exactly similar in their proportions, and that there is more in common between the architects of Chartres and Paestum than ever the measurers of diameters and modules dream of.'[11] 'Ornament is as much a matter of feeling as poetry.'[12] True enough. But such outbursts merely threw the apprentice back to the task of finding himself a good eye and thanking God for it.

More helpful was his insistence on the place of figure-drawing in architectural education.[13] Its method must not be the rigmarole of Dyce's *Outlines*, but the study of the live model, the antique, and anatomy.[14] Its basis was his belief in the necessary integration of architecture and sculpture. 'No good architecture', he once noted, 'without figures.'[15] From the study of the human figure stemmed an understanding not only of sculptural form and naturalistic ornament but ultimately of all three-dimensional design. He quoted Haydon's dictum with approval: 'a man who draws a figure can always draw a leaf, but the converse by no means holds good'.[16] 'The great and crying defect of the art-architect at the present day is the want of the knowledge of the human figure; and until that is obtained I am afraid that there will be but little progress. I say art-architect, to distinguish him from the surveyor-architect.'[17]

Such opinions mark Burges as an out and out Ruskinian. Rickman had popularised an elementary Gothic classification. Blore had been the leader of a generation dedicated to topographical accuracy. Pugin had preached the dogma of function and the doctrine of 'the true Picturesque'. And the Ecclesiologists had 'at last drilled architects into building churches by recipe'. But 'all this was mere architecture, or rather, the bones of the building without the flesh. Mr Ruskin arrived to supply the deficiency, and to point out the intimate connection between good sculpture and good architecture'.[18] In short, Burges adopted wholeheartedly the Ruskinian doctrine of architectural expression: function alone 'tells no story'. Gothic 'architecture was (and it always must be) eminently an architecture of figures and subjects . . . part . . . [of] the great poem of Christian art'.[19] Figure-drawing was the basis of art; construction was only half the art of architecture. Any architect who lacked the training and instincts of an artist was forced to take 'refuge in foliage, notches, chamfers, and other specimens of misapplied ingenuity'.[20] Hence, he thought, the weakness of much mid-Victorian Gothic.

But what of architectural drawing? Burges had been trained under Blore and Digby Wyatt, respectively perhaps the most meticulous and the most versatile of early Victorian architectural draughtsmen. About the time of his Long Journey, however, he rebelled against nearly everything they had taught him. He had come to believe that architectural drawing must be essentially diagrammatic, that is explanatory rather than pictorial. 'Drawing, after all', he told his students, 'is only a sort of writing; and in a letter it is not a question of how you write, but what you write.'[21] A 'dozen . . . dirty pieces of paper', laboriously drawn, during a month abroad, 'in dirty roofs or at the feet of ladders', were worth any number of 'elegant-coloured perspectives with fashionable ladies and children in the foreground – not put in by the architect'.[22] 'To understand the construction of a building thoroughly, it is necessary to go on to the roofs and into the gutters, and there commence one's study.'[23] 'Telling sketches [are] the curse of architecture.'[24] Instead, let a young architect measure: measurement is to the architect what dissection is to a medical man.[25]

> The manner in which a man draws does and must affect the nature of his design . . . if he use strong thick lines, he will . . . be induced to make his design massive and simple, and not give way to the vanities of crockets and pinnacles. . . . He likewise sees his design in its most severe and unfavourable light, and ten to one the building will turn out much better than the drawing. . . . If, however, the architect draws in a moderately thick line, and puts in stone joints and etches the walls . . . he simply deceives not only his client, but still worse, himself; for the building is almost certain to come out worse than the drawing. . . . As to the third style of drawing, with very fine hair-like lines, relieved by what is termed black lining, whereby small fillets are made to look like hollows, and hollows like fillets – this style, in fact, is scarcely worth mentioning, for it means nothing, and hardly anybody employs it in the present day; and, indeed, one is almost tempted to believe it to have been invented by some instrument-maker. I may likewise observe that it was generally employed in the worst days of architecture – the eighteenth century.[26]

Such specious practices still survived on the Continent, particularly in Italy.[27] But the pursuit of Gothic art was hampered rather than helped by techniques of draughtsmanship more familiar to Palladio than to William of Wykeham. Worse still was a device of recent introduction: 'the comparatively modern system of etching. . . . Probably no one thing has done so much harm to architecture . . . [For] the truth is not in it.'[28]

Brass rubbings, he allowed, could be amusing and instructive: Burges must have been a dab hand with Ullathorne's Heelball or Richardson's Metallic Rubber.[29] But perspective drawings were the curse of architectural training. Drawings for *display* merely created a mood. A young architect should 'measure with his own hands every detail he is desirous of studying'. On his trips abroad, therefore, Burges avoided pretty sketches and tried instead 'to dissect architecture – in other words, to make careful drawings, measured and plotted on the spot'.[30] This may have been as much a matter of necessity as of choice. Burges was so short-sighted that he found the preparation of perspective drawings uncommonly difficult. He fell back, therefore, on large-scale, diagrammatic details. It was a trick he seems to have learnt from C. Bruce Allen.[31] And the results were electric.

'He was one of the most rapid and brilliant draughtsmen I ever met with,' Aitchison recalled; he 'had the most inexhaustible fund of invention; illustrations of literary incidents, designs for chalices, croziers, knives, scent bottles, comic alphabets, caricatures, Medieval towns or buildings, came forth from his pen, pencil or brush without a moment's reflection.'[32] In his study he drew fast. On site he moved faster still. With his drawing board balanced on the backs of two chairs, his T square, set square, plummet and measuring rods at the ready, note book in hand, a 'tax-gatherer's bottle' of indelible brown ink attached to his button-hole, Billy Burges went into action, pince-nez swinging, watch-chain rattling, instruments clanging; climbing ladders, tapping stonework, feeling sculpture, probing mortices, peering short-sightedly at undercut mouldings, measuring dim-lit timber roofs and – grimy as a chimney-sweep – shouting gleefully to his companions at each new find.[33]

Burges's own drawings consciously followed what he took to be medieval practice. Fifteenth and early sixteenth century drawings in the British Museum, for King's College Chapel, Cambridge;[34] for Henry VI's tomb;[35] for a royal gallery[36] and ceremonial tents;[37] as well as a vellum representation in the College of Arms, showing the funeral of Abbot Islip at Westminster Abbey[38] – these were just a few of the models upon which Burges based his style of drawing. He admired their bold, freehand lines; their use of strong colour and dark ink, their lack of shading and fussiness. These too were some of the qualities he admired in Dürer's drawings, and in the architectural sketches supposedly by Michelangelo – perhaps by Vasari – which he examined at Lille.[39]

The Elizabethan ichnographer, John Thorpe, had been almost the last to follow the simple rules of explanatory drawing. 'With Thorpe we take leave of the Middle Ages',

Burges concluded; 'it [was] reserved to us moderns to make our drawings at once ugly and scientific' by hatching, etching, shading and other devices designed to increase verisimilitude at the expense of clarity. Georgian architects had made great play with thin lines, geometrically drawn and blacked in: 'a practice destructive of all breadth of effort, and absolutely perplexing to the eyes'. Even the elder Pugin had followed this fashion. And the younger Pugin, though 'the first to change the system in his plates', had 'made things look too well by his marvellous etching; indeed, there is a fizziness and action in all his plates which you look in vain for in the real thing.[40] The present system of etching up a drawing is an offshoot from this style, and is, I am afraid, open to nearly the same objection. We have, for its use, to thank competition committees, who, forbidding the employment of colour, have obtained a much more seductive style of perspective; for I think I would any day back a good etched drawing against a coloured one [in competition]'. Either way, this pursuit of pictorial effect had depreciated the status of working drawings: 'the success of a design in stone and mortar must depend upon the working drawings, for nobody sets out work or chisels stones from perspectives; and it is in these that I hope to see good, strong, thick, bold lines employed, so that we may get into the habit of leaving out those prettinesses, which only cost money and spoil our designs.'[41]

For such purposes, illuminated MSS. seemed to Burges very often the best models. And they were models he loved to study. 'No one who has ever visited Siena Cathedral', he wrote, 'can forget the vast number of manuscript choral books which are ranged about the beautiful sacristy.'[42] In one notebook he lists details of forty-eight illuminated MSS. in the British Museum which he had consulted.[43] One MS which Burges particularly admired was the so-called Queen Mary's Psalter, an early fourteenth-century document known to *cognoscenti* as BIB. REG. 2B. vii.[44] Much less elaborate than the fifteenth-century *Roman de la Rose* or the exquisite *Splendor Solis*, it was nevertheless an ideal source. In clear inked outlines heightened with touches of purple, brown, sepia, green and yellow, it began with Bible stories from the creation and fall of Lucifer down to the death of Solomon. Then followed a finely illuminated calendar, the signs of the zodiac, the labours of the year, the psalter and the litany. Some of its marginal themes – legends of the Madonna and the saints, bestiaries, games, etc. – were not unlike those of another manuscript Burges knew well, the *Roman d'Alexandre* in the Bodleian. The stylised poses, the actual evidence of costume and architecture, the 'life and energy' of the figures – which Burges believed that among his contemporaries only John Leech of *Punch* could match – all these supplied practical sources of inspiration. The Keeper of Manuscripts at the British Museum, Sir Frederick Madden, had forbidden tracing.[45] Nevertheless, first Westlake and then Purdue had proved indefatigable copyists.[46] And Burges acknowledged at least one instance when the authority of BIB. REG. 2B. vii was brought into play: his restoration of the sculptures in the chapter house at Salisbury.[47]

But it was the drawings of Wilars de Honecort which constituted Burges's favourite model.[5] This famous thirteenth-century sketchbook – rediscovered in the Bibliothèque Nationale by Quicherat, edited by Lassus and Darcel and re-edited by Willis[48] – consisted of fifty-four pages of coarse vellum, of which twenty-one had been torn out, bound in a limp, folding cover of dirty pigskin. Notre Dame de Cambray, Laon, Lausanne, Lucerne, Rheims, Chartres, Vaucelles, St-Etienne de Meaux – these were the chief monuments illustrated, all drawn with crude details and naïve geometry.[49] These drawings Burges found 'curiously in unison with the stern, severe, local character of the thirteenth century architecture of Flanders and Picardy'.[50] In perspective and anatomy they were weak: bears, swans, crawfish, cats, grasshoppers, lions, men and women, all drawn in outline in a simple, gawky, angular way. In matters of mechanics and primitive engineering, however, the drawings were at least curious. For Burges they were hypnotic.

> The sketches were first made with a leaden or silver pencil, either of which would perfectly mark on the vellum. . . . If the subject were an architectural one, the straight lines were ruled, and the circles put in with a compass, one end of which had a leaden point. These lines were afterwards gone over with a blackish brown ink, by means of the hand alone, no instrument being employed. . . . There is no faltering or wavering, but the line is just as thick and as firm where it ends as where it begins. Again, in drawing things in small, mouldings and foliage become simplified so as not to break up the breadth of the composition. Clearness is got by blacking hollows where they occur, and the grounds of ornaments, such as capitals, etc. The walls of the plans, however, are not etched, and we shall find this practice obtaining even in the time of Thorpe, the majority of whose plans are not etched, although not devoid of colour. One would imagine that Wilars might have etched them up with his leaden point as he often did his drapery; but nothing of the kind occurs. Another peculiarity of our architect was, that, when he copied any executed work, he copied it not as he saw it, but with variations of his own, as he would execute it himself. . . . But with all his peculiarities, Wilars presents us with a decidedly good style of drawing, and which, it strikes me, might eventually be developed into something much better than that in use of late years. I mean, that we should join our improved knowledge of perspective and of the figure to the energy, simplicity, and firmness of our confrère of the thirteenth century.[51]

Such was the model Burges kept in mind: the model for his own Vellum Sketchbook, filled with hand-drawn outlines, drawn in with a crow-quill pen and brown indelible ink.[52] This Vellum Sketchbook, which he christened 'Wilars', contained his favourite Gothic 'dodges', the cream of his archaeological travels. In conception indulgent, in style archaic, it sums up much of Burges's quirky genius. Indeed, it became something of a legend in the profession. When part of Burges's library was sold soon after his death, 'Wilars' alone fetched £285.[53]

To classicists of a slightly older generation – men like T. L. Donaldson and J. B. Papworth – the yardstick of good architectural drawing was its precision and high finish. Romantic Goths of Burges's persuasion – J. P. Seddon, for instance – preferred vigour and simplicity: allusion rather than illusion.[54] Of course, exhibition drawings were different. Since about 1815, architectural exhibitors at the Royal Academy had submitted perspectives in full colour.[55] According to convention, therefore, exhibition drawings required the full apparatus of pictorial technique. For such purposes Burges preferred to employ artists like E. S. Cole[56] or Axel Haig. But it was, on the whole, in plain working drawings that he pinned his hopes for the future of British architecture: 'When the profession generally begins to draw the figure and make bold architectural drawings, and generally to think for themselves, instead of going to past ages and precedents, we may then hope to have an *Architecture*.'[57]

'The drawing of the thirteenth-century architects', Burges concluded, 'was queer; their perspective worse; their knowledge of mechanics, and the application of geometry to masonry very limited; but they have left us Amiens, Westminster, Cologne and Beauvais. The late ingenious Mr Peter Nicholson and his followers drew beautifully and scientifically; they filled whole books with the most abstruse problems of conic sections and wonderful dog-leg staircases; and they have left us in brick and stone – what?'[58]

Such fondness for the crudities of thirteenth-century drawing was nicely satirised in a mock-heroic epistle to the *Builder* by one John de Camden Town (né Tomkins). Very much in the manner of Carlyle, it pokes fun at the medievalists' cult of architectural manliness:

Youth! Study old Wilars. Dig deep into the Crookedness of him; his Things do not tally. Learn to draw like Wilars. Nature throw to the Dogs. Elegances, Symmetries, Tee-Square Simulacra, have none of them. Perspective, Photography, Proportion, Common Eyesight, put far from you, and stick to grand old Norse Thoughts and Things awry. . . . Saw-mills, Catapults, Wheels of Fortune, does old Wilars draw; right primitive Carpentry, work of old Hatchets and Adzes – scorning your Jack-planes, Triangles, Mortice-and-tenon-apparatus, Twopenny-nails, Tee-square-totalism, Elegancies, Symmetries, Peter Nicholsonisms. . . . A comrade for Ruskin in the Shades, this same Wilars. A pair of big-fisted fellows there. Fists clenched to smite down all Tee-square Jotuns. . . . Fists clenched, I say, therefore, for the Pitching-into and Punishment of Classical-Cockerell Jotuns; Harlicarnassian Tites; Roman Ashpitels; Donaldsons, Ph.D. – Philhellenist Donaldsons, that is; Owens Jones, Digbies Wyatt, Crystal Palace Jotuns; old effete Jotuns of Saint Paul's, Whitehall, Somerset House, and other Wren-Jones-Chambers work; Vitruvian, Palladian, Cinquecentine, Michelangeline Jotuns – the Noses of them knocked awry, demolished . . . by better than Torrigianine mallets, by knuckles of big-fisted Norse Fellows; Barries, too, Westminster Jotuns; Pugins, even, Jotuns of Short-coming, who failed to dig deep enough into the Crookednesses, and have hearts, therefore, that would not fill a nutshell!...[59]

Absurd? Of course. But such Romantic vapourings tell us much about the emotional dynamics of High Victorian Gothic. Burges may not have carried the whole profession with him: Scott was sympathetic,[60] but Street, for instance, remained a prolific and unrepentant sketcher. 'What a pity', Burges is said to have remarked, 'that he cannot build his cross-hatchings.' Still, Burges had many followers in matters of draughtsmanship, men like E. W. Godwin,[61] J. P. Seddon and E. J. Tarver. Philip Webb, for one, always regarded the 'ability to make picturesque sketches' as 'a fatal gift to an architect'.[62] And years later Paul Waterhouse reminded students: 'Never draw to make a pretty sketch-book – Burges taught us that. ... To draw is to learn.'[63]

Such a blank rejection, by Burges and his followers, of all shading and perspective, inevitably produced a reaction. And this reaction in favour of expressive draughtsmanship naturally coincided with the return to classicism heralded by the Queen Anne Revival. As early as 1870 voices had begun to urge a return to classical draughtsmanship.[64] By 1874 R. Phené Spiers, Architectural Master at the Royal Academy, was openly advocating the revival of classical techniques, spiking Gothic guns by citing Viollet-le-Duc, and turning the achievements of Godwin and Burges upside down: 'in such [Gothic] designs ... in which there is rhythm and symmetry and what I may be allowed to call Greek feeling, the projection of the shadows brings out the qualities of the design.'[65] This return to pictorial values in architectural draughtsmanship was consummated by the vigorous etchings of Norman Shaw – and their obvious suitability to developing techniques of photolithography.[66]

Photography was an aid which Burges employed with caution. He saw the obvious benefits of accuracy and speed: 'what figures can draw or engrave like the sun?'[67] But he also saw the dangers. He was well aware that architecture might die from a surfeit of negatives. Pullan was all in favour: 'an architect should travel about with a pistolograph ... and bag his sixty pieces of detail per day.' Lamb was less enthusiastic: 'photography is but too often substituted for sketching.' Burges was even more damning:

Both photography and sketching are but too often substituted for drawings measured on a ladder, and plotted at the foot of it. ... The measurer will know all the ins and outs of the building – why this detail is treated in a particular manner, and why that method of construction was employed; while the sketcher will simply have an idea that such and such elements form a picturesque group, although he will probably be quite ignorant of the construction which determines the form of such elements and the necessity for their particular grouping. As to the photographer, poor fellow! the extent of his knowledge will probably be, that under certain circumstances the honey process is the best, and that under others the collodian answers better. Indeed the sum of my advice ... would be – Measure much, sketch little, and, above all, keep your fingers out of chemicals. ...[68]

Generally speaking, therefore, Burges used photography as a recording device and as an aid to compositional massing, not as a means of multiple plagiarism. As for the *camera lucida*, he thought it an even more dangerous instrument than the camera. Its use involved the suspension of thought without the compensating benefit of accuracy: mere 'laborious idleness'.[69]

Burges's book of *Architectural Drawings* was formally begun in 1864,[70] discontinued in 1865 when his draughtsman W. S. Barber left London, and resumed in 1869 when Barber was replaced by E. J. Tarver and H. W. Lonsdale.[71] Twenty years before – at the start of his Long Journey – he had abandoned pretty sketches as fit only 'for the inspection of parents, friends, and idiots'.[72] He had realised that what was needed was a collection of measured medieval details: 'a sort of grammar of thirteenth-century architecture.' Alas, he had scarcely begun when the advertisement appeared for Viollet-le-Duc's *Dictionnaire*.[73] All hope of publication was abandoned; the drawings were reserved for his own use. Pressure from friends, however, induced him to reconsider the idea, and the book eventually appeared in 1870.

Only two hundred and ten copies were printed, of which one hundred and sixty were for advance subscribers. The lithographic plates were at once destroyed, and no copies were allowed 'to go into the trade'. Dissection rather than delineation was, of course, the avowed aim. There is no hint of aesthetic theory.[74] Structure is all. 'My object', he once noted abroad, 'is not so much to tell what was employed in the thirteenth century, as *how* it was employed.'[75] Reviewers found the plates of the flèche at Amiens particularly impressive: 'An Herculean labour ... drawn to $\frac{1}{4}$ in. scale, with every tenon and pin.' 'They were not pretty sketches; some people called them ugly; but they were sketches made with the intention of getting at the heart of the detail ... finding out how and why it was made ... not fair-weather work, but made ... on the top of ladders, with stumps of pencil, on paper wet with rain and held down against the wind. ... They were drawn for publication in an equally downright and almost defiant contempt of architectural prettiness, and to any but architects were hardly comprehensible.'[76] It was in fact a book for working architects. And one hundred and thirty-one of them subscribed. When E. W. Godwin reviewed it, he called it 'one of the most useful architectural works ever produced in this country'.[77] The scale of drawings doubled that of its rivals. The plates of Amiens and Beauvais were triumphs of draughtsmanship. So were those of Châlons-sur-Marne and the Hospital at Beaune. But of more 'practical value to the modern architect' were the lesser items: finials, timber roofs, timber houses, tiled roofs at Mantes, Dijon and Troyes; the Grange at Beauvais or the dormers on the Hospital at Beaune, besides chalices, altars, buttresses, doors, windows, fountains, capitals, cornices, crosses, canopies, brackets, balconies and battlements. Only a handful of errors were noticed: a few beams mismeasured at Beaune; a few drawings of costume incorrectly transcribed.

Such precision, such deadpan understatement in drawing, was however only one side of Burges's style of presentation. He had another string to his bow: the fantastic.

It was in 1858 that Burges first revealed to the public at large his capacity for architectural fantasy. In that year he exhibited a design, on vellum, for a fountain commemorating the legendary Sabrina, to be placed in Southgate St, Gloucester.[78][6] He had been working on the design since 1856.[79] And he had been thinking about 'dodges' for fountains since he gaped at the Pretoria Fountain in Palermo in 1854.[80] The story of Sabrina – King Locrin's unhappy daughter who began her days in an underground cell and ended them in the River Severn – had been celebrated by Milton in *Comus* and related in detail by Geoffrey of Monmouth. Such a saga gave Burges ample opportunity for significant ornament and symbolic sculpture. There was even some etymological evidence that 'Severn' and 'Sabrina' derived from the same root.

The *Builder*'s description of this particular dream is too good to abridge:

> Mr. Burges has endeavoured to work out the story by representing the early part of the history in the groups under the lower basin. Those shown [here] represent Estrildis brought captive to Locrin – the marriage of Locrin and Gwendoloena – and Locrin visiting Estrildis and Sabrina in the underground apartment. At the extreme top we see Gwendoloena ordering Estrildis and Sabrina to be thrown into the water; while quite at the bottom are bas-reliefs of the Undines, or water-spirits, who rejoice over the prey that awaits them. The tributary streams are placed in the capital, immediately over the top group ... [Now for] the animals, fish and insects abounding or supposed to abound on the banks of the stream. Uppermost of all is the otter holding a shield emblazoned with the arms of Gloucester; below are the frogs, firstly in their natural position and secondly developed as gargoyles. Then come the fish; and lastly, intermingled with the foliage running round the lower basin, the lizards, the insects, and the shells. The lizards are made use of as a means of pouring extra jets of water. The background shows an imaginary view of ancient Gloucester at the beginning of the thirteenth century. On the right is the armourer's shop, on the left the pillory; behind is the town hall with a lofty belfry tower. An arched opening gives us a view of the town, while at the crown of the arch is hung a sabre taken from some Saracen by one of the Earls of Gloucester during a crusade.[81]

It was indeed a design 'intended and calculated to challenge attention'. The *Ecclesiologist* blanched at the drawing's 'Pre-Raphaelite crudeness of colour'. But there was praise for the 'boldness' of its Gothic forms and the 'quaint grotesquerie' of its sculpture. 'Let Mr Burges', their critic concluded, 'with his great ability and

8 John, 3rd Marquess of Bute (1847–1900): heir-apparent.

9 Bute in adolescence: surrounded by a web of intrigue.

knowledge, avoid as he has hitherto done, mistaking eccentricity for power, and he is on the high road to lasting eminence.'[82]

Nothing came of the Sabrina Fountain. All that the citizens of Gloucester could bring themselves to do was to erect 'a miserable little parody ... a dribbling little fountain' by some unknown hand.[83] Nevertheless, it was the Sabrina Fountain which first drew E. W. Godwin to Burges. 'In this', Godwin recalled, 'I noted a realisation of the Middle Ages, such as no modern pencil had ... produced.'[84] It was not a piece of precise archaeology: the scene looked more like Southern France or Spain than medieval Gloucester. But the spirit of the Middle Ages was there. Still more so in Burges's bird's-eye fantasy: 'St Simeon Stylites.'[7] Burges was proud of both: he chose to exhibit them in the Paris Exhibition of 1867.[85] After all, they were conceived before Viollet-le-Duc, before Rossetti's illustrations to Tennyson's 'Palace of Art', and above all before the popular medievalism of *Once A Week* and *Good Words*.

'St Simeon Stylites' was drawn in 1860 and first exhibited in 1861.[86] It was received quizzically by the *Ecclesiologist*: 'The whole drawing looks like a woodcut ... from the *Nuremberg Chronicle*.'[87] Indeed it does. Here Burges has captured something of the terrible vision of Albrecht Dürer. It was a style with many imitators: E. J. Poynter's 'Castle By The Sea' (1862) for instance.[88] It was a style carried into the next century by Beresford Pite.[89]

Dürer was an artist Burges collected – at least in print form[90] – along with Holbein and Lucas Cranach. All three were much admired by the *avant garde* in the 1860s, and by the fashionable in the 1870s. Dürer for his capacity to idealise 'the roughness of reality'; Holbein for his Italianate softening of the 'harshness and angularity ... of the German school'. Lucas Cranach, however, was often condemned for the very qualities which must have attracted Burges: his 'mystic symbolism', his minimal classicism, and the immediacy of his technique.[91] Of the three it was undoubtedly Dürer who impinged most directly on the artistic consciousness of the architectural world. 'Death on the Pale Horse',[92] 'The Great Dragon Cast Out',[93] 'The Vision of the Throne',[94] 'Satan Bound'[95] – these woodcut echoes of a Sublime Apocalypse lent themselves admirably to lithographic processes. In the 1870s they also supplied a grim Gothic counterblast to the omnipresent flaccidity of the Queen Anne Revival. Their landscapes boast ruined towers, misty cities and fortified towns.[96] They even included useful examples of the domestic arts: 'quaint and practical details of a bygone age.'[97] Burges must have been especially struck by the way in which the German School fused the graphic and metallic arts, in particular the arts of woodcut and goldsmithing. Metallic forms, religious and secular, are translated into the media of wood, copper plate or panel. But though made softer and freer, the lines of foliage and drapery frequently betray the hardness and angularity of the goldsmith's hand.[98] Dürer's 'realism' is a favourite theme in contemporary criticism: 'Luther was a Dürer in theology, whilst Dürer was a Luther in art'.[99] Reality – and fantasy too. It was a potent combination. And nowhere more potent than in Burges's architectural dreams.

But 'who was St Simeon Stylites?', 'a student' asked the *Building News* in 1873. 'Was he a kind of Medieval Diogenes, or a mere anchoretical Christian – a saint of real or supposed existence?'[1] Back came several elaborate replies describing the career of this fifth-century Syrian monk who spent more than thirty years on a column sixty foot high, fasting, praying and working miracles – such as ridding the land of wild beasts.

> Crowds of pilgrims came from Gaul and India. . . . The tribes of Saracens fought for the honour of his blessings. The Queens of Arabia and Persia acknowledged his supernatural virtues. Theodosius the younger consulted him constantly . . . [Once] the arch-fiend, in disguise as an angel of light, came to proffer him translation with a chariot and horses of fire; he raised his left foot in order to mount, but added the sign of the cross, when the unholy pageant vanished, and he remained standing on one leg for a whole year until mortification set in. . . . Song-birds came to lament around his grave. . . . He was canonised immediately after his death with great pomp at Antioch by the Master General of the East, in presence of six bishops, twenty-one counts, and 6000 soldiers. . . .[2]

It was a vision memorably pictured by Tennyson;[3] a vision which matched even the fevered imagination of young Burges.

For Burges's Heavenly City was not the city of Saint Augustine but the city of Albrecht Dürer, seen through the misty eyes of Alfred, Lord Tennyson:

> . . . a city of Enchanters, built
> By fairy Kings . . .[4]
> . . . a city all on fire
> With sun and cloth of gold.[5]

Burges's sketchbooks, particularly those compiled during the waiting period of his early thirties, are littered with fragments of unbuilt dreams: 'A Fantasy Castle';[6] 'A City in Heaven' complete with Gothic vistas and an endless procession of the Blessed;[7] 'Dante at the Gate of Purgatory';[8] and – most Wagnerian of all – 'Changing Guard in Heaven'.[9] His was a

> . . . city . . . built
> To music, therefore never built at all,
> And therefore built for ever.[10]

An architect's Camelot:

> . . . [a] dim rich city, roof by roof,
> Tower after tower, spire beyond spire,
> . . . our Camelot,

> Built by old kings, age after age, so old. . . .
> So strange, and rich, and dim . . . where the roofs
> Totter'd toward each other in the sky. . . .
> And . . . the spires
> Prick'd with incredible pinnacles into heaven.[11]

For an underemployed architect such daydreams are the stuff of life. By his mid-thirties Burges was – in architectural circles at least – an international figure. He had travelled more widely than any of his contemporaries. His learning was incontestable. His eclecticism was more broadly based than any of his rivals; Romanesque, Gothic, Islamic, Greek, Japanese – even Florentine and François Premier – were all grist to his mill. His Gothic dreams were images of genius. His restoration of Waltham Abbey had shown his talents as a church builder. He had executed minor works – at Gayhurst, Bucks, for Lord Carrington; at St Augustine's, Canterbury, for Beresford-Hope – and they showed immense promise. And how he could draw.

> A design, says Georgius, 'ought by rights to set one's hair on end'. His plans are 'done on a great many sheets of Whatman's best double elephant paper, in highly muscular drawings, highly coloured for the distinguishment of stone from brick, ash from fir, and even brickwork in cement from brickwork in mortar. Elaborate tile paving is painted on the floors. Figures of the heavenly host are delineated on the walls. The sacrarium is a perfect mob of saints and angels. The mimic altar is adorned, not only with the very drapery of the cloth, but with the precise folds in which it is to be arranged. The reredos is a blaze of colour impossible to be described. The very candelabra and other ornamented furniture are shown in Indian yellow to signify fine gold. And there are priests, monks, acolytes, and pages represented here and there . . . holding up ten foot rods to give everything its proper scale. Nor are inscriptions wanting. Edifying texts by way of ornament occupying every architectural band and frieze. Monograms are planted like a crop of sacred riddles on every boss and bracket. And where the paper is not covered by drawing, it is covered by descriptive particulars, memoranda, and observations, obscure because illegible, but manifestly as prodigiously adventurous as the rest. The *ensemble* is quaint beyond expression; and it may certainly be owned . . . that the ordinary beholder can scarcely help having every hair on his body permanently on end.[12]

No wonder Viollet-le-Duc was nearly fooled. When he first saw the winning Lille competition drawings, he thought they were real thirteenth-century work – until he spotted the Whatman watermark in the paper.[13]

But at the age of thirty-five Burges had yet to produce a single major building. Lille (1855) and Constantinople (1856) had been won and lost. Brisbane Cathedral

(1859–60) turned out to be little more than a mirage. Then in 1863 he won the competition for Cork Cathedral, and in 1865 he was introduced to Lord Bute. Billy Burges had arrived.

TALKING

Burges was clearly a clubbable man. Temperamentally he may have been an outsider. But professionally and socially he was an insider through and through.

Burges was elected to the Institute of British Architects in 1860.[14] He was quickly involved in its running battles between Goths and Classics: in 1864 over the award of the Royal Gold Medal first to Ruskin, then to Viollet-le-Duc;[15] and in 1865 over Beresford-Hope's election as President.[16] As a young man, however, he had doubted the Institute's value. Although he was never formally a member of the Architectural Association, he much preferred its atmosphere: its informal, unstuffy ethos was very much his métier; he was always a friend to the young.[17] 'I can well remember,' he recalled, 'in my younger days, how the Institute was considered as a sort of Sleepy Hollow, especially in the possession of what was termed "Classic" architecture.' But the young Goths joined in the end, and 'in due time [we] had our fair share of the government'.[18] The headquarters of the architectural profession grew in strength, its library expanded, its examinations were accepted, its studentships prized, its professional mores established. Burges had little time for the annual Gold Medal. But he believed in the Institute's status. He even saw it as a House of Lords to the Architectural Association's House of Commons.

> [I wish] to strengthen the Institute in every manner ... [to] have all the other architectural societies and exhibitions collected under the same roof ... the Architectural Museum ... a more or less permanent exhibition of working architectural drawings (the pretty perspectives going as usual to Somerset House) ... an exhibition of ordinary building materials, another of models, and a third of new inventions; in fact, there should always be some exhibition – free if possible – on hand. The lower parts of the building should be converted into shops for trades connected with the profession, i.e. for the sale of books, bronzes, goldsmiths' work, etc.; and I would even have the Arts Club – the real Junior Athenaeum – in an adjoining house.[19]

J. P. Seddon was a strong supporter of this idea of amalgamation.[20] Nothing came of it, of course. But Burges kept a watchful eye on the Institute's proceedings – too watchful for the Institute's comfort. Despite his genial manner, he must have been a thorn in the Secretary's flesh. In 1862 he was appointed to the Council.[21] In 1871–2 he was a member of the Professional Charges Committee and took part in a discussion on professional charges at the General Conference of Architects.[22] In 1878 he was pressing

William H. White to produce a Secretarial ruling on connections with trade and on the ownership of architectural drawings.[23] White replied with an evasive obscurity worthy of the Circumlocution Office itself. So Burges tried the same question on the Irish Institute, and there found a readier response. Irish members were even asked their opinions.[24] In 1880 he not only corresponded with White on the administration of Institute funds, but published the correspondence in the *Building News*.[25] And a few weeks before his death – in fact only a few hours before his fatal collapse – he wrote a vigorous protest about R.I.B.A. elections: too many Councillors had become 'household words' by holding office too long; and the election of President had become merely a matter of 'routine, like the election of the Lord Mayor'.[26] This particular controversy raged round Burges even as he lay dying. For the question at issue was personal as well as constitutional: should Horace Jones become President by virtue of seniority, or should the prize go to G. E. Street, 'by sovereignty of nature'. Burges claimed Jones as a 'friend'. But he admired Street as a true Goth. His solution was therefore pragmatic: call a general meeting, ditch the dull mechanism of seniority, and return to the 'old mode of election'. His advice went unheeded. There was a public squabble between both factions before Street emerged as President.[27] Throughout, Burges was in a tricky position. Street was a Goth, but Jones was a fellow FAB.

The FABS were a select, semi-secret coterie, founded in 1859 and limited to fifteen members: the archaeological élite of the R.I.B.A.[28] Nominally, their role was the circulation, discussion and sale of architectural works published abroad. They were the Foreign Architectural Book Society.[29] But their real purpose was simply architectural fun. Burges was not a founder-member.[30] But after his election he quickly became its leading spirit. In August 1863 the annual two-day Recreation Meeting was inaugurated with a visit to Hatfield. Burges and Seddon were guests, plus a third person – probably the self-important Edis – described simply as 'Big Wigg'. Within weeks Burges had been elected, and the minutes take on a new hilarity. The bibulous Nesfield and the bonhomous Digby Wyatt had been elected in 1860. C. F. Hayward[31] and John Norton[32] were already founder-members. So was Burges's friend J. Stevenson Barber.[33] Burges shared their interests and their style. With classicists like F. P. Cockerell, Charles Fowler, Octavius Hansard, Horace Jones and Professor J. Roger Smith and T. Hayter Lewis he must have had many a tussle. But they were, after all, all gentlemen and scholars. And the elections over the next two decades clearly show which way FABS voted in the Battle of the Styles: Arthur Blomfield, Somers Clarke, Aitchison, J. L. Pearson, Devey, Waterhouse, Pullan, Stevenson and Eastlake. In May 1865 Burges invited the group up to Oxford to look over his work at Worcester College; afterwards they dined happily at the Star Hotel. In July he was one of 'ye FABS doing the staircase' at Knole, and staying at the Crown, Sevenoaks.[34] In September 1866 he invited them to Waltham, to 'freely discuss' his Abbey restorations, and to feast at the Four Swans on stuffed pike and Michaelmas goose. Perhaps Burges was host again in 1870 when they took an omnibus from Winchfield to Bramshill and dined together at Basingstoke. And once again in 1874 at Harrow, when Aitchison dismissed the architectural fare, and carried *nem.con.* an immediate adjournment for dinner. Burges certainly invited the FABS down to Windsor in 1869.[35] And in 1878 came a high point in his career: the FABS met at his new house in Melbury Road.[36] Burges seldom missed a meeting. Almost the last entry in his diary relates yet another session of his favourite club: 'Waterhouse FABS, March 9, 1881'.[37]

Street was a guest when the FABS visited Canterbury in 1866; Waterhouse when they went to Penshurst, Chiddingston and Hever in 1867. T. H. Wyatt and Stacy Marks went with them to Winchester in 1868; Leighton to Cambridge in 1869; and Woolner and Eastlake to Guildford in 1870, bumping uncomfortably together in an unnecessarily small carriage. Millais and Du Maurier were guests on the 1873 trip to Newark and Southwell. Trollope and Keane joined them at Maidstone and Leeds Castle in 1874. In 1871 they met at Hansard's house in Dulwich, played bowls and ate a capital supper. In 1872 Browning, Lord Exeter's architect, took them over Stamford and Burghley and arranged a sumptuous luncheon. In 1878 they were at Stonehenge. In 1879 the FABS descended on Oxford again, driving out to Blenheim in a coach and four. Alma Tadema was a guest of honour. And Horace Jones – 'the personification of a City magnate'[38] – arrived separately in a hansom cab, having missed the early train.

Such were the traditions of the FABS: disorderly book-sales, hectic travelling, light conversation, and heavy meals. Such junketing was by no means cheap. All FABS were men of means. Most of them lived near the Strand or Regent Street. In 1863 Digby Wyatt's book fines alone amounted to £5 11s. 4d.[39] In 1859 Norman Shaw decided he could not afford to join. 'I have no dibs to spare,' he told Hayward; 'I have not paid my tailor for ever so long, and I live such a long way off. . . . However you will without doubt easily find a dozen fellows ready to join you, and stump up their guineas like bricks. . . . With best wishes for the success of the FABLIMBBS (Foreign, Architectural, Book lending, interchanging mutual benefit burial society). . . .'[40] John Lockyer joined under pressure: 'What with the Institute, Arch. Exhibition, Arch. Publication Soc., Arch. Museum, Arch. Benevolent, Arch. Photographic and the Arundel – the guineas altogether mount up.'[41]

Burges certainly stumped up his guineas like bricks. Besides the R.I.B.A. and the FABS, he was active in the Hogarth Club, the Arts Club, the Verulam Club,[42] the Athenaeum, the Arundel Club, the Architectural Photographic Association, the Architectural Museum Society, the Architectural Exhibition Society[43] and its parent Architectural Association, the Royal Archaeological Institute, the Medieval Society, and eventually the Royal Academy. There is only one obvious gap in the list: the Society of Antiquaries.

With the Royal Academy Burges maintained a tenuous, love-hate relationship. 'Academies', he used to say, 'are the death of art.'[44] Before 1870 he preferred to exhibit at the Architectural Exhibition Society. After that date, he exhibited often enough at Burlington House, mostly atmospheric competition drawings from the hand of Axel

Herman Haig. But he disapproved of the Academy's influence on architecture, its encouragement of pictorial perspectives. The fact that he was not afraid to say so, often and in public, must surely have hampered his own election. Quite unjustly, Norman Shaw and J. L. Pearson became A.R.A.s years before him, in 1872 and 1874. So did E. M. Barry: he became A.R.A. in 1861 and R.A. in 1869. Shaw became a full R.A. in 1877. In 1868 there were two vacancies at Associate level, and Burges was nominated along with P. C. Hardwick, E. W. Pugin, T. H. Wyatt and Charles Barry Jnr.[45] Hardwick and Barry were chosen. Three years later he was kept out once again. By 1880 Burges's omission had become a scandal. It was rumoured that Pearson's prospective elevation as R.A. was designed to ease the log-jam: Burges, Bodley and Arthur Blomfield were all eligible, but Burges was the logical choice, on grounds of seniority and talent.[46] At last, on 28th January 1881, Burges was elected A.R.A., together with two painters: John Brett and Andrew Gow.[47] Almost the last entry in his diary reads: 'Signed roll at Academy, March 1.' He was proud of his election. But he felt rather more at home in less prestigious, more ephemeral organisations.

The Hogarth Club, for instance. Although it existed for less than four years, between 1858 and 1862, its Friday meetings in Waterloo Place became both a focus and a stimulus for the whole Pre-Raphaelite generation. It derived its name not from the eighteenth-century artist but from Mr Hogarth, the fashionable printseller in Haymarket, eponymous hero of the 'Hogarth frame'.[48] Burges recorded its formal foundation in 1859, his own election in 1860, and its break-up at the end of 1861.[49] Morris and Burne-Jones, Madox Brown and Holman Hunt, Ruskin and Rossetti – the Pre-Raphaelite stars were mostly members; and there was a whole secondary constellation of painters as well: Arthur Hughes, Val Prinsep, Leighton, G. F. Watts, John Brett, G. P. Boyce, Fripp, Inchbold and Lear. There were architects too: Bodley, Street, Webb and Woodward. And artists who defied any classification, like J. R. Clayton, William Bell Scott and John Hungerford Pollen. Once at least the Hogarth met at Morris's place in Red Lion Square. 'In the room,' Boyce noted, 'were some interesting drawings, tapestry and furniture, the latter gorgeously painted in subjects by Jones and Morris and Gabriel Rossetti.'[50] Burges must have been in his element. But, alas, the club's purpose proved unclear and its finances unsound. The Hogarth failed to survive the 'fickle tempers of its artistic members'.[51]

The life of the Medieval Society was even briefer. It was founded in 1857, and Burges was a committee member. His colleagues came from the same Pre-Raphaelite catchment as the Hogarth Club: Morris, Holman Hunt, Madox Brown, Ruskin, both Rossetti brothers, W. Bell Scott, J. R. Clayton and Coventry Patmore. The list includes five other architects: Street, Seddon, White, Woodward and Bodley; and four of Burges's personal friends, his travelling companion Frederick Warren; his brother-in-law R. Popplewell Pullan; Tom Taylor the critic; and one clergyman of Pre-Raphaelite sympathies: the Rev. J. F. Russell.[52] On at least one occasion the committee of the Medieval Society met in Burges's own rooms.[53] Its membership suggests not only a Pre-Raphaelite ginger-group, but a caucus of Burges's closer friends. Unfortunately no record of its existence survives after 1858.

The Architectural Museum had a rather longer life too. Its membership constituted much more than a particular clique or côterie. It was founded in the euphoric year 1851 as a craft-based supplement to the Institute of British Architects. Its object was an improvement of taste through the provision of decorative models in the form of drawings, tracings, photographs, casts and fragments. From the start it supported the Gothic Revival, and Burges was a stalwart patron. 'Though it has no obligatory credo', Hope admitted in 1863, 'it is mainly Gothic. It does not exclude other styles, but it has a strong Gothic bias.'[54] Hope became its President, Bute and Ripon Vice-Presidents. Its collection was housed in a shabby mews in Cannon Row, Westminster.[55] Burges must often have clambered up its rickety outside staircase to attend lectures and committee meetings. After 1869 – as the Royal Architectural Museum – it occupied rather more spacious premises at 18 Tufton St, Westminster, designed in appropriately Gothic style by Ewan Christian and G. Somers Clarke.[56] Architectural Art Classes were regularly held, in conjunction with the A.A. and R.I.B.A.[57] Among the exhibits were several presented by Burges: carved fragments from Southwell, Winchester and Ely; casts of Ghiberti's door-panels in the Baptistery at Florence; a facsimile of a Limoges enamel plate from Amiens; fragments of cut velvet from Beauvais and stamped leather from Châlons-sur-Marne; a brass-rubbing from King's Lynn; pieces of painted plaster from Pompeii and Seluntium; the cast of a jewelled book cover from Troyes; and a decorated iron door-handle, with its original scarlet underfelt, picked up by Burges while travelling with Aitchison.[58] As the Gothic Revival waned, however, so did the Architectural Museum. Its collections were eventually absorbed in 1916 by the Victoria and Albert Museum.

Unlike the Medieval Society and the Architectural Museum, the Architectural Photographic Association cut across stylistic barriers. Its first and second Presidents were both staunch classicists: C. R. Cockerell and Sir William Tite. But Burges felt at home on the committee with stalwart Goths like Scott, Seddon, Street, Norton, Ferrey and Truefitt, as well as FABS like Hansard, Hayward, Lewis and Wyatt. Exhibitions were held annually, at least between 1857 and 1861, at a gallery in Conduit St.[59] Subscribers could order copies of prints, by Alinari for instance, or Roger Fenton. Membership must have been well worth a guinea.

The Archaeological Institute was rather more expensive. But then it played a much more central rôle in Burges's career, and indeed in the lives of a whole generation of Gothic Revivalists. Founded as the British Archaeological Association in 1843; re-founded as a separate Institute in 1845; 'Royal' from 1866, it supplied a focus for the study of British medieval antiquities.[60] Unlike the Society of Antiquaries, which had something of a bias towards Romano-British remains, its particular sphere of interest was the Middle Ages. And preservation was as much its concern as documentation. Burges's key patrons – Bute, Hope and Ripon – were all members. So were lesser patrons like W. Cunliffe Brooks,[61] W. R. Cusack Smith, Dr Robert Wollaston[62] and the Spurrells. So were many of his friends: antiquaries, collectors, historians, architects. Among the leading spirits at its foundation were Albert Way, Edward Blore, G. G. Scott, Thomas Willement, Benjamin Ferrey and Charles Winston, all from London; E. A. Freeman and J. H. Parker from Oxford; Dr Whewell and Professor Willis from Cambridge; Dean Mereweather from Hereford; J. L. Petit from Shropshire; Gambier Parry from Gloucestershire; and Ambrose Poynter from Dover. The first President of the Institute was the Marquess of Northampton, patron at Castle Ashby of three fellow-members: Digby Wyatt, Burges and E. W. Godwin. The second President was the eccentric Lord Lyttelton. Corresponding members included a formidable Gallic quintet: Didron, Daly, De Caumont, Lassus and Viollet-le-Duc. Later on, more of Burges's friends joined too: Pullan, Stephen Tucker and N. H. J. Westlake. Among their colleagues were a trio of great historians: Stubbs, Round and Green.

Burges's loyalty to the R.A.I. – perhaps stemming from its early split with the British Archaeological Association – seems to have been intense. For his generation, its membership really constituted an élite corps of medievalists. And this exclusive loyalty to a comparatively junior body may perhaps explain his exclusion – or rather, self-imposed abstention – from the senior and more prestigious Society of Antiquaries. Burges was a member for thirty years, and a councillor for twenty. And one of his last undertakings was the organisation, with Baron de Cosson, of a major R.A.I. exhibition: 'Ancient Helmets and Examples of Mail.'[63]

Besides attending conferences in different parts of the country, Burges exhibited and spoke regularly at the R.A.I.'s London headquarters. The list of objects which he explained to his fellow-members makes curious reading. In 1852 he exhibited a piece of Roman tessellated pavement.[64] In 1856 he showed a fourteenth-century betrothal ring adorned with a crowned heart;[65] two fourteenth-century fragments of bone carving;[66] and two fourteenth-century Florentine paintings on panel, representing St Barbara and St Agatha.[67] In 1857 he showed a drawing of a fifteenth-century ivory tablet, engraved with figures of Morris-dancers and Maid Marian, which he had found at Vercelli;[68] a drawing of a false right arm, made of iron and preserved in the Museo Correr at Venice; sketches of Queen Theodolinda's jewels at Monza;[69] and a cast from a German ivory mirror-case, representing the assault on the Castle of Love.[70] In 1858 he exhibited a shell (*Murex trunculus*) used by the ancients in the manufacture of purple dye, discovered at Athens in 1857 during excavations in the Odeum of Herodus Atticus; as well as a small ornamental fountain and several pieces of metalwork damascened in gold and silver which he had brought back from Constantinople.[71] In 1859 he exhibited a *Portiera*, or stamped-leather door-curtain, brought back by him from Italy, and decorated with silvered and gilt foliated patterns on a colouring of dark bronze green;[72] a collection of fourteenth and fifteenth-century locks, hinges, knockers and door-handles;[73] drawings of roof paintings added about the time of Richard II to the Chapelle des Pêcheurs adjoining the ancient church of St Brelade in Jersey; and drawings of thirteenth and fourteenth-century mural paintings – St Nicholas and other Saints, and a favourite mural admonition, *Les Trois Vifs et les Trois Morts* – brought to light by his own restorations for the Rev. T. Burningham in the South aisle of Charlwood church in Surrey.[74] In 1861 he exhibited two cinerary urns from a barrow on the Wiltshire Downs.[75] Next year it was a Saxon iron spear-head found in the River Lea, and a collection of medieval daggers, knives and spurs dredged from the Thames during the construction of the embankment for the Houses of Parliament.[76] In 1863 he showed several more objects: a fragment of linen wall-hanging, painted in water-colour with representations of boar-hunting in a country estate;[77] two pieces of seventeenth-century embroidery, one embossed with images of Charles II as Orpheus charming the animals and a mermaid holding a mirror of talc, the other representing a shepherd, shepherdess, lion and stag, with a city in the background;[78] a Chinese ewer enriched with *cloisonné* enamel;[79] some steel chain-mail, probably Oriental but fished out of the Thames, and some ladies' scissors, supposedly medieval, of brass edged with steel, dug up near St George's Chapel, Windsor.[80] His exhibits for 1864 included examples of oriental plate, medieval metalwork and seventeenth-century cutlery.[81] And in 1867 he showed a tryptich attributed to Mabuse.[82]

Now most of these objects came from Burges's own collection. Here is antiquarian eclecticism with a vengeance. Such a rum list of curiosities prepares us for the magpie hoard in his own home. But before we even approach his office, a few more glimpses of clubbable Billy Burges at bay.

The Arundel Society, founded in the Pre-Raphaelite year of 1848, for the propagation of Pre-Raphaelite principles and the publication of Pre-Raphaelite art, clearly had Burges's sympathy and – presumably – his subscription.[83] But it is the Arundel Club – less famous and less serious – to which he refers in his diary.[84] Founded about 1862 by Frank Talfourd – an Inner Temple lawyer known for his burlesques in the manner of J. R. Planché – it operated close to Burges's rooms, first in Salisbury Street and then at Adelphi Terrace.[85] Its members were mostly journalists, actors and men of the theatre, denizens of what G. A. Sala christened 'Great Brain Street'. Its hours were late, its customs Bohemian. Burges was on his home ground.

Still more so at the Arts Club.[86] Established early in 1863 by refugees from the Garrick, its headquarters were at 17 Hanover Square, once the home of 'Hell Fire' Dashwood. In 1876 it moved to Dover St. Burges was practically a founder-member.[87] He involved himself in its refurbishment.[88] He may even have designed a set of cups.[89] Laughing with Prinsep; smoking with Whistler; singing with George Du Maurier or Stacy ('Marco') Marks; joking with Rossetti; quarrelling with Albert Moore; drinking with Swinburne (he was nearly expelled, in a drunken frenzy, for stamping on members' hats)[90] – membership of the Arts Club was almost an education in amiability. As an architect, Burges dined mostly at 'the Bricklayers'

Table' with friendly rivals: Owen Jones, Sir T. N. Deane, George Aitchison, and Digby Wyatt; Street, Ferrey, Hardwick and Hayward; sporty Arthur Blomfield, genial Horace Jones; the jovial F. P. Cockerell, the lordly Col. Edis, or the mettlesome E. W. Godwin. Some of Burges's closest friends were members: G. P. Boyce, practically a room-mate in Buckingham St; Charles Augustus Howell, 'that remarkable factotum of uncommercial artists';[91] J. M. Jopling, crack-shot husband of lovely Louise; and Horatio Walter Lonsdale, his draughtsman, illustrator and cartoonist, playing billiards after dinner with grave precision. Some nights the drink was stronger and the singing louder. Those were the nights of a new election at the Royal Academy. No wonder Burges christened it 'the junior Athenaeum'.

The Athenaeum was, of course, clubland's academic summit. After waiting for fourteen years – a normal probation period at that time – Burges was elected in 1874 by 208 votes to 19.[92] His application was endorsed by the signatures of fifty-one supporters. That list – friends, colleagues, patrons – constitutes almost an epitome of his public career. The key name is Beresford-Hope, judiciously appearing as seconder after a non-contentious architectural proposer, Joseph Clarke. With Hope went the Tory, Church and Gothic lobby: the architects Gilbert Scott, G. E. Street and T. H. Wyatt; the Reverend ecclesiologist Benjamin Webb; F. T. Palgrave of *Golden Treasury* fame; the Rev. Charles Lyndhurst Vaughan, a ritualist from St Leonard's-on-Sea;[93] Sir Frederick Williams Bt., Tory M.P. for Truro;[94] Sir Francis Sharp Powell, Fellow of St John's College, Cambridge and Conservative M.P. for that City;[95] William Henry Stone, a Liberal M.P., but like Hope from Harrow and Trinity College, Cambridge;[96] and – last but not least – another Trinity man, George 4th Baron Lyttelton, once a Liberal M.P. but better known as a suicidal, melancholic enthusiast for church and empire, colonies and cricket, and a champion chess-player who translated Tennyson's *Lotos Eaters* into Greek.[97]

Next on the Athenaeum list comes a group of non-partisan, establishment architects: F. C. Penrose, F. P. Cockerell, E. M. Barry, Charles Barry Jnr and T. L. Donaldson; plus one architectural rogue theorist, James Fergusson. And next three names without which no Victorian pantheon of the arts would be complete: Charles Landseer, Frederick Leighton and Richard Redgrave. Then there are the antiquaries and collectors: Sir Augustus Wollaston Franks, P.S.A., Keeper of British and Medieval Antiquities at the British Museum,[98] and his archaeological colleague, Major Rhode Hawkins;[99] Frederick Ouvry, P.S.A., bibliophile, the original of Dickens' 'Mr Undery' in *Household Words*;[1] J. S. Hodson, who organised the quatercentenary Caxton Exhibition at South Kensington in 1877;[2] Sir Frederick Locker-Lampson, poet, bibliophile and clubman;[3] and Sir Julian Goldsmid Bt., a Liberal M.P., millionaire and collector.[4] Another group were all linked with the saga of Burges's greatest unexecuted commission – the decoration of St Paul's Cathedral: the learned and sensitive Dean Church, the learned and formidable Dean Milman, the silver-tongued Canon Liddon, and Prebendary Plumtre, whom Burges also knew as

Chaplain of King's College, London, Dean of Queen's College, Harley St and translator of Dante.[5]

Finally comes a random group, linked to Burges only by accidents of acquaintance and patronage. Solomon Hart, R.A., architectural artist and antiquary;[6] Henry T. Wells, R.A., a miniaturist and portrait painter who married Joanna Mary Boyce;[7] Sir Henry Longley, son of Archbishop Longley, for whom Burges designed a memorial plaque;[8] Col C. H. Luard and W. R. Cusack Smith, both minor patrons; Sir George Scharf, bachelor, topographer, socialite and Director of the National Portrait Gallery who had worked with Digby Wyatt on the Crystal Palace and with J. B. Waring on the Manchester Exhibition of 1857;[9] Sir Charles Gregory, railway engineer;[10] Sir William Drake, chairman of the Burlington Fine Arts Club, who refounded Salviati & Co. in 1869 as the Venice and Murano glass and mosaic company;[11] E. W. Cooke, R.A., of Glen Andred, Kent, a topographical artist who had studied under A. C. Pugin and travelled for Earl de Grey;[12] Thomas Chenery, a shy bachelor barrister who became first *The Times*'s correspondent in Constantinople, then Professor of Arabic at Oxford, and finally Delane's successor as editor of *The Thunderer*;[13] and Francis Jeune, Bishop of Peterborough, an evangelical university reformer who preached in French at Westminster Abbey on the opening of the 1862 Exhibition.[14]

Such, then, were Burges's supporters at the Athenaeum. Each name suggests a commission received; a connection maintained; a link in the network of patronage. Several of Burges's key patrons are on the list, and many of his friends. But the two men who were to provide him with some of the greatest professional opportunities of his career are missing: Lord Ripon and Lord Bute. And the men who actually helped him in his work, day by day, are of course missing too: his pupils and assistants.

TEACHING

Burges never ran a large office. He was never in the same mass-production league as Gilbert Scott, Arthur Blomfield or Ewan Christian. His few pupils became personal friends, his assistants life-long colleagues.

He first 'had a clerk' in 1851.[15] An 'improver' arrived in 1855: W. Aitchison.[16] During the 1860s and 1870s there must generally have been at least half a dozen people working in the small office in Buckingham St, clerks, pupils or assistants. Numbers fluctuated according to the pressure of work. One pupil, Salles, for instance, seems to have been taken on in 1869–70 to help with Cork Cathedral.[17] In 1874 there were four assistants; in 1880 there were three pupils.[18] In 1874 Burges took on extra staff to deal with the design for Trinity College, Hartford, Connecticut. One of these new assistants was Walter Millard (1879–1936). Another was W. G. B. Lewis. Another was W. F. Unsworth. And another was Josiah Conder. Thanks to Millard we can catch something of the atmosphere. All four worked long hours at their drawing boards, under the direction of the office manager J. S. Chapple. Punctuality was prized; silence generally observed. 'We learnt,' Millard recalled, 'what it was to work while we were at it, and to work together.' As they worked, Burges's friends would call in and offer advice: Godwin's advice, in particular, 'set one thinking'.[19] In the evenings they might study figure-drawing at the Slade School, or drill with the Artists' Rifles.[20] The Franco-Prussian War was still in everybody's mind.

When Trinity College was finished, Millard transferred to Street's office.[21] But Lewis (d. 1913) stayed on. In fact Lewis remained in Buckingham St for six years, from 1874 to 1880.[22] He thoroughly absorbed the *genius loci*: his 'Design for a Royal Academy of Arts' (1884) combines memories of Cork, Cardiff and Dover, with echoes of the Sabrina Fountain in front and Castell Coch behind.[23]

Lewis's contemporary, W. F. Unsworth (1851–1912) had come to Burges after spells in Paris and in the office of G. E. Street.[24] His career was transformed when he won the Shakespeare Memorial Theatre competition while still in Burges's office. A Gothic theatre had always been one of Burges's dreams. He had plotted one with Godwin for years. And we may suppose that Unsworth's scheme embodied many of the ideas that were floating about Buckingham St. An extraordinarily eclectic design, Franco-German in origin with touches not only of Burges (sculptured panels by Lonsdale)[25] but of Street, Butterfield and Norman Shaw as well, Unsworth's theatre, library and art gallery complex survived to dominate Stratford-on-Avon until the fire of 1928.[26] He never matched that form again.

Josiah Conder (1852–1920) had a rather more persistent talent. He came to Burges from the office of Professor T. Roger Smith. In 1876, after two years at Buckingham St, he emigrated to Japan, married a Japanese girl, and settled down to become the leading architect in his adopted country. The Anglo-Japanese nexus was, of course, basic to progressive aesthetics in the 1860s and 1870s – witness the work of Burges, Godwin and Dresser. Conder, therefore, hardly felt aesthetically out of place. In the service of the Imperial Japanese Government he was successively Professor of Architecture in the Engineering College, Architect to the Public Works Department, Consulting Architect to the Imperial Palace Bureau and Lecturer in Architecture at the Imperial University, Tokyo. Palaces, embassies, clubs, villas and colleges flowed from his office. And he ended his days as Honorary Chokunin, a member (fourth class) of the Order of the Rising Sun, and a member (third class) of the Order of the Sacred Treasure.[27] Despite its infusion of Japanese vernacular, Conder's work remained essentially Burgesian. His Soane Medallion 'Design for a Country House' (1876),[28] had been more Burgesian than Burges himself, bursting with symbolic sculpture, bristling with towers from Cardiff, and peppered with mullioned windows from Knightshayes and timbered gables from Viollet-le-Duc. His Tokyo University (1879 onwards), in a kind of Anglo-Franco-Japanese, unmistakably recalls Burges's Trinity College, Hartford, Connecticut.[29] His Shintomiza Theatre, Tokyo (1879) is confessedly traditional in form, but with occasional touches which Burges would have relished.[30] Indeed Conder maintained connections with Burges despite the huge distances involved. In 1878 he sent Burges some china.[31] And in 1880 he arranged for Burges to take on one of his Tokyo pupils, a young Japanese named Kingo Tatsuno.[32] In due course Conder and Tatsuno represented Japanese architecture at the Worlds Fair in Chicago (1893).[33] It is perhaps not too fanciful, therefore, to see Burges in yet another seminal rôle: as godfather to the Western architectural tradition in Japan.

But Burgesian principles went further still. Another pupil, the future Sir William Emerson (1843–1925), P.R.I.B.A., translated Burgesian Gothic into Indian. After training with Habershon and Pite, Emerson entered Buckingham St in 1865.[34] He was put to work on the Bombay Art School project, and sent out to India in 1866.[35] Burges had given him a style. Now he found his métier as architect to the Raj. His principles of design were boldly eclectic. Just as Mohammedan builders had absorbed the art of the Hindoos, so British architects must absorb the native architecture of India. Hybridity in Europe – Santa Sophia, Monreale, San Miniato in Florence, St Mark's Venice, St Front at Périgueux, even the apse at Canterbury – indicated the infinite flexibility of the eclectic process. 'Indeed are not many of the most lovely flowers and plants hybrids, and has not the intermingling of the different families of the human race produced some of the noblest types of men?[36] By mingling Early French, Romanesque, Byzantine, Egyptian, Moorish, Hindoo and Mohammedan elements Emerson hoped to strike out a style for the future. And in doing so he made himself master of one of the more extraordinary styles of the nineteenth century: Anglo-Indian Gothic.

In England Emerson designed little of importance: a church in Brighton,[37] a tomb in Yorkshire,[38] houses in Queen's Gate, Kensington,[39] his own house in Chiswick.[40] His greatest schemes – the Berlin Parliament House (1872)[41] and Liverpool Cathedral (1885),[42] both strikingly Burgesian – remained paper projects. His most conspicuous works were all far away in India, and he ended his career appropriately with the Victoria Memorial, Calcutta (1904–5).[43]

At Bombay Emerson designed the Girgaum Church (c. 1870–73),[44] the Arthur Crawford Market (1865–71)[45] and the market fountain (1874);[46] at Allahabad the Cathedral of All Saints (c. 1869–93)[47] and Muir College (1872–8);[48] and at Bhavnagar (or Bhownugger) the Takhtsingi Hospital (c. 1879–83)[49] and the Maharaja's Palace (1894–5).[50] Allahabad Cathedral transports the spirit of St Finbar's, Cork into the diocese of Lucknow. The structure of Crawford Market has echoes of Skilbeck's warehouse and Cardiff Castle stables, while its fountain inevitably recalls the visionary Sabrina Fountain, Gloucester.[51] But Muir College is most Burgesian of all.[52] In fact Emerson's description of its eclectic basis is so characteristic of Burges's methods – and of 'progressive' Gothic thinking in general – that it is worth quoting at length:

> I determined not to follow too closely Indian art, but to avail myself of an Egyptian phase of Moslem architecture, and work it up with the Indian Saracenic style of Beejapore and the north-west, combining the whole in a western Gothic design. The beautiful lines of the Taj Mahal influenced me in my dome over the

hall, and the Indian four-centred arch suggested itself as convenient for my purpose, as working in well with the general Gothic feeling. The details show how the Gothic tracery is blended with the Indian geometrical perforated stonework in the windows, and the Caireen Moucharabyeh wood-work; Gothic shafts and caps are united with Indian arches; and the domes stand on Gothicised Mohammedan pendentives and semi-circular arches; the open staircase is also a Gothic feature adapted to Oriental requirements. The pavement of the hall is a combination of marble and stone inlays, mosaic work and *opus alexandrinum*. . . .[53]

We shall hear that voice again, but next time it will be the voice of William Burges.

Now for Ernest Lee (1845–90).[54] Lee was a pupil of Edis rather than Burges; a consumptive and a clergyman's son of private means. He soon fell under Burges's spell. With Lonsdale he revelled in Early French: in the office in Buckingham St, and in the field at Amiens and Chartres.[55] Together they designed a chancel for St Mary's, Whitechapel, so heavily sculptural and elaborately polychromatic as to be almost a Burgesian pastiche.[56] In 1869–70 Lee won both the Soane Medallion and the Pugin Travelling Studentship, and soon became one of the pillars of the Architectural Association.[57] His Soane Medallion 'Design for a Railway Station' was indeed a Burgesian performance, criticised at the time for excessive 'stumpiness'.[58] In the mid-1870s he worked closely with another of Burges's pupils: Thomas Manley Deane. As the fourth in a great dynasty of Irish architects, young Deane stayed several years (*c.* 1872–7) in Buckingham St before returning to his family practice.[59] The designs with which he won the R.A. Travelling Studentship (1876), and the Soane Medallion (1877) are both robustly Burgesian.[60] Thereafter, however, the master's influence diminishes amidst a welter of Renaissance and vernacular forms.[61] Lee proved less independent. After Burges's death he did branch out into Anglo-French Gothic and Anglo-Dutch Queen Anne.[62] But he was always Burgesian at heart, and even carried loyalty to Burges's circle so far as to marry Lonsdale's sister.[63]

Two of Burges's staunchest allies were William Frame and J. S. Chapple. Frame was not a pupil, but an assistant[64] in Burges's office who from 1873 onwards maintained an independent practice while pursuing his master's style tenaciously. His Soane Medallion 'Design for a Public Hall' (1873)[65] has many Burgesian mannerisms: the wheel window, the gabled fenestration, the lead-patterned towers, the sculpture and the mosaics. In fact they are the mannerisms of the whole 'Early French' school which Burges dominated: compare E. W. Godwin's design of 1871 for Leicester Town Hall.[66] Frame's work occasionally takes the form of *ersatz* Burges: the Bute Dock Building in Cardiff, for instance. But at his best he was an effective practitioner of that muscular style which J. P. Seddon (among others) christened 'Burgesian'.

John Starling Chapple joined Burges in 1859[67] and stayed with him to the end. Indeed he stayed beyond the end, for he continued to work in Buckingham St for two years after Burges's death.[68] Their relationship was close: 'skittles with Chapple', 'bought watches, self and Chapple' are typical entries in Burges's diary.[69] For many years Chapple acted as office manager, clerk of works and executant, involving himself with furniture and stained glass[70] as well as with architecture. And in the end it fell to him to complete the interior decoration of Castell Coch, as well as the structure of St Michael and All Angels, Brighton, and the town hall complex at Dover. Burges's death left him desolate. 'My very dear master', he calls him, looking back on 'a constant relationship of twenty-two years'; 'one of the brightest ornaments of the profession.... I have hardly yet got to realise my lonely position yet – he was almost all the world to me.'[71] Burges was clearly capable of inspiring extraordinary devotion among his colleagues. And in Chapple's case the sudden shock of Burges's early death was made worse by his own approaching blindness.[72]

Only two associates were as close to Burges as Chapple: his chief artist, Horatio Walter Lonsdale; and his brother-in-law, Richard Popplewell Pullan. Pullan was a fine scholar and archaeologist in Greek, Gothic and Byzantine fields.[73] He had a facility for design in almost any style, except of course Baroque. But he lived his life in the shadow of greater men. As a youth he trained with Alfred Waterhouse in the Manchester office of a local classicist, Richard Lane. In 1844 his design for the Queen's Robing Room at the House of Lords was naturally eclipsed by Pugin.[74] In 1853 his work on the Byzantine and Medieval Courts of the Sydenham Crystal Palace was naturally overshadowed by that of their progenitor, Matthew Digby Wyatt.[75] In 1855–6 his design (with George Evans) for Lille Cathedral was beaten into second place by Burges and Clutton.[76] In 1856–7 his design for the Memorial Church at Constantinople was eclipsed by Burges and Street.[77] His scheme for the decoration of St Paul's Cathedral joined a number of others in limbo.[78] His designs for the Memorial Church at St Petersburg (1882) were beaten by a Russian;[79] his designs for Truro Cathedral (1878) by J. L. Pearson;[80] for the War and Foreign Offices by William Young and G. G. Scott;[81] for the Liverpool Exchange Buildings by T. H. Wyatt;[82] for the Natural History Museum by Waterhouse;[83] for the Glasgow Municipal Buildings (1882) by William Young;[84] for the English Church in Rome (*c.* 1871) by G. E. Street;[85] for the Dublin Science Museum by T. N. Deane;[86] and for Hamburg Town Hall by Gilbert Scott.[87] As if that wasn't enough, he married Burges's sister in 1859, published Burges's designs after his death in 1881,[88] worked from Burges's office, and lived on to a bronchitic old age in Burges's Tower House, Kensington. His greatest works of scholarship were all editorial: Newton's excavations at Halicarnassus[89] and Texier's Byzantine and Grecian discoveries[90] might never have seen the light of day without him. And by continuing the Dilettanti Society volumes on Ionian Antiquities, he placed himself almost anonymously at the service of a famous archaeological tradition.[91]

Pullan's career as an architect ended almost equally anonymously: he completed several of Burges's unfinished works. And, to crown a life of anonymity, his only executed works of any substance are all abroad: churches at Pontresino (1879)[92] and

10 Bute aged 17: Lothair.

11 Bute as Rector of St Andrews' University (1892–7): scholar, mystic and millionaire.

Baveno (1873);[93] some elaborate gates in Nice;[94] and the conversion of a castle on Lake Maggiore into an English Gothic mansion.[95]

Lonsdale's position was one of even closer dependence. He was undoubtedly a draughtsman of exceptional precision,[96] and a fluent designer of occasional power.[97] He had been trained as an architect under H. E. Kendall,[98] and his earliest published drawings are of the South Kensington Museum's casts of the sculptured doorway at the Cathedral of Santiago de Compostela, Spain.[99] Under Burges's influence he learnt to admire Wilars and to love Dürer. In 1871 he won the R.A. Travelling Studentship with a design for 'A National Mausoleum'.[1] But at that point he was diverted by an invitation from Burges to work at Studley Royal and Skelton. He threw up his career as an architect and became an architectural artist. Wherever Burges went, Lonsdale went too, designing stained glass and mural decorations in profusion. Independently, he also executed commissions for furniture,[2] metalwork,[3] sculpture,[4] and heraldic illustration.[5] But his best work was all for Burges. Without the master's control, much of his later figurative work tends to be mechanical and vapid.[6]

With Lonsdale – a quiet, dignified fellow – Burges's relations were easy. Things were very different with Fred Weekes (1833–93), son of the sculptor Henry Weekes, R.A. Weekes taught figure drawing at the Architectural Museum.[7] He occasionally exhibited in oil at the R.A.[8] And he seems to have gone on producing cartoons for stained glass into the 1890s.[9] But the bulk of his work, for glass or on panel, was executed for Burges. At its best, his stained glass has a vigour and originality which Lonsdale never matched. And conscious perhaps of his own talent, he seems to have chafed unhappily as Burges's satellite.

Millard, Unsworth and Lewis; Conder and Tatsuno; Sir William Emerson, Ernest Lee and Thomas Manley Deane; William Frame and J. S. Chapple; Fred Weekes, H. W. Lonsdale and Richard Popplewell Pullan: not a dazzling list, but a group of talented men, moulded in their master's image, art-architects and medievalists to a man – jokers and jesters too[10] – devoted above all to art rather than business. Burges attracted men of ability rather than ambition. It says much for his pre-eminence in the later 1860s that he was able to enlist, as a temporary assistant for the Law Courts competition, one of the ablest and most scholarly architects of the next generation: Richard Phéné Spiers (1838–1916), a future Master of the R.A. School of Architecture.[11]

There were other artists too. Frederick Smallfield (1829–1915), who grew up with Burges in Digby Wyatt's school,[12] travelled with him on the Continent,[13] and served him well as a decorative artist on a small scale.[14] Axel Herman Haig (1835–1921), an immigrant Swede and a pupil of Ewan Christian, taken up by Burges and allowed full rein as a topographer and etcher of superlative talent – the perfect expositor of Burges's special genius.[15] Henry Stacy Marks (1829–98), wittiest of artists and happiest of companions, one of Burges's team of friendly furniture painters;[16] another was Charles Rossiter (1827–91).[17] Albert Moore (1841–93), an outspoken Yorkshireman with a real gift for figurative composition.[18] Ill-fated Thomas Morten (1833–66), a talented illustrator whose career ended in suicide.[19] W. F. Yeames (1835–1918), a friend of Burges before he became famous for 'And When Did You Last See Your Father?'[20] J. A. Fitzgerald (fl. 1845–93), a prolific artist of anecdotal and fairytale themes.[21] N. H. J. Westlake (1833–1921), who at Burges's suggestion took up glass-painting and became not only a leading stainer-glazier but an authoritative writer on its art.[22] Henry Holiday (1839–1927), who began as a minor Pre-Raphaelite and – with Burges's encouragement – ended as perhaps the most prolific late Victorian stainer-glazier of all.[23]

Finally, two names greater than any of these: Edward Burne-Jones and E. J. Poynter (1836–1919).[24] To Burges must go the credit for guiding Burne-Jones's earliest efforts in stained glass, and for arranging his post with Powell's of Whitefriars – a first step on the climb to Olympus. In return, it was Burne-Jones who helped to make Burges's restoration of Waltham Abbey such a triumph. As for Poynter, Burges deserves the credit for sponsoring the earliest phases of his career. Poynter had been known to Burges in the early 1850s through his father, Ambrose Poynter the architect. They were in Rome in 1853–4, and probably visited Sicily together.[25] They were almost certainly in Paris together in 1856[26] – the Paris of Du Maurier's *Trilby*. In 1857 Burges began to secure his fellow artist a series of commissions for decorative painting and stained glass. Poynter's career – which took him eventually to the Presidency of the R.A. – had been launched.

Smallfield, Haig, Stacy Marks, Rossiter, Moore, Morten, Yeames, Fitzgerald, Westlake, Holiday, Burne-Jones and Poynter: they were all Burges's friends, mostly a little younger than he. The majority – like Burges himself – had trained together at Leigh's Drawing School (later Heatherley's) in Newman St. Several of them contributed sketches to *Once A Week* in the 1860s. From Burges they received advice, encouragement and employment.

Such, then, were Burges's pupils and assistants, his friends and colleagues, his allies in art, his postillions on the road to Parnassus.

But, whether for architects or artists, Burges founded no school. As we shall see, he built up a team of manufacturers and craftsmen: almost an Arts and Crafts movement in microcosm. His style was to have many imitators. But his followers were devotees rather than disciples: their links were personal rather than professional. To them – as to all his friends – he was always 'Billy'. And as Robert Kerr pointed out, no one ever called G. E. Street 'Georgie'.[27]

LAUGHING

What was life like at 15 Buckingham St, Strand? And how was Billy Burges at home? His rooms [166–167] were on the second floor of a seventeenth-century house immediately overlooking the Thames.[28] Peter the Great may once have lived there, and Dickens certainly did. The light was good and the air bad. Before the days of the Thames Embankment, high tides lapped the pavement steps. Artists, architects, surveyors and engineers were thick on the ground: in 1857 there were at least twenty in Buckingham St, and by 1879 more than thirty.[29] It was a professional quarter, but near enough to Soho to preserve the illusion of Bohemia. How Burges and his Pre-Raphaelite friends must have scoffed at its Georgian ambience: Robert Adam's Adelphi was but a stroll away; the York Water Gate – then popularly attributed to Inigo Jones – lay just below Burges's stained glass windows. In the rooms immediately above him lived G. P. Boyce (1826–97). And it is thanks to Boyce's diary that we can picture Burges at home.

Boyce had begun as an architect, working in the office first of George Devey, then of Wyatt and Brandon. Pre-Raphaelites were his friends. But he himself was never a Pre-Raphaelite. His métier was water-colour landscape, precise, sunlit, calm. A perennial bachelor – he did not marry until the age of forty-nine – Boyce lodged in Buckingham St until, on Lizzie Siddal's death, he moved into Rossetti's old rooms in Chatham Place, Blackfriars. Rossetti, Philip Webb, William Morris, Charles Keane and William Bell Scott: they were perhaps his closest friends. But – like Burges – his friendships ran the full gamut of the Hogarth Club: Madox Brown, Leighton, Street, Woolner, Burne-Jones, Sir Frederick Burton.[30] Philip Webb designed him a home – West House, Chelsea – close to Cheyne Walk.[31] His diaries conjure up images of a comfy, bohemian, slightly raffish world: the Pre-Raphaelites at play.

There he is, joking in Rossetti's studio, overlooking the river, with J. P. Seddon, Clayton, Hunt, Hughes, Millais or Ruskin – munching 'sweet chestnuts and coffee, honey and hot spirits'.[32] Rossetti and Morris call round for tea in Buckingham St.[33] Allingham and Munro come to breakfast; afterwards, Boyce reports, they 'skirmished and rhapsodied and *ecstasied* over [Moxon's] new Tennyson, and Millais' and Rossetti's illustrations'.[34] One night we find him rendezvousing with voluptuous Fanny Cornforth at the Argyle Rooms, taking her to supper at Quinn's, and being found there *à deux* by Rossetti.[35] And there he is again, at Simeon Solomon's 'weekly re-union', consuming 'tea and fish, wine and cake'.[36] Another day, he calls on Rossetti at Tudor House, Cheyne Walk. The house has been newly furnished 'most picturesquely, mostly with fine old Renaissance furniture bought of a man at 8 Buckingham St'.[37] At other times we can picture him dining, amidst masses of blue and white china, with 'a gallicised Yankee' named Whistler.[38] Or lounging in a tent after dinner at Rossetti's, with 'Topsy' and Janey, Philip Webb and Burne-Jones.[39] Their talk is jokey and boisterous. 'Spiffy', 'cheesy', 'jammy', 'nobby', 'stunning', 'jolly', 'splendacious': the in-language of the Pre-Raphaelites.[40]

Burges is part of this world. Their language is his language. Breakfasting with Swinburne,[41] dining with Rossetti,[42] travelling down with Col. Edis to visit William Morris at Red House,[43] taking Turkish baths,[44] reading Edgar Allan Poe[45] – Burges is one of the set.

A few more entries in Boyce's diary[46] convey something of the atmosphere:

12 Dec. 1857.   Went down to Burges. Miss Cook was sitting to him for the figure in his [Sabrina] fountain.

7 Feb. 1858.   Gave Burges (in exchange for something he is to do for me) a sketch I made of Llyn Crafount in North Wales in the autumn of 1856, which he persists in calling the 7th Hell, as it reminds him of Dante's Inferno. The only alteration I made on it (to suit his fancy) is giving a red flush as of flame in the horizon.

13 Feb. 1858.   Miss Cook came to sit for me. Little Simeon Solomon called and stayed a long while and jawed and bored us considerably. Burges came up and I introduced them.

15 Feb. 1858.   Miss Varley sat to me. Discovered Burges had sent on to me the Valentine she had sent to him, followed by another. I enclosed them both again in an envelope for her to post to him. Went to a dancing and musical 'shine' at Clayton and Bell's . . . Jovial and unceremonious. . . .

29 May 1858.   . . . Rossetti called to see me while Burges was taking tea with me. After a while he got Annie Harrison (the landlady's daughter) to sit to him. Burges bullied him into using vellum when he wished simply for paper. Consequently he didn't make so good a sketch as he would have done had he been left to his own bent. It was in pen and ink, and he gave it to me before leaving, which was at a very late hour. He told me some amusing anecdotes about Thackeray, and repeated some most ludicrous exclamations of Morris'. He read a lovely little MS. poem of Browning's about a portrait of a golden-haired beauty on a golden ground that he had copied from some lady's album. Burges asked him how he would lay in a head in oil colour [While he explained] I made a slight sketch of Annie. . . .

30 April 1859.   Found Simeon Solomon and Poynter in Burges's room and appropriated (by leave) a caricature by Simeon of Morris and his wife.

5 June 1860.   Called on Fanny Cornforth who, I heard through Burges, was ill. Found her so in bed. . . .

19 July 1862.   Rossetti and Swinburne called on me. We went down and tea'd in Burges's room. After tea Burges, Seddon and Rossetti went off to 'Judge and Jury'. Swinburne and I to get some ices.

24 April 1867.   To Arts Club to dine with Edward Godwin. The others invited were Street, Madox Brown and W. Burges. Tremendous political discussion arose after dinner, Swinburne frantically joining in.

With the Judge and Jury Club we enter the Victorian underworld.[47] From 1841 to 1869, 'Judge and Jury' were bywords for obscenity and scurrility. First in Bow St, then in the Strand, then in Maiden Lane, and finally in Leicester Square, the club moved on, a few steps ahead of the police. Thackeray described it twice: as 'The Cave of Harmony' in *The Newcomes*, and as the 'Back Kitchen' in *Pendennis*. The star of the show was 'Baron' Renton Nicholson (1804–61),[48] a pawnbroker turned impresario who presided over nightly parodies of salacious legal cases. Adultery, rape, incest and indecency: 'evidence' was supplied by witnesses in drag; cross-examinations were conducted by ribald counsel; the drunken audience acted as jury; then Nicholson himself, clad in judicial garb, prescribed a suitably indecent sentence. Occasionally the performance was enlivened by Tableaux Vivants or Poses Plastiques: semi-nude women posturing on a revolving wheel. Behind the scenes, private rooms – and their occupants – were available for hire. Imagine the audience: drunks and gamblers mostly, leery business men from upcountry, a scattering of guardees, clubmen and young bloods out for a night on the town, plus a handful of inebriated Pre-Raphaelites in hazy pursuit of reality. No wonder Burges was 'one of those rich men who never have any ready money'.[49]

Another of Burges's haunts was Jemmy Shaw's in Westminster, a low pub notorious for rat-hunts. Ratting – gambling on the rat-killing talents of favourite dogs – was particularly popular with the 'fast' set in the 1850s and 1860s. Apprentices at the Westminster Pit,[50] undergraduates in Christ Church Meadows,[51] men-about-town at Jemmy Shaw's:[52] ratting was the sport of bohemians and rakes, the next best thing to cock-fighting. And Billy Burges seems to have been an addict.[53] On at least one occasion he staged an impromptu rat hunt in his office. 'The office boy was sent out . . . for a sack of rats: a rat-pit was extemporized out of drawing boards, architectural folios . . . and an elderly and distinguished client who chanced to call . . . found the rat-hunt in full cry, and the eminent architect and his . . . sporting friend in their shirt sleeves, hallooing on their respective champions to the slaughter.'[54]

At times dogs seem almost to be his closest friends. Three pet puppies – Bogie, Pinkie and Dandie – haunt his diary. Bogie arrives in 1865, has four puppies in 1867, five in 1869, an uncounted number in 1870 and five more in 1871, before dying in 1876.[55] Pinkie (a poodle) arrives on the scene – presumably as a borrowed pet – in 1867, nearly drowns in 1868, is finally bought in 1870–71, receives an enamelled collar designed by Burges in 1876,[56] and dies in 1880.[57] Dandie's career (a terrier) is more adventurous, arriving in 1867, biting Fanny Cornforth, Godwin and Mrs Emerson in 1870–73, surviving an operation in 1877, and being lost and found in the year of his death, 1879.[58] Pinkie survives in mosaic at the entrance to Tower House. And all three, immortalised by Rossiter, gaze out – fluffy and unconcerned – from a piece of Burges's painted furniture.[193] Dandie II survived his master: purchase is recorded only a few weeks before Burges's death.[59]

Besides dogs, there were parrots. This was a taste which Burges seems to have shared with W. E. Nesfield – a rumbustious Goth who sacrificed his talents to women and drink. Nesfield's notebooks include a sketch of 'Poor Polly lying in state at 30 Argyll St, Feb. 25, 1863'.[60] Burges's sketchbooks supply more detailed evidence of devotion: a design for a gabled sarcophagus, a tulip vase in front, candles at its corners, 'P.P.P.P.' along its frieze, feathered friends 'Jane' and 'Tommy' looking on, and an inscription to the effect that 'Poor Polly died Feb. 19, 1863. She was a gentle bird'.[61]

Visitors to Buckingham St – clients even – clearly had to beware of this menagerie. Burges used to joke that guard-dogs were necessary, otherwise he would have too many clients.[62] Once across the threshold, however, their welcome was warm. With a parrot perched on his shoulder, Burges was invariably affable, and usually jolly. E. W. Godwin recalled how he was received on his first visit: 'I introduced myself; he was hospitable, poured wine into a silver goblet of his own design, and placed bread on the table. With few words on either side we ate and drank, and thus began a friendship which was more intimate and sincere than any friendship of my life.'[63]

In the later 1860s no one was closer to Burges than Godwin. Their tastes were parallel: Japanese and Early French. Burges once sketched Godwin as playing Peter de Corbie to his own Wilars de Honecort.[64] After a career in Bristol as a promising Ruskinian Goth – winning competitions for Northampton and Congleton Town Halls – he had moved to London in 1865.[65] In the metropolitan air his talents as a wit and interior decorator, as a furniture designer, littérateur and man of the theatre, flourished. In fact they flourished so well that his early promise as an architect remained unfulfilled. With Burges he travelled in Wales and Ireland.[66] With Burges and a succession of ladies, he visited the theatre.[67] With Burges he spent a week hidden in Alfred Burges's house in Blackheath, preparing an astonishing scheme for the Law Courts competition of 1866.[68] Burges often stayed with Godwin and Ellen Terry in their secret love-nest near Wheathampstead. Ellen even traced out Burges's drawings for the interior of Cardiff Castle Clock Tower.[69] And it is Burges, close enough to both lovers to be trusted as a witness, who supplies one vital piece of information, the date and circumstances of the break-up of that famous romantic alliance. In his diary, late in 1874, he notes simply 'N[Nellie] left Godwin'.[70] In the 1870s Burges and Godwin disagreed over style and colour. As the years passed, Godwin became less of a Goth, and more – in Max Beerbohm's phrase – 'the greatest aesthete of them all'.[71] He came to think that Burges's designs suffered from an 'excess of strength'.[72] But rows never spoilt their friendship. Right to the end they would take tea together in the garden Burges planned at Tower House.[73]

With Burges there were always plenty of rows. 'Row with Clutton';[74] 'row with Barkentin';[75] 'Row with D. Brandon';[76] 'Row between Edis and Woolner';[77] 'Burne-Jones row and dinner at Rossetti's';[78] 'Swinburne twisted spoon....'[79] Burges often, as he put it, trod on people's toes.[80] But he stood by his friends. Odd friends too. Witness the case of James Thomson (1834–82), poet – under the pseudonym 'B.V.' – pessimist, insomniac, dypsomaniac and radical free-thinker. With him Burges goes to the theatre; together they even go shopping for an armoured breast-plate.[81] Or witness the case of Farrell Hogg, a gentlemanly trickster probably known through Edwin Walford.[82] When Hogg was 'brought up' before the magistrates, Burges tried to persuade Rossetti to join him in court. Burges went, but the great Pre-Raphaelite was too busy – or, rather, found it difficult to get up in time.[83]

Rossetti's trouble was chloral. Thomson's trouble was alcohol. With Burges – occasionally at any rate – it was opium. A laconic entry in his diary for 1865 is revealing: 'Too much opium, did not go to Hayward's wedding.'[84] Now Burges regarded this entry as significant: the phrase 'too much opium' is repeated as an important happening in that year's summary of events. Moreover, 'too much' implies that he was used to taking more moderate, ordinary doses. Evidently he went beyond his usual limit on this occasion, presumably at a stag party the night before C. F. Hayward's wedding.[85] What effect opium had on his work one can only guess. But it is hard to resist the conclusion that it reinforced the dreamier elements in his artistic make-up.

Smoking,[86] drinking, laughing, banting. . . . Banting was a London cabinet maker whose dietary nostrums swept fashionable society in 1864. His recipe for weight-reduction included the avoidance of fat, starch and sugar.[87] Burges was one of the first to Bant: 'tried Banting', he notes in his diary, under the category of important events.[88] Not that it seems to have done much good. Billy Burges was always inclined to be plump. Plump, jolly and short-sighted. As he grew older he grew more irascible. In Poynter's portrait of 1858 he wears a puckish look; in a photo taken just before his death he stares out at posterity like some petulant bulldog. Burges's humour was childish and ingenuous, impish, almost Chaucerian. He seems to have been, alternately, as gleeful and as bumptious as an overgrown schoolboy. And perhaps as naïve: in his notebooks bawdy sections – and the names of certain female models – are disguised in Greek.[89]

It was Rossetti, of course, who immortalised Burges as a Pre-Raphaelite Peter Pan:

> There's a babyish party named Burges
> Who from infancy hardly emerges:
>   If you had not been told
>   He's disgracefully old,
> You'd offer a bull's eye to Burges.[90]

And it was Edmund Gosse who, in a letter to Austin Dobson, penned a glorious description of Billy Burges at tea:

> He used to give the quaintest little teaparties in his bare bachelor chambers, all very dowdy, but the meal served in beaten gold, the cream poured out of a single onyx, and the tea strictured in its descent on account of real rubies in the pot. He

was much blinder than any near-sighted man I ever knew, and once, when with me in the country, mistook a peacock seen *en face* for a man! His work was really more jewel like than architecture, just because he was so blind, but he had real genius I am sure.[91]

We shall come back to that judgement again. Meanwhile, let Lady Bute have the last word on Billy Burges as a person: 'Dear Burges ... ugly Burges who designs lovely things. Isn't he a duck.'[92]

Perhaps she was thinking of him in his own medieval kit: a specially designed costume, complete with hood and liripipe.[93] Of course, at bottom, such affectations stemmed from an excessively theatrical instinct, an instinct he shared with his hero Pugin and his friend Godwin. With Godwin and the young Ellen Terry, Burges was an enthusiast for play-reading.[94] Tom Taylor, playwright and theatre critic of *The Times* was a close friend. References to theatrical events pepper the pages of his diary. Listening to Dickens or Brandreth; watching Irving in 'The Bells' and going behind the scenes at Covent Garden; 'Snapall' at the Gaiety, 'Caste' at Cardiff, 'Zoo' at the St James's, 'Salvini' at Drury Lane, 'Antigone' at Dublin, the 'Golden Dustman' at Astley's; watching a Punch and Judy show, or 'Joseph in Marionettes' at Bourges; listening to 'The Rose of Castile', or the Westminster School Play in Latin – Burges's taste seems to have been catholic if nothing else. On one occasion he makes up a foursome with Godwin, a Miss Charlton and Mrs S.[95] Another time he organises a party consisting of Louise Jopling and her sister Alice, the Marcus Stones, and himself and sister Mary, to see 'A Voyage to the Moon'.[96] And on another occasion, just before his death, he visits the Lyceum with Lord Bute.[97] But perhaps the outings he enjoyed most were the annual office parties on Boxing Day. From 1873 to 1880 he never misses a year: dinner first at a tavern – the Sol or the Maid and Magpie – then on to a show at the Savoy or the Gaiety, or at Astley's Amphitheatre. And the last occasion was perhaps the best: dinner this time at Melbury Rd, and afterwards one last theatrical night out with his clerks and draughtsmen, and pupils from Buckingham Street.[98]

But such jollifications were only relaxation from the serious business of life: archaeology and architecture. As an antiquary, Burges was formidably well equipped. 'Archaeology', he wrote 'is the true magic mirror', revealing to man not 'glimpses of the future', but 'images of things past.'[99] He combed the libraries of England. He scoured the treasuries of Europe. His range was extraordinary. In January 1862 the *Gentleman's Magazine* trusted him to report on a Florentine exhibition of Renaissance and medieval art: marble medallions attributed to Simone Memmi; bronze and terracotta work by Donatello; bas-reliefs by Lucca della Robbia; fifteenth-century marriage coffers, painted with the stories of Narcissus, Pyramus and Thisbe, Ulysses, Lucrezia and Boccaccio's Torello; paintings attributed to Raphael and Correggio; and silver representations of the Passion, supposedly by Albrecht Dürer.[1] In July he was reporting on the Loan Museum at South Kensington – an extensive display of medieval treasures in private hands.² In July on the International Exhibition, in September on its Japanese section.³ In November he wrote on Swedish ecclesiastical polychromy in the Middle Ages.⁴ Next year came reviews of a battery of French publications on recondite themes:⁵ Didron on a tenth-century Milanese ivory diptych published by the Arundel Society; Viollet-le-Duc on some figured gargoyles at Milan cathedral and a famous door-knocker at Troyes; Darcel on Nicholas de Verdun's twelfth-century Klosterneuburg dossal, Cellini's celebrated salt-cellar at Vienna, and Wilars de Honecort's drawings for the towers of Laon and Bamberg cathedrals; Loriquet on some Roman mosaics at Rheims; Baudot on the Merovingian cemetery at Charnay; Labarte on the old palace of Constantine at Constantinople; de Linas on early medieval vestments; Verneilh on champlevé and cloisonné enamels; Didron Jnr on painted glass; Renon *versus* Viollet-le-Duc on the drawings of Wilars de Honecort. ... All this in the year of the Cork cathedral competition. And 1862–3 was by no means unusual. In 1865 he was reviewing de Lasteyrie on the seventh-century Crown of Reccesvinthus; Delacourt on the jewellery found in the so-called tomb of Theodoric, King of the Visigoths; and de Linas on the Merovingian treasures attributed to the legendary St Eloi.⁶

Such wide-ranging critical exercises were more than virtuoso performances.

> There are two great uses of antiquarian studies. One ... is to enable us to conjure up as if by the magician's wand the dress, furniture, architecture etc of past ages. ... The other ... is to restore disused arts, and to get all the good we can out of them for our own improvement.⁷

Fantasy and utility, therefore, stemmed equally from the labours of research and criticism. And such criticisms were all the more effective for being delivered with wit. Thus, on the iconography of Gambier Parry's painted ceiling at Ely:

> I am rather surprised that so eminent an ecclesiologist should have violated one of the first laws of iconography, by painting his angels with coverings on their feet. Angels are God's messengers, and are represented barefooted with wings. The angels of the Old Testament up to the time of the Babylonian empire have no wings, while the angels under the Christian dispensation have wings as an emblem of celerity; the Greek angels have sandals, but not shoes. I am sorry these matters should not have been observed by Mr Gambier Parry.⁸

Burges was indeed impatient. He often complained about the service in the British Museum.⁹ Once he was forbidden to make a tracing at Sir John Soane's Museum until the next Trustees' meeting. 'Something should be done with this ... very useless institution', he exploded. 'An Act of Parliament might surely be obtained for handing over the pictures to the National Gallery, the library and the librarian (salary included) to the Institute of British Architects, the sarcophagus, manuscripts, and antique gems to the British Museum ... the rest of the collection is of very little value.'[10] 'His temper', one contemporary recalled, 'was certainly volatile.'[11]

Temperamentally an outsider, professionally independent, stylistically *sui generis*, Burges never hesitated to speak out, and to speak out boldly. His fondness for repartee could be expensive: his remarks on Wren probably cost him St Paul's, and his comments on professional malpractice must have made him many enemies. He had no firmer friend than his brother-in-law, Pullan. But his review of Pullan and Texier's *Byzantine Architecture* is sternly critical.[12] Few younger followers were closer than E. J. Tarver. But one of Tarver's frontispieces is briskly attacked for its cult of excessive variety.[13] H. H. Statham, later editor of *The Builder*, jokingly remarked in 1876 that Burges had the reputation of being 'a kind of architectural Ishmael'[14] – a professional outlaw who lived only to attack his fellows. E. W. Godwin remembered a number of 'bruises'.[15] And Aitchison admitted that 'when angered [Burges] was like the bee, *ponit animam in punctu*'.[16] But his attacks were spiced with humour and diluted by good nature. He enjoyed the cut and thrust of journalism, but he had no truck with anonymous malice.[17] When he criticised young contributors to the *A.A. Sketchbook* for concentrating on hatching and perspective rather than plain measurement and constructive detail, he apologised for hurting their feelings.[18]

As a lecturer he easily established a 'rapport' with his audiences. Street's style of lecturing was apparently 'grandiose': formidable learning, dressed up in arcane language, and delivered at 'a galloping rate'.[19] When members of the A.A. visited the Law Courts in 1876, the architect's public manner was described as positively 'repellant ... Mr Street is not the most communicative of men'.[20] In contrast, Burges was friendly, informal and fun. When he spoke to the A.A. in the same year he provoked so many questions and comments that he felt 'like Martin Chuzzlewit on the eve of his departure for America'.[21] By 1875 he had obviously become an established favourite on the rostrum. When he was billed to speak 'On Things in General', the *Building News* facetiously suggested he deal with a whole series of serio-comic themes dear to his heart:

> Reasons why figure-drawing should form a portion of primary education in order that the millennium may be hastened. . . . Touch on the melancholy but growing desire for scarlet buttons, blazing furniture, and highly-seasoned soups.
>
> Trace the historical connection between the Tower of Babel, the Palazzo Vecchio, Florence, and his own Temple Bar tower to the Law Courts. The evolution theory in relation to Hotel d'Ecoville and Mr Whichcord's design for St Stephen's Club, and the law of development as evinced in the Hotel de Ville, Compiègne, and Mr E. W. Godwin's premiated design for the Bristol Assize Courts.
>
> Wind up with a dissertation on the intimate connection between Venetian

Gothic architecture and a fancy for pet-dogs, and an offer to back his latest canine acquisition at any odds against all comers in his next rat hunt.[22]

Burges's lectures are purposely palatable. But his antiquarian and historical writings tend to be factual and unvarnished. When it came to architectural books, for example, he much preferred G. Bonet's strictly archaeological analysis of Caen to Dean Farrar's 'eloquent ... cheerful and gossiping' history of Westminster.[23] He wrote carefully, but he spoke easily. In fact he spoke fast, and often, and to big audiences.[24] An architect's business, he once remarked 'is to act, not to talk'.[25] But he denied his own prescription in private and in public. He was not one of those lecturers who use audiences as sounding-boards for the arrogance of their own egos. Still – intellectually speaking – he obviously enjoyed his own company. That his audiences relished this projection of the lecturer's *persona* was due, as much as anything, to his obvious honesty, his transparent love of art. One extract from an after-dinner speech at Freemasons' Hall, to the Architects' Conference of 1871, will suffice:

> The acquisition of art and its cultivation is not easy; it requires sleepless nights, many hours of laborious work, much watching, and thought; and [even] then a student knows that he is only a child in comparison with the giants of antiquity (Applause). People complain because in the country they cannot get works of art; that there are no books and no museums. [But] a man of energy will always have a museum in the beauties of nature, in studying God's work in its most picturesque and loveliest forms; ... a book or two he can always get, but I believe the less books the better (Cheers).[26]

HOARDING

Burges seems to have been largely apolitical. Unlike Viollet-le-Duc, who was both anti-clerical and republican,[27] he regarded both the established church and the established social hierarchy as indispensable patrons and guarantors of the arts. He hardly needed telling that the creation of beauty is a costly business. Building churches in poor neighbourhoods, he remarked, was always easier than building churches in middle-class areas: there were always 'rich proprietors who take a delight in doing things properly'.[28] Not surprisingly, during the Chartist troubles of 1848, he enrolled as a Special Constable.[29] He had little time for those who harped on 'the social and political failings of ... the Upper Ten Thousand'. Real-life peers were seldom as worthless as 'that very gentlemanly but half-idiotic nobleman, Lord Dundreary'.[30] When he voted, he probably voted for Gladstone; at least, Gladstone's victory of 1880 is the only election he records in his diary.[31] His attitudes to class were really rather naïve: 'When Her Majesty, the Duke of Devonshire and Mr Beresford-Hope ... send their jewels to a public museum for months together, a very practical answer is given to those people who try to set one class against another.'[32] But any architect in private practice acts as a professional conduit for the distribution of surplus value. Burges was a very expensive architect. He had a vested interest in conspicuous consumption. 'Money,' he noted firmly, 'is only a secondary concern in the production of first-rate works. . . . There are no bargains in art.'[33]

A collector himself, Burges championed the autonomy of private collectors. He rejoiced in a free market in art. And in mid-Victorian England – 'that "Gouffre de l'Europe",' as he christened it[34] – he found himself in a magpie's paradise.

Burges started to collect armour in 1865, and re-started in 1869.[35] His collection was housed in Buckingham St until 1878, when it was moved to Melbury Rd.[36] A number of favourite pieces in his collection were bequeathed to the British Museum at his death. One was a fifteenth-century German helmet, or salade, which he photographed in 1870,[37] coveted for nine years, and eventually persuaded his friend J. Davidson to exchange for a piece of jade.[38] Another was a breastplate ornamented with an image of the Blessed Virgin, bought in 1873.[39] Other items are more elusive. In 1876 he notes: 'Pig-faced bascinet offered me';[40] in 1878: 'Saw Helmet Majendis';[41] and in 1880: 'Bought Bajazet's helmet.'[42] In 1874 he is examining armour at Gurney's.[43] Several of these items can probably be identified with pieces now in the British Museum, or rather in the Tower of London Armouries, where most of Burges's armour is at present kept.

It was in 1875 that Burges began to acquire a number of pieces in conjunction with Fred Weekes. This was a partnership full of acrimony. Two diary entries follow each other in quick succession: 'Weekes and I bought armour. . . . Weekes in trouble about armour.'[44] What the nature of the trouble was, one can only guess. But within a year we find Burges is trying 'to sell armour' and then having his collection turned down by the Armourers' Company.[45] Perhaps with Weekes's encouragement, Burges had spent unwisely. Perhaps Weekes grew restive as Burges's agent. All we know for certain is that Burges had scarcely been in his grave four months before Weekes launched a bitter personal attack on his qualifications as a collector. The news that the British Museum – that is Sir Augustus Franks – had accepted Burges's armour roused him to fury. The pieces did not amount to a 'collection'; they were merely a 'medley of odds and ends, accumulated by an eccentric, and on these points perfectly ignorant individual'. Even 'the few really good pieces' had been 'ruined by vulgar burnish and tinsel – the donor's besetting sin in everything'. Weekes claimed to be greatly relieved when Franks rejected several items. He even turned the knife in the wound by announcing that Burges had been his 'pupil' in this sphere of antiquities – and 'not an apt pupil . . . his knowledge to the last was nothing on this point'.[46]

Weekes's accusations were not only malicious but largely irrelevant. Of course Burges was an amateur. But he was by no means ill-informed. Of the 153 items[47] from his collection of arms and armour now in the British Museum or the Tower of London – English, French, German, Turkish, Polish, Italian, Japanese, Indian, Burmese,

Singalese or Chinese – several are by any standards outstanding. It is not, and never was, a major collection. Burges would never have ranked himself in the same league as S. R. Meyrick, although he had the good sense to acquire more than a dozen items from the Meyrick Collection.[48] But he felt, and felt keenly, the magic of medieval mail, the thrill of antique weapons. It was he who rescued the famous Broadwater Helm, and revealed it to the R.A.I. in 1878.[49] As for his scholarship, his article on the Broadwater Helm[50] and his catalogue, written jointly with Baron de Cosson, for the R.A.I. Exhibition of 1880,[51] will stand comparison with the work of any of his contemporaries in this field. The R.A.I. Exhibition was his own idea. He even designed its fittings.[52] More than 60 items came from his own collection. And he intended its catalogue to form a preliminary to a full-scale study of the subject. The catalogue's entries are crisp and critical. One of Burges's chief objectives in staging the exhibition was to demonstrate the number of forgeries currently in collections and on the market.[53] And afterwards de Cosson had no hesitation in paying tribute not only to Burges's well-known 'geniality', but also to the 'power . . . and . . . great originality of his mind'.[54]

Besides Burges's armour, the British Museum also received a number of precious objects from his collection of metalwork and ivory. First came four separate gifts: a fourteenth-century ivory sculptured head, once in the Meyrick Collection;[55] a fifteenth-century painted glass panel from Dijon;[56] a fifteenth-century ivory mirror case and rosary;[57] and a sixteenth-century gold ring with a turquoise cameo of Hercules.[58] Then came two dozen items by way of bequest.[59] Among these, some of the most valuable were a group of caskets ornamented with carved animals;[60] a sixteenth-century sapphire ring;[61] some gold Byzantine earrings;[62] several carved ivory devotional tables;[63] a Saracenic water bowl inlaid with silver fishes;[64] and a pair of Saracenic writing boxes inlaid with medallions and arabesques.[65] Burges's tastes were surely as catholic as his style was eclectic.

His private library was extensive and idiosyncratic. After his death two sales were arranged, in 1882 and 1918, comprising well over seven hundred titles – and many of these represent items in several volumes, or multi-volume runs of periodicals.[66] As might be expected in a lifelong FAB, his collection was particularly strong in Foreign Architectural Books. Even then, a number of them were very rare; today many are simply unobtainable outside copyright libraries.

But it is Burges's collection of medieval MSS which would now be deemed a veritable treasure-hoard. After his death no less than sixteen illuminated volumes found their way into the British Museum. A fifteenth-century Venetian volume of Petrarch's poems;[67] a French fifteenth-century Book of Hours, once the property of Henry VIII's sister Mary, its crisp vellum exquisitely decorated with arabesques;[68] another fifteenth-century Book of Hours, Italian this time, from the library of Cardinal York, painted with birds, insects and animals;[69] a thirteenth-century Bible, Italian or Southern French, illuminated with grotesques;[70] an early thirteenth-century biblical text written in the monastery at Citeaux;[71] a thirteenth-century French psalter, bound by Burges in dark green velvet, its margins bursting with wonderful anthropomorphic beasts;[72] more grotesque animals in a book of alphabets from sixteenth-century Germany;[73] a late fifteenth-century Petrarchian codex;[74] a fifteenth-century French missal[75] and a fifteenth-century Juvenal;[76] three Books of Hours[77] and a volume of poems by Christine de Pisan,[78] all fifteenth-century; and finally two items of which Burges must have been especially proud: a fourteenth-century 'Roman de la Rose', rebound in plush purple velvet, with miniatures carefully restored by Lonsdale;[79] and an early fifteenth-century psalter, once the property of Brunisande, daughter of Archambaud V, Comte de Périgord, lavishly rebound in royal blue velvet, embossed and studded with Burgesian symbols.[80] And there were others too. A manuscript Koran which he bought in 1879, for example.[81] How he must have pored over margin and miniature. How he must have fondled their bossy bindings and glittering clasps.

DREAMING

Burges never married. Perhaps he preferred to express his ego in art rather than offspring; to beat the grave by creation rather than procreation.[82] He did not shrink from family ties: he dutifully records family Christmasses in his diary, as well as details of births, marriages, deaths, christenings and confirmations. And when he designed his dream-house in Kensington he included a nursery in its plan. Maybe, like his friend Didron, he proposed to fill the vacancy by adoption. He certainly approved of a life like Didron's devoted to scholarship and art, iconography and architecture; a life well spent in the company of 'romantiques' like Victor Hugo, Théophile Gautier and Sainte-Beuve.[83] There were one or two girls for whom he developed a sentimental attachment, Emma Crocker, for example, and Louise Jopling. The Crocker sisters were distantly related to Burges: the eldest was married to his uncle; and he immortalised Emma – his little 'Auntlet' – in the centre portrait of his Crocker Dressing Table. According to Holiday, Burges 'had been "sweet" on his "auntlet", but ... marrying would not agree with his favourite tastes, such as drinking sherry at lunch out of a silver chalice of exquisite form and workmanship', the sherry 'poured into the chalice from a flagon of rock-crystal mounted in silver set with precious stones', and 'all designed by himself'.[84] As for Louise Jopling, Burges admired her for years, and designed her a Chelsea studio in 1879.[85] In 1881 she noted sadly: 'Poor Billy Burges is dead. . . . He was a very nice little fellow, and it was a well-known joke of his at the [Arts] Club that he was only waiting for Joe's decease to be my No. 3.'[86] Alas, it seems to have been no more than a joke. Louise had many other admirers, including Millais, Whistler and Oscar Wilde. When Burges bumped into her in 1876 at a party at Lady Bethune's he was so busy talking to 'a long-haired critic' named J. Beavington Atkinson that he failed to recognise her.[87] But, really, there was never time. Time

Burges regarded as precious: 'a commodity that can never be regained'.[88] And art had first priority.

Burges's approach to religion was aesthetic rather than theological. He was not christened until he was thirteen.[89] This may suggest that he was brought up as a Baptist. Certainly his father had no love for Roman Catholics: according to his will, his granddaughters were to lose half their inheritance if they became papists. Perhaps as a reaction against such restrictive thinking, Burges certainly emphasised, in his art and in his writings, the visual rather than the metaphysical side of religion. He loved ceremony almost for its own sake. This attitude may help to explain one last dimension of his *persona*: Burges was also a Freemason, and – like Robert Browning – he may well have been a Rosicrucian.

It was on 2nd May, 1866, that he was 'initiated as a "Free and Accepted Mason" in the Westminster and Keystone Lodge, No. 10'.[90] It was a fashionable lodge, some 140 strong, mostly composed of Oxford graduates. They met regularly at Freemasons' Hall and feasted annually at Greenwich or the Star and Garter, Richmond. Five of the members were among Burges's closest colleagues: F. P. Cockerell, Col. Edis, W. E. Nesfield, R. Phéné Spiers and Robert Willis.[91] 'Made a Freemason', he mentions in his diary for 1866, noting it twice as an important event.[92] On 7th June he was raised to the Second Degree, and on 4th July to the Third.[93] He had passed quickly through the first three degrees – 'Entered Apprentice', 'Fellow Craft' and 'Master Mason' – acknowledging at each step his faith in the Grand Architect of the Universe. In 1868 he visits the provincial lodge at Cork,[94] and in 1874 the lodge at Stratford-on-Avon.[95] So much is clear. But is there more?

The implications of Burges's masonic career are obscure. Links between architecture and freemasonry are traditionally strong. And we know that the freemasons of Cork were among the principal patrons of Cork Cathedral. Lord Ripon, Burges's patron at Studley Royal (and indirectly at Skelton) was Deputy Grand Master in the 1860s, and Grand Master between 1870 and 1874.[96] Burges was sufficiently involved to design a coat of arms (Chatterton) for the Cork masons in 1878.[97] In 1868 he notes twice in his diary a single mysterious phrase: 'Rouge Croix'.[98] And from 1854 onwards, in many of his designs, there appears and reappears a device which he seems to have adopted almost as a trademark: the Rosicrucian or Alchemical Alembic.[99] Was Burges, therefore, not only a Freemason but a Rosicrucian?

Mother Grand Lodge, England, dates only from 1717; Ireland from 1725 and Scotland from 1736. But specific records relating to previous lodges go back to the sixteenth century; traditions to the Dark Ages; and legends even to prehistory. The oldest MS copy of the *Old Charges*, or Constitutions,[1] was one Burges may well have known: a document dating back to 1390 and once mistitled *A Poem of Moral Duties*.[2] The second oldest MS, a fifteenth-century document, Burges may also possibly have known.[3] These and other MS Charges make clear that before the Grand Lodge era the context and content of Freemasonry was essentially Christian. Indeed Anglo-Saxon

Freemasonry – unlike the more political Latin Freemasonry of Continental Europe – remained and remains at least para-Christian: 'a peculiar system of morality veiled in allegory and illustrated by symbols.'[4] It was its politics as much as its potential pantheism which caused it to be condemned by Pope Pius IX, himself an ex-Freemason.

But if the roots of Freemasonry are mysterious, the origins of Rosicrucianism are positively impenetrable. Legend and mythology cloud the air. One tradition traces both societies back to King Arthur's Knights of the Round Table.[5] The legendary Christian Rosenkreuz is supposed to have made a pilgrimage to the East in 1422, bringing back the mysteries of his cult. True or false, the Rosicrucians played a powerful, if shadowy, role in Reformation Europe. In the seventeenth century they seem to have been a brotherhood of hermetic philosophers whose cult was obfuscated rather than clarified in the fantastic writings of J. V. Andreä. Alchemy, elixirs of life, sylphs, gnomes, undines, salamanders – these were the stock in trade of the Brethren of the Rosy Cross. And they were to be symbols Burges often employed in decoration.[6] But in the seventeenth century, at least, behind the allegory, the fantasy and the myths, lay a serious purpose: a humane reformation of science. And in the eighteenth century it may even have been the Rosicrucians who played a vitalising role in the modernisation of ancient Freemasonry.[7]

All that can be said with confidence is that the Rosicrucian idea surfaces, vanishes and re-surfaces over the centuries as part of the evolving mystique of speculative masonry. John Dee, the Elizabethan magician, and Andreä, the early seventeenth-century Bohemian mystic, certainly have parts to play. In 1676 a Brotherhood of the Rosy Cross undoubtedly existed in England.[8] About 1754 the Grade of the Rosy Cross made its appearance as the eighteenth Grade of Freemasonry: a grade specifically Christian and chivalric in intention.[9] Whether or not this development was due to Jesuit infiltration, it may well represent a Rosicrucian permeation of an increasingly secular masonic tradition.[10] Anyway, it was to this eighteenth Grade that Burges was elevated in the Grand Metropolitan Chapter No. 1 in 1868.[11] Meanwhile, if Rosicrucians survived in England as a separate sect, they survived underground. They surface in 1859, in Manchester of all places, as a respectable antiquarian society.[12] And one of their publications found its way into Burges's library, along with several others on masonic subjects.[13] Then in 1866 they surface again, with the full panoply of mystery and ritual, as the Masonic Rosicrucian Society, or Societas Rosicruciana in Anglia – *Soc. Ros.* for short. Their re-founder on this occasion was Robert Wentworth Little (d. 1878), an ex-clerk from Freemasons' Hall who became 1st Grand Magus in 1867. With this society – the *Soc. Ros.*, or Rosicrucians reborn – Burges almost certainly had links.

Now Little had apparently been fortified in his position by 'orders' from one of the last survivors of the old English Rosicrucians, and by secret documents found in 1810 in the vaults of Freemasons' Hall by William H. White (d. 1866), Grand Secretary to

12 Bute's Coming of Age, 1868: Mount Stuart before the Fire.

13 Bute (standing, fourth from right) and Mgr. Capel (sitting, fourth from left) with officers of the Pontifical Zouaves, 1870. The central figure is probably Mgr. Edmund Stonor, and the seated figure on the left Bute's future biographer, Abbot Sir David Oswald Hunter Blair Bt., O.S.B.

the Freemasons of England.[14] The society's purpose was so wide as to be almost cosmic: 'to investigate the meaning and symbolism of all that now remains of the wisdom, art and literature of the ancient world'.[15] Its journal *The Rosicrucian* appeared regularly from 1868 onwards. Ritual was its language and astrology its diet. By 1871 there were 144 Fratres, including 72 in London.[16] All brothers had to be already Master Masons, that is Freemasons of the 3rd Degree. The Grand Patron was Lord Lytton.[17] Members included frauds like Kenneth Mackenzie (d. 1886);[18] eccentrics like Hargrave Jennings;[19] drug addicts like Frederick Hockley (d. 1887); well-meaning scholars like W. R. Woodman and W. W. Westcott (1848–1925) – 2nd and 3rd Magi respectively; J. L. Thomas, a dim architect who was at school with Burges and Rossetti;[20] and Stephen Tucker, a genealogist friend of Burges who acted as J. R. Planché's assistant at the College of Arms.[21]

To a man like Burges, the Rosy Cross must have been irresistible. No matter that the cult's most famous figures – Andreä and Cagliostro – may both have been frauds; that Descartes and Leibnitz both tried and failed to make any contact with the supposed society; that its nineteenth-century career as an offshoot of Freemasonry had little or no connection either with the fabulous origins of the movement in the Crusades, or with its mysterious heyday during the Reformation and Counter-Reformation. The Rosy Cross was as intriguing to Burges as it was to Shelley, or Walter Scott, or Bulwer Lytton. Appropriately, he was to die in a bed decorated with Rosicrucian or Alchemical symbols, painted by Holiday with a theme from one of Tennyson's poems: 'The Day Dream.'

In the 1890s the *Soc. Ros.* seems to vanish in a masonic mist[22] only to rise again – in Paris this time – as the Ordre Kabbalistique de la Rose-Croix. Founded by the Marquis Stanislas de Guaita (1861–97), it was much concerned with the Holy Grail, and seems to have been taken up by the French Symbolists. In 1892–7 they held a series of exhibitions at their Salons de la Rose-Croix. In the hands of artists like Moreau, Klimpt and Puvis de Chavannes, the old Rosicrucian legends are reshaped to serve new purposes: an exploration of the subconscious through allegory and dream. Indeed the Symbolist manifesto sums up all the hazy aestheticism of latter-day Rosicrucian mythology: 'The Order favours first the Catholic Ideal and Mysticism. After Legend, Myth, Allegory and Dream, the Paraphrase of great poetry and finally all Lyricism. . . .'[23] By that date it was too much for Burne-Jones. 'I don't know about the Salon of the Rose-Cross,' he wrote to G. F. Watts; 'a funny high falutin . . . silly . . . piece of mouthing.'[24] Forty years earlier he might have been less dismissive – in Oxford, Chelsea or Buckingham Street, Strand – when the Pre-Raphaelite dream was new.

Chapter Three

IN SEARCH OF STYLE

'The great question is, are we to have an architecture of our
period, a distinct, individual, palpable style of the 19th century?'

T. L. DONALDSON, 1847

THE DEBATE

For painters, poets or musicians, the Dream might be an end in itself. For architects –
even for Burges – vision had to compromise with reality. Their dream became the
quest for a New Style, a style which would unite the beauties of the past with the
necessities of the present: an architectural Holy Grail.

Now this concern with the idea of a New Style was itself new. Never before had
architects searched – collectively and self-consciously – for a New Style. Before the
nineteenth century, style had always been the accepted language of the age, even if that
language had itself been historically based – like the Renaissance or Palladianism – or
subject to private interpretation, like the Baroque or the Rococo. For the mid-
Victorians, however, such easy acceptance was inconceivable. Progress was in the air.
Evolutionary thinking had gripped the minds of a generation. The impact of
historiography was inescapable. And once the habit of looking back, for comparative
or inspirational purposes, was established, spontaneous development became
impossible. Innocence had been driven out by the dilemma of choice. Architecture
could no longer evolve naturally because architects were aware of their own
evolution. 'The peculiar characteristic of the present day, as compared with all former
periods', confessed Gilbert Scott, 'is this – that we are acquainted with the history of
art.'[1] 'In primitive times,' wrote Viollet-le-Duc, '*style* imposed itself on the artist; today
the artist has to rediscover style.'[2] Mid-Victorian architects faced a challenge wholly
unprecedented in scale and scope: new materials, new structural processes, new
building-types. ... New Style? The logic of discovery and progression seemed
irresistible. Science and technology, theology and metaphysics, breathed alike the
same evolutionary ethos. Only architecture seemed to lag behind, limping along in the
cast-off clothes of more creative generations. The evidence of discontent is
overwhelming. Again and again, in lectures and letters, in books, pamphlets and

periodicals, the cry goes up: 'Are we to have an architecture of our period, a distinct, individual, palpable style of the nineteenth century?'[3]

Burges will speak in this debate. He will speak often and impulsively. What he has to say contains no blinding revelations. But his very confusion is valuable: he speaks on behalf of the mid-Victorian generation, a generation bewildered by novelty and confused by change, a generation of architects whistling in the dark.

Burges was hardly an original thinker. He was strong on instinct and weak on ideology. He had no time for 'the various theories of . . . the Ideal and the Beautiful'.[4] He believed in the potentialities of education: the Government Schools of Design, the Architectural Museum, the future Victoria and Albert Museum. But apart from the therapeutic value of figure-drawing for designers, and the dissemination of sound technique for artisans, he was blithely uninvolved in the definition of educational goals. He summed up 'the whole practice of architecture' as just 'the exercise of common sense and good taste'.[5] His judgements of exhibitions and competitions were intuitively rather than conceptually based.[6] At bottom he had a naïve faith in the intangibles of artistic inspiration: 'those gifts of God, a correct eye and a good taste, are better than all the rules of all the schools of design in the world.'[7] 'No rules,' he felt, 'will ever teach a man the value of one tone of colour as compared with another.'[8] Taste, he maintained, 'is a question on which volumes have been written, and on which they may be written with no earthly profit; for the only way to improve taste, or rather to improve the talent God has been pleased to give us, is not by dissertations, but by seeing beautiful objects'.[9] 'A good eye was the gift of a good God. This appeared to him the most rational conclusion on the subject.'[10]

So we must look elsewhere for our leading speakers. Billy Burges will just interrupt us as we go along. The battle lines of the debate follow the customary division in mid-Victorian thinking: those who look backwards and those who look forwards. But the burden of this battle – the struggle of Past and Future – pressed with particular urgency on the architect. For him evolution was not a hypothesis but a necessity, not an abstraction but a daily challenge. 'His science,' noted one critic in 1864, 'is continually urging him onward . . . his art . . . is ever bidding him to look . . . back.'[11] Not surprisingly, therefore, whether he looked backwards or forwards, or backwards *and* forwards at the same time, the mid-Victorian architect, Janus-faced and ambidextrous, hovered in a state of vacillating eclecticism.

PAST v. FUTURE

First, let James Fergusson speak. He speaks as a critic and an amateur. He speaks as a scholar who wields his learning like a club. His dogma is the dogma of utility and function. He speaks for science, for engineering, for Progress.

'Within the last hundred years,' he announces in 1863, apropos Samuel Smiles,[12] 'engineers have doubled the mechanical power, and more than doubled the productive resources of mankind.' Linked by steam and telegraph, 'a thousand millions of human beings ... can combine to ... effect any given object'; the world looks forward to 'results ... such as have not yet been dreamt of in our philosophies'. Most wonderful of all is 'the express engine, rushing past at a speed of 50 or 60 miles an hour, making 1000 or 1200 pulsations in a minute, consuming coals with reckless wastefulness, and casting its vital heat and life's blood to the four winds at each beat of its valves. Nothing that man has done comes so near to the creation of an animal as this ... especially when we see the monster fed with great spoonfuls of cooked black vegetable food, from which it evolves the vital heat of its capacious lungs, which, after circulating through its tubular veins, is launched into the air with the waste products of combustion ... the great steam-engine factories ... are the glory of the mechanical engineer, and ... are among the most remarkable triumphs of mind over matter that the world has yet witnessed'. In the cotton mills of England, thirty million spindles ply; 'fairy fabrics are spun and woven by an iron beast as heavy and as strong as fifty elephants'. At sea, paddle steamers give promise of ocean-going vessels almost without 'practical limit'. Vast harbours and cyclopean breakwaters create 'calmness and shelter in the midst of tempest'. Lighthouses – 'the most perfect specimens of modern architecture' – 'send their rays through the darkness with a space-penetrating power that a few years ago would have been deemed impossible.' Viaducts, tunnels and bridges of stupendous size had been achieved, annihilating the Menai Straits or even the Alps. 'If any one had proposed twenty years ago to throw a railway bridge over ... Niagara, he would have been looked on as a madman. Yet this has been accomplished.' In railway stations, too, the engineer has 'conquered space ... there is no practical limit to the extent of our roofs'. As for the electric telegraph, it has made 'London and New York ... within speaking distance' of each other. 'Before many years are over we may see recorded in the morning's *Times* events that happened at Sydney, or Shanghai, or San Francisco on the previous day. Surely this is a wonder and a triumph of scientific skill if anything ever was; and surely the men who do these things are giants!' All honour, therefore, to 'that noble example of the dominion of man over the earth – the science of Engineering'.

But what of architecture? In Fergusson's eyes, the ablest architects of the mid-century were enmeshed in the pursuit of 'a chimera': the Gothic Revival. Pugin had given spurious justification to this whole 'aberration'. He preached not Truth but 'falsehood'.[13] 'Thirteenth-century' Gothic was 'an anachronism, as little suited to our wants and as little expressive of our feelings as the armour or the weapons of the same age. It would be as reasonable to build our warships after the pattern of the galleys in which our Edwards and our Henrys went to Crecy and to Agincourt, and to reintroduce the bows and arrows with which they fought and conquered, as to reproduce their architecture for our dwellings and civic buildings'. As it is, 'we have no Style of architecture', and 'of the two absurdities [Greek and Gothic Revivals] the Gothic is perhaps the less absurd'. Still, 'the Gothic mania'[14] is 'a standing insult to the age in which we live'. In reviving thirteenth-century Gothic, an architect like G. E. Street was attempting the impossible: 'he might as well attempt to restore the Heptarchy!' 'According to this Joshua of architects, the sun of art stood still when Edward III died in 1377. . . . [Barry and Pugin's] Palace of Westminster is not perfect, but it at least has this merit, that its style is two centuries nearer our time than Mr Street's. . . . Where is all this to end? . . . One step backward we can still see our way to – there is the Saxon. . . .' After that, 'there will only then remain the . . . Druidical style'. Even so, 'a stuccoed Stonehenge, with a glass and iron roof' might be 'a better representation of the architecture of the nineteenth century' than the new Law Courts in the Strand. The Gothic Revival was 'a thoroughly vicious system', justifiable on this occasion only 'if the Strand were the bed of a pellucid mountain stream, and this building were designed to be placed on its banks in some remote sparsely inhabited Midland valley, for the accommodation of a congregation of barefooted friars'. There was only one hope: the R.I.B.A. 'must write over its doors, "Archaeology is not Architecture".'[15]

Alas! Fergusson concludes, 'the building profession is divided against itself'. While engineers challenge the future, architects cower in the past. 'They aim at restoring an artistic heptarchy in the midst of the progress of the nineteenth century. . . . Instead of following out principles, [they] are content to copy forms. . . . Greek mouldings and Gothic pinnacles . . . dreaming of reproducing the elegance of classical times, or the blundering enthusiasm of the Middle Ages, while the engineers are spanning our rivers with structures such as the world never saw before – bridging our valleys with viaducts, arching under our mountains, and roofing acres for stations.' And who is to blame for this deplorable dichotomy? 'Architects,' he concedes, 'would delight in' the reunion of architecture and engineering. 'It is the public . . . their employers who do not see the necessity for it, and cannot understand its bearing.' The task therefore is twofold. Firstly, persuasion: Fergusson neutralising Ruskin; secondly, example: Stephenson and Brunel neutralising Burges, Street and Butterfield. The grand strategy is clear: 'To call architecture back within the domain of logic and common sense.'[16]

So much for the Future. There is a naïve simplicity about Fergusson's faith in technology. His optimism does not extend to concrete suggestions about style. In fact his speculations on the future of architecture add up to little more than bombastic hypotheses. Those who looked to the Past were rather more sophisticated, but, alas, equally confused. Let their spokesman be Beresford-Hope. Hope was the son of Thomas Hope – Neo-Classical Hope of Deepdene – an independent High Tory M.P., an articulate High Churchman, the patron of Butterfield, Carpenter and Burges, and for many years President of the Ecclesiological Society.

'We are a medieval party,' he reminds the ecclesiologists in 1862. 'Why? because we find that there are many things which make medieval art the most serviceable to the present nineteenth century. We greatly respect archaeology and we gladly study antiquities; but we study medieval art with a view to the benefit of the present age, and the edification of succeeding generations.'[17] 'We took up the Gothic movement because we believed that that was the movement most practicable for the material, and the social and the political, and the religious needs of this progressive and agitated century.'[18] 'Liberal' or 'progressive eclecticism' is 'the very key-stone of our system . . . it . . . makes the [Ecclesiological] Society a living power.' What we hope to develop is a 'type of art . . . which, though called medieval, is still modern and progressive'.[19] In its origins the new style will be universal, but in its formulation it will be English: 'this style, while boldly eclectic in its details, must, in its main principles, vividly embody the historical characteristics of England, for whose material uses it will come into being.'[20] Nationalist feelings and evolutionist thinking will both have their part to play. 'The only style of common sense architecture for the future of England, must [therefore] be Gothic architecture, cultivated in the spirit of progression founded upon eclecticism. But here our difficulties only begin . . . [for] what are we to eclect?' In the 1830s and early 1840s, we chose English Gothic as 'our point of departure', 'the starting point for that which was then our only dream, the development and perfecting of our English Gothic'. In the battle between 1st, 2nd, and 3rd Pointed, victory went to 2nd – Decorated – 'the golden mean of English Gothic'. 'It certainly flattered our insular pride. We were the best men in the world – nobody was like us – nothing like our style.' In the 1850s the basis of the revival broadened: Italian, French and German Gothic were all absorbed. But still we need a foundation, 'more broad and comprehensive. . . . To be truly eclectic, we must be universally eclectic – we must eclect from everything which has been eclected; and we must assimilate and fuse everything that we eclect, for without such fusion the process remains after all only one of distributive collection. . . . And even then we may only be storing up material for our successors. Ours is only an eclecticism of the past. . . . I imagine there will be an eclecticism of the future'. New materials, both decorative and structural, 'must in time revolutionize all architecture; but I believe it will be a peaceful . . . revolution [supplementing] . . . the good tradition of the old time'.

And where will all this stop? 'I will stop', Hope concludes sagely, 'where common sense tells me to stop. When I can no longer assimilate I will cease to absorb.' Meanwhile the motto is: 'progress through eclecticism'.[21] And this eclecticism must be 'conservative . . . not destructive, retrospective no less than prospective, national rather than cosmopolitan, and yet encircling its native tradition by the imported and assimilated contributions of other lands'.[22] In that respect Hope speaks for the bulk of his generation in England. In France voices were still heard demanding absolute fidelity to a single style. In 1856 Lassus denounced eclecticism as 'the Plague of Art[23] . . . the common enemy . . . the scourge of our epoch'. In England he found few supporters.[24] 'Englishmen,' announced the *Building News* in 1858, 'are the most eclectic of the human race.'[25] And their ultimate, collective, aesthetic goal was still that same eclectic goal set out by Beresford-Hope's father in 1835: 'an architecture . . . at once elegant, appropriate, and original. . . . "Our Own".'[26]

Hope's trumpet call to eclecticism, *The Common Sense of Art*, appeared in 1858. Four years later current design was put under a microscope at the Exhibition of 1862. What was the result? The Exhibition building had been designed by Capt. Fowke, an engineer not an architect, and a very different sort of eclectic. Fergusson welcomed Fowke's characteristic *mélange*: 'neither Grecian nor Gothic, but thoroughly nineteenth century.'[27] But for Beresford-Hope the building was an 'architectural fiasco': its walls displayed 'that particular combination of Venetian and emasculated Byzantine which might be termed the Cosmopolitan-Governmental architecture of this century';[28] its brick-based glass domes were 'the basest and most purposeless crystallo-chalybeate bubbles which earth has yet egurgitated'.[29] Its interest lay in its modern exhibits, and in their relationship to the medieval exhibits simultaneously shown in the Loan Exhibition at South Kensington.

The Archaeological Institute and the Society of Antiquaries had already sown the seed of a new taste for medieval workmanship. But the art of the Middle Ages had only recently been revealed to the general public: first by the Society of Arts exhibitions of 1849 and 1851; then by the Manchester Loan Exhibition of 1857. Now, in 1862, the South Kensington Museum – 'the British Museum of post-classical art' – was bidding fair, by its own eclectic example, to revolutionise the art workmanship of the nation. Any museum must contain examples of good and bad taste. But Beresford Hope had no fear of corruption. Let South Kensington 'freely expand into the realms of ugliness' – provided students are kept safely at a distance.[30] The modern manufactures displayed in the neighbouring 1862 Exhibition seemed to substantiate his confidence in medieval inspiration. In bronze, tapestry and stained glass England was still weak. But he took comfort in the progress of Gothic: the architectural metal-work by Skidmore, the tiles and mosaics by Maw, the ceramics by Minton, the brass by Hart, the embroidery by Jones and Willis, the decorative metalwork by Hardman.

In architecture, from many different routes, 'a new style' seemed to be germinating, 'derived from, but not servilely following, existing systems'. Lined up in 1862, facing each other 'like rival armies', the British exhibition of architectural drawings emphasised that the mid-Victorian age was indeed 'an epoch of vast material and intellectual activity in the pursuit of architecture'. There they were, 'the Gothic on one side, the classical and the renaissance on the other, but peacefully commingled in the external galleries ... partially devoted to the Scotchmen'. Scots Baronial was indeed eclecticism with a vengeance. Still, here was historicism in labour: 'the eager, sometimes exuberant, oftener healthy, search for originality'; the battle of ideas from which, one day, One Style would come. 'It is progressive art; and as true progress must ever be putting itself to school, it seeks to learn of every style which ever loved the beautiful, in order to adapt and to assimilate, heedless of the parrot reproach of eclecticism, provided only that the eclecticism be one of fusion and of development, and not merely of juxtaposition.'

Such was the Hope of English Architecture – and the Goths, in their eclectic mood, were best placed to realise that Hope.[31] The Gothic Revival had indeed moved on from its ecclesiological phase to the eclectic. In 1842 the first volume of the *Ecclesiologist* had proclaimed: 'It is no sign of weakness to ... copy ... perfection.'[32] That perfection had been thought to be Decorated or Middle Pointed. Twenty years later the net had been flung far wider. 'Whatever beauty any other style possesses', Beresford-Hope concluded, 'that beauty we embrace; and we hope, or dream ... that in some later day the hidden link that joins it to the seemingly rival developments may be discovered. Art we believe is one, only man has not yet mastered the secret of its unity'.[33] For Beresford-Hope – as for Burges and Lord Bute – the discovery of that secret, the achievement of 'Pure Art', was the ultimate object of the High Victorian Dream. This was their philosopher's stone, its identification as desirable as the finding of the Holy Grail, as inevitable – and as distant – as the Second Coming. For architectural theologians – and for ecclesiologists the border-line between architecture and theology was by no means clear – the attainment of a Victorian Style was indeed that

> ... one, far-off divine event
> To which the whole creation moves.[34]

But how to translate such dreams into architectural reality? The materials were there in abundance, but where was the Messiah who would weld them into Pure Art? Gilbert Scott had already called for 'a master mind' to create the new synthesis.[35] Beresford-Hope agreed: 'The science of criticism has attained a philosophic amplitude hitherto unknown. All that is wanting – a great deficiency, we willingly own – is a man of genius.'[36]

ARCHITECTURE v. ENGINEERING

For thousands of educated Victorians that man of genius was John Ruskin. But Ruskin's contribution to the search for style was, to say the least, confused. In 1857 he bravely addressed the young iconoclasts of the Architectural Association on what he called their chief 'head-problem in these experimental days': the quest for a style 'worthy of modern civilisation in general, and of England in particular; a style worthy of our engines and telegraphs; as expansive as steam, and as sparkling as electricity'. With the aim of a skilled debater, he fired straight at their Achilles Heel. What exactly was to be the form of this New Style? And, anyway, who was to form it, and for how long? Was each 'inventive architect' to 'invent a new style for himself, and have a county set aside for his conceptions, or a province for his practice? Or must every architect invent a little piece of the new style, and all put it together at last like a dissected map?' Anyway, what next? 'I will grant you this Eldorado of imagination – but can you have more than one Columbus? Or, if you sail in company ... who is to come after your clustered Columbuses? ... When our desired style is invented, will not the least we can all do be simply – to build in it? – and cannot you now do that in styles that are known?' Whatever happens, that New Style will not be final. 'You shall draw out your plates of glass and beat out your bars of iron till you have encompassed us all – if your style is of the practical kind – with endless perspective of black skeleton and blinding square or – if your style is to be of the ideal kind – you shall wreathe your streets with ductile leafage, and roof them with variegated crystal – you shall put, if you will, all London under one blazing dome of many colours that shall light the clouds round it with its flashing, as far as to the sea. And still, I ask you, What after this? ... if you cannot rest content with Palladio, neither will you with Paxton. ...' No, Ruskin concludes, 'if you think over this quietly by yourselves, and can get the noise out of your ears of the perpetual, empty, idle, incomparably idiotic talk about the necessity of some novelty in architecture, you will soon see that the very essence of a Style, properly so called, is that it should be practised *for ages*, and applied to all purposes; and that so long as any given style is in practice, all that is left for individual imagination to accomplish must be within the scope of that style, not in the invention of a new one'.[37]

That was well said. But the problem of style was not so easily brushed aside. After all, the Crystal Palace was a great ineradicable fact.

J. C. Loudon, horticulturalist and landscape gardener, had foreseen in 1837 that the coming age of iron would mean an end to all established architectural systems: 'all habituated notions of ... proportion ... must, of course, be discarded'. Instead of adapting 'the new material to their designs', architects would have to 'adapt their designs to the new material'.[38] Pugin thought otherwise. For him, architecture and engineering were poles apart. 'No engineer', he wrote, 'ever was a decent architect, and if they attempted Gothic it would be frightful.'[39] When Pugin was introduced to Sir Joseph Paxton, he was asked what he thought of that knighted gardener's Crystal Palace. 'Think', he replied, 'Why that you had better keep to building green-houses, and I will keep to my churches and cathedrals.'[40] In private he talked of that 'glass monster', that 'crystal humbug'.[41] Burne-Jones put it more eloquently in 1854. 'Poor fools! ... As I look at it in its gigantic wearisomeness, in its length of cheerless monotony, iron and glass, glass and iron, I grow more and more convinced of the powerlessness of such material to affect an Architecture. Its only claim to our admiration consists in its size, not in those elements in which lies the true principle of appreciation, form and colour: its form is rigid and mechanical, its colour simple transparency and a painful dazzling reflection: it is a fit apartment for fragrant shrubs, trickling fountains, muslin-de-laines, *eau-de-colognes*, Grecian statues, strawberry ices and brass bands – but give me "The Light of the World" and the apse of Westminster.'[42] In 1855 the Duke of Devonshire, Paxton's patron, arrived at Lismore Castle in Ireland, and saw for the first time its new-built battlements bristling high above the Blackwater. 'Go, Crystal Palace', he scoffed, 'What are you to this quasi-feudal, ultra-regal fortress?'[43]

One of the few thinkers to grapple with the aesthetic implications of new structural techniques was Edward Lacy Garbett. His *Rudimentary Treatise on the Principles of Design in Architecture* (1850) divided the whole of recorded architectural history into three phases: 'the DEPRESSILE, the COMPRESSILE, and the TENSILE methods. – the *beam*, the *arch*, the *truss*; of which the two former have been made the bases of past systems [Greek and Gothic]: the third is ours. ... To this third system of constructive unity, there is no old style adapted. ... Let us not mistake what we have to do. It is that which has been done only twice before; in the time of Dorus, and in the thirteenth century. ... Let us not deceive ourselves: a style never grew of itself; it never will. It *must* be sought, and sought the right way. ... A new style requires the generalised imitation of nature and of *many* previous styles; and a new system requires, in addition to this ... the binding of all together by a new principle of unity, clearly understood, agreed upon, and kept constantly in view.'[44]

Garbett's logic was impeccable. His thinking might have supplied a bridge between the rationalists and the eclectics, between Fergusson and Hope. Ruskin considered his arguments weighty enough to justify a separate reply in an appendix to *The Stones of Venice*, vol. i (1851). But that is the last we hear of Garbett. He ended his days a forgotten guru, writing pamphlets on biblical exegesis.

'Engineering of the highest merit and excellence, but not architecture.'[45] That was the *Ecclesiologist*'s view of the Crystal Palace. It was also the opinion of John Ruskin. Iron he was willing to accept, but only in disguise: as a cement but not as a support, for binding but not for propping. In one unguarded moment he confessed that 'the time is probably near when a new system of architectural laws will be developed, adapted entirely to metallic construction'.[46] But in general his thinking entirely denied such a possibility. A real architecture of glass and iron, he claimed, was 'eternally impossible'. His reasoning ran as follows. Colour and form were the only 'means of delight in all productions of art. ... Form is only expressible in its perfection, on opaque bodies, without lustre. ... All noble architecture depends for its majesty upon its form: therefore you can never have any noble architecture in transparent or lustrous glass or enamel. Iron is, however, opaque ... and, therefore, fit to receive noble form' – but only 'as noble as cast or struck architecture can ever be: as noble, therefore, as coins can be, or common cast bronzes, and such other multiplicable things – eternally separated from all good and great things by a gulph which not all the tubular bridges nor engineering of ten thousand nineteenth centuries cast into one great bronze-foreheaded century, will ever overpass one inch of'. Thus the Crystal Palace was not Art – the expression of genius, labour and love. Its value as an emanation of humanity was negligible. Its worth consisted merely in one 'single ... thought' by Paxton, plus 'some very ordinary algebra'.[47]

In this even Fergusson came close to concurring: 'A work of art is valuable in the direct ratio of the quantity and quality of the thought it contains.'[48] And that thought must be aesthetic rather than technological. Hence the necessity for architects as well as engineers, 'to elaborate Building ... into Architecture'.[49] Lacking that additional quality, the Crystal Palace cannot really be Architecture at all: it is 'not ornamental to such an extent as to elevate it into the class of the Fine Arts'.[50] 'Architecture', it could therefore be claimed in 1879, 'is educated engineering.'[51] That was the nub of the matter. Educational apartheid set up social and linguistic barriers which were then piled high with cultural luggage. William White put the case for separate professions simply: engineering consists 'in the science and art of construction'; architecture in 'the science and art of composition and design'.[52] Behind barricades labelled Function and Beauty, architects and engineers fought out a sterile battle for the spirit of the age. To the church architect, and the 'Art-Architect' in particular, most engineering was simply 'uncivil'.[53]

Such thinking carried the day in the 1850s. Those who campaigned for a wholly new 'Metallurgic Architecture', like William Vose Pickett in England or Jean-Baptiste Jobard in France, were dismissed as eccentrics.[54] 'I do not believe', Street announced flatly in 1852, that such systems 'constitute architecture at all.'[55] L. A. Boileau's 'synthetic' churches of stone and iron aroused only vicious hostility among English and French critics.[56] Paxton remained the only major prophet of what Fergusson called 'Ferro-Vitrous Art'. And even he happily compromised with historicism in partnership with G. H. Stokes. The architectural establishment was embarrassed by the whole subject. Gilbert Scott admitted that metallic construction opened out 'a perfectly new field for architectural development'.[57] But it was not a field which he ploughed with either consistency or conviction. At Brighton, his Brills' Baths building boasted an iron-framed Gothic dome.[58] And along the platforms of St Pancras Station he forced Gothic arcades to mingle with the ribs of Barlow's gigantic train shed on terms of heroic equality. But, in general, Scott played safe. His decorated iron girders at Kelham Hall, Notts. (1858–62), scarcely go beyond the principle of Butterfield's Gothicised iron beams in the presbytery at All Saints, Margaret Street (1850–59).

Such major experiments as there were, to integrate new materials and old forms, proved disappointing. In 1855, for example, the new Oxford Museum, opposite Butterfield's Keble College, was hailed as 'an experiment ... of the greatest importance to architecture'; an attempt 'to try how Gothic art could deal with those railway materials, iron and glass'.[59] Alas, the result was yet another pastiche, this time in metal rather than stone. 'We consider the principle [of Skidmore's iron roofing] to be erroneous', the *Ecclesiologist* concluded in 1861. 'After all this is merely a stone-vaulting system in iron. The shafts, arches and ribs all follow the type of a stone construction. The effect is fairy-like, we admit; and some of the perspectives are exceedingly novel and striking. But the doubt recurs whether after all this is a proper metallic construction. ... The domical treatment of [Sydney Smirke's] magnificent [domed] round reading room of the British Museum (1851–7) is far more satisfactory. ... [Besides] the iron roof and the ... sides of the quadrangle ... are not blended together, but are planned in crude juxtaposition. . . . The problem has been beyond the powers of the gentlemen, Messrs. Deane and Woodward, who have been entrusted with the perilous honour of developing the unknown capacities of a new style.'[60] It had also been beyond the capacities of the ecclesiologists themselves: their Iron Church, designed in 1855 by Carpenter, suffered from much the same defects.[61] Perhaps Beresford-Hope was wisest to admit that a New Style based on Paxton's Crystal Palace was simply beyond his understanding: 'As to the Crystal Cathedral, I must humbly say that I cannot grasp so novel an idea.'[62] Gottfried Semper put the matter in a nutshell: 'faced with such a material, a stylist's mind ceases to function.'[63]

Now Burges recognised his own era as 'the real age of iron.[64] 'The Civil Engineer,' he admitted, 'is the real nineteenth century architect.'[65] He had absorbed Pugin's gospel of function, and could see its relevance to metallic construction. He would even have appreciated Thomas Garner's admiration, in 1858, for the constructional integrity of the Hansom Cab: it's 'so truthful, so-so-so medieval'.[66] But on the whole he lamented the unrelieved ugliness of much contemporary technology: 'engineering works are generally so ugly, that one is apt to be thankful even for small mercies' – even the gilded rivets of Hungerford Bridge.[67] Despite his engineering background, Burges's aesthetic was essentially atectonic. He would have applauded Lutyens's aphorism: 'architecture begins where function ends.' A machine without decorative expression was no more beautiful than a skeleton without flesh and blood. It was the artistic imagination which turned building into architecture, utility into beauty. Such was the alchemy of art. But the logic of that mystical process beckoned enticingly towards the absurd. 'One is very much tempted', he admitted, 'to imagine and try and think out how our ancestors of the twelfth and thirteenth centuries would have treated a royal locomotive with its tender and carriage – say one for William Rufus, or King John, or Henry III, all of whom were fond of magnificence: perhaps they would have converted the locomotive into the form of a dragon vomiting the smoke through his upraised head; his body and wings being rich with gold, colour, tin and brass, and perhaps even great crystal balls would do duty for eyes. Again, how would they have treated a steam-boat? Would the funnel have been made into a sort of tower? Would the sails have been painted with coat-armour? Would shields have been hung all round, and would the paddle-boxes have been historiated with subjects on gold ground?'[68] Such images are the stuff of dreams. And, true to form, Burges produced at least one sketch of a Gothic paddle-steamer.[69]

In the 1860s, most of Burges's friends lost what little faith they had in new materials. Some, like George Aitchison, continued to chew at the problem.[70] Most threw in their hands. After 1855, and still more after 1870, building regulations in London actively discouraged the use of exposed iron construction. G. E. Street dismissed the search for a new, metallic architecture as 'a wild goose chase'. If people really wanted to see logical and characteristic examples of metallic design, they had only to visit a few of the public lavatories of London.[71] Better for an architect to stick to 'the materials which God had given him – brick, stone and wood'. There was something almost sinful about an architect employing iron girders: 'whenever he had introduced them he felt conscious of having done something which he ought not to have done.'[72] William White felt much the same: iron was suitable only for the baser sort of building, the lower ranges of the architectural hierarchy; large-scale, utilitarian structures – factories, for instance. 'Where was the massiveness so essential to architecture – the bulk – above everything else, the shadow? How could there be architecture without shadow?'[73] 'Ferrotecture' and architecture were fundamentally different systems: 'ironwork must always be rigid, cramped and attenuated in its proportions, and, from its nature as a metal, was unfit for domestic uses ... the massiveness, the bulk, the play of light and shade, the superposition, which were essential features of architecture, could only be given to iron construction by destroying its leading characteristics. Indeed, were iron generally used for building, architecture would be extinguished.'[74] Iron may well be the key to the future, White concludes, but 'so far as I am concerned, it may predominate in Utopia'.[75]

Such attitudes help to explain the apparently destructive atavism of the mid-Victorian architectural profession. We need not be too surprised at their intellectual blinkers. Like representational painters after the invention of photography, they could hardly be expected to jettison the accumulated wisdom of several thousand years in return for a few crumbs of experimental science. Victorian architects clung to pre-industrial aesthetics in a post-industrial world, just as today we cling to Christian ethics in a post-Christian society. Burges and his fellow architects turned their backs on the implications of contemporary technology, and sought salvation in an eclecticism of the past. But that decision was only the start of their problems, for – as Beresford-Hope put it – what were they to eclect?

ANGLO-VENETIAN v. EARLY FRENCH

In 1849 Ruskin had argued, in his *Seven Lamps*, for the rejection of styles and the pursuit of style: 'we want no new style of architecture. . . . But we want some style.'[76] Once a single style had become universally accepted, its adaptation would eventually produce a new style suitable to a new world. There was certainly a germ of truth in that opinion. It was precisely by narrowing his terms of reference, and sticking to the rules of Greek construction, that 'Greek' Thomson eventually produced – by a process of reduction and abstraction – a style which was both original and relevant. And it was chiefly through the universal adoption of Early French that progressive Goths of the 1850s and 1860s hoped to precipitate the birth of a new style. Unfortunately, in 1849, Ruskin had recommended not one style, but a choice of four: Pisan Romanesque, as in the Baptistery and Cathedral at Pisa; Early Gothic of the Western Italian republics, as at Sta. Croce, Florence; Venetian Gothic – Sta. Maria dell'Orto, for example; and early English Decorated, as in the North transept at Lincoln. Of these, he claimed to favour the last, 'fenced from [any] chance of again stiffening into the Perpendicular'.[77] But in practice his influence was all in favour of the third alternative, Venetian Gothic.

In years to come, haunted by suburban Venetian villas, Ruskin bitterly regretted this. His famous *volte-face* on Anglo-Venetian Victorian deserves to be quoted again.

> I am proud enough to hope . . . that I have had some direct influence on Mr Street . . .[78] But I have [also] had indirect influence on nearly every cheap villa-builder between [Denmark Hill] and Bromley; and there is scarcely a public house near the Crystal Palace but sells its gin and bitters under pseudo-Venetian capitals copied from the Church of the Madonna of Health or of Miracles. And one of my principal notions for leaving my present house [and fleeing to Brantwood in the Lake District] is that it is surrounded everywhere by the accursed Frankenstein monsters of, *in*directly, my own making.[79]

In the 1855 edition of *Seven Lamps* Ruskin went out of his way to deny his supposed commitment to Venetian Gothic. 'The Gothic of Verona', he wrote, 'is far nobler than that of Venice; and that of Florence nobler than that of Verona. [But] for our immediate purposes that of Notre Dame of Paris is noblest of all.'[80] By 1859 he was in full agreement with Street: Chartres was ten times as fine as St Mark's, Venice.[81] The focus of medievalism had already moved from England to Italy; it was now moving from Italy to France. Both shifts represented a move from Puginian to Ruskinian thinking.

By the end of the 1840s, Pugin's 'true Picturesque' had carried the day in architectural circles. In the 1850s the Palace of Westminster was regularly denounced for excessive regularity. James Parker described it scornfully as 'a Gothic skin stretched over a Palladian skeleton'. E. A. Freeman talked of 'Gothic panels nailed to a Palladian frame'.[82] And it was chiefly aversion to the memory of Barry's regular river frontage which prompted so many competitors in the Law Courts competition of 1866, to pin their faith in Picturesque values. Nevertheless, the 1850s witnessed a progressive rejection of this Puginian vision. The 'true thing', the 'perfect revival', was no longer enough. When David Brandon exhibited a design for St John's Lansford, Hants., *The Builder* commented tartly: 'it might pass for an old church; and, so long as that is by far the most prominent attribute of a building, we hold the design cannot be accepted as in every respect satisfactory, or, indeed, as at all the illustration of art architectural'.[83] Novelty had replaced authenticity as the *sine qua non* of fashion. More important, the Picturesque had given way to a renewed concern for the Sublime. Instead of variety of silhouette and irregularity of plan, architects strove for horizontality, breadth of outline and massive simplicity. It was Ruskin's *Seven Lamps* which – under the heading of 'The Lamp of Power' – revived such Burkeian concepts in a world where they had been largely forgotten.

Popular explanations of the Sublime usually made a hazy subject hazier still.[84] All the same, a striving for Sublimity is almost invariably there, below the surface of High Victorian design. In this, the transition from Early Victorian to High Victorian, from Puginian to Ruskinian values, William Butterfield led the way. In Butterfield's restorations, the ecclesiologists saw 'the stamp of reality'.[85] In his original designs, the same pundits identified not the stigmata of streaky bacon or veal-and-ham, but the eternal verities of the Sublime.[86] Where Butterfield led, the next generation followed. But whereas Butterfield always relied on English precedents for the bones of his designs, Street and Burges, and the young men of the 1850s, turned elsewhere, to Continental Europe. In pursuit of Sublimity, the massive austerity of early Continental Gothic turned out to be a richer source of inspiration than the 'hectic flush' of English Decorated.[87]

This switch from English to Continental sources in the 1850s was partly due to an increasing concern with the problems of urban, and particularly secular, Gothic. In those fields, Europe was richer in its remains than England. Hence the frenetic travelling of Burges's generation. Burges's own travels we have already noted. Street made his first foreign tour – to France – in 1850. In 1851 he was in Germany, in 1853 Italy. In 1855 he revisited Germany; in 1857 Italy and France. In 1861, 1863 and 1868 he was touring Spain. Scott had been in Germany in 1844–5 in connection with the Hamburg Nikolaikirche competition. In 1847–8 he was in France, in 1851 in Italy. Butterfield had probably been abroad in the later 1840s. He was certainly in Germany and Austria in 1851, 1855, 1862, 1870 and 1872; in France in 1852, 1854, 1855, 1857, 1859 and 1868; and in Italy in 1854 and 1868.[88] All four men, at different levels and in very different ways – Butterfield remained English at heart – were to carry the gospel of Continental Gothic throughout Britain in the 1850s and 1860s.

Burges respected, but never fell under the spell of Italian Gothic. Street admired and synthesised it.[89] Scott plundered it in pursuit of 'a chastened eclecticism'.[90] But all three agreed on the innate superiority of English, and especially French, Gothic. German Gothic lacked the necessary 'nervous manliness'.[91] The study of Italian Gothic had been pioneered by Thomas Hope, Didron and Willis. Even Pugin had dabbled in it – though his bold brickwork is East Anglian rather than North Italian in origin.[92] Between 1842 and 1847 the *Ecclesiologist*'s attitude to brick changed – under the influence of Benjamin Webb – from contempt to approval.[93] In the latter year publication of a pamphlet by Thomas James, *On the Use of Brick in Ecclesiastical Architecture*, stimulated interest in Italian medieval brickwork. It may even have triggered off Butterfield's addiction to bricky patterns.[94] The repeal of the brick tax in 1850 gave the new fashion a flying start. But the breakthrough had already occurred in 1849: Butterfield's Italian polychromy made All Saints, Margaret St, a mecca for progressive Goths. And Ruskin – 'the hierophant of Gothic'[95] – made North Italy sacred to the English.

Burges regarded that event as a disaster. First Palladian, then Greek, then Perpendicular and Early English, then Decorated, then Geometrical – Georgian and early Victorian architecture had slipped into a series of fashionable straitjackets, each new garment as inflexible as the last. Then 'one day Mr Ruskin published his *Stones of Venice*, and . . . a rush was made for Italian Gothic . . . the details of which, never very fine, were nearly as unsuitable for our purpose as those of Greek architecture itself. I do not for one moment wish to deny the wonderful massiveness, beauty, and strength of the larger Italian works; on the contrary, I think them deserving of the most careful study, although they are precisely the features most difficult to introduce in these days of leasehold tenures and large fenestration; but the details of Italian Gothic are worse than useless. For the most part they are executed in marble, which requires just as different a treatment to stone as stone does to brick' – and modern Italian Gothic confounds the mouldings of all three.[96] The beauties of Italian Gothic consist not in its picturesque details, but in 'its large and broad masses, its strong arches, with their deep voussoirs and strong soffits, and its very sparing use of mouldings'.[97] When Benjamin Ferrey – a Puginian rather than a Ruskinian Goth – was shown round Venice in 1851 by young Gilbert Scott, he kept muttering. 'Batty Langley! Batty Langley!'[98] Burges would have echoed that exclamation, no doubt with an additional expletive. Scott himself was cautious: 'I never fell into this mania.'[99] Italian Gothic was merely one ingredient in the new eclecticism. 'Italian Gothic must not be used in England, but . . . the study of it is necessary to the perfecting of our revival.'[1] Even Street voiced serious doubts. He praised Venetian Gothic's unique capacity for 'the harmonious combination of colour and form in architecture'. But he regretted its insufficient concern for 'truthful construction'. And he warned against the danger of excessive polychromy: 'this hot taste is dangerous'.[2]

So for Burges, Ruskin's writings were both an inspiration and a trap. In the eyes of ecclesiologists their greatest achievement had been to rescue the Gothic Revival from the smear of Popery. Pugin – that 'wonderful man', as Burges always thought of him – had tainted the movement with a whiff of incense. Ruskin supplied an anti-papal deodorant. So anti-papal, in fact, that in years to come he went out of his way to recant: the 1880 edition of *Seven Lamps* is prefaced with a public apology for such 'rabid and utterly false Protestantism'.[3] But Ruskin never specifically apologised for both plagiarising and insulting Pugin. Nor did he apologise for his grotesque misjudgement of Burges.[4] Still, Burges always respected him. 'No man's works', he wrote in 1865, 'contain more valuable information than Mr Ruskin's, but they are strong meat, and require to be taken by one who has [already] made up his mind. . . . [For] to one in search of a style and just beginning his architectural life it is almost destruction.'[5] Thus Burges himself – anchored to Early French – could absorb the occasional Italian 'dodge': the trilobe roof from the twelfth-century Lombardic church of San Zenone, Verona, for instance.[6] Or the tower of the Palazzo Vecchio in Florence; or the domelet ceilings of Messina; or the gilded and painted beams of Monreale in Sicily; or the honeycomb vaulting of the Capella Palatina at Palermo; or

14 The marriage of Lord Bute and Gwendolen Howard at Brompton Oratory, 1872.

15 Bute's funeral, October 1900: the cortège arrives on the Isle of Bute.

16 Upper Gallery, the Great Hall, Mount Stuart, Isle of Bute, *c.* 1914.

17 The Garden Front and Chapel, Mount Stuart.

the great bronze doors of Monreale and Pisa. Such Italian or Sicilian details – or, for that matter, motifs from Cairo or Constantinople – could be absorbed by an *aficionado* of Early French like Burges. They were all grist to the eclectic mill. But architectural tyros must beware. 'The architecture of Venice is a marble architecture, and not a stone one; it is suited to a totally different climate to ours, and it is under totally different conditions. Thus the sea bathes the feet of almost every building, and forms a very different base to kitchen windows and area railings – the latter, by the way, one of the most absurd modern eyesores. I shall never forget my horror on coming upon a Venetian bank built in freestone in a quiet, dull cathedral town – it was simply an impertinence.'[7] 'Nearly all our faults in modern architecture may be traced to the misuse of Italian examples.'[8] 'Modern Venetian – Gothic freely treated' was enough to destroy the good name of Medieval Art forever.

In the quest for a Victorian Style, therefore, Venetian precedents seemed to Burges to be misleading. He came to think the same about thirteenth and fourteenth-century English Gothic. 'The details', he wrote in 1865, with reference to London, 'are too small and the masses too cut up, for this great smoky city, where everything becomes covered with a coat of black after a few years'. Early French, however, 'is a style which very nearly answers our conditions, and if we go a little further back and examine what is called the Transition style, as developed in England and France, but especially the latter, we shall find almost everything we want. In the first place it is an architecture of great broad masses – it requires few or no mouldings, it employs round and pointed arches indifferently, the large arches generally being pointed and the smaller ones circular; it is capable of any amount of carving or sculpture, and this carving or sculpture can be omitted or added without calling for constructive alterations, for it is often taken out of the mass itself, more especially in the strings and voussoirs. Thus a building can be decorated after it has been erected, but yet it is perfect even without the decoration. The great opportunities for figure sculpture should also be taken into account. The tympana of doorways, the spandrels of arches, the spaces within the arcades, and the pediments of gables, can all be made to tell stories from our history, poetry or literature. ... [Transitional Gothic in fact possesses an] applicability to sculpture probably greater than any architecture since that of Greece'. Exterior decorative painting would be impractical in modern conditions, and deplorable if covered with plate glass. Exterior mosaic calls out for marble settings rather than stone. So sculpture is the wisest medium for modern decoration, that is sculpture integrated in a modern development of Early French. For all these reasons, English Gothic 'certainly won't do'.[9]

There was no doubt at all in Burges's mind that thirteenth-century Gothic represented the peak of medieval achievement. That century was 'the golden period of Christian art and poetry – the age which presented us with the Cathedral of Beauvais, the Abbey of Westminster, the Niebelungenlied and the Divine Comedy'.[10] Canterbury, for example, he thought 'the best of our cathedrals, always excluding the

Perpendicular parts'.[11] It was an age innocent of Vitruvian theory.[12] But thirteenth-century English work did not bear comparison with Early French. 'The mouldings in English thirteenth-century work', he noted, 'are far more beautiful in their sections than successful in their perspective, looking too much like bundles of reeds separated by hollows.' Whereas 'the French architect of the same period looked more to the effect and less to the section; he left more plain surfaces . . . thus his mouldings, where he did use them, have a more telling effect'.[13] These differences gradually increased. Before the reign of King John, France and England were one empire, with one architectural style. After that date, England 'drifted into a distinctive architecture . . . with its conventional three-foil foliage, its lancets, its triplets, its round abaci, and its reedy mouldings. . . . We find no height in the churches; on the contrary, they are low, and have long and irregular plans. They are admirably suited for small towns, and for small, pretty landscapes. . . . The mouldings are always very small, so are the window spaces, or rather the lights between the mullions, and at last we come to such productions as the West front of Windsor Chapel Royal – a most dreary specimen of architecture. . . . We have nothing like the great Town Halls of Flanders, and our cathedrals are very second-rate affairs after those on the continent'.[14] So much for Lincoln; so much for Salisbury. Alas, like the west window at Cologne, they marked 'that unhappy turn in medieval art, when men designed tracery, not to contain figures or to sustain the glass, but simply for its own sake; as if art could be produced by the compasses instead of the pencil'.[15]

For Burges, therefore, in the 1850s and even into the 1860s, Early French represented both a basis for the architecture of his own age and a springboard for the architecture of the future. 'Early French art [is] more suited to the requirements of the present day than any other phase of Medieval architecture. We live under different conditions to our [medieval English] ancestors. They delighted in small pretty buildings, with delicate details, which would be out of place in our smoky atmosphere. In French art everything is upon a larger scale, and it is usually suited to our large warehouses and for high houses, such as are being sown broadcast in old London.'[16] French Gothic was nobler, cheaper and characteristic of the modern age. 'The distinguishing characteristics of the Englishmen of the nineteenth century', Burges concludes, 'are our immense railway and engineering works, our line-of-battle ships, our good and strong machinery . . . our free constitution, our unfettered press, and our trial by jury. . . . [No] style of architecture can be more appropriate to such a people than that which . . . is characterised by boldness, breadth, strength, sternness, and virility.'[17]

ARCHAEOLOGY v. INVENTION

Besides Burges, who were the evangelists of Early French? In France it was Arcisse de Caumont, Ludovic Vitet and Prosper Merimée who initiated a more sympathetic approach to medieval buildings. De La Saussaye and Delaquerière were also influential. But it was three members of the Didron family – Adolphe or Didron the Elder, founder and editor of *Annales Archéologiques*;[18] his brother, the publisher Victor Didron; and Adolphe's adopted son Edouard – who together played the educative and controlling role of the Ecclesiologists in Britain, and paved the way for the greatest of French Goths, Viollet-le-Duc. It was the elder Didron in particular who gave the Early French movement its first major triumph when he made sure that Lille Cathedral would be built in the style of thirteenth-century France.[19]

Annales Archéologiques began publication in 1844, two years after the *Ecclesiologist*, and ceased in 1870, again two years after its rival.[20] From the start, however, its emphases were very different. Its chosen field was thirteenth-century rather than fourteenth-century; its expertise was symbolism rather than liturgy. Its interests were not only architectural but decorative: the minor arts – metalwork, needlework, tiles, enamels, woodcarving – were treated seriously and at length. Above all, it was Catholic, not Anglican. Monstrances, thuribles, chrismatories and reliquaries were all permitted. Viollet-le-Duc and Lassus[21] were among the earliest contributors. The Abbé Texier[22] and Felix de Verneilh[23] wrote regularly in the 1850s and 1860s. Pugin and Willement were subscribers from the start. So was J. H. Parker of Oxford. So were antiquaries like Thomas Stapleton, Albert Way, Thomas Wright and Roach Smith. Before long Whewell and Willis of Cambridge were on the subscription list along with Beresford-Hope. Wrought iron hinges at Vézelay[24] and Chablis;[25] the chalice of St Remi at Rheims;[26] the church of Notre Dame at Châlons-sur-Marne;[27] Orfèvrerie;[28] 'The Gothic Style in the nineteenth century';[29] 'The [fourteenth-century] Armoire at Noyon';[30] the thirteenth-century church at Montréale (Yonne);[31] thirteenth and fourteenth-century pavements, decorated in elaborately geometrical fashion;[32] Paganism in Christian Art[33] – these were the sort of items for which Didron's *Annales* were famous. Publications were exchanged; information shared. The *Annales* carried regular commentaries on the state of medieval studies in England.[34] In a sense, the movement of the *Ecclesiologist* towards thirteenth-century Europe, and away from fourteenth-century England, was a measure of the influence and success of its French rival.[35] Beresford-Hope's progression is typical: he begins as a Puginian apostle of 'the real thing', and ends as the Pope of eclecticism, a veritable High Priest of syncretists.[36] Archaeology upstaged ecclesiology, and both outflanked invention. Didron had much to be responsible for.

Like the *Ecclesiologist*, Didron's *Annales* were confessedly confessional. Secular buildings hardly fall within his terms of reference. For these we must look, for example, to Aymar Verdier's *Architecture civile et domestique*, a short-lived periodical which began in 1852. But for secular Early French precedents the most influential publicist was undoubtedly Eugene Viollet-le-Duc.

Burges made no secret of his admiration for Viollet-le-Duc, at least as regards the Frenchman's scholarship. He regarded the *Dictionnaire* – 'that wonderful monument of human knowledge and human industry'[37] – as quite invaluable. The speed of research and illustration amazed him.[38] The woodcuts were *tours de force*.[39] However, 'he draws too well for a practical architect', Burges complained, 'for a man who has this fatal gift makes his designs look so well on paper', that they far outshine the final result.[40] Viollet's *Entrêtiens* aroused less enthusiasm: he thought the woodcuts 'excellent', but the essays 'long-winded' and some of the theories about geometrical composition positively pernicious.[41] He certainly felt little sympathy with Viollet's fantasies of metallic vaulting. Nevertheless, Viollet's volumes were really Burges's Bible. 'We all crib from Viollet-le-Duc,' he admitted disarmingly, 'although probably not one buyer in ten ever reads the text.'[42] Burges's final judgement on Viollet-le-Duc, delivered in public at the R.I.B.A., was characteristically candid: he was a great scholar, an average architect, and a disastrous restorationist.[43] Posterity has endorsed his verdict.

But apart from a few big names – Lassus, Didron, Viollet-le-Duc: 'that brilliant knot of art-writers', as Beresford-Hope called them[44] – it was not the French who led the field in pursuit of Early French, but the English. French commitment to medievalism was less generalised than English. 'It is true', Burges noted in 1865, 'that they spend large sums (or rather the State does) in very equivocal restorations of their glorious cathedrals, but they don't build their country houses in the Pointed style. With them that style is essentially a *hors d'oeuvre*, and even the clergy, who in our country have been the great leaders of the movement, are more than suspected of having their affections fixed upon the bastard pagan style of modern Rome than on the art glories of their forefathers.' England was different. The country of Pugin and Ruskin had 'taken up the subject of Medieval art and architecture more seriously than any other nation'.[45] So it happened that the leading pundits of Early French were English: Burges, Clutton, Street, Norman Shaw, W. E. Nesfield, R. J. Johnson, T. H. King and W. Galsworthy Davie.

Clutton's *Domestic Architecture of France . . . from Charles VI to . . . Louis XII* (1853), for which Burges supplied several drawings,[46] could only loosely be categorised as Early French: it was concerned with fifteenth-century work and, by 1852, fifteenth-century French domestic architecture already seemed 'comparatively debased'.[47] The book, however, was well received in France.[48] So was Norman Shaw's *Architectural Sketches from the Continent* (1858). But this time the sources of inspiration had been firmly pushed back to the thirteenth century. Many of the ecclesiastical items must have been well known to Burges.[49] Some of their details were clearly of great interest to him.[50] Some of Shaw's secular examples anticipate details of Burges's later work.[51] And the plates themselves – unlike Clutton's – are expository rather than illustrative, just as Burges preferred. They lack, however, the diagrammatic clarity of Burges's own *Architectural Drawings* (1870).

Nesfield's *Specimens of Medieval Architecture* (1862) covered much the same ground.[52] So did Johnson's *Specimens of Early French Architecture* (1866)[53] and

Galsworthy Davie's *Architectural Sketches in France* (1877).[54] But none of these was nearly as popular as the works produced by Thomas Harper King. King was almost the John Britton of this post-ecclesiological phase of the Gothic Revival: the man who brought Early French to the drawing-boards of a whole generation. An English Catholic convert, King spent most of his life in Bruges, translating Pugin into French and collecting drawings for publication. His four-volume *Study-Book* (1858–68), to which Burges contributed, contained a mass of examples, all carefully drawn to a uniform scale. Burges must particularly have approved the choice of Laon,[55] Chartres,[56] Rheims,[57] Braisne,[58] Etampes,[59] Toulouse,[60] Dijon,[61] Semur,[62] and Auxerre.[63] Here indeed are a number of minor ingredients in the Burges style: foliage mouldings, capitals, tympana, spires and spirelets, stylised ball-flowers, finials and diapers – all these can be approximately traced in King's meticulous plates. But even as one turns those crisp pages today, one wonders perhaps whether the geometric vigour of High Victorian Early French did not owe something to the diagrammatic way in which its prototypes were necessarily set out in measured form. All those fragmented wheel window segments; all those foreshortened piers in which capital and base seem to meet head-on, with little or no intermediate shaft. Perhaps gazing at such lithographs encouraged the gestation of those abstract, abbreviated, geometrical forms which, in the 1850s and 1860s, seem almost to caricature their medieval originals.

Anyway, such were the principal published sources for Early French. As a short cut Burges recommended the following: Willis on the East end of Canterbury; Parker on Glastonbury and the great hall at Oakham; Viollet-le-Duc on Poitiers, Angoulême, Arles, Vézelay and Moissac.[64] But any 'thirteenth-century man' worth his salt would undoubtedly go on pilgrimage himself, to Normandy, to Picardy and to the Isle de France: Bayeux, St Quentin, Amiens, Noyon, Chartres, Notre Dame de Paris, Rheims – the cathedral *and* the church of St Remi – Soissons, Laon, Châlons-sur-Marne and Beauvais. Those were the high points of Early French, singled out, for example, by George Edmund Street.[65]

Street expressed the credo of 'a thirteenth-century man' with a passion equal to Burges. In 1858 he praised thirteenth-century Gothic for its 'energy, life, purity of form and colour, and rigid truthfulness in the treatment of every accessory in every material'. Then he adds: 'Who that really has worked heartily at his work will venture to deny that in stonework and the science of moulding; in sculpture – whether of the figure or of foliage; in metal-work – whether iron or silver; in embroidery, in enamelling, and in stained glass, the northern art of the thirteenth century is infinitely more pure, more vigorous, and more true than the work of later times? . . . its great lesson to us is that of earnestness and reality . . . just the kind of earnestness which will enable men possessed of its principles to grapple with the difficulties of nineteenth-century inventions and thoughts in the most real and simple manner – just the kind of art which will impress itself upon a practical age like the present.'[66]

Such convictions excluded whole areas of medieval architecture from any form of appreciation. King's College Chapel, Cambridge, for instance, gave neither Street nor Burges much pleasure. Burges called it 'that wonderfully overpraised building', and considered it a very poor example for budding Goths. 'The glass is good of its kind,' he conceded, 'so are the Renaissance west stalls and screen, while the roof is a pretty puzzle in stone-cutting; all the rest of the building is, however, positively bad.'[67] When challenged to substantiate his opinion by an anonymous M.A. from Trinity College, he produced a characteristically 'facetious' reply:

> my business at present in this world is to build, and not to argue ... *de gustibus non est disputandum*. ... [But let] M.A. ... go to Paris for a fortnight, and then spend every morning in studying the Sainte Chapelle, and every afternoon ... before the West front of Notre Dame. He may then come home with the recollection of those two buildings fresh in his mind, and look at King's College Chapel. ... Perhaps he will then understand why I do not admire [it]. ... If, however, he object to the discomfort of crossing the Channel, or should his long vacation be pre-occupied, I shall be most happy to endeavour to convert him at Cambridge itself, by rebuilding his college chapel, or indeed that of any other college at Cambridge, for there are several which are in great want of it.[68]

Ruskin would have agreed. He dismissed King's College Chapel as 'a piece of architectural juggling'.[69]

Of course Early French did not go unchallenged. There were always voices to be raised in defence of English Gothic – 'delicate, subtle ... refined' – so unlike the 'coarse, rude and barbarous' thirteenth-century French.[70] 'Everything Gothic done at this moment is French,' complained one correspondent in *The Builder* of 1863, adding '... or would-be French. The Gothic of France is very beautiful and expressive of French thought; but to transplant it to England is as absurd as to suppose the English language could ever convey the beauties of Molière, or French the character of the writings of Shakespeare. The noblest of distinct manly traits is lost in this effete struggling after sensation by the use of strange forms. ... It does not please except by its novelty and strangeness. ... English architecture ought to be English'.[71] In the same year the *Ecclesiologist* hailed Bodley's All Saints, Cambridge, as a portent – a swing back to Puginian purity: 'The time for a reaction from exclusively French or Italian types has at length arrived.'[72] Such judgements were only a little premature.

For the confidence of even the fiercest Goths in the validity of Early French was never absolute. To them, as to High Victorian architects right across the spectrum, that New Style still seemed as far away as some 'undiscovered Cape of Good Hope'.[73] Archaeology had turned out to be a substitute for, rather than a stimulus to, invention. Gilbert Scott spoke for the middle-of-the-road man when he justified Gothic *faute de mieux*: 'I am no medievalist; I do not advocate the styles of the middle ages as such. If we had a distinctive architecture of our own day, worthy of the greatness of the age, I should be content to follow it; but we have not.'[74] Students hungered for instruction, and found only confusion. Listen to the professoriat. 'This is a most critical period', announced Professor T. L. Donaldson, 'we are all . . . in a state of transition; 'there is no fixed style now prevalent. . . . We are wandering in a labyrinth of experiments . . . trying by . . . amalgamation . . . to form a homogeneous style.'[75] 'It is useless to deny', confessed Professor Sydney Smirke, 'that aesthetics generally have not kept pace with either physics or with the exact sciences. . . . [Architecture] has not kept pace with time.' And the aesthetics of engineering offer no solution: 'The mere dry, unimpassioned beauty resulting from the quality of fitness, however it may satisfy the engineer, will hardly suffice to meet the aspirations of the architect [for] as artists . . . we desire something more.' Only a cautious eclecticism held out any hope: there lay 'the best chance of ultimately arriving – it may be after a long purgatorial period of folly and excess – yet ultimately arriving at a sound, consistent and original style, worthy of the genius and civilisation of the nineteenth century'. [76] In the 1850s and 1860s Early French had been chosen by the *avant-garde* as a chrysalis from which the butterfly of a New Style might emerge. By 1870 such hopes had proved illusory. Professor T. Roger Smith fell back on *rundbogenstil*.[77] Professor E. M. Barry fell back on platitudes. 'What, then, is to be the architecture of the future? . . . [It is to be] true, original, and scientific.'[78] 'About as satisfactory,' commented Andrew Dewar of Nova Scotia, 'as if some one had asked him what style he would have a coat made, and he had answered, "Of good taste, true colour, and machine-made".'[79]

The triumphs of High Victorian architectural achievement were shot through with uncertainty. Sated with archaeology, they still hungered after invention. And even Burges – the most belligerent supporter of Early French – could not escape the disease of his generation: doubt.

'GO' v. GOTHIC

In the 1860s Burges had no doubt at all as to what was bad in British architecture. His *bête noire* was the 'modern Gothic' produced by that group of architects immortalised by Goodhart-Rendel as 'The Rogues': E. B. Lamb, Samuel Sanders Teulon, Joseph Peacock, R. L. Roumieu, F. T. Pilkington, E. Basset Keeling, Thomas ('Victorian') Harris and – in a class by himself – William Butterfield.[80] Their style – and still more that of their less talented followers, the 'ignorant and untutored rabble',[81] was a rebarbative cocktail based on the harshest, most primitive components of Anglo-Venetian and Early French. In the slang of the day, it had GO. In many ways it was a popular parody of that muscular Gothic language which Burges himself had helped to create.[82] His criticisms, therefore, were appropriately biting.

Burges grouped his objections to 'modern Gothic' under ten headings:[83]

i) *Rhythm*. 'If we look at the facade of any large building of the Middle Ages, we shall find nearly as much regularity as in a Classic building. . . . Modern buildings look very much as if they had been shaken around in a hat.'

ii) *Colour*. 'No one is satisfied unless the building presents a most piebald appearance; red bricks, yellow bricks, black bricks ... tiles.' Constructional polychromy – and incised ornament – was most effective when used sparingly in constructive fashion.[84]

iii) *Marble*. This, the richest of materials, should be limited to large slabs and columnar shafts, not used in semi-spherical form to punctuate Caen stone with piebald blobs like inset cannon-balls.[85]

iv) *Tiles*. These should be used economically, even for floors; 'walls should be painted'.

v) *Chamfers*. 'The great delight of the modern architect is in his chamfers: he chamfers everything he can possibly get hold of, whether there is any necessity for the process or not.' Whatever its applicability to woodwork, there was no visual justification for chamfering the lines of a pointed arch or the angles of an archivolt. 'Chamfers are very good things in their way ... but it is quite possible to have too much of a good thing.'

vi) *Notchings*. 'Notchings in a huge spire may do duty for dogtooth.' But they should never be employed on archivolts or on 'the upper edges of the abaci of columns, where a straight line is most imperatively demanded by the eye'. Worse still, 'the lower edges of mouldings are notched, till they look like what milliners call inserted work'. Worst of all, 'even our furniture is notched', in gross defiance of utility. 'One of my friends possesses a table where the lower edge of the top is thus decorated, greatly to the discomfort of his visitors' knuckles. After all, this notching, although very cheap, is very barbaric, and I believe is indicated by Mr Owen Jones as among the very earliest of the attempts of the savage mind for the decoration of the war-club.'

vii) *Arches*. 'Every kind of arch in itself is so very beautiful that it would appear almost impossible to make an ugly one; but, thanks to modern ingenuity, a great deal has been effected towards that end.' Top-chamfering, segmental arches and stilted tympana should all be avoided. Still more so, 'Saxon straight-sided arches',[86] those anti-constructive and 'inexpressibly ugly' attempts at spurious muscularity. 'This endeavour to get apparent strength by the employment of straight lines where our ancestors would have used curved, is one of the greatest faults of the present day, and of all is the most painful to the eye ... no man who has ever properly studied the figure would be guilty of such a thing'.

viii) *Small Columns*. Street's 'excellent' use of miniature columns in place of ornamental buttresses has been copied 'to death'; 'we even see columns mast-headed on the tops of our highest gables, and figures on top of them'.

ix) *Stonework*. Architects have learnt to avoid foliage 'covering the building or object until it looks like a petrified arbour', and strings 'jumping up and down in a most spasmodic manner'. But they still frequently employ 'crude and ugly foliage' consisting of truncated leaves and right-angled stalks, all in a misplaced 'endeavour to get strength'.

x) *Woodwork*. Church furniture is 'generally very poor and miserable', not 'sharp and solid' like the stalls at Amiens. And the whole concept of an open roof had become an inhibiting cult: the majority of thirteenth- and fourteenth-century church roofs had been boarded, ceiled and painted.

To these ten criticisms, Burges added an eleventh: the use of sash windows and acres of plate glass instead of small panes and Gothic casements. He described plate glass windows surmounted by Gothic arches, hipped gables and high-pitched roofs – as for example in Butterfield's Milton Ernest Hall (1856) – as 'pretentious and ugly'.[87] Burges was never friendly with Butterfield. He disapproved of his excessive polychromy, and his cavalier attitude to Gothic precedents. Besides, they were worlds apart, socially and intellectually. But then Butterfield was *sui generis*. He was never the leader of a school. And Burges would have been the first to admit that the excesses of GO could not be heaped upon his head.

High Victorian GO was in fact an attempt to construct a brand new style out of the pulverised fragments of the Gothic Revival. As such, it was doomed to reflect the egoes of its own practitioners. Burges called it 'the Original and Ugly School'.[88] Teulon, for instance, is an architect of undoubted talent. But at Elvetham, Hants. (1859–60), his frenetic pursuit of originality in pattern and colour comes near to destroying all unity and coherence of design. Again, Pilkington's churches at Edinburgh (Barclay Church, 1862) and Kelso (1863–6) have their own explosive merit. But J. T. Micklethwaite's criticism of 1873 comes very near to the truth.

> The common symptoms [of GO] in our churches are harshness, even to brutality of general design, with studied ugliness and systematic exaggeration and distortion of details, stumpy banded pillars, stilted arches, a profusion of coarse carving, notches, zigzags, curves ... and long wiry crockets bursting out of unexpected places ... like hatpegs. ... GO is in fact architectural rant, and may be defined as the perpetual forcing into notice of the personality of the architect. ... 'See', he says in his work, 'what a clever fellow I am'.[89]

Burges put it more simply: 'Ugliness is not strength.'[90] He was even ruder about Basset Keeling. Anglo-Venetian and Early French may have been the starting points for Keeling's 'acrobatic Gothic' Music Hall in the Strand (1864). But excess had become his basic principle, and vulgarity – in colour, material and form – his besetting vice.[91] E. B. Lamb belonged to an earlier generation. He was a hangover from the Regency, an architectural laggard from the age of Loudon. His sins, therefore, stemmed from frenzied pursuit of the Picturesque rather than over-indulgence in the Sublime.[92] As for 'Victorian' Harris, his famous design for a terrace at Harrow 'in the Victorian style', seemed to Burges to sum up all the chaotic pretensions of popular architecture in the 1860s.[93]

'Victorian' Harris was not the first to call for a Victorian Style. But he did call loudest. He demanded a universal style which would 'realize the spirit of our own time . . . an indigenous style of our own, embodying the spirit of the good of every age, and springing out of ourselves . . . an honest independent simple expression of the true God-fearing English character'.[94] Take away the 'cant', snorted the *Ecclesiologist*, and he was merely calling for the same thing as 'nearly all architecturalists have learned to desire, viz., a characteristic development of the National Pointed, so as to meet all the wants of the age, and to assimilate all the new processes and materials which are now available'.[95] It was the old High Victorian dilemma all over again. And in the hands of 'Victorian' Harris the result was catastrophic. 'Eclecticism! Eclecticism!', wailed J. P. Seddon, 'what horrors have . . . been perpetrated in thy euphonious name.'[96]

GO certainly cured Burges, as it cured most of his contemporaries, of any lingering belief in the imminence of a New Style. But during the early 1860s he still retained a fund of confidence in eclectic theory. One day it would supply 'the basis of our future architecture'.[97] In 1861 he thought – such was the rate of progress – that in twenty years time England would be ready to rebuild the Western towers of Westminster Abbey.[98] Reviewing the 1862 Exhibition, he takes heart from a fountain by Nesfield with panels by Albert Moore, a design which combines Greek and Gothic forms. On behalf of 'the rising school' of Goths, he addresses – rather rhetorically – the pundits of classicism:

> We will take your drawing, we will take your sculpture, we will take your way of decorating your myths; but we will have nothing to do with your eternal Doric, Ionic and Corinthian . . . your low pediments and shallow mouldings, fitted for a hotter and sunnier climate than ours. We are the descendants of Adam, and have eaten of the tree of good and evil, and we will exercise the knowledge thereby acquired by taking the good and leaving the bad.[99]

Thus spake the eclectic. As the 1860s progress, however, Burges's optimism weakens. In 1861 he admitted that his generation would be unlikely to see the New Style: 'that good time will not be in our day.'[1] By 1865 he had to confess openly the nineteenth century's 'fatal . . . want of a distinctive architecture'. 'In every age of the world except our own, only one style of architecture has been in use. . . . [Today] the student . . . is expected to be master of . . . half-a-dozen.' 'Until the question of style gets settled', he concludes, 'it is utterly hopeless to think about any great improvement in modern art'.[2] At present debased Classic is used for public, secular buildings, and debased Gothic for private and religious ones.[3] One day both schools may disappear. Only then may we 'get something of our own of which we need not be ashamed. This may, perhaps, take place in the twentieth century, it certainly, as far as I can see, will not occur in the nineteenth.'[4] Meanwhile the architect must take his cue from the engineer: 'our viaducts, our bridges, and some of our railway stations are really worthy of a great people; so are our docks and our piers ... from these ... we must take the keynote of our future architecture. If once we build solidly and with masses of good material, there will be no fear of the final result.'⁵ A New Style will emerge from the structural process. But how is the advent of this aesthetic paradise to be accelerated? Burges can only invoke the aid of 'some kind fairy' to 'make a clean sweep of all our existing buildings and all our books on architecture, to say nothing of our architects', and 'to hide our museums and picture galleries for at least a couple of hundred years'.⁶ Billy Burges grasped the historicist nettle all right, but perhaps he rather enjoyed being stung.

Anyway, that was Burges in 1865. Two years later, his gloom has deepened still further. He still believes in the linguistic analogy: 'the various styles are to really beautiful architecture ... what languages are to a poem.' But he has begun to doubt the validity of architectural poems, however beautiful, composed in archaic tongues: 'this cannot go on.'⁷ 'We have no real vernacular in architecture', he tells a young audience at the Architectural Association. 'Neither of the two great styles belongs to our own days. We have to learn them painfully and imperfectly as we should learn languages ... we are seeking for an architectural language suited to our times. ... We have taken many points of departure [Perpendicular, Decorated, Venetian, Early French], and thrown them away, one after another, until it must be confessed that we have got a little confused.'⁸ When the students press him for a prediction – what is the style of the future to be? – he curtly replies: 'I cannot tell.'⁹

The following year, 1868, he is gloomier still. 'For three centuries', he tells an audience of churchmen, 'the Pagan revival ran its course, and now we have travelled far into another revival, *viz.* that of our National Medieval Architecture. The question is, How far have we succeeded? Perhaps in mere servile copying we have succeeded better than has been the case in the other revivals. We have had more books, greater facilities for travel, new processes of reproducing our drawings, improved machinery for striking off the plates; and, lastly, all the wondrous aid of photography, by which the artist and the machinery are superseded. But, somehow or other, we have not been very successful, either in our copies or in our own efforts. If we copy, the thing never looks right, however servilely the mouldings e.g. may have been copied. The same recurs with regard to those buildings which do not profess to be copies: both they and the copies want spirit. They are dead bodies; they don't live. We are at our wit's end, and do not know what to do. It is bad enough to see our faults, and to know how to correct them in future work; but there is probably no more depressing sensation than to feel the presence of faults and not to know how to correct them'.¹⁰

By 1876, Burges had really given up hope: the choice of one style (Early French) had failed; the choice of several styles (Eclecticism) had also failed.

If we take up any of the architectural publications, we are simply astonished at the number of various styles which are all being practised concurrently. There probably never was such a complete architectural masquerade as we see at the present time. ... If we are ever to have a style in architecture it will certainly not come from the exclusive choice of any of the existing ones, neither will it come in our own time, although certain writers as early as thirty years ago were calling out for no copying but for the creation of a new style. They might as well have asked for the millenium. Nobody can or ever will invent a style; it must come by common practice and common consent. In the meanwhile we may help it on by becoming better artists, and being better read. No one can predict how the new style will be evolved or when it will come: perhaps some day we may wake up and the law of leasehold may be abolished; then it may be discovered that it pays to make ... our house or warehouse the best of its kind. Then may follow the consideration that dirty brick and decaying stone are not the most suitable materials in a city like London, with its atmosphere saturated with gases; then may follow the reflection that granite, porphyry and majolica are the only substances which will resist the acid gases. But majolica can be decorated and painted and made to tell histories, and to speak like the living statues of the Medieval artists, and then, if we have not neglected our opportunities, and if we have studied the arts – both the great and the subsidiary – in a monumental spirit, then indeed we may see the beginning of a new style – a style founded upon common sense, and construction in our own materials combined with beautiful and monumental art.[11]

Those words, and those which preceded them, were spoken even as Cork Cathedral – Burges's greatest masterpiece in the Early French style – was rising to completion. When we come to look at that extraordinary work, and at others by Burges more extraordinary still, it will be as well to remember the doubt and mental turmoil which lurk behind such apparent confidence. Burges's own words give the lie to his text-book reputation as a happy-go-lucky Goth.[12] Even at its zenith, at the end of the 1860s, the Gothic Revival was riven with uncertainty. And rebellious younger Goths, younger than Burges, bored with ecclesiology, tired of GO, weary even of the thirteenth century, were already sharpening their T squares for a palace revolution.

GOTHIC v. QUEEN ANNE

It was during the mid-1860s that the weekly architectural press began to record rumblings of rebellion within the Gothic empire, 'quiverings of the Gothic earth-crust from the pent-up smouldering fires below'.[13] In his introduction to the 1862 Exhibition Catalogue, F. T. Palgrave – later immortalised as editor of *The Golden Treasury* – had dismissed classicism as 'galvanised pedantry'; Gothic was 'best': 'the Architecture of Heaven and the Architecture of Home.'[14] In the same year Burges had announced triumphantly that 'the Medieval school ... comprises nearly every rising architect'.[15] Such complacency was quickly shattered. Gothic orthodoxy was soon eroded – on the secular front at least – in two ways.

First came Old English, a revived form of rustic, Home Counties vernacular, complete with tile-hanging, hipped gables, casement windows, half-timbering, ribbed brick chimneys, and pargetting.[16] Eden Nesfield and Norman Shaw were the leading culprits, renegades both of them from Burgesian Gothic. Nesfield a protean gentleman-genius; Shaw 'a Scotsman on the make', but the most talented Scots architect since Robert Adam. Then came Queen Anne, a flexible urban argot, sash-windowed, brick-ribbed, based on late seventeenth-century vernacular classicism, Dutch, French, Flemish, German and English – seasoned with a dash of Japanese.[17] Nesfield and Shaw were again the leaders, backed up this time by a group of rebels from Gilbert Scott's office: G. F. Bodley, J. J. ('Jock') Stevenson, E. R. Robson, G. G. Scott, jnr, Basil Champneys and T. G. ('Anglo') Jackson. And hovering in the background, godfather to the new eclecticism, was Morris's own architect, Philip Webb, glancing backwards over his shoulder to parsonages by Pugin, Butterfield and Street. From Red House, Bexleyheath (1859–60) to The Red House, Bayswater (1871); from Kew and Kensington to the City and the Thames Embankment; from School Board domestic to Pont Street Dutch, the bricky tide swept on.

Warington Taylor (Morris's business manager) had been one of the first – in 1862–4 – to question the omnipotence of Gothic, and to call for a Georgian revival. He was followed by the Rev. J. L. Petit. In 1867, Petit, previously known as a maverick Goth, publicly praised the domestic architecture of Queen Anne's reign as both practical and handsome.[18] By 1868 Philip Webb's London houses had established Queen Anne as a fashionable fact, and – according to Burges – Thackeray was bidding fair to do for the new style what Lord Byron had done for the Greek Revival and Sir Walter Scott for Gothic.[19] By 1870 'the Queen Anne Mania' had almost broken free from its Gothic Revival parentage: it was a style with only a few 'lingering hankerings after the fleshpots of Gothic tradition'.[20] First the furniture, then the plaster, then the wrought iron, then the woodwork, and finally the exterior fabrics of Queen Anne houses themselves, had been revived. Queen's Square and Queen Anne's Gate, with their warm red bricks, their rectangular sash-windows, their thick glazing-bars, their shell-headed doorways, had become accepted as domestic models of convenience and propriety.

1870 was the year in which *The Architect* printed a devastating critique on 'The Consequences of the Gothic Revival'. Its effect was only partly offset by spirited replies from J. P. Seddon and E. W. Godwin.[21] *The Builder* had never been committed to Gothic. But *The Architect*, dominated by Seddon, Godwin and Burges, played down Queen Anne and stayed true to the Gothic cause, at least until the mid-1870s. In 1873 – 'the First Year of the Queen Anne Revival'[22] – its editor, T. Roger Smith, commissioned E. B. Ferrey to refute the polemics of young T. G. Jackson,[23] and William H. White to resuscitate some of the principles of Gothic composition.[24] The following year battle was joined between Robert Kerr and J. P. Seddon,[25] and White produced a splendidly malicious parody of a Queen Anne facade.[26] In 1874 G. E. Street summed up the attitude of the Old Guard: Queen Anne buildings were merely 'bad copies of bad originals'.[27] But within a year the tide had turned.

The battle for the *Building News* was fiercer, but equally brief. Throughout the 1860s its editorials are profoundly troubled by the absence of a viable Victorian style. But on the whole they follow the progressive Gothic party line: if a New Style is ever to emerge, its most likely parentage will be Early French – but Early French purged of excessive archaeology and uncorrupted by the fatal virtuosity of the later middle ages.

> One after another we have tried them all – Greek, Roman, Italian, and Renaissance; English-Gothic, French-Gothic, Italian-Gothic, Gothic of all periods – Early, Middle and Late; Romanesque, too, and Byzantine; not to speak of Moorish and Arabian. We have tried them separately, and we have tried them mixed. . . . 'Early Gothic' [may indeed be the germ of a Modern Style] but Early Gothic may mean two very different things. . . . Which of these two is the best foundation for modern work – the incompleted Geometrical, or the perfected Lancet style? . . . Tracery once allowed, it is not easy to stop its development. Some of our leading architects [e.g. G. F. Bodley], having started years ago with its best and earliest forms, have been, and are still, going through a 'decline and fall' of Gothic in their own practice. Their plate tracery has grown up into bar tracery – and this into more and more complex forms; the rest of their detail has kept it company, and their work has passed on from Early to Middle Gothic, or later. The breadth and freshness and simplicity which characterised their work are gone. The hopefulness has vanished from it; the germs of a nineteenth-century building style are no longer to be sought there; its authors have given up thinking for themselves, and have swallowed the Medieval system whole. They 'make it' A.D. 1371, and ignore the trifling fact that their clock is 500 years too slow. It is the natural result of having accepted the principles by which Middle Age art grew old and died. . . . A pointed style, free from . . . the slightest germs of tracery, does not . . . contain the seeds of its own ruin. It will . . . harmonize with a higher class of painting and sculpture, and will not demand an exaggerated quaintness in their productions in order to assimilate them to itself. It is strong, beautiful and severe – natural and reasonable; fit for an age whose best characteristic is earnest study of facts rather than wild fantastic redundance of imagination[28]

That editorial was almost the swansong of Early French. It was written in 1871, just at the moment when belief in the style collapsed.

Two doughty Goths, J. P. Seddon and J. D. Sedding, refused to surrender their medieval banner. When in 1874 Dr G. G. Zerffi accused the Gothic Revivalists of trying to do the impossible – reviving the form of medieval Gothic without the tyranny and superstition which created it – Sedding vigorously denied this facile equation of Christianity and barbarism and concluded: 'Modern Gothic ... has achieved many noble things, and is steadily advancing in freedom and power.'[29] A year later Seddon and Sedding were equally impenitent – dismissing Queen Anne detail as mere 'gibberish' and 'garbage', a prostitution of art pursued by a band of aesthetic Adullamites – though Seddon's attitude was somewhat compromised by his own address: No 1, Queen Anne's Gate.[30] 'The Queen Anne style', wrote Sedding 'answers to the Tudor of Gothic: it is the tail not the head of English Renaissance, and the ... adoption of this effete period as a model for the nineteenth century ... has given a freakish and transient character to the movement. ... [Its basis is a conflation of] choice morsels of the Renaissance of all dates and all countries. ... [Its result is] licentious eclecticism ... a mongrel style facetiously called the Free Classic. The conduct of some of the designers of this class is like unto a child in a garden picking the tops of flowers ... to make a promiscuous but malodorous nosegay.'[31] 'Will you go back to the prattle of childhood,' J. P. Seddon asked the students of the Architectural Association, just 'because you like baby-talk. For goodness sake, if you will be eclectic ... choose the best ... [not the] barbaric'.[32]

Seddon and Sedding were among the last to employ such confident language. By 1875 most Gothic Revivalists seem to have lost their nerve. Few dared to echo Lacy W. Ridge's toast: 'Queen Anne is dead';[33] or to follow Blashill's downright dictum: '"Queen Anne" is a copyism – and a copyism of ugliness to boot.'[34] That year, many readers of the *Building News* laughed heartily at a wheeled Gothic coal scuttle by W. Wilkinson of Oxford.[35] By 1876 the revived Queen Anne style was sufficiently orthodox to attract temperate and constructive criticism.[36] By 1877 even J. D. Sedding was toying with the fashion, albeit in Jacobethan form.[37] In 1878 the *Building News* actually devoted an editorial to the Five Orders.[38] And in 1880 there even appeared a new edition of *The Works in Architecture of Robert and James Adam*.[39] The Goths were clearly in retreat.

At least part of the steam in the Queen Anne controversy stemmed from the parallel debate in the mid-1870s over J. T. Emmett's vitriolic articles in the *Quarterly Review*.[40] Emmett attacked the whole basis of historicism with a rationality equal to Fergusson and a vehemence equal to Ruskin. In particular, he pilloried the 'Art-Architect' as a product of professional and social fragmentation. Academic exclusiveness and class divisions had created a mandarin architecture, wholly divorced from any vernacular tradition. The newly enroyalled Institute of British Architects responded violently. The whole structure of professionalism seemed to be at stake, as well as the supremacy of orthodox style. The very idea of aesthetic freedom produced an Establishment *frisson* in a generation horrified by the terrors of the Paris Commune. Emmett's vision of the inspired, autonomous artisan seemed to threaten the foundations of Victorian bourgeois professionalism. 'From the Empire of Classicism,' wrote one *Building News* correspondent, 'we have drifted through Gothic down to the communism of Queen

Anne; which may, indeed, be termed a reign of terror, wherein the hands of the workman have more power than the head of the designer.'[41] In the same year, during a discussion at the Architectural Association on 'The relationship between the Artisan and the Architect', 'a working man' named Ramskill dared to question even the need for an architectural profession: 'The architect, as he at present fulfils his functions, is an individual not wanted in the social economy . . . [architects] are mere ornaments.' He sat down to outraged cries of 'Order!'[42]

The names given to the new fashion reflected the confusion of its origins. 'Dutch William', 'Free Classic', 'Mystic', 'Neo-Classic',[43] 'Re-Classic',[44] 'Stuart',[45] 'Re-Renaissance'[46] – these were by no means the only labels suggested. Still, whatever its title, there was no mistaking the new mood: a return, devious and tentative, but a return none the less, to the long-neglected fount of classicism. By 1877 even the Judge Advocate General, George Cavendish Bentinck, felt free to harangue his constituents at Whitehaven on 'The Decline and Fall of British Architecture'. Pugin had initiated the Decline; Ruskin the Fall. Renaissance was now at hand: a revival of the classical tradition, a Renaissance of the Renaissance.[47] One symptom of this aesthetic counter-revolution was a new sympathy for the work of Sir Christopher Wren. The threatened destruction of several Wren City churches aroused protests in 1877–9.[48] And Burges bore the full brunt of the new taste when he attempted to refurbish St Paul's.

During the later 1870s, the Queen Anne Revival became first a cult and then a craze. To 'manly' Goths of the old school, its advocates seemed precious and prissy: 'Queen Enne', they lisped in affectation.[49] Out in Bedford Park, some of the more zealous Queen Anneites even dressed the part: cloak, silk stockings, buckle shoes, knee breeches, silk coats and hair powder.[50] Thackeray, Burges muttered darkly, was indeed a guilty man.[51]

The flight from the thirteenth century had certainly been quick in gathering momentum. By 1873 Norman Shaw, Bodley, Nesfield, Webb, Stevenson, G. G. Scott, jnr, R. W. Edis, T. G. Jackson, Basil Champneys – even Butterfield and Rossetti – had all deserted, either to Old English or to Queen Anne.[52] One of the few popular designers to hold fast to the old line was that protean pundit of the grotesque, J. Moyr Smith. Why bother, he asked in 1875, to exchange evolutionary Gothic for a stylistic mess of pottage?

> A patchwork of Japan,
> And queer bits of Queen Anne,
> All mixed upon the plan
> Of as you like, or as you can.[53]

Initially, Pearson, Brooks, Street and Scott remained steadfast. But Scott died in 1878. Then Brooks and Street dallied with vernacular classicism at Londonderry House[54] and Marlborough College.[55] J. L. Pearson stayed pure, and mute. Only Burges, Sedding and Seddon held fast to the Gothic credo, and spoke out. More prudent critics kept their powder dry, and waited for that intangible New Style to emerge.[56] By 1876 even Burges's loyal assistant, E. J. Tarver, had gone a-whoring after Queen Anne – though discreetly and far away – with a red-brick hunting-box in the Ardennes.[57]

E. W. Godwin seems to have had mixed feelings about the new vogue. In general he endorsed the *deus ex machina* argument: eclecticism giving birth to a New Style.[58] But as late as 1875 he was still arguing the futility of any return to Classicism, however Free.[59] In 1871, at Beauvale House, Notts., he combined an exterior in Nesfieldian Old English with an interior in the Anglo-Japanese taste.[60] Yet in 1877 he was still designing in Gothic, for the Manchester Baths competition.[61] In 1874 he took a fateful step in designing a parsonage house at Moor Green, Notts., with sash-windows and plate glass.[62] In Burges's eyes, Godwin had betrayed the Gothic cause. There was no turning back. In 1876 he produced furniture 'in the revived Queen Anne style'.[63] And in 1877 E. W. Godwin – Burges's staunchest ally in the 1860s and architect of Gothic town halls prominent in Northampton,[64] Congleton[65] and Retford[66] – finally went over to the enemy. That was the year he was found shamelessly mixing Old English and Queen Anne, not only on the Chelsea Embankment[67] but in the aesthetes' own suburb of Bedford Park.[68] By 1878, in Tite Street, Chelsea, he had practically rejected the historicist yoke.[69] He had finally shaken off Burges's influence. He had broken free of Early French. He had lost his faith in eclecticism. 'What then is left?', he asked in 1875. 'Nothing but the vernacular, the builder's work, naked of ornament, void of style, and answering only to one name – Utility.'[70]

Burges refused to capitulate. By 1875 he found that all the evils of GO had merely been replaced by a new set of aesthetic vices known generically as the Queen Anne Revival.

The receipt for this invention [he told a student audience at the Architectural Association][71] is simply to take an ordinary red-brick house, and put as many gables, dormers, and bay-windows as possible; in fact, to cut up the outlines: the great object being to get the picturesque by any and every means. The windows should be long and narrow, and filled with lead glazing, or with small frames divided by straight bars painted white. One professor of the style (if not its inventor) used to put in some twelfth-century features, such as a very severe pointed arch, like those found in the South of France. This may have been done for conscience's sake, but it is only fair to observe that the other professors, who are, for the most part, deserters from the Gothic camp, keep very clear of any such eccentricity. The ornamental parts consist of a few scrolls in the brickwork, and coarse woodwork, occasionally verging on the Jacobean, dull green and white being used for the interior painting. It cannot be denied that there are sundry advantages connected with this arrangement, which fully accounts for so many good men throwing over their own style and adopting it. In the first place, there is the picturesque outline, which, by the way, has but little to do with the real 'Queen Anne' style. In the second place, the small panes of glass and thick bars supply in some part the use of tracery, and give scale to the building. In the third place, it saves a very great deal of trouble – the mouldings, such as they are, are those in common use; and above all, the style, if so it can be called, is fashionable. ... Medieval architecture was a perfect system; it had its own development, and was surrounded by all the subsidiary arts. [But] in Queen Anne's time we were at the very dregs of the *Renaissance*. ... [As for today], it is impossible to go on building dwelling-houses in the 'Queen Anne' style, and parsonages and town-halls, and domestic buildings of the better class, in the Gothic style. One must swallow up the other; and what would happen if the former were the victor? ... I, for one, would be very unwilling to give up the Gothic school, not only because I have been brought up in it, but because I think it has more capabilities for our climate than any other ... the 'Queen Anne' fashion, like other fashions ... will have its day. I do not call it 'Queen Anne' art, for, unfortunately, I see no art in it at all.

That was Burges's last stand. In the discussion that followed his lecture he was curt and uncompromising: Queen Anne was an illiterate 'negro-language'; 'he had been brought up in the thirteenth-century belief, and in that belief he intended to die.'[72]

What especially hurt Burges was the fact that this rejection of Gothic purity spread not only among benighted classicists, but within the ranks of renegade Goths, and younger Goths in particular. Moreover, the same contagion had infected even Pre-Raphaelite artists. That was one theme in an explosive paper which J.J. Stevenson delivered at the R.I.B.A. in 1874. The Pre-Raphaelites 'have abandoned the purity and restraint [along] with the stiffness and imperfection of Medievalism, and glory in the fulness of physical life, and the richness and freedom of Classic ideas.'[73] In painting, E.J. Poynter had already begun to play the role of Richard Norman Shaw in architecture. At the same time 'Free Classic' or 'Re-Renaissance' represented a return to something Fergusson had long been groping for among the fragments of Italianate tradition: a 'combination of classicality and common sense'.[74] 'Commonsense reasons and conventional ideas', noted the *Building News* in 1877, 'were looked upon, only ten years ago, as vulgar, and as indicating a low taste. ... It is extremely amusing to see how the spirit of the dream has changed.'[75]

To a certain extent, the Queen Anne movement embodied a truce between the two warring traditions, a compromise between Gothic and Classic: Gothic in planning and composition, Classic in the language of its forms. It was this fusion which reconciled even William Morris to the new style.[76] Pragmatism seemed to have triumphed over dogmatic principles. Oddly enough, however, the new vogue also represented a return to the pursuit of 'Truth'. In the eyes of a new generation, the Gothic Revival had lost its integrity; its Puginian virtues had sunk beneath a mass of erudition and eccentricity. Once more the young Turks of architecture were hot on the trail of 'Truth'. 'Truth' had been the cry which brought down Palladianism in the last quarter of the eighteenth century; 'Truth' again had destroyed the Greek Revival – in England if not in Scotland – in the 1830s. Now the Gothic Revival itself – once the hallmark of integrity – had succumbed to the virus of established attitudes, and fallen victim to the gospel of *reality*.

For the rationale of the Queen Anne revolt grew out of the Gothic Revivalists' own search for a revived vernacular. The Queen Anne brigade wished to substitute a Georgian builders' vernacular for the artificially resuscitated vernacular of Gothic. In a sense it was also an attempt to secularise the Gothic Revival, to dispel the suffocating religiosity of medievalism. Even as early as 1862, Warington Taylor had not been alone in believing that 'a square-arched window is the want of the age'.[77] Butterfield had used sash windows in parsonage houses and secular buildings since the 1850s. Scott was not averse either to sash windows or to plate glass.[78] Burges was horrified. But such pragmatic modifications of the Gothic mode proved irresistible. 'The Gothic style,' complained 'Jock' Stevenson in 1875, 'is, in fact, *the artistic expression of an obsolete mode of construction*. . . . The interest of refined and educated minds for the last thirty years has been directed not to improving the vernacular style, but to the hopeless attempt of supplanting it by another, which appeared at first to flourish, but has not taken roots in the soil of the country.'[79]

> The [Queen Anne] style in all its forms has the merit of truthfulness; it is the outcome of our common wants picturesquely expressed. . . . The [very] success of Gothic . . . [has been] one cause of this reaction. Its advocates urged that it was good not only for churches, but for every kind of building, that it ought to become again, as it had once been, the vernacular architecture of the country. The wish has been granted. The nineteenth century has expressed itself in Gothic; and, in gin-palaces, rows of houses built to sell, semi-detached villas, chapels and churches, Gothic, which of old was simple and unpretending, by means of its boasted freedom from restraint has lent itself with fatal facility to the expression of loudness, vulgarity, obtrusiveness, and sensationalism more objectionable far than the dreariest Classic of Gower Street or Wimpole Street. *That* may be very dull prose; the other is screeching sensational poetry or *Daily Telegraphese*.[80]

Of course it was unfair. He was talking of GO rather than Gothic. But such an outburst, in public, at the R.I.B.A., required – as Robert Kerr admitted – considerable 'moral courage'. Edmund Sharpe, a learned Goth, became first speechless, then angry. H. Heathcote Statham, a learned Classic, was scornful. Wyatt Papworth, learned in all styles, was doubtful. Waterhouse and Eastlake were cautious. E. J. Tarver conceded the utility of the new fashion as regards domestic interiors. But Robert Kerr announced that 'the sooner we get out of the "Queen Anne" mania the better'; history would show that its only function was that of a stepping stone to a better form of classicism.[81] And of course that loquacious Professor was right: Norman Shaw ended up as an apostle of Edwardian Baroque.

In the short run, the only effective *riposte* from the Gothic school lay in the resuscitation of a period of Gothic long neglected: the sixteenth century.[82] Queen Anne had scarcely triumphed before the pointed arch reared its head once more. By 1876 Perpendicular was back on fashionable drawing boards, for the first time since the 1830s. 'Shall we', asked the *Building News*, 'see another Gothic Revival?'[83] J. D. Sedding firmly answered 'Yes'.[84] The 'rising school of late Gothicists' made claims less sweeping than the High Victorian Goths of the 1850s and 1860s: early Gothic for the country, late Gothic for country towns, and free Renaissance for the city.[85] But late Gothic represented a veritable life-line for last-ditch Goths like J. P. Seddon. As late as 1880 he was still invoking the spirit of Viollet-le-Duc, and still refusing to touch Queen Anne: 'I can't dabble with dirt.'[86] Norman Shaw's 'Queen Antics' might 'be making his fortune, but such architectural absurdities – neither Gothic nor Classic – were 'treason to the profession'.[87]

Seddon and Sedding had their reward. The Gothic Revival was not extinguished by Queen Anne. In the 1870s its empire lost whole swathes of territory marked 'urban' and 'secular'. But even there, after temporarily retreating underground, the medieval style re-emerged, transformed. 'Late and flat' became the watchwords of the movement's last phase: Arts and Crafts Gothic. Its flexibility was admirable; its adaptability incontestable. Even so, to any Goth worth his salt, it must have seemed a poor substitute for the stern geometry of Early French. The search for a Victorian Style, Gothic in inspiration and eclectic in form, had apparently been abandoned.

A WAY OUT OF THE DILEMMA

Burges never suffered from delusions of absolute novelty. He came to agree with Gilbert Scott: 'No age has ever deliberately invented a new style ... [it is] morally impossible to do so.'[88] But as a young man he willingly subscribed to Beresford-Hope's doctrine of progressive eclecticism. During the 1860s and 1870s his optimism gradually evaporated, leaving him with only one last vestige of evolutionary dogma: the future of architecture must reside not in the resolution of historicist/functional riddles, but in a renaissance of the minor arts; the style of tomorrow must lie in the hands of the craftsman of today. If dress, fabrics, ceramics, furniture, glass, metalwork and domestic artifacts generally could regain their erstwhile vitality, then the salvation of architecture would follow in due course. Hence the primacy of decorative art in Burges's aesthetic cosmology. He would certainly have endorsed G. E. Street's Ruskinian dictum: 'three-fourths of the poetry of a building lies in its minor details.'[89] 'I am afraid', he wrote in 1865, 'that if any improvement is to be expected, it must be got by working up to our architecture, not by working down from it. In fact, we have no architecture to work from at all; indeed, we have not even settled the *point de départ*. ... Our art ... is domestic, and ... the best way of advancing its progress is to do our best in our houses ... if we once manage to obtain a large amount of art and colour in our sitting rooms ... the improvement may gradually extend to our costume, and perhaps eventually to ... architecture.'[90]

So, to Burges, architecture might still be the mother of the arts, but its future lay in its less arthritic progeny: the arts applied. Hence his position as proto-high-priest of the Arts and Crafts movement. His advice might well have been: 'think small'; art, like charity, begins at the domestic level. Interestingly, it is precisely this approach – the search for an alternative architecture through a renaissance of the minor arts – that is today being looked to as an escape route from the ruins of the Modern Movement. Our dilemma in the 1980s – an age of post-brutalist uncertainty – closely parallels the dilemma of the 1880s.

For Burges, therefore, towards the end of his life, the short-term future of architecture seemed bleak. To outsiders, at any rate, he seemed to have opted out of the debate. By 1876 he appeared – at least to observers across the Atlantic – not only England's 'most rigid medievalist', but also an architect immured by his own obstinacy in 'a position of somewhat Druidical isolation'.[91] Scott was more flexible, of course: he believed instinctively in architectural compromise, the *via media*; E. M. Barry called him 'the Dr Hook of the Gothic Revival'.[92] But then 'the wilfulness and spontaneity of true Gothic were ... not in him'.[93] Not so Burges. He remained a 'rabid Medievalist',[94] a veritable Ultramontane among Goths. During the 1870s, therefore, he moves out of the mainstream of architectural fashion and into a luxurious backwater. While London architects jostle each other for leadership of the Queen Anne revival, Burges toils away happily on churches for Lord Ripon and Lady Mary Vyner, on castles for Lord Bute, and on a miniature fantasy palace for himself. He appears less frequently in building journals. And when he does appear – as architect to St Paul's – he is no longer a cult figure, but a target for criticism and abuse.

In effect, Burges had already resolved the problem of style in his own private fashion. He had escaped into a world of architectural fantasy. He faced up to the historicist dilemma, and then preferred to look the other way. His bluff manner, his mercurial temperament, his private income, his rich patrons, his saving sense of humour, his endless capacity for private fantasy, his fondness for alcohol and opium – all these factors helped to exclude him from the more serious preoccupations of his rivals. So when Burges ducks the issue of style, we need not be too surprised. By limiting his recommendations to the practice of figure-drawing, the cult of colour, and the encouragement of the decorative arts, he shrugs off the intellectual burden, and leaves the creation of a New Style to future generations. In doing so he moves away from the High Victorian Dream towards Art for Art's sake and the *fin-de-siècle* syndrome. The creative process becomes its own justification; architecture, like any other art, sloughs off the straitjacket of utility and finds its own validity in the wider realm of aestheticism. Hence Burges's status as a link between the Pre-Raphaelites and the Symbolists.

Burges's withdrawal from the whole stylistic debate was by no means unique. In fact it was typical of the 1870s. Broadly speaking, the Battle of the Styles – Gothic *versus* Classic – characterised the 1850s; the Battle for a Style was a phenomenon of the 1860s. After 1870 a whole generation of architects gave up battling. They lost their faith in Gothic; they lost their taste for GO. They fell back into the arms of Queen Anne – 'that vexatious disturber of the Gothic movement'[95] – an architecture without rules, without illusions. The heroic age of High Victorian architecture was over. Burges despised Queen Anne as an architecture of desperation, 'the very dregs of the Renaissance'.[96] But he did share in the general flaccidity of the 1870s. He gave up wrestling with eclectic theory, and concentrated on private rather than public, decorative rather than structural design. 'Some years ago', noted Andrew Dewar of Nova Scotia in 1872, 'we had great hopes of Mr Burges becoming a leader, because his designs were all characterised by a boldness and originality that promised great things – that seemed destined to take well with the profession, and have numerous followers. But lately he has almost forsaken architecture, and become – in heart at least, if not in practice – a painter. . . .'[97]

That came uncomfortably near the truth. Some of Burges's unexecuted decorative schemes – Knightshayes, Devon, for instance – already suggest a private world of fantasy. His designs in furniture, glass and metalwork seem less a public performance than a private miracle. In his work for Lord Bute, architectural and decorative, vision at last floats free from reality. And in his own secret dream-world – Tower House, Kensington – Burges finally found his architectural *nirvana*. He had abandoned doubts for dreams.

But even dreamers dream at second hand: their images derive from the dregs of their own subconscious. Burges's art sprang ultimately from the Middle Ages. But its resulting images are vivid, personal and new. How did he do it? The next four chapters answer that question in detail. But perhaps one example may serve as a preliminary explanation. On his drawing-room table at Tower House, Kensington, sat a most extraordinary object: Burges's elephant inkstand (1862–3).[226; 227] Let E. W. Godwin explain its construction and significance:

> Do you desire to make an inkstand? Take a Chinese bronze elephant incense-burner, with dumpy legs that are hardly more than feet, remove the pierced howdah-like cover, and in its place put a low circular tower of green porcelain, domed with a *cloisonné* cup reversed, and crowned with a Japanese *netzuki*. Combine these things with metal mouldings and machicolated parapets fashioned after the manner of the thirteenth century; arrange the ivory finial, the dome and tower so that each may turn on a pillar at the back, uncovering receptacles for

matches, red ink and black; mount the whole on a slab of marble and suspend chains, and rings, and seals from tusks and trappings, and you have the inkstand. ... Observe the power of adaptation: the things he is dealing with are Chinese and Japanese, but the whole is thirteenth-century – Burgesesque. A few pieces of metal in his favourite style to unite them, and lo! This strange group of Eastern things fall into their places as if they had originally been designed for the purpose. ... As one looks at it in admiration of its rich colour, its usefulness, its elephantine strength, one never thinks of its lovely dome as a cup reversed, or of the ivory figure group that crowns it as a Japanese button. But it is in the bronze elephant itself that we are chiefly interested. This short-legged, thick-set beast exhibits the power of conventionalising a natural object in a very remarkable degree. The thing is so like and yet so unlike; so false in detail, so true in essence. It was this power of the artist, whether exhibited in Chinese bronze or Egyptian granite, in Pentelic marble or Caen freestone, that Burges was so quick to recognise, to appreciate, to enjoy. And it was this mastery in conventional treatment, this power of governing natural form so that it could best serve the artificial purpose for which it was selected, that he possessed in a remarkable degree. Nesfield, Shaw and Street, each in his own way, has produced architectural designs more beautiful and far more graceful than any building Burges ever designed or could design; but no one of the century in this country, or any other that I know of, ever possessed that artistic rule over the kingdom of nature in a measure at all comparable with that which he shared in common with the sculptor of the Sphinx and the designer of Chartres.[98]

Godwin did not exaggerate. That elephant inkstand is not only a paradigm of the eclectic process. It is the very epitome of its creator's special genius: Burges's answer to the dilemma of style.

PART TWO

Chapter Four

RENAISSANCE

'Italian work will not do with a *little* decoration. It must either be
properly done or left alone.'

WILLIAM BURGES, 1872

In a way there was no such thing as the Renaissance. It developed not as a 'movement'
but as an episodic sequence of attempts, widely different in time and place, to
rejuvenate the arts of the middle ages by an infusion of antique forms. Like Ruskin,
therefore, Burges was sensible enough never to condemn the Renaissance out of hand.
What he did condemn was its degenerate descendant, the mumbo-jumbo of post-
Renaissance classicism. By accepting the early Renaissance as a last flowering of the
Middle Ages he commandeered a store of high calibre ammunition for the artillery of
the eclectic process. And by thus enlarging his professional reach, he was able to tackle
several commissions which would otherwise never have come his way – including
perhaps the most ambitious design of his whole career.

FLORENCE CATHEDRAL

Appropriately, Burges first wrestled with the Renaissance at the very shrine of its
birth, Santa Maria del Fiore, in Florence[92]. It was not a building he regarded as
perfect. Like Pugin, he dismissed the exterior of cathedral, baptistery and campanile as
'magnified Brighton workboxes'. In this respect he felt that Giotto's was a genius
flawed. And as for Arnolfo di Cambio, Burges refused to consider him 'a first-rate
architect, much less a genius . . . the marble placage of the old Lombard churches, rife
with historiated carvings and inlays, representing hunts, fights, men, monsters, etc.
becomes in his hands a mere succession of angles and panellings in black and white
marble'. What redeemed the baptistery was its detail: the mosaics of the dome,
glowing in gold; the zodiac pavement incised in white marble; the glorious gates of
gilded bronze by Pisano and Ghiberti; and the gleaming silver altar dossal by
Pollaiuolo and Verrocchio. The interior of the cathedral seemed initially 'disappointing': he thought the square rib-vaulting 'starved and mean'; the white-washed walls

insipid; the gallery 'clumsy'; the marble choir enclosure by Baccio Bandinelli awkward; and Vasari's painting of Brunelleschi's dome 'simply as bad as it can be'. What rescued the interior from mediocrity was its 'wonderful' stained glass, especially the great circular window at the West end.[1]

But the Duomo had never been finished. The great competition organised in 1490 by Lorenzo the Magnificent for the completion of the Western front – the first architectural competition on record – had proved abortive. The original, incomplete West end had been dismantled by Benedetto Uguccione in 1586 – an 'act of vandalism', as Burges put it, 'under the pretence of doing something more modern. Luckily this something was never done'. What was destroyed, however, was not a façade designed by Giotto or Arnolfo di Cambio but a fragmentary accretion, 'a mass of sculpture intermixed with bad architecture, both Pointed and Renaissance. In fact it was the dregs of the Pointed school, and by no means so pure as the [old] schools at Oxford, or any of our own late Pointed buildings'. It was this unfinished West front which had been temporarily covered up in 1514 by a wooden façade designed by Sansovino. To replace it, two successive competitions were set in motion. But repeated squabbles – 'the avenging manes of Giotto' – ensued. Designs were prepared by Buonalenti, Cigoli, Dosio, Giovanni de'Medici, Passignano and Silvani. Baccio del Bianco's design was actually begun, but the townspeople, Burges noted, 'generally grumbled so much at it, that it was never carried out. Then in 1661 a design painted on canvas was put up and remained until a high wind kindly blew it to pieces. Then in 1688 [Grazioni and some] ten painters from Bologna perpetrated the present sham in fresco, which I am happy to say has nearly disappeared'. In 1842 a scheme was prepared by the architect who restored Santa Croce, the Chevalier Matas, as part of a general restoration. But this too was nipped in the bud by the troubles of 1848. Yet another design was produced soon afterwards by the Swiss architect, J. G. Muller. 'And finally', Burges concludes, 'in this present year of grace, 1862, we are to have another competition, open to all the world.'[2]

Here, then was a revivalist's dream: a chance to place oneself in direct succession to the immortals; to complete a temple hallowed by the names of Giotto, Brunelleschi and Ghiberti. The springtime of the Renaissance was to revive in the spirit of Risorgimento. Three successive international competitions were held, in 1863, 1864 and 1866. It was the first of these which Burges entered – the only Englishman to do so. There were forty entrants, but only two from North of the Alps. The judges included the architects Edouard van der Nüll, Malzezzi and Monti; the art historians Paolo Selvatico of Padua, Ernst Förster and Massimo d'Azeglio; and the sculptor Giovanni Dupré. Viollet-le-Duc and Professor Bertini of Milan acted as assessors. Conditions of entry were sent out in September 1861. Burges had, of course, already studied in Florence. But during that Autumn he made a particular study of the cathedral's complex history in the archives of the Uffizi and the Opera del Duomo. During the Summer of 1862 he continued to work on his designs. And on Christmas day Barber took them to Florence.[3] Early in 1863 the drawings were shown to the committee of the Ecclesiological Society.[4] The result of the competition was quick, and 'negative'.[5] The jury withheld all three premiums. Burges did not even receive one of the nine consolation prizes.[6] A second competition, limited this time to ten architects, followed quickly. Again the result was deadlock.[7] Not until the third competition did a clear winner emerge: Emilio de Fabris, of Florence.[8]

The root of the trouble was uncertainty in the minds of judges and competitors alike. Should the new façade follow the existing roofline, with its shallow central gable and flat-roofed aisles? Or should it create its own, triple-gabled silhouette – in the manner of Siena or Orvieto, or Santa Croce – independent of the main structure? Burges adopted the latter procedure. This approach he shared with many of the competitors, including – initially – the eventual winner. What marked out his design as unique was its treatment of fenestration and decorative sculpture. Burges claimed that documentary evidence in the cathedral archives postulated the existence of two vertical central openings, in addition to the three surviving circular windows.[9] His design therefore incorporated traceried Gothic fenestration, echoing the famous false windows on the inside of the Western wall. Little evidence supporting Burges's thesis seems to have come to light during subsequent work. So the judges may well have felt justified in eliminating his entry on archaeological grounds. What probably swung the jury against his design, however, was its heavy concentration of sculpture. Ranging his figures in broad tabernacled bands, with a mighty Jesse Tree in the centre, Burges supplied a densely three-dimensional, positively cisalpine scheme which might well have resulted in a *tour de force* of sculptural iconography. On the other hand it might not. The judges evidently decided not to take the risk. And in de Fabris they identified a competitor who proved flexible enough to modify his design at least three times – increasing its sculptural content and eliminating gables and pinnacles – in pursuit of architectural consensus.[10] As a result, the Duomo of Florence boasts a Western front, erected 1875–87, which looks no more than it is: the product of the deliberations of an international committee over a period of a quarter of a century.

GAYHURST, BUCKINGHAMSHIRE

Burges first built in the Renaissance style at a Jacobean seat in Buckinghamshire. Its name was Gayhurst, and it had been erected from 1597 onwards, chiefly by one of the Gunpowder Plotters, Sir Everard Digby, father of Sir Kenelm Digby. In the mid-eighteenth century the house had been extended by the Wright family, who also employed Capability Brown and Humphry Repton to landscape its riverside setting. It was in 1856 that Robert, 2nd Baron Carrington (1796–1868) took a twenty-one-year repairing lease on Gayhurst from Lady Macdonald of Slate, the last representative of the Wrights.[11] Carrington already had two houses in the county: Wycombe Abbey, and Tickford Park, near Moulsoe. He also owned Deal Castle, Kent.[12] At

Tickford he employed Burges, in 1859, to make minor alterations.[13] At Wycombe Abbey Burges seems to have been called in to examine a Roman pavement, to alter a conservatory and perhaps to install panelling removed from Gayhurst.[14] At Carrington's town house, 8 Whitehall, he probably supervised alterations.[15] And at the parish church at Moulsoe, Burges was responsible for the reconstruction of the chancel (1861)[16][40] and for the installation of Carrington family tombs, robustly guarded by a Gothic palisade.[17] But it was at Gayhurst that Burges's efforts for Lord Carrington were concentrated. Carrington hated Wycombe.[18] And Lady Carrington seems to have been so fond of Gayhurst that she was determined to buy the property outright. Much to her regret, she failed to purchase the freehold. That privilege eventually fell in 1882 to J. W. Carlile (d. 1909) of Ponsbourne Manor, Herts.[19] It was he who belatedly completed much of the work which the Carringtons had begun.[20] Since then Gayhurst has been first institutionalised and then despoiled.

Carrington was Burges's first major patron. Officially, he was a staunch Whig of Conservative disposition, Lord Lieutenant of Buckinghamshire, Fellow of the Royal Society, and an enterprising landowner who left £70,000.[21] Unofficially, he was known in clubland as 'a maniac, who believed that an honourable part of his person was made of glass, so that he was afraid to sit thereon, and used to discharge [his] legislative and judicial functions . . . standing'.[22] It was Grenville Murray, illegitimate son of the 2nd Duke of Buckingham, who mischievously revealed Carrington's 'laughable hallucination' to a wider public in 1869. Writing in a libellous journal called *The Queen's Messenger*, he jokingly described Carrington as:

> a harmless lunatic . . . who . . . persistently refused, during the whole of his uneventful life, to sit whenever it was possible by any exercise of ingenuity to stand up or lie down. He suspended himself, indeed, upon rare occasions, in a curious chair of his own contrivance, but he did so in fear and trembling. . . . He even adopted a recumbent posture with many precautions; and when he retired for the night was accustomed to go gingerly down on his stomach in order that the lower part of his body might be uppermost. He then trusted that, if lightly covered, it might escape crack or damage. When he walked abroad, he could never hear the sound of approaching footsteps from behind without emotion [23]

For this, Murray was horsewhipped by Carrington's son on the steps of the Conservative Club, challenged to a duel, and eventually forced to flee to Paris.[24]

Such gossip cannot be dismissed as worthless: some supporting evidence survives among Carrington's own letters.[25] And such eccentricities are by no means irrelevant to Burges's architectural career: Gayhurst turned out to be a very strange house, and to accommodate its owner's peculiarities it was fitted up with one of the most curious lavatories ever built.

Burges began work at Gayhurst in 1858 with the insertion of new mullions,[26] closely followed in 1859 with a bookcase and blinds for Lady Carrington.[27] At the same time, however, he was working on a full-scale scheme of renovation. This slowed down work considerably. 'That little Burges', Carrington complained to his son, 'irritates me with his protracted decorations.'[28] This scheme was drawn out in detail and entered in a presentation folio which seems to have survived in the house until 1950. In its absence we can only guess at its overall effect. But the whole scheme was to have climaxed in 'a state staircase of much grandeur'. This was the design with which Burges made his *début* at the Royal Academy,[29] and it remained unexecuted. But what was completed was grand enough. The bill was rumoured to be in the region of £20,000.

Besides a formal garden, geometrically planned with stylised pedestals and yew hedges, Burges created a succession of exotic interiors. A stone-built back staircase – the Caliban Staircase (1859–61) – vaulted in panelled wood and stencilled with 'quaint inscriptions'.[30] A Guard Room (1859), its entrance guarded by a monstrous male caryatid – Caliban – crouching, prognathous, menacing.[100] A dining room (1861) with twin chimneypieces, ceiling-high, bearing *alto relievos* by Nicholls of *Paradise Lost* and *Paradise Regained*[31][101]. A bedroom with a specially designed wardrobe for Lady Carrington (1865).[32] One reception room with a mermaid chimneypiece (1860); another – the Peacock Room (1860) – with refurbished panelling; another with a chimney sculptured with monkeys stealing apples (1865).[33] A drawing room – the Abbess's Room (1861 and 1872) – in green, blue, Venetian red and gold, panelled throughout in the style of Catherine de Medici's *cabinet* at Blois, and elaborately painted with fruit and flowers, birds and inset medallions, by Frederick Smallfield[34][133]. A kitchen 'fit for a college', with an open roof and 'a well-ventilated lantern for the escape of culinary fragrance'. Apartments for the *chef*, approached by a separate staircase in the dinner-bell turret and fitted with an internal oriel for observing the activities of servants. A brew house; a bake house; a dog kennel (1860). And finally lavatories of a curiosity rarely equalled. Plumbing seems to have been something of an obsession with Lord Carrington. Perhaps the fact that his lovely first wife had died of cholera, in the epidemic of 1832, induced him to take sanitation seriously. At any rate, he installed portable chemical closets in each of the main bedrooms. Female servants had their own 'retiring rooms' next to their apartments. Menservants were supplied with an extraordinary multiple water-closet, with accommodation for five, next to the butler's pantry and footmen's rooms. Half-way between a Cotswold dovecote and the Abbot's Kitchen at Glastonbury, it consisted of 'a quaint stone circus lighted and ventilated by roof dormers, and surmounted at the apex of the roof by a boldly sculptured Cerberus with red glass eyes in each of his three heads'.[35] Designed in 1859–60,[36] exhibited in London in 1861[37] and again in Paris in 1867,[38] Carrington's Privy was surely one of Burges's happiest inventions: a picturesque convenience, dedicated to a cloacal demon with billiard-ball eyes, for a patron with plumbing on the brain[73].

Burges's first choice of sculptor for Gayhurst had been J. L. Tupper (*c*. 1826–79), a minor Pre-Raphaelite poet who earned a living first as an anatomical draughtsman at Guy's Hospital, and then as a drawing-master at Rugby School.[39] His poems never sold well; neither did his sculpture. But he had contributed to *The Germ* in the heady days of Pre-Raphaelitism, and Rossetti always remained his friend. It was Rossetti, indeed, who in 1860 interceded on his behalf with Burges when Carrington rejected one of Tupper's sculptured reliefs. Tupper had threatened Burges with legal action. Burges had apparently cut Tupper at the Hogarth Club. Rossetti eased the tension by suggesting that the offending *bas-relief* be returned to the sculptor, and the down-payment returned to the architect. He also explained that in any case Burges was not the cutting sort: he was simply too short-sighted to notice anybody.[40] Nevertheless, Tupper remained dismissed. His place was taken by Thomas Nicholls. Thus began a partnership between architect and sculptor which lasted for twenty years.

In its choice of style, Gayhurst was a curious *début* for a committed Goth. Pullan called it 'a style bearing affinity to Renaissance'.[41] Part of its flavour is Jacobean: Burges's notebooks indicate visits in 1859 to Hatfield and Hollingbourne. They also reveal another source of inspiration: the staircase at Harlaxton Manor, Lincolnshire. That amazing Baroque performance, by Salvin and Burn, with its Michaelangelesque giants and frolicsome putti, must indeed have set Burges on fire. Alas, his own great staircase at Gayhurst remained a dream. Even its design has now been lost. What survives is really no more than a collection of fragments. Still, the style is extraordinarily interesting. Its matrix is early French Renaissance, the eclectic François Premier manner of the Château de Langeais, the royal Château at Blois – which Burges visited in 1853 – and the Hotels Lasbardes and de Vaillac at Toulouse.[42] But Burges has made the language his own. Outside, the formal garden is punctuated by stone pedestals in a kind of geometricised Franco-Jacobean.[43] Inside, the famous mermaid chimneypiece echoes, perhaps, a motif in the Musée de Cluny, Paris.[44] His grotesque Caliban nods distantly to the muscular herms by Pierre Puget which flank the portal of Toulon Town Hall (1656). But its bizarre exaggeration is unmistakably Burgesian. Only Burges would have dared to make it the dominant feature of a staircase, and to combine it with a more orthodox late Gothic motif: the tasselled ropework from the Tristram l'Hermite house at Tours.[45] Finally, the Abbess's Room has more of Burges than of François Premier.

At Gayhurst several leitmotifs of the later Burgesian mode are already present: Smallfield's miniature floral panels; Nicholls' figurative sculpture in high relief;[46] the proto-*art nouveau* metalwork of the back staircase; the mermaid chimneypiece; the syncopated silhouette of the outbuildings. The *Ecclesiologist* astutely described the idiom as 'a sort of free Gothicising renaissance, which displays much playful fancy'.[47] It was not a style he chose to use again in its entirety, except perhaps in his vanished, unexecuted scheme for the Long Gallery at Castle Ashby (1875).[48] Elements from Gayhurst, transmuted by Burges from motifs at Blois, were to reappear in the Octagon Staircase and Chaucer Room at Cardiff.[49] Smallfield's floral panels re-emerge at Castell Coch. More generally, the decorative language of the early Renaissance – François Premier plus a strong dash of Florentine – formed the basis of Burges's work at Worcester College, Oxford, and ultimately at St Paul's Cathedral. It was a style both original and flexible, and Gayhurst was its testing ground. For Burges it was a *début* worth waiting for. And he remained grateful to the Carringtons. To Lady Carrington he presented a triple jewelled pendant, set with cornelian, pearl, emerald, sapphire and carbuncle;[50] and to Lord Carrington, the first of his great patrons – and in some ways the oddest – he dedicated *Architectural Drawings* (1870).[51]

WORCESTER COLLEGE CHAPEL, OXFORD

Worcester College Chapel[132] had been designed by James Wyatt in 1776–90, designed moreover in the linear, understated manner of his work at Heveningham Hall, Suffolk. Burges was called in to turn this ecclesiastical drawing-room into a chapel, to medievalise a Neo-Classical interior, and to Christianise a pagan system of decoration. All this he managed to do. And he did it without altering Wyatt's structure, indeed without altering more than a few feet of Wyatt's chastest mouldings. First he refashioned and accentuated the compartments of Wyatt's ceiling. Then he filled the niches with statues, the windows with stained glass, the floor with mosaic and the walls with painted imagery. Finally he added furniture of superlative quality: stalls of walnut inlaid with box; a lectern and candelabra of bronze and alabaster; even an organ-seat bulging with leopards' heads. And all this for a college whose funds were lower than its churchmanship.

Gilbert Scott had been first on the scene. Early in 1863 he submitted a scheme for completely remodelling the chapel. Instead of Wyatt's 'modern assembly room', he proposed an apsidal design in the Byzantine style.[52] Byzantine, he explained, was 'the connecting link between Classic and Gothic; its interiors excepting Gothic are the most beautiful in existence, and offer without any exception, the finest field for decorative purposes'.[53] The Fellows of Worcester were not convinced: Scott's estimate was £5/6,000. They turned instead to Burges, tying their invitation to a ceiling of £1,200–1,500.[54] During the Summer vacation of 1864 the transformation of Wyatt's 'sordid', 'woe-begone and dismal chapel' began.[55]

In Oxford Burges already had a firm friend in the shape of J. H. Parker.[56] But he had other allies in the Worcester S.C.R.: the Rev. H. C. O. Daniel (1836–1919), a future Provost of the College;[57] and the Rev. J. D. Collis (1816–79), a genial, hard-drinking Freemason, Headmaster of Bromsgrove School, Vicar of Stratford-on-Avon, and later Bishop of Nova Scotia.[58] Like Burges, Daniel had been educated at King's College School. He had also been a Lecturer there in 1859–63, at the time of the King's Chapel reconstruction scheme. Like King's, Worcester had a very strong church tradition. And the clerical-family nexus between King's and Worcester was reinforced in 1865: another Daniel, the Rev. W. E. Daniel (1841–1924), also educated at K.C.S., became first Chaplain of Burges's redecorated Worcester College chapel.[59] 1864 is the date on the Worcester chapel ceiling; 1864 the date of the Rev. H. C. O. Daniel's college Fellowship; 1864 is also the date when Burges judiciously augmented the college plate by presenting a silver beaker inset with nineteen, seventeenth-century German crowns.[60] Clearly, Burges's friends secured him the commission. And having secured it, they guaranteed its completion by private generosity. Collis presented the alabaster candelabra and one of the windows; Daniel the silver-backed Testaments for the lectern. Appropriately, in Burges's mural iconography, the prophet Daniel presides in a central, dominating position above the altar.

In employing Burges to rejuvenate Wyatt, the Fellows of Worcester were feeling their way towards a synthesis of Gothic and Classic. Inevitably their architect looked for inspiration to Florence, to Raphael, to that cultural watershed where the Middle Ages meet the Renaissance. There are echoes here of Raphael's arabesques in the Vatican *loggie*, and in the Villa Madama, Rome. There are reminiscences, perhaps, of the Uffizi in Florence. There are hints of Urbino: Luciano Laurana's pilasters and friezes in the Palazzo Ducale.[61] There are also signs of Pompeian inspiration, particularly in the decoration of the ante-chapel.[62] And early Christian motifs appear in the mosaic pavement. Such eclecticism demonstrated Burges's capacity to assimilate a variety of sources: what Ernest Lee described as 'the wondrous flexibility of the ultra-Goth'.[63] References like these were not wasted on mid-Victorian Oxford. But it was not so much the style as the iconography which caused the greatest stir.

When the Oxford Architectural and Historical Society visited Worcester College in 1886, Daniel showed the party round, explaining how hard put to it the Fellows had been to restrain Burges's enthusiasm. Grappling gallantly with the iconography, he expounded the theme of the whole scheme: Man and Nature combine in the worship of God.[64] The roof illustrates the Temptation and the Fall, the walls the Te Deum and the Benedicite. The words of the Te Deum run around the dado, those of the Benedicite around the cornice. Natural and Revealed religion join in decorating the roof: the theological virtues and the natural virtues. Around the dome, the royal ancestors of Christ. And in the interstices 'the different genera of birds, beasts, and fishes, creatures inhabiting ... the air, the water, or the earth'. At eye-level were groups from the Te Deum: on the North side the heavenly host, on the South representations of the earth, or human society; next to these twelve prophets, and opposite them twelve apostles. Last, on the South side, the martyrs, the holy innocents, Stephen, Polycarp, Perpetua and others, down to Huss, Jerome of Prague, Latimer and Hooper. The opposite series represents the Church in its various manifestations: Augustine and Ambrose, the Empress Helena, and Chrysostom, Monica, Charlemagne and Benedict, Catherine of Siena and Elizabeth of Hungary, Thomas Aquinas and Wycliffe, Luther and Pascal. On the floor the history of the Church. Within the sacrarium the Parable of the Sower: Our Lord scatters grain, and from the ground rises a vine, its tendrils encompassing images of the Confessor, the Martyr (St

George), the Virgin (St Katherine, patroness of learning), the Evangelist (St John), the Apostle (St Peter) and the Holy Woman (St Mary Magdalen). In the body of the chapel – beyond the lectern – the four doctors of the Western Church; and before the lectern, the English Church: kings, martyrs, builders, saints.[65] The theme of the windows is 'Christ the Light of the World'. And in the four corners stand the four evangelists, accompanied by legendary scenes from their lives. The stalls are inlaid with tokens of redemption. Even the finials of the seats bear emblems of brute creation praising the Lord. No wonder Professor Westwood remarked that 'there was no English building extant in which so much study had been devoted to a scheme of ornamental decoration, and such care given to the execution of the designs'.[66] Burges's scheme can be read on three horizontal levels, and vertically as well as horizontally. It adds up to a display of High Victorian iconography – what German critics call a programmatic exercise – which is rivalled only by G. E. Street's American Church in Rome.

The material of the pavement caused almost as much comment as its symbolism. During the Summer vacation of 1865, the sanctuary was paved with *opus vermiculatum*, that is with small cubes of coloured marbles arranged in figurative patterns: probably the first major use of this technique in England since Roman times.[67] Next year the main body of the chapel was paved with *opus sectile*, that is with larger segments of marble shaped according to pattern: a technique little used in the West since the Renaissance.[68] Rouge Royale from Belgium, Genoese green, and Welsh marbles were all employed. Burke & Co. were responsible for the sanctuary, Harland and Fisher for the remainder.[69]

Burges's use of mosaic was based on a knowledge of medieval techniques unique in his generation. The revival of mosaic flooring had begun with pavements at Deepdene, Surrey (1839) and the Reform Club, Pall Mall (1840), designed by H. S. Hope and Sir Charles Barry, and made by Blashfield and Singer and Pether respectively.[70] Then came new discoveries by Blashfield, Prosser and Minton, and the writings of Owen Jones and Digby Wyatt. It was from Wyatt that Burges first learnt the principles of mosaic manufacture and design. But this knowledge was more than supplemented by his own research. He studied *opus tesselatum*, or *opus vermiculatum*, at Pompeii. He studied *opus sectile* (or *opus Alexandrinum*)[71] in England and abroad: the pavements of the high altar and of St Edward's chapel at Westminster;[72] the pavement adjoining St Thomas à Beckett's shrine at Canterbury; pavements in the churches of Navara and Vercelli, and in the churches of S. Sabina and S. Lorenzo Fuori le Mura in Rome. He studied *opus Greconicum* – that is, geometrical glass mosaic set in marble – at Westminster as well: in the tomb of Henry III and in the shrine of the Confessor. This was a technique Burges later employed in several altar dossals. Finally, he studied *opus musivum* – that is, figured glass mosaic on large-scale wall surfaces – in Venice, Monreale and Palermo.[73] Worcester College, Burges conceded, was hardly the place for such extravagance. But his chance would come soon enough: at St Paul's

Cathedral. Meanwhile, the revival of lithostratic art had made a major step forward in the pavement of an Oxford chapel.

Early in 1864 Burges determined on 'a professional artist' for the six stained glass windows at Worcester. Millais was chosen, and produced a cartoon for 'The Adoration of the Magi'. The experiment was not a success. 'Mr Millais', Burges decided, 'is almost our first artist . . . but this [window] has been done in a hurry, and I think some apology is due for it.' The architect let it be known that he would not have the offending window in the chapel 'at any price'.[74] Burges clearly required a more tractable artist, and the Fellows of Worcester required more speed. So Lavers and Barraud agreed to employ Henry Holiday instead.[75] By the end of the year Holiday had produced a cartoon for 'The Annunciation'; by the following Spring four windows had been installed.[76] The remaining three followed soon afterwards. Together these windows made up a single theme – 'The Light of the World' – based on seven incidents in the life of Christ, each foreshadowed in Old Testament prophecy, each glazed scene being related to its painted prophet in the lunette above: the Annunciation (Isaiah), the Adoration of the Magi (Zachariah), the finding in the Temple (Malachi), the Baptism (Joel), the Crucifixion (Daniel), the Empty Sepulchre (Hosea) and the Ascension (David).[77]

Holiday was responsible for all the mural decorations except those forming part of the arabesques around the windows. These fell to Smallfield: endless miniatures of the works of creation, illustrating the Benedicite. The contracting decorator was Fisher of London. It was not until 1870 that the painted frieze of the Te Deum – Holiday, assisted by Ellis Wooldridge – was complete.[78] Its multiplicity of biblical figures gave ample scope for dispute. It was difficult, for instance, to prevent the processional groups from looking like rows of 'charity children'. One scrap of banter among the Fellows survives:

'What women would you suggest here?'
'Two good queens?'
'Miss Burdett-Coutts would be too recent, I suppose!!!!'[79]

Holiday, indeed, must have come to regret his commission. He was refused even the slightest room for manoeuvre. When he ventured to lighten the colour scheme of the borders, the architect pulled him up short. 'Burges', Holiday complained toDaniel, 'says I have no right to meddle with his decoration'. Holiday's interference, Burges replied, was 'a most monstrous and unheard-of thing'.[80]

Friction of that kind must occasionally arise even when architect, artist and craftsman share the same aesthetic assumptions. Much depends upon the architect's tact as coordinator. And Burges was neither a consistent nor a tactful man. The animal finials[102] of the chapel stalls, for instance, were probably sketched by Burges, modelled by Nicholls and then carved by Robinson. One day, while the carving was in progress, Burges bustled in and flew into a temper, telling workmen the whole business was 'abominable'. A little later, in quieter mood, he agreed that everything was in order.[81]

But dealing with dons was even trickier. Among the Fellows of Worcester was Edmund Oldfield, the college librarian. He was to emerge as one of Burges's sternest critics in the battle for St Paul's Cathedral. At Worcester the part he played is by no means clear. But the ingredients for a full-scale controversy were there from the start. It was the gilded corner statues of the four evangelists which aroused the bitterest feeling. Protests against these 'idolatrous images' began in November 1865. Acting on behalf of the Fellows, William Stebbing of Lincoln's Inn explained the problem:

> Our architect has, I fear, involved us in some embarrassment with his very ugly statues. . . . Had Mr. Burges set up statues to Faith, Charity and the like, or had he even omitted the names . . . the case would have been different.

In July 1866 the Attorney General, Sir Roundell Palmer, was called in to give an opinion. Diplomatically, he denied neither the illegality of images, nor the penalties attached to their use. He merely queried whether these objects were in fact images at all. He concluded they were not: their purpose was decoration not worship. Alas, that did not satisfy the 'iconoclastic urge' of the Rev. Charles Browne. In November 1868 he despatched an epic protest to the Provost: these 'abominations' in chapel were an encouragement to 'sensuous and carnal worship'; there was an 'unprecedented crisis' in the Church of England, mariolatry was rampant, there was 'flagrant use of the crucifix'; this 'Romanising leprosy' was 'fostering in our students idolatrous thoughts'. The epistolary battle raged on for no less than ten years. But Browne and his Evangelical kind were swimming against the ritualistic tide. Lichfield Cathedral; the chapels of Magdalen and Trinity College, Oxford; the case of the Exeter reredos; the report of the Ritual Commission – battle-honours, all of them, in the ascent of the new ritualism. In vain did Browne, taking the waters with his mother at Cheltenham, endorse his letters to the Provost of Worcester: 'to be pondered with prayer.' Burges's statues stayed. And Browne refused to pay the Attorney General's bill.[82]

In December 1864 Burges secured authority for several key additions: a lectern, two candelabra, six gas standards, a marquetry dado, parquetry flooring, painted panels flanking the altar, and baldaquined desks for the Provost and Vice-Provost. These extras added up to more than £800.[83] A year later he was encouraging Daniel to press for an altar inset with marble, bronze and lapis lazuli.[84] Nothing came of the idea. No doubt for both financial and liturgical reasons it was thought imprudent. But in 1865 the leopard-headed organ seat did appear.[85] By Michaelmas that year the panelling had been installed, along with the lectern, credence table, candelabra and organ case, and the mosaic pavement had been begun.[86] In 1869 the Chapel Committee agreed to authorise silver bindings for both Old and New Testaments[219], to be made by

Barkentin to Burges's designs but incorporating seventeenth-century Flemish panels, at £25 each.[87] The alabaster lectern and candelabra[104] were modelled in Quattrocento style by Nicholls, and carved by Jacquet of London.[88] With them came six bronze gas burners, each echoing the exquisite metalwork of St Sebald's shrine in Nuremburg (1508–19).[89] For the inlaid woodwork – probably executed by Walden – Burges perhaps had in mind the elaborate intarsia work in the cathedral stalls at Lucca and Perugia.[90] Years later Emerson called this some of the best modern inlay he had ever seen.[91]

There were those who disagreed. Fergusson, predictably enough, dismissed Burges's chapel as 'a failure': 'an infinite number of small details, some classical, some medieval, some modern ... harmonized by darkening the windows.'[92] And in a violent letter to *The Times* one critic, sheltering under the pseudonym 'Paulinus', pitched into the whole scheme with gusto: he described the parti-coloured columns – 'striped ... red ochre and gold' – as no better than 'the drop curtains to a Bartholomew Fair show'.[93]

But Burges's allies stood firm. Collis replied to Paulinus with force:

> Burges ... has covered walls, architraves, tympana, roof, niches, floor with exquisite designs, every one with a significant meaning. He found 'a room', and he has left 'a chapel' full of thought, of genius well applied, of symbolism. ... It is a perfect study from end to end. It is the only building in England where the walls were designed for the windows, and the windows for the walls. There is no floor like it in England of elaborate mosaics; the massive seats of dark walnut inlaid with box simply unrivalled, the stall ends, each an artistic study in zoology or ornithology; the six smaller candelabra, suggested by, but not servilely copied from, St Sebald's shrine at Nuremburg; the noble altar candelabra and the lectern of alabaster, of most original design, the very binding of the volumes of solid embossed silver. ... On this side of the Alps there is no sacred building of the kind, not excepting the Sainte Chapelle itself in Paris, so beautiful and so suggestive. ... Mr. Burges knew what he was about: he demanded and he wisely obtained *carte blanche*, and a judgement suspended until the work was completed, and we are proud of the result ... [all] proof that he can handle an Italian building in the spirit of the style, *without the introduction of a single Gothic detail*.[94]

Perhaps Collis protested too much. But, by any standard, the chapel is a remarkable room. In its elaboration and its completeness, Burges's iconographic programme remains almost unique among High Victorian ecclesiastical interiors. The interplay between stained glass and mural paintings is particularly unusual. Even if the standard of Holiday's work falls below the highest level, the fittings – in wood, bronze and alabaster – are superb. In the end, the Fellows of Worcester – severally and collectively – paid out much the same sort of sum as Gilbert Scott had originally suggested: at least

£6,000.[95] Burges had turned Wyatt's Neo-Classical box into a treasure-chest of ecclesiastical art. The spirit of Neo-classicism had been exorcised, and James Wyatt – the Destroyer – destroyed.

WORCESTER COLLEGE HALL, OXFORD

Meanwhile, in 1872 Daniel had begun to press for the redecoration of Wyatt's hall. Burges produced a rough estimate and design[131] in June of the following year, plus a detailed report in November. The ceiling was to be built up in compartments, filled with arabesques, like the chapel. A new dado was to be installed, of walnut inlaid with box and decorated with armorial bearings. The upper walls were to be painted red, with simulated white draperies. A new chimneypiece – which Burges regarded as 'crucial' – was to rise in front of a blocked window to the full height of the hall; it was to be decorated with medallions of benefactors, ornamented with the college arms supported by amorini, and crowned by a statue of St Laurence. The entrance columns were to be covered with marble; the windows filled with grisaille glass with coloured insets – banqueting scenes from Homer, Vergil, Shakespeare and Milton – modelled on 'the charming windows of the Certosa near Florence, which are said to be the work of Giovanni da Udine'. One window, to the East of the chimneypiece, was to be a dummy, like the West windows in the Duomo at Florence. 'This can be managed so well by means of painting and tinsel,' Burges explained, 'that the deception in certain lights is very difficult to detect.' A massive walnut sideboard was to be inlaid with tarsia, like the woodwork in the chapel.[96] And all the portraits were to be removed, or copied, or cut down to uniform size: 'Nothing would be so destructive to the effect of any scheme of decoration as a number of irregular sized dark pictures.' The estimate was £3,035. 'Italian work', Burges sternly reminded the Fellows, 'will not do with a *little* decoration. It must either be properly done or left alone.'[97]

During the Summer of 1873 work began with a surprise: a medieval reredos was discovered behind Wyatt's plaster. But in the Spring of 1874 the Fellows were still negotiating with their architect. They were themselves divided. Collis stayed loyal to Burges; Oldfield remained hostile. But they were agreed on the need for economy. And they decided to put pressure on Burges. Would he modify his design? Would he preserve the portraits and lower the cost? No, he would not. 'My duty as I understand it', he explained, 'is to give you the best design my ability enables me to do – not to try how much I can do for a certain sum.' When one Fellow bearded him in Buckingham St, he was informed that the Senior Common Room were '*horribly cantankerous*'. Whatever happened, those portraits must go: 'I really do not see,' he expostulated, 'how the present pictures can by any ingenuity be made to harmonize with any system of decoration.' As for cutting down the chimneypiece: 'I should be most unwilling to alter a work which I think is pure art for the mere debased Vitruvian of the last century.' Much Oxford opinion was hostile. The Dean of Christ Church told Burges:

'If executed your Hall will be a florid representation of the cinquecento decoration. But I think it somewhat too florid. . . .' Even Collis admitted 'it will *never* do to banish the pictures'.

So the Fellows played their trump card. In June 1874 they called in the ubiquitous J. D. Crace. Crace's scheme⁹⁸ consisted of a series of sub-Raphaelesque clichés, liberally inscribed with platitudes: 'Welcome is the best cheer'; 'Hunger is the best sauce'; 'Contentment makes a feast'; 'Summum bonum in intellectu non in sensu consistit.' Burges capitulated in November 1875. The college was to have plain, washed walls and ceiling; grisaille glass; a simpler panelled dado and a smaller, uncoloured chimneypiece. 'I much prefer no colour at all', Burges admitted, 'to what newspaper correspondents call a chaste effect.' The Hall Committee emphasised that, come what may, the chimneypiece must be 'somewhat modified both in form and character'. Taking no chances, the General Committee struck out the word 'somewhat'.⁹⁹

As executed, therefore, between 1876 and 1879.¹ Burges's hall was at best a pale shadow of his original scheme, some $\frac{5}{8}$ Wyatt and $\frac{3}{8}$ Burges. As a stylistic exercise the work went well: prototypes from Florence or Verona were adapted freely and creatively.² But economy ruled. Fucigna's chimneypiece[103] was truncated, losing its cowl and statue in the process, as well as its gilding and colouring. Campbell and Smith's painted decorations were simple in the extreme, just a stencilling of red on buff-yellow. Walden's sideboard duly made its appearance, but his armorial panelling was paid for only by drumming up contributions from armigerous collegers at £10 a time.³ Burges had been outmanoeuvred. After his death successive alterations – in 1909, in 1927–8 and again in the 1950s – created just that 'chaste' effect which he despised. This progressive transformation, from Florentine to Neo-Georgian, was completed in 1966–7. Thanks to Mr Woodrow Wyatt, every trace of Burges was removed: *Wyatt redivivus.*⁴

THE MAGNIAC MONUMENTS, SHARNBROOK, BEDFORDSHIRE

Between his two commissions for Worcester College, Burges executed two minor designs which serve as an epilogue to this phase of experiment in Renaissance forms: the Magniac monuments at Sharnbrook, Bedfordshire.

A Huguenot family of clockmakers, grown prosperous in the China trade, the Magniacs of Colworth expanded in influence, as financiers and Liberal party supporters, as the nineteenth century progressed. They were also collectors and patrons. Hollingworth Magniac (d. 1867) was a connoisseur of medieval art, an accumulator in the tradition of Beckford and Bernal. His son, Charles Magniac M.P. (1829–91) was more of a public figure.⁵ He secured Waterhouse's appointment as architect of Bedford Shire Hall.⁶ And it was he who gave Burges the chance to execute two of the more curious designs of his career: a memorial and mausoleum for the

Magniac family, both in free versions of Sicilian Renaissance.[7]

In 1863–6 Hollingworth Magniac had altered Colworth Hall extensively.[8] Perhaps it was he who installed fittings and display cabinets in a mixture of Florentine and Rococo styles.[9] But Charles Magniac had an equally eclectic appetite. Speaking to the R.A.I. in 1881, he affirmed his belief in progressive eclecticism with all the fervour of Beresford-Hope:

> I have no faith in revivals. I have very little faith in copies. . . . I have no faith in imitations whatever. I believe the great secret of art to be originality, and unless it is original it is nothing. If you cannot apply the principle of Archaeology as you would the principles of Euclid to the science of art, I believe we shall come to nothing. . . . What we want is a national architecture.[10]

National or not, the Magniac monuments are certainly original. Using the Magniac insignia to good advantage, Burges's designs gaily interchange cheery cherubs, bulging brackets and grotesque, anthropomorphic masks. The material is white statuary marble, flecked with coloured insets, orange and red, blue-grey and pink. Sicilian Baroque has been rusticted. The swirling, riotous forms of Monreale in its latest phase have been thinned down and refashioned to adorn a village church in Bedfordshire.

Sharnbrook was perhaps a *jeu d'esprit*. Burges's designs for Florence Cathedral had been a disembodied dream. Other projects for King's, London and King's, Cambridge had been minor schemes of minor interest. But Gayhurst had marked a stylistic breakthrough. And Worcester College was a double commission of real stature. All seven schemes, however, pale into insignificance in comparison with Burges's next Renaissance work: his programme for St Paul's Cathedral.

St Paul's Cathedral

On Christmas Eve, 1838, Lord Macaulay was strolling in St Peter's, Rome, and bumped into young Mr Gladstone.[11] Both of them – Establishment Anglicans in the citadel of Popery – were reluctantly overcome by its splendour. And both of them felt the comparative inadequacy of England's equivalent, St Paul's Cathedral. 'I should like', Macaulay thought, 'to see the walls of St Paul's incrusted with porphyry and verde antique, and the ceiling and dome glittering with mosaics and gold.'[12] Thirty-two years later, in 1870, Gladstone launched a public appeal to rescue St Paul's – dirty and unfinished, but still 'the noblest church of modern times' – from the 'repulsive condition' produced by one and a half centuries of neglect.[13] He led an appeal for the completion of St Paul's in a manner worthy of the greatest 'temple of . . . our Faith[14] . . . the only cathedral built by Protestant hands and money[15] . . . the cathedral church of London, the mightiest of cities, the heart of England, of a vast empire, the capital of the whole civilised world'.[16]

By the mid-Victorian period the filthy state of St Paul's was a national scandal. And the vast acreage of its unfinished interior was a standing challenge to every architect and artist in the kingdom. That is easy to understand. But we have to make a mental effort to realise that in the 1860s Wren's reputation – and still more that of his contemporaries – stood at rock-bottom level. During the previous hundred years, the reputation of St Paul's had been twice destroyed: firstly by the rationalism of Neo-Classical theory; secondly by the fundamentalist medievalism of the Gothic Revival. To both Classics and Goths of the mid-nineteenth century, Baroque was anathema and Wren was a great architect, corrupted by the depraved taste of his age. His Baroque devices – the triple-layered dome, the two-storey portico, the clerestory screen walls hiding the flying buttresses – were all seen not as ingredients in an expressive discipline, outward signs of inward strength, but as a series of illusionistic deceits, worthy only of corrupt art. In 1879 *The Architect* called St Paul's 'the most audacious and unmitigated building-sham upon the face of the earth'.[17] So when Burges talked of Wren's 'abominations', he was merely reflecting the prejudices of his contemporaries.[18] When in 1871 he joked of making 'that old wretch Christopher Wren turn in his grave', and of restoring St Paul's 'off the face of creation', he was being irresponsible rather than outrageous.[19] The pendulum of taste only began to swing back in Wren's favour during the mid-1870s. But it swung back with sufficient velocity to knock Billy Burges clean off his Gothic pedestal.

The saga of the decoration of St Paul's differs fundamentally from all the other sagas of Victorian cathedral restoration. For in the case of St Paul's what was involved was not restoration but completion. Alas, that did not make the way smoother. The story is long and complicated. In the eighteenth century there were two attempts to complete the unfinished interior. In 1773 a grand Royal Academy scheme, with Reynolds, West, Barry, Cipriani, Dance and Angelica Kauffmann all taking part, was rejected by Bishop Terrick as too Popish. Then a less ambitious scheme, by Reynolds and West, for painted panels over the Sanctuary entrances, was also abandoned.[20] The early nineteenth century was a period of inertia. Nothing was done until 1853–6, when Thornhill's painted dome was restored by E. T. Parris. That created a precedent for action. And the rest of the century is a period of almost continuous agitation. There are three major phases, each associated with a particular Dean: 1858 onwards, under Dean Milman; 1870 onwards, under Dean Church; and 1890 onwards, under Dean Gregory. Milman was Broad Church; Church was fairly High Church; and Gregory very High Church. He was also a strong Conservative: Disraeli made him a Canon, and Lord Salisbury made him Dean. The battle for the completion of St Paul's was, therefore, as much theological and political as aesthetic. In that respect, the debate goes to the heart of the Anglican dilemma. As it stands today, St Paul's is a post-Reformation cathedral, built on a pre-Reformation plan; designed for Anglicans, re-planned for Evangelicals, and then re-decorated for Anglo-Catholics. Hence the complexity of the story.

Now in the beginning clerical pressure had forced Wren to change his design from a Greek cross plan to a Latin cross: Ely Cathedral became the model instead of Santa Sophia. In other words, he was forced to change his design from a plan suited to a Protestant ministry of the Word, to a plan suited to a Catholic sacramental system. He was also forced to change from a plan which rivalled St Peter's in its fluency, to a plan involving a necessarily awkward conjunction of dome and crossing. As built, the cathedral was divided by a prominent organ screen, a 'box of whistles' as Wren called it.[21] There were two sections: the choir for daily services for the Dean and Chapter; the transepts, nave and aisles for a public promenade; for clerical and choral processions in and out of the choir; and occasionally for a remote, half-listening congregation. It was a medieval arrangement without the justification of medieval liturgy. Except on rare state occasions, St Paul's was very rarely used to its full capacity. It was cold, bare and empty. In 1833 Canon Sydney Smith described it as an icy Hell – his vision of Heaven, incidentally, was 'eating *paté de fois gras* to the sound of trumpets': 'To go to St Paul's is certain death. The thermometer is several degrees below zero. My sentences are frozen as they come out of my mouth.'[22] Until 1851 the public were not even admitted unless they paid 2d.[23] A thorough visit could cost as much as 4/4d. And as for Christian symbolism, even a simple cross did not make its appearance over the altar until Easter 1869.[24] It was only in 1858 that the theatrical Milman, 'the great Dean', set out to bring the people in. He began evening services, services under the dome.[25] And from 1870 onwards, the sermons of the silver-tongued Liddon regularly filled that great cavernous space for the first time.

By the mid-nineteenth century the Evangelical Movement had made the planning of St Paul's seem restrictive; by the mid-Victorian period the Oxford Movement had made its decoration seem inadequate. 'I would see the Dome', vowed Milman in 1858, 'instead of brooding like a dead weight over the area below, expanding and elevating the Soul towards Heaven. . . .'[26] That was not to be. Instead there was an endless debate, leading to institutional deadlock and aesthetic compromise.

The architect to the Dean and Chapter since 1852 had been Francis Cranmer Penrose (1817–1903).[27] Penrose was perhaps the most learned classical architect of his generation. Burges bracketed him with C. R. Cockerell as 'the last of the Romans'.[28] The blood of Archbishop Cranmer flowed in his veins. His first cousin was Matthew Arnold: his aunt was Dr Arnold's wife. At Cambridge he had been a triple rowing blue and a friend of Charles Kingsley. His credentials as a fervent classicist and a muscular Protestant were impeccable. His R.I.B.A. portrait by Sargent shows him bewhiskered, bookish and benign. What better custodian could there be for London's Anglican headquarters? Alas, he was a scholar in a job which required a politician.

On the exterior, Penrose was responsible for one small but important improvement. Wren's successor, the rascally William Benson, had given the entrance steps of the West front curved balustrades. Penrose restored Wren's original right-angled design.[29] But inside, far from leaving Wren's arrangements inviolate, almost the first thing he did – in 1861 – was to remove the screen and return stalls, placing the organ in one of the Northern arches of the choir. One of the chief supporters of this move was Sir Charles Barry.[30] At the same time, a theatre organ – from the old Alhambra Music Hall in Leicester Square – was placed in the South transept.[31] Penrose failed to get Wren's screen placed there as well. But this extraordinary organ stayed in place until 1873, despite a death-bed protest from Barry.[32] Penrose claimed that the foundations of the crypt indicated that Wren never intended a screen, and merely bowed to clerical pressure. But removing Wren's screen made nonsense of his Latin cross compromise. Anyway, it was a move with Evangelical overtones. As the 1860s progressed, the cathedral's governing body became rather more High Church. The screen came back into fashion. At first an open screen of metal and marble was envisaged.[33] Then in 1871 – largely on James Fergusson's advice – a decision was taken to reinstate the organ screen, one bay nearer the Dome, but to divide it into two halves, thus maintaining a continuous vista while restoring the division between clergy and laity. A real Anglican compromise.

In the early 1870s there were other compromises in the air too. Micklethwaite and Somers Clarke proposed another altar in front of the screen, under the rim of the dome, thus making two altars: one for the clergy and one for the laity.[34] Burges thought there was something in this plan, and put forward Florence Cathedral as a model.[35] So did G. E. Street.[36] So did Basil Champneys.[37] Another idea was for an altar with a semi-circular screen, modelled on that of St Fermo, Verona.[38] Such suggestions were indeed sensible. They accepted the fact of Wren's reluctant decision to divide the space into two parts; they emphasised the basic duality of the plan; and they provided St Paul's with not one climax, but two: the dome and the choir. But Penrose persisted in his own compromise on acoustic grounds. The organ was divided, and the original organ case on the North side of the screen was replicated on the South.

Meanwhile, surplus woodwork from Wren's screen was used as an interior porch for the North transept.[39] In 1860 a new pulpit had been installed, designed by Penrose in Early Christian taste, after a design by Butterfield had been abandoned.[40] Gilding was begun in the domes and arches of the choir.[41] Two paintings by G. F. Watts were hung in the nave (*c.* 1867).[42] Stone-coloured paint, temporarily authorised by Wren as a preservative and later renewed by Cockerell, was removed.[43] A competition was held, in 1863, for decorating the apse. Baron Trinqueti defeated Watts, Leighton and Stevens. But the outcry against a foreigner – who might even be a Catholic – was deafening.[44] For all these matters Penrose was generally responsible. More important, he also made a start on filling the windows with stained glass, and the vaulting with mosaic.

Probably the least satisfactory of these changes was the installation of stained glass from 1861 onwards: three windows in the apse, including a central Crucifixion;[45] a great West window of the Conversion of St Paul;[46] two windows at the West end of the aisles; six in the drum of the dome; and one on the South side of the choir. The glass chosen was Munich glass. Now Munich glass had recently been used in Glasgow Cathedral. Its dark colours, fussy borders, heavy shading and inadequate firing had raised a storm of abuse. Undaunted, Milman and Penrose visited Glasgow and commissioned Julius Schnorr von Carolsfield as designer. The outcry was strident, not least from Burges.[47]

As for the mosaics, Penrose favoured 'Roman mosaics' – that is, the flat, Renaissance variety – and exhibited a scheme for covering the great dome and its spandrels in 1860.[48] In 1864 four mosaics were placed in the spandrels: St Matthew and St John by Watts; Isaiah and Jeremiah by Stevens. And in 1866, 1873 and 1875 Penrose exhibited full-scale designs for covering every vault in the cathedral with Roman mosaic, plus marble inlay on the upper walls, intarsia work in the apse,[49] more stained glass windows, and a great bronze West door.[50] The dome mosaics were to take the form of a Te Deum, by Woodington. With all this, Burges disagreed fundamentally. He never doubted that, as regards mosaic technique, Byzantine precedents were the ones to follow: 'What building would NOT look well, covered with mosaics on a gold ground?' But Renaissance mosaics – petrified pictures – would only produce 'the boudoir effect of St Peter's ... which always struck me as having been originally executed as a reception room for Her Royal Highness the Princess of Brobdingnag'.[51] It was probably through his influence that in 1870 Messrs. Powell of Whitefriars submitted, free of charge, a single panel of glass mosaic modelled on some mosaic of the third century A.D. found in the Palazzo Albani, Rome.[52]

During the 1860s and early 1870s, therefore, there had been no clear direction. Penrose seems to have been buffetted between Evangelical and High Church pressures. More important, as Gilbert Scott pointed out,[53] he was, confessedly, not competent to deal with problems of iconography and decorative art. 'This is the grandest project of modern times', the *Building News* announced in 1870; we need 'a master mind.'[54] *The Architect* said the same thing in 1872: 'It needs only the finishing touch of some master-mind to make it one of the finest churches in Christendom.'[55] Burges's supporters were starting to move into place.

At the outset, there had been a wide measure of support for the Appeal of 1870; more enthusiasm in fact than for the Appeal of 1861.[56] Contributions poured in from all levels of churchmanship.[57] Both Liberals and Tories were represented on the Committee. There were three Liberal M.P.s: John Walter, proprietor of *The Times*; George Cavendish Bentinck, and Sir William Tite. There were three publishers: John Murray, Henry Butterworth and William Longman. James Fergusson spoke for architectural theory; Gilbert Scott for architectural practice; Gambier Parry for decorative painting. But one man inevitably took the lead: Beresford-Hope. He vowed to clothe the 'manifest nudity' of St Paul's.[58] And with him went the Rev. Benjamin Webb, Dean Church, Canon Gregory and Canon Liddon. That High Church quintet were determined on a programme of polychromy and Christian symbolism. All four were committed ecclesiologists, and Webb was the movement's high priest. Liddon was a fervent Puseyite; he preached at the opening of Keble College Chapel; he was also at school with Burges and Rossetti. Church was a friend of Newman, and had been brought up in Florence. Together they secured Burges's appointment in several stages between 1871 and 1874. Dean Church publicly defended the decision in ominously well-chosen words: he called Burges 'a man of genius . . . who will treat St Paul's as a great Christian Cathedral . . . the noblest Italian church on this side of the Alps'.[59] Many of the subscribers to the Appeal were rather taken aback.[60] And Tite, Bentinck and Fergusson – respectively Classical, Protestant and Rationalist – set to work to destroy Burges's position.[61]

On the face of it, it was an extraordinary appointment – like Robert Kerr being appointed to restore Westminster Abbey[62] – almost an insult to the ghost of Christopher Wren.[63] Although he had worked in Florentine style at Worcester College, Oxford; in François Premier at Gayhurst; and in Sicilian Renaissance at Sharnbrook, Burges was known to the public at large as an out-and-out Goth. And although he had sat on an R.I.B.A. committee concerned with improving the approaches to St Paul's,[64] he had evinced no special interest in Wren. Indeed, back in 1861 he had made his intentions with regard to St Paul's only too clear. After commiserating with Penrose on his fiendishly tricky task, he remarked that perhaps

> the best thing to do with the interior would be to chisel off all the projections, mouldings, foliage, etc., everything, in fact . . . and then to cover it all over with painting, or better still, mosaic on a gold ground like St Mark's, at Venice; the piers and walls below the windows being plated with precious marbles. The exterior might be refaced with new ashlar and the upper storey taken down, so as to show the flying buttresses. While, the sham lead dome being destroyed, the brick cone could be decorated like the dome at Chiaravalle, near Milan, which Mr Fergusson, with great reason, I think, supposes to have been the original design for the dome at Florence. I am afraid, however, that both these suggestions are rather too sweeping. . . .[65]

It seemed a nice joke at the time. Ten years later the problem was rather less amusing.

According to Church, the aim was 'to render the interior of the Cathedral worthy of its unrivalled exterior, and to carry out the intentions of its great architect'.[66] According to the Appeal, 'Sir Christopher Wren's intentions, his mode of treatment, and, as far as can be authenticated, his very designs, will be scrupulously kept sacred and followed'.[67] Unfortunately, as E. W. Godwin pointed out, 'no one [had] the remotest knowledge of any detail drawings by Wren setting forth his intentions'; so the whole episode became simply 'a fine opportunity for an antiquarian squabble'.[68]

In July 1870 Burges had been asked – through Hope's influence – to draw up a preliminary iconographic scheme for the decoration of St Paul's: no drawings yet; just iconography.[69] The report was submitted in February 1871. 'Iconology', *The Architect* helpfully told its readers, 'is the philosophy of sacred imagery; iconography the art of its design; and an iconographic scheme a sketch for the embellishment of a sacred edifice with figure subjects.'[70] Burges's scheme consisted of the following principal elements: in the Eastern apse, above the altar, Christ in Majesty; in the spandrels of the choir and transept vaulting, the Angelic Hierarchy – Cherubim, Seraphim, Angels, Archangels, etc.; at the West end, the Creation and Fall; in the nave, transepts and aisles – walls and windows – scenes and figures from the Old Testament; in the transepts and choir, scenes and figures from the New Testament;[71] and in the great dome, the multitudinous images of the Heavenly Jerusalem and the Apocalypse. Finally, the South West Chapel, at that date still occupied by Stevens's Wellington Monument, would appropriately boast the Cardinal or Manly Virtues. And the North West chapel, perhaps to be dedicated to the memory of Albert the Good, would be decorated with emblems of the Theological or Christian Virtues.[72]

It was a vast scheme, owing more than a little to the writings of Didron, Mrs Jameson and Lady Eastlake,[73] and involving hundreds of figures of saints, prophets, patriarchs, martyrs and priests – 'weeded out', of course, to suit Protestant sympathies. There was no image of the Virgin Mary. Still, it seemed a High Church, not to say Anglo-Catholic scheme. And given the Broad Church leanings of the bulk of its own congregation, an impossible one. Burges was its creator, but its sponsor was Beresford-Hope. Even *The Architect*, loyal to Burges and devoted to Gothic, shook its editorial head sadly. 'Not one man in a thousand will believe it possible that the project can ever be carried into effect. ... The day is fortunately gone by for disposing of the question by an insurrection in the streets, the breaking of Mr Burges's windows, and the burning of the corner of Edgware Road. The utmost, probably, that will be attempted is to insinuate, in various forms of smart writing, that the thing has been overdone.'[74]

And so it happened. But not at once. The first step was the appointment by the Executive Committee for the Completion of St Paul's, of a Fine Arts sub-committee. Then, on 22 April 1872, while James Fergusson was out of the way, convalescing on the Continent, the sub-committee agreed, by the narrowest of margins, to appoint Burges as architectural consultant. Burges was given the title of 'Architect'; Penrose remained 'Architectural Adviser' and 'Surveyor of the Fabric'.[75] The anti-Goths protested in *The Times*.[76] On 19 May Burges submitted a report. On 8 August – after weeks of manoeuvring – he was formally appointed. And on 6 November he was instructed to prepare designs. In Spring 1873 he set out for Italy, visiting Genoa, Florence, Arezzo, Rome, Ferrara, Padua, Venice, Mantua, Milan, Chiaravalle and Turin.[77] His mind was filled with images of the early Renaissance. That Summer and Autumn he worked steadily on designs. On 7 December 1873 a first model, for one bay of the nave, was officially inspected; on 27 March 1874 a second model[135] for the choir. But, alas, the Fine Arts committee rejected both by four votes to three.[78] So on 19 May 1874 the Executive Committee overruled the Fine Arts committee, voting ten to four to accept Burges's scheme, and to dissolve the troublesome sub-committee for good. At that point the recalcitrant four – Cavendish Bentinck, James Fergusson, Edmund Oldfield and Gambier Parry – launched a counter-attack, denouncing the designs as vulgar, extravagant, Jesuitical and – above all – in 'the style of Mr Burges rather than that of Sir Christopher Wren'.[79] Led by *The Times*, the press lashed itself into a frenzy of aesthetic indignation. Most of the criticism was pseudo-theological rather than architectural. Many of the attacks were simply absurd.[80] But the Dean and Chapter lost their nerve. A general meeting, specially summoned in November 1874, bowed to the storm and suspended operations.[81] Burges simply noted in his diary: 'St Paul's all over.'[82] When his designs[83] went on show at the Royal Academy a few months later, the die had already been cast. On 24 March 1875 Burges noted in his diary: 'St Paul's finally paid' – that is, the final instalment of his total payment of £1,175, plus £571 for expenses.[84] On 11 June 1877, he recorded his formal removal: 'Dismissed from St Paul's.'[85]

Well, was his dismissal justified? Burges's instructions had been superficially precise: to 'have reverent regard to the intentions of Sir C. Wren, either as indicated by his known style, or as evinced by any designs or models of his which may be in existence; and, failing these, the style of architecture and decoration adopted by the best Italian architects and artists of the sixteenth century'.[86]

Now knowledge of Wren's intentions was slim. Hard evidence was limited to a flimsy sketch, a couple of dubious engravings, and a posthumous footnote in *Parentalia* (1750). This crucial footnote read as follows:

> The judgement of the Surveyor was originally, instead of [Thornhill's] painting [in the dome] . . . to have beautified the inside of the cupola with the more durable ornament of mosaic work as is nobly executed in the cupola of St Peter's at Rome. For this purpose he had projected to have procured from Italy four of the most eminent artists in that profession; but as this art was a great novelty in England, and not generally apprehended, it did not receive the encouragement it deserved. . . . The painting and gilding of the architecture of the East end . . . over the communion table was intended to serve the present occasion, till such time as materials could have been procured for a magnificent design for an altar, for which the respective drawings and a model were prepared. . . . An altar-piece of the richest Greek marbles, with wreathed and sculptured columns supporting a canopy hemispherical.[87]

In other words, Wren disapproved of Thornhill's grisaille-painted dome.[88] His decoration of the East end in painted marbling was only temporary. And he intended to install mosaics and a baldacchino in the manner of St Peter's. To support this, a sketch by Wren for a baldacchino survived.[89] And two engravings showing decorations for the dome and spandrels: one in the style of Verrio, published in 1702;[90] and one in the style of Borromini, published in 1755.[91] But Wren had no experience whatever of Byzantine or Oriental mosaic. He had never been to Venice or Istanbul. He had never even been to Italy. In fact he never travelled further than Paris and Versailles. His intentions as regards mosaic, therefore, must have been nebulous in the extreme. As regards carving and painting, the construction of the cupolas in the nave and aisles, as well as the spandrels and soffits of the arches, indicated some intention on the part of the architect to insert decorative work at a later stage. 'There are compartments', Dean Newton explained in the 1770s, 'which were originally designed for bas reliefs or suchlike decorations, but the Parliament, as it is said, having taken part of the fabric money and applied it to King William's wars, Sir C. Wren complained that his wings were clipt, and the Church was deprived of its ornaments.'[92] Wren made no mention at all of stained glass. But as regards polychromy in general, there was one extra piece of supporting evidence. The 1870 Appeal quoted Wren's quotation from the French theorist Roland Freart [the Sieur de Cambray]: Painting and Sculpture are the key to architecture; 'all must be lame without it'.[93]

If knowledge of Wren's general aim was therefore slim, evidence as to his precise intentions was negligible. Precedents from Wren's style elsewhere were, of course, available. Burges was able to model his aisle and nave domelets, for instance, on an elaborated version of the dome of St Stephen's, Walbrook. But the presumptive evidence of Wren's preferences in decorative painting was quite unacceptable to mid-Victorian taste. 'Sprawling allegories, splashes of fore-shortened figures, clouds and cupids. ... Are we prepared', asked Godwin, 'to have "reverent regard" to such debased and corrupt work?'[94] So much for Verrio; so much for Laguerre. As Eastlake put it, 'to plead for the decoration of St Paul's in a style which shall be synchronous and consistent with the style of the architecture itself, is to plead for what we do not hesitate to call bad taste'.[95] So much for Grinling Gibbons, Tijou and Thornhill. In all the hubbub about Burges's designs, no one ever suggested that St Paul's should be painted in 'the vicious taste of the age', that is in the style of Wren's contemporaries.[96] Late Baroque art had no place in the High Victorian pantheon. Burges, therefore, had in practice no choice. Gothic and Byzantine seemed quite unsuitable for St Paul's, and Baroque was simply unacceptable. He was forced back on precedents from 'the best' architects and artists of sixteenth-century Italy.

But who were 'the best'? After all, the cinquecento ran all the way from Raphael in Sta Maria del Popolo to Vignola's Gesù. Burges preferred the 'sculpturesque severity ... of ... the Umbrian school of the first quarter ... of the sixteenth century' – that is, Perugino and Raphael – to the work of Correggio or Vasari, or the 'luxuriant naturalism' of the Venetian school of the last quarter of the sixteenth century.[97] The art of Raphael he regarded as 'the purest version of classic art the world has seen since the days of ancient Greece'.[98] But there were two phases of Raphael. And Burges preferred the earlier, 'Giottesque' phase, rather than the later work in the Vatican *loggie*. Burges's models and exhibited drawings for St Paul's indicate the influence of

Giotto's decoration in the Arena Chapel at Padua;[99] Perugino's work in the Sala del Cambio, Perugia;[1] as well as Raphael's arabesque, reticulation and inlay at Sta Maria del Popolo, Rome.[2] And there is evidence of further eclectic sympathies in Burges's designs for mosaic paving in the choir: *opus sectile* in the manner of Sta Maria dei Miracoli, Venice; and *opus vermiculatum*, with Early Christian emblems reminiscent of Ravenna.[3] Such combinations of marble, mosaic and gilding, could be paralleled, of course, in churches which Burges himself found difficulty in praising – the 'Scalzi' in Venice (Sta Maria in Nazaret), for instance, designed in 1680 by Longhena and Sardi. In his choice of materials, however, he plumped for practicality: mosaic, majolica, bronze and marble were more or less imperishable; could all be easily cleaned; and would reflect rather than absorb light. Finally, he was determined to replace the Munich windows with lighter glass, early Renaissance in style. Burges made no attempt to estimate the cost. 'I entirely put aside . . . the question of expense. . . . [It is just] a question of time.'[4]

In the early stages of the debate, there was qualified approval – from Penrose, for instance – for Burges's preliminary proposals.[5] But when Burges's models actually appeared, Penrose decided that the whole scheme was 'overdone'. The subdivision of the nave and aisle domes – indeed the alteration of so many profiles and mouldings – could not be justified by Wren's intentions: the attic figures were 'trifling'; the gilding 'excessive'; and the polychrome fluting of the pilasters, after the manner of the Annunciata in Genoa, was a mistake. Better to follow the Certosa at Pavia, which was plain below and rich above. The design was fine 'in the abstract'. But, in actuality, so much 'incrustation' might make the cathedral 'lose dignity'. Wren was aiming at 'the coloss'.[6]

This private debate at the R.I.B.A. was reflected in a public debate up and down the land. It is hard to think of any single architectural issue which attracted more popular coverage in the mid-Victorian period. The press was divided, and divided violently. In quarterlies, monthlies, weeklies, dailies, the battle raged on. On the whole, the *Ecclesiologist*, the *Saturday Review*, the *Church Builder*, the *Art Journal*,[7] the *Athenaeum*[8] and the *Architect* supported Burges. The *Builder* was consistently hostile. The *Building News* prevaricated at first,[9] and then joined the opposition.[10] And *The Times* acted as an Establishment megaphone for the belligerent Protestantism of the popular press.[11] Superficially, it was a matter of 'Goth versus Classicist'.[12] But below the surface it was a religious and political battle as much as an aesthetic one. The *Ecclesiologist* was not only Gothic but Anglo-Catholic and Tory. The *Builder* was not only Classical but Protestant and Radical.

On the Anglo-Catholic side, the *Church Builder* dreamed of a cathedral which was not only liturgically functional but decoratively expressive. 'The whole [design] should be a great Christian poem to be offered up as an act of worship'; St Paul's was not just an 'architectural monument', but 'a Christian cathedral'.[13] On the Protestant side, the *Builder* attacked Burges's mosaic angels as theologically suspect: 'we might prefer not to see these shadowy hierarchical terms transformed into visible and permanent figurations'. The great figure of Christ in Majesty was a 'ludicrous . . . *fetish* of the barbarous ages of Christianity'. The emblems of Paradise in the pavement of the apse were 'like a child's Sunday puzzle, and a poor amusement even for children'. St Paul's, the *Builder* concluded, 'more than any other cathedral, embodies the spirit of the Reformation'. Burges's design should be rejected by all who 'have not willingly shut their eyes to the intellectual history of Christianity'.[14]

Like Scott over the Foreign Office, and Street over the Law Courts, Burges became the victim of a Classical witch-hunt.[15] But unlike Scott and Street, he also had to face the full fury of the Protestant lobby. The most fanatical of Burges's Protestant enemies was J. T. Emmett, the *Quarterly*'s vitriolic and anonymous critic.[16] But scarcely less fierce was Professor T. L. Donaldson, a senior classicist and an Evangelical Protestant, a great power in the R.I.B.A., 'the Father of his Profession'.[17] He called Burges's mosaic figures 'semi-barbarous. . . . Medieval monstrosities'. This was 'polychromy with a vengeance'.[18] 'The type of the Roman Catholic [cathedral] must not be adopted. There must be a sober majestic treatment' – like Baron Trinqueti's work at Windsor. Let Burges heed 'the fourteenth homily of our Church: "The outrageous decking of temples and churches with gold, silver, pearl and precious stones shall be confuted"'.[19] St Paul's, he thought, was in grave danger of becoming 'a mass-house', clothed by Burges in 'the sensuous allurements of the harlot . . . tawdry, meretricious and luscious'.[20]

By comparison, the chromatic criticisms of J. G. Crace were mild. He merely remarked that while Burges's scheme might suit the Certosa in Pavia, in London it would be a 'calamity'.[21] But it was the clash between Burges and Fergusson which produced the hottest sparks. As one paper put it, the two men 'were like flint and steel'.[22] Fergusson, as usual, showed himself a dogmatic rationalist. Overall marble veneering would be a sham: 'For chimney pieces or console tables such a mode of treatment may be legitimate; but in monumental buildings it was only adopted in Italy by the worst architects in the worst age . . . [in] architecture so capricious and bad that one shudders to think of it. . . . Bernini, Borromini [and] Iuvara . . . were the men who used marble most, and their works are simply frightful.' Stained glass would produce 'undesirable gloom'. Polychrome vaults would seem to bring the roof 'down on our heads'. Figurative schemes would be archaic anachronisms. Mosaics would be unwise, since the techniques were as yet insufficiently understood. And the whole scheme – to cost perhaps £400,000 – was 'absurdly extravagant . . . one of the most fantastic proposals . . . ever submitted in seriousness to any body of men'.[23] For that sort of money, Fergusson would have preferred to rebuild St Paul's altogether. He had always liked Wren's Great Model better than the 'architectural bathos' of the executed version. Now, with breathtaking self-confidence, he proposed a reconstruction of the whole choir, giving the cathedral a second, octagonal dome, decorated with Ravenna mosaics – a more outrageous suggestion than anything Burges ever dreamt of.[24]

Several of Burges's personal friends, notably Gilbert Scott,[25] J. P. Seddon,[26] T. Roger Smith,[27] and William H. White, rushed to his defence. One particular ally who stood by him – though not uncritically – was E. W. Godwin. He had minor criticisms: the aisle domelets were over-divided; the bronze cupids and wreaths over the nave capitals were unnecessary; the pendentive figures were too small; the great figure of Christ in Majesty was awkward; and – most of all – the colour-scheme of choir and apse was too rich. But on the whole he was surprised to find that he approved: 'the design for the nave emphasises and develops the better parts of Wren's work, is not opposed to the work of some of the best artists of the sixteenth century, is magnificent without being intemperate, rich without being gaudy, and bright without being garish'; even in the choir, 'I expected magnificence of colour, and I looked for thorough archaeological knowledge. . . . But I did not expect to find such brightness, freshness, and light'.[28]

More enthusiastic still was the *Saturday Review*.[29] But then its proprietor was Beresford-Hope. Still, Burges's brother-in-law, Pullan, was quite right in calling the scheme 'the most important undertaking on which [Burges] was ever engaged'.[30] He devoted months of study to it and thousands of miles of travel. He even kept a separate diary, annotating the scheme's progress over the best part of a decade.[31] As soon as he was appointed, he justified – quite honestly – his previous condemnations of Wren's style: my earlier remarks, he explained, 'had reference to our present and future architecture . . . not to the preservation and completion of the works of past ages. . . . I have studied colour decoration in Italy, and classic architecture in Athens . . . and whatever opinion I may hold respecting his details, I have never been so blind as to deny to Sir Christopher Wren his just position as one of the greatest of our architects'.[32] In adopting Raphael as his model, Burges had fulfilled his instructions to the letter: 'I was told to fall back upon the "best architects and artists of the sixteenth century", and surely', he protested, 'there can be no comparison between the merits of Raphael and Correggio.'[33] To modern eyes, his mortal sin was lack of caution. But that by no means ruled him out in the eyes of contemporaries. Even Cockerell approved of the insertion of stained glass.[34] Even Fergusson was in favour of filling the great dome with mosaics, on the model of St Peter's.[35] And it was Fergusson who first considered the complete reconstruction of the choir, and then sanctioned the insertion of a gigantic marble reredos in the 1880s.[36] In three decades of public debate scarcely a single voice was raised in favour of leaving St Paul's completely alone.[37]

It was Burges's intention – perhaps naïvely – to complete St Paul's 'in the same manner as Sir Christopher Wren would have [worked] had he lived at the present time. . . . I do not think that [he] would have indulged in sprawling Cupids and rococo ornament . . . he would have avoided all such things and have worked out the problem in the purest phase of Italian art. . . . The general effect . . . would probably have resembled . . . St Peter's at Rome'.[38] As William H. White put it, 'Mr Burges has attempted to think as . . . Wren would have thought had he enjoyed the advantages of the present day'.[39] And that was not quite as bizarre a viewpoint as it may sound to us. Even Penrose allowed that any design for completing St Paul's should give Wren 'credit for the enlarged acquaintance with the subject of decoration which modern travel and research would have afforded him'.[40] It was Burges's tactics which were at fault rather than his strategy. In producing an overall scheme at the outset, he was no doubt artistically correct. But it was bad tactics to show his hand all at once. As a *Punch* cartoon put it: 'Si Ornamentum Requiris, Circumspice: If you require ornament, be circumspect.'[41]

From a personal point of view, Burges came out of the controversy surprisingly well. His design was attacked as inappropriate rather than intrinsically bad. And his ability and learning were taken for granted, even by some of his sharpest opponents – J. J. Stevenson,[42] or Robert Kerr,[43] for instance. The weak link in Burges's defence lay not in his own talent, but in that of his assistants: a St Paul's decorated on the basis of cartoons by H. W. Lonsdale might well have been a dispiriting place.[44] But there is evidence that he intended to employ Leighton and Richmond as well.[45]

But perhaps, after all, the whole idea was impossible: to complete the decoration of England's only Baroque cathedral, using any style *except* the Baroque; to complete the interior of England's only Protestant cathedral, using forms which would not offend the Puritan eye; and, in any case, to proceed with only the flimsiest evidence of the architect's original intentions as to colour, design or even materials. Gambier Parry admitted it was impossible: 'like draining the Bedford fen.'[46] Or as Robert Kerr put it, 'If an angel from heaven had come down with a plan for St Paul's, it would have met with precisely the same treatment'.[47] In 1891 G. F. Bodley invited Burne-Jones to design mosaics for the semi-domes of the choir. He turned the invitation down.

> I couldn't face it, and yet I love mosaic better than anything else in the world. It's nonsense to put mosaic there – nonsense I think to try to do anything with it but let it chill the soul of man and gently prepare him for the next glacial cataclysm. It wants carpets hung about, and big, huge, dark oil pictures, and hangings and rich stuffs, and the windows let alone, no stained glass anywhere, no colour except black and silver, no chilling surplices, Bach always being played, and me miles away. Me miles away. . . .[48]

Anyway, impossible or not, for Burges the operation was a *fiasco*. The irony of it all was that he had been unjustly robbed of Lille Cathedral and the Crimea Memorial Church, thus outraging the architectural profession. And now he had almost been manoeuvred into St Paul's, thus outraging the public. He had emerged as the dupe of a faction-ridden and inconsistent committee of taste.[49] In the process he became the Puritans' Aunt Sally, a whipping boy for the aesthetic guilty conscience of mid-Victorian England. Beresford-Hope's plot had failed.

But not for long. After a two-year truce, Beresford-Hope was back in the fight, calling for a scheme of decoration which was both Early Christian and Early Renaissance, Classical and Byzantine.[50] First came a slow propaganda build-up: the Ecclesiological Society was re-founded on a 'non-professional' basis as the St Paul's Ecclesiological Society. Dean Church became President. Hope, Webb, Gregory and Liddon were all Vice-Presidents.[51] Direct action discreetly descended to the crypt: St Faith's Chapel was fitted up in 1877; and the Wellington tomb was surrounded with mosaics designed by Penrose and made by female convicts in Woking Goal.[52]

But what about the dome? And all those acres of undecorated space? By 1876 Edmund Oldfield – one of Burges's opponents – had come round to thinking that after all the Early Renaissance was the best precedent. He suggested a competition between Watts, Poynter and Leighton.[53] In April 1877 Burges and Hope were already thinking of resuscitating Burges's scheme.[54] But Burges had to be finally dismissed before any new start could be made. Dismissed he was, therefore, and in 1878 a new sub-committee of the Dean and Chapter agreed to commission Leighton and Poynter – who was also Trinqueti's nephew – to begin work on the basis of Stevens's old model. Stevens's pupil, Hugh Stannus was to be the executant artist. Estimates for mosaic were to be obtained from the Murano Glass Co. (formerly Salviati & Co.) and Messrs. Powell of Whitefriars. And patient Penrose was to supervise the whole thing.[55] Stevens, Leighton and Poynter made a formidable trio. And their collective scheme was not deficient in power. Poynter said of Stevens's scheme that 'Michaelangelo himself never did anything finer'.[56] But J. P. Seddon was not alone in thinking that the inset panels in the dome might produce a distorting effect. Perhaps it was safer to stick to Thornhill.[57] The *Builder* claimed that subdividing the dome destroyed its 'real grandeur and mystery ... by cutting it up into sections like an orange'.[58] Pullan said that Stevens's design was 'the dream of a man who had Michaelangelo on the brain'.[59] And next year Pullan himself produced a scheme with C. Heath Wilson of Florence which countered the criticism of sub-division by treating the whole inner domed surface as one great coned sphere – like Correggio's dome at Parma Cathedral – a mighty domical Te Deum.[60] It was designed for fresco, tempera *or* mosaic. 'Fortunately', commented *The Architect*, 'there are some men who are blessed with sanguine temperaments.'[61] None of these schemes aroused much support. Still less did a maverick design by J. P. Seddon 'founded on a painting by Botticini in the National Gallery'.[62] Meanwhile, as if to reinforce the public's sense of *déja vu*, the *Architect* confused everyone by choosing to republish Burges's design of 1874.[63]

Then in 1883 Dean Church tried a new tack. He invited Bodley to design a new high altar and reredos. In 1886–8 the reredos was installed, a monster construction in pink marble, towering as high as the clerestory. Its justification was based on the fact that once the screen had been divided, the dual nature of Wren's plan had been destroyed: the focus and climax of the whole cathedral must now be an enlarged high altar. But of course it was far too massive. Happily it was partly destroyed in the Blitz, and has now been replaced by a baldacchino designed by Stephen Dykes Bower and Godfrey Allen in 1958. In 1888, however, Bodley and Garner's reredos was the talk of ecclesiastical England. The Dean and Chapter were arraigned in the House of Lords on charges of erecting a superstitious symbol. They were eventually acquitted: the Lords ruled that the Calvary centrepiece was not a superstitious symbol but merely a representation of historical fact.[64] That gave the green light for further 'Popish plots'. The sanctuary pilasters had already been plated with marble by Farmer and Brindley.[65] Next came the altar itself, and the Jesus Chapel behind it in 1891–3.[66] Finally, statues were placed in the drum of the dome, designed by Kempe and executed by Winnington for Farmer and Brindley. That just left the mosaics.

In 1890 Canon Gregory became Dean. A bulldog cleric of adamantine disposition – his predecessor described him as like 'cast iron'[67] – Gregory was perhaps the only man who could have carried the scheme through in the teeth of public rage. It was Bodley who seems to have suggested Sir William Richmond.[68] And Richmond was a match for Gregory in what one journal called his 'colossal self-confidence, verging on insanity'.[69] By this time Penrose had become 'a frail old soul', whiling away his last years in the study of astronomy. Richmond 'had the bit between his teeth' before Penrose's effective successor, Somers Clarke, could halt him.[70] Fergusson was dead by now, and so were Tite and Donaldson and Gambier Parry. Even without Beresford-Hope, the High Church brigade seemed to have it their own way. At the Diamond Jubilee Service in 1897, copes were worn for the first time since the seventeenth century.[71]

First came the completion of the eight spandrels of the dome, using designs by Stevens and Watts, worked up by W. E. F. Britten, in Salviati's Renaissance mosaic.[72] Then, between 1892 and 1894, Richmond's mosaics began to spread steadily across the apse, through the sanctuary and into the choir.[73] Millions of glass tesserae were employed, made by Powells of Whitefriars, in the ancient manner of Ravenna. And there was still $\frac{7}{8}$ths of the cathedral to go. . . . It was estimated that completion would take fourteen years. Then in 1899, just as Richmond was beginning to start gilding, painting and stencilling the periphery of the choir, the Protestant storm burst. Once again *The Times* girded its editorial loins. Petitions were signed in the name of Reformation. There were protests in the House of Lords. The Earl of Wemyss – without seeing them – attacked these 'barbarous, anachronous ... Byzantine mosaics'.[74] The *Spectator* pleaded: Spare the Nave![75]

Richmond was unrepentant: 'That I am a Vandal is not true; I may be a Heathen or a Goth.' In a letter to *The Times* of 'prodigious length',[76] he produced one last, impassioned plea – Pre-Raphaelite in tone, Ruskinian in spirit, Burgesian in vigour – for colour, colour at all costs. In its bare, frigid emptiness, St Paul's embodied the soul of Puritan England. Richmond saw himself fulfilling the High Victorian rebellion against a philistine tyranny of 'the barbarous followers of John Knox and mobs of Puritan savages'. In calling for mosaics, Wren, he thought, had been 'a man far in advance of his time in England'. Appropriately, he was backed up by the aged Holman

Hunt, writing – inevitably – from Ravenna.[77]

Quite consciously, Richmond was working in Burges's shadow. His father, George Richmond R.A., had served on the Appeal committee back in 1870. He himself had been one of the artists Burges had in mind in 1874. Quite logically, therefore, he now used Burges's model to display his own proposals.[136] Some of Burges's ideas – the winged-angel spandrels for instance – reappear in Richmond's designs. Richmond fully endorsed Burges's commitment to Byzantine rather than Renaissance mosaic. The best work, he believed, occurred in the fifth to ninth centuries, and again in thirteenth-century Italy. 'After that mosaic went off, and eventually the pictorial system began to come in, and it is against that that I have been fighting.'[78] As one of Richmond's apologists put it: Burges had sketched out a grand scheme, 'but that true Gothic architect was nipped in the bud'.[79] It was Burges's early Christian lead which Richmond chose to follow rather than the High Renaissance manner favoured by Stevens and Poynter. The validity of Burges's scheme had thus been posthumously vindicated.

In 1974 Burges was vindicated once again. By that date the mosaics had grown dim with the dust and soot of three-quarters of a century. Careful cleaning revealed their true glory. Today Christ towers in majesty with his angels above the new baldacchino in purple, red, white and gold. Birds, beasts and fishes of the earth praise their creator across the triple domes of the choir. The four apses of the crossing glow in green and gold, russet and blue. Richmond had fulfilled Burges's ambition – but with one important difference. Burges's figures had been damned as too archaic. Richmond's – being twenty years later – have an *art nouveau* attenuation which escapes accusations of archaism by advancing towards abstraction. Lit obliquely, with electronic brilliance, the jagged tesserae glitter and sparkle with the warmth of electric sunshine. Thornhill's dome recedes into subfuse obscurity. The evangelists and prophets, by Stevens and Watts, look down opaquely from the eight spandrels of the dome. The nave's subsidiary domes, still unfinished, stare white and vacant.

Granted the premise that Wren's work should be completed – admittedly a pretty big premise to grant – then Burges has been proved right, triumphantly right.

Chapter Five

GOTHIC

'Whatsoever thy hand findeth to do, do it with all thy might.'
ECCLESIASTES ix, 10

ECCLESIASTICAL BUILDINGS

For Burges Gothic meant above all, Early French: that noblest and truest of styles, born in the springtime of the Middle Ages. Its origins lay in structure, its fulfilment in decoration. And in both fields – architecture and the applied arts – its greatest triumphs were ecclesiastical. In designing churches, therefore, whether Early French or not, Burges could meet the Middle Ages on its own ground. Now Burges was not a religious man. His allegiance to 'Continental notions' of religious observance,[1] seems to have been largely aesthetic. He once went on record as a supporter of public rather than private prayer – but only because public worship made for elaborate churches.[2] His religion was the art of the Middle Ages, not its theology. The bulk of his church work was Anglican, but two of his greatest patrons were Catholics. As Robert Kerr put it, 'Butterfield was High Church, Scott Low Church, and Burges no church'.[3] Still, his learning made him official adviser on church metalwork to the Ecclesiological Society. And no man entered into the spirit of medieval church design more wholeheartedly than Burges. His vision encompassed the whole spectrum of visual art: sculpture, painting, metalwork, stained glass, mosaic, textiles and woodwork as well as architecture itself. His dream was the church candescent, an aesthete's version of the church militant: Faith made manifest in Art.

LILLE CATHEDRAL

The chronology of the Lille competition is clear enough. The programme was announced in December 1854: a competition open to all the world, for a cathedral bigger than Noyon and almost as long as Rheims. There had been nothing quite like it since the Renaissance. The *Ecclesiologist* hailed the competition as a beacon of light in the aesthetic darkness of Flanders.[4] Architects in France, England, Germany and Belgium took to their drawing-boards. 'Everything', announced the Comte de

Coulaincourt, 'presages a brilliant competition.'[5] At first the contestants were given one year to prepare their designs. Later the deadline was extended from 1 December 1855 to 1 March 1856.[6] Between 13 and 25 March 1856, the forty-one designs were exhibited in the Halle au Blé. After the exhibition, solemn High Mass inaugurated the jury's deliberations. On 25–30 March and 10–13 April the jury met in preliminary and final sessions. The entries were first reduced to nineteen and then placed in three classes. On 13 April, at a ceremony with choral accompaniment, the decision was announced: Clutton and Burges were the winners.[7] Both men had visited the site in 1855.[8] Accompanied by Pullan, Burges had personally delivered the competition drawings on 28 February; and on 17 March – in company with Aitchison – he had paid a special visit to the exhibition.[9] On 14 April the news reached England.[10] On 26 April both the victors arrived in Lille to be publicly acknowledged. The euphoria, however, was brief. On 13 May occurred the mysterious 'row with Clutton'. The laying of the foundation stone, however, went ahead on 9 June. And the winning architects pocketed their prize money. But the sum amounted to only 6,000 Francs instead of 10,000: their design was not to be built.

So much is beyond doubt. What is rather less clear is the explanation of the dénouement: the fact that the cathedral was eventually constructed, in 1856–79, not to the designs of the winning architects but in accordance with a composite scheme concocted by one of the judges with the help of one of the defeated competitors. *Perfidia Gallia*? The *Land and Building News* blamed the Ultramontanes and the Emperor.[11] The *Saturday Review* blamed old-fashioned chauvinism.[12] The *Ecclesiologist* put it all down to 'the divided factions of the judges and the executive committee, to political, to national, to ecclesiastical influences, to individual timidity, to corporate unconscientiousness, to *clique* and to backstairs'.[13] Whatever the reason, the Cathedral of Notre Dame de la Treille, ill-starred at its birth and bungled in design, was never completed.[14]

The competition specification left little room for any surprise designs.[15] Each scheme had to include one or two towers surmounted by spires 300 feet high; three portals, a nave and two aisles; a triforium, transepts, choir, sanctuary and apsidal chapels; a lady chapel, baptistery and funeral chapel as well as sacristies and meeting rooms. Inside, the programme specified a full range of Gothic fittings: stained glass windows, incised paving, font, stalls, lectern, screens, grilles, organ, confessionals, ambones, and a high altar of painted stone complete with tabernacle and ciborium or baldacchino. Brick was recommended as cheaper than stone. And the cost was not to exceed £120,000 including fittings. Architecture and fittings were to be separately submitted and judged. And in that respect the precise parameters of the Competition Commission could hardly have been better tailored to the talents of at least one joint entry from England: that of Messrs. Clutton and Burges. There was only one snag, apart from the usual trouble with raising money: there was no guarantee that the winning design would in fact be executed.

It was the Commission, composed of seventeen of Lille's leading citizens, who set out the terms of the competition. In this they were advised by the elder Didron and the Abbé Martin. That was as far as the Commission went. Judgement was delegated to a separate jury. Now the jury consisted of six well-known Goths: de Contencin, the French Directeur-Général des Cultes; Lemaistre D'Anstaig, who had been responsible for the restoration of Tournay; Arcisse de Caumont, the lexicographer of Gothic; the elder Didron; the Abbé Martin (1801–56), editor of *Mélanges Archéologiques*; and Reichensperger, 'the Montalembert of Prussia'. Beresford-Hope declined. Alas, all six were pundits rather than architects. In the early stages, at least, Didron was the key figure. It was he who suggested the competition. It was he who fixed upon early thirteenth-century as the style,[16] and he who – as editor of *Annales Archéologiques* – joined with Beresford-Hope – the power behind the *Ecclesiologist* – to publicise the competition at European level. But there were no practising architects on the jury. Supplementary advice had to be sought from Questel (architect in charge of Versailles); from Danjoy (architect in charge of Coutances); and from E. W. Pugin, who happened to be in Lille at the appropriate moment.[17] According to Didron, it was the architects, rather than the archaeologists, who carried the day for Clutton and Burges.

Of the 41 entries, 15 were French, 14 English and 8 German, plus one each from Scotland, Holland, Belgium and Luxembourg. From the start – despite their pledge of 'entire fair play' – the Commission had been obviously inclined to choose a Frenchman, a Catholic, and preferably a Lillois. But the jury awarded first prize to 'Foederis Arca' ['Ark of the Covenant'] by Clutton and Burges [18–19; 29a]; second prize to 'Quam dilecta tabernacula tua Domine virtutum' ['How glorious are thy tabernacles, O Lord of might'] by G. E. Street; and third prize to 'L'Eclecticisme est la plaie de l'art' ['Eclecticism is the plague of art'] by J. B. A. Lassus. Of the nineteen awards – three prizes, seven medals, nine credits – English architects took eight.[18] The result was indeed 'an extraordinary compliment to English art'.[19] 'At Lille', confessed Didron, 'the architecture and archaeology of France have met with their Agincourt.'[20] French pride had been mortally wounded. Aymer Verdier and Lassus, in particular, started to intrigue in earnest.[21] There was talk of the French Government – who in any case would have to pay for the bulk of the work – recalling the competition to Paris. The French competitors pressed for a second exhibition in Paris to redeem their honour. Failing in that, they managed to exhibit their designs privately in Lille, after the result had been announced – this time excluding all English entrants.

In the end French honour was compromised rather than saved by a devious strategem: the Commission rejected the decision of the jury, placed the matter back in the hands of the Abbé Martin, and encouraged him to prepare a new design, on the basis of several winning schemes, to be executed by a young competitor who, though defeated, was at least a local boy – Charles Leroy (d. 1879).[22] The architectural world exploded: instead of 'the chivalric spirit of the thirteenth century', the competition had been conducted in an atmosphere of intrigue and 'blarney'.[23] 'What we have won in the open battle field,' announced the *Ecclesiologist*, 'we have lost in the cabinet, not to say the *coulisses*. Intrigue has done its work.'[24] The *Building News* described the whole affair as a monument to 'injustice, bad faith and intolerance'.[25] Beresford-Hope protested in vain.[26] The 'hodge podge' design of Martin, Leroy, Clutton, Burges and Street went ahead.[27]

Now Didron had recommended Normandy and Picardy as a suitable hunting-ground for Early French prototypes.[28] Clutton and Burges knew the area well. In mass, horizontality and much of its detail, 'Foederis Arca' derived from Noyon. Noyon too supplied the conical chapel roofs and – with a touch of Montreale in Burgundy[29] – the cartwheel transept windows. But it was Châlons-sur-Marne which provided close precedents for those soaring twin spires, diapered with lead and bristling with pinnacles.[30] The mighty rose window was perhaps a conflation of Châlons, Laon and Braisne.[31] From Chartres came the Western doors and the spread of the apsidal chapels; from Notre-Dame de Paris the gallery above the Western portal; from Rheims the doorway embrasures and sacristies, the paired lancets and spirelets; from Amiens the porches and central flèche;[32] from Laon the serried niches. From the transepts of St-Jacques, Rheims, came the galleries and clerestory;[33] from Châlons, Chartres, Soissons and Auxerre came the basic proportions of the nave arcades.[34] As for iconography, from Amiens and Basle came the theme of the North window sculpture: 'La Vie Humaine' or 'La Roue de Fortune'; from Rheims, the theme of much of the interior sculpture: 'La Divine Liturgie'.[35]

All these sources were very well known to Burges. But as regards the exterior, at least, Clutton seems to have had an equal say. Their drawings are joint productions. It was the Houses of Parliament competition all over again, with Burges playing Pugin to Clutton's Barry. At Hatherop church, in 1855, Burges seems to have been responsible for details in the mortuary chapel: bands of richly foliated carving, grotesque gargoyles, stumpy columns and perhaps stained glass. The same must also have been true at Dunstall church, Staffs., and St John, Limehouse. In the latter church, however, the design of the sculptured Jesse Tree tympanum was striking enough to convince any observer that a major talent had arrived on the architectural scene.[36] In all these early works, Burges is content to play second fiddle. Not so at Lille. The exterior is a joint work. Inside, Burges ruled. And here the prototypes are not only French but Italian. The figured paving in the sanctuary and choir derived from St Remi at Rheims, from Canterbury, Amiens, Siena and St-Omer;[37] the maze in the nave derived from Chartres, St-Quentin, Rheims and Amiens. The confessionals[176] recalled late thirteenth-century armoires at Noyon and Bayeux. The organ[177] was lettered in the manner of Wilars de Honecort, and painted with allegories – the King of the Air, the four elements, the four winds, the nine muses; Jubal, Pythagoras, David, Orion, St Cecilia, Amphion, Orpheus, etc. – partly derived from manuscripts at Rheims.[38] The retable conjures up memories of Basle, the lectern of Rheims.[39] But the baldacchino is obviously Italian in style; the sculptured pulpit embodies echoes of Siena, Pisa and – most of all – Pistoia; and the stained glass glows with memories not only of Chartres but of Florence. In vain had Lassus flown his anti-eclectic banner.[40] 'Foederis Arca' was a triumph for progressive eclecticism.

Viewed historically, the Lille competition can be seen as a watershed: the moment when the *imprimatur* of ecclesiology was transferred from Decorated to Early French. As Gilbert Scott recalled, it was 'the first occasion on which the Ecclesiological Society's law as regards Middle Pointed was set at nought'.[41] When the drawings were examined by the Ecclesiological Committee in 1856, and again when they went on show in London in 1858, there was no shortage of praise.[42] The victors were English. But in a way it was also a victory for the *Annales Archéologiques* over the *Ecclesiologist*, for Didron over Beresford-Hope. At first the pundits of the Ecclesiological Society were rather taken aback.[43] They preferred Street's design, stylistically later in its detail and less dogmatic in its conception. 'Foederis Arca' was 'rather austerely conceived', with 'ungainly and underdeveloped forms'. The sculptured choir screens were a trifle archaic. The four-bay nave was over-short; its conception almost too 'broad and massive'. 'The general effect is grandiose but one regrets constantly that some of the rudeness and eccentricity of a too early style have not been abandoned'. But Burges's fittings won them over. Every sheet of drawing was a *tour de force*, a triumph of re-creative archaeology. In the curious words of the jury's verdict, the drawings displayed not only 'fertility of invention' but 'the abundant sap of a living poetry'.[44] Maybe that multi-storey 'New Jerusalem' font was 'grotesque' enough to grace the Benedictional of St Ethelwold.[45] Maybe that organ, towered, battlemented and painted, was 'needlessly archaic'. But on the whole the 'ameublement' was admired without exception. In particular, the richness of the baldacchino[95] was irresistible: glittering with 'coloured mosaics, jewellery, and a *repoussé* retable, of gilt metal, after the old Basle type'.[46] The composition might be heavy. But the decoration – what the *Ecclesiologist* called its 'symbolical and hieratic art' – carried the day. That had been the jury's opinion, and the opinion of no less a critic than César Daly as well.[47] That, evidently, was Didron's opinion too: the real quality of the scheme lay in its iconography.[48] Didron did not approve of the closed screen on liturgical grounds, but there was no denying its sculptural impact.[49] And as for that extraordinary organ, it inspired at least one of Burges's followers – William Emerson – as well as one young architect of genius: Richard Norman Shaw.[50] With his drawings for the decoration of Lille Cathedral, Burges's reputation as the outstanding artist-architect of his generation had been established.[51]

So the Lille commission was lost. The winning designs were not even published: no seductive perspectives had been allowed. But details of 'Foederis Arca' echo down the years in a number of Burges's schemes. The cartwheel window in the transept reappears at Cork, and again at Lowfield Heath. The lectern eventually made its début at Cork, the reredos at St Michael's, Brighton. The spires reappear – tantalisingly – in another winning but unexecuted scheme: St Mary's Cathedral, Edinburgh. The *flèche* appears again at Cardiff Castle. The confessionals[52] are eventually transmogrified into painted furniture at Tower House. The stern lancets and richly sculptured bands reappear at Waltham Abbey. And the organ appears again at Cork – in a preparatory scheme at least. Burges's Lille drawings may have been unexecuted, but they did not remain unused. Designed to grace an industrial town in Northern France, they became instead – *faute de mieux* – a seed-bed of ideas for the future.

THE CRIMEA MEMORIAL CHURCH, CONSTANTINOPLE

The idea of a national Crimean memorial was launched at a meeting in London on 28 April 1856. The memorial was to take the form of an Anglican church, built in Constantinople, on a site presented by the Sultan. As at Lille, there was to be an international competition. This time there were five judges: the Bishop of Ripon; Sir Charles Anderson Bt.; George Peacock, Dean of Ely (a friend of Beresford-Hope); Professor Robert Willis; and Beresford-Hope himself. Inevitably, Willis and Hope emerged as key figures. The Society for the Propagation of the Gospel was charged with guardianship of the funds. Instructions to competitors were issued on 4 June.[53] Designs were to be submitted by 1 January 1857. There were forty-six entries, all of them English apart from two Frenchmen, four Germans and one American. The results were announced on 3 February.[54] As at Lille, Burges – under the motto *Vita Nuova* – was placed first, and Street second.[55] In 1857–8 the winning designs[20; 21–22; 30a] were exhibited in London three times over: at the Royal Academy;[56] at the Architectural Exhibition Society's Gallery in Suffolk St; and at King's College, London.[57] On 19 October 1858 Lord Stratford de Redcliffe laid the foundation stone.[58] Burges was there.[59] But, ominously, his name was missing from the inscription.[60] When the Crimea Memorial Church was eventually built in 1864–8, it was built to designs by G. E. Street.[61].

The instructions issued by the Memorial Church Committee had stipulated: 'the designs must be a modification to suit the climate, of the recognised ecclesiastical architecture of Western Europe, known as "Pointed" or "Gothic". . . . Numerous and beautiful instances . . . of this modification [exist] in Southern Europe. . . . Any approximation to the specific features of Byzantine architecture is prohibited. . . . Still more [so] . . . the imitation of any forms connected with the religious architecture of the Mohametans. . . . [But out of deference to Islamic taboos] no representations of the human form, or the forms of animal life, are to be introduced, either externally or internally.' The cost was limited to £20,000. Finally, architects were reminded of the availability of local marbles, and the incidence of earthquakes in the neighbourhood.[62]

Such instructions were only superficially precise. Was the church to be primarily a memorial to English soldiers? Or was it – in the words of Professor Willis – a 'manifesto . . . of the Anglican Church . . . on the borders of the Bosphorus', a home for stranded Anglicans, marooned 'in the far-off territory of the Turk'.[63] The site itself had yet to be chosen. And the nominated style clearly gave competitors considerable latitude: was it to be English, French, Italian or Islamic? Burges decided on a synthesis of all four.

The climate of Constantinople clearly ruled out the broad tracery and rich mouldings of English Decorated. The sterner Gothic of Southern France would be more appropriate. And most suitable of all would be the narrow windows, clear surfaces and patterned polychromy of medieval Italy. It was to Italy, therefore, that Burges went for inspiration – at least in the first instance.

Burges claimed that his Crimea design was based on the church of San Andrea at Vercelli, a building recently illustrated by Grüner,[64] and a building he made a point of visiting.[65] He chose San Andrea as a model because the circumstances of its construction corresponded closely to those of the Crimea Memorial Church. It had been built in the thirteenth century in Italy. But – according to legend – it had been built by English workmen and English money.[66] It therefore combined the Gothic of Northern and Southern Europe. Its 'foliage and mouldings retain their northern nature, for the climate little influences these: but the windows become more narrow to keep out the excess of light; the roofs are lower, to suit the local tiles; the walls are of brick, with bands of stone to relieve the somewhat sombre colour; and, lastly, the different coloured stones and marbles are employed on the façade with the same readiness with which an artist would apply the colours of his palette'.[67]

At the very least, Vercelli supplied Burges with models for gable, cornice and roof line. It also gave him the idea of a free-standing campanile, skewed out at an angle from the body of the church. Vercelli had, however, one identifiably English feature: a square East end. This Burges did not follow. He chose instead to adopt a characteristically French plan: an apsidal chancel and ambulatory. This enabled him to stamp his design with the lineaments of Early French. The arcades opening from the choir into the ambulatory, for example, were inspired by Beauvais.[68] The 'chevet' itself recalled Notre Dame in Paris.[69] And the rose window and angle pinnacles were also obviously Gallic motifs. Together they more than counterbalanced the Venetian billet-moulds around the ambulatory windows. Only one source had been recognisably translated from England to Turkey: the trefoiled triforium of New Shoreham church.[70] And only one German source was suggested for the interior of the double-columned apse: the Church of Heisterback, near the Drachenfels on the Rhine.[71] On the whole, French and Italian Gothic formed the matrix of the design. There were to be two distinctly Constantinopolitan features, however: firstly a projecting penthouse, shading the triple portals of the Western front; and secondly a separate tower which – bearing in mind Turkish hostility to the sound of bells – was cunningly designed to recall in its appearance both an Italian campanile and the look-out of the *muezzin*.

Burges's design, therefore, was necessarily Western in origin. But in its structure and materials his church set out to adapt itself to, and express, its Eastern locality. The effect of earthquakes was to be minimised not by thickening walls and buttresses but by tying the building together with a system of tie-rods and chains. To lighten the load and diminish the thrust, vaults were to be filled with light concrete, like that used at Salisbury Cathedral and in the cloisters at Rouen. The core of the walls was to be black rubble limestone. The facings were to be of terracotta and brick, or white and blue-black masonry. These coloured materials were themselves to be coloured: by decoration with glass mosaics exported from London, and with mastic-filled incisions executed on the spot. The roof was to be constructed of spruce fir from the shores of the Black Sea. Inside, the dado of Marmora marble was to be inscribed – in the manner of Assyrian palaces – with the names of every officer and man who fell in the Crimean War. The same marble – cloudy white in colour – was to be carved in the capitals of the columns and the tracery of the windows. The columns themselves were to be of red Balaclava marble with gilded capitals. Eventually, Burges hoped, the interior was to be filled with 'the local arts of mosaic and marqueterie, for which the Orientals have, in all ages, been famous'. Meanwhile, the vaulting ribs were to be of banded stone and terracotta; the bosses carved and gilt. Glass mosaic and mastic patterns were to chequer the blind triforium with colour. The windows were to be 'filled with very thick sea-green glass, disposed in grisaille patterns on a cross-hatched ground'. The nave pavement was to be of white Italian marble; that in the choir might well be richer: either *Opus Alexandrinum* or else incised marble along the lines of Siena Cathedral. 'The monumental aisle round the apse', Burges concluded, 'is studded with small windows, so as to produce the effect of a crown of light round the more sacred portion of the edifice. In the nave, on the contrary, there is ... very little light, no less than three of the aisle windows being suppressed ... by ... the vestry, and ... by ... the porch.'[72]

Burges's synthesis did not please everybody. Some thought it insufficiently speluncar – that is, insufficiently dark and cave-like for a semi-tropical climate.[73] The judges themselves took exception to Burges's Early Christian baldacchino.[74] The *Ecclesiologist* thought the whole scheme 'thoroughly un-English', and much preferred the 'unmodified Teutonism' of Street's design. An English memorial should be neither French nor Italian, nor Byzantine. Burges's design was not only 'quasi-Pointed' and Romanesque in flavour. It suffered from excessive 'horizontalism'. It was, in fact, just the sort of church 'one might find on the shores of the Adriatic'.[75] Certainly Burges's perspective presentation, aligned on a domed mosque and thronged with figures in Turkish garb, emphasised the Oriental context of the commission.[76] Certainly his details were un-English. But by combining an aisled nave with a monumental apse he neatly satisfied the dual requirements of community church and memorial chapel. Anyway, the *Saturday Review* admired the catholicity of the exterior.[77] And the interior – as the *Building News* observed – actually managed to be 'Oriental without being Mohammedan, and ... Christian without being idolatrous'.[78]

Within a year of winning the competition, Burges had been forced to modify his design. Not until a year after the announcement of the award was a site procured on land presented by the Sultan – high up on the Pera side of Constantinople, overlooking the Bosphorus and Scutari. Forced in any case to adapt his plan to a sloping site, Burges seems also to have been caught out by an inflation in Turkish prices.[79] For the sake of economy he agreed to lop off the Southern transept and the flying buttresses of the ambulatory, as well as one or two bays of the nave.[80][23] In 1859 the work was reported to be in hand.[81] But in 1860 there came a further call for the 'retrenchment' of the clerestory.[82] That was the year in which work was said to be 'really in hand', and contracts were drawn up promising completion by 1863.[83] The following May work actually did begin, and completion was promised inside two years.[84] By now the judges of the Memorial Committee had been reinforced by James Fergusson, and Willis had retired in favour of J. G. Talbot. Between 1856 and 1861 Burges produced three, if not four, modifications of his original design.[85] First the nave had six bays, then five, then four, then three; and then two bays plus a triple-columned narthex modelled on St-Germain l'Auxerrois.[86][24] The portals were reduced from three to one. Ribbed groin-vaulting was replaced by cheaper Roman groining without ribs, surrounded by barrel-vaulting which was cheaper still. But in 1863 even this drastically modified design was turned down by the S.P.G.[87] Burges had economised enough, and would clearly go no further. In 1866, therefore, Street was called upon to produce a totally new design. Even his minimalist performance was not completed until 1868. The whole affair, as one correspondent to the *Builder* put it, had been 'a mystery and a muddle from the beginning'.[88]

Burges's final plan took the form of a simple horseshoe, tight and muscular.[89][30a] By paring down his original dream he produced a design of manifest solidity and power. But the polychrome flush was missing. Monochrome Early French turned out to be cheapest of all. English parsimony – as well as 'Turkish chicanery'[90] – deprived Burges of one of the best chances of his career. According to Pullan, the final straw came when he was asked to forgo his stone vaulting.[91] He had to rest content with his original £100 prize, plus £150 for modifications, plus $2\frac{1}{2}\%$ on the final design of 1863.[92]

In the context of Burges's own *oeuvre*, his first Crimean design stands out in at least one respect: never again did he indulge in so much polychromy. Horizontal bands in red and white Marmora marble, diapered patterns in blue, black, white and red, brilliant glazed tiles, ribbed voussoirs, geometrical devices, mosaic, *sgraffiti*, *intarsiatura* – 'Vita Nuova' was Ruskinian almost to excess.[93] Far away in Constantinople, Burges clearly felt at liberty to outdo Butterfield. On home ground his exterior designs suggest that he preferred a more sombre palette. With the sole exceptions of Fleet church and the Harrow Speech Room, he henceforth consistently avoided structural colouration. Between 1856 and 1863, his Crimea scheme became smaller and cheaper; more French and less Italian; harder, sterner and self-consciously plainer. In that respect Burges echoed the changing predilections of his own generation. Ruskin had been supplemented by Viollet-le-Duc.

BRISBANE, EDINBURGH AND TRURO CATHEDRALS

Lille had been a crushing disappointment, Constantinople a long-drawn fiasco. By comparison, the Brisbane episode came as something of an anticlimax. The first Bishop of Brisbane was appointed in 1859. And it was in that year, thanks to the Ecclesiological Society, that Burges was commissioned to prepare designs.[94] The scheme was at most conjectural. And it was not until 1867 that building began – not to Burges's designs, but to those of D. W. Ryan.[95]

For Brisbane, Burges chose Early French again, but Early French adapted to the semi-tropical heat of Northern Australia.[25 ; 29b] Now there were two theories of tropical church design current in the mid-Victorian period: the permeable (draught-admitting) and the speluncar (cave-like). For Colombo, in Ceylon, in 1847, R. C. Carpenter chose the first of these methods. At Brisbane Burges chose the second. The result was a design which shared a few of the characteristics of both Lille and Constantinople. Nave and aisles; short transepts; a saddle-back bell tower on the South West; an apsidal choir and apsidal North and South chapels; cartwheel windows; geometrical tracery; massive piers and square abaci; stumpy columns; broad buttresses; low roofline: the elements of Early French are there, but simplified to the point of primitivism.[96] Semi-tropical conditions supplied an excuse to exaggerate the naturally massive forms of the style. The saddle-back tower echoed Bièville, near Caen in Normandy – a precedent he had learned from Clutton at Hatherop. Across the West front, as at Notre-Dame de Paris, were to run a series of royal statues ('Queensland') set in a trefoiled arcade. But the clerestory and triforium have been thrown into one, arcaded, round-windowed band: 'a masterstroke', commented the *Ecclesiologist*.[97] The walls are four feet thick. And the resulting depth of shadow across the window bays accentuates the cathedral's cave-like character. As in the Lille and Crimea designs, however, there are one or two hints from south of the Alps. The ceiling of the nave, coved and boarded, with massive tie-beams – designed to separate roof and ceiling with a volume of cooling air – turned out to be Burges's first essay on an Italian theme which soon became almost a signature-tune. The pulpit, raised on minatory hounds, was a gargantuan version of a Pistoian precedent: Durandus, after all, had likened an effective preacher to a barking dog.

'Solid and massive' indeed; 'bold and original' even.[98] The architect, wrote one critic, 'is not an ordinary man but one who from the fact of having thoroughly mastered what he attempts, has the boldness to throw aside the trammels which are too often allowed to embarrass the architectural designer, and is thereby enabled to produce legitimate and genuine originality'.[99] Perhaps. But even the faithful Pullan thought Brisbane 'the least satisfactory of his ecclesiastical designs'; its proportions 'squat' and its gabled tower 'heavy'.[1] The *Builder* was also hostile, but for the wrong reasons: the windows were minuscule, and the mouldings archaic; 'the elevations appear as if copied from an old manuscript'.[2] But then the *Builder* was still looking for that elusive Victorian style. Burges had settled for a tropical adaptation of thirteenth-century Gothic. And Brisbane Cathedral, had it seen the light of day, would certainly have been a curiosity: a cathedral church for a semi-tropical colony, in semi-speluncar Early French.

Burges's chance to create a great Gothic cathedral came, of course, at Cork. But towards the end of his short career, he had two other opportunities: at Edinburgh and Truro.

Unlike Lille and Cork, the Edinburgh competition was limited, limited to six architects: three English and three Scots. Such symmetry was, however, more apparent than real. In the first place, St Mary's was to be Episcopalian, not Church of Scotland. Anglicanism was therefore in the air. In the second place, an English assessor was appointed, namely Ewan Christian. In the third place, the three Scottish entrants were comparative lightweights: Lessels of Edinburgh; Peddie and Kinnear; and Alexander Ross of Inverness. The three Englishmen were all heavyweight Goths: Scott, Street and Burges.

The eclecticism of Early French was certainly apparent in all the leading entries. Ross's clerestory echoed the Ste. Chapelle; his Western spires were modelled on Notre Dame, Etampes – via Burges's Cork Cathedral and T. H. King's invaluable *Study Book*.[3] Street's clerestory recalled Notre Dame, Dijon.[4] For his spires Burges went to Noyon; for his flèche to Amiens; for his transept gables to Ely; for his plan to Sens and Langres, Dijon and Lisieux – a plan he himself used before at Cork and Constantinople.[5] But it was Scott, doyen of so many competitions, who hit upon the winning combination. Some saw in his designs several 'old French friends' like Coutances Cathedral and St-Aubin, Angers. That may well have been so. What is certain, however, is that for his plan he went to Ely; for his lancets to York; for his mouldings to Dunblane and Elgin; for the bulk of his nave to Glasgow; for his Chapter House to Margam Abbey; and for his soaring central spire to Chartres and Senlis.[6] Such a dazzling display of erudition clearly 'captivated the good folk of Edinburgh'.[7] If the London Law Courts competition marked the climax of Gothic eclecticism in the secular sphere, then the competition for St Mary's, Edinburgh might be said to hold much the same position in ecclesiastical design.

But by choosing Scott, the Episcopalians of Edinburgh played safe. Street's design was more like a parish church than a cathedral. Scott's was a cathedral alright, but a cathedral dedicated to the goddess of caution. Burges's design might well have proved a masterpiece.[8][26; 27; 29d] Pullan thought it the best of his ecclesiastical designs.[9] Lighter than Cork, simpler than Lille, subtler than Brisbane, it embodies all Burges's experience in full-scale Gothic design. At the time critics were unanimous in praising its originality, balance and force. Years later they regretted bitterly that St Mary's,

Edinburgh – sublimest of all his Gothic dreams – had remained unbuilt.[10] As Ewan Christian put it, 'Mr Burges's designs were all remarkable; but . . . that was a lovely one'.[11]

Whether Truro would have equalled Edinburgh as Burges's best unbuilt cathedral it is quite impossible to say. His design was never completed, let alone submitted. In 1878 eight architects were invited to submit drawings: St Aubyn, Bodley and Garner, Burges, Pearson, Pullan, J. O. Scott, Street and J. M. Brydon. But the drawings they were invited to display were not necessarily to be for Truro Cathedral. Only St Aubyn, Bodley and Pullan prepared drawings expressly for the purpose.[12] And none of these proved to be the winner: the prize went to J. L. Pearson.

Fragmentary sketches[13] suggest that Burges was thinking of an orthodox thirteenth-century composition – two West end towers, three portals and a crossing spire – enlivened by a free use of sculptural ornament. The reredos at least would have been an impressive display of sculptural pyrotechnics.[14]

The Chapter House, Salisbury Cathedral

If he could not build new cathedrals, Burges might at least restore old ones. And two of his early works were important instances of restoration.

Restoration of the Chapter House at Salisbury had been recognised as necessary in 1843.[15] But apart from a survey by T. H. Wyatt, nothing was done until 1854. In that year the project was revived as a memorial to Bishop Denison. Clutton was the architect chosen, and he immediately staked his claim as an authority by reading a paper on chapter houses to the Wiltshire Archaeological Society.[16] But he needed an assistant, an art-architect to deal with iconography and polychromy. Burges was the man.

When Clutton and Burges began work in 1855 the Chapter House was 'neglected . . . ruinous . . . delapidated and even dangerous'.[17] The whole structure, as Burges put it, 'had got a twist'.[18] The central column had lurched five inches out of perpendicular. The Norman tiles, supposedly brought from the Cathedral of Old Sarum, had been broken and scattered. And the 'greater part' of the stained glass had been 'used to fill up the city ditch, in the time of J. Wyatt Esq'.[19]

The first stage of work – largely structural, and supervised by Clutton – was completed by July 1856. Work on the vestibule, and the bulk of the sculpture and polychromy, had yet to be begun. Even so, nearly £5000 had already been spent.[20] The windows alone would cost another £1607.[21] These were not finally installed until 1860, executed by Ward and Hughes, under the direction of Gilbert Scott. Their grisaille glass in pale, geometrical patterns, excluded heraldic images and followed, therefore, only half of Burges's recommendations. For Burges had been involved in the decorative part of the work since the start.[22] In particular, he had been responsible for the restoration of the sculpture, and for the design of a mosaic pavement for the vestibule.[23] It was in the autumn of 1856 that Clutton decided to become a Roman

Catholic.[24] That decision made his position at Salisbury impossible. His consequent resignation, however, threw the commission not into Burges's eager hands, but into the capacious grasp of Gilbert Scott. Hence the fact that Burges's part in the restoration programme is so confusingly documented.

Architecturally, Burges thought the Salisbury Chapter House not quite 'up to the mark ... of Westminster, Canterbury, or Wells'. Iconographically, however, it was almost unique: 'one of the very few illustrations of English iconography which have escaped the violence of the Puritan'. Its sculpture and stained glass had been arranged in three broad themes. The vestibule sculptures represented the triumph of the Seven Virtues over the Seven Vices, that is the oft-repeated epic of the Psychomachia of Prudentius. The Chapter House arcades contained no less than sixty sculptural representations of the Old Testament cycle, from the Creation of the Universe to Moses' Receipt of the Decalogue. And above these, in the eight windows of the Chapter House, shone the Angelic Liturgy and the armorial bearings of royal and noble benefactors. Sufficient evidence remained for Burges to tabulate these themes in detail: a considerable body of partially mutilated sculpture; a few fragments of stained glass, redistributed elsewhere in the cathedral; and vestigial indications of a full-scale programme of polychromy. Using related evidence in illuminated manuscripts – notably Queen Mary's Psalter, Bib. Reg. 2 B VII – he was able to reconstruct most of the sculptural details as a prelude to restoration. The story of Joseph's Dream in Queen Mary's Psalter 'came in most usefully for the restoration of the missing feet, arms, costume, weapons, utensils, etc'.[25]

Here of course, was the nub of the problem. How accurate, indeed how justifiable, was such a recreative process? Clutton had admitted that the restoration of the arcades would be 'to some extent arbitrary'.[26] In the West and North West arcades only the silhouettes of figures survived as evidence. Inevitably there were critics who feared for the 'integrity' of the fabric.[27] Yet both the *Builder* and the *Ecclesiologist* supported the whole scheme to the hilt.[28] In one particular case – the sculpture at the base of the central pillar, for which Burges suggested as 'a guess' the saga of Reynard the Fox – the original mutilated marble was preserved in the cloister so that posterity could judge the accuracy of his reconstruction. Comparing both items today, the most neutral adjective that comes to mind is 'imaginative'. Yet given the assumption of the age – the prevailing ethos of creative restoration – what else should we expect? The leading pundits were unanimous. 'These reliefs', the *Ecclesiologist* explained, 'were in many places so obliterated and decayed that little remained in many places but the impressions ... of the shadows of the departed statuettes on the wall. Considerable ingenuity ... has been displayed in recreating a group from the disjected members of a single head or foot .... Perhaps we are not wrong in thinking that Mr Burges's well known archaeological knowledge has been brought to aid in these cunning recreations.'[29] 'Mr Burges', nodded the *Gentleman's Magazine*, 'has thoroughly mastered ... the study of Iconography ... and has brought to bear upon it a degree of learning and research which few could equal.'[30] 'The restoration', *The Guardian* concluded firmly, 'is not conjectural but is undoubtedly a facsimile of the original design.'[31] At the very least, in 1855, Burges had recorded meticulously all fragments of colour and sculpture prior to restoration. His tabular programme of the building's polychromy and carving survives, therefore, as an indispensable document for the student of medieval iconography.[32]

Two artists assisted Burges in the Chapter House restoration: the sculptor J. B. Philip (1824–75) and the painter Octavius Hudson. Salisbury Cathedral was one of Philip's earliest commissions. He went on to execute the reredos at both Ely and the Chapel Royal, Windsor, and ended with what must surely rank as a triple blue for any Victorian sculptor: statues decorating the Houses of Parliament, the Royal Academy and the Albert Memorial.[33] His daughter Beatrice even managed to marry first Godwin and then Whistler. Hudson's career was rather less meteoric. But under Burges's direction, Philip and Hudson had at least produced a more than interesting exercise in the revived polychromy.[138] Minton tiles in floor and arcading followed original Norman patterns; the central column of Purbeck marble was 'polished up to a lustrous glass, and the light vaulted roof . . . garlanded . . . with an elegant wreath of painted foliage, an exact revival of the original colouring, with gilded tufts at the inter-section of the ribs'. 'The walls of the arcade', the guide book explained, 'are diapered in rich and harmonious colours, and profusely embellished with *fleurs-de-lis*, birds and various devices similar to those on the pavement. The marble shafts dividing the niches are polished to a "silvery lustre", and the gilded foliage of their capitals shines out with a most splendid effect. The arch-mouldings of the canopies re-appear in their primitive hues; and the judicious application of colours and gilding to the sculptures has been attended with the happy effect of rendering the grouping more distinct, and imparting additional animation and expression to the figures of the frieze . . . The . . . windows . . . are glazed with richly diapered glass, the tracery . . . being relieved by some figures in brilliant colours . . . [Even] the ancient [round] table of the Chapter House [has been] restored at the cost of the late Miss Wickins of the Close.'[34]

Apart from the round table, the greater part of that description must now be transposed into the past tense. As early as 1874 Hudson's paint was beginning to flake. Towards the end of the century the Minton tiles in the arcading were removed along with the rest of the lower polychromy. Half a century later worse vandalism took place. In the main body of the cathedral Scott's reredos, screen and chancel paving were torn out in 1959–60. Then in 1966–7 the Dean and Chapter decided to expel the stained-glass windows of the Chapter House. Two windows were thrown down before the operation was cut short by public outrage.[35] Alas, the coherence and harmony of that 'noble and luminous octagon'[36] had been destroyed. The Chapter House at Salisbury survives, therefore, as a medieval torso. But the incrustations of mid-Victorian scholarship and taste, which once made it a doubly valuable document, have largely vanished.

WALTHAM ABBEY

Burges's first contact with Waltham Abbey was tantalising. 'Had a chance at Waltham', he noted in his diary for 1853, but 'Poynter got it.'[37] It was not until 1859 that the *Ecclesiologist* was able to announce with satisfaction: 'Mr Burges has been called in to restore that noble architectural fragment.'[38]

Ambrose Poynter's contribution had been limited to the restoration of the West portal and the Western end of the South aisle.[39] The great eleventh-century church – last resting place of Harold, King of the Saxons – approached its octocentenary in a state of miserable decay. Truncated in the sixteenth century, barbarously cut up in the eighteenth, the fabric was plainly in need of help.[40] But help did not necessarily mean the same thing as restoration. 'With regard to the . . . nave', Burges explained in 1859, 'I should totally deprecate any attempt at what is called restoration, i.e. I should not attempt to restore the vaulting or the filling-in of the triforium, or to raise the roof to its ancient pitch. An architectural fragment of [this] interest should, it appears to me, be kept as a fragment, and as untouched as possible beyond the necessary structural repairs.'[41] What was immediately necessary was the removal of all pews and galleries on the West and South; and the strengthening of the damaged piers of the nave, one pier in particular having to be rebuilt.[42] There could be little controversy on that score. Much more contentious was the next phase: the insertion of a new ceiling; the rebuilding of the North aisle and the South clerestory; the rescue of the Lady Chapel; and – most of all – the construction of a new chancel.

For the ceiling of the nave Burges chose Peterborough as his model, and young E. J. Poynter as his artist.[43] But the thirteenth-century Peterborough prototype has been simplified. Poynter's twenty-nine canvases, set in lozenge-shaped panels, represent 'The Economy of the World': the Four Elements, the Past and Future, the Signs of the Zodiac and the Labours of the Months.[44] Their reticulated setting, painted by Campbell,[45] deftly multiplies the vista of the nave without losing lateral tension. The *Ecclesiologist* had no complaints.[46] And the result certainly pleased both Freeman[47] and Lethaby.[48]

It was the chancel at Waltham which was really the problem. Thanks to the vandalism of the Reformation period, there was in fact no Eastern focus at all, merely a crude filling-in of the chancel arch.

> The East end [Burges explained][49] is in a very unsatisfactory state, being lighted by a large ugly square window. The question then arises, what would be the best thing to do with this Eastern wall. Now there are two courses open, viz. either to fill it with a composition in the Norman style, so as to accord with the rest of the building, or to do as an architect would have done in the Middle Ages, and indeed in every age except our own, viz. to fill it with a composition of the most beautiful architecture known to us. After much consideration, I am inclined to lean to the latter course, for the following reasons.

1st. By having the east end in a different style, the extent of the old work will be visible to the most superficial spectator, and nobody, either now or hereafter, will be deceived as to the extent of the old work.

2nd. It will show the church to be what it is, a fragment of a larger one, for it will then have no pretensions to completeness.

3rd. Nothing will then be restored or made good for which there is not ample authority in the church itself.

As the architecture of the early half of the thirteenth century is now universally considered the best, I should therefore propose to make the new East window in that style. . . . [Throughout] I have been guided by one great consideration, viz. to destroy no old work and to add nothing of my own but what is absolutely necessary, and even then to do it in a manner so that it would be easily distinguished from the old work.

Above all, he concludes, 'the history of the building [should be allowed] to show itself'. In other words, Burges's approach was the same as Gilbert Scott's at Kirkstall Abbey, Leeds: the result should indicate that the fabric 'has been a *ruin* and has been restored'.[50] The difference was that Scott reported in 1873, Burges in 1859. No wonder E. W. Godwin referred to Burges's report as 'a model'.[51]

Burges probably began work on his design for the East end at Waltham in 1859.[52][33] Next year he revealed his proposal to the Architectural Exhibition Society.[53] And in the following year, soon after its structure had been completed, he exhibited his design at the Royal Academy.[54] The reredos, however, took fifteen years longer. An engraving published in 1861 shows an earlier, much simpler scheme.[55] Nicholls' final cartoon, and a model of its central section – a Nativity flanked by the Shepherds and the Magi – formed a high-point of the Medieval Court at the 1862 Exhibition.[56] At this stage only one of the figures had been carved in alabaster and coloured.[57] Further designs for the Eastern wall were exhibited at the Paris Exhibition of 1867,[58] and again – in the form of Cole's final perspective – at the Architectural Exhibition of 1870.[59] Installation of the reredos, with the Annunciation and the Flight into Egypt added to left and right, was not completed until 1876.[60] But the finished work was worth waiting for. Modelled by Nicholls with robustly three-dimensional vigour; coloured and gilt by Charles Campbell of Harland and Fisher, it was indeed a reredos rich and ripe – even by High Victorian standards.[34] Parts of this composition had already been anticipated in a parallel commission: the dossal in All Saints Episcopal Church, Edinburgh.[61][96,97] There the same team cooperated – Burges, Nicholls, Harland and Fisher – and on a similar theme: the Annunciation flanked by Moses and Gideon. Burges explained that he was aiming at a more vigorous style than the much-copied Ghiberti gates at Florence. There is certainly no absence of vigour in either piece. But the Edinburgh dossal is almost too rich for its small-scale setting. At Waltham there is no such difficulty. The peripheral sculpture – scenes from Aesop's

Fables – is equally assertive, and the architectural superstructure positively cyclopean. Punchy columns compressed like flexed muscles; capitals overscaled with uncanny skill; spandrel carvings taut and sinewy. One's gaze is drawn upwards, again and again, past those three muscular lancets, to that great rose window, abstract and compelling – for all the world like the eye of some giant, geometrical cyclops. Burges has caught and distilled the essential sublimity of Early French. At Waltham, High Victorian and Romanesque meet and compete on terms of heroic equality.

But without their stained glass, those windows would be blind. Now the history of the re-glazing of Waltham Abbey is worth unravelling. Not only are the windows fine in themselves, they form part of a much wider story: the High Victorian renaissance of stained glass manufacture. And in that renaissance Burges played an important role.

When Burges reviewed the 1862 Exhibition, he was horrified by most of the stained glass exhibits. 'What horrible juxtapositions of colour', he complained, 'what sharp and glaring tints!' The cramped method of display hardly helped: to appreciate its 'brilliancy', stained glass had to be studied 'at a distance'.[62] Even so, the weakness of much contemporary manufacture was obvious. 'We fill our churches with stained glass which future generations will probably break to pieces.'[63] 'The old work looks like jewels ... the new work resembles a bad kaleidoscope.' 'A really good piece of glass', Burges considered, should 'look, if near to the eye, and of small dimensions, like the windows of jewels we read of in the Arabian Nights, and which we see in reality if we go to Constantinople or Jerusalem. If up high, and composed of large pieces, it [should] look as if chopped out of gigantic sapphires and rubies, as we see in the great Italian churches.'[64] In Florence, the windows of the Duomo were 'made of thick metal ... as if composed of slices of gems'. At the Suleimanyeh in Constantinople the glass was 'as thin as an eggshell', resembling 'a number of small jewels arranged as a pattern'.[65]

Burges experimented with both types, Italian and Oriental. In 1857 he designed a window of Islamic type for the Architectural Exhibition. It was not a success: its network of protruding frames impeded oblique viewing.[66] Burges hoped to see a window of this 'oriental' type placed in Ely Cathedral, that 'museum of stained glass'.[67] But such glazing remained a curiosity. Burges recognised that the future of stained glass lay in a development of West European forms. And here his ideal was the 'jewel-like' glass of the Duomo in Florence. In those 'incomparable' windows, he recalled, 'the colours are few and massed together, yet every one is made up of no end of pieces of different tints of the same colour; these, again, are toned on both sides, but there is very little shading, properly speaking'.[68]

Until the early 1860s, at any rate, Burges had confidence in only four stained glass firms: Powells of Whitefriars, Lavers and Barraud, Clayton and Bell and – to a lesser extent – Heaton, Butler and Bayne. All four contributed to the glorification of Waltham Abbey.

Since the seventeenth century glass-making had been conducted, continuously and successfully, in the Whitefriars Studios between the Thames and Fleet St. James Powell (1774–1840) of Bristol bought the firm in 1834. Ten years later the tax on glass was repealed and business increased rapidly. Between 1852 and 1872 the window department's turnover doubled.[69] Not far away, in lodgings in the Inner Temple, lived Charles Winston (1814–64), a patent lawyer whose amateur interest in medieval windows transformed the production of Victorian stained glass. Winston was a close friend of Burges and well known to the Pre-Raphaelite circle. Burges described him as 'one of the kindest of men and the best of friends' – a friend, moreover, with 'that keen sense of the comic which is generally found in all superior men'.[70] By establishing a systematic classification of medieval glass, Winston made himself a veritable Rickman in his field.[71] Burges likened him to Pugin.[72] Others compared his influence on decorative art to that of Ruskin. Certainly, it was thanks to Winston that the eighteenth-century style of pictorial transparency gave way so universally to the Victorian revival of the mosaic system. Winston, too, was the man whose chemical investigations in the early 1850s – in conjunction with Powell's chemist, Edward Green – reestablished the technology of medieval 'pot metal' glass. It was Winston's discoveries, historical and chemical, which made possible the deep-tinted glory of Powell's best windows. Now Whitefriars and the Temple were within strolling distance of Burges's rooms in Buckingham Street as well as Rossetti's studio in Chatham Place. Burges was Winston's friend, and Rossetti introduced Burne-Jones to Powell. From this triangular relationship emerged some of the finest stained glass of modern times.

The firms of Lavers and Barraud, Clayton and Bell, and Heaton, Butler and Bayne were all formed in the years 1855–58. N. W. Lavers (1822–1911) and F. B. Barraud (1824–1900) were both cartoonists who had worked for Powell's around the time of the Great Exhibition.[73] So had two of Gilbert Scott's assistants, J. R. Clayton (1827–1913) and Alfred Bell (1832–95). Clement Heaton (1824–82), a chemist, joined James Butler (1830–1913), a cartoonist, in 1858; R. T. Bayne (1837–1915), another cartoonist, arrived in 1862.[74] In those heady years, after the repeal of the glass tax, there were so many commissions to be had that easy interchange between rival firms was quite acceptable. Burne-Jones worked for Lavers and Barraud and for Powell's before joining Morris. Both Clayton and Bell also worked at different times for Lavers and Barraud. Heaton, Butler and Bayne shared Clayton and Bell's premises in Cardington St, Euston, before moving into a purpose-built Ruskinian Gothic factory, designed by Arthur Blomfield in King St, Covent Garden.[75] Meanwhile, Lavers and Barraud had set up in equally Ruskinian premises, designed by R. J. Withers, in Endell St, Covent Garden.

With all these firms Burges had close contacts. He probably secured E. J. Poynter his first work at Powell's.[76] It was certainly he who introduced N. H. J. Westlake (1833–1921) – a hungry young artist from Hampshire – to Lavers and Barraud in

1860.[77] Soon afterwards it was he who monitored Holiday's first cartoons for Powell's. On both a personal and a professional level Burges emerges as a pivotal figure in that Pre-Raphaelite revolution which swept over English decorative art – and especially stained glass design – in the mid-nineteenth century. With two firms, however, he had very little connection: Hardman and Co. of Birmingham,[78] and Morris, Marshall, Faulkner and Co. of London.[79] While he would have been the first to acknowledge Pugin's genius, the products of Hardman and Co. – virtually Pugin's family firm – must have seemed too brash and too Perpendicular for Burges by the later 1850s. And although he certainly shared Morris's commitment to the revival of medieval crafts, the stained glass produced by that famous firm (1861 onwards) must have seemed to him increasingly tainted with Renaissance freedom. That was his only cause of disagreement with Winston.[80] It was the nub of his gradual estrangement from Westlake and Holiday. And it was also the reason why he eventually transferred his commitments in stained glass manufacture first to Saunders and Co., and then to Worrall and Co., both firms in whose finances he was more directly interested, and in whose unflinching medievalism he had absolute confidence. W. Gualbert Saunders had arrived in Buckingham St in 1865.[81] With brief interruptions because of ill health,[82] he worked with Burges – or with Burges's satellites, Holiday,[83] Chapple [84] and Lonsdale[85] – for fifteen years. It was probably at Waltham that he executed his first glass for Burges, in 1868. And when he finally left England in 1880,[86] it was his old assistant William Worrall who carried on both the firm and its Burgesian traditions.

By the mid-1850s, therefore, Winston had resuscitated the technique of early medieval glass manufacture. Henceforward pot metal, fired according to ancient prescriptions, formed the basis of the mosaic method. The science was there, but not the art. 'If we look at a modern window', Burges complained in 1861, 'it generally appears to be all right as long as the spectator is just in front of it; but when the said window is put in its place, say at the end of a chancel, where you can obtain a good view, it loses all its transparency, and looks like a painted deal board'. There were two reasons for that: the lack of properly coloured cartoons, marked so as to guide the glazier in his cutting; and a certain monotony of texture in both the colouring and the glazing itself. Before 1862, at least, Burne-Jones was almost unique in supplying finished coloured cartoons for the glass painter. A revival in that sphere, therefore, depended on the emergence of a capable school of cartoonists.[87] As to colouring and glazing, improvement in that field depended on an informal cooperation between artist and manufacturer.

> It is very desirable [Burges believed] to make the background of a highly coloured window of a greyish, greenish blue, so that the brighter glass of the figures may tell out against it, above all to vary the tints of the same colour; i.e. if it is a question of a green garment, to make it up of as many tints of green as possible, and not to cut the whole affair out of the same piece of glass. Again, more variety may be got

by a judicious use of toning, the which toning may be made of the powdered glass, burnt on with a flux; but by far the most valuable results are obtained where the colour varies in the same piece of glass, when, in fact, it is streaky.[88]

Thanks to Winston, Powell's had got the colour right. Their light blue and ruby glass could not be faulted. Their products were even being distributed in the form of uncut glass sheets to other manufacturers. What had yet to be consistently produced was that cloudy, opalescent texture Burges was looking for. To achieve it he had, in effect, to set up his own firm: Saunders and Co.

It was late in 1859, or early in 1860, that Burges chose Westlake to prepare cartoons for an East window at Waltham – probably to be produced by Lavers and Barraud – portraying the death of King Harold.[89] Within a few months, however, the commission had been transferred to Powell's and – more important – to Powell's new cartoonist, Edward Burne-Jones. The reason for the change is unclear. But 1860 was the year of Burne-Jones's glorious 'Annunciation' window at Topcliffe, Yorkshire. It had been prepared at Butterfield's behest. And when that austere architect took exception to the 'sensuous' nature of the Pre-Raphaelite Madonna, Burges gleefully commissioned a second version for his own study in Buckingham St.[90] Now this 'Annunciation' had been produced by Lavers and Barraud. But in 1859 Burne-Jones had also been employed by Powell's on the St Frideswide window at Christ Church, Oxford. Perhaps it was that mesmeric performance which swung Burges in favour of the Powell–Burne-Jones combination. Anyway, at Waltham, Burne-Jones and Powell it was to be. The result was a triumph: some of the finest Pre-Raphaelite glass ever executed.

Burne-Jones prepared his cartoons in 1860–61. Accounts survive for a second version of the central lancet, produced for the 1862 Exhibition. These indicate that Powell's glass painter Grieve must take most of the credit for the actual process of production. He and his daughter spent a total of 401 hours in painting and sorting the glass.[91] The central lancet commemorates the incumbent's sister Elizabeth (d. April 1859); that on the left Louisa Banbury (d. Nov. 1867); and that on the right the incumbent's sister Susanna (d. Oct. 1878). Now it seems unlikely that these three windows were actually installed at such disparate dates. Presumably the incumbent, the Rev James Francis, advanced full payment to Powell's out of his own pocket. More intriguing than the dating, however, is the distribution of responsibility for the design. Morris is reputed to have had a hand in the cartoons.[92] Did Burges? In his diary, at the crucial moment, he notes three guests in immediate sequence: 'Rossetti, Jones E. B., Morris'.[93] It is hard to resist the conclusion that those windows were the subject of some conversation. In the St Frideswide window at Oxford, Burne-Jones's figures overload and fragment the overall design. At Waltham he uses the Jesse Tree almost literally as a framework on which to hang his figures. As a result, the design 'reads' far more coherently. Now the Jesse Tree is a recurrent theme in Burges's *oeuvre*. It appears hardly anywhere else in Burne-Jones's.[94] What could be more natural than for Burges to guide and encourage the young Burne-Jones, just as he did the young Poynter, the young Holiday,[95] the young Westlake, the young Stacy Marks,[96] the young Charles Campbell, and so many others.

Anyway, there is no gainsaying the success of the final product. Burges rightly thought the Waltham windows a great improvement on those at Oxford: 'exceedingly rich and jewel like',[97] he called them; the result of 'perfect material and a first-rate artist'.[98] Perhaps the figures are too small. But from the distance of the nave they dissolve into splashes of pure colour, a cascade of dappled light which gluts the eye and spins the brain. Higher up, Christ rides in abstract majesty, encircled by the Days of Creation. The subjects liquefy into chromatic shapes. Their colours melt in a sea of green and blue. By comparison with contemporary work elsewhere – and comparisons have been made between Burne-Jones's glass at Waltham and windows by Gerente at All Saints, Margaret St,[99] and others by Ingres at Dreux and Neuilly[1] – these windows are indeed extraordinary.

The rest of the stained glass at Waltham Abbey was mostly destroyed in the Blitz. Before that catastrophe, however, there were examples of windows made by nearly every major mid-Victorian firm. From Powell's – apart from the great East window – came the Colvin window, from cartoons by Holiday, in the East wall of the South aisle.[2] From Lavers and Barraud – with Westlake as cartoonist – came the Edenborough window in the North aisle.[3] From Clayton and Bell came the Carr[4] and Thomas[5] windows, also in the North aisle, and the two Francis windows in the South aisle.[6] From Saunders came two more North aisle windows: the Saunders window of 1868, from cartoons by Rossiter;[7] and the Banbury window, from cartoons by Lonsdale.[8] Finally, from Heaton, Butler and Bayne came the window in the tower portraying the Four Quarters of the Day. It had been the bells of Waltham Abbey which inspired the 'wild bells' of Tennyson's *In Memoriam*. Now they inspired Burges to produce one of his more engaging conceits: a quartet of ringers tolling bells representing Morning, Noon, Twilight and Night, amid a flurry of angels with butterfly wings.[9] Lonsdale was the cartoonist for this window, but he worked directly from Burges's designs. The same held true for Rossiter's Martyrdom of St Stephen in the Saunders window.[10] Again, Westlake's cartoons for the Edenborough window's Good Women were prepared under Burges's supervision;[11] and Lonsdale's musical angels in the Banbury window represent a standard Burges device. Last but not least, Holiday's false window between the Lady Chapel and the nave represented one of Burges's recurrent obsessions: an attempt to realise in one process the 'translucid pictures' of Theophilus and the shimmering falsities in the aisles of Florence Cathedral.[12]

Such fragments of evidence remind us forcibly of Burges's controlling role. To say that a stained glass window is 'by' any one particular person is always most misleading. In the Victorian period at least four people could be involved in the process of design and manufacture: architect (scheme and supervision), glass-manufacturer (material), artist (sketch and cartoon) and glass-painter (enamelling, firing and assembly).[13] Those glorious East windows, therefore, are 'by' Burges, Powell, Burne-Jones and Grieve. At Waltham there were in all at least four different stained glass manufacturers, and at least five different cartoonists. But there was only one architect. Thanks very largely to the efforts of Winston and Burges, the quality of English stained glass had been transformed. In the early 1850s, stained glass design had often been left to glaziers or architect's clerks. By the early 1860s a whole generation of artists – men like Burne-Jones, Rossiter, Stacy Marks, Smallfield, Holiday and Westlake – had emerged, capable of producing cartoons of quality and precision. That they did emerge was due, at least in part, to Burges.

Like the stained glass, the fittings of Waltham Abbey only appeared gradually. The organ was installed in 1860;[14] the beamed aisle roofs in 1867;[15] the gasoliers in 1875.[16] The enamelled brass lectern of 1872 was presumably not from Burges's design. One hopes he had no hand in the drastic alteration of the font. But both altar and sedilia are certainly his doing. Low and chunky, carved in black American walnut, their spare geometry echoes the controlled muscularity of their setting. So does the pulpit: a plain hexagon of dove grey marble, inset with coloured rectangles, sage green, buff and pink, in Irish, Tunisian and Italian marbles, picked out with Venetian gold mosaics.[17]

The rescue of the Lady Chapel had to wait until 1874–5.[18] Built in 1316, perhaps as a charnel-house and Chapel of Resurrection, its fabric had fallen into a deplorable state. Used as a coal cellar, a cloakroom, a privy, a boiler-house, and even a kindergarten – Waltham's Lady Chapel had suffered, as Burges put it, 'every injury that a building could sustain short of actual demolition'. Its tracery had been destroyed, its parapets fractured, its walls pierced, patched and plastered. 'Such is the state of one of the most beautiful buildings of the Middle Ages', Burges noted in 1872, that 'I may observe that during my experience I have never seen any other which has endured such barbarous treatment.'

But that did not give the restorer *carte blanche*. Burges was adamant in maintaining that there should be no refurbishing without necessity, and – more important – no restoration without evidence. A few fragments of the West window, with its double plate tracery, survived. Reconstruction was therefore permissible. Nothing whatsoever survived of the four South windows. But without them the chapel would be meaningless. Recreation, however conjectural, was therefore inevitable. On the other hand, the parapet was missing altogether. Its purpose was not vital to the fabric. Therefore its restoration, which would necessarily be an exercise of imagination, was impermissible. 'The fact is', he concluded, 'that we have not the least hint to guide us in the restoration of the parapet, and it is not an essential part of the composition like the tracery of the windows. Both the church and the chapel are, after all, but mere wrecks, yet still precious in the history of our national art; and upon the principle of destroying as little evidence as possible, I would leave both the roof and the parapet of the chapel in their present condition.'[19] Despite his fantasies, despite his impulsive temperament, when it came to restoration Burges knew when to stop.

The restoration of the Lady Chapel was paid for by the Lord of the Manor, Sir T. Fowell Buxton.[20] The first phase of work in 1859–60, on the main body of the church, had cost £5,000. That money had been raised partly by public subscription; partly through a donation from Sir Charles Wake Bt, then Lord of the Manor; and partly through a subscription from the War Department: the abbey had to be kept up for the spiritual good of men employed in the gunpowder and munitions factory nearby. Reredos, altar and pulpit cost Col. Edenborough another £1,500. Apart from the East window – estimate £1,000 – no figures survive for the cost of the stained glass. Several of these windows were paid for by the Rev Francis, vicar from 1846 to 1885; and their total cannot have been far short of £3,000. The lectern was valued at £100. The carved stalls were doubtless several hundred more. Over a period of twenty years, therefore, something like £10,000 must have been spent.

When his friends in the St Paul's Ecclesiological Society visited Waltham in 1879, Burges was already too ill to show them round.[21] The whole protracted operation – culminating in the re-slating of the roof in 1877[22] – had been a remarkable exercise: not so much in restoration, but in what he called 'conservation and repair'.[23] At the time of the octocentennial celebration, one newspaper commented: 'We should be wrong if we regarded [this] . . . great national work . . . as one of restoration. It has been simply a repair judiciously conceived and admirably carried into effect with but one view, the conservation of the severe and massive style of the early Norman period in all its simplicity and grandeur'.[24] Quite so. Outside, smooth-faced ashlar and rocky rubble demarcate the archaeology of the site with surgical precision. Inside, all the arts are mustered under one controlling mind. At Waltham, Burges does not copy. He meets the Middle Ages as an equal. Unbelievably, the current guide book fails even to mention his name.

St Augustine's College, Canterbury

After several major disappointments – notably Lille and Constantinople – Burges must have been glad to receive even minor commissions. In 1859–60, two fortunately arrived, at Canterbury and Fleet.

Founded by St Augustine, destroyed by Henry VIII, reconstituted as a Victorian missionary college for the conversion of the Empire – the site of St Augustine's Abbey is almost a microcosm of the history of English Christianity. 'St Augustine's Abbey', wrote Dean Stanley, 'was the Mother School, the Mother University of England, the seat of letters and study, at a time when Cambridge was a desolate fen, and Oxford a tangled forest in a wide waste of waters.'[25] By the early nineteenth century its ruins were a disgrace, occupied by the 'Old Palace Pub' and a Kentish version of Vauxhall Gardens. In 1843 a Tractarian surgeon, Dr Robert Brett of Stoke Newington, protested in the *English Churchman*: 'These hallowed and time honoured ruins are now converted into a Brewery, Pothouse, and Billiard Room. These walls which once resounded with the solemn Chant, and swelling Anthem, now re-echo the wild, fiendish revelries of the bacchanalian, or the maddening curses of the gamester. [The whole site is a] scene of sordid, revolting profanity and desecration. [May God] dispose some pious and wealthy Catholic to purchase and restore the sacred edifice.'[26] Beresford-Hope was the man. In 1844 he purchased the site. In 1845 he commissioned Butterfield to design a new Missionary College. And in 1858 he charged Burges with the design of a monument to its first missionary martyrs.

Now Hope took a personal interest in St Augustine's. He failed to persuade Benjamin Webb to become one of its founding Fellows – 'Just look at yourself and ask if you are not a medieval Fellow.'[27] But, as at All Saints, Margaret St, he did control much of the building and decoration. And its style embodied several important trends. In a letter to Webb about the upper chapel, for instance, in September 1845, he noted for the first time: 'we introduce polychrome'.[28] All decorative details were carefully considered. Willement's windows were praised by the *Ecclesiologist* in 1848 as 'the best modern specimens we have ever seen'.[29] And the same journal, in 1859, picked out Burges's *alto relievo* in the lower chapel as 'almost the only' item of 'Christian sculpture' worth reporting.[30]

Burges's missionary memorial[94] took the form of 'a sculptured diptych':[31] a pair of boldly modelled groups in identical architectural settings. One portrayed the meeting of Pope Gregory and the English Slaves – 'Not Angles but Angels'; the other the conversion of King Ethelbert by St Augustine. One was paid for by the sister of the Rev J. H. Hutchenson; the other by the missionary students themselves – out of money saved through not taking sugar in their tea over a period of several years.[32] Both groups were designed in 1858[33] and carved in Aubigny stone in 1859. The sculptor was Theodore Phyffers (fl. 1840–72). A Belgian immigrant, Phyffers had already worked under Pugin at the Houses of Parliament, and under Matthew Digby Wyatt in the Byzantine Court at the Crystal Palace.[34] At St Augustine's his figures are indeed 'pure and expressive'.[35] But it is their setting which rivets the attention. Those protuberant rosettes; those stumpy columns compressed like biceps – here Burges has distilled into a few square feet of masonry all the latent muscularity of Early French. Of course the effect is exaggerated. But it is the exaggeration of genius.[36] By comparison, Beresford-Hope's altar piece[37] – with its standing figure of the Good Shepherd, executed under Burges's direction by Nicholls – seems competent enough, but really rather tame.

All Saints, Fleet, Hants

The Lefroys were a clerical tribe of Huguenot extraction, distantly related to Jane Austen. They enter the Burges story by marriage. In 1845 Charles Edward Lefroy (1810–61), barrister-at-law, Secretary to the Speaker of the House of Commons, married Janet Walker, daughter of Alfred Burges's great engineering partner. Lefroy was on the way up: he even changed the name of his Hampshire seat from Ewshot House to Itchel Manor. Twelve years later his heiress wife was dead, and Lefroy planned a church in her memory. There was no doubt about the parish: his brother was the first vicar of nearby Church Crookham. And there was little doubt about the architect: young Burges was the obvious man. The foundation stone was laid in August 1860.[38] At the same time (1860–61) Burges was working on a village school – gabled, red-brick – not far away at Winchfield, for Lefroy's brother-in-law, the Rev Charles Frederick Seymour (1818–97).[39] Before the church's consecration in April 1862, however, Lefroy himself was dead.[40] Walker stepped in to complete the project as a joint memorial. His own death occurred within a few months of the ceremony.[41]

Fleet, therefore, is essentially a memorial church, almost a family shrine. Burges had himself contributed an embroidered altar frontal. Red-brick and cheap – it cost only £3,323 – the church's apsed, basilican plan is simple in the extreme. Its construction is simpler still: a concrete core faced with brick. The plate-traceried wheel-window; the arcaded narthex; the sturdy buttresses; and the broad pairs of unfoliated lancets in rubbed red brick – all have a bold Burgesian stamp.[39] Particularly effective is the exterior cornice, trefoiled in terracotta; and the West door, with its tympanum sculpture of Christ in Majesty framed by concentric brick arches.[42] The exterior is an essay in under-statement, the interior an excursion in polychrome abstraction. Taking Ruskin half-literally, Burges produced an overall scheme of coloured geometrical patterns which accentuated the interior structure without being in the least constructional. Mouldings are limited to the shape of the plainest brick. The brick-pointed piers are clean and bare. Coloured brick bands, painted white and blue on red; stencilled geometrical motifs, scattered on capital and cornice; a vaulted ceiling boarded and painted, dappled with appliqué signs – North Italian and Sicilian sources have been diluted without distortion. Here, as the *Ecclesiologist* put it, is living 'proof that the simplest and plainest designs *need* not be hackneyed or commonplace'.[43] It is an unpretentious church, simple and plain-spoken. Burges's pulpit is multi-columned and enriched with foliage; but his font is no more than a combination of the purest cylindrical forms.

The richness of the church is concentrated in the founders' monument (1861).[44][98] At St Augustine's Burges had already tried out the sculptural qualities of Early French. Those extraordinary monuments – right at the start of his active career – had revealed that Burges was already pursuing a theme which would haunt him for the rest of his life: the cult of strength. At Fleet, Burges carried the idea several stages further. Here the sculptor was probably Nicholls. The marble effigies of Lefroy and his wife – Lefroy holding a model of the Church of the Holy Sepulchre – rest beneath a gabled arch of gargantuan proportions. This time, the supporting columns are not merely squat: they are apparently crushed by their superincumbent burden. Six censing angels swing their way around the canopied arch, in heavy counterpoint to the thrusting sprockets of the gable's base. As always with Burges, the animal forms catch and hold the eye. The pet dogs at the Lefroys' feet are irresistible. Nicholls has interpreted his architect-master well. But perhaps the architect himself has gone a little too far: the Lefroy monument is not so much muscular as muscle-bound.

Unfortunately, the squat proportions of the Lefroy tomb have been accentuated by its removal from the chancel to a corner of the North aisle. In 1934 Burges's narthex was destroyed; the nave was extended two bays further West; a new vestry was added to the North East; and the West doorway, with its sculptured tympanum, was transferred as a new entrance to the South aisle.[45] Worse still, Burges's carefully patterned apse has been whitewashed, destroying at one blow the visual coherence of the interior. One lonely protest deserves to be re-quoted:

> There can only be one reason why William Burges has so few admirers to-day, and that is because few people know his works or take the trouble to understand his curious and highly individual point of view. Soon, no doubt, there will be a revival of interest in the unique and fascinating qualities of this Victorian genius; but meanwhile .... alas! .... Fleet ... is 'merely Victorian'. And so a work by a none too prolific genius is irreparably spoiled.[46]

CORK CATHEDRAL

'Got Cork', Burges noted excitedly in his diary early in 1863.[47] His luck had turned; he had landed his first major commission at the age of thirty-five. The competition for a new cathedral of St Finbar had been launched in April 1862.[48] There were sixty-eight competitors. Drawings arrived from Cologne, London, Edinburgh, Dublin, York, Liverpool, Bristol, Eton and Belfast, as well as from Cork itself. Few, however – apart from E. W. Godwin, T. N. Deane and J. P. Seddon – were candidates of any real weight.[49] Prizes were limited to £100 and £50.[50] And winning seemed a small trophy anyway: expenditure was limited to £15,000. But thanks to a little gamesmanship and a lot of luck, Burges managed to turn a minor provincial scheme into a project of international importance.

Cork was the first new cathedral to be built in the United Kingdom since Wren's St Paul's. By the early 1860s, moderate High Churchmanship – and even a measure of prosperity – had been successfully exported from England to Ireland.[51] But in the same decade, the Anglican Church of Ireland was struggling for its very existence.[52] In 1868 readers of the *Southern Reporter* were warned: 'The eyes of the whole world are fixed on the Irish Church'; she must not 'wax faint or grow cold'.[53]

After being twice cheated in major competitions, Burges was hardly in a mood to be too scrupulous about the conditions of entry. Other competitors took the conditions literally and produced a pinchbeck cathedral for £15,000. Burges offered a

Gothic dream, a fully-fledged thirteenth-century French cathedral complete with aisles, towers, spires and sculpture. He admitted it would cost at least twice as much. And he made his admission clear in a printed statement attached to his design. But defeated competitors were understandably furious.[54] They complained that Burges had competed on unequal terms. By doubling his scale of operations, he had offered the judges no more than half a cathedral, banking on local enthusiasm – 'the piety of future generations' – to make up the deficiency. One defeated competitor, J. P. Seddon, stood by him: competitions were 'absurd' anyway, and this one had at least produced a potential masterpiece. In effect, Burges had gambled on the zeal and gullibility of the selection committee. And he won.

By the mid-nineteenth century Cork's twelfth- and fourteenth-century cathedral had become a subject of some embarrassment to the town. Battered by siege and shot in 1689–90; rebuilt in meagre classical style in 1735, the medieval building survived only in the shape of a single steeple. In 1865 the *Builder* dismissed it as 'an unsightly old structure, wholly unworthy of the city of Cork, of the age, and of the sacred purpose to which it was dedicated'.[55] Burges certainly cared little for it: he claimed that only the Western doorway was worth keeping, and even that was not indigenous to the cathedral but a later insertion from the Dominican Abbey of St Mary.[56] Today, apart from dismantled panelling and scattered tombstones, almost the only vestiges of the old cathedral are the early eighteenth-century gatepiers at the Western approach – and even these Burges had intended to replace by a Gothic 'Parvise'.[57]

In the late 1860s, over Ireland as a whole, the established Anglican church amounted to about 12% of a population of just over five million. But in the province of Munster it was little more than 5%.[58] Still, it was the landowners' church; and in urban areas, in business and in the professions, it remained strong. As a city Cork was second only to the urban strongholds of Dublin and Belfast. It was controlled by Anglicans. And its Bishop was one of the most forceful Evangelicals on the Irish Bench: John Gregg. He was an electrifying preacher in armswinging, barnstorming style. His advice to country parsons was succinct: 'Short sermon, thirty-five minutes, explain text, reason on it, urge it home strongly, exhort warmly, conclude prayerfully and close simply'.[59] Such techniques were to prove useful when it came to raising funds for Cork Cathedral.

The foundation stone was laid amidst 'all the pomp of ecclesiastical and masonic arrangement'. It was 12 Jan. 1865, or 5865 according to masonic reckoning. The nobility and gentry of the neighbouring counties were there in full force. Thousands thronged the churchyard. Five hundred Freemasons attended in ceremonial dress. Burges himself walked in the procession – between the Earl of Bandon (Chairman of the Building Committee) and the Provincial Grand Master of Munster. The Deputy Grand Master wore 'pendant to a blue riband the invincible Masonic relic, the jewel belonging to *Sister* the Hon. Mrs Aldworth' – Freemasonry's only female member.[60] Dedicated 'to the glorious principles of the blessed Reformation', the new cathedral was hailed as 'the dawn of a new era ... which will contradict the miserable calumny that the Church in Ireland is dead (Cheers)'. Bishop Gregg wound up the ceremony by throwing Burges a challenge: 'We are guaranteed both taste and beauty by our architect ... he ought to be hung in chains if he disappoints us'.[61]

Burges did not disappoint. But then his clients gave him *carte blanche*. Right from the start, his designs had presumed a more lavish level of expenditure than any other competitor dared to expect. And even that presumption was not enough. One by one alterations were inserted in his original design,[62] each more lavish that the last. First another bay was added to the choir. That cost £600. Then barrel vaults were decided on for the aisles, in place of wooden ceilings. Then ashlar facing was adopted instead of rubble. Then white limestone instead of sandstone for the exterior.[63] Then Stourton stone instead of Portland for the interior crossing piers. Then the Western towers were raised, and the number of portals was increased from one to three.[64] Later on there would be a separate vestry (1896) and chapter house (1904).[65] Again, foundations needed to go deeper than expected: rock levels turned out to lurk as much as 25 ft. below the surface. That added another £2,500 to the total. Burges's original estimate had even excluded the cost of fees for architect, quantity surveyor and clerk of works. These added another £1,500 to the bill. All these extras, however, were only the beginning. There was also the matter of the exterior and interior decorations. Burges's competition scheme had scaled these down to a minimum.[66] He guessed that future piety would guarantee ornament on a lavish scale. He guessed correctly.

The sums of money raised were indeed extraordinary. A cathedral scheduled to cost £15,000 ended up by costing £100,000.[67] Burges himself had occasionally to do some 'touching up', as he called it. But in Bishop Gregg Cork possessed a fund-raiser of genius. He arrived in Cork in 1862, and immediately made the construction of the new cathedral his life's ambition. Within two years £9,000 had been subscribed. Beresford-Hope himself sent £500. Then, at a public meeting in March 1864, at the Imperial Hotel in Cork, the call went out for more. Appeals were made to religious rivalry and civic pride. In Belfast and Dublin, in Tuam and Kilmore, in Down and Connor, Protestant cathedrals were being planned or rebuilt. Why not Cork? 'Now my friends', urged Bishop Gregg, 'I hope you will give something today towards this work – I can place something at your disposal. Would you be satisfied if I put down £100? Would that be a good beginning? Take £1,000 (Great cheering). ...' The Earl of Bandon promptly promised another £100, and the rest of the audience another £158.[68] At the laying of the foundation stone in January 1865, prayers concluded with a shower of private donations. As usual, Gregg topped the bill with a performance worthy of an auctioneer:

'How much did you get Mr Dean?'
'£1,700.'
'I say make it two thousand .... (Cheers). How easy it is to please you .... What!

build a cathedral for Cork, and amid the gentry and the people there is only £2,000
... Make it £3,000 I say then (Great cheering). Make it £4,000. ...'[69]

And Gregg's efforts continued for another twelve years. Subscription lists reveal
that the Duke of Devonshire gave £400; the Early of Bantry £200; the Earl of Cork
£600; the Earl of Egmont £900; the Earl of Shannon £100; William-Bence-Jones (a
friend of Burges) £1,000; and Burges's father £100.[70] The cathedral was consecrated
on 30 Nov. 1870. But at that date no more than its carcass had been built. Those towers
and spires still soared only in their architect's imagination. Work continued slowly and
expensively. Then, on the fifth anniversary of consecration, came the great moment.
Bishop Gregg stepped into the pulpit. He had amazing news. Some time before, he
had written to a local merchant, Francis Wise, asking for a large donation towards the
cost of the central tower. Gregg read out Wise's reply:

> I shall subscribe £10,000 towards that object – (Bishop: 'That is good is it not?
> Wait now until you see what he further says) – or I will give you £20,000
> provided [another] £10,000 be subscribed by – (Bishop: now here is the puzzle) –
> Jan. 1st next.

The congregation waited, breathless. Bishop Gregg was about to play his trump card.
Mitre – figuratively speaking – in hand, he had called on another rich Corkagian, a
Freemason named W. H. Crawford.[71] According to legend, he told Crawford of
Wise's generosity and then thundered: 'Go and do thou likewise!' Playing off one
magnate against another, the Bishop had asked plainly for the vital £10,000, and got it
.... £30,000 at a stroke! Interrupting his sermon, Gregg called on the choir: Burges's
new-built walls shuddered to the sound of Handel's Hallelujah Chorus.[72] Two years
later Crawford parted with another £8,300 for the sculpture of the West front.[73]

If fund-raising was a problem, so were the logistics of construction. The first
contractor, Robert Walker, proved a broken reed.[74] His withdrawal in December
1866 precipitated nine months' delay. Not until August 1867 did Gilbert Cockburn of
Dublin step into the breach.[75] Financial support seemed to waver. But a contribution
from the Ecclesiastical Commissioners helped fund-raising to regain momentum. In
1867–8 building proceeded fast. By 1868 the *Ecclesiologist* could report: 'The aisle and
ambulatory walls are up to the eaves; the nave pillars are set, and some of the arches
turned. The arches from the transepts to the nave and choir aisles are completed; the
coupled pillars of red marble in the sanctuary are fixed, and the triple West doorway
has been erected'.[76] By 1870, £36,000 had been spent.[77] That was the year in which a
local civil engineer named W. H. Hill replaced Adams as clerk of works or executant
architect. It was a difficult time: there were riots in the streets, and labourers were
striking for 15s. per week instead of 12s.[78] Hill and Burges worked closely together
during 1870–74; Burges spent a good deal of time in Cork in 1870 for instance. In
August 1873 Delany of Dublin took over from Cockburn. And in the Summer of

1876 he contracted for the completion of all three spires, with Sier as Clerk of Works.[79] By 1880 some £62,000 had been spent. All this on the fabric alone. Decorative sculpture and the gorgeous fittings of the interior would add at least £40,000 to that total. Of course such a level of expenditure was not without profit for Burges: on structural work he took 5%; on decoration 10%. At last, on 6 April 1878, the aged Bishop Gregg performed the ceremony of laying the topmost stones of both the Western spires.[80] Less than two months later he was dead. The privilege of topping off the central spire – a ceremony performed on 23 Oct. 1879 – went to his successor.

In its plan,[29c] Cork realised Burges's Crimea and Brisbane schemes; in its elevations[28;32] it retrieved the lost designs for Lille. Its prototypes run through the roll-call of Early French: Sens for the East end and Laon[81] for the West; Nesle,[82] perhaps, for the great rose window; Laon or Etampes[83] for the angle-columned towers; Chartres or Amiens for the angel on the apse;[84] Amiens for the Western portals and the internal vaulting shafts which run continuously through all three levels – arcade, triforium and clerestory.[31] But the wrought iron hinges of the Western doors stem from an English source: Merton College, Oxford.[85] And the mighty wooden roof of the apse – trilobe in section, with corbelled kingposts and illuminated coves – echoes the church of San Zenone in Verona.[86] Each prototype, however, has been simplified – distilled almost – in pursuit of abstraction and sublimity. The East end – compositionally speaking – is Sens without its buttresses; the West front is Laon without its towers. If Cork is indeed 'the apotheosis in the British Isles of Early French',[87] it is Early French as visualised in Burges's own peculiar way. The story goes that the Royal Academy's hanging committee of 1868 mistook Burges's West front design for a topographical drawing of a French cathedral.[88] They cannot have looked very closely. A comparison between Cork and the church of Notre Dame at Dijon, for instance, emphasises the extraordinarily personal nature of Burges's synthetic style: Cork is 'more Burgesian than Burgundian'.[89]

Cork is a small cathedral. It crouches, heavily-muscled, like some tumescent beast waiting to spring. Its rocky geometry makes Scott's Edinburgh Cathedral look pedestrian, and Pearson's Truro antiquarian. Despite its miniature scale, its design exudes weight, power, majesty .... Or does it? The *Ecclesiologist*, at least, had no reservations: 'We have never seen a design which more entirely embodies the special features of the Minster'. Here was a 'typal example', a cathedral *par excellence*.[90] Other critics were less sure. Some thought it awkward and insufficiently Irish.[91] Warington Taylor thought it looked 'stumpy'.[92] Even E. W. Godwin worried about its 'exaggerations', its 'elephantine' touch.[93] In 1863 one local pundit, Robert Rolt Brash, summed up the burden of criticism then and since:

> In dimensions it is but the size of an ordinary parish church, being only 180 ft. in length, while it exhibits all the external features of the largest existing cathedrals, whose length runs to 500 ft. or more. The effect of this is to make the building look

exceedingly short, and disproportionately high; for those features which produce grandeur in a structure of large extent have a contrary effect on buildings of small size. A church 180 ft. in length, 70 ft. in height to the ridge, and having three towers and spires, would look a perfect abortion of a cathedral, a swelling attempt to look big, contrary to every principle of proportion and optical effect.[94]

Now Burges was well aware of the problem. And he produced a solution which was thought through at every stage. His thinking began with the necessary economy of the plan. Cork would never be able to afford a really large cathedral. He consciously designed the spires to offset the modest dimensions and inevitable horizontality of his design: 'to carry off the height and shortness of the building'.[95] Given the necessity of spires, then – ideally – there had to be three: 'One would look bad', he noted, 'and two would be seen in a line.'[96] To have no spires at all would be to reduce a cathedral to a meeting house, and to throw away the finest site in the city. Burges's logic is hard to fault. And – granted 'the theoretic perfection of Early French'[97] – so is the excellence of his design.

Much of the pleasure in our appreciation stems from the texture and colour of the masonry. Cork limestone: dug along the valley from Cork to Youghal, it quarries violet grey, and weathers off-white.[98] Red sandstone – from the Brickfield Quarry at Glenmire – was used only for foundations and invisible walling. Apart from the gutter-course and columns – in a slightly darker limestone from Kilkenny – the whole structure is faced in the locality's own limestone, quarried in this case at Ballintemple.[99] On damp, gloomy days it takes on a marmoreal, almost luminous quality; in sunshine it sparkles like salt. Red sandstone would have absorbed what little light there is: Cork is not the sunniest of cities; mouldings would have melted in the mist. But this hard-edged silvery limestone, in carefully-pitted ashlar, reflects and multiplies the light. Rock-hard, grainy, non-porous; it resists the sulphurous air of the city and shrugs off the threatening grime. Not so the crystalline limestone from Ballinasloe, imported by Burges for the statuary of the portals.[1] The four Evangelistic Beasts stand out sharp and clean, but the saints and virgins of the Western front are dusky-faced, mantled in dark grey soot.

The West front of Cork[32;112] became almost a testing ground for Burges's theories on the relationship of architecture and sculpture. Sculpture, he made it known, was 'the one indispensable attribute of architectural effect'.[2] He was well aware of the weakness of architectural sculpture in his own day. 'We are doing a work', he explained in 1878, 'which has not been attempted since the West front of Wells cathedral.'[3] If the standard was Wells, the model – at least for those three great portals – was Chartres. Without the experience built up by his twenty-year partnership with Nicholls, the task would have been impossible. 'It is certainly difficult', he told Gregg, 'to get people like Mr Nicholls .... Such men are not to be got every day. The Western front of Cork Cathedral should be a specimen of the best architectural sculpture the age can produce.'⁴ Thanks to the munificent Crawford, that was indeed the result.

   In all there were 1,260 pieces of sculpture built into the cathedral's fabric.⁵ Every one was personally designed by Burges. Every one was modelled in plaster by Nicholls.[113] And – except for the figures in the Western portals, and the four Evangelistic emblems around the rose window – every one was carved *in situ* by R. McLeod and his staff of local stone-masons. The overall standard is consistently high and occasionally outstanding: just look at that ten-horned rhinoceros menacing the great tower from its bulbous corbel at the junction of transept and chancel; or, in calmer vein, study the vestry tympanum of St John and the Angel Measuring the New Jerusalem.⁶ On the cost of Nicholls' model-making and carving – executed in London – Burges felt justified in charging 10% commission, so close was his 'personal superintendence and his own special design and instruction'. On McLeod's carving – executed from Burges's designs, but at long range – he charged 5%.⁷ It was a painstaking and protracted operation covering the best part of a decade. Burges took immense care in ensuring, by regular visits, that every piece was 'up to the line'. Well might he remind the Bishop in 1879 that 'carving and sculpture are not bricklaying'.⁸

   It was Dean William Connor Magee – himself a Freemason – who suggested that the Freemasons of Cork present the four Evangelistic Beasts carved around the rose window.[112] Burges took particular trouble over their design.

> The architect, in the first instance, [he explained in 1869] made sketches to a half-inch scale. The models were then partially executed by Mr Nicholls, of Lambeth, under the superintendence of the architect. Then both sculptor and architect repaired to the British Museum to see how the Ninevites treated similar subjects, and the figures were finally finished from the information then obtained. It is true that this is a very troublesome process both for the sculptor and for the architect; but the art of sculpture in connection with architecture has been so forgotten that it is only by such painful processes ... that we can obtain work which, when executed, we should not wish to see altered. Of course ... there are plenty of sculptors who can copy nature more or less correctly; but far higher qualities are demanded when it becomes a question of arranging the lines of the figures with due regard to the lines of the building; and when it also becomes a question of properly filling up a certain space, and, above all, of making those modifications of nature which are imperatively demanded in such work. Thus the eyelids and other details have often to be exaggerated, and the outline, if the subject is a bas-relief, be cut square and not rounded off, or occasionally it must be strengthened with an incised line, or some parts of the drapery must be undercut or the reverse. Now, Mr Nicholls has attended to all these points, and, although at present we have only the half-sized models from which to judge, there is every probability of the real work turning out a success.⁹

Success indeed. In 1870 the carving on site – in the solid masonry of the wall – was entrusted to C. W. Harrison of Dublin, a sculptor trained in the school of Ruskin's hero, O'Shea. The resulting integration of architecture and sculpture is masterly. The visual impact stunning.

> The round window [wrote Handley-Read], an epitome of Early French, draws the eye like a target. The encircling rim is tough enough to confine the explosive force of the radiating shafts, but it transfers their outward thrust by squeezing the [four] beasts ... into their exiguous corners: trapped between square and circle, and almost Assyrian in conception, they are carved with rocky surfaces suited to their monumental scale. Even the beasts are diminished by the sheer weight and rather harsh geometry of the window, but the group as a whole, extra forceful for being compressed into an exact square, threatens to overwhelm the gables and porches lower down. Everything here, except the four gargoyles, again rocky and monumental, is crisp and dapper to the point of elegance – a '13thc' addition to an 'Early French' church.[10]

At half a glance it looks easy enough. But how rarely such a combination of architecture and sculpture occurs in nineteenth-century art. One contemporary failure will suffice as a comparison. Wilton church (1841–5) by Wyatt and Brandon is a milestone in England's rediscovery of Continental prototypes. But the evangelistic beasts around its rose window cling on precariously, thrown off balance by the rotating thrust of an overmighty rim. On the West front of Cork architecture and sculpture meet on level terms, reciprocal forces in a joint creation. 'It is not too much to say', Eastlake concluded, 'that no finer examples of decorative sculpture have been produced during the Revival.' Burges's evangelistic beasts 'exactly represent that intermediate condition between natural form and abstract idealism which is the essence of Medieval and indeed of all noble art, and they possess the further merit of being admirably adapted to their position'.[11]

The rate of payment for stonecutters and carvers was a recurrent problem. McLeod tended to pay his masons higher wages – 7s. for a 10½-hour day, or £2.2s.6d. for a 60-hour week – much to Delany's annoyance.[12] Burges declined to intervene: rates of pay were 'a little out of the architect's province'.[13] The truth of the matter seems to have been that McLeod was 'a most troublesome person',[14] but a craftsman after Burges's own heart. In executing the carving – the capitals in the chancel for instance had to be done twice over – McLeod willingly risked bankruptcy. 'I knew from the first I was losing,' he explained in 1877, 'but thought it would be wrong to stop the work for the sake of money. I believed I would be treated honourably as ... the cost ... should not be grudged to make the ... carving beautiful.'[15] 'This loss', he reminded Burges a year later, 'has harassed me more than you can imagine, or know, or may be inclined to believe.'[16] That did the trick. 'I do not consider the price for the sculpture too high',

Burges explained to the Bishop, 'considering the extremely hard nature of the stone and the degree of finish we shall require .... We are very fortunate in having Mr McLeod, who has worked in sculptor's studios, and is accustomed to the hard and brittle limestone. To such men the only course is to give their price because you would not be able to get anyone else who would do the work so well ....,[17] McLeod was certainly expensive: at £60 the gable angel was reputed to bring him a profit of 100%.[18] But his four mighty gargoyles on the West front[110–111] – the Triumphs of Virtue over Vice[19] – are a noble achievement. 'We should have to search hard in Victorian architecture', Handley-Read concluded, 'for finer animal sculpture carved to a large scale.'[20]

Burges, Nicholls and McLeod were, in fact, a good team. And Burges was particularly anxious to complete the great West front while all three were still alive. 'This work is a most important and difficult one', he explained in May 1878; 'it cannot be done in a year or two.' Indeed 'the designing and building of the Cathedral, in point of difficulty and of art, is child's play to what is now contemplated'.[21] 'I do not think anybody concerned except myself has any idea of the length of time the work will take and the immense amount of labour involved .... Life is short and uncertain, and I want Nicholls to begin at once.'[22] Again, 'we shall have to depend on one or two men such as Mr Nicholls who has been twenty years training for this sort of work, and therefore considering the instability of human life both in his case and my own, to say nothing of Mr McLeod, I am very anxious that no time should be lost.'[23] Those words proved prophetic. Bishop Gregg died within a fortnight; Burges's brother died within a month; and Burges himself was dead within three years. Nicholls' ten Virgins and sixteen Saints, as well as the tympana of the three portals – writhing with figures and flashing with golden mosaic – all turned out to be posthumous works, directed by Chapple and Pullan. They were not finished until 1883.[24] Smooth without insipidity; naturalistic without pedantry, the full-size figures fall only a little short of Pre-Raphaelite greatness. By any yardstick, the central tympanum of the Resurrection is outstanding.

In designing the interior fittings Burges ignored all questions of cost. In distributing contracts he went for 'the best labour and the best materials rather than the lowest price'. As he explained to Bishop Gregg, 'the question fifty years hence will be, first: "Is this work beautiful?" and secondly: "Have those to whom it has been entrusted done it with all their heart and ability?" . . . Good art is far too rare and far too precious to be cheap.'[25] Nor could it be produced in a hurry. 'I am getting on with the furniture', he assured Caulfield in 1876, 'but it is a dreadfully long affair, it requires so much consideration and care.'[26] His labour was well justified. Even as early as 1863, the *Building News* recognised its stamp of genius: 'Its gorgeousness lies not in a confusion of carving, elaborated tracery, crowds of statuary, or crude colouring, but in well-directed lines, boldly-sectioned mouldings, justly balanced masses, and harmonious simplicity'; here is 'real *architectural* power'.[27]

From the outset Burges aimed at a unified and coherent programme of stained glass. In a report of 1868 he dismissed the bulk of contemporary glass as 'utterly bad'. Even where individual windows were good in themselves, lack of coordination destroyed their effect. At Ely, for example, the juxtaposition of windows by an assortment of different makers produced all the 'discordant colours of a gigantic pattern card'. At Cork, therefore, Burges precluded any possibility of random insertion, firstly by drawing up an overall iconographic scheme; secondly by establishing his own control over all three stages of design – sketch, cartoon and manufacture; and thirdly by setting up a procedure for gradual donation.[28]

The iconography of the stained glass mingles with that of the interior sculpture in a characteristically Protestant theme: Revelation. The crossing piers carry heads of the Four Beasts; the pulpit the Four Evangelists. And the glass runs in a cycle from the Creation in the Western rose window to the vision of God's throne – beast-bound, as in the Apocalypse – in the most Easterly window of the ambulatory. In all, the seventy-four windows, executed from the mid-1870s onwards from slightly earlier designs, must have cost at least £5,000. Burges himself produced cartoons for all but six of the twenty-seven clerestory windows, for the glorious wheel window at the West end and, perhaps, for the round window in the North transept.[29] Fred Weekes was his cartoonist for the three central windows in the apse clerestory and, perhaps, for the small roundels in the transepts.[30] All the remainder fell to H. W. Lonsdale, and very faithfully did he follow his master's sketches.[31] Saunders and Co. were the manufacturers, Worrall their stainer-glazier, 'under the immediate superintendence of the architect'.[32] Burges earned his 10% commission.

The stained glass at Cork[33] may not be the best that Burges produced, but it is very fine indeed. The clerestory lancets burn darkly high above: deep-eyed zodiac figures, pierced by translucent stars.[34] In the great West window the Days of Creation – abstract, incorporeal – shimmer in circles of prismatic light. The transept glass has an almost opalescent finish. And the eighteen windows around the ambulatory of the apse glow strong and richly, even on the dullest day. These ambulatory windows, Handley-Read concluded, 'are in their way faultless. The scale and treatment of the figure subjects, grouped throughout the series in three frames to a light, are exactly suited to observation at close range; the lines of the lead sub-divisions are rationally placed to emphasise the units of design in a way which at the time was distinctly advanced; and the colours, notably high-pitched and full-blooded, could be said to burn, given a little sunshine, with a hard, gem-like flame – they would, however, have been rather too hot, too visceral for Mr Pater. These windows are High Victorian, not *fin-de-siècle* . . . . [and] they are among the best of their period'.[35]

Now for the metalwork. The nine wrought-iron screens, separating chancel and ambulatory follow sinuous patterns first evolved for the Lille competition. They were executed by Hart and Co. in 1876–7.[36] The David door[114] – cast in bronze by Hatfield and inlaid with silver by Barkentin and Krall – was posthumously executed according to Burges's designs in 1889.[37] Its broad-spreading voussoirs are alive with grotesque beasts; its tympanum is filled with sculpture of rare felicity and grace. Those top-heavy voussoirs reappear frequently in Burges's work. Their inspiration seems to have been Sicilian: a Moorish exaggeration of an Italian prototype.[38] Burges adopted the idea early on, and adapted it again and again. At Cork the David door carries tremendous punch. And nothing could be more Burgesian – except perhaps the lectern.

This lectern[217–218] was presented by the women of Cork. Nine hundred pounds of solid brass, 9 ft. 9 in. high, it is decorated with profiles of Moses and David and ornamented with forty-eight drops of polished glass, set in clusters like crystal grapes.[39] Nicholls was responsible for the modelling. The design is both Puginian and High Victorian: Puginian in its upper details – the cresting, the 'crystal' drops, the sconces; and High Victorian in the design of its lower section, particularly the Early French forms of stump-column and knot. This combination of 1840s and 1850s, reappearing in the 1870s, can be explained, quite simply, by accidents of design and manufacture. Burges merely re-used in 1877 a design prepared for the Lille competition in 1856. The manufacturers, Jones and Willis, worried so little about keeping up to date that they happily exhibited their lectern at the Paris Exhibition of 1878.[40]

As always with Burges, inlay and mosaic are prominent at Cork. The low choir wall[140] is composed of veined white marble, set with moulded alabaster, red and green marbles and gold mosaics. A grotesque human head stares out through alabaster leaves: its design mingles Gothic and Renaissance; its execution blurs the boundary between High Victorian and Arts and Crafts design.[41]

The altar – of carved oak, resting on black marble inlaid with mosaic – was erected in Gregg's memory in 1879.[42] For the reredos, Burges proposed two alternative designs: a marvellous Jesse Tree, with sculpture and mosaic, echoing a prototype in Worms Cathedral;[43] and a geometrical crucifix mosaic, panelled and gilt.[44] The executed version (1879) is a variant of the second of these, deprived of its crucifix, presumably on Protestant grounds.[45] The credence table (1880) is composed of marble and alabaster, inlaid with gold mosaic and lapis lazuli, and decorated with four storks in high relief, their plumage coloured *au naturel*.[46]

The mosaic pavement of the apse[139] was designed by Burges and made in Paris from Lonsdale's cartoons by Burke and Co. in 1877.[47] Italian artists[48] from Udine were employed, using marble segments mined in the Pyrenees. The theme is a text from St Matthew: 'Again, the kingdom of Heaven is like unto a net that was cast into the sea and gathered of every kind'. On the periphery of the design, corks – Burges could never resist a pun – float upon the sea green pavement between curling waves of white Parian. Within the folds of the net appear all sorts and conditions of men: Soldier, Child, Rustic, Fisherman, King, Hunter, Doctor, Merchant, Husbandman, Artisan and Slave. Between them lurk the creatures of the deep, floating bright-hued in multicoloured marble. Upon the approaching step appear the Parables of the Sower and the Grain of Mustard Seed: the Sower scattering corn, the Good Shepherd rescuing sheep, and between them, birds, butterflies, branches and leaves – a veritable tapestry of marble. The cost was £400.[49]

All these items – the mosaics and inlays of the chancel – are handled with understatement and restraint. The thunderbolts occur in the nave. First the organ. Originally at the West end, Burges made its setting uncompromisingly, almost brutally, austere.[50] The corbels of the gallery – Architecture and Sculpture – and the vaulting sculptures of the staircase – Bishop, King, Soldier, Farmer – make no concessions to prettiness. And in the font[109] geometry is carried still further, almost to the point of Euclidian purity. Seven squat columns – reduced by compression almost to the status of symbolic supports – link circular bowl to octagonal base. The materials are white, red and green marble, set with letters of polished brass, and a cross of polychrome abstraction.[51]

Most ruthless of all is the pulpit.[108] Designed in 1873 and finished in 1874,[52] but not painted until much later, by Eileen Dann, it is hard to interpret and harder still to like. At the time, several critics thought it ugly.[53] A writer in the *Limerick Chronicle* was aghast at 'its vast redundancy of diameter'; it looked like 'some large vat'; the ugliest thing he 'ever beheld in a place of worship'.[54] Even Handley-Read thought it 'aggressive ... defiant ... a shock, an onslaught ... undeniably ugly'. 'Carved out of huge blocks of stone and marble, a minor High Victorian thunderbolt, it has the massive bulk of a well-head scaled, apparently, for Stonehenge ... and ... embodies inflations and abstractions which are almost caricatural. No one would suppose, looking at those exaggerated finials, that Burges was a learned archaeologist, and in the drum of the Pulpit he has all but sacrificed style to geometrical shape'.[55] Indeed he has. Here is a link between the 1860s and the 1960s, between the grotesque 'realism' of the Pre-Raphaelite and the cruel 'functionalism' of the New Brutalist.[56] Once again Burges defies an easy label. Clearly this is not a matter of stumbling ugliness: it is a closely calculated performance; an essay in abstract shapes and exaggerated forms; as overwhelming in its impact as one of Bishop Gregg's own sermons. Ugly or not, that pulpit matches the sublimity of its setting.

Among the woodwork, the Bishop's Throne stands out. Rearing 46 ft. into the air, two thirds as high as the mighty crossing piers, it was constructed towards the end of Gregg's lifetime and erected immediately after his death. Besides symbolic beasts and birds, its carvings glorify a score of Cork's own Bishops, beginning with St Finbar and ending with Gregg himself. Executed by Walden in solid oak, from models by Nicholls, it cost £1,463, and was exhibited at the Royal Academy in 1877 and at the Paris Exhibition of 1878.[57] The Sedilia[115], too, came from Walden's workshop in 1879–80. Their canopies are carved with crockets, and crowned with figures from a celestial choir: winged angels playing musical instruments, one of Burges's favourite conceits.[58] Walden seems to have been not only a good joiner but a cheap one. His tender for the stalls – carved with animals and insects – was so much lower than those of his competitors that Chapple decided to keep the figures secret: it is most 'undesirable', he told Caulfield, 'that Mr Walden should get the information, either now or in the future'.[59]

Few could cavil at the quality of Burges's fittings. But there were occasional criticisms of the interior as a whole. In 1878 one critic found only 'extreme narrowness and vast height ... an oppressive air of heaviness and tremendous solidity, and a painful want of architectural lightness and grace.'[60] Such judgements wilfully misunderstand the architect's intentions. Cork should be measured not by the criteria of Decorated and Perpendicular Gothic, but by the canons of Early French. Compression, certainly; narrowness and extravagant height, perhaps. But in actual fact the proportions of the interior are controlled by the structural exigencies of the great central tower. 'The four colossal piers at the crossing ... dictate both the width and height of the entire vessel; faced in absolutely plain stone, they define the tall, high-shouldered slit which so dramatically heightens the spectacle of the apse – the glittering climax to an all but monochrome sequence. Seen from the West end, it is framed between walls and piers of masonry which shore up an unforgettable parallelogram of towering space'.[61]

Burges's polychromatic scheme was never completed. Even so, there is plenty of colour at Cork. In the first place, there are the structural materials. The great piers which support the central tower are of grey-brown Stourton stone. Tawny Box-ground Bath stone supplies the rest of the internal dressings.[62] The reddish columns are, naturally, of Cork red marble.[63] Elsewhere Burges budgeted for marble shafts from Languedoc, Devon and Switzerland – but in the end he settled for Irish green.[64] The nave and aisles are quiet, almost monochrome. The sanctuary explodes in a crescendo of colour: green and red columns; gilded capitals; walls, arches and ceiling patterned in red, blue, gold, white and green. The actual painting of the great trefoiled roof – a host of angels, if not the angelic host itself – was only completed in 1935, but to Burges's designs, by Prof. E. W. Tristram (1882–1952). Mounting the sanctuary steps is like stepping inside some giant's jewel casket. But the colours never distract from the iron logic of the structure. There is an 'athletic strength',[65] a blunt-edged swagger, about the interior which defies disagreement. The balls of foliage in the capitals are hard as a clenched fist. Sir Ninian Comper used to say that a great church 'should bring you to your knees'.[66] Maybe. But there are various ways of inducing genuflexion: Burges knocks you flat.

Bishop Gregg had dreamed of a cathedral to crown the city, to 'strike the human mind with its sublimity'. Sublime indeed: the Western towers rise to 180 ft.; the central spire soars 240 ft. into the clouds. And it is the sight – first and last – of that glorious trinity of spires which transfixes the memory:

Exquisitely proportioned as regards their component parts, exquisitely proportioned in relation to each other ... Beautiful ... under all conditions of atmosphere and light – rearing their graceful forms, strong and unflinching, whilst the storms of winter rave around their heads, soaring into the summer blue, gleaming pinnacles of snowy white, 'fired from the west' by the setting sun and boldly flashing back his splendour, or in the gloaming seen as dark blue spires on the fading gold of a daffodil sky . . . .[67]

Its consistency of style makes Cork almost unique among cathedrals. And it was this sense of *completeness* which contemporaries especially admired: one rightly called it 'one of the most perfect churches of modern times'.[68] At Cork Burges managed to keep both his principal talents in equilibrium: an unerring sense of mass and scale, and an unflagging zest for the minutiae of design. As the *Irish Builder* admitted, the style might not be everyone's favourite; its cost and richness of decoration might even seem offensive; 'as an architectural monument', however, 'nothing could possibly be better'.[69]

But for legal difficulties, Burges would have been buried in his own cathedral. Instead of burial, there was a memorial service and a eulogy by the Bishop: 'It is a solemn thought that the creating mind . . . of that gifted man – is now at rest, that no more work will be done by the genius who, before one stone of this magnificent cathedral was laid, planned it all, and saw it in his own mind.'[70] The Bishop's text was appropriate for the greatest art-architect of the Gothic Revival: 'Whatsoever thy hand findeth to do, do it with all thy might'. That day the bells of Cork were silent.

SMALLER IRISH CHURCHES

Bishoprics are not normally hereditary, even in Ireland. But so powerful was John Gregg's identification with Cork, that it cannot have seemed unnatural for him to be succeeded in 1878 by his son Robert – already Bishop in the neighbouring see of Ossory – *en route* to the Archbishopric of Armagh.[71] Burges must have been delighted: completion of Cork Cathedral was now guaranteed. Besides, the Gregg dynasty had already supplied him with two commissions elsewhere, at Carrigrohane and Kilkenny.

Robert Gregg was Rector of St Peter, Carrigrohane, not far from Cork, between 1865 and 1874. As soon as he arrived, he commissioned Burges to design an additional South aisle and vestry.[72] It was a small commission, in an obscure Irish village. But Burges made the most of it. The slit windows, the curved mullions of the vestry, the polygonal shafts set into the thickness of the low arcade wall: all reveal an original architectural mind. And the stained glass (1867) – presumably by Saunders and Holiday, in rich Pre-Raphaelite vein – is predictably good.[73]

At Kilkenny Cathedral – seat of the Bishop of Ossory – Burges was commissioned to supply a memorial window to John Hugh Bainbridge, Robert Gregg's son-in-law. Bainbridge, one of the chief sponsors of Cork Cathedral, had been drowned at sea on

10 June 1877.[74] The two-light window, at the West end of the North aisle, was produced by Saunders, from cartoons by Lonsdale, and follows the dark-hued, reductive patterning of that combination's work at Cork.[75]

One of the distinctive features of Kilkenny was its ancient round tower. It was a feature Burges eagerly adopted at Templebrady: Georgius Oldhousen had a passion for round towers as sheer as chimney stacks.[76] At Holy Trinity, Templebrady (1866–68)[77][41], high above the harbour at Crosshaven, he concocted a design which ingeniously combined Early French with Irish Vernacular. Celtic round towers – at Glendalough, Co. Wicklow, for example, or the twelfth-century church of St Finghin, Clonmacnoise, Co. Offaly – sometimes performed the double function of defensible landmark and perfunctory vestry.[78] Burges revived this ancient idea, but translated it into Early French with the help of a crowning arcade and conical dome from the towers of Notre-Dame La Grande in Poitiers.[79] The fact that he felt able to try the same 'dodge' in his Bombay School of Art designs says something for the catholicity of Early French. But in neither case did the idea come to fruition. Templebrady was never to see its Hibernian campanile.[80] Even so, the body of the church is more than enough to identify its architect. The smooth plate tracery, the low-slung, battered porch, the overscaled voussoirs, the emphatic string courses: these are all Burgesian trademarks. Seldom, however, did Burges achieve such flinty geometry, such controlled muscularity. And the surviving interior fittings certainly measure up to the quality of the exterior – notably the pelican-dragon corbels of the chancel arch,[81] and the stained glass at the East end, presumably by Saunders and Weekes: a triple-figured Jesse on a background of streaky green.

Another Irish commission, springing indirectly from Cork, involved the extension and alteration of the parish church at Newtownbarry, Co. Wexford, now known as Bunclody. In March 1876 Robert Westley Hall-Dare, squire of Newtownbarry, died at Rome aged 35. Two months before, his brother Charles had died at the age of 15.[82] Burges designed a memorial: a new West front to the church, pierced by one rose window and two lancets. The exterior wall was broken by a boldly arched doorway and decorated by a diapered gable. The windows – made by Saunders from cartoons by Lonsdale – have the usual clarity of outline, and a tonal scale similar to the windows at Cork.[83]

St Michael and All Angels, Brighton

The church architecture of Brighton owes everything to the Wagner family. In the seventeenth century Wagners were tailors in Silesia. In the eighteenth century they were hatters in Pall Mall: hatters to the Hanoverian Court, capmakers to the army, and outfitters to the gentry of England. In the nineteenth century they gave up trade, took up religion and emerged as clerics on a heroic scale.[84] The scope of the family's ecclesiastical empire was indeed Wagnerian. When the Rev H. M. Wagner

(1793–1870) became vicar of Brighton in 1824 there was only one church – the medieval parish church of St Nicholas – and two private chapels. At his death forty-six years later there were seventeen churches and five chapels of ease. But there was still only one parish, and Wagner was its master. His territory was once described as 'a Bishopric within a Bishopric'. Not for nothing was he son-in-law to the greatest church-builder of the Regency, Joshua Watson (1771–1829). Eighty thousand souls lived under his dominion.[85] From a score of clergymen he exacted absolute obedience: his battle with one firebrand preacher – the celebrated Robertson of Brighton – became a *cause célèbre*.[86] And in truly patriarchal style, this clerical emperor of the South Coast created several colonies for his own family. His nephew, the Rev George Wagner (1815–57) – 'a pale ascetic youth, with the character of a medieval saint'[87] – was appointed in 1851 to a church built by a spinster sister, Mary Ann Wagner (1791–1868). And his eldest son, the Rev Arthur Wagner (d. 1902) – the legendary Fr Wagner of Brighton – was installed in 1850 in a new church of Tractarian splendour even before he had been ordained.

At Trinity College, Cambridge, in the 1840s Arthur Wagner first tasted the heady wine of ecclesiology. He was never, in fact, an orthodox ecclesiologist; but he remained a ritualist all his life. He grew up a plump, cherubic bachelor, a fervent Anglican sacramentalist, a rich priest whose life was dedicated to the poor. His first church, R.C. Carpenter's St Paul's, Brighton (1846–8), gave him a taste for building, a taste which quickly became obsessional. Mission huts; chapels; churches; cathedrals in all but name – he built or rebuilt at least a dozen Brighton landmarks. G. F. Bodley, R. H. Carpenter, George Somers Clarke Jnr., Edmund Scott: these were his principal architects. And Brighton's churches are his memorial: the high-shouldered belfry of St Paul's; the dazzling reredos of St Martin's; the dizzy bulk of St Bartholomew's. As lofty as the vault of Amiens; wider than the nave of St Paul's, Scott's St Bartholomew's was tougher than Teulon, bolder than Butterfield and highest of the High. It cost Wagner £18,000. His churches were daubed with Protestant slogans; his curates were charged with Popery; his rituals were investigated by the Privy Council; his veracity was questioned in a murder trial; he was even beaten up in the street. But under Fr Wagner's benevolent protection South Coast Anglo-Catholicism became a religious phenomenon of national interest. No wonder his father, a High Churchman but never a Tractarian, once preached a kindly – but cautionary – sermon on the subject of his son's obsessions: 'Lord, have mercy on my son, for he is lunatick and sore vexed'.[88]

This, therefore, was the world of supercharged Highchurchmanship into which Burges found himself drawn in the early 1860s. For Fr Wagner himself he designed only a temporary church. But for two of Wagner's epigoni, the Rev John Purchas and the Rev Charles Beanlands, he designed a major church and some church plate of extraordinary quality.

'Wagner's church', Burges noted in his diary for 1863. Alas, it was no more than a temporary structure – near Somers Clarke's later church of St Martin's – 'to be used hereafter as a hall'. Its area was only 144 × 36 ft. Even so, Burges managed to give it the stamp of his own style.[89] The high-pitched gable, the cartwheel window, the lean-to narthex, the tie-beamed roof, the plate-traceried lancets, the buttressed apsidal chancel: each feature is characteristic of Burges's cheaper churches. The style itself is minimal Early French. But the plan, as the *Ecclesiologist* noted, is a miniaturised, Protestant version of the Dominican churches of Italy.[90]

Much larger and more elaborate was the church Burges designed for one of Fr Wagner's curates, the Rev Charles Beanlands (1823–98). Beanlands began as an *avant-garde* ritualist, and ended as confidant and chaplain to the family of the 24th Earl of Crawford.[91] He seems to have been especially friendly with Crawford's ecclesiologist son, Colin Lindsay (1819–92), and Crawford's genealogist grandson, William Lindsay (1846–1926). As an undergraduate at Cambridge, Beanlands had caught the Cam-denian fever: he even designed the first post-reformation chasuble on a non-fiddle-back pattern.[92] William Lindsay eventually went over to Rome, but Beanlands stayed within the Anglican fold – just. Throughout his life his links with the art world were strong: he travelled, he collected, and he had his portrait painted by G. F. Watts. In 1859 Wagner presented him with the new ecclesiastical district of Montpelier, Brighton, and made him responsible for the erection of a new church, St Michael and All Angels. Bodley was the architect chosen. The foundation stone was laid in 1861, and consecration followed in 1862. Now Bodley's church was his first major design, boldly Ruskinian, in plum-red brick with bands of buff Bath stone.[93] 'A boyish, antagonistic effort', he called it, years afterwards when he had long forsaken Italian and French Gothic for English Perpendicular, suave and smooth.[94] Its exterior was severe; the glory lay inside. Its windows were filled with early Morris glass from cartoons by Ford Madox Brown, Burne-Jones, Philip Webb and Morris himself. Its roof was painted by Morris and Webb. And its altar fittings were designed by Burges.

These fittings for St Michael's show Burges in a new light, as a master of metal-work design. In woodwork there is less to see. The carved walnut choirstalls, echoing those at Cork, are less arresting than those at Waltham. And the vestry cupboard – if it is by Burges – is cheap and unpretentious. The textiles, however, are intriguing, and the metalwork superb. In the textile field comparatively little of Burges's work survives. His altar frontal for Beanlands, therefore, made *c.* 1861 by Miss Anderson, a member of the Society for the Advancement of Ecclesiastical Embroidery, is particularly interesting.[95] It features the seven archangels, framed by fantastic turrets and Gothic arcades, embroidered in colour against a white background. Its companion set of vestments and banners is less indicative of an architectural or sculptural mind, and much less conclusively Burgesian.[96] In any case, all these items are overshadowed by the metalwork.

As an artist in church metalwork, Burges undoubtedly chafed under the aesthetic bonds of Protestantism. Pugin had been able to design reliquaries, chasses, thuribles, pyxes, ciboria, chrismatories and all manner of monstrances. To a designer like T. H. King, the sacristy was his oyster.[97] But Burges – at least while executing Anglican commissions – was forbidden to indulge in the bric-à-brac of Popery. In practice he was limited to chalice, paten, flagon, cross, candlestick, service-book bindings, altar frontal, dossal and alms-dish. Still, that was enough. And the reformed church did have the advantage of placing greater emphasis on lecterns. Indeed, Burges's career more than demonstrates the validity of his own dictum: 'a man may show his talent in designing and executing goldsmith's work quite as much as in architecture, painting or sculpture.'[98] As in stained glass, so in metalwork, however, Burges suffered the excitements and frustrations of the pioneer. For some time his own designs were hamstrung by the quality of workmanship available.

Between 1843 and 1856 Butterfield was the Camden Society's accredited metalwork designer. Its chosen manufacturers were John Keith and Son of Britannia Terrace. Between 1856 and 1864, Street held the same position and Keith remained as manufacturer. In 1864 Burges succeeded to the position previously held by Butterfield and Street. His favourite manufacturers were Hardman & Co.; Hart, Son and Peard; and Barkentin and Krall.

John Hardman & Co. of Birmingham were a firm Burges never employed for stained glass. As silversmiths, however, he employed them to make several remarkable chalices in the early 1860s. After Pugin's death in 1852, their chief designer was J. Hardman Powell. Powell in turn trained a number of assistants, notably several members of the Pippet family. But the Hardman silver made at Burges's behest was designed by Burges himself. Hart, Son and Peard were a firm with whom Burges had a long-standing arrangement. Charles Hart (d. 1880), a Bible-trained ironmonger, took up ecclesiastical metalwork in the 1840s and joined the Ecclesiological Society in 1863. He was partnered by Thomas Peard, an ironmonger from Bideford, in 1853. Separated in 1860, they joined up again – along with Frederick Jackson – c. 1870. Hart superintended the Birmingham works, Jackson the finance, and Peard the factory in Drury Lane, the showroom in Regent St, and the production of the firm's catalogue.[99]

Jess Barkentin (?1800–81), 'the Danish Cellini', jeweller to the Court of Denmark, had worked with Hunt and Roskell before making his name with the Alexandra Vase (1864).[1] He succeeded Keith as silversmith and goldsmith to the Ecclesiological Society in 1867.[2] Carl Krall (1844–1923) was a German, of Czech descent – Norman Shaw called him 'the balmy German'[3] – who had been apprenticed in Switzerland, studied in Munich, Berlin and Paris and arrived in England c. 1866. He joined Barkentin c. 1869, and became a member of the Art Workers' Guild in 1885. The firm partly re-emigrated to America and ended up designing the Coca Cola sign.[4] Burges employed Barkentin and Krall for some of his most dazzling work.

At St Michael's, Brighton, Burges employed all three manufacturers in turn: Hart, Hardman and Barkentin. Hart was responsible for the silver, pear-shaped wine flagon of 1862,[211] its handle studded with agates.[5] Presumably the same firm produced the ring-handled alms-dish.[6][212] And it was presumably Hart who made Burges's original altar cross of silver and ivory, and the six silver candlesticks, modelled on specimens in the Cluny Museum.[7] It was Barkentin, however, who produced, in 1867, Burges's specimen scheme for an elaborate dossal,[210] silver gilt, shimmering with 'enamels and filigrees ... exquisitely wrought'.[8] Finally it fell to Hardman to produce 'Beanlands' chalice'.[213] That is the description which appears in Burges's diary for 1862. With conical bowl, leaf-shaped calyx, spherical knop and circular foot, its form owes something to both Gothic and Byzantine prototypes. Its materials are equally eclectic: parcel-gilt silver, malachite, lapis-lazuli, crystal, amethyst, agate, topaz, turquoise, pearl and cinnamon stone. And its iconography is a Burgesian *tour de force*: the vesicas of the calyx are engraved with winged seraphim in Byzantine manner; around the rim is inscribed an extract from an eighth-century 'Hymn for the dedication of a church'; and the foot is engraved with allegories of the Four Rivers of Paradise, the Tree of Life, the Tree of Knowledge, and the Heavenly Jerusalem – 'a wall great and high', pierced by 'twelve gates, and at the gates twelve angels, and names written thereon, which are the names of the twelve tribes of the children of Israel'.[9]

A year or so later, Burges designed a second chalice[214] for St Michael's, a second chalice richer even than the first. With hexagonal bowl, flourettes, spherical knop and circular foot, its form is compact and geometrical. But its surface coruscates with colour: the flourettes are enamelled in black and green; the stem is malachite above and cornelian below; the knop is of rock crystal caged with filigreed straps studded with diamonds, turquoise, garnets, moonstones, amethysts, sapphires and pearls; and the foot is set with ogee-shaped niello panels of Christ and the archangels Gabriel, Michael and Raphael, studded with gems. Hardman again was the maker, and the chalice was presented to the church in 1864.[10]

The glitter and solemnity of Beanlands' services attracted large crowds. One of the censers – probably designed by Didron – had been brought back from Paris by Beanlands and William Lindsay. Summoned by a bell retrieved from Sebastopol, the congregation grew. Swelling numbers prompted dreams of expansion. And this time, in 1868, Beanlands turned to Burges: he had fallen out with Bodley over a fifteenth-century Flemish triptych.[11] 'St Michael and All Angels', noted the *Building News*, 'is about to be enlarged, we may say reconstructed'.[12] But the money had yet to be found. For the time being, Burges's work in Brighton remained small-scale, limited perhaps to another chalice connected not with Beanlands but with an even more dogmatic ritualist, the Rev John Purchas (1823–72).

As one of Fr Wagner's more enthusiastic curates, Purchas might just have merited a footnote in a sub-parochial history. As the author of *Directorium Anglicanum* (1858, 1865, 1866, 1879), however, he is sure of at least a mention in any history of Anglican ritual. And during the last four years of his life, between 1869 and 1872, Purchas entered the ranks of the immortals. His love of ritual became notorious, even in

Brighton: he was known to hang a stuffed dove above the altar at the feast of Pentecost. Pursued first by a retired colonel, and then by an ex-Indian judge, he appeared before the Canterbury Court of Arches and the Judicial Committee of the Privy Council, charged with a whole cluster of offences against the rubric: 'using a cope (otherwise than during a communion service), chasubles, albs, stoles, tunicles, dalmatics, birettas, wafer bread, lighted candles on the altar, crucifixes, images, and holy water; ... standing with his back to the people when consecrating the elements, mixing water with the wine, censing the minister, leaving the holy table uncovered during the service, directing processions round the church, and giving notice of unauthorised holidays'.[13] Fined, suspended and very nearly imprisoned, Purchas carried on censing, a willing martyr to the cause of Anglo-Catholic ritual.

Perhaps it was this martyr's crown which prompted the creation of a suitable memorial soon after his death: the Purchas chalice, silver-gilt, set with precious and semi-precious stones, and made by John Hardman & Co. in 1874.[14] Now the attribution of this chalice to Burges is by no means clear. In fact, documentary evidence of any sort has yet to come to light. All we have are enigmatic references in Burges's diary for 1865–6.[15] But in terms of style the 'Purchas chalice' is indeed Burgesian. Its knot resembles that of Beanlands' chalice; its collet that at Kingsbury; and its jewelled base arcading – derived perhaps from a thirteenth-century chalice at Rheims[16] – echoes the decoration of another chalice made by Hardman from Burges's designs.[17] If it is not Burges, it certainly belongs to his school.

Meanwhile, back at St Michael's, Beanlands had not given up hope. Throughout the 1870s, however, Burges's plan remained in abeyance. The fabric of Bodley's church alone had cost at least £4,000. But services were conducted with great panache: there were even drums to accompany masses by Beethoven, Mozart or Gounod.[18] Beanlands seems to have been a formidable fund-raiser, especially with the ladies. Two spinsters named Windle made the Bodley building possible.[19] Chalices and vestments glittered with jewels cast into the collecting plate by several of Beanlands' parishioners. When the time at last came for extending St Michael's, Bodley had left the scene. But Burges was still in favour: for Beanlands' mother's family he had virtually re-designed a house in Yorkshire in 1865. In 1868, therefore, he produced a dramatic scheme for the aggrandisement of Beanlands' church. Bodley's building was transformed into a South aisle, dwarfed by a new Burgesian nave, and echoed on the Northern side by another aisle and vestries.[37] Over the whole composition towered a vast campanile.[20] Alas, funds were still insufficient. Work was not to begin in earnest for another quarter of a century, long after Burges was dead. Execution fell to the faithful Chapple. The new nave[38] was at last begun in 1892, and structurally completed in 1895. The roof was added in 1899. Not until the turn of the century, however, was the sanctuary finished, with its banded alabaster walling and elaborate reredos by Romaine Walker. Kempe's windows in the North aisle and Beanlands' tomb in the chancel, appeared about the same time. Some of the carving –

the cherub's-head capitals in the sanctuary – were still in hand in 1914, the year when Temple Moore's marble altar-piece was finally installed.[21] In this final phase, 1892 onwards, more than £17,000 was spent.

Chapple's version of Burges's grand design is in substance faithful enough. But the surface seems somehow too suave. The touch of the master is missing. The East and West windows – Jesse Tree and Creation by Lonsdale and Saunders – are perhaps a little too bright.[22] Nicholls' carving of St Michael is a little too smooth. Still, the bones of the building are nobly shaped. Those ringed piers; that double-plated tracery; that masterly linking of arcade, triforium and clerestory; that gargantuan cartwheel window. There are echoes here – right at the end of the century – of triumphs of long ago: Lille and Constantinople; Brisbane and Edinburgh. Bodley's earlier work is overshadowed but not suppressed. Goodhart-Rendel understood. 'Magnificent in conception and noble in size, the new church is as faithful to the traditions of Northern France as the old is to those of Southern Italy, and is perhaps the finest of those few precious works that testify for all time to the genius of William Burges. New St Michael's, with its cathedral-like nave of arcade, triforium, clerestory and vault is as grand in its way as anything that the nineteenth century has produced.'[23] That is pitching it a little high – but only a little.

LESSER ENGLISH CHURCHES

Burges had the reputation – which he never denied – of being an expensive architect. But he was also capable of working in a style which was economical in price as well as form. Several of his smaller churches illustrate this capacity: a talent for cutting costs by concentrating ornament only where it was necessary.

At Chiswick, for example, in 1861, he designed a church which would have rivalled Templebrady in miniaturised muscularity. Plate tracery, low-sprung vaults, square soffits, compressed colonnettes: Early French at its simplest.[24] Work was begun but remained incomplete, until the arrival of J. L. Pearson in 1882. Pearson incorporated some of Burges's work, rather to the disadvantage of his own additions. The contrast between the 1860s and the 1880s – between thirteenth-century and fifteenth-century mouldings – is telling. Still more so the stained glass. Burges's two surviving windows – perhaps by Holiday for Lavers and Barraud – are minor miracles of design, glowing with deep, lustrous light.[25]

Lowfield Heath (1867–8)[26][43] cannot have been a very expensive commission. But the details are handled with rare skill. On the outside, roughly textured sandstone laid in narrow bands contrasts with smooth plate tracery and smoother facings. Inside, a modest chancel is converted into an architectural experience by a double-planed, triple window of staggering power. A whole clutch of the architect's trademarks reappear: the lean-to porch, the louvred tower, the top-heavy window surrounds, the nail-head studding, the wheel window with compass-point sculpture, the tie-post boarded roof, the 'Church' and 'Synagogue' heads, the triple-decker corbels of the nave, the stumpy columns of the chancel arch, the iron hinges wrought like pomegranate fingers – even the half-hidden joke: a puppy-dog corbel lurking between gable and tower. No one but Burges could have designed the fleshy tendrils of the pulpit,[27] still less the evangelistic beasts of the font.[28] Lowfield Heath is a veritable anthology of Burgesian 'dodges'. The basic elements of the design had been anticipated in his unexecuted scheme for Bewholme church, Yorkshire (1861).[29] The Four Ages of Man sculptures had been used before for Florence, and would be used again at Skelton. Nicholls' sculpture, inside and out, has been drawn with verve and placed with unerring tact. These were the details Goodhart-Rendel admired for their 'extraordinary vigour'.[30]

By comparison, the nearby church at Outwood (1869)[31] is plain-spoken to the point of bluntness. The timber altar-rail, for instance, is rude and rustic, the masonry rough and crumbly. The timbered roof and mosaic reredos are recongisably Burgesian. But the saddle-back tower (1876 by W.P. Manning) must have been altered in execution.[32]

Murston (1872–3)[33][42] is equally simple. Rose window, plate tracery, lean-to porch, lobed roof, apsidal chancel: it is a pattern common to Burges's earlier church at Fleet and his later church at Cumnock. But being in Kent rather than Hampshire or Ayrshire, Murston is faced not with brick or stone, but with knapped flint. As at Cumnock, the spire – 135 ft high – was never built. £2,000 was subscribed, but £3,000 was needed.[34] So the tower appears truncated; the composition awkward and unbalanced. But the interior – presumably designed with polychromy in mind – is effective; and the multi-columned font develops the Lowfield Heath prototype with success.

All these were country churches. For Burges, no modern town church worth naming had been built before 1864. 'We want churches', he told ecclesiologists, 'something like Angevin churches, with great thick walls, domed or vaulted, filled with mosaic inside, and perhaps majolica or mosaic or marble outside. As to putting a little village church in London it is simply absurd. London at the present day is very different from London in the middle ages. England in the middle ages was something like a third-rate kingdom; at present it is first rate, if not the first. London has increased enormously: we are rebuilding it as rapidly as we can, and getting houses five or six storeys high. We might get churches quite as high, and also get great masses, so as to distinguish them from private houses. The only way to ornament them will be by the assistance of such men as Dr Salviati, Mr Fisher, and other artists who work in mosaic. It is an imperishable kind of ornament. If the Angevin type is taken, we can get large broad surfaces, and the mosaic can be done so many square feet a year. It is never finished, but always going on'.[35] New materials, new wealth, new processes, should dictate the type of structure and the form of decoration. 'We should not be building little copies of thirteenth-century village churches with Kentish rag-rubble walls in the heart of the nineteenth-century commercial metropolis. On the contrary, we should build thick and high walls, of good sound stone or brick, so thick that they should bear vaulting or domes, and so high that they should over-top the huge warehouses which surround them. In them we should place great columns and slabs of precious marbles brought from afar and polished by that real slave of the lamp, the steam engine. The domes and upper parts of the walls would glow with imperishable mosaics from our glass-houses, and the same source would supply the gems for the windows. The dossal would shine with gilded metal and gems, and a whole history would be carved in the stalls'.[36] Ecclesiology had begun the battle. Now it was time for Art.

Those views were hardly original. In enunciating them, Burges did less than justice to the ideas – and achievements – of Butterfield, Street and Beresford-Hope. But, at least as regards decoration, he alone was able to envision the totality of the dream. Paradoxically, he was never able to actualise that vision. Burges's town churches – that is, if we exclude Cork Cathedral – are not major works. And he made only two contributions to the ecclesiology of London, both begun in 1872–3: St Thomas's, Upper Clapton, and St Faith's, Stoke Newington.

At Clapton Burges inherited a nondescript Georgian church of 1776, with a Regency tower of 1827. Between 1873 and 1878, he transformed its interior into a glittering basilica. Bumpus records the process:

> Taking as his ideal ... San Clemente, at Rome, [Burges] turned old St Thomas's inside out. ... The galleries which surrounded the church on three sides were taken away; the two rows of windows, lighting the sides, were reduced to one; tracery, of a kind seen in some Greek basilicas, was inserted in the windows; a flat, deeply coffered roof of wood was placed over the huge pillarless expanse; a low, Western narthex, opening into the church by a colonnade of square pillars was added; and a *chorus cantorum*, fenced on its North, South and West sides by a wall of beautiful white marble, with ambone-like erections for the reading desk and pulpit of the same material, was formed in the centre of the area towards the East. Frescoes now enrich the semidome of the apsidal recess containing the altar, and portions of the walls in other parts of the church, and stained glass of deep rich tinctures has been inserted in several windows. In short, the transformation under the magic wand of Burges was marvellous, and is well worth minute inspection.[37]

Burges had translated a Protestant conventicle into an Early Christian basilica. The result was very much more impressive than his earlier attempt to Gothicise a similarly dull box at Hoddesdon, Herts (1861).[38] But little or nothing of Burges's work at Clapton survives. The nave was destroyed in the Blitz. And what little of Burges survived has in turn been remodelled by N. F. Cachmaille-Day.[39]

'Stoke Newington', Burges notes enigmatically in his diary for 1868; and again 'Stoke Newington drawings' in 1871, and 'Stoke Newington begun' in 1872.[40]

Consecration followed in 1873, when only the chancel and two thirds of the nave had been built.[41] Not until 1881 was the West front begun, several months after Burges's death.[30b; 35–36]

The chronology is important. Not only was St Faith's completed by another – James Brooks – but the cardinal features of its great West front reappear in one almost exactly contemporary church by J. L. Pearson (St Augustine's, Kilburn, 1870–80),[42] and in two later designs by Brooks (St Peter, St Leonard's on Sea, 1883; and Liverpool Cathedral, 1886).[43] There are three possible explanations. Either Burges cribbed from Pearson, and Brooks in turn cribbed from Burges; or else Brooks refashioned Burges's designs in Pearson's image, and then re-used Pearson's idea twice more; or else the West front of Stoke Newington grew out of the same eclectic matrix as the West front of Kilburn, and so impressed Brooks when he came to complete it that he absorbed portions of the design into his own vocabulary. Of these alternatives only the last is really feasible. Burges needed no lessons in Early French from Pearson. And Brooks would hardly have treated Burges cavalierly within months of his death; the West front was conceived as a Burges memorial, and Brooks acted free of charge, in his capacity as churchwarden of Butterfield's neighbouring church of St Matthias.

St Faith's, therefore, is essentially a Burges church; his only complete town church; and doubly interesting as his sole attempt to answer the aesthetic and liturgical demands of an urban parish with the language of progressive eclecticism.

St Faith's originated as a High Church protest. The Bishop of London appointed a Low Church vicar at Butterfield's neighbouring St Matthias. The congregation replied by setting up their own liturgical kingdom. Their leader was Dr Robert Brett (1808–74), the 'Pope of Stoke Newington'. His assistant was Richard Foster.[44] Between them they made possible a church which might have ranked among Burges's most extraordinary creations.

Even in its unfinished state, it merited a special visit by the Architectural Association.:

> St Faith's is a fragment of what promises to be a church of monumental character. The site being bounded by roads on two sides, the problem was to plan a church which should extend to the verge of the ground, without loss of space by external buttresses, and that would afford an uninterrupted view to all worshippers. The manner in which these requirements have been met has been by an edifice of brickwork, of great height, consisting of a nave and spacious semicircular chancel; massive buttresses being carried inside the building. ... The buttresses are so arranged as to allow a passage, 5 ft deep, to be formed in the thickness of the wall. This is carried behind the apsidal chancel as an ambulatory leading to a vestry in the rear. About 10 ft above the floor-level of the church, a kind of triforium, wide enough to place two rows of seats, is formed upon the buttresses. On this triforium a tier of cast iron columns is placed to support the roof. This is barrel-shaped, boarded, and very lofty. ... The style adopted is 13th c. French, but there are few

details. The effect is novel, if not beautiful, but the building, incomplete even so far as the portion erected is concerned, evidently does not do justice to the designs.[45]

That plan – Albi translated into Early French – had come down to Burges via Clutton's *avant-garde* St Jude's, Bethnal Green (1845–6). The apsidal sweep of the great coved roof derived perhaps from Tillard, near Beauvais. The coupled arches of the nave arcades from St Jacques at Rheims. The broad lancets echo those at Sens or Auxerre, or the East end of the choir at Canterbury. Other elements have been traced to the Chapel of the Archbishop's Palace at Rheims, the partour of the choir of St Jean at Sens, and the early thirteenth-century church of Nun Monkton near York.[46]

Burges treated these historical elements in a ruthlessly functional way. The yellow brick walls were stark and sheer as a warehouse. The cast iron columns might well have graced a pumping station.[47] Ecclesiology had put on its working clothes to do battle in the streets of Stoke Newington. Early French had been industrialised. Unfortunately, the 'Pope of Stoke Newington' died in 1874, and – despite Brooks's West front – St Faith's remained an unclothed skeleton. 'It is truly grievous', Bumpus noted, 'to see a church of the structural claims of St Faith's so spoilt. Properly fitted and decorated in a style such as Burges would have approved ... this most striking and abnormal of London churches ... might have become one of the most remarkable raised in England since the Revival.'[48] In 1944 the skeleton bacame a torso. A German flying bomb ripped open the roof, creating 'a spectacle of incredible grandeur ... the fragment of something infinitely magnificent. The remote apse was patinaed with sunlight sprayed through open rafters; and the west wall had been torn aside just sufficiently for the noble and still fresh interior to gain by contrast with its rough-hewn shell. Nothing', Sir John Summerson recalls, 'could have been more moving – and nothing less stable.'[49]

St Andrew, Wells St, London

A short stroll from Oxford Circus – not far from All Saints, Margaret St – stood the mecca of ecclesiology: St Andrew's, Wells St. Beresford-Hope became its churchwarden in 1853; Benjamin Webb its vicar in 1862, its congregation was rich and fashionable. Its services 'High Church without being in the least Anglo-Catholic'.[50] Twice daily the psalms were sung. Each Sunday the choir sang masses by Beethoven, Cherubini, Schubert, Haydn, Mozart or Hummel. In the early 1870s, Charles Gounod himself was a frequent attender, and his Passiontide motets were adapted from the Latin by Benjamin Webb. Outside, it looked rather a dull church, designed by Hamilton and Daukes in 1845–7. Inside, it was a veritable treasure-house of High Victorian design. Stained glass by Pugin and Hardman, and Clayton and Bell; an altar frontal by Pugin; a font-cover by Pearson; a reredos carved by Redfern; a lectern designed by Butterfield; a font, pulpit and open screens designed by Street; a gallery painted by Alfred Bell; and a litany desk, tomb, window and full set of altar plate all designed by Burges. In 1933 the church was dismantled, transported stone by stone, and re-erected at Kingsbury, Middlesex. Despite their curious career, however, nearly all the church's treasures survive.

Webb's predecessor as vicar of St Andrew's had been the Rev James Murray (d. 1862). And it was Murray's memorial which gave Burges his first commission for this prestigious church. The memorial, designed in 1862,[51] took the form of a recumbent effigy, set in a recessed, canopied tomb, backed by a mural painting, and surmounted by a stained glass window. The form of the tomb – raised up and set into the wall – was Italian, perhaps from prototypes in Padua or Verona.[52] But the calculated over-scaling of the sculpture – beasts, birds and foliage – reveals at once the identity of its designer. Nicholls was the sculptor; Harland and Fisher executed the colouring;[53] Smallfield was the artist responsible for the inset Christ in Majesty;[54] and Smallfield – apparently in conjunction with Poynter – produced the cartoons for the grisaille glass window executed by Lavers and Barraud.[55] Architecture, sculpture, painting, glass: once again, Burges emerges as coordinator-in-chief, master of all the arts.

Next came the litany desk, designed by Burges in 1867. Such an item of ecclesiastical furniture was, in any case, *avant-garde*: it only became rubrically respectable in 1857.[56] Burges contrived to make it not only respectable but symbolic. It features not only St Andrew, St George and St Michael, but the emblems of the Passion and figures symbolising penitence and prayer: censing angels, Zacharias and the Prophet Joel.[57] Here, then, is a veritable 'Altar of Innocence'. Modelled in clay by Nicholls; carved by Robinson of High Holborn in chunky, blackened walnut, inlaid with maple *intarsiatura*, the St Andrew's litany desk is a prime example of Burges's talent for compressed, highly charged, almost overwrought, design.

Still more so the altar plate. Burges's designs consisted of a chalice, two vases, two candlesticks and a crucifix, all made by Barkentin and Krall.[58] The vases – for lilies – have Burges's characteristic tulip-vase necking. Their silver gilt bowls are set with enamel medallions in blue and green. Candlesticks (1871) – silver gilt, gem-set and enamelled – are decorated with pearl drops. Like the candlesticks and vases, the crucifix (1875) was presented by W. R. Cusack Smith (1832–87), a London barrister of Irish descent.[59] Silver gilt, set with enamel and crystal, decorated with an image of St Andrew, plus four sacrificial emblems (Abel, Abraham, Melchisedec and Esca Angelorum), this crucifix resembled one made for Lord Bute in 1871 and cost Cusack Smith £340.[60] But the chalice (1867–69) was more elaborate still. Not only was its stem composed of malachite, and its surface studded with jewels; it was richly decorated with figured enamels. Its wide bowl was set in a double calyx decorated with enamelled symbols of Christ: 'the Agnus Dei, emblem of His innocence; the Pelican, emblem of His meritorious Death; the Lion, emblem of His Resurrection; the Eagle, emblem of His Ascension; the Antelope, emblem of His loftiness of soul; the

Phoenix, emblem of His new Life; the Ox, emblem of His Sacrifice; and the Swan, emblem (by its dying song) of the voluntariness of His Death.' Below this symbolic band, the knop was decorated with enamel roundels representing the Church, the Synagogue and the Four Rivers of Paradise. And below this again, the circular foot was filled with quatrefoil enamels representing the Angel of the Annunciation, the Virgin Mary, the Crucifix between Sun and Moon, St John the Evangelist, St Andrew, plus a fragment of fourth-century gilded glass from the early Christian catacombs, presented by Burges himself.[61]

At St Andrew's, Burges's mastery of all the decorative arts is incontestable. When the A.A. visited the church in 1875;[62] when the St Paul's Ecclesiological Society visited it in 1881,[63] what was particularly noticed was Burges's close involvement with every stage of design and with the actual process of manufacture.[64] The vocation of art-architect was not a responsibility he took lightly. And at St Andrew's, Wells St, his work – until its dispersal – was in a sense on permanent exhibition. His last connection with the church came just before his death, when he designed a tomb for a leading member of the congregation: Emma Jane Knight Watson, wife of the Secretary of the Society of Antiquaries.[65]

ALL SAINTS, SELSLEY, GLOS

The donor of the glorious St Andrew's chalice had been John Baker Gabb, Superintendent of the Alliance Marine Insurance Co. from 1851 to 1870. The Gabbs were clothiers of Ebley, near Stroud. And Ebley – improbably enough – was a centre not only of the Gloucestershire woollen industry, but of ecclesiology and Pre-Raphaelitism too. At Ebley Mills lived Sir Samuel Stephens Marling Bt. (1810–83), the area's Liberal M.P., a rich mill-owner who died in his own counting house.[66] His neighbours included two artistically-minded clerics: the Rev Samuel Lloyd, Vicar of Horsley; and the Rev John Gibson, Rector of King's Stanley.[67] All three joined forces to create All Saints, Selsley (1861–2), a shrine of High Victorian art. High up on Selsley Beacon, its French saddleback tower – 107 ft tall – looks out over the Stroud valley, echoing the French Gothic tower of Marling's factory below.[68] Next to the church stands Lloyd's Picturesque house, Stanley Park. And not far away is Gibson's rectory, rebuilt in 1858 by R. Reynolds Rowe. Here, then, was a Cotswold nucleus of 'progressive' Goths. Selsley church is their achievement. Bodley was the architect; the stained glass was designed by Morris, Webb, Ford Madox Brown, Burne-Jones and Rossetti; the altar plate was designed by Burges.

Burges's Selsley chalice was designed in 1860, and made in silver in 1862 by Hart. With its broad bowl, calyx of stylised leaves, fluted stem, lobed knop, and high circular foot, the chalice is broadly thirteenth-century in style. But the double-tiered engravings on the foot are characteristically Burgesian: at one level, Christ the King, Christ the Sacrifice and the Four Evangelists; at another, the Agnus Dei with chalice and pelican, and the four evangelistic symbols.[69] It was a design Burges used elsewhere: at Holme-upon-Spalding-Moor, Yorks (1861: Keith); at Elvetham, Hants. [208] (1873: Barkentin),[70] and at Cuddesden College, Oxon (1873: Hart). At Selsley the matching flagon, of the same date, is also by Hart. In form it is almost identical to Burges's flagon at St Michael's, Brighton. The Selsley flagon, however, is engraved with portraits of David, Melchisedec, Abel, and Noah: Old Testament prefigurings of the Eucharistic Sacrifice.[71] Chalice and flagon reappear once more at Freeland, Oxon (1868: Hart).

The new parish of Selsley had been carved out of the older parish of King's Stanley. And at King's Stanley rectory lived Burges's friend, the Rev John Gibson. For Gibson's wife, Burges designed a bracelet and other items of jewellery, executed by Wakeman.[72] Gibson seems to have designed the choir stalls in his own parish church.[73] He certainly subscribed to Burges's *Architectural Drawings*. And – most intriguing of all – he is reputed to have had a hand in the design of Selsley's wonderful Creation window.[74] Now the deep-tinted abstraction of that great wheel window – the stylised wave patterns for instance – is more than a little reminiscent of some of Burges's own glass at Cork or Studley Royal. Perhaps Burges was involved here as well – along with Morris, Webb, Gibson and the glass-painter Campfield. The suggestion is tempting. But there is no proof.

THE DUNEDIN CROZIER

In 1865 the Rev H. L. Jenner (1820–98), Secretary to the Ecclesiological Society, was appointed first Bishop of Dunedin in New Zealand. The Society decided to present him with a crozier. Now at that time Arthur Blomfield was designing a crozier for the Bishop of Calcutta, and R. H. Carpenter a crozier for the Bishop of Chichester. But Burges's Dunedin crozier[215] was more ambitious than either of these. In fact, in terms of artistry and originality it was one of the best designs he ever made.

At first it was to be a pastoral staff in ebony and ivory.[75] Then it became silver and ivory, set with gems. Barkentin was the maker, and with it he won the title of goldsmith to the Ecclesiological Society.[76] First a model was prepared to Burges's designs, for display to the committee.[77] Then the work was executed in 1866–67, photographed by Francis Bedford and Frank Good, shown at the Architectural Exhibition, and presented to the departing Bishop.[78]

Burges's design represents 'the delivery of the virtuous from the power of the Evil One, through the instrumentality of the Champion of the Church, symbolised by the combat between St George and the Dragon'.[79] The dragon's reptile scales erupt with cabochon jewels; the princess, hair flowing, struggles vainly while a mustachioed St George forces open the mouth of the beast and plunges his broadsword deep into its gullet. Burges must have been enjoying himself. He re-drew the design in 'Wilars' – his vellum sketchbook – with the arch annotation: 'This is the staff of the Lord Bishop of the isles where they eat one another'.[80] And in 1875 he pulled the ultimate trick on posterity: with the crozier itself far away in the Antipodes, he published his design as a thirteenth-century original.[216] The vehicle of publication was a popular French periodical called *L'Art Pour Tous*.[81] Within twenty years the crozier had made its way not only into a German textbook, but into its English translation.[82] What a 'dodge'!

SMALLER RESTORATIONS

About the middle of the nineteenth century two attitudes towards restoration were in conflict: the destructive and the conservative. Burges supported the conservative.

The destructive theory – which its supporters would have preferred to call creative – was chiefly developed in France. It starts with Prosper Merimée's definition of 1845: 'By restoration we understand the conservation of that which exists and the recreation of that which has definitely existed'; it concludes with Viollet-le-Duc's dangerous dictum of 1866: 'To restore a building is to re-establish it to a completed state which may never have existed at any particular time'. The slogan of this school was 'Unity of Preference', and in England in the 1840s and early 1850s, the style preferred by ecclesiologists tended to be fourteenth-century Decorated. In the 1860s and 1870s the choice of style widened: this new freedom was known as eclectic restoration. But it was a freedom which still boded ill for medieval fragments. All over the country churches were destructively restored according to thoroughly Procrustean principles: between 1840 and 1873, no less than 7,144 of them, that is about half the Anglican churches of the land. 'One *perfectly longs* after an untouched church, admitted Gilbert Scott in 1862; adding shamefacedly: 'We are all of us offenders in the matter.' Indeed he was. What Wyatt began, Scott completed. His bag was said to include 26 cathedrals, 15 abbeys and 182 churches. 'The great difficulty', he confessed, 'is to know *where to stop*.'[83]

It was in reaction to such excesses that the theory of 'conservative restoration' developed. E. A. Freeman had invented the term as early as 1846. 'It would reproduce in repairing a building', he claimed, 'the exact details of every [surviving] piece of ancient work,' in other words, the creation of 'a new facsimile'. Such an attitude represented a new caution, and a novel catholicity of taste: a 'preferred style' was no longer to be imposed. Among the converts to this way of thinking were Street, Morris and Burges.

Burges frequently attacked 'the French mania for destructive restoration'.[84] 'No such edifice as the Abbey of St Denis now existed', he complained in 1861; 'It was utterly spoiled many years ago.'[85] Equally alarming was the headlong 'restoration' of St Patrick's Cathedral, Dublin, over-lavishly subsidised by Guinness.[86] But then criticism, he admitted, was easy enough. Who could confidently draw a line between repair and restoration? And where, in the end, did archaeology lead?

Westminster Abbey was a case in point. Burges thought the North portal, as 'restored' in Wren's time, 'a crying shame ... a disgrace to London'. But a modern re-restoration of that offending transept would pose problems delicate in the extreme. As Burges confessed, it was 'a very difficult matter to handle'.[87] Things had been easier for Viollet-le-Duc at Carcassonne. There, 'there was no art to destroy. It had been restored in the most perfect manner, and afforded a good idea of the military architecture of the Middle Ages. ... [Now] it was a page to learn from.' But that did not absolve him from responsibility at St Ouen; still less at Pierrefonds. There Viollet's fundamental insensitivity stands revealed: 'antiquarianism and archaeology do not make an architect'.[88] That night at the R.I.B.A., 'in the excitement of the moment', Burges spoke more honestly than he later thought wise.[89] Still, he was right.

Unlike many Victorian architects, Burges was at least well-qualified to tackle the ticklish problems of restoration. He was, in effect, a professional archaeologist. When Pearson wanted a bibliography on Westminster Abbey, it was to Burges he went for advice.[90] Burges's judgement with regard to the original roofing of London's medieval Guildhall has been fully vindicated by modern research.[91] And his cautious advice at Llandaff Cathedral – against Prichard and Seddon's re-roofing – was remarkably progressive for its date.[92] But it was not a field of practice he entered with relish:

> There is really no more difficult problem in the whole practice of architecture ... for a man to succeed thoroughly in it, he must be not only versed in modern and ancient construction, but must also be an antiquarian and something of an artist. [Each time an inexperienced architect] with good connections [tackles a work of restoration] we run a chance of losing some landmark in the history of architecture. [Since the triumph of Camdenian principles, too many churches had been restored.] I do not know whether ... to call this a restoration or a destruction, for so much injury has been done under this pretended restoration, that I do not hesitate to declare that we have lost a great deal more than we have gained. ... What really is wanted in the restoration of a church, is to do as little as possible. Keep it together if it is possible. If an aisle or a tower is tumbling down, rebuild it, using as much of the old materials as possible. ... Should there be any money to spare, employ it in a work of art as good as you can get for your money, i.e. one stained glass window, a dossal, or a painting on a wall or roof: but then get it good, and let it tell some story.[93]

WINSCOMBE AND FORTHAMPTON

Burges's talent for the cautious embellishment of medieval churches is confirmed by evidence at St James's, Winscombe, Somerset, and St Mary's, Forthampton, Gloucestershire. Both commissions were the product of family connections. Both seem to have been begun in 1863–4. Both involved the refurbishment of medieval churches which had suffered from repeated alteration. And both resulted in stained glass of superlative quality.

In 1855 the Rev John Augustus Yatman (1817–94) – a bewhiskered gentleman – cleric and amateur architect – retired from his Yorkshire curacy to become squire of Winscombe, near Weston-super-Mare. On Winscombe Hill, overlooking Glastonbury Tor, he began to build a house appropriate to his position. William Railton – designer of Nelson's column – was the architect employed. But by 1858 Yatman had abandoned Railton's faded Neo-Classicism: he had succumbed to William Burges. That was the year of his marriage, and also the year of his father's death. William Yatman Snr. (1786–1858) had been a successful London barrister. Another of his sons – Herbert George Yatman (d. 1911) – was already Burges's principal client for painted furniture. When the Rev Yatman decided to design himself a memorial, therefore, Burges was an obvious choice as adviser.[94] And work at the house led naturally to further work at the church. In 1862 a new vicar arrived at Winscombe. Yatman – who never progressed beyond the status of deacon – commissioned a restoration of the chancel. Its principal feature took the form of three stained glass windows in memory of his mother (d. 1858). When Pevsner wrote these up in 1958 he described them as 'much better aesthetically' than the church's medieval glass; 'splendid glowing colours, pretty apple and apple-leaf ornament, understanding use of leading ... one of the best examples of Morris glass in existence and quite unrecorded'.[95] But Morris was neither the artist nor the manufacturer. Those glorious lancets are by Burges, Weekes and Saunders (*c.* 1870). Their ten angular figures – in stylised Jesse form – echo sketches for Cardiff, Lowfield Heath and Skelton. Burges may even have been his own cartoonist. And the chromatic arrangement – shaded purple, gold and green on a background of watery blue and white – follows exactly his own recipe for successful design. Deep-set, dark-hued, these windows rank among his very best.

The chancel window at Forthampton is scarcely less important. In 1863 Augusta Emmeline Yorke died within weeks of producing an heir to the Gloucestershire estate of Forthampton. Her husband Reginald and her father-in-law Joseph Yorke called on Burges for a memorial.[96] First came a set of almshouses (1863), and then a sculptured dossal and triple window worthy of one of the few stone altars to have survived the Reformation.[97] The dossal (1866)[98] – a crucifixion with eight flanking figures – has Nicholls' boldly three-dimensional stamp. It forms both foil and base for a truly dazzling window. Like the Winscombe windows, the Forthampton glass is divided by leaves and russet apples. The range and intensity of colouring is also similar. But the nine Virtues are more conventionally Pre-Raphaelite, and their backgrounds and borders heavily diapered. Dating from 1866 – the pulpit window is 1869 – this glass must stem from the workshop of Saunders and Weekes, or else from the brief Holiday-Saunders partnership.[99] Either way its balance and tone are superb. At

Forthampton, as at Winscombe, Burges transformed a modest parish church into a focus of Pre-Raphaelite art.

LAMBETH PALACE CHAPEL

Burges held strong views on the subject of interior polychromy. In the first place its colour-scheme must be limited in range and controlled by precedent. In the second, its iconography must pursue a systematic programme. In great churches, he explained, 'what we want ... are light, beautifully coloured pictures on a deep background, say either of greenish blue or gold, and confined within ornamental borders, which will at the same time correct the lines of the architecture'. 'Snug' parish churches, however, had no need of a latter-day Giotto. There, 'lamp-black, and red and yellow ochre' were sufficient. And in great cathedrals, glowing with stained glass, extra colour need only appear in the form of moulded hollows tinted dull red, or capitals spiked with gold.[1]

> No one in his senses supposes that all the Medieval churches were decorated in brilliant gold and colours, like the Sainte Chapelle of Paris, or St Stephen's at Westminster. Yet they were painted, and in this manner; the rubble of the walls was dubbed out to a plain surface; the angle jambs of windows and doors were made of stone. ... The whole of the walls were then covered with a coating of gesso (whiting and size) $\frac{1}{8}$ in. thick, which was gradually thinned off as it approached the stone jambs, which were covered with only a thin coating of it, so they did not show as stone. Upon this gesso, the artist painted his subjects with a red outline and shaded them up with black and red and yellow, using white for the high lights. ... The seas of diaper we see in modern churches were unknown to the old artist, who, when he did employ diaper, did so only as a background. [Such was the decoration of] nearly every church in the thirteenth century.[2] The dead walls spoke and a story was told.[3]

Burges based these conclusions on extensive archaeological study. It was he – via J. H. Parker – who analysed for the Society of Antiquaries the cycle of fourteenth-century wall paintings discovered at St Mary, Chalgrove, Oxfordshire, in 1858.[4] It was he again who – in the same year – guided the uncovering of another cycle of thirteenth-century mural paintings at St Nicholas', Charlwood, Surrey. The paintings had been discovered by a friend of his, the Rev T. Burningham. Burges supervised their cleaning, recorded their form, and explained their significance to the Royal Archaeological Institute.[5] He was able to compare them with murals in the Campo Santo at Pisa, and with others which he had previously recorded on the roof of the thirteenth-century 'Chapelle des Pécheurs' adjoining the church of St Brelade in

Jersey.[6] And that by no means exhausted his terms of reference: he was even able to compare the iconography of medieval Swedish churches with his favourite illuminated manuscript, B. M. Royal 2 B.VII.[7]

A rare opportunity to translate theory into practice occurred at Lambeth Palace Chapel. Thanks to the generosity of Lachland Mackinstosh Rate, Burges was able to carry through a complete programme of polychrome decoration. In a detailed report of 1876[8] he set out the list of necessary exterior repairs: decayed freestone – polluted by the nearby pottery works – was to be replaced by ground Box stone; gables and parapets were to be renewed in Bath stone; and a new roof of higher pitch was to be covered with Westmorland slates. Straightforward enough. His real interest centred on the interior. Blore had already substituted plaster groining for the panelled ceiling of Archbishop Laud. Burges decided to keep it, but only as a base for painted decoration. Laud's elaborate woodwork, however, survived. Burges decided it should stay. After all, it was 'historical' and 'very picturesque'. But 'the varnish should be removed and boiled oil freely applied. When the wood shall have obtained its proper colour, partial gilding might be applied, and the arms ... emblazoned'. As for the rest of the fittings, Burges noted sharply: 'there is no dossal and the altar and movable pulpit are unworthy of such a building'. The new altar should rest on a sanctuary pavement of *opus vermiculatum*. And all the windows should be replaced, and filled with themes previously used by Archbishop Morton. 'I have taken the subjects', Burges explained, 'from the Biblia Pauperum, of which a list will be found in the Life of Our Lord by Lady Eastlake. I propose to follow the ancient rule of beginning at the Western window with the Creation, reserving the Eastern window for the Crucifixion and finishing at the South Western window with the Last Judgement. In the jambs of the windows and in the plain spaces [surrounding them] ... I would represent the prophets and messengers, while the vault itself would be filled with the Angelic Host playing instruments of music.'

As it happened, Fisher executed the painted work, Saunders the glass. And Rate's estimated bill came to £7,140: £710 more than the first estimate, and £2,140 more than his original offer.[9] The result must have been – at the very least – a complete and coherent example of High Victorian church decoration. Alas, its quality can only be judged from old photographs. Lambeth Palace Chapel was gutted by fire bombs in 1941.[10]

THE RICKETTS MONUMENT, KENSAL GREEN CEMETERY

Among the cryptic references in Burges's abbreviated diary, one is particularly enigmatic. 'Bonnor's tomb', he noted in 1867, and again in 1868. But who was Bonnor? And where was his tomb?

Well, George Bonnor (1822–93) was a lawyer who in 1852 secured a partnership in a firm of West End solicitors.[11] Within a year he had married Julia Anne Ricketts, a descendant on her mother's side of the Aubreys of Glamorgan. This hypergamous marriage produced no children. But it did – indirectly – produce a tomb: one of the most extraordinary tombs in London. The Bonnors set up house at 42 Queen's Gate Terrace, a large Italianate property crammed with works of art and staffed by seven servants.[12] There, in his old age, lived Julia's father, Capt Charles Spencer Ricketts, R.N. (1788–1867), a relic from the age of Nelson.[13] Ricketts had served in a hard school. His commander had been Thomas Cochrane, 10th Earl of Dundonald (1775–1860), 'the Blue-Jacket's idol', 'El Diablo' to his enemies, the man Napoleon nicknamed 'Le Loup de Mer'. Having joined the Navy at the age of seven, Ricketts married an heiress at twenty-six, and promptly retired. Thanks to his wife – Elizabeth Sophia Aubrey – he became landlord of Dorton and Boarstall, Bucks, and even High Sheriff of the County.[14] He fathered four children, set up a country spa, and wrote crusty polemics on the necessity of flogging.[15] But the marriage did not run smoothly. Mrs Ricketts waited until she was a widow and then became the fourth wife of a neighbouring squarson, the Rev George Chetwode.[16] Mrs Bonnor inherited £30,000 from her errant father,[17] and commissioned a tomb which would match his wild career – and eclipse the wounded dignity of the Aubreys. Burges was the lucky designer.

Tombs and monuments supplied Burges with some of his best opportunities. For Beresford-Hope's friend J. D. Cook (1811–68), editor of the *Saturday Review*, he designed a massive granite tomb above the rocky cliffs of Tintagel.[18] For the Hon Frances Mitford (1804–66) – sister of the proud and eccentric Lord Redesdale – he designed a glittering monument in Batsford church: creamy white marble, inset with gold mosaic and carved with birds, lions and green-eyed griffons.[19] But Ricketts' monument was to be more extraordinary than either of these.

Among Burges's drawings, there are several sketches for an elaborate canopied tomb incorporating a draped bier in the shape of a ship.[20] The ship remained a flight of fancy. But the sculptured canopy and bier were built: raised on sixteen stumpy columns, bristling with gargoyles, and groaning with a surfeit of crockets. Ricketts' monument[99] makes the Magniac tomb look tame. Hunched like a porcupine, fattened to the point of obesity, its reptilian silhouette is almost a parody of Early French. Pevsner called it 'atrociously rich' without realising its authorship.[21] But all the hallmarks of its architect's Gothic style are there to see: the ringed colonnettes, the studded trefoils, the muscular soffits, the mastic-filled inlay, the foliate masks, the compressed proportions, the overscaled sculpture. Billy Burges was having fun.

'If a building is all crockets', Burne-Jones once remarked, 'you go mad.' But like the poetry of William Morris, Burges's architecture makes demands on the spectator which are total. To accept is to surrender – or at least to suspend one's rational faculties for a moment. To quote Burne-Jones again: 'you cannot find short quotations in him, he must be taken at great gulps'.[22] Anyway, sipping or gulping, we are now ready to taste Burges's finest Gothic churches: Skelton and Studley Royal.

Skelton and Studley Royal

George Frederick Robinson, 1st Marquess of Ripon, P.C., K.G. (1827–1909)[4] was a Romantic Socialist, rich enough – almost – to translate the Dream into reality.[23] He was born in 10 Downing St, the son of Prime Minister 'Goody' Goderich, Disraeli's 'transient and embarrassed phantom'. Embarrassing – to his Liberal colleagues – Ripon may have been, but transient he was not. In a political career stretching over more than half a century he became successively Secretary of State for War, Lord President of the Council, Governor-General of India, First Lord of the Admiralty, Colonial Secretary and Lord Privy Seal. 'I started', he claimed in 1908, 'at a high level of radicalism. I am a radical still.'[24] He began as a Socialist, and emerged as a Gladstonian, but he was never a true Liberal: his radicalism had a strongly paternalistic streak, and he remained profoundly hostile to *laissez faire*. Appropriately, he came nearest to greatness as a reforming Viceroy who sowed the seeds of Indian independence.[25] A pint-sized, shrill-voiced idealist, he gazes quizzically out of Herkomer's portrait: a monocled, bushy-bearded patriarch with an eye vaguely fixed on the millennium. Granville dismissed him as 'a very persistent man – with wealth'. But in his ideological progression from Christian Socialism to Neo-Feudal Whiggery, Ripon never betrayed his fundamentally humanitarian impulse. Writing to W. E. Forster in 1881, from the Viceregal Lodge at Simla, he 'rejoiced' that 'despotic power' had not diminished his reforming instincts: 'I get more Radical every day.'[26]

What marked Ripon out as an ideal patron for Billy Burges was his romantic medievalism. When he became Marquess of Ripon in 1873 he had hoped to revive the ancient title of Mowbray. As a young man his Christian Socialism had been too Christian for F. D. Maurice, and too Socialist for Charles Kingsley.[27] In 1852, for instance, he gave £500 towards the Engineers Strike. In 1833 he was lecturing on Tennyson to the Hull Mechanics' Institution.[28] When he inherited Fountains Abbey his first thought was the re-creation of its community in modern form. 'If only I could get half a million of tin,' he wrote to Tom Hughes in 1853, I would 'turn that Fountains Abbey, restored and beautified, into a Working-man's University – don't that make your mouth water!'[29] When he built a private chapel in his house at Studley Royal, he dedicated it to Our Lady of Fountains, so that she 'should have something of her own again'.[30] With a flourish of gold sovereigns he rescued the shrine of San Damiano near Assisi, after reading Augustus Hare's *Cities of Northern and Central Italy* (1876).[31] And when in 1896 he sponsored a pageant at Fountains Abbey, Lord Bute was one of the party, and Ripon's private secretary J. Hungerford Pollen wrote down what all three felt: 'I wept when I remembered the days when the Abbey lived, and was the glory of the country; when the poor were fed and warmed in the wintry cold, when "hospitality" was kept, and all men rejoiced in the Catholic Faith. The times were rude, violence and injustice were not unknown, but heroic penances, noble works of charity, loyal service, were known also.'[32] Pugin himself could not have put it better.

As for art and architecture, Ripon's sympathies were clear. Writing to Hughes from Venice in 1856, he announced: this is 'the best place in the world to disgust one with Renaissance architecture – the churches built by Palladio are simply and perfectly *hideous*.'³³ And in 1852 he echoes Burges's admiration for Millais' *Huguenot*, but with sentiments which were rather more naïve: 'I can't get [it] out of my head. There's true democratic painting in them flowers and bricks ... it looks after the little things as much as the great.'³⁴ Ripon had clearly moved a long way from the classical taste of his uncle, Earl de Grey, first President of the R.I.B.A.

Ripon was also a Freemason and a Catholic, or rather a Grand Master who became a Roman Catholic, amid intense publicity – resigning his seat in Gladstone's Cabinet – in 1874. In 1853 he had been initiated in the Lodge of Truth at the Rose and Crown Hotel, Huddersfield. By 1870 he had risen to Grand Master. His defection was widely regarded as betrayal. The *English Independent* called him 'the pervert Marquis'. *The Times* talked of his 'fatal demoralisation', his surrender of all 'mental and moral freedom'.³⁵ 'The world has been much scandalized', K. R. H. Mackenzie wrote to Swinburne, 'and the Masonic Fraternity (of which I am a member) in particular, by the obvious insanity of the Marquis of Ripon in going into the Whore of Babylon. As the Pope is the Devil's doorkeeper, I hope he'll get his deserts.'³⁶ In fact Ripon's temporary break with Gladstone was as much political as religious: he opposed the extension of the franchise in the counties.³⁷ And at least two previous Grand Masters had managed to combine Freemasonry with Catholicism: Viscount Montacute in 1732 and Lord Petre in 1772. But the anti-papal stance of Gladstone's Ministry did put Ripon in a particularly tricky position. Indeed, he often found a certain incompatibility between his political and religious friendships: 'Dined at the [Brompton] Oratory', he noted in 1878; 'found the Fathers very Tory'.³⁸ As politicians, even as Catholics, Ripon and Bute were poles apart: Ripon preferred Low Mass to High.

It was the murder of his close neighbour and brother-in-law, Frederick Grantham Vyner, in 1870 which seems to have galvanised Ripon into a new religious awareness.³⁹ He had previously been an earnest Evangelical, interested in the ethical side of Freemasonry. Now he developed a new enthusiasm for the sacramental aspects of Christianity. Vyner had been kidnapped by Greek bandits during an expedition to Marathon. A ransom of one million drachmas was demanded in return for his release and that of his seven companions. After a fortnight's negotiations, armed troops were sent in to rescue the hostages. During a running gun battle near Dilessi, Vyner and three of his friends were shot dead.⁴⁰ Vyner's mother, Lady Mary Vyner, and his sister, Lady Ripon, decided to use the unspent ransom money for the construction of two churches on their neighbouring estates. The twin results of Vyner's murder, therefore, were Christ the Consoler at Skelton-on-Ure, near Newby Hall; and St Mary, Aldford-cum-Studley, near Studley Royal.⁴¹ Burges was already not unknown to the Yorke-Compton-Vyner-Carrington family network. Besides, Vyner had been a close friend of Bute's at Oxford. Burges was an obvious choice as architect. Ripon naturally filled the post of co-patron and intermediary. Ironically, before either church was finished, he had become a Roman Catholic. That, however, did not prevent his burial in the family vault at St Mary's.

Both churches were commissioned in 1870,[42] and begun in 1871.[43] Skelton was consecrated in 1876, Studley Royal in 1878. Both churches shared the same builder, J. Thompson of Peterborough. But Burges imported different Clerks of Works: J. Thomas of Cardiff for Studley, and Sier of London – who worked at Cork – for Skelton. Both churches are similar in scale and plan[30c]: a short nave and equal aisles; a deep, square-ended chancel; a South porch and South West baptistery area; a single tower and spire; and a prominent organ over the North aisle. But Studley Royal is the richer in decoration: Skelton is reported to have cost £25,000; Studley Royal £50,000 – although the first estimates seem to have been £10,000 and £15,000 respectively.[44] And in site, massing and compositional effect, both churches could hardly be more different. Skelton is Picturesque; Studley Royal approaches the Sublime.

Skelton is a memorial church, in a pastoral setting, hung round with drooping willows[44]. It is approached on a double diagonal axis: from South East the chancel crouches, traceried, pinnacled, against up-rearing nave and spire; from the South West porch, aisles, nave and spire take on a jagged pyramidal silhouette shot through like a target by the great rose window. Nicholls' sculpture draws in the shadows of the slanting light: the Consoler in the East gable; the Good Shepherd in the porch[50]; armorial shields along the buttresses of the nave; the Four Ages of Man at the rose window's compass points. But the real richness occurs inside[45–46]. Nave, clerestory and aisles are coloured with shafts of Irish black marble. The chancel[48–49] is vaulted in limestone and panelled in multi-coloured marbles. Nicholls' sculpture of the Ascension bulges overpoweringly above the chancel arch[45]. And the stained glass[143] – manufactured by Saunders under Burges's direction, from sketches by Lonsdale and cartoons by Weekes – girdles the whole interior with jewelled light: in the aisles, the Parables and Miracles, in the clerestory, the Prophets; in the rose window, Christ the Consoler and the Conditions of Life; in the East window, the Crucifixion and its pre-figuration in Old Testament lore; and in the chancel's lateral windows, scenes from the Old and New Testament.[45] The pulpit of red and white marble bulks geometrically large. The font[107] – of Tennessee marble, given by Lord Ripon in memory of his only daughter – sits squarely on its dumpy columns beneath an open, crocketted tabernacle-cover containing figures of Christ and John the Baptist.[46] The organ loft (1873)[105] leans forward menacingly, corbelled out over grotesquely sculptured animals.[47] The congregation is indeed bombarded with sculptured images. The corbels are alive with carving. But the chancel's impact is in no way diminished: in fact its richness dominates, a focus of moulded form and dappled light. Its ribbed vault is low-slung on compressed shafts of red, green and black marble; its entrance screen of white marble is panelled with porphyry, mosaic and alabaster; its stalls are cut in American walnut; its reredos[137] carved with medallions of the magi and the prophets in white alabaster;[48] its pavement chequered with red and yellow tiles; its window tracery deep-set, double-planed, trapping the sanctuary in a meshed marmoreal web.[49]

In style, Skelton represents a decisive shift in Burges's eclectic repertoire, from a French to an English base. The *Builder* dated it precisely: 'c. 1270'.[50] English thirteenth-century Gothic certainly supplies the matrix: the exterior tracery of the chancel, for instance; or the capitals and arches of the nave arcade; or the rose window.[51] But French influences are by no means absent. The finials of the spire's pinnacles, for example, are French. And the bulging balcony of the organ loft echoes the fourteenth-century Gothic chimney-wall, designed by Giu de Dammartin, in the Great Hall of the Palais de Justice at Poitiers.[52]

At Skelton Pevsner sees only 'tremendous ornateness, glitter . . . excessive relief . . . and . . . great opulence . . . of a somewhat elephantine calibre'.[53] Goodhart-Rendel was rather more appreciative: 'This church is one of the most remarkable churches of the nineteenth century, and to my thinking one of the most beautiful. . . . The chancel is a dream of richness and beauty.'[54] In fact, almost alone of his generation, Burges managed to seem sweeter after 1870, without becoming sugary. Massiveness is tempered with grace. A comparison with Bodley's near-contemporary chapel at Clumber Park, Nottingham, is telling. Both employ English rather than French sources. But Skelton's details are boldly cut; Clumber's are thin and flaccid.

Victorian architects worked within an overall framework of architectural hierarchy and decorative propriety, a framework summed up in Aitchison's dictum: 'Decorate up to the presence that fills the house.' Burges took that injunction literally: this is the house of God, so Skelton is decorated to the hilt, from door hinges to prayer book.[55] The team was the usual one: Nicholls, Lonsdale, Weekes, Saunders, Barkentin, Walden, Campbell and Hart – though Fucigna also makes a brief appearance, with sculptured garden ornaments at nearby Newby Hall.[56] The same team were employed at Studley Royal, and with even greater success.

The great park at Studley Royal had been laid out *c.* 1716–40 by John Aislabie, Chancellor of the Exchequer at the time of the South Sea Bubble. His son William added the Fountains estate in 1768. Lakes, avenues, canals, temples, grottoes, follies – plus the Jacobean mansion of Fountains Hall, the Palladian seat of Studley Royal, and the mighty ruins of Fountains Abbey itself – all these made Studley the finest man-made landscape in the North. To this Burges added one more architectural ingredient: a church which in its purpose, setting and design serves almost as an epitome of the High Victorian Dream. In 1815 an obelisk had been placed at the head of a mighty avenue aligned – through Colen Campbell's Palladian arch – on the axis of Ripon Minster. After 1870 the pagan obelisk gives way to a Christian church: 'The secular private elysium of the eighteenth century is invaded by, and made to serve the purposes of, the religious fervour of the High Victorians.'[57] The Aislabies had re-created Arcadia in the image of Claude or Poussin. Ripon and Burges interrupted that idyll by reasserting the values of the Middle Ages. After all, the climax of Disraeli's *Sybil* had occurred midst the ruins of Fountains Abbey. St Mary's, Studley Royal, was not just a church. It was a denial of Neo-Classical virtues; a pointblank rejection of the Railway Age; a Gothic portent of the New Jerusalem. Even the attendant estate cottages (1873) proclaim the new paternalism – and the new eclecticism.

According to legend, the church 'was designed at a moment's notice on the spot by Mr Burges, single-handed, the T square and drawing-board having been provided by Lady Ripon, so that the design might be made, as she said, by her architect, and under her influence'.[58] Burges was certainly friendly with the Marchioness, and she seems to have taken particular responsibility for the church after Ripon's conversion to Catholicism. But there is no sign of haste or improvisation. Quite the reverse. The whole scheme must have been meticulously prepared. And it was in Lord Ripon's name that several particularly expensive pieces of metalwork were commissioned from Burges and Barkentin: a gold cross in 1871;[59] a reliquary in 1876, symbolising the Salutation of the Blessed Virgin;[60] a jewelled crucifix in the same year;[61] and another reliquary in 1877, containing perhaps a fragment of the true cross.[62]

As at Cork, Burges took great care in the choice of stone. Both Skelton and Studley were built of the same stone: interior limestone of creamy white from Ripon's own quarries; pale grey Catraig stone for exterior facing; and a fine-grained stone of similar hue from Morcar quarry for exterior facings and mouldings. In March 1871, Burges reported to Ripon, then in Washington, U.S.A.:

> I went to sundry quarries with Mr Thompson, as we are rather puzzled about our stone for the fine work, window jambs, doorways etc. The Hudfall stone won't do. Its colour is so dark and so different to the Catraig that it would make the church look spotty. Besides the colour is bad in itself. After a good deal of investigation both in the various quarries and of old buildings, I found that the local limestone came nearest in colour to the Catraig. It also appears to stand remarkably well. Mr Mason told us [Ripon's] white quarry was only fit for inside work, but there was another quarry near Markinfield Hall called the Morcar quarry. This stone is much more lasting and more difficult to work than the white quarry, and will I think suit our purpose admirably.[63]

One or two of Burges's contemporaries would have been better advised to follow suit. By mixing sandstone and freestone Bodley destroyed the visual impact of his chapel at Clumber. And by mixing sandstone and limestone at All Souls, Hailey Hill, Halifax, Gilbert Scott set up a chemical reaction perfectly calculated to destroy the building altogether.

Like Skelton, Studley marks a movement away from Continental to English sources[51 ; 54]. Early French – almost within the shadow of Fountains Abbey – was clearly inappropriate. Even so, English, French and Italian colloquialisms mingle to produce a rich and idiosyncratic vocabulary. The crocketted gables over the chancel windows are evidently French in derivation; so is the rose window at the West end; so are the louvred openings of the tower and the sculptured tabernacles at the East end – perhaps deriving from the gable of the central portal in the West front of Bourges. The idea of a lean-to porch at the West end[53] derives, very distantly, from one of Burges's favourite churches, St Lucien near Beauvais;[64] but it also has a Cistercian flavour: one existed at Fountains. Again, the South porch shows Burges in Early French mood; so does the spirelet-flanked junction of tower and spire. The geometrical tracery, however, is more English than French. And inside, the English sources take command – in essentials, though not in details.

The main piers of the nave derive their Purbeck shafts from Beverley or Salisbury, and their capitals from Salisbury or Wells. The double tracery of the chancel is also English in origin: the East end of Ripon, or the Angel choir at Lincoln.[65] But the square soffits of the tower arch, the chancel arch and the sanctuary arch are all French, from Laon or Beauvais. The spiral staircase comes from Poitiers.[66] And the tri-lobe roof of the nave – so often a hall-mark of Burges's church designs – is Italian in origin, from the church of San Zenone in Verona. The winged lion in the chancel is also Italian, but handled in a very Burgesian way. Then there is the chancel roof, the nearest thing possible to a Gothic dome. Now a Gothic dome was a recurrent mirage for nineteenth-century architects. It appears, for example, in Schinkel's dream cathedral.[67] It appears in two competition designs of 1869: Lockwood and Mawson's designs for Bradford Town Hall,[68] and J. Oldrid Scott's scheme for Manchester Town Hall.[69] It was something Gilbert Scott often dreamed of doing – in his Berlin Parliament House design for instance[70] – but never succeeded. Sir T. G. ('Anglo') Jackson did succeed, in Romanesque vein, at Giggleswick School, Yorkshire.[71] Burges could have found a Romanesque dome at Angoulême.[72] But for Studley Royal he seems to have gone to Italy for his source, to the sacristy of Padua Cathedral, built in 1260, which in turn may have formed the basis of Brunelleschi's old sacristy in Florence, at the church of San Lorenzo.[73] The ogee profile of the apsidal roof at Cork runs right round at Studley, turning 180 degrees – Verona and Padua combined. One final 'dodge': Billy Burges always talked about a clever crib as a 'good dodge'. Underneath the organ is a tiny domelet, trefoil in section. That reappears time and time again in Burges's ceilings, from Kensington to Cardiff. It came from Sicily, from the cathedral at Messina.[74]

Entering the church from the West end, one instinctively ducks to avoid the arch above the entrance, seemingly splayed – flattened almost – by the formidable bulk of the tower[53]. The doorway is wrapped in shadow. But inside the body of the church is suffused with tinted light. The colour increases in density as one moves eastwards. The shafts of the nave piers are of plain black marble; but in the chancel black alternates with green, and green with red and orange. The chancel's walls are lined with Egyptian alabaster, purple, white and yellow; its floor is paved with mosaic; and it rises to a crescendo of painted and gilded decoration. Entering the sanctuary[56–59] is like stepping inside a reliquary or jewel casket. On three sides a battery of stained glass windows is set in tracery double-planed for depth. Above, the Gothic vault – dome and honeycomb – rises in layers like gilded lace. Perfectly placed, delicately wrought, that dome is less a vault than a baldacchino. Indeed the sanctuary itself is less an architectural construct than a gilded tabernacle of the Blessed Sacrament.[75]

The interior of Studley Royal is an elaborate exercise in iconography, linking stained glass, fresco and mosaic. The overall theme is 'Paradise Lost and Paradise Regained': earthly paradise is lost in the nave and aisles; the vision of heaven is regained in chancel and sanctuary. Beneath the tower are the Ancestors of Christ and the Beasts of Daniel. The steps dividing chancel and sanctuary are of triple-coloured porphyry marble: white, black and red – symbolic of man's original state; his fall; and his redemption, sanctification and purification.[76] At the chancel steps is a quotation from the Psalms: 'We will go into the House of the Lord, Our feet will stand in thy gates, O Jerusalem.' And indeed they do. The mosaic floor of the chancel depicts the shrines of the Holy City: the Tomb of David, the Golden Gate, the Temple, the Dolorous Arch, the Holy Sepulchre, Golgotha, the Church of the Resurrection, Gethsemane and the Tomb of the Virgin. A few steps further on, the sanctuary pavement represents the Garden of Eden: an armed angel guards the gates, and the four rivers from Genesis – Gihon, Pishon, Hiddekel and Euphrates – flow symbolically from vases at the four corners. As Pullan put it, 'pavements were always Burges's strong point'.[77] The winged lion of Judah gazes across the choir, from the web of window tracery, with red-eyed, basilisk stare.[78] Solomon and David look on from bench ends close by. Frescoes in window surrounds represent the Visions of St John the Divine as stated in the Book of Revelation. The wagon roof in the chancel[142], painted on canvas, conjures up prophets, apostles and martyrs in Te Deum procession. Four golden angels in the spandrels of the vault trumpet forth their message on the winds. And the sanctuary dome[144] blazes with cherubim and seraphim, tier upon tier, star upon star, into the empyrean.[79]

One of the first moves Burges had made on obtaining this double commission was to secure Lonsdale's employment. 'My friend Mr Lonsdale', he explained to Ripon in March 1871, 'who generally draws the small sketches for my stained glass has just got the Travelling Studentship of the R.A. But inasmuch as the sum he would gain from your work and that of Lady Mary would be double what he would obtain from the Academy, he has consented to remain and do your work. If the Academy will grant him an extension of time, say six months, well and good. If not he will throw the Academy overboard.'[80] Never was the Royal Academy spurned to better effect. Lonsdale stayed behind, and worked for Ripon with Burges, Weekes and Saunders. The result was one of the great triumphs of modern stained glass design.

The Western Jesse window contains scenes from the Life of the Virgin, interspersed with Burges's favourite musical angels. The clerestory lights contain medallions of the Angelic Hierarchy. The aisle windows depict scenes from Bible history. As at Skelton, the colours are warm and streaky, the backgrounds cool, and the outlines as firm as leading can make them. The stylised figures are less successful than their animal counterparts. But that is a general weakness of stained glass and sculpture in the mid-Victorian period. And the windows of the sanctuary and chancel more than make up for any deficiencies in the aisles. These are filled with scenes from the Book of Revelation[145]. Temples and battlements rear upwards.[81] Winged horsemen scour the heavens, hair flying, sabres flashing. A crowned virgin 'clothed like the sun' shimmers in flames of fire. A 'great beast' rises up out of the sea, its seven crowned heads baying at the sun; its brown scales lashed by silver waves. A woman jewelled and robed rides upon another beast, 'scarlet coloured, full of names of blasphemy'. A winged dragon fights 'a war in Heaven, 'gainst Michael and all his angels'. Another dragon menaces a virgin.[82] And yet another dragon spews unclean spirits from its many mouths – spirits in the guise of frogs.

These formalised monsters exude a kind of playful menace. 'Burgesian' is the word which springs naturally to mind. But their impact is almost puny compared with that of two adjoining windows on the Southern side of the sanctuary. 'The first angel sounded, and there followed blood and fire mingled with hail': plants, flowers and branches twist and jostle in nightmare profusion, lurid, almost luminous, in a sunset of blood. 'And the second angel sounded, and a great mountain burning with fire was cast into the sea': galleons sink, trees cascade in avalanche, confounding wood and water, earth and air, in a veritable tornado of light. The fragmentation of these windows is masterly. The essence of the medium – a translucent mosaic held together by lead[83] – is not only understood but emphatically expressed. The vocabulary is old, the language startlingly new. These windows, in fact, leap the boundary between formality and abstraction, between Pre-Raphaelitism and the Modern Movement. The palette, even the perspective, of Samuel Palmer has been translated into splashes of vitrified light [XI].

Studley Royal is not a large church. In its dimensions it is scarcely bigger than Skelton. But every inch is stamped with its architect's special genius. Two items in particular: the vestry door and the font. The vestry door (1876), sumptuously bound in brass, was the architect's personal gift. Low and narrow, double-shouldered for strength, it bears an image, in sharp relief, of the Virgin and Child against a typically Burgesian background of diapered and woven patterns.[84] The door is fine. The font[106] is unforgettable: a veritable meteorite of Tennessee marble, in rich, faintly speckled purple, punched with carvings of gilded bronze. Nicholls was the sculptor. His Four Ages of Man – struck from models which reappear again and again in Burges's sketches[85] – memorialise the phases of mankind with images of timeless dignity.

Studley Royal comes right at the end of Burges's career as a church designer. It combines Puginian articulation – in clarity of plan and separation of units – with a thrust which is High Victorian and a three-dimensionality which is essentially Burgesian. The plan[30c] echoes Pugin's St Giles, Cheadle, almost exactly. But in modelling and spatial effect it is wholly different. What he tried to do all his life, and what he undoubtedly succeeded in doing at Studley, was to break out of the Ecclesiological straitjacket without falling into excess. The quality of the interior decoration makes it, in Pevsner's words, 'a Victorian shrine, Early English in style, but a dream of Early English glory'.[86] At the time, Pullan called it 'one of the most perfect churches in the kingdom'.[87] Cork Cathedral may well stand as Burges's greatest Gothic work, but Studley Royal remains his 'ecclesiastical masterpiece'.[88] If he had built nothing else, his claim to greatness would still be incontestable.

As one approaches the church, along the avenue from Ripon, it takes on an almost cathedral grandeur[54]. Viewed from the South[55], its silhouette is roughly triangular: its sloping profile picks up the ascent of the sloping site. And it is this carefully calculated gradation – chancel, nave, tower and spire – which dramatises the long approach from the East. From the entrance lodge, one is struck by siting and composition. At this distance, the body of the church acts merely as a podium for the spire. As one passes under the Palladian arch, the shape is an elongated pyramid: the details have yet to emerge from the mass. But towards the foot of the sunken boundary wall, as one swings left at the cottages, the design of the East front[52] suddenly becomes intelligible. Burges had to produce a façade which could be 'read' from one hundred yards away. He succeeded by overscaling his mouldings, piercing the wall with niches, and cramming each cavity with sculpture. The buttresses supply the framework, demarcating the proportions and squeezing inwards the tracery of the central window. Most architects would have stopped there. But in the triangle of space between window and gable, Burges inserts three tabernacles.[89] Each is filled with sculpture and blank tracery. And each is locked into the design by its own flanking finials: these spring from the buttresses below and thrust their barbed lances through the coping stone above. In designing this facade Burges gambled, and gambled well. Could he produce a design which exploited the sublimity of the approach without killing the rest of the church? He could: his design was a triumph of three-dimensional balance. Pevsner calls it 'crazy'.[90] But its madness is merely the belligerence of genius.

In 1975 the Historic Buildings Council visited Studley Royal, by then in the care of the Department of the Environment. The late Lord Holford had defied his doctors in order to be there: his first sight of the church was to be his last architectural excursion. The black government car sped along the avenue. Stage by stage, Burges's optical genius was revealed. Holford kept silent. Then, as he stepped outside and breathed the majesty of that setting, he spoke quietly: 'Here was an architect who understood scale.'

SECULAR PUBLIC BUILDINGS

Church-building was a challenge for any Victorian Goth. But the challenge of secular commissions was greater still. Here the problem of style was crucial. Now the bulk of Burges's secular Gothic work, architectural and decorative, was designed under special circumstances, for Lord Bute or for himself. The results were – respectively – feudal and fantastic. And they deserve separate chapters to themselves. One group of his Gothic designs, however, remains for consideration: secular buildings for public rather than private purposes. These never formed a large part of Burges's practice. But each posed, in varying form, the eternal conundrum of style. A City of London warehouse; a set of Soho lodgings; a home counties' town hall; an Indian art school; a public school theatre; an American college; and a monumental scheme for London's new Law Courts: it would be hard to think of a group of projects more dramatically diverse. Here, surely, was a multiple test for the viability of Gothic in the mid-Victorian age.

Skilbeck's Warehouse

For a Gothic revivalist there could hardly be a greater test than a warehouse. How could medieval forms adapt themselves to the requirements and materials of nineteenth-century commerce? 'There are as yet few warehouses and shops in any purely Pointed style', the Ecclesiological Society noted in 1859. 'While the sumptuous character of new constructions in London and other great towns for commercial purposes denotes the growth of public taste, they have as yet unfortunately scarcely travelled out of the beaten track of Italian and Renaissance.'[91] Six years later, in 1865–6 Burges was commissioned to remodel Skilbeck's drysalters' warehouse at 46 Upper Thames St, London.[92][71] His brief was mundane: re-fit a nondescript storage depot; reface its street frontage, adding a top storey, while retaining the four-storey floor levels below. The result was astonishing. First he divided the new façade vertically into two and horizontally into three. Then he linked the twin arches of the attic storey with a pierced gable, filled its spandrels with sculpture, and topped its parapet with finials. So far all is deceptively easy. But each item in the composition had to be functional as well. The ground floor became an essay in glass and iron: plate glass windows, wrought iron guards and a massive cast iron beam, exposed and stencilled. Above, pulleys, crane, ropes and loading tackle festoon, without embarrassment, the symbolic sculpture of the façade.[93]

Skilbeck's warehouse was an immediate hit, and remained a firm favourite with the critics. J. P. Seddon was delighted.[94] E. W. Godwin thought it 'strikingly clever'.[95] R. W. Edis thought it good enough to adapt, if not to copy.[96] Indeed variations of Burges's prototype soon appeared far and wide.[97] Eastlake noted that it was 'one of the very few instances of the successful adaptation of Gothic for commercial purposes at the East end of London'.[98] Even 'Victorian' Harris had to admit that its use of exposed iron was 'plucky'. The *Ecclesiologist*[99] called it 'a great success'. Besides being necessarily simple, inexpensive, and adapted to 'the most severe business purposes', it displayed 'great solidity and firmness, plenty of light, every accommodation, and very considerable artistic effect'. 'Under the gable, under two projecting corbels, stand two stout lions, which support the pulleys for drawing up the smaller parcels. The great crane is supported by a corbel which is carved into a bust of a fair Oriental maid, symbolising the clime from which so many of the drysalter's materials are brought; and over a circular window in the gable is a ship bringing in its precious freight. Mr B. has made good use of ironwork in the window frames. The iron girder which stretches across the front of the building is left open and painted, the bolt-heads being gilt. The effect is capital.'[1]

That iron girder remained an architectural 'lion', although its aesthetic viability – according to Laugier's doctrine of apparent utility – remained in doubt.[2] Years later one of Burges's obituarists remembered this warehouse as 'probably the most successful attempt ever made to unite the requirements of art and mercantile convenience'.[3] For all that, Godwin felt obliged to point out that here, in Upper Thames St, his friend was still wrestling with the dilemma of style. And the outcome – at half-way point in Burges's career – was still in doubt.

> Mr Burges ... has spent his early life, not in doing, but in learning *how to do*. His real architectural works are very few and far between. He has built a small church somewhere in Surrey, restored Waltham Abbey Church, and one or two others, built a model lodging-house, begun a cathedral, and erected a small warehouse; and this temperance, some people would call it *slackness* of business, has enabled him to make himself master of his art, so far as he has gone. The question is, How far has he gone? My own opinion, and I think no one would be more ready to subscribe to it than Mr Burges himself, is, that he has only attained to the knowledge of how they worked in old times, more particularly in his favourite period of history – the close of the twelfth and beginning of the thirteenth centuries. Out of this *may be* developed a good strong nineteenth-century architecture; but as yet neither Mr Burges nor anyone else has shown us how. The warehouse in Upper Thames St is essentially a Medieval warehouse, if we omit the lower storey, which has nothing in common with the rest of the superstructure. ... Had a thirteenth-century architect used an iron girder he would not have reduced the pier supporting it to less dimensions than the pier immediately above it. It has, to say the least, an awkward look, and will always remind one of a modern insertion in a Medieval front. ... But ... at any rate, we have to thank Mr Burges for giving us in the city a piece of genuine thirteenth-century construction, and two or three pieces of carving better than any modern carving with which I am acquainted.[4]

St Anne's Court, Soho

The model lodging-house Godwin referred to was St Anne's Court, Soho[70; 72]. Now almshouses in the country presented no real stylistic difficulty. When Burges designed almshouses at Worthing (1860; 1866)[5] and Forthampton (1863)[6] he was able to adapt traditional cottage prototypes, Home Counties and Cotswold respectively. But a lodging-house in London was rather more of a challenge. It was a challenge Burges took up at the behest of Lackland Mackintosh Rate, the Anglican philanthropist for whom he refurbished Milton Court, near Dorking,[7] and the Archbishop of Canterbury's chapel at Lambeth. The 'model lodgings' movement – the operation sarcastically known as 'five-per-cent philanthropy' – was more concerned with squaring conscience and profit than with creating a new style.[8] The planning of St Anne's Court, therefore, was dictated by mundane considerations. For an outlay of £2,900 Burges supplied a total of thirty rooms which could be let at 3/- per week each or 5/6d. per pair, to tailors or carmen in the neighbourhood of Wardour St earning an average of £1.15.0d. per week. Additional facilities included a school room, shop, kitchen, scullery and lavatories. The annual average return on Rate's investment was $4\frac{1}{2}$%.[9] Chapple collected the rents.

The *Ecclesiologist* called the style 'a kind of Pointed'.[10] In fact Burges has pared to the bone his favourite thirteenth-century French, added a hint of North Italian polychromy and rounded off the whole design with vigorous strings and labels. The method of construction – simple brick walling with cast iron piers – seemed appropriately industrial. Eastlake was not alone in thinking it a 'simple, well-proportioned and judicious design, admirably adapted for its homely purpose'.[11]

Dover Town Hall

Dover Town Hall[63] was a curiously protracted commission which Burges inherited from Ambrose Poynter and bequeathed to Pullan and Chapple. In 1835 Dover Corporation decided to rescue their thirteenth-century Maison Dieu; but their new town hall, incorporating this historic hostel, was not completed until nearly fifty years later.[12] Poynter began work on the medieval hall in 1852, and was succeeded by Burges in 1859.[13] By 1863 J. P. Seddon was able to examine the restoration and report in glowing terms: 'the vigorous design of Mr Burges ... is visible in the nervous ironwork in the doors, the grotesque animals forming the label terminations (which are *grotesques* of right good sort, and not caricatures or monstrosities as too usual now-a-days), and in the noble gasolier standards on the dais, as well as in the thoroughly Medieval carvings above.'[14] The six great Decorated windows of the hall were gradually but dramatically filled with stained glass made by Heaton, Butler and Bayne to cartoons by E. J. Poynter.[15]

By 1880, however, Hove and Hastings were planning elaborate new town halls.[16]

Not to be outdone, the Mayor of Dover, a grocer named Richard Dickeson, forced through a comparable scheme, much to the indignation of his ratepayers.[17] Burges prepared plans for a new public hall running parallel to the medieval structure, plus attendant offices on the site of an adjoining prison.[18] Economy was clearly an overriding aim. And Burges seems to have suppressed his stylistic preferences in order to match the ragstone walls and Decorated tracery of the Maison Dieu. Still, his silhouette is undeniably Picturesque; Nicholls's carving is more than competent; and the interior of the Mayor's Parlour and Connaught Hall – by Pullan and Chapple – though utilitarian in the extreme, contains a few good Burgesian 'dodges'.[19] Dover broke no new ground. But then the commission itself was hardly conducive to new thinking.

BOMBAY SCHOOL OF ART

Not so the School of Art, Bombay. Founded in the 1850s by a rich Parsee, Sir Jamsetjee Jeejeebhoy, Bombay Art School was a flourishing institution. One of its first instructors was Rudyard Kipling's father.[20] In 1865 Burges, Street, Roger Smith and Trubshawe were invited to submit designs for a capacious new building. Burges seems to have been the only one eager to accept. William Emerson was at Buckingham St at the time, and worked directly on the plans. It was Emerson who went out early in 1866 with the first thirty-eight drawings. Another ninety-one followed soon afterwards, along with Burges's formal report.[21] Unfortunately, the Indian officials were so used to dealing with engineers that they refused to offer any more than $2\frac{1}{2}\%$ commission. Burges baulked at such unprofessional pay, and Bombay School of Art fell into the hands of the sappers.[22]

Burges's design[64], however, was by no means wasted. It caused a major stir in the architectural profession. The *Ecclesiologist* christened its style 'a kind of . . . quasi-Orientalizing Gothic'.[23] What exactly did Billy Burges have in mind?

The Schools of Art at South Kensington were not a very helpful precedent. 'The building itself', Burges explained, 'and the mode of lighting would entail the very greatest inconvenience if copied in a tropical country.' Far more helpful were studies which Burges had previously made in Italy and Constantinople. He sought a style 'which without involving any very difficult masonry [would] admit of either much or little ornament, and [would] present those broad masses and strong shadows we all admire so much in Eastern architecture'. He found it in 'the architecture of Europe at the end of the twelfth century'. 'It associates with the Eastern pointed architecture more than any other style,' he noted, while retaining 'a distinct and well defined European character.' It could also be adapted to the climate of Bombay – to accommodate, for instance, flat, double roofs with deep eaves, and lintels fit for window blinds. Burges's design was essentially practical. A garden supplied botanical specimens. An outer courtyard supplied parking space for 'carriages and palanquins'.

'The great object', he explained, 'is to exclude the sun, while admitting the air freely. This is effected by double walls in the shape of corridors which run round the whole building with the exception of the ends of the wings.' The wings themselves were to be lighted by 'pierced slabs of stone'. Elsewhere the windows were as small as possible. Doors were located opposite each other 'so as to secure a through draught of air'. The ground floor was vaulted throughout, and raised on terraces to guard against the monsoon.

In plan the building was E shaped, axially based on a central hall and communicating corridors which divided up room space for 'the various art industries: silver workers, stone and wood carvers, lithographers and wood and copper engravers', plus those engaged in glass painting, or in using the kiln. 'The more dirty industries of modelling and casting in plaster' were placed between the main building and the smithy. Differentiated circulation was guaranteed by six entrances and five staircases. The great staircase, with its multiple balconies, was modelled on Blois. But the dome above it nodded towards Istanbul by way of Périgueux and Angoulême. The corner domelets were to be covered with small stone tiles, like those on the side turrets of Notre Dame at Poitiers. Inside, communicating doors were to consist either of Venetian blinds, or of 'turned fret-work, such as may be seen at Cairo' – and was later seen at Cardiff Castle. Lecture rooms, studios, a museum, a library, plus staff bedrooms and accommodation for native servants in the attic, completed the arrangements. The façades were finished with armorial carvings, and with sculptures representing the Arts and Sciences – nimbused in the Eastern manner – as well as those symbolic Virtues thought to accrue to citizen artists. Interior sculpture was to be supplied by future generations of students. But models might initially be exported from England: capitals carved by Lewis and Jacquet, and statues sculpted by Nicholls. Detailed drawings were in fact sent out for all significant mouldings, especially the ribbed Gothic vaulting which Burges presumed to be quite beyond the capacity of native workmen. The materials were to be basalt rubble and squared Coorla stone.

The school's great feature, of course, was its smithy. Burges called it 'a circular domed building somewhat in the shape of the old medieval kitchens . . . divided into three parts, the largest devoted to the smithy, the other two to the kilns'. 'We should say', remarked the *Building News*, 'it was very much . . . in the shape of a medieval kitchen; . . . in fact, just as if it had walked out of the pages of M. V. le Duc.'[24] And so it had. Burges's Bombay smithy refashioned in monstrous form the Benedictine kitchen at Marmoutier,[25] [65] a conceit eventually realised in miniature in a tulip vase for Lord Bute. Among the *cognoscenti* Burges's Bombay project became a legend. E. C. Lee called it 'perhaps the most marvellous design that he ever made, compelling rigid thirteenth-century Gothic to fulfil the requirements of the torrid zone, and to harmonize with its surroundings'.[26] At the very least it would have been a formidable High Victorian export, and a worthy addition to the Anglo-Indian buildings of Bombay.[27]

TRINITY COLLEGE, HARTFORD, CONNECTICUT, U.S.A.

Burges's plan for Trinity College was twice as big as his Bombay scheme, and half as interesting. It had, however, the advantage of being begun, if not completed.

It was in the summer of 1872 that Abner Jackson, Trinity's formidable President, visited Britain. He had come to choose an architect, and a model, for a new university college which would rival the buildings of Yale, Harvard and Oxford. It would also put the American Episcopalians at least on a par with the Congregationalists and Baptists. Taking the traditional tourist route, he visited Westminster Abbey, the British Museum, Eton, Oxford and Stratford-on-Avon. In Oxford he consulted J. H. Parker, who naturally recommended Burges.[28] With Burges as guide, Jackson examined several colleges. He particularly admired Brasenose, Pembroke, All Souls and Butterfield's Keble. Then away he went to Scotland, to Scott's Glasgow University – which he disliked – and Scott and Henderson's Trinity College, Glenalmond, Perthshire – by which he was much impressed. Like Trinity College, Hartford, Glenalmond was an Episcopalian foundation. 'It is', Jackson noted, 'a most noble pile of buildings.'[29] With Burges he later surveyed Butterfield's St Augustine's College, Canterbury, and Rickman's Jesus College, Cambridge. And next year, 1873, he returned again to work with Burges on the plans. But it was above all that first view of Glenalmond which Jackson took back with him to America as the model university of his dreams.

And what dreams. For the first time, a full-blown English quadrangle was to be introduced to an American campus. Burges's first plan (1873–4)[30][74] envisaged a mighty quadruple-quadrangled structure, complete with chapel, library, museum, dining hall, art gallery, theatre, observatory, and blocks of rooms for students and professors topped with many a soaring tower and spire. Even Burges's second plan (1874–5) – a mere three quadrangles in extent, with a frontage of only 1,300 feet: one and a half times the length of the Houses of Parliament – was bigger than any comparable university building on either side of the Atlantic. No doubt such fantasies were primarily a fund-raising device. One contemporary writer even compared their scale to the Capitol at Washington. $400,000 (£80,000) was the target in 1875.[31] But the sum raised can never have approached that figure. Jackson himself died early in 1874. Detailed drawings were prepared for only one third of the scheme. And less than one sixth of Burges's master plan survived the transition from drawing board to campus.[32]

The executive architect employed was a local man, F. H. Kimball.[33] He visited England in December 1873 and worked on the plans with Burges until October 1874.[34] Together they visited the British Museum to examine the fittings of the library.[35] Kimball was given responsibility for detailed specifications. But he seems to have been assisted by another local man, G. W. Keller (1842–1935).[36] Foundations were begun in July 1875. Frederick Law Olmstead was called in to lay out the grounds, a fine site known as Rocky Ridge.[37] By 1878 two blocks were completed, in rough red local sandstone with creamy Ohio facings: Seabury Hall for teaching and administration, and Jarvis Hall for dormitories. Between them, a linking gateway block – Northam Towers[75] – was eventually added in 1882.[38]

> O Trinity! thy turrets gleam.
>   In proximate suburban space
> Like vast cathedral towers, and seem
>   Suggestive of some holy place. . . .
> Grand metamorphosis of rocks![39]

But for all the exuberance of Hattie Howard, the Hartford poetess, Trinity College remained but a fragment of a grand design.

In style, the *New York Herald Tribune* observed, Burges's plans were 'Early French Gothic'.[40] So they were, although the square towers and the theatre façade have more than a touch of North Italy. But the bulk of the scheme was Early French in a characteristically Burgesian way. The apsidal chapel recalls his scheme for Trinity College, Cambridge. The semi-circular theatre recalls the Harrow Speech Room. The triplet windows recall Cork. The soaring towers and bulging bays recall his Cardiff Castle and Law Courts designs. The mullioned windows anticipate Tower House. And the serried dormers – with their cast iron casements, their punchy plate tracery and their diapered patterns – recall Knightshayes, as well as the Strand front of Burges's Law Courts scheme. Inside, the stone chimneypieces, the robust geometrical woodwork, and the tie-beamed timber roofs echo half a dozen Burgesian designs. Even the finials of the towers are familiar from Castell Coch. And the result is a success. By comparison, Seddon's Aberystwyth is frantically Picturesque,[41] and Blomfield's Selwyn College, Cambridge positively insipid.[42]

Yet there is something unsatisfactory about Trinity. Somehow the magic is missing. As early as 1877 it was regarded as rather a 'conundrum'.[43] Burges's work always depended heavily on his personal supervision of detail. On this occasion, supervision was ruled out by distance, and detailed finish was ruled out by cost. Very little of Nicholls's sculpture – his owl of wisdom tympanum, for instance – was ever executed.[44] Plans were sent back to England for Burges's confirmation.[45] But his most ambitious ideas – notably a variation of the Cardiff Castle dining room chimneypiece[46] – remain paper dreams. Burges's involvement with educational buildings seems indeed to have been ill-fated. His designs for King's College, Cambridge (1877–8),[47] and Ripon Grammar School (1873–4),[48] both remained unbuilt. And his great American venture never reached fulfilment. In the final analysis, the importance of Trinity College, Hartford, lies not in its subsidiary place in Burges's *oeuvre* but in its key position in the development of late nineteenth-century American architecture. Through Kimball, through Keller and – most of all – through H. H. Richardson, not a little of Burges's genius lives on across the Atlantic.[49]

HARROW

The speech Room at Harrow School was a smaller commission, but rather more prestigious. It was Beresford-Hope who secured it for Burges.[50] Hope was a loyal Harrovian, and it was probably through his influence that Burges secured two other commissions with Harrovian connections: a memorial brass for Archbishop Longley, and a crozier for Bishop Jenner. 1871 marked the three-hundredth anniversary of the school's charter, given by Queen Elizabeth I to John Lyon. A Lyon Memorial Fund was set up, and by 1875 it contained some £38,000.

Burges's initial commission was for a speech room, a museum, a laboratory, two science lecture rooms, an art room, four classrooms and a gymnasium. The Headmaster quickly pointed out that the old Speech Room – by C. R. Cockerell – would not be wasted: it could be converted into a museum, art room and class room. Burges's report,[51] therefore, proposed to rebuild one boarding house as laboratories, science lecture rooms and class rooms. The gymnasium – with galleried interior and porched exterior – would take up a site to the north of the new Speech Room. And the 'Speecher' itself, the focus of the entire scheme, would occupy a dramatic position on the bend of the High St[76]. Burges took full advantage of this steeply sloping site, adapting the raked section and semi-circular plan of an antique Greek theatre. 'I have endeavoured', he explained, 'to employ the native material (brick) in the most advantageous manner and to work to the style of the best building in Harrow, viz. [Scott's] Vaughan Library.' Faced with a requirement for one thousand seats, Burges happily endorsed the need for 'a huge mass'. But to mitigate the size he chose a flat-roofed, semi-circular plan: a rectangular 'hall type' would have required enormous height. This semi-circular plan, Burges reported, also 'lends itself to the introduction of many [exits or] *vomitoria*, thus facilitating escape in case of accident or panic'. 'I have clothed it', he concluded, 'with our national architecture and availed myself of modern science to cover it over from the air.'[52]

Throughout the operation Burges found himself hampered by the need for economy. He probably relinquished the laboratories and gymnasium to his friend C. F. Hayward[53] with some relief – though a Burgesian gymnasium, with turrets from Angoulême and a trilobe roof from Verona, might have been intriguing. But the Speech Room was more important altogether. Burges and Hope had long dreamt of a Gothic theatre.[54] Burges particularly admired the great auditorium at Parma.[55] Designing a modern theatre in the Gothic style demanded, at the very least, 'ingenuity and resource'.[56]

Burges started drawing in 1871. Thereafter work proceeded fitfully. There were formidable engineering problems involved in excavating the site: £4,000 was spent in sinking piles forty feet deep. The first stone was laid in July 1874; the opening followed exactly three years later.[57] His original plan[76] had been dramatically Ruskinian, with vaulted arcades and polychrome voussoirs. The concealed flat roof presented difficulties of construction, and the dogmatic horizontality of the whole scheme seems to have aroused opposition. Burges was forced to trim his sails. He inserted a pitched roof and introduced compositional modifications which exchanged the open arcades for asymmetrical towers[77]. The smaller, North tower, was not finished until 1919. The tall South tower was never completed at all. In its place stands a tamer structure by Herbert Baker, erected as late as 1925. The present exterior of Burges's Speech Room is therefore an unhappy compromise: it lacks the Sublime horizontality of his first design, and the Picturesque asymmetry of his second.

Inside, Burges's compromises with economy were equally unfortunate. The roof structure – rolled steel trusses radiating from a central steel drum and supported on cast iron columns – was novel and adventurous. Indeed the ceiling stands as testimony to Burges's constructive skill. But the decoration[134], by which as always he set great store, remained unfinished. Nicholls did execute a number of corbels,[58] but the capitals of the pillars were not carved until 1923. The timber vaulting – and then only the gallery vault – was not painted until 1924. The stained glass (by C. F. Bell) did not appear until 1925. The processional frieze, filled with Grecian authors and allegories of the muses, was never even begun. Burges's favourite jelly-mould domelets – much magnified from their Messina prototype – remained unadorned. And the figurative sculpture on the proscenium wall remained uncarved. Burges's hopes for 'the future application of both high and decorative art' never materialised. His vision of a Grecian theatre, rendered in a Gothic style suitable for the nineteenth century, can only be fully appreciated in Haig's eloquent lithograph.

In its heyday, at the end of the nineteenth century, the Harrow 'Speecher' was a stage setting for the full panoply of late Victorian public school *esprit*. Each year the July Speech Day followed a pre-ordained pattern: the school's brass band parading on the lawn; an exultant audience one thousand strong; schoolboy monologues; prize medals; 'cheering on the steps' as visiting celebrities emerged; then luncheon for boys and guests alike, with salmon and claret cup; and school songs after tea.[59] Burges's Speech Room still retains a little of this votive atmosphere. But Beresford-Hope's dream that it would also embody the New Style of the Victorian age remained largely unfulfilled.

THE LAW COURTS

In 1835 and 1866 London was the scene of two great architectural competitions, for new Houses of Parliament and for new Courts of Law.[60] They mark, clearly and dramatically, two distinct stages in the development of the Gothic Revival: Early Victorian and High Victorian. In the first contest Barry was the official winner, Pugin the genius in the shadows. In the second – after devious manoeuvres galore – Street was awarded a technical knock-out, but most of the cheering and applause was reserved for Billy Burges.

The Law Courts competition was limited, by invitation, to eleven competitors, each guaranteed a fee of £800: H. R. Abraham, E. M. Barry, Raphael Brandon, William Burges, T. N. Deane, H. B. Garling, H. F. Lockwood, J. P. Seddon, Gilbert Scott, G. E. Street and Alfred Waterhouse.[61] Apart from Abraham, who was the Attorney-General's brother-in-law, every competitor was a seasoned competition wallah; and, apart from Garling, Lockwood and Barry, all of them were committed Goths. By general agreement, it seemed only natural that the majesty of the law should find expression in the greatest secular Gothic building of the later nineteenth century. As Beresford-Hope put it, 'for the temple of traditional British law, the law that produced a Lyttelton and a Bracton, and a Gascoyne, an Italian or a Grecian edifice would be a startling anachronism'.[62] The result however – professionally if not artistically – was a fiasco. The judges were divided: the lawyers and laymen (including Mr Gladstone) placed Scott first and Waterhouse second; the architectural judges placed Barry first and Scott second. So a compromise was suggested to the Treasury: a combination of Barry's plan and Street's elevations. That proved unacceptable all round. Scott took umbrage. And a third round of negotiations ensued. In 1868 Street at last emerged with the commission, though his prize was to be whittled down over the years by government parsimony. Barry was fobbed off with the prospect of rebuilding the National Gallery; Waterhouse with the Natural History Museum, South Kensington. Burges was left with the praise of the press, and the admiration of his colleagues.

Burges took the challenge seriously. With E. W. Godwin he retreated to Blackheath to work at his drawings in peace.[63] He took on young Phéné Spiers as a specialised draughtsman. His Report (1867)[64] went to some length to explain and justify his choice of style: French in detail; English in composition; Italian in silhouette; Victorian in synthesis[60–61]. His belief in the universal viability of Gothic would never be tested on as grand a scale again: his estimate was £1,584,589. Alas, the competition turned out to be not only the climax but the swan-song of the Gothic Revival.

Now the Law Courts fiasco coincided with the demise of the *Ecclesiologist*. The Gothic Revival was never the same again. But initially at least, ecclesiologists hailed the competition as a triumph for the pointed arch: all eleven designs were Gothic. 'How much thought and trouble, what hours of labour and brain-work. . . . We look to this immense edifice as a future art teacher . . . of generations of Englishmen.'[65] True to its tradition, the *Ecclesiologist* unleashed a quiverful of thunderbolts before handing out its bouquet. Abraham's design was weak: 'ordinary . . . sham Gothic, of thirty or forty years ago'. Seddon's was impossibly extravagant; Garling's old-fashioned and feeble. Lockwood's elaborate perspectives failed to hide the emptiness of his 'fancy Gothic'. Deane's design lacked 'power'. Barry's managed to recall both St Paul's Cathedral and the Houses of Parliament. Brandon's scheme was 'very striking', but quite inappropriate and fundamentally copyistic: his Gothic Valhalla was 'a direct plagiarism of Westminster Abbey apse and all'. That left Street, Scott, Waterhouse and Burges. Street, so often the darling of the ecclesiologists, was dismissed for contrived originality, 'quasi-monasticism and confused composition'. 'His fenestration is terribly faulty'; his pierced gables 'extraordinary and weak'; his 'canopied lancets . . . are repeated *ad infinitum*'; his 'blank constructional arcade . . . is not true art'. So much for the eventual winner. What of those two sturdy competitors, Scott and Waterhouse? Both schemes were hard to fault in functional terms. But Scott's design betrayed a fatal 'admixture of styles'. Unnerved, perhaps, by his experience at the Foreign Office, he had diluted the purity of Gothic with touches of Italianate and even Indian. 'I should be quite ready,' he admitted uneasily, 'if thought too ornate, to adopt a severer tone.'[66] Waterhouse went still further in his efforts to compromise with modernity: his vast covered central court was a veritable 'Crystal Palace sort of thing. . . . It is all very well calling the style a development; it appears to us to be far from a healthy one'.[67]

But with Burges the *Ecclesiologist* had no doubts. 'It is quite refreshing to turn to the exquisite and pure art of Mr Burges's charming drawings. We have no slovenly half-thought-out work here; no attempt at effect by quaint notching or irregular arrangement; . . . [no] patchwork and piecing. . . . No [other] design . . . [is] so perfectly congruous in all its parts . . . it is the work of a master mind, an original work of an accomplished artist, who [has] so thoroughly learned the style . . . as to make it truly express his own thoughts and intentions.' Burges had admirably filled out the irregular site, 'like a true medieval artist'. His architectural vision had 'immense strength'. Even without its soaring towers, 'it would still stand pre-eminent . . . for artistic feeling and power'. Only Burges had produced a design in which sculpture formed 'an integral part of the architecture . . . in almost all others it is treated as an adventitious ornament'. Both gateways – over Strand and Carey St – scored high marks for 'simplicity of outline, . . . beautiful sculpture, and a total absence of rubbish or tawdriness'. Nothing surpassed the majesty of Burges's entrance towers in the Strand. Most of all, his plan displayed an elemental lucidity. He rejected outright the idea of a central concourse: there was no medieval precedent for a vaulted hall, and the very idea was but a naïve echo of Westminster Hall. Instead, he arranged his building in concentric zones, with the public on the periphery and the judges immured in a central keep, linked by flying passages to their attendant courts[62]. Symbolically and artistically, Burges's design was irresistible. It is 'the very best architectural work we have seen since the commencement of the Gothic Revival. . . . [In] architectural power, artistic talent, and ability to plan . . . none . . . can compete with Mr Burges'.[68]

Why then did he fail? Perhaps the judges were wedded to the idea of a central public hall. Perhaps they took fright at all those machicolations. More likely, the lawyers and politicians just could not bring themselves to take him seriously. Street's 'executive power' was undeniable. Barry had an inherited reputation for competence. Scott and Waterhouse were legendarily business-like. But Burges . . .? A truculent Goth, who drank claret out of rock-crystal and ate whitebait off *cloisonné*? No, that would never do. Beresford-Hope had taken him on one side and told him: 'Well now Burges, you've got this chance; I know what sort of fellow you are; you mustn't spoil your chance by any of your jokes.'[69] Obediently, Billy Burges limited his tricks to a recording angel over the Record Tower. But still the judges didn't trust him. He seemed as eccentric as one of his own gargoyles. In a way, it was the Houses of Parliament saga all over again. Neither Pugin nor Burges were committee men; Barry and Street were men of affairs. In rejecting Burges's scheme, the judges rejected the designer rather than the design.[70] In fact there is some evidence that Street was chosen merely to keep Burges out.[71]

There were few serious criticisms of Burges's project.[72] Perhaps those eighteen towers were a little 'overwrought and missal-like'. Perhaps their conjunction of square bases and circular superstructures was 'unworthy' of a master. Perhaps the dormers were finished with 'angular abruptness'. Perhaps the multiplication of window reveals to add depth and shadow was 'rather overdoing it'. Perhaps the elevations were enriched to the point of top-heaviness. Perhaps in modelling so many towers on the Palazzo Vecchio at Florence, the palace at Poitiers and the château at Pierrefonds, the architect had 'rather gone beyond himself'. Perhaps the tower machicolations would have seemed an outdated 'frolic' even in 1395. But on the whole it was judged a vision of 'architectural power', 'beautiful ... grandly simple ... and ... truly magnificent'.[73] Haig's sepia-shaded bird's eye view hardly did it justice. But then Burges alone of the competitors followed the rules to the letter, and sent in a plan[62], a bird's eye view[60] and a detailed elevation[61] rather than a series of pretty perspectives.[74] His plan required no window dressing. By abandoning a central hall and redistributing the space upon a zoning principle, he secured not only grandeur but light, silence and fresh air. Reviewers were amazed at this evidence of practicality on a large scale: if it had been 'a goblet or a grotesque', then Burges might have been expected to lead the field; but here it was the utility of his plan which was so striking. He had managed 'to repress the grotesque', to disguise his 'cloven hoof'.[75] Burges's design 'was the one generally approved by the profession at large'.[76] His colleagues would have greeted its victory with 'jubilation'.[77] Even his fellow competitors acknowledged its superiority. Scott thought Burges's design 'eccentric' and even 'wild'; but he conceded that 'his architecture exceeded in merit that of any other competitor'.[78] 'How the government could have passed him over', recalled Aitchison, 'when they had such a genius to their hand, is difficult to understand.'[79] 'I wouldn't mind', mused Street, 'being beaten by drawings like those.'[80]

The *Builder*'s attitude is interesting. From the start, predictably enough, it favoured the laggard Neo-Classicism of E. M. Barry's plan. And that turned out to be the preference of the judges too.[81] What the *Builder* did not bargain for was the seduction of those same judges by 'Street's style-laden pencil'.[82] Editorial policy tacitly backed an article by a dyed-in-the-wool classicist, W. Watkiss Lloyd, which dismissed Street's over-punctuated composition as sheer 'anarchy'.[83] Logically, therefore, the same journal played down the drama of Burges's scheme, concentrating on its clarity and convenience of plan.[84] Illogically, however, the *Builder* failed to draw the obvious conclusion of its arguments, a conclusion towards which the judges themselves were groping: a marriage of the best plan and the best elevation was most likely to occur not in a conflation of two architects, Barry and Street, but in the designs of the one outstanding competitor, Burges. Only Scott was a serious rival on that score. But, unlike Scott, Billy Burges was never the establishment's favourite architect. And the fact that he was Beresford-Hope's candidate cannot have helped. Years later Hope himself put his finger on the problem: Burges was too good-natured, too self-deprecating, to do himself justice; 'he was too real and natural a man to pose for posterity' – or for a panel of competition judges.[85] In Kerr's words, 'Scott was a laborious and pushing man of business. ... Street a fighting ecclesiastic; Burges an enamoured boy.'[86] Men of the world took him at his own valuation. The public felt differently. The throng of spectators and 'fair spectatresses' at the 'architectural tourney' in Lincoln's Inn Fields took Burges to their hearts. 'Eager gazers took in [his] wealth of towers and turrets, and refreshed themselves in a dreamy sense of power.'[87]

The *Architect* had no doubts: Burges's design was 'artistically magnificent'.[88] Street's first (competition), second (Embankment) and third (executed) designs were all disastrous: a concatenation of unrelated elements, 'painful to even the most advanced Goths'. *The Times* said out loud what even devoted Goths were murmuring: the winning scheme was merely 'a chaos of ill-distributed masses'.[89] Of course that was an exaggeration. Street was an architect who well understood the twin bases of thoroughfare design: perspective and detail.[90] Ruskin, Roger Smith, Paley and Godwin all rallied to his defence. Nevertheless, on this occasion, Street pursued obliquity to excess and variety beyond the point of reason. Summerson concludes that Street's 'exterior design is as totally incoherent as [his] great hall is eloquent. It represents the pathetic collapse of an overstrained imagination'.[91] Burges's scheme, however, in planning and silhouette, would have combined lucidity and drama to an exceptional degree. By joining up the outer, inner and innermost zones of his plan with flying paths and passages; by integrating Chancery Lane and the Strand itself in his scheme – by means of subways, bridges and a flamboyant Temple Bar – he created a fantasy city, a neo-medieval Troy, piercing the clouds with its turrets, bruising the heavens with its battlements. His vision of a medieval city, topped by a tower 335 ft high, would have dominated the Western approaches to the City of London. His Judges' Hall would have exploited to the limit the massy qualities of Early French. His Clock Tower would have become one of London's best known symbols. All in all, his unexecuted design must take its place with Inigo Jones's Whitehall – and a whole string of unbuilt Hanoverian palaces – as one of the greatest missed opportunities in English architectural history.

No design by Burges was more widely – and ruthlessly – imitated. Now Burges's style was distinctive, and copying it could be a hazardous business. Plagiarism could be so easily exposed. The defeated design for Leicester Town Hall by Robins and Roper (1871) was a fairly obvious crib from Burges's Law Courts.[92] So was Speakman and Charlesworth's Manchester Town Hall design. And so was Burnet's Glasgow Stock Exchange (1877): so much so that E. W. Godwin made public accusations of 'architectural poaching'.[93] But the design which revealed professional plagiarism on a grand scale was Lockwood and Mawson's Bradford Town Hall.[94] In this case Burges had not entered the competition in 1869: he had learnt his lesson with the Bradford Exchange fiasco of 1864.[95] But Lockwood and Mawson's winning scheme was such a blatant paraphrase of Burges's Law Courts design that E. W. Godwin felt forced to protest. 'If Mr Burges has acted as consulting architect,' he asked sarcastically, 'why is it that his name is not attached to the design?'[96] To that, Lockwood and Mawson had two replies. Firstly, that Burges's Law Courts scheme had itself had a consulting architect in the shape of Godwin himself.[97] And secondly that Burges, anyway, had no monopoly of – or copyright in – the medieval sources used in both designs: the Palazzo Vecchio campanile, the upper windows from the Galerie des Rois and the Galerie Intermédiaire at Amiens.[98] No doubt the barb went home. Still, Billy Burges cannot have been wholly displeased by this envious form of flattery. His own copy[99] of his Law Courts Report contains two cuttings tipped in as illustrations: a view of Burnet's Glasgow crib, and another of the offending Bradford Town Hall design by Messrs. Lockwood and Mawson, plagiarists.[1]

Scott and Street were never copied in quite the same way as Burges. 'Imitations of Burges's peculiar style', Pullan recalled, 'were to be seen . . . in many streets of London. . . . True the style was open to all the world, but the plagiarism . . . extended to features which Burges had made essentially his own, and which were sometimes bodily appropriated.'[2] One motif which seems to have entered the aesthetic consciousness of a whole generation was Burges's adaptation of the Flamboyant dormers from the Cluny Museum.[3] Another was his use of paired conical towers.[4] As for that Tuscan campanile, it came to be regarded as Burges's signature, and was copied in competitions up and down the land. 'Its influence on architects has been such,' noted Andrew Dewar of Halifax, Nova Scotia, 'that not a month passes without one of the professional journals having an illustration with one of those towers as the leading feature. Judging from those periodicals, we would say that Mr Burges is at present exerting more influence on architecture than any other man living.'[5] Throughout Britain, public buildings still bristle with the epigoni of Burges's Law Courts campanile. And the cult of Burges's scheme long outlived its author. In the 1880s the *Builder* remembered his Strand front as displaying 'more of real genius' than anything else in the whole competition.[6] The *Building News* thought it 'beyond all question, the most artistically conceived design submitted'.[7] And several architectural students still thought it *avant-garde* to submit sub-Burgesian prize drawings.[8] Phéné Spiers's elevation of the Strand front was eventually presented by the Office of Works to the

Architectural Association as a model of draughtsmanship and design.[9] As Burges put it, modestly: 'I got a certain amount of reputation from the drawings.'[10]

At least one obituarist reckoned the Law Courts as Burges's 'greatest work': 'the marvellous beauty of the ... Strand front and Temple Bar – bridge would have handed his name down to posterity as the greatest English master of the style in which they were conceived.'[11] Godwin always considered 'the façades, the clock tower, and the bridge ... among ... the best compositions of our age'.[12] Here indeed were massed together the principal attributes of the Burgesian style: 'force and massiveness ... of composition, combined with great picturesqueness of detail.' More than any other large-scale, secular design which he produced, it met the problem of style head on. Perhaps, recalled the *Builder*, 'it was too square – we might almost have said, too grim and stern – in its general aspect, and strongly feudal in character; but the treatment of the detail bore the impress of great power, and a contempt for anything slight or filagree in style. It would have been a building which no one could have seen without being impressed ...'.[13]

The Law Courts competition was perhaps the saddest of the many missed opportunities of Burges's career. But then, as Westlake put it, years later, 'competitions are *seldom* given to the best man – look at the number poor Burges won and should have won, and I think he only executed one'.[14] That one, of course, was Cork Cathedral. In some ways, lack of success was his saving grace: it saved him from Scott's prolixity, from Street's overproduction.[15] Successful architects are worldly men. Burges was notoriously unworldly. He was Pugin reborn; Pugin without the incense.

> His work was not day-work, but soul-work; it was not done for profit, but for love. That such an artist should be what is called a prosperous man of business is impossible; and posterity will rejoice to know that Burges was a disappointed man. The world has never at any time been able to get on very well with such men. They are what is called impracticable fellows. ... It is your smooth and pliant, cautious and (as the Scotch say) *canny* gentleman who suits the 'building owner'. Burges was not canny; in fact he was emphatically uncanny. ... To [such a] poetic soul ... the world ... is ... not worth the winning.[16]

The Law Courts scheme was the closest Burges ever came to realising his wildest dream of all: a Gothic city. 'If all the Gothic buildings which have been executed these last thirty years', he sighed in 1875, 'could be collected together in one or two cities, what glorious cities they would make!'[17] That metropolis of dreams would never be built by government action, still less by public subscription. To realise even a tithe of his vision, Burges needed a great patron, a veritable Maecenas.

Chapter Six

FEUDAL

'Lothair rose, and paced the room with his eyes on the ground. "I
wish I had been born in the middle ages," he exclaimed. . . .'

DISRAELI, *Lothair*, 1870

'Cardiff', Burges noted in 1865; 'Introduced to Lord Bute.'[1] Billy Burges had landed
the greatest Victorian romantic of them all: John Patrick Crichton-Stuart, 3rd
Marquess of Bute (1847–1900)[11], heir to a giant industrial fortune, scholar, mystic,
multi-millionaire, High Tory, philanthropist, compulsive builder, archaeologist,
herald, linguist, theologian, historian, liturgiologist, astrologer, philologist,
ethnologist, traveller, Celticist, psychical researcher, convert to Roman Catholicism,
landlord of 117,000 acres, inheritor of thirteen titles, owner of half a dozen major
seats, sponsor to some sixty building projects, patron of a dozen architects. . . . An
extraordinary man. And yet a man remembered by many only for the one thing he
longed to forget: he was reputed to be the richest man in the world.[2]

Well, what was the origin of his wealth? Lord Bute was 16th in line from Robert II,
King of Scotland. But the first real founder of the family fortunes was John Stuart, 3rd
Earl of Bute (1713–92), George III's much-maligned Prime Minister. Courtly talents
brought him a wife who turned out to be an heiress, Mary Wortley-Montagu, and a
political empire based on influence over the young King and the young King's mother.
Taste and learning also established him as a leading patron of the arts, with an Adam
mansion at Luton Hoo, two Adam houses in Berkeley Square and South Audley
Street, an Adam seat at Highcliffe, Hampshire, and a formidable collection of books,
manuscripts and paintings.

The second founder of the family's fortunes – the Prime Minister's son, the 1st
Marquess of Bute (1744–1814)[3] – also owed his position partly to popularity with the
ladies. Known in his youth as a profligate and dandy, he married not one heiress but
two: firstly the 'rich ugly Miss Windsor', who later inherited great estates in Cardiff
and South Wales long owned by the Herberts, Earls of Pembroke;[4] and secondly
Frances Coutts, a member of the famous banking family – her dowry was a six-figure
sum. Like his father, the 1st Marquess was also a collector and bibliophile. His son,

Lord Mountstuart – the Prime Minister's grandson – died as the result of a riding accident at the age of twenty-seven. He too married a minor heiress, Elizabeth Crichton, heiress to the Ayrshire and Wigtownshire lands of the Earls of Dumfries.

It was the 2nd Marquess of Bute (1793–1848) – the Prime Minister's great-grandson – who consolidated and developed this vast accumulation of property. He too married twice: firstly a daughter of the Earl of Guilford – a childhood friend who eventually became yet another heiress, with lands in Cambridgeshire and Oxfordshire – and secondly a daughter of the Marquess of Hastings. He is, however, famous in his own right as 'the maker of modern Cardiff', the man who built Cardiff Docks. He was, in fact, one of the most remarkable people ever to be omitted from the *Dictionary of National Biography*.⁵ Like the celebrated Duke of Bridgewater, he not only profited from but actually helped to create the industrial revolution. An earnest, solitary, myopic, evangelical Liberal Tory, he had all the confidence and resolution of an early nineteenth-century industrialist, tempered by an inborn sense of paternalist responsibility. He inherited, or acquired by marriage, largely underdeveloped and widely separate properties in Ayrshire, Bedfordshire, Bute, Cambridgeshire, Durham, Glamorgan, London and Oxfordshire. And he turned them into an efficiently coordinated business concern with an immense potential income. His Glamorgan estates formed little more than one sixth of his whole property, and each year he was able to stay there only about one month. But the development of these Glamorgan lands proved crucial to the making of the Bute fortune – and to the making of modern Cardiff.

When an Edinburgh surveyor, David Stewart, first surveyed the Glamorgan estates in 1818 he had a sorry tale to tell. 'I never saw', he wrote, 'an estate in a more neglected condition. The neglect of centuries cannot be corrected in three or four years ... the Marquess will not, during his life, be able to repair the consequences of the neglect of his predecessors.'⁶ But Stewart reckoned without the demonic energy of his new master. The 2nd Marquess set out to make Cardiff another Liverpool; it ended by eclipsing Newcastle as well.

His scheme had a massive simplicity about it. First, turn Cardiff into a major port. That would provide an outlet for the mineral wealth of the Welsh hinterland. Then ground rents would rise, port duties would flow from the new-built docks and mineral royalties would stream in from mining estates leased out to the thrusting ironmasters of Merthyr.⁷ And so it happened. But not during his own lifetime. The grand design of the 2nd Marquess was essentially a long term programme. Between 1814 and 1848 his Glamorgan estates produced some £260,000. But his investments – £150,000 on land purchase and £250,000 on dock-building – exceeded his revenue by £140,000. During the 1840s he sold his London house on Campden Hill and his seat at Luton. But at his death in 1848 debts and mortgages on his Glamorgan property stood at £493,887. Four years previously, however, the 2nd Marquess had told his London solicitor: 'I am willing to think well of my income in the distance.'⁸ What magnificently understated optimism! By 1868, the year his son came of age, debts had been reduced to £235,000; annual interest payments had been nearly balanced by investment dividends; and income from the Glamorgan estates alone stood at £100,000. By 1880 that figure had been nearly doubled. During the 1870s debts rose again – as high as £500,000. But interest charges on such sums represented less than a quarter of annual disposable income.[9] After having been subsidised for some years by the rest of the Bute property, Cardiff's bounding prosperity had more than reversed the process.[10]

First came the Bute West Dock in 1830–39.[11] Then in 1841 came the Taff Vale Railway,[12] supplementing the canal which in 1794 had in turn replaced the old mule train as the link between the coalfields and the sea. Then came the Bute East Dock in 1855–59,[13] the development of the Roath Dock in 1868, 1874 and 1887,[14] and finally the Queen Alexandra Dock in 1897–1907. During the whole Victorian and Edwardian period, first the Bute Trustees and then the 3rd Marquess and his lieutenants raised the 2nd Marquess's investment in dock-building to something approaching £6,000,000.[15] The results were staggering. Cardiff's population went up from 3,521 in 1821 to 39,546 in 1871; and from 82,761 in 1881 to 164,333 in 1901. Coastwise exports of coal rose from less than 100,000 tons in 1830 to 400,000 in 1845, 500,000 in 1850 and 1,000,000 in 1865. Foreign exports of coal rose from 20,000 tons in 1845 to 200,000 in 1850, 1,000,000 in 1860 and 2,000,000 in 1870. By 1900 – the year the 3rd Marquess died – the total coal exports from Cardiff amounted to 7,500,000 tons. Cardiff – a grimy Eldorado – had truly become not only 'the emporium of South Wales', but the greatest coal-port in the world: a town created not only in one reign, but by one family. On an isthmus at the harbour entrance William Frame's Bute Dock Building (1896) proudly symbolised the triumph of enlightened paternalism.[16]

When the 2nd Marquess died suddenly in 1848 – the crowds at his funeral were greater than those at the funerals of George IV and William IV – his son was only six months old: the richest baby in Britain[8–9]. During his long minority the investments continued to pile up under the able direction of his Trustees. When he came of age as 3rd Marquess in 1868 amid scenes of feudal joy – at least two oxen were publicly roasted in Cardiff – his gross *income* was in the region of £300,000 per annum. Much of this derived from ground rents and mineral royalties: the Bute revenue from dock dues was – compared with the massive scale of investment – surprisingly small.[17] Even so, the young Marquess was 'portentously rich'.[18] And *The Times* asked solemnly: 'What will he do with it?'[19] The answer was soon quite clear: he became the very embodiment of the High Victorian Dream.

Now Bute's obsession with the magic of the past and the mystery of the future, his genuinely medieval feeling for imagery and symbolism, can only be understood in a religious context. As a child he had been baptised an Anglican but brought up a Presbyterian. Even so, his instincts were entirely Catholic. A journal dictated by him during a Continental holiday at the age of nine already reveals his future interests. . . .

'Then the voices grew louder, and the censer was flung in the air, and the bell was rung furiously ... and the organ roared louder. ...'[20] He was converted to Roman Catholicism while an undergraduate at Oxford – or 'perverted' as the newspapers put it.[21] In the autumn of 1866 he had sought out the tiny chapel at East Hendred. There the sanctuary lamp had glimmered since the Middle Ages, even in the darkest days of Reformation.[22] 'Vavasour, Tresham, Bigod, Englefield, Arundell, Hornyold, Plessington, Jerningham and Dacre':[23] such names must surely have echoed in young Bute's brain as he knelt before the altar. Pressure, however, was brought to bear on him to delay the actual moment of conversion for two years, until he was twenty-one.

During the previous twenty years, the aristocracy had been 'going over' in increasing numbers: the tally runs to seventy-five conversions between 1850 and 1910.[24] Abingdon, Beaumont, Buchan, Dunraven, Gainsborough, Denbigh, Braye, Holland, Donington, Emly, the Marquess of Granard, Orford – and now Bute: the trickle of lordly converts was becoming a stampede. The clinching agent in Bute's conversion – as in so many others – was the mysterious Mgr. Capel.[25] Protestants began to scent a Popish Plot. Victoria's richest subject had been 'ensnared' by a foreign power. One Glasgow newspaper referred to him as 'his perverted Lordship'. *The Times* merely announced: 'for our part we are sincerely sorry for him.'[26] The battle for Bute's sensitive soul, England *versus* Rome, forms the main plot of Disraeli's novel, *Lothair* (1870).[27] Only the *dénouement* is different. In the book – despite the machinations of Cardinal Grandison (Manning) and Monsignor Catesby (Capel) – Lothair forsakes Rome for the Duke's Anglican daughter, Lady Corisande. In real life, Bute fell in love with the mysterious Maria Fox, adopted daughter of Lady Holland;[28] was then almost engaged to an Anglican daughter of the Duke of Abercorn;[29] before finally changing his faith and marrying into the Catholic Howard family.[30][14] His conversion to Catholicism seems to have taken place on two levels, intellectual and aesthetic. He needed the certainty of Catholic faith, and the visual therapy of traditional Catholic ritual. Either way, his conversion was historically based: his Catholicism was the product of his medievalism.[31]

When Augustus Hare met the young Marquess in 1874 he wrote:

> It was like reading *Lothair* in the original, and most interesting at first, but somewhat monotonous, as he talks incessantly – winding into his subject like a serpent, as Johnson said of Burke – of altars, ritual, liturgical differences; and he often almost loses himself and certainly quite lost me, in sentences about the unity of the Kosmos. ...[32]

For Bute the content of religion was inseparable from its symbolic expression, the operation of the sacramental system, the due observance of the liturgical calendar. Christianity in its 'modern' form, secularised, demythologised, politicised – a kind of supercharged Red Cross – would have struck him as absurd.[33] He thought a cathedral without sung office was a mere 'nut-shell without the nut'.[34] Even his friend and biographer, Abbot Sir David Oswald Hunter Blair – a plump Benedictine baronet with a passion for old families and good claret – was slightly bemused by ejaculations like 'Isn't it perfectly monstrous that St Magnus hasn't got an octave'.[35]

Bute later became a Vice-President of the Society for Psychical Research. And in the late 1880s and 1890s, 'the golden age of British spiritualism', he was closely associated with some very extraordinary people and some very peculiar happenings.[36] In particular, he seems to have been completely deceived by a fake medium known as 'Miss X'. Her real name was Ada Goodrich Freer (1857–1931). She was apparently mistress to F. W. H. Myers, and is described as 'going from man to man' in spiritualist circles, until she was ultimately exposed. Bute subsidised her dubious investigations and actually wrote a book with her called *The Alleged Haunting of B[allechin] House, Perthshire*.[37] He even encouraged Miss Freer and another medium named Miss Wingfield to help him elucidate the original plan of St Andrew's Priory.[38] In a sense spiritualism is the polymath's last resort: as Faust put it, 'I have learnt everything, and nothing now remains but magic'. But Bute's interest in the occult certainly had its academic side. He acquired a unique collection of documents concerning trials by the Inquisition for witchcraft and sorcery.[39] Perhaps it all began as a Romantic pose. As an undergraduate at Christ Church he once threw a fancy dress party in the college morgue, and appeared as host dressed as the Devil in wings, horns and tail. In later years, however, his pursuit of the occult certainly became a serious business. Even as a young man 'he spoke much of Antichrist'.[40] By 1886 he was 'experimenting in thought transference'.[41] By 1889 he was 'trying crystal vision'.[42] By 1891 he was conducting 'crystal vision experiments' in his exotic Summer Smoking Room at Cardiff.[43] By 1894 he was hearing footsteps at Falkland and seeing 'black and white visions' in a crystal ball at Mount Stuart.[44] And by 1895 he had made contact – via 'Miss X' – with his lost love, Maria Fox.[45] Spiritualism, he found, had robbed death of its terrors.[46]

'The Bute' certainly cuts a bizarre figure. As Rector of St Andrew's University for instance, his bulky shape swathed in robes of his own designing, purple and pink, modelled on a Benedictine habit.[47][11] Or again, with his chaplain, Mgr. Capel, posing for a studio photograph with a posse of Papal Zouaves[13]. But some of the other figures who weave their way in and out of his career were far, far stranger. Frederick Rolfe, 'Baron Corvo', for one, Bute's choir schoolmaster in the 'Tin Tabernacle' at Oban.[48] Corvo's tenure of office was brief. But he remembered Bute as 'the Marquess of Mount Stuart' – and Hunter Blair as 'Fr. Benedict' – when he came to write *Hadrian VII*.[49] Stranger still was 'Fr. Ignatius' – the Rev. Joseph Leycester Lyne, O.S.B. (1837–1908) – the maverick monk of Llantony Abbey. To him Bute was an indulgent landlord, never a patron.[50] Strangest of all – at least in this context – was Edmonia Lewis (1843–c.1910), the daughter of a Negro father and Red Indian mother, who migrated to Rome in the 1860s as one of that exotic band of American women sculptors who – in Henry James's phrase – 'settled upon the seven hills in a white marmorean flock'.[51] In 1867 Miss Lewis carved a 'Madonna and Child' for Lord Bute. Around the same time she modelled a bust of the Pope. Thereafter she vanishes into obscurity.

Figures like Baron Corvo, Fr. Ignatius, Edmonia Lewis, 'Miss X', Mgr. Capel and Abbot Hunter Blair lend perhaps an air of melodrama to Bute's life-story. They should not be allowed to do so. For Bute himself was by no means a melodramatic figure. In fact he was painfully serious, excruciatingly conscientious and terrifyingly industrious. By the end of his life he is said to have mastered twenty-one languages. His libraries were packed with rare manuscripts and books. His list of writings is by any standards prodigious. His entry in the British Museum catalogue runs to thirty items: commentaries on Greek, Latin and Coptic prayers; studies in heraldry, topography, hymnology and hagiography. But besides his own works, he edited the writings of other scholars and subsidised many more. The universities of St Andrews, Glasgow and Cardiff rank him among their greatest patrons. He was the mainstay of the *Scottish Review* almost from its foundation in 1882. He contributed no less than thirty-six articles to its pages, ranging from Celtic history to translations from Turgénieff and commentaries on Wagner. Predictably, it ceased publication on his death. Innumerable Catholic schools were indebted to his generosity. He was the leading patron of the Byzantine Research Fund. But his academic *opus magnum* was undoubtedly his translation of the Roman Breviary, his 'beloved child', a massive work on which he laboured for ten years.[52] Its second edition (1908) contains 1,330 pages, each closely printed in three columns. Bute used to say, as George Eliot remarked of her translation of Strauss, 'I began this work young and finished it old'. Critics were generally impressed by the integrity of his scholarship; Rosebery – for one – praised the nobility of his style.[53]

Finally, Bute was a polymath with a sense of humour. That was one of the reasons for his friendship with Burges. His public pronouncements are spiced with wit; his private letters suggest a sense of fun which is positively Rabelaisian.[54] Did he also possess a sense of the absurd? That would be asking too much. He was hardly the sort of man to see the point of Max Beerbohm's jibe: 'A man must be really mad if he takes himself seriously.'[55]

Bute took himself very seriously. That was inevitable, given his temperament and position. More than most men, he walked alone. He laboured all his life under a crushing sense of isolation. His shyness was legendary. '"Oh!" was an exuberance with him. Twice repeated, and he felt he had been talkative.'[56] His speeches – and they were generally very good ones – threw him into preparatory despair. In his first speech, at a dinner for three thousand in Cardiff, at the age of twenty-one, he spoke movingly of his 'loneliness', his 'absolutely crushing' responsibilities. Hence his retreat into a private world: 'an antiquarian universe ... of great writers, theologians, poets, philosophers, and barons and abbots and monks long dead.'[57] His love of seclusion was positively monastic. But the public were there, and would not go away. In 1887, at the opening of the Roath Dock, there was luncheon for four thousand, dinner for two thousand eight hundred and tea for thirteen thousand children. So he sailed the seas in search of peace. To Iceland in 1867,[58] to Scandinavia and Russia in 1868 – indeed to most accessible parts of the globe. In 1865 he was in Palestine and Egypt. In 1866 in Palestine, Malta, Sicily, Greece, Kurdistan and Armenia. In 1869–70 he was in Italy, Sicily and the Holy Land. In 1874 he fled to Nazareth: 'No one can get at us there.'[59] In 1878 he was back in Italy; in 1879–80 in Cairo, a place he returned to in 1892. In 1882 he returned to the Mediterranean; in 1884 to Athens and the Greek Islands. In 1886 he was in Germany; in 1888 in Italy and Sicily. In 1891 he was in Teneriffe – studying the language of the Canary Islanders. Some of these trips were in the nature of archaeological excursions; others were health cures. Others – notably the visits to Oberammergau in 1871, 1880 and 1890 – were essentially pilgrimages. But, in a very real sense, they were all voyages of escape. On occasion he had to be dragged back to the boardroom by telegram from archaeological digs in the north of Scotland, or from even further away – from Athens, Jerusalem or Oberammergau. He bought land in Palestine and Syria, Egypt and Turkey. But even his remotest travels failed to satisfy 'this noble hermit, this scholarly and cultured recluse'.[60] He had to take refuge in the past: 'he loved the past and lived in it.'[61] And only one man could re-build that vanished world for him – the 'soul-inspiring Burges'.[62] Their private creation was a tangible dream – a feudal fantasy – as bizarre in its way as anything conjured up by Edward Lear or Lewis Carroll, or even by Ludwig of Bavaria.

When they met in 1865, Bute was eighteen and Burges thirty-eight. Bute the orphan nobleman at Christ Church, intense, shy and solitary[10]; Billy Burges, the eternal schoolboy[1], the 'Lutyens of his generation', brimming with enthusiasm, full of jokes and puns and outlandish schemes; both of them, architect and patron, born romantics, drunk with learning, in love with the Middle Ages. Bute's potential as a patron was vast: Burges released the spring.

It didn't take long for Burges to establish himself as a family friend of the Butes. He was always 'more of a trusted friend ... than a paid servant',[63] certainly more than Bute's court jester. In 1870 it was already 'skittles with Lord Bute'.[64] By 1873 he is 'the soul-inspiring Burges'. By 1875 'the great man'.[65] In 1874 he stays with Bute at Bendinat, in Spain,[66] in 1877 at Baveno on Lake Maggiore.[67] Bute even takes him to the theatre, and to the House of Lords.[68] And Lady Bute was even friendlier. She found Burges's company a tonic.[69] In 1873 'dear Burges' presents her with 'a most beautiful brooch'[253]. 'Ugly Burges', she writes to her sister, 'who designs lovely things. Isn't he a duck.'[70] By 1874 we find Burges presenting her with a pet dog, 'a charming small thing', which she christens 'Lady Scamp'.[71] The very last work of his life was a 'Pearl Shell Bottle for Lady Bute'.[72] Billy Burges was almost one of the family – even falling asleep over dinner. In 1879 Bute sends his wife a charming vignette of 'the great man' *in extremis* at Harrogate:

Whether it was the consequence of the champagne ... or what, I don't know, but the soul-inspiring one was a Martyr to the collywobbles this morning. He told me, about 10 A.M. that he had already visited his aunt six times. Pill-box had to be sent for, who complimented him on his boyish appearance, considering his age, and gave him medicine and chicken broth. He was supposed to be fit to start (and did so) for London about 4 P.M. His only remedy seemed to be eating very strong peppermint lozenges, so that the room smelled of them even more than it does of tobacco, which is saying a good deal.[73]

Eighteen months later, Burges was dead – 'a great loss', as Lady Bute put it, 'in more ways than one'[74] – and the Butes were choosing treasures from his collection.[75] By that date, however, mementoes of 'the great man' were really superfluous: the Butes already had Cardiff Castle and Castell Coch.

CARDIFF CASTLE

Cardiff was the commission of a lifetime: the chance of creating a dream castle for Maecenas himself. By the late 1860s Burges was already working at full stretch, but Cardiff took priority. As he explained to Bute in 1873, 'I consider your business as paramount to other considerations'.[76] Between his meeting with the great patron in 1865[77] and his own death in 1881, Burges was never free of Cardiff. And he continued the project – posthumously speaking – well into the twentieth century. For after Burges's death work continued in strict accordance with his designs under the direction of William Frame. At Frame's death in 1905 the 4th Marquess appointed another architect named H. Sesom-Hiley; and in 1921 Sesom-Hiley was succeeded by J. P. D. Grant (1890–1976).[78] The latest works, therefore, notably the Roman gateway and battlemented outer walls, were conducted at two or three removes from Burges, but very much in the Burgesian spirit, and following the advice of one of Burges's archaeological contemporaries, G. T. Clark (d. 1898).[79]

In one of his earliest public speeches Bute declared himself 'painfully alive to the fact that [Cardiff] Castle is very far indeed from setting anything like an example in art'.[80] After generations of neglect the 1st Marquess had in 1774 begun the clearance and landscaping of the central court – employing 'Capability' Brown – and the reconstruction of the residential section in the West wing, under the direction of Henry Holland. That was after an elaborate but abortive scheme had been prepared by Robert Adam.[81] Work was abandoned, however, in 1794 on the death of Lord Mountstuart.[82] And it was not until *c.* 1817 that these operations were completed, possibly by Sir Robert Smirke.[83] All this work was conspicuously pre-Puginian, and something of a torment to young Bute's aesthetic sensibilities. He had, in effect, inherited a semi-reconstructed ruin. An ancient castle – Roman, Norman and Plantagenet – had degenerated into a 'Picturesque seat'[80; 82]. Bute called in Burges as regenerator in chief.

The ancient site of Cardiff Castle took the form of a vast rectangle more than 600 ft square, surrounded by a moat and divided internally into three wards.[84] Burges's report of 1866[85] was limited to the South West angle of the Middle Ward: the Black Tower facing Castle St; the boundary wall fronting Llandaff Rd; and the right-angled section of wall running towards the castle residence and the old Town Gate. He had already determined to make that right-angled corner the site of a new tower, a strong vertical accent which would dominate the whole composition. So much is clear in his advice to the Bute Trustees, despite a smokescreen of objectivity.

'There are three distinct ways,' he began rather disingenuously, of dealing with the problem: '1. The Strictly Conservative, 2. The Antiquarian, and 3. The Modern.' The *Conservative* method was indeed austere: 'finding out what features really did exist in ancient times and . . . strictly preserv[ing] them . . . with no additions excepting such as might be imperatively demanded and [even these] should be made as different to the old as possible'. Such an approach would only be justifiable 'were the remains of high interest in the history of architecture or precious on account of their art'. The *Antiquarian* method gave the architect a little more latitude: it involved 'an archaeological restoration, i.e. the replacing of everything that a study of archaeology would lead us to suppose had been lost'. The moat, for example, would have to be excavated; the battlements replaced according to thirteenth-century models at Conway or Caerphilly[86], or – better still – along the lines indicated in an eleventh-century MS of Caedmon in the Bodleian; wooden galleries would have to be constructed; some peripheral cottages would need to be restored, others removed; and 'the ditch would be separated from the road by a very stout palisade of painted wood'. The third course – the *Modern* – was much more drastic. Burges described it as 'like the two former . . . a conservative [method] as far as the preservation of old work is concerned, but it would involve sundry additions which are to a certain degree demanded by the fact of the castle being used as a nobleman's residence'. Neighbouring cottages could be cleared. A formidable corner tower could be erected – 'a handsome object at the present entrance of the town [which would] cut up the long line of unbroken wall'. The Black Tower could be rebuilt – 'not [as] a copy', but as 'a really handsome piece of architecture'. And the moat could be planted as a medieval garden. 'We must never', Burges concluded, 'lose sight of the fact that Cardiff Castle is not an antiquarian ruin but the seat of the Marquis of Bute.' In effect, the architect had come near to giving himself *carte blanche*.

Bute came of age in 1868, and work began straight away. During the three years since Burges began his design, he had been involved in the great London Law Courts competition. There he had envisaged a miniature city, bristling with towers, spires and turrets[60]. At Cardiff that vision came close to reality: the dream castle was to be a dream city in microcosm[81; 83]. The site of Cardiff Castle is flat: so Burges gave it a syncopated silhouette. Its position is hemmed in by the city: so Burges made its towers overtop their tallest neighbours. Burges wanted to create an image both municipal and feudal – appropriately Bute also became Mayor of Cardiff – and here the obvious source of inspiration was North Italy. The clustered towers of San Gimignano; the campaniles of Florence and Siena; the jagged skyline of the fifteenth-century Castello Sforzesco at Milan:[87] all these Burges had visited, and all these are metamorphosed into the silhouette of Cardiff Castle. But there are touches of Nuremberg,[88] and Franco-Swiss elements too: the Palace of the Popes at Avignon;[89] the thirteenth-century Castle of Chillon on Lake Geneva;[90] the fifteenth-century Château L'Aigle near Villeneuve;[91] and the fourteenth-century tower at Constance.[92] All these Burges had visited, several with Somers Clarke in the summer of 1869. Finally, there is the vernacular castellated element: in 1869–70 Burges made a particular study of Conway and Caernarvon;[93] and in 1878 he visited Durham 'to study the keep approaches'.[94]

Now Pugin always remained a hero to Burges, and Burges must have known Pugin's dramatic skylines at Alton Towers and Scarisbrick, as well as the Pugin-Barry silhouette at Westminster. But Pugin was a master of linear, flat surface patterns. He never matched Burges's volumetric vigour. Pugin's is almost an engraver's architecture, Burges is a sculptor at heart. Moreover Pugin's range of sources was, on the whole, limited to English prototypes. Burges had all France and Italy, Sicily and Turkey to draw on, too. Cardiff Clock Tower, therefore, has moved several stages onwards from Big Ben: Pugin, plus Ruskin, plus Viollet-le-Duc, plus Burges. Here is romantic eclecticism triumphant. The Cardiff skyline is a High Victorian fantasy, a belligerent rejection of Georgian harmony, balance and coherence: Billy Burges kicking Henry Holland and 'Capability' Brown in the teeth. Seen from its Western side, reflected in water and framed in foliage, that silhouette is unforgettable: five towers in profile – Bute Tower, Beauchamp Tower, Herbert Tower, Guest Tower and Clock Tower – an explosion of archaeology and romanticism.

As late as April 1868, Burges's plans for rebuilding the entrance gate and Black Tower were still vague. In that month he sent Bute 'a rough idea of the masses of the new [twin-towered] gateway. I have not had time to think out this last work, and I should hardly like to call it even an idea.'[95] By that time, however, the Clock Tower was beginning to crystallise. In 1866 its details were still fluid. There was no sculpture, no heraldry, not even a clock, merely a boldly machicolated arcade immediately below the galleried Summer Smoking Room. The Winter Smoking Room was vaulted and furnished with exterior balconies, but the Bachelor Bedroom had yet to be created. The two lower floors were destined for the gardener, as sitting room and bedroom. From here he was to tend the sunken medieval garden, and watch over the citizens of Cardiff as they sniffed the scented plants or sunned themselves beneath the ramparts. This moat garden must be counted one of Burges's happiest devices.

> The public [he wrote] might be admitted at certain hours. The paths would be gravelled, but the beds would be raised some 18 inches and enclosed with their

walls of stone, some would only contain grass, others flowers and some grass with holes for the insertion of flower pots . . . One long bed would run at the foot of the wall, and on it would be placed a trellis for creeping plants and espaliers. A bed would run along the centre but more raised than the others, at the extremity of which would be placed fountains and in the centre a statue. The garden would be separated from the road by an ornamental wrought or cast iron railing and strong handsome stone piers.[96]

Those piers were the origin of Burges's famous 'Animal Wall' – now the last surviving fragment of something which must surely have been unique: a municipal Pre-Raphaelite garden.

The laying of the Clock Tower's foundation stone on 12 March 1869 was not without its comic elements. Burges was present, along with Mc. Connochie. 'The stone was duly laid at the North East corner, but owing to the party being so sparingly possessed of the current coins of the realm, the usual deposition of money etc. had to be postponed. . . . The company afterwards adjourned to the Cardiff Arms Hotel, and, over a champagne luncheon, wished success to the undertaking.[97] Soon work was progressing rapidly. And within two years the structure of the tower was complete.[98] Cardiff had been given a new skyline.[91]

The Clock Tower[79;91] – appropriately enough – has a single iconographic theme: Time. Inside and outside, its decorative images portray the heavenly bodies and temporal divisions. The clock itself is flanked by statues – painted by Weekes and Smallfield[99] – representing the seven planets, standing on pedestals carved with their respective signs of the zodiac.[1] In the Winter Smoking Room[146; 150] the windows – the work of Weekes and Saunders (*c.* 1870) – represent the six days of the week, as enshrined in Saxon or Norse mythology: Moni, or the moon (in Scandinavian mythology Sol, the sun, is female and Moni, the moon, male); Tyr, a one-handed Northern Mars; Wodin, or Odin, the terrible lord of Valhalla; Thor, son of Odin, armed with a wondrous mallet and gauntlets of iron; Freyja, the Scandinavian Venus; and Satur, chief participant in the Ragnorök, or twilight of the gods.[2] The seventh day is of course represented by the Sun, carved on the central boss of the room's vaulting. On the four walls and in the eight spandrels of the vault, are Weekes's paintings of the twelve signs of the zodiac.[3] The four seasons appear in pictorial form on the walls, as well as Lonsdale's murals of the origins of music and painting.[4] Dawn, Sunrise, Sunset and Moonlight are depicted in the four corners. And the amusements of winter appear in sculptured form in the chimneypiece: Diana the Huntress, the Goddess of Heaven, being frequently identified with the Greek Artemis and Goddess of the Moon.[5] In the Bachelor Bedroom above[149], we move from astrology to alchemy. The twelve signs of the zodiac appear in proxy form as their respective precious stones.[6] The walls are labelled with thirty-two types of gem. Mineral rocks from the Bute estate are inset in the chimneypiece – itself a miniature mountain. And the mineralogical theme is continued in portraits of goldsmiths and jewellers in the vaulting – Cellini, Ghiberti, etc. – and in stained glass allegories of six precious jewels: ruby, topaz, diamond, emerald, sapphire and pearl.[7] Each stone is linked to a musical instrument, and ancient instruments appear again in the corners of the walls. Finally, in the Summer Smoking Room[II; 152], the tiled floor depicts the five continents, and the Holy City, and the life cycle of the birds and beasts of the earth. Inlaid with silver, bronze and copper, and set in enamelled tiles, it embodies a model of the world – *Globus hic monstrat microcosmum* – and incorporates the date of its conception: 1871.[8] The chimneypiece is carved with the amusements of Summer – lovemaking being common to Summer and Winter.[9] The frieze of painted tiles illustrates the legends of the zodiac: above, Apollo and Cupid, Venus and Jupiter; below, Hercules, Castor and Pollux, Jupiter and Ganymede, Europa and the Bull, Phryxus and Hellen, etc[10] Figures of the four elements – earth, fire, air and water – fill the spaces between the ribs of the dome. The eight winds of Greek mythology – Africus, Auster, Zephyrus, etc. – appear as giant, anthropomorphic corbels, each clad in appropriate garb.[11][123] Around the walls paintings by Weekes represent seventeen different types of metal.[12] Astronomers of the past look down from the spandrels: Kepler, Herschel, La Place, Copernicus, Newton, Ptolemy, Tycho Brahe, Aidenmehev. The stars on the ceiling are boldly marked, each with its name and symbol. And right in the centre, a sun-burst chandelier in the form of Apollo – reflected below in tile and glass, marble and alabaster; mirrored aloft in star and dome – shimmers above this whole extraordinary scene.[13][154]

Eight years after its design was conceived,[14] Lord Bute's tower was complete. 'We had luncheon today for the first time in the lower room of the tower,' wrote Lady Bute in September 1873; 'Dear Burges was present and quite content with his own work'.[15] Bute must have been equally content: those astrological complexities were surely of his own devising. The topmost ceiling of the Summer Smoking Room was his special joy. 'It seems to remind me', he wrote, 'of the real stars glittering on a fine night.'[16]

These rooms are really intellectual exercises. No wonder Burges was accused of sacrificing comfort to art.

> 'Your rooms', says Monsignore, 'seem to be made almost as uncomfortable as they can possibly be.'
>
> 'Why, of course!' exclaims the astonished artist, fixing his glass somewhat indignantly in his eye, 'what you call uncomfortable I call quaint. . . . I want to get rid of the idea of modern cosseting, you know, and drainage and wood floors, and so on . . .'
>
> 'You don't go in for beds, do you?'
>
> 'No, they're later . . .'[17]

In fact, the Clock Tower boasted at least one bed, painted and patterned like

Burges's own bed in Buckingham St.[18] There were also at least two sets of chairs. In the Winter Smoking Room, Burges modelled his six spartan, steel-framed chairs directly on drawings by Viollet-le-Duc.[19] In the Summer Smoking Room, however, there were luxurious ottomans; and the ten chairs seem to be very much his own design, Jacobean in shape, Romanesque in decoration, of ebony inlaid with ivory.[20] Six more chairs follow the same pattern, but in different materials: oak inlaid with mother-of-pearl. In the Bachelor Bedroom, the wash-stand, dressing table and sofa are all plain-spoken versions of standard Burgesian designs – so spartan as to seem almost temporary. But the chiffonier in the Winter Smoking Room is neither temporary nor plain: its massive mahogany carcass is inset with mother-of-pearl.[21]

Among the decorations of the Clock Tower, the tiles are particularly striking. Burges had been involved since the 1850s in the revival of encaustic tiles. In 1858 he drew and described some thirteenth-century tiles recently discovered at Chertsey Abbey in an article entitled 'What we learn from the Chertsey tiles'.[22] During the 1860s he worked closely with two manufacturers: William Godwin of Lugwardine, Herefordshire;[23] and George Maw of Broseley, Shropshire.[24] Technically, both depended largely on earlier discoveries by Herbert Minton. Archaeologically, the ground had already been prepared by Pugin, Shaw, Willement, Nicholls and Cottingham.[25] Minton's had been Pugin's favourite firm, contractors for the Houses of Parliament. Indeed Herbert Minton's position in the field of ceramic tile manufacture is comparable with Charles Winston's in the field of stained glass.[26] But in the 1860s – thanks to designers like Digby Wyatt, Owen Jones, Street, Seddon and Burges – the initiative passed to Maw.[27] 'Floreat Maw Salopia' is stamped on many a mid-Victorian interior. In particular, it was Maw who developed the use of 'Majolica tiles for architectural purposes'. These Majolica tiles – moulded tiles covered with opaque or transparent glazes – came to be preferred to the encaustic variety which were flat-patterned with inlaid coloured clays. They were especially suitable for tiles in the Islamic style. Maw's London agents were W. B. Simpson & Sons of the Strand.[28] Simpson's 'art tiles', blanked out in Shropshire, hand-painted and fired in London, are outstanding even in the crowded field of High Victorian ceramics.[29] The achievements of Morris and De Morgan in the 1880s should not detract from Simpson's contribution in the 1870s. And Simpson's never produced anything finer than the floor tiles in Burges's Summer Smoking Room at Cardiff.

Burges unveiled the Tower exterior, and the Summer and Winter Smoking Rooms, at the Royal Academy in 1870.[30] 132 feet and seven stories high; 25 ft square, with walls five feet thick, built of Caerphilly stone from Lord Bute's own quarry, Cardiff's Clock Tower became a London sensation. Gardener's sitting-room, gardener's bedroom, winter smoking room, private bedroom and bathroom, clock-room, servant's room, summer smoking room and gallery – each apartment richer than the one below it; here was a veritable skyscraper among palaces.[31] A skyscraper, moreover, clad in the garments of progressive eclecticism. The decoration of the outer roof – stars tinned on lead – was inspired by the church of Notre Dame at Châlons-sur-Marne.[32] The painted vaults of the Winter Smoking Room and Bachelor Bedroom derive from Palermitan prototypes: the thirteenth-century Torre di Santa Ninfa;[33] or apartments in the twelfth-century Palazzo Vecchio.[34] The tiled floor of the Summer Smoking Room was inspired by that before the high altar in Westminster Abbey.[35] The four tulip vases (1874)[155] in the same room were miniaturised versions – via Viollet-le-Duc – of the Abbot's Kitchen at Marmoutier, near Tours[65], remodelled along the lines of vases from Beauvais and Java.[36] The elaborate door[251] to the Bachelor Bedroom was 'deeply cut like . . . Arab and Norwegian doors'.[37] The device of mounting their pierced hinge-plates on red and black velvet ('Marouflage') was a 'dodge' Burges learnt at Constantinople. Nothing could be more eclectic. Even Lord Bute's bath was itself a Roman antique, its marble surface inset with fishes and lizards in copper, silver and brass.[38]

But despite their historical prototypes, these rooms seemed so original, so outlandish, that they baffled the critics. No record has been found of their reception at the Paris Exhibition of 1878.[39] But the *Builder* called them 'truly fearful and wonderful'.[40] The *Architect*, staggered by their iconography, agreed that at least they were 'thoughtful art'.[41] The *Archaeological Journal* thought the mass of detail 'overpowering'.[42] The *Building News* admitted defeat altogether: the 'portentous corbellings' in the Summer Smoking Room, 'are of a character of design which we honestly allow we fail to comprehend'.[43] 'Surely, Mr Burges', observed the *Builder*, 'the colouring, the *tout ensemble*, is not the most harmonious in the world'.[44] On one characteristic, however, all the critics agreed: the element of unabashed theatricality. Appropriately, some of Burges's drawings for this enchanted tower were traced by the young Ellen Terry, while she was living with E. W. Godwin.[45]

It was, however, not Godwin but William H. White – writing pseudonymously – who produced the most telling argument in favour of this abstruse iconographical exercise.

> All these *motifs* and decorations are to Lord Bute's tower what fittings are to ordinary people's houses. You, Brown (the South Wales branch of the Browns) are pleased to sneer at Wodin and Thor, at love in all weathers, at the elements, at the Zodiac and all other signs, at the precious metals which do not belong to you, at all and everything connected with ornament designed in a style with which you are not familiar, and the details of which you do not care, or do not know how, to decipher. But, pray, when you have made your fortune, how will you decorate your rooms? . . . [With] gewgaws filched from the fashions of three of the French Louis [?] . . . [Or with] a plaster combination of acanthus leaves, a plant which you have never seen, and of which you know nothing . . . [?] And very likely all these things which you are pleased to think ornament will cost you as much in proportion as the decorative furniture in Cardiff Tower has cost Lord Bute.[46]

At the time of Bute's marriage in 1872 the reconstruction of Cardiff Castle had really only just begun. 'Pray don't imagine, my dear,' he writes to his fiancée, 'that the house is all done up as if we were living in the reign of Henry III. There is only my sitting room, the oratory and the new tower. The rest is by no means satisfactory, and has been the victim of every barbarian since the Renaissance'.[47] During 1872–3 a model was prepared showing the scope of future improvements. Bute seems to have been rather 'doubtful' about Burges's ideas: the form of the future Bute Tower and Guest Tower were still vague.[48] 'The house', Bute complained in 1873, 'is all topsy-turvy'.[49] But by the summer of 1874 the new skyline was beginning to take shape.

This phase of activity, however, was abruptly curtailed by the financial crisis of 1874–75, a book-keeping crisis in the Bute fortunes which temporarily threatened the whole operation.[50] In 1871 and 1873 there had been major coal strikes. The capital value of agricultural land was falling, and with it the scale of rentals. The bulk of Bute's capital was tied up in dockland development. The Trustees naturally looked askance at Burges's feudal extravaganzas. Cardiff Castle and Castell Coch had, therefore, to be paid for out of Bute's personal income; much of their cost must have been floated on borrowed money.[51] On 16 Nov. 1874, Burges noted: 'Cardiff works very nearly stopped'.[52] Bute seems to have suffered from a neurotic misapprehension of bankruptcy. 'Affairs are, I must say, looking as black as night', he tells his wife in spring 1875; 'and if we can still cash up to the butchers and bakers we can't to other tradesmen employed by Mc Connochie'.[53] 'I hardly know what to say or do. . . . If the money can't be raised, the workmen . . . will have to be paid off, and I fancy we shall have to send away some of the servants, and sell perhaps the horses. . . . Telegrams are flying backwards and forwards several times a day. . . . We shall have to consider . . . living abroad . . . St Malo is a beastly hole, but there are . . . many nice places to be found further South . . . say at Cintra or the Azores. . . .'[54] But with credit like Bute's, there was really no problem. 'Another £100,000 from the Equitable' saw them through. Their budget was temporarily cut to £15,000 p.a., and Burges even managed to reduce building expenses to £25 per week.[55] Work was soon in full swing again. By September 1876, there were twenty-seven workmen back on site.[56] Throughout, Bute's confidence in his chosen architect never wavered. 'Burges is very clever', he assured his fiancée in 1872, 'and his company is amusing, which is always such a luxury'.[57]

During the early 1870s work was gradually proceeding. In 1868–9 Burges had designed a new set of stables to the North of the castle compound.

> It forms an entire quadrangle, entered by gateways on opposite sides; a lean-to roof, on wooden supports, gives shelter cloister-wise all round the interior. A fountain, which, if it would not frighten the horses, would certainly form an effective feature, occupies the centre of the quadrangle, and the inevitable turret, dedicated to pigeons, sticks up at one corner, but hardly so as to gather the

grouping together as well as it should. [Still] the design is one we should be glad to see carried out.[58]

Carried out it was, in 1872–5, in red Newbridge stone and green Welsh slates.[59] But the skyline was shorn of its staircase turret and pigeon tower, to say nothing of the fountain. The result is plain and unexciting: Lord Bute was not interested in horses.

He was interested in oratories. Cardiff Castle was to have had two, if not three. In 1868 Burges produced designs for altering the castle's domestic chapel, apparently situated just to the North of the Beauchamp Tower.[60] Only its Byzantine Gothic dome, painted with angels by Smallfield, survives.[61] It seems to have been regarded as temporary.[62] And Bute dreamed ultimately of completing his rejuvenation of Cardiff by restoring the keep as a receptacle for a greater and more elaborate chapel. This visionary scheme centred on a circular, two-storeyed, arcaded courtyard, topped by a domed 'Domestic Oratory' – the whole structure soaring higher than the Clock Tower itself.[63] As late as 1895, in a codicil to his will, Bute recalled this extraordinary fantasy. By that date Burges's altar, bronze crucifix and candlesticks had been transferred to Falkland House. From there they were in turn removed to Edinburgh, to adorn the Archbishop's private chapel.[64]

Meanwhile, Bute had created his own private oratory[156] in the tiny room where his father 'fell asleep and woke in eternity'. This 'little mortuary chapel', between the Beauchamp Tower and the Herbert Tower, was planned at the end of the 1860s, but not completed until the later 1870s. In 1873 it was still 'all a skeleton'.[65] In 1874 the rib vault was still being carved.[66] Westlake's windows only appeared in 1875.[67] In transforming a dressing room into a chapel, Burges achieved a powerfully vaulted space which is almost claustrophobically rich. Here, as one writer put it,

> there is not a square inch of idle space. . . . The floor, . . . is of inlaid marble tesserae, the dado of dove marble inlaid with shields enamelled with arms. . . . The altar is a perfect gem. Below it, and inside a sepulchre of open bronze tracery-work, rests [Fucigna's] figure of Jesus in sculptured marble.[68] Externally sleep the guards [modelled by Fucigna and cast in bronze by Hatfield],[69] whilst above is painted the figure of Christ, with the angel and holy women. Above the dado are various pictures [by Westlake], all bearing upon the Resurrection. The light is transmitted through stained glass figures [by Lavers and Barraud] representing the Evangelists, and their reflections fall upon the jambs, painted with figures of the Greek and Latin Doctors of the Church. The vaulting is covered by the archangels and angels holding the instruments of Our Lord's passion.[70]

The bronze door (1876) is one of Burges's finest, cast by Hart and damascened in silver, with the Virgin and the Tree of Life.[71] The minor fittings are all worked out with immense skill: the crucifix of barbed bronze with crystal mounts; the aumbry of cedar wood and bronze, inlaid with polished brass; the heraldic enamels;[72] the piscina of dove grey marble. The altar even miniaturises portions of Orcagna's shrine at Orsan-michele, Florence.[73]

While the oratory was progressing, the foundation stone of the new Bute Tower had been laid on 24 April 1873. Designs for the exterior, with its four giant figures sculpted on high, were prepared the previous autumn.[74] Inside, the Small Dining Room had been planned as early as 1872. Its decoration introduces us to yet another member of Burges's team: Charles Campbell. It was in 1873 that the firm of Campbell, Smith & Co. was founded, largely under Burges's aegis. Campbell had worked for Harland and Fisher.[75] Burges had taught him to draw, and trained him in the principles of colour and composition.[76] The firm prospered. Indeed it became the most prestigious private firm of architectural decorators in Britain. But they never executed anything more dazzling than this Small Dining Room. The chimney-piece[121], for example, is a polychrome *tour de force*. As so often in Burges's work, it takes the form of a design originally proposed for a previous commission: in this case, for Trinity College, Hartford, Connecticut.[77] Its design, indeed, forms a recurrent theme in Burges's *œuvre*.[78] On this occasion, the richly modelled lower frieze was carved by Nicholls in Painswick sandstone; the upper figures in Caen stone or Corsham Bath stone. These figures relate the Old Testament story of the angels' announcement of a child to Sarah and Abraham: hence the Greek inscription 'Entertaining Angels Unawares'. Campbell's colouring is almost electrifying.[79] But the rest of the room is not eclipsed. The oak panelling glitters with inset silver and coloured glass.[80] Winged dragons flank the firegrate. The frieze floats free with swooping angels.[81] The windows, by Lonsdale and Saunders (*c*. 1873), glow richly with scenes from the life of Abraham.[82] Their shutters are alive with quirkish patterns.[83] Even the bell-push consists of a monkey with an acorn in its mouth. The furniture, a little heavy, was added in 1890 by William Frame.[84] But the ceiling takes the breath away.

Burges's painted ceilings, at Cardiff and later on at Tower House, stemmed principally from two decorative traditions: Moorish and Arabic. Both traditions were themselves synthetic: Moorish influence in Sicily, Arabic influence in Cairo. Sicily was for Burges irresistible in its amalgam of different styles. 'In Sicily, and only in Sicily', Gally Knight had noted, 'the Greeks, the Saracens and the Normans were united, and by their fortuitous conjunction, the northern, the classic and the oriental styles were blended together; the Romanesque, the Greek and the Saracenic. Nothing of the sort is to be seen anywhere else.'[85] The Cathedral at Messina Burges found particularly intriguing: its painted woodwork, stemming from antique Greek traditions of polychromy, with beams and domelets blazoned in gold, azure and scarlet.[86] The basilica of St Paul outside the walls of Rome, and the Cathedral of Monreale near Palermo, were stylistically comparable.[87] But both of these had been partly burned. The polychrome ceiling at Messina survived unscathed. For Burges its decoration – its jelly-mould domelets, it painted beams – supplied evidence of the compatibility of

Classical, Gothic and Oriental traditions in art. In that respect, the Sicilian synthesis was not unlike the Spanish.[88] Synthetic in its origins, might it not form the basis of yet another synthesis? It might, in conjunction with other sources. So to it Burges added Cairéan elements: that is, motifs from houses in Cairo decorated by Arab craftsmen. One example which must have appealed to him was the seventeenth-century Mosque D'El-Bordeyny, with its beamed, coffered and painted ceilings.[89] Ceilings such as these, multicoloured, mirrored and almost oppressively rich, were surely in Burges's mind when he conceived the exotic ceilings of Cardiff's Bute Tower.

Above this dining room, the Bute Tower contains Bute's sitting room, bedroom and roof-garden. In the sitting room, the chimneypiece (1874) has a brass-columned overmantel set with marble.[90] The windows contain four roundels enclosing allegories of the Seasons. The ceiling is beamed and gilded, with sixteen of Burges's favourite Messina domelets. The frieze is painted by Rossiter with legends from the life of St Blane.[91] And the door glows with images painted by Sir William Douglas[92] on the theme of the Seven Deadly Sins[148]. Two of Burges's favourite medieval texts – the *Psychomachia* of Prudentius and the *Rota Alternationis* of the Arundel Psalter – supply the imagery. Pride and Avarice are there, in the form of an empress and a miser; so are Lust and Anger: a voluptuous matron and an angry knight. But the other three symbols show a variation on the usual list: Indulgence in the form of a bacchante; Idolatry in the form of a negro and golden ram; and Discord in the form of a warrior amazon. Over all seven vices triumphs a winged god, Wisdom.

Lady Bute's sitting room, bedroom and bathroom – adjacent to the Bute Tower, but located within Holland's section – are largely Georgian. From an artistic point of view they are comparatively small beer. Bute's bedroom[149], however, is a virtuoso performance in wood and marble. Above the heraldic chimneypiece Burges placed a gilded statue of St John the Evangelist (1874–76), modelled by Fucigna, cast by Barkentin, glittering with enamel and semi-precious stones.[93] And above the evangelist rears a gilded bronze eagle, with 'silver beak, claws and real eyes'.[94] The adjacent bathroom is guarded with Turkish wooden grilles (1875);[95] the clothes cupboards are set with mirrors.[96] The washbasin itself, enamelled with a mermaid menaced by monsters, is a variant on Burges's own Mermaid Bowl.[97] And the windows of the bathroom were originally screened with onyx-studded lattice,[98] and filled with translucent slabs of alabaster – a conceit Burges may have learned at San Miniato al Monte in Florence.[99] The bathroom wall was inset with thirty-six types of marble: Siena and Amaranth, Languedoc, Caserta, Cashmere Onyx, Emperor's Red. ...

> There were lumps of marble that you wanted to eat, and the very names of some of them should be enough to make one happy. ... When I shut my eyes last night I could see nothing but the petrified waves and tide-marks and signs of shimmering winds on wet surfaces.[1]

The bedroom's stained glass – executed by Lavers and Barraud, perhaps from cartoons by Westlake – illustrates the Seven Churches in the Book of Revelation.[2] The corbels bulge with angels by Fucigna.[3] And all around, panelled walls and panelled ceiling – beamed, coffered, mirrored, painted, domed – glittering with a thousand facets. Lady Bute was understandably impressed: 'I am writing in your beautiful bedroom – with your wonderful St John – and the seven churches – it is all so lovely.'[4]

At the top of the Bute Tower, up a domed spiral staircase,[5] lies the Roof Garden or Peristyle, erected in 1873–6:[6] a delicious bower, silent, sweet-scented, high above the noisy city[147]. A colonnade of slender pillars surrounds a miniature cortile, inlaid with marble, mosaic and tile.[7] A splashy fountain (1875–9), alive with bronze otters, lions and fish;[8] a bronze Madonna (1876–8), calm and still, conjuring up memories of Rheims or Amiens;[9] four castellated bronze flower boxes (1877), styled on trophies from ancient Pompeii;[10] tiled walls, inscribed in Hebrew, flashing with stories from the Book of Kings;[11] deer's head corbels, hung with chains;[12] and a massive bronze door (1876)[250], featuring an incarcerated otter, moulded with three-dimensional wit.[13]

> [Here] one may almost imagine [oneself] sitting in the court of some nobleman's house in the South of France in the twelfth century, ere what we call Gothic Art had ceased to be somewhat Greek. There, laid out in symmetrical forms, are beds of choice azaleas and camellias, and standing in the midst a beautiful bronze figure of the Virgin and Child, whilst around the loopholed wall is covered with enamelled paintings of ancient stories.[14]

Here indeed is a tiny, private world, open to the sky, but closed to the distractions of humanity.

Should Lord Bute wish to leave his tower, cross over the moat, and stroll across the park towards his excavated Black Friars Monastery – then a rustic bridge[89] was at his disposal. Bridge and summerhouse combined; raised on stilts and roofed over with exaggerated eaves, it seems to have been modelled on a structure noticed by Burges on Lake Lucerne.[15] Alas, this rustic *jeu d'esprit* – 'unique in this country'[16] – bristling with exaggerated finials, was dismantled in the 1930s. In 1875 the estimate had been £1,108.[17]

Inside the castle, between the Bute Tower and the Beauchamp Tower, a narrow lobby known as Lord Bute's Passage provides access to a servants' staircase, and ties both towers to the Banqueting Hall. It is an awkward space, tortuous and dim. Burges made it a bruising experience. The plain staircase erupts into three square columns of Rhondona marble, crowned with bulbous capitals, linked by anthropomorphic lamp-holders and lit by tinted glass.[18] The doorway had first appeared, in much more elaborate form, at Cork;[19] the lamp-holders at Knightshayes;[20] and the glass – 'Undine', 'Gnome', 'Sylph' and 'Salamander' – at Winscombe Hall.[21] A back-stairs lobby had been turned into a Burgesian anthology.

Climbing into the Chaucer Room[158], at the top of the Beauchamp Tower, is like stepping into an upturned kaleidoscope. Its base is the medieval octagon; its summit the towering forest of Burges's timber flèche. Chaucer himself presides over an alphabet chimneypiece, and all around him are images of Chaucerian fancy. On the floor is a vine-leaf maze of encaustic tiles; on the lower walls oak panelling (1884) inlaid with wild flowers and mother-of-pearl. Higher up are paintings of legendary ladies – Cleopatra, Thisbe, Phyllis, Philonella; eight painted heads and eight corbels sculpted by Nicholls: Chaucer's *Legend of Good Women*.[22] Higher still, a network of painted branches gives shade to the birds of the air: Chaucer's *Parlement of Foules*. Then comes the gilded balcony, breaking forward on timber vaulting: a miniaturised version of the octagon at Ely crowned by a miniaturised version of the flèche at Amiens. The balcony's stained glass illustrates the *Canterbury Tales*: thirty-two windows,[23] each filled with a Chaucerian character or theme, massed and tangled like a ribbon of flowers, glowing with filtered light. [III] The flèche was conceived in 1872, begun in 1877 and finished in 1879.[24] Structurally speaking, the room dates from 1877–9, decoratively from 1879–81 – although painting seems not to have been completed until 1890. Burke supplied the chimneypiece,[25] Simpson the tiles,[26] Hart, Son and Peard the metalwork,[27] Campbell and Smith the painting, and Worrall the glass (1880–85) – working from cartoons by Lonsdale.[28] The inlaid panelling was executed by Thomas John Jnr.[29] The Chaucer Room came within Lady Bute's personal domain, and she took particular care to ensure that the decoration was more 'carefully' done than that at Castell Coch.[30] The result, certainly, is fantastic – even by Burgesian standards. Here the High Victorian Dream has been actualised, within the shell of a fifteenth-century guard chamber. And where did the general idea come from? In the very year of its beginning, 1877, Burges wrote to the Rev. J. Willis Clarke at Cambridge and commented on the library at the Castle of St Angelo in Rome: its shape an octagon; its lighting from above; and its floor a labyrinth.[31]

While the Chaucer Room was slowly progressing work was also in hand on the Guests' Tower, and on the Library and Banqueting Hall. The bulky Guests' Tower, as its name implies, was designed to accommodate rooms for visitors. It replaced the domestic quarters in Holland's Southern wing. Comfort rather than display was therefore the primary consideration.[32] The exterior was certainly Burges's design: its arcaded parapet recalls work he had studied at Swansea and St David's.[33] But much of its furniture and interior decoration – the Nursery, for instance, painted with images from fairy tales – was not completed, nor was the adjacent Tank Tower, until the Edwardian period.[34] The Library and Banqueting Hall, however, were from the first conceived in terms of display. They are the largest rooms in the castle. Their windows recall the Donjon of the Palace at Poitiers.[35] One above the other, they occupy the site of the fifteenth-century Great Hall. Holland and Smirke had divided this Great Hall into a Staircase Hall and Dining Room. Burges abolished this division. And by creating a new entrance hall several bays to the South, he managed to expand the space available without altering either the Western line of the Roman wall or the Eastern front of the medieval Lodgings. As the programme of work moved into its second decade, architect and patron showed no signs of faltering. If Burges's inventive powers began to flag, they could be supplemented by Bute's encyclopaedic knowledge, biblical, genealogical or astrological.[36] If Bute's resolution wavered, he could always seek 'refreshment . . . from several hours with . . . the great man . . . the soul-inspiring Burges'.[37] Together, they made a formidable team.

The Library is Cardiff's academic engine room. It is low and darkly toned. A place of wood and leather, and bay-windowed recesses, designed for reading and concentration. Drawings date from 1873 onwards.[38] Completion occurred just after Burges's death.[39] The symbolism is redolent of scholarship and learning. The bookcases bear the names of Greek authors. Over the doors appears the Tree of Knowledge, with two apes struggling for possession of the Book of Truth. The stained glass windows are filled with images of Prophets, Apostles and Kings.[40] The corbels are painted with legendary devices of Roman emperors and Welsh princes. On the walls appear the names of some thirty poets and writers, from Sophocles to Schiller. And above the fireplace are five sculptured figures.[41][122] Four represent the Greek, Assyrian, Hebrew and Egyptian alphabets. The fifth apparently represents Lord Bute himself, in the guise of a Celtic scholar-monk. He is shown in profile – Myers used to flatter him by saying: 'You have a profile like one of the Fathers of the Universal Church.' Campbell and Smith did the painting, including, for example, the doorway chameleons;[42] Simpson the tiles; Barkentin the armorial heating grilles;[43] Nicholls the carved bell-pulls;[44] Lonsdale and Worrall the stained glass; and Gillow the mahogany bookcases, inset with Californian marble and marquetried tulip wood devices carefully drawn out by Lonsdale.[45]

The Banqueting Hall[159] is the largest room in the castle. Its style is appropriate to its fifteenth-century structure: a Flamboyant Perpendicular of Burges's own invention. The vaulted hammer-beam roof, however, has a more precise origin: it was borrowed by Burges either from the parish church at Framlingham, Suffolk, or else from St Peter's, Norwich.[46] The room is entered from its Southern end, through a Screen's Passage – completed under Frame's direction – which positively writhes with carving.[47] High above, the vaulting glints with heraldic shields: fifteen generations of Crichtons, Stuarts and Herberts.[48] The vast murals were, as usual, conceived by Burges and executed by Lonsdale – assisted on this occasion by R. W. Maddox and A. Robertson.[49] Twenty-six subjects in oil on canvas portray the exploits of Robert the Consul, a twelfth-century Norman lord of Glamorgan, during the troubled reigns of Matilda and Stephen.[50] In the giant chimneypiece, Robert rides forth to battle; his lady waves him farewell; trumpets sound from the battlements; and his imprisoned uncle, Robert, Duke of Normandy, peeps through the bars of a lonely dungeon.[51] The form of this chimneypiece derives perhaps from one in the Hôtel Jacques Coeur at Bourges: La Cheminée de la Salle-du-Rez de Chaussée.[52] But Burges has inflated and allegorised its elements, as he did previously at Knightshayes. There the French prototype became the Castle of Love, here the Castle of War – the Black Tower at the entrance to Cardiff Castle. Begun as early as 1875,[53] the painted decoration of the Banqueting Hall was not completed until 1881,[54] its wood-carving not until 1893.[55] Simpson and Godwin were responsible for tiles,[56] Fisher and Campbell for colouring and gilding,[57] Barkentin for metalwork.[58] Twenty-eight stained glass windows complete the room. Manufactured by Saunders, from cartoons by Lonsdale *c.* 1873, they depict successive lords of Glamorgan and their consorts.[59]

After a while, the prodigious mass of ornament in these rooms begins to sate the eye and blunt the judgement. On his drawings for the Banqueting Hall windows Burges wrote: 'Note. The colour is kept light as the glass is for a domestic building.'[60] 'Domestic' is hardly the adjective which springs to mind. These rooms manage somehow to be both palatial and spartan. And some of the figurative decoration is undoubtedly weak. Lonsdale's cartoons for the Chaucer Room windows, for example, do have a rather sub-Tenniel look. His expansive murals in the Banqueting Hall are certainly no more striking than his Magna Carta window in the Barons' Hall at Arundel.[61] At heart he was a miniaturist, ill at ease with overblown murals. None of these rooms was designed for the hanging of pictures. Hence the survival of the Drawing Room (next to the Library) in its eighteenth-century form. There the Bute family portraits had to be crammed from dado to frieze. The only other room where pictures were permitted seems to have been the Bachelor Bedroom in the Clock Tower. In that strange eyrie, competing with shoals of Burgesian ornament, were hung the pictures which once decorated young Bute's rooms at Christ Church, Oxford.

In general, the impact of the Cardiff rooms varies inversely with their size. The sixteenth-century Herbert Tower contains two of Burges's finest small-scale interiors: the Study and the Arab Room. Both belong to the later phase of operations, the early 1880s.[62] In the Study – originally the Librarian's room – the rib-vaulted ceiling is painted with birds and fruit on branches; the canopied chimney – carved by Nicholls – is bright with butterflies and parrots. Sophocles, Homer and Aeschylus look down from the walls. And six stained glass windows relate the story of Hercules and the golden apples. According to legend, the Hesperides were the 'daughters of the evening'. In their garden grew the apples, guarded by the dreadful dragon Ladon. Hercules slew the dragon, picked the apples, and delivered them to Eurystheus.[63] In these windows, Hercules and the Hesperides shine with Burges's customary clarity of outline. But the dragon glimmers with menace, scaly, bat-winged, pop-eyed, multi-fanged[X]. Charlie Campbell seems to have been the cartoonist, and perhaps the manufacturer too.[64] Documentation is sparse. But there is no doubt about the quality: that dragon is an astonishing performance.

Islamic influence at Cardiff culminates, appropriately enough, in the Arab Room[I; 160–161] near the top of the Herbert Tower. Now Burges's fascination with

Islamic art was by no means unique. The Paris Exhibitions of 1867 and 1878 had aroused curiosity about the style[65] – not least in the mind of Ludwig II of Bavaria. European interest in the Middle East stretches from Delacroix to Edward Lear; from *Omar Khayyam* to *Schéhérazade*. In a sense, the world of Islam was a Romantic discovery. 'Are we never to get out of Egypt any more?', complained Ruskin: 'nor to perceive the existence of any living creatures but Arabs and camels?'[66] But Burges seems to have found a particular delight in *kayf*: that intangible quality which Sir Richard Burton described as 'the savouring of animal existence, the passive enjoyment of mere sense; the pleasant languor, the dreary tranquillity, the airy castle-building, which in Asia stand in lieu of the vigorous intensive passionate life of Europe'.[67] This is the world of J. F. Lewis (1805–76), an artist gone native in Cairo, living – as Thackeray put it – 'like a languid Lotus-Eater, a dreamy, hazy, lazy, tobaccofied life'.[68] A world which survives only in the sun-lit dreams of Thomas Allom (1804–72), David Roberts (1776–1864) or Thomas Seddon (1821–56). Seddon in particular – the 'purest Pre-Raphaelite landscape painter', as Ruskin called him – belonged to the inner circle of Pre-Raphaelite Orientalists: Lear, Lewis, Leighton, Holman Hunt.[69] Burges surely knew him. Through Leighton, Aitchison and J. P. Seddon, Burges ranks as a peripheral member of this fraternity. So does another of his acquaintances, that sad-eyed laureate of darkest London, James Thomson. It was an Oriental tale, 'Weddah and Om-el-Bonain', which in 1872 first brought Burges and Rossetti into contact with the mysterious 'B.V.'[70]. Those cryptic initials stood for 'Bysshe Vanolis': Thomson's homage to Shelley and Novalis. Like Burges, 'B.V.' mingled Dante with Islam. The two men met each other at the theatre, and even went shopping together.[71] But unlike Burges, Thomson was a victim of melancholia: his pessimism drove him to alcohol, and alcohol brought him to the grave.

Thomson's 'City of Dreadful Night' seems far away from the opulence of Cardiff. Still, the Arab Room matches even B.V.'s strangest fantasies. In designing its honeycomb vault Burges no doubt dreamt of re-creating the shimmering vaults of Siculo-Norman Sicily – the Capella Palatina; the Zisa, or House of Delights – as well as Arabic interiors in Egypt.[72] But this generalised Islamic influence can be measured more exactly. Burges's library included several key works on Arabic architecture and decoration. From Pascal-Xavier Coste's *L'Architecture Arabe ou Monuments du Caire* (1837–9) he may well have derived the first spark which led him towards those trellis-bobbined screens, those beamed and multi-domed ceilings.[73] In 1877 there also appeared in Paris three mighty folios by A.C.T.E. Prisse d'Avennes, entitled *L'Art Arabe d'après les monuments du Kaire, 7ᵉ–18ᵉ*. Burges bought a copy. So perhaps did his friend George Aitchison. Anyway, within months of its publication the Arab Room at Cardiff and the Arab Room at Leighton House, Kensington, had both been begun. Burges's stalactite vaults, his honeycomb glass, his 'meshrebêyeh' trellis, and his kufic inscriptions, can all be traced to the gilded plates of this exotic publication.[74] At Cardiff, perhaps, the lily suffers from a surfeit of gliding. But then, suffocating richness was the aim. The dado is lined with Italian dove marble.[75] The upper walls are faced with tiles by Simpson of almost iznic quality. Wall cabinets are built of cedar wood and mounted in silver. Around the walls Burges inserted niches for statuettes of Eastern gods.[76] And along the fretted cornices he placed eight gilded parrots flanked by glittering crystals. The windows can be shuttered into pinpoints of light. Above the fireplace, mosaic and lapis lazuli glitter in a sea of milky marble.[77] And as for the stained glass: 'sliced jewels'.

There are other Arab rooms in English houses: Rolleston Hall, Staffs.;[78] Sledmere, Yorks.;[79] Rhinefield, Hants.[80] There is an Indian room at Osborne and another at Elvedon. There is even a Turkish room in Lady Waldegrave's Strawberry Hill.[81] But Burges knew none of these. He may have known Boeswillwald's exotic church interiors at Biarritz and Pau, and Duthoit's at Roquetaillade.[82] He certainly knew the Turkish Baths in Jermyn St,[83] the East India House Museum,[83a] and the Alhambra Music Hall in Leicester Square.[84] But Burges's oriental vision is richer than any of these. Its materials are costly, its workmanship superb. 'If a thing is worth doing', Oscar Wilde remarked, 'it's worth doing to excess.' Appropriately, it was on this room that Burges was working when he paid his last visit to Lord Bute's dream-castle.[85] Bute inscribed the chimneypiece as their joint memorial

Paradoxically, Bute's dream-castle lacks its triumphant climax. The great staircase was never completed: the present entrance hall, a sad apology, dates only from 1928.[86] The only staircase of any grandeur is the Octagon Staircase in the Beauchamp Tower.[87][157] This embodies two characteristic Burgesian conceits: at the top of its parapet lurks a crocodile (1874) about to gobble up a baby;[88] at the bottom a marble lion (1876) snarls through the grille of an heraldic vizor – a 'dodge' picked up in the cortile of the Bargello in Florence.[89] Intriguingly done – but no substitute for the great staircase. That would indeed have been an experience of 'barbaric splendour',[90] a fitting overture to a palace of dreams. All we have is Axel Haig's perspective[162], shown at the Royal Academy in 1874.[91] Its vaults are spangled with Saints, Kings, Prophets and Poets. Its arcades swell with sculptured images of the seven churches in the Book of Revelation. Its walls are hung with legends, its windows filled with heraldic glass. Evangelistic beasts prance along the balustrade, and writhing serpents entwine each candlestick. The polished steps are of rose-coloured granite. The stellar-painted vault rests on a newel shaft of Purbeck marble, girt with a moulded annulet.[92][223] And at the foot of the stairs a giant horseman greets us, mailed in burnished bronze. Critics and commentators were left gasping. As the *Builder* put it, the spectator is left speechless, like the Queen of Sheba when she saw Solomon in all this glory.[93]

But even with the great staircase, Cardiff Castle would still have been a series of dazzling episodes rather than a coherent architectural programme. Architecturally and decoratively, each room is an autonomous unit, grafted on to – or hewn out of – a medieval structure. How should we interpret them?

At the time, critical opinion was mixed. The *Architect*, for instance, just let Bute and Burges have their own way:

> The thoughts and occupations of the owner are translated in the things surrounding him; there is style in them – not the style of the multitude, but of a *grand seigneur* who, from circumstances, has more sympathy with the past than the present; who is poet enough to choose poetical illustrations for the decoration of his favourite rooms; and who, blest with vast hereditary possessions, chooses to make a little world of them and live in it.[94]

That was insufficient for Andrew Dewar of Halifax, Nova Scotia. He praised Burges for endowing his buildings with 'meaning'; for showing an understanding of semiotic design well 'in advance of the age'. But he also accused him of subordinating architecture to painting and sculpture: 'Instead of an architect, he has become, and would have us become, mere canvas-stretchers for the painters.' That was no way to advance the style of the future.[95] By the 1870s, the *Building News* was beginning to agree: 'Mr Burges evidently labours under the extraordinary impression that the main purpose of architecture is to serve as a basis for the display of colour.'[96] And James Fergusson, of course, was implacable. He found in Cardiff ample confirmation for his belief that Burges's genius for design – which he readily admitted – was magnificently irrelevant to the needs of the nineteenth century.

> Being almost unrivalled as a draughtsman, [Burges] has been able to reproduce the forms and details of medieval architecture in a manner that has never been surpassed. What he is doing now at Cardiff Castle is perhaps the most truthful reproduction of medieval baronial art in modern times. In all the ancient castles fitted up hitherto for modern habitation, the owners have insisted on something like modern feelings and modern refinement . . . in spite of the archaeologists; but at Cardiff nothing of the sort is tolerated . . . [Here is] an art congenial to the tastes of an illiterate baron surrounded by his blood-stained ruffian retainers, who, when not engaged in fighting or plundering, spent their time in drinking and debauching in their fortified dens. Time and romance have thrown a halo over these times, and mosses and ivy have so softened the harsher features of their art, that few can realise the utter barbarism of these ages. Mr Burges has done so in a manner no other man has approached, and deserves all possible credit for his achievement; but. . . .[97]

Fergusson is nothing if not predictable. But how should we formulate our own judgement today? How should we interpret these extraordinary rooms? Not as exercises in spatial control: that is an explanation of architectural form better suited to Baroque. Certainly not as an expression of structure: that is a rationalist view of design taken over from Neo-Classicism by the Modern Movement. No, the explanation must be Ruskinian: architecture as a vehicle for the decorative arts, eclectic, didactic; plus a special Burgesian gloss: architecture as fantasy, architecture as fun. These rooms are not machines for living in. They are fantasy capsules, three-dimensional passports, to fairy kingdoms and realms of gold. In Cardiff Castle we enter a land of dreams.

When the dream fades – when we re-cross the drawbridge and return to industrial Cardiff – we are left, as so often in the aftermath of dreams, with a jumble of haunting details. Burges was, above all, a master of detail. And it is for its details – apart from its silhouette – that Cardiff Castle will be remembered. In the Bute Workshops at Cardiff a whole generation of craftsmen – particularly woodcarvers and joiners – grew up in the Burgesian mould. Their foreman was Thomas John, father of the future Sir William Goscombe John.[98] Their work is invariably accomplished, and occasionally outstanding: for example, the inlaid doors (1872) to the Winter Smoking Room and Bachelor Bedroom.[99][251] Under Burges's eye, details sprout and multiply in the hands of his trusted lieutenants: door-handles by Hart; key-plates by Barkentin; animal bell-pushes by Nicholls and John; animal 'gurgoyles' along the battlements;[1] armorial central heating grilles; and the weird, anthropomorphic creatures which jump and slither over every available surface.[2] These rooms glow and shimmer with the sparkle of heraldic glass, the glitter of steel-hinged shutters, the gleam of mosaic and polished marble. In sheer self-defence, the eye of memory recoils, holding fast to a few landmarks in a veritable sea of images: the fang-toothed pop-eyed devil (1872) above the doorway of the Winter Smoking Room; the silver lizards in Lord Bute's bath;[3] the chained dragon guarding the entrance to the Clock Tower's topmost storey; the stained glass visage of Arachne – turned into a spider by Athena – squinting down in Lady Bute's boudoir;[4] the roots and tendrils which worm their way round the Octagon Stairs, penetrate the Dining Room chimney piece, and positively permeate the Library; the alabaster section set in the winding gloom of the Clock Tower staircase, glowing in sunset like a pillar of fire; or, more vivid than any of these, those lovable animals designed to peer across the outer parapet of the moat – lion, sea-lion, lynx, monkey, bear – designed by Burges and modelled by Nicholls, with all the gusto of Wilars d'Honecort.[5][119]

Cardiff is obviously memorable. But is it unique? Certainly in Victorian Britain there is nothing to match its obsessive exoticism. A. W. Pugin at Alton Castle, Waterhouse at Eaton Hall, Godwin at Dromore, E. W. Pugin at Carlton Towers, Salvin at Alnwick and Peckforton – all these produced Picturesque silhouettes, but none approaches the Burgesian Sublime. And none has comparable interiors.

What about Europe? Here a number of nineteenth-century dream castles float into mind: Schwerin in Germany, Miaramare in Italy, Bussaco in Portugal, Pierrefonds in France, Neuschwanstein and Hohenschwangau in Bavaria. But Miaramare is backdrop architecture, Schwerin an overblown château; Bussaco owes everything to its setting; and as for Pierrefonds, though its sheer bulk is awesome, Viollet's interior details lack

Burges's fluency and thrust. That leaves the Ludwigian fantasies of Neuschwanstein and Hohenschwangau. Their settings are certainly Sublime. But their interiors are somehow both derivative and meretricious. Burges had a qualified admiration for Viollet-le-Duc, but none at all – as far as we know – for Ludwig of Bavaria. Bute's enthusiasm for Wagner was limited to opera: his High Tory Catholicism had no truck with Ludwigian megalomania. Neither Bute nor Burges could be described as a voluptuary. Aesthetic indulgence is kept at bay by Bute's asceticism and by Burges's sense of humour. The aura of Ludwigian indulgence is wholly missing at Cardiff. One final difference. The Bavarian castles are mountain fantasies. Cardiff is an urban dream – or rather a dream-castle implanted in a city. As such it is surely incomparable. Conceived as a neo-feudal vision, it now performs a municipal, indeed national function: its silhouette has become the skyline of the capital of Wales.[6] The dream of one great patron and one great architect has almost become the symbol of a whole nation.

CASTELL COCH

Not far from Cardiff stands Castell Coch: the 'red castle' in the 'red forest'. It was originally built early in the thirteenth century by Gilbert the Red, Earl of Gloucester, to guard the Taff valley 'gainst the Welsh.[7] Since the fifteenth century it had been in ruins. By the 1860s it must have been irresistibly Picturesque:

> Here stood a shatter'd archway plumed with fern;
> And here had fall'n a great part of a tower,
> Whole, like a crag that tumbles from the cliff. . . .
> And high above a piece of turret stair,
> Worn by the feet that now were silent, wound
> Bare to the sun, and monstrous ivy-stems
> Claspt the gray walls with hairy-fibred arms.[8]

'There are two courses open with regard to [these] ruins', Burges advised Bute in 1872; 'one is to leave them as they are and the other to restore them ... as ... a country residence for ... occasional occupation in the summer.'[9] Bute hesitated during his financial crisis of 1873–5. Then came the decision. Castell Coch was to rise again in Burgesian glory – not as a charge on the Bute Trustees, but paid for out of the Marquess's 'own pocket'.[10]

Archaeology was a passion with Bute, second only to liturgy. At Whithorn Priory in Galloway he excavated the earliest Christian church in Scotland.[11] During the 1880s he excavated the site of the Grey Friars church at Cardiff, and restored a tiny twelfth-century church at Cogan. During the 1890s he excavated the Black Friars monastery, under the shadow of Cardiff Castle.[12] But his archaeological *tour de force* in the Cardiff area was undoubtedly Caerphilly, the largest castle in Wales. Bute began the restoration of the central keep during the 1880s, and work has continued ever since: a record of nearly one hundred years of restoration.[13] 'Some of Bute's happiest hours', recalled Hunter Blair, 'were spent standing by, wrapped in his big cloak and smoking innumerable cigarettes, while a band of workmen, directed by one of his many architects, dug out the foundations of a medieval lady chapel, or broke through a nineteenth-century wall in search of a thirteenth-century doorway.'[14]

Castell Coch supplied an opportunity not only for excavation but for recreation. As such it has become a text-book classic. But a very similar scheme, produced by Burges at exactly the same time, 1871–2, is almost unknown. This was a project for the reconstruction of another of Lord Bute's ruined properties, Rothesay Castle on the Isle of Bute, legendarily founded in 1140 by the Viking invader Magnus Barefoot. If anything, the result would have been even more spectacular than Castell Coch, with twice as many round towers. Burges produced an elaborate historical and archaeological report, illustrated by visionary schemes of reconstruction.[15][87] No doubt he hoped that Bute would find the prospect beguiling. But work stopped short at excavation: after 1877 Bute's energies in that part of the world were concentrated on the rebuilding of Mount Stuart. Rothesay Castle was destined to be no more than a trial run for its Welsh counterpart.

Burges's report on Castell Coch was prepared in 1871–2. Work began in August 1875. The structure was finished by the end of 1879.[16] But when Burges died in 1881 the interior had hardly been begun.[17] It was completed – under the direction of William Frame and J. S. Chapple – only in 1891.

Bute's second dream-castle did not emerge fully-fledged from Burges's imagination. Its design evolved gradually, becoming more austere outside, and more dramatic within. Originally Burges envisaged a more complicated silhouette: a battlemented Watch Tower bursting through the core of the Keep Tower; a chapel and defensive 'Hoard' clinging to the perimeter of a double-coned Well Tower[78]. These features were not abandoned until after 1877.[18] The result was a smoother, less syncopated skyline. Inside, the Keep Tower was originally to have been divided into four sections – plus two lower service stages – arranged in vertical sequence. In 1878–9 four became two – two double-decker rooms – a vast improvement in terms of spatial impact.[19] By denuding inside and outside of superfluous structure, Burges moved away from archaeology towards abstract, timeless shapes[84–86; 88]. A comparison with Carcassonne is telling. Viollet-le-Duc has recreated the simulacrum of a medieval fortress: the apparatus is there, but somehow the poetry is missing. Burges has travelled one stage further, dissolving his prototypes in the crucible of the creative process. Castell Coch is not a sham, despite its portcullis and drawbridge. It is as much a work of art in its own right as *Lohengrin* or *Ivanhoe*. In a very real sense, by idealising the feudal past, by concentrating its images in novel form, Burges has surpassed the Middle Ages – just as Tennyson upstaged Mallory. He inherited the plan; he invented the superstructure. Art has added an extra dimension to archaeology: debris translated into dreams.

Castell Coch is perhaps the most spectacular example of what Handley-Read called Burges's translations 'from High Gothic into High Victorian'. Not, of course, the linear intricacy of ecclesiastical Gothic, but the massy impact of medieval militarism: 'Study the great broad masses, the strong unchamfered angles.'[20] Here indeed is an exercise in solid geometry. The rocky shapes, smooth and hard, crash into one another like boulders on a beach. 'The whole building', writes Dr Girouard, 'exudes a pride in the weight and power of stone'[21]: stumpy chimneys melting into towers; towers merging into battered abutments – circle dissolving into square; the masterly variation of conical and rectangular masses; the marriage of cylinder and cone. Burges's stylistic sources for the exterior strike one at first as obviously French.[22] But it was the Swiss castles of L'Aigle and Chillon on Lake Geneva which supplied the closest prototypes for those towers and parapet walks. He also made use of English details – the drawbridge and portcullis, for instance, and the bretache over the entrance – from Carlisle, Caerphilly, Winchester and the Tower of London.[23] And he went to great pains to demonstrate that pointed towers could also be seen in many English illuminated manuscripts – notably the invaluable B.M. Bib.Reg. 2 B VII.[24]

Even more than Cardiff Castle, Castell Coch is not a case of restoration but of re-creation. It looms aloft, a medievalist's fantasy in wood and stone – almost a stage-set for *The Sleeping Beauty* – set in woodlands garlanded with wild garlic and surrounded by the Marquess's own vineyards. From the choicest grapes Lord Bute personally directed the making of altar wine, and from the surplus (1885 and 1893 were vintage years) good commercial sales were reported – though his Lordship admitted that people were unlikely to switch from Hock to Coch, or even to 'Cocheimer'.[25] The vines have gone. But the beech trees remain: a dark, cavernous forest of gnarled trunks with roots like ivy-mantled tentacles. And the wild garlic is still there too – traditionally used to ward off vampires.[26]

Burges had described Castell Coch as a 'country residence … for occasional occupation in the summer'. In fact it was all gloriously impractical and was very seldom used. The projected stables and offices were never built.[27] And the main rooms are neither military nor domestic. Across the drawbridge, under the portcullis, and into the courtyard: so far all is martial. Only Fucigna's entrance statue of the Virgin – echoing the Vierge Dorée at Notre Dame – adds a softening touch of decoration.[28] Then up the steps, and into the Castellan's quarters: we enter the enchanted castle.

In effect, there are only two 'reception rooms': the Banqueting Hall[164] and the Drawing Room[163]. The first of these is unexciting in shape and anaemic in detail. The tie-beamed, pine and cedar-panelled roof has the right baronial swagger. Chapple's furniture – made in the Bute workshops at Cardiff – is plain-spoken and boxy.[29] But Lonsdale's murals[30] and Nicholls's sculpture of St Lucius definitely lack the Burgesian touch. The impact of the Drawing Room is therefore all the greater.

This octagonal room had been originally planned as two apartments, one on top of the other. Throwing them into one, with gallery and vault, was a happy afterthought of 1879.[31] Here, Burges explained, 'I have ventured to indulge in a little more ornament'.[32] Indeed he has. The panelling is painted with no less than fifty-eight different floral patterns. Snails, lizards, and caterpillars; butterflies, mice and birds worm their way around the doorways. Scenes from Aesop's Fables illuminate the walls. The theme is Life and Death in Nature: the butterfly, the chrysalis, the bird's nest, the egg – symbols of regeneration. Heraldry and nature combine. Bute and his ancestors float within the flux of time, below the blue sky of eternity. Nicholls's three Fates above the chimneypiece spin out the destiny of mankind, framed by the frayed and twisted rope of life. In Campbell's murals family portraits mingle with the leaves, and hang by ribbons from the boughs. Simpson's tiles embody the insignia of the zodiac. And around the walls the panelling is alive, threaded through with plants, roots and tendrils.[33]

But the glory of the Drawing Room is the great rib-vault[165], executed in stone, spangled with butterflies and

> .... birds
> Of sunny plume in gilded trellis work.[34]

None of the motifs is accidental. Each plays its part in the overall iconographic scheme.

> Here ... is a rich world of gold and blue, of carved butterflies and painted animals and flowers. The dominant feature is the vault, suspended over the room like an immense glittering starfish, or a fireworks display, with the gilded flickering rays of the sun like a Catherine wheel in the centre, and the ribs falling down from it in lines of gold; filled with the movement of the wings of butterflies, and of flying birds, and with stars twinkling between them on a background of rich and deep blue. The vault represents the sky; below the gallery one is back on earth, the birds and butterflies are still there but they are now fluttering and settling amongst the branches of trees and gigantic hollyhocks and sunflowers, and have been joined by foxes, monkeys, squirrels and other animals: lower still there is dark green panelling with panels of flowers painted on a rich gold ground. The whole scene is surveyed by the three Fates, spinning and clipping their thread in an alcove above the fireplace....[35]

It is magnificent, but it is not Burges – at least not all of it. The bulk of the moulded work is his.[36] But the painted decoration is only Burges diluted, Burges at second hand. Fireplace and tiles were ready before his death.[37] But the insertion of sculpture, and the execution of painting and panelling, are all posthumous, dating from 1886–7.[38] Their execution, by Nicholls and Campbell, was supervised by William

Frame. The furniture is by J. S. Chapple. Bute was unhappy about some of the details. The butterflies on the ceiling had to be 'tickled up' in an 'artistic' way by Charlie Campbell's cousin Tom.[39] Not until November 1886 could Frame say that at last 'we have done with parrots and cockatoos'.[40] By that date no one could deny the overall richness of effect.

If anything, the Drawing Room is eclipsed by Lady Bute's Bedroom[IV; 204]. Lord Bute's Bedroom (1888) is a spartan performance: chunky furniture and stencilled walls.[41] His consort's apartment is a place of soft, Tennysonian languor. Except for the later chandelier, nothing has been touched since its completion in 1891. Here the interior shape is pure Burges: an arcaded circle, punched through by window embrasures, and topped by a trefoil-sectioned dome. Again, the chimneypiece is by Nicholls, the painting by Campbell, the grate by Hart, and the wardrobe, dressing table and bizarre castellated washstand – dragon-topped, fish-enamelled – by J. S. Chapple (1891).[42][205] The symbolism of this room's decoration – monkeys, pomegranates, nesting-birds – allegorises the sequence of courtship, conception and infancy. The winged figure over the chimneypiece is Hope: it recalls a flying figure in Lorenzetti's frescoes at the Palazzo Publico, Siena. But the dominant theme, of course, is the Sleeping Beauty: the mirrored sections of the dome are entwined with thorns and brambles. Detailed drawings by Burges for much of the moulded work survive.[43] Nicholls's carving must have followed Burges fairly closely.[44] But Campbell's painted panels are definitely post-Burges: Bute took exception to the monkeys, perhaps because they seemed too lascivious.[45] All the movable fittings had to be executed in the Burges manner – at one remove from 'the great man' – by his devoted office staff. Chapple's furniture was only executed ten years after the master's death. But the Burgesian idiom is mimicked perfectly. We find, for example, Frame writing to Nicholls in 1887 about the chimneypiece, and asking – 'Would Mr Burges have done it …?'[46] Well, indeed he would. The only comparable setting is Burges's own bedroom in Melbury Rd, Kensington. Lady Bute's bed – a framework of scarlet and gold, glittering with crystal-ball bed knobs – is medieval to the point of acute discomfort.[47] This room is surely a retreat for some lovelorn Tennysonian maiden – or for Dame Edith Sitwell, playing the Lady of Shalott.

The Well Tower Chapel was never completed. For it Burges designed many a

> . . . . casement . . . .
> Flame-colour, vert and azure.[48]

But the project languished in 1879. Otherwise Castell Coch sums up to perfection the learned dream world of a great patron and his favourite architect, re-creating from a heap of rubble a fairy-tale castle which seems almost to have materialised from the margins of a medieval manuscript. The structure alone must have cost more than £25,000.[49] Burges worked for Bute elsewhere: a convent chapel in Cardiff (1870), converted from an old barn, and dignified by a baldacchino;[50] a village church at Cumnock, Ayrshire (1878–80), a cheaper version of his church at Murston.[51] But these were small commissions. Castell Coch – that 'enchanted castle'[52] – was the final flowering of a great partnership. Here indeed is a vision of Pre-Raphaelite precision. Here the Dream verges on hallucination. The achievements of Ludwig of Bavaria had been rivalled in miniature in the hills of Glamorgan.

MOUNT STUART

While Burges lived Bute was reluctant to employ other architects. John Prichard (1818–86)[53] and John Oldrid Scott (1832–1913)[54] appear as the recipients of particular commissions. But it is not until the early 1880s that new names feature regularly on the scene, three in particular: John Kinross (1855–1931), Robert Weir Schultz (1861–1951) and Sir R. Rowand Anderson (1834–1921).[55] To Kinross fell the restoration of Pluscarden Priory, Morayshire; the Greyfriars near Elgin Cathedral; the Augustinian Priory at St Andrews; and Falkland Palace, Fife. Falkland in particular – 'the most luxurious of my palaces', as Bute called it – was restored with immense skill and rare discretion.[56] To Schultz – among many lesser works – fell additions at the House of Falkland and the Old Place of Mochrum; the restoration of Sanquhar Castle, and Kames and Wester Kames Castles on the Isle of Bute; as well as additions at Dumfries House, Ayrshire; the Garrison, Millport; and St John's Lodge, Regent's Park, London.[57] Later on he was responsible for St Andrew's Chapel in Bentley's Byzantine masterpiece, Westminster Cathedral. Finally, to Anderson fell Paisley Abbey, Renfrewshire; St Margaret's, Dunfermline; the domed Byzantine church of St Sophia at Galston, Ayrshire, and – a bigger prize than any of these – the reconstruction of Mount Stuart on the Isle of Bute.

In several of these schemes Burges had a preliminary involvement. He did no work at Dumfries House – an Adam building which Bute described as 'the homeliest' of his seats. Nor did he work at St John's Lodge. But in 1879 he was responsible for a small chapel at Chiswick House, Bute's previous London *pied à terre*.[58] And at Mochrum, in 1876, he may just possibly have had a hand in the restoration of what must then have been a semi-derelict Peel Tower.[59] Bute thought it 'an exceedingly pretty place'.[60] But Hunter Blair remembered it as 'a queer two-storeyed tower set in the middle of a wild Wigtownshire moor, on the edge of a gloomy lake ... in very ugly country ... almost inaccessible by road or rail'. Thither Bute retreated to correct the proofs of his mammoth translation of the Roman Breviary:

> We lived on trout and grouse caught and killed by the keepers. ... Proofs arrived from the publishers by every post. We used to take long walks, often in pouring rain, through the sodden moors; and in the middle of our walk Bute would extract from his pocket long sheets of proof, and read to me in sonorous tones his

admirable translation of collects, lessons or hymns, and invite my criticism, which annoyed him if in the least unfavourable. . . . In the evening, as we sat in slippers, after our frugal meal, over a good peat fire, my host would be in lighter vein, and would entertain himself and me by reading (in a far from impeccable French accent) one of some French novels which he had brought to recreate us during our solitary evenings in this weird abode. An English friend of mine who was staying there became bored almost to frenzy by these strange days and nights, and implored Bute to . . . take him away. . . .[61]

Mount Stuart was rather more comfortable.

The eighteenth-century Mount Stuart, where Prime Minister Bute had lived, consisted of a plain classical house with flanking wings. Its architect was Alexander McGill, its date 1718–22.[62] It was finely sited and well planted. But to High Victorian eyes, insufferably dull. So much so that when Bute came of age[12] the island was agog with rumours of imminent reconstruction.[63]

During the early 1870s Bute made some internal improvements to the main body of the house, including ceiling designs from his own hand. Harland and Fisher were employed in painting figures of the four seasons as well as panels of birds. But Burges seems not to have been consulted. At any rate, when he visited Mount Stuart – perhaps in 1872, perhaps in 1876 'in consequence of Hornet'[64] – he glanced at the panelled mirrors, painted grapes and vine leaves in the drawing room, shrugged his shoulders and muttered: 'I call that damnable.'[65] In 1873–5 Burges had in fact been responsible for the insertion of an oratory in McGill's northern wing. 'The designs', Bute assured his wife, 'are really very good, and will look remarkably well.'[66] The design was Burges's: a gilded miniature, columned, panelled and beamed, hung with icons, glittering with fresco and mosaic, faintly echoing in its details three Early Christian shrines at Ravenna: St Apollinare in Classe, St Apollinare Nuovo, and the Tomb of Galla Placida. But the iconography was Bute's: a galaxy of fifty-six saints, each bearing appropriate symbols; and below the altar, flowers from Gethsemane, a sculptured relief of the Agony in the Garden, maps of the Holy Land, and stones from the Holy Places mounted in Mother of Pearl.[67] Campbell was responsible for the painted work, again under Bute's detailed direction. 'As to Charlie Campbell', he reminded Lady Bute, 'what I wanted painted was a little mound, with four streams running out of it, and stags drinking. . . . He had better sketch roe deer for the purpose, but begin the rock first and I'll talk about the deer when I arrive.'[68]

So far, Bute had merely tinkered with the Georgian house. Then came a providential disaster. The central section of Mount Stuart was ravaged by fire in December 1877.[69] Bute had always regarded his island retreat as 'a great deal nicer than' Cardiff.[70] Now he had an excuse to make it not only nice but Sublime.

Rebuilding began in 1879 and concentrated first on replacing the central block. Then came the refurbishing of the old wings, ending up with yet another chapel – the climax of Bute's architectural career. Over a period of thirty-five years, between 1879 and 1914, the mammoth design slowly approached completion.[71] Workmen enjoyed a topping off 'soirée' in 1881.[72] But as late as 1894 Bute's daughter was reporting: 'The house is in a fearful mess – no proper floor in the hall, only concrete. We are just getting the boards down now.'[73] The staircase was built by 1888, but the gallery balustrade was still unsettled in 1897. Only in 1898 was the chapel structurally complete, and decoration was still in progress at the outbreak of World War I.[74] By 1900 some £600,000 had apparently been spent.[75] The final total was rumoured to be in the region of £1,000,000. That must be an exaggeration. Even so, here was Romantic extravagance of almost Ludwigian proportions. Peacocks roamed in the gardens of Cardiff Castle. But the grounds of Mount Stuart were peopled with kangaroos.

Mount Stuart was a *coup* for Anderson. He probably won the commission on the strength of his *Municipal, Commercial and Street Architecture of France and Italy* (1878). He had worked in Holland under J. H. Cuypers and in London under Gilbert Scott; and had then become a partner of David Bryce before setting up practice independently. He was a very poor draughtsman, and relied heavily on assistants. Still, his scholarship was considerable, his stylistic range extensive and his constructive skill impressive. Today he is chiefly remembered for his public buildings: the French Renaissance Central Station in Glasgow; the French Gothic National Portrait Gallery, Edinburgh; the classical dome of Edinburgh University. But some of his finest works were restorations: Jedburgh and Culross Abbey, and Dunblane Cathedral, for example. This easy affinity with both the Renaissance and the Middle Ages must have appealed strongly to Lord Bute.[76] To modern eyes, however, his work somehow lacks fire. His obituarist put his finger on it: 'his . . . work is that of the head rather than the heart.'[77] At Mount Stuart the head may indeed have been Anderson's; but happily the heart belonged to 'the soul-inspiring Burges'.

Inside and outside, Mount Stuart is a belated monument to High Victorian eclecticism[16–17]. Its interior planning is vigorously expressed in the exterior silhouette.[78] Its formidable pink bulk bulges with 'muscularity' and erupts in skyward protuberances and 'functional' excrescences. But it is certainly not 'Scots Baronial': its source of inspiration is Southern Europe. Spanish Gothic, in particular, aroused Bute's enthusiasm. And there are several echoes of Segovia's Alcazar in the upper storeys of Mount Stuart.[79] 'Never in England or out of it', Bute wrote in 1870 after a quick visit to Cádiz, Lisbon, Cintra and Seville, 'have I seen cathedrals worked so splendidly as the few Spanish ones I saw. I could not have conceived the grandeur of the fabric, establishment, and functions of Seville – *infinitely better than St Peter's*.'[80] The cathedral at Palma he found especially 'impressive, and very Spanish'.[81] And the cathedral of Saragossa struck him so powerfully that he used it as the model for his new chapel at Mount Stuart. Bute had a special reason for admiring the architecture of Peter de Luna. 'That the famous Spaniard was an architect, or a discriminating patron of architecture', Anderson noted, 'Saragossa testifies; but he was more to Lord Bute, he was the Pope, the Benedict XIII, whose papal bull confirmed the foundation charter of St Andrews University. He was not acknowledged as Pope by England or Italy, but he was acknowledged by Scotland, and that went a long way with Lord Bute.'[82]

The interior of Mount Stuart is an object-lesson in the eclectic process. The precedents seem chiefly to have been North Italian, Flemish, French and Spanish. For the chapel, inspiration was sought in the lofty Gothic windows of the Sainte Chapelle; the tripartite groining of the upper church of St Francis at Assisi; and the great octagonal lantern of the cathedral at Saragossa. Lined with white Carrara marble and suffused with tinted light, the chapel has as its focus an elaborate bronze altar decked with silver statues of Celtic saints.[83] But the eye inevitably strays to the high-vaulted roof pierced by lead-lined tabernacles; to the floor of glistening Alexandrian mosaic; to the silver icon made for Lord Bute in the Tsar's Imperial Academy;[84] and to another 'Russian trick', the blood red glass of the clerestory.[85] Such an extraordinary range of precedents underlines Bute's progressively catholic taste. In the great hall, for instance, the railings of the gallery are copied from the tomb of Charlemagne at Aix-la-Chapelle.[86] Anderson had prepared a different design. Bute countermanded his proposal and sent him off to Aix to make 'measured drawings ... on the spot'.[87] Precise historicism like that emphasises Bute's personal involvement in the whole programme. He regarded archaeology as the only hope for art – 'for we have ceased to be inventive' – 'and we are happily losing that timidity which has been making people afraid of a too faithful imitation'.[88] He had learned this archaeological approach at the feet of Billy Burges. But Burges's brand of eclecticism had been less dogmatically derivative.

At Mount Stuart Anderson was the nominal architect. But the interior decoration seems to have been largely outside his control. His patron was Burges's patron; his team of craftsmen was Burges's team. It was Nicholls who was responsible for carving; Campbell for painting.[89] It was Lonsdale who created the Days of Creation above the stairs and the frieze of Lady Bute's sitting room.[90] It was Lonsdale who drew the cartoons from which Worrall (Saunders & Co.) executed the stained glass windows in the hall. And it was Burges's faithful, if choleric, deputy William Frame who acted as coordinating executive. Frame 'designed' the chimneypieces, the panelling, the doorcases, the ceilings.[91] In particular, Frame must take the credit for the design of Bute's astrological sitting room – known as the 'Horoscope Room' – glowing with the horoscope of Bute's nativity. Frame designed the sub-Burgesian domelets, the bulbous castellations, the 'glass stars, and coloured glass globes', and the 'birds, flowers, etc. in bright colours, as Lord Bute seems to have a failing for it'.[92] Finally, it was Frame who made last-minute, detailed alterations to the stained glass of the great hall.[93] But the supervision of this team fell to Bute. Indeed some of the details of the decoration are very clearly his. For example, he supplied Lonsdale with no less than 'seven sheets of notes' to guide him in designing the staircase windows.[94]

Compared with Cardiff, the quality of design at Mount Stuart is sometimes weak, and the level of execution poor. Nicholls was urged on by Frame – 'the work will be just to your taste, foliage and grotesques all referring to dining'[95] – but without Burges's guiding hand his invention seems to have flagged. Frame's own designs here – the hall chimneypiece, for instance – lack the real Burgesian punch. As the 1880s progressed, he seems to have declined into bibulous torpor. In 1890 Bute notes sadly in his diary: 'Frame . . . drunk again . . . had to dismiss him.'[96] And where does Anderson fit into the picture? Contemporaries were accustomed to remark that he was not at his best with Gothic. Certainly his Renaissance work has a stronger 'feel' about it.[97] Perhaps the influence of Bute – and through him, the magnetism of Burges – was just too strong for him. The interior of his Catholic Apostolic Church in Edinburgh certainly bears an uncanny resemblance to Burges's defeated Edinburgh Cathedral design.[98]

One man raised the interior of Mount Stuart to the highest level: Burges's trusty ally, H. W. Lonsdale. He did the same at St John's Lodge and the House of Falkland. At St John's Lonsdale covered the ceiling with constellations of stars and astrological symbols, the signs of the zodiac, the four seasons and the three fates; and in an apse he placed a grand Aurora, holding a crystal ball among the clouds. At Falkland the great staircase explodes with colour; its wooden barrel vault swims with giant emblems of the four winds – 'the Bute' appearing himself, blowing a conch shell. But at Mount Stuart Lonsdale surpassed all his previous efforts. There the great hall soars up-wards in cathedral splendour – twelve mighty marble piers; a galleried triforium [16], its vaulting pierced by translucent bosses; a clerestory of stained glass, blazing with the light of heaven; and overall a painted vault, scored with the constellations of the universe.[99] This hall is 60 ft square and 80 ft high – as grand as the saloon in Barry's London Reform Club. Bute made a point of demanding that its glass be above all 'brilliant'.[1] Brilliant it is: those 'zodiacal windows' (1889–90) – by Lonsdale and Saunders – are a veritable maelstrom of colour, forming and re-forming in changing patterns of light. By day their rainbow tints flash and glimmer with the movement of cloud and sun. By night their zodiac figures dissolve in blackness, but their constituent stars shine out like silver in the moonlight.

On 29 May 1891 Bute noted in his diary that he saw these windows for the first time. Lonsdale was there to receive his patron's congratulations. But the conception belonged to Bute, and the inspiration – ultimately – to Burges. As at Falkland and St John's, as at Cardiff and Castell Coch, heraldry, allegory and symbol combine in simulating the unity of space and time. Burges had instructed Bute in the unity of art. Bute had taught himself to seek out, through art, through faith, the ultimate unity of the universe. In the hall of Mount Stuart the Dream came closest to fulfilment.

Myers well remembered Mount Stuart's 'strange-illumined vault . . . encircled with a translucent zone which pictured the constellations of the Ecliptic; the starry lights represented by prisms inserted in that "dome of many coloured glass". Therethrough, as through a fictive Zodiac, travelled the sun all day; with many a counterchange of azure stains or emerald on the broad floor below, and here and there the dazzling flash of a sudden-kindled star'.[2] Hunter Blair arrived there one foggy night and wonderingly recorded his impressions:

> We stand in a vast hall gleaming with light. The walls are lined with rarest marbles, pavonazetto, emperor's red, and pink-flushed alabaster; all round runs a Gothic arcade, cipollino columns crowned with daintily-carved capitals of purest white, and arches of grey Sicilian. Above is the great gallery, four-square, groined in cedar-wood, with massy gilded railings copied from the tomb of Charles the Great. On the azure vaulted roof, eighty feet above our heads, shine the 'stars in their courses', all in orderly array, glittering points of prismatic light. The floor is of inlaid marble and mirror-polished oak, and over all streams the radiance of a hundred shaded electric lamps.[3]

Beneath the stairs, an organ.[4] And from its keyboard, the magic strains of Wagner. Bute visited the Bayreuth Festival for the first time in 1886. He attended twelve performances in seven weeks,. punctuating the music with bouts of mineral-water drinking in Karlsbad.[5] He returned again in 1888 and 1891. He was not a naturally musical person. He regarded a performance of *Parsifal*, for instance, as primarily a religious experience, to be received in silence – and he protested vigorously to Cosima Wagner about the 'revolting' applause, by 'the illiterate part of the audience', after Acts II and III.[6] By 1894 he had been completely Wagnerised: 'Wagner spoils one for most other operas.'[7] He had come to realise that through music – as through all art – mankind derives faint glimpses of divinity. That, as he saw it, was the patron's *raison d'être*: to reveal the transcendent power lurking dimly in the creative process; to place, in Redon's words, 'the logic of the visible at the service of the invisible'.[8]

Towards the end of his life, tortured by skin disease, impeded by strokes, Bute retreated to Mount Stuart – his 'real home'[9] – working in the library, praying in Burges's miniature chapel, walking alone by the shore. In lighter moments, he had a cache of Burgesian treasures to cheer him. Silver soup plates (1868)[255; 256] and fish plates (1867), engraved with visual puns – Smelt: a fishmonger holding his nose; Perch: a winged fish upon a branch; Salmon: the crowned king of fishes; Scotch Broth: a sheep dressed as a Highlander; Turtle: a City gent, wearing his chain of office.[10] Or again there was 'Lord Bute's Cup and Cover', a secular chalice, made to Burges's designs by Barkentin in 1875[259]: silver gilt, ringed with bands of turquoise and lapis lazuli, set with gems and decorated with heraldic enamel.[11] Or 'Lord Bute's Water Bottle', made by Barkentin in 1880: its clear glass cased in a silver gilt container, decorated with wonderfully Burgesian fishes with gem-set eyes, topped with amethyst and ringed with translucent enamels.[12][V] Or 'Lord Bute's Claret Jug', made by Barkentin in 1869–70[258]: clear glass mounted in silver and silver gilt, with leopard handle, masked spout and figured crown; set with turquoise, pearl and amethyst; decorated with translucent and opaque enamels in bright heraldic colours, illustrating the legendary career of Dionysus.[13] Finally – happiest of all – there was 'Lord Bute's Cruet', a deliciously Burgesian object made, like the cup and the water-bottle, as a birthday present from Lady Bute in 1877[254; 257]. This consists of no less than ten detachable sections: the base with two figures in medieval garb, straining to lift their burden of condiments above the checkered floor; the pierced litter or tray-container; the salt and pepper cellars, each with detachable lids; and the mustard casket, with its minute coral handle enamelled 'J.S.', and its own separate spoon in the shape of a tiny claw. Every detail is worked out with exquisite skill and truly obsessive care.[14]

Such trinkets may have lightened Bute's last days. But his wealth had become a burden to him; its responsibilities crushing. Towards the end he lived 'a life simple and almost solitary', Myers remembered; a life of 'slow meditative brooding ... of long walks and long conversations on the mysteries of the world unseen. ... That same yearning for communion with the invisible which showed itself in his Prayer Books and Missals, his Byzantine churches restored, his English churches built, showed itself also in the great crystal hung in his chapel at St John's Lodge; as it were the mystic focus of that green silence in the heart of London's roar; and in the horoscope of his nativity painted on the dome of his study at Mount Stuart; and in that vaster, strange-illuminated vault of Mount Stuart's central hall'.[15]

It was on the Isle of Bute that he was laid to rest[15], in a little eighteenth-century chapel, within sight and sound of the sea:

> ... not as one unknown,
> Not meanly, but with gorgeous obsequies,
> And mass, and rolling music.[16]

Chanting voices drifted softly in the mist; pine torches guttered in the gloom. Once he had grown 'wealthier – wealthier – hour by hour'.[17] Now he was beyond the reach of envy, 'with Lazarus, who once was poor'.[18] His body was placed in a marble sarcophagus. But his heart was taken to Jerusalem and buried on the Mount of Olives.[19]

Temperamentally and intellectually, Bute was closer to the fourteenth century than to the eighteenth or the twentieth. He belonged to the Age of Faith not the Age of Reason, still less the Age of Progress. He believed implicitly in the validity of the hierarchical system – social, political, religious. His Disraelian Toryism was reinforced by religious conviction and a profound historical sense. For him society was merely a microcosm of the ordered world of creation. And within that structure he practised fervently the patrician virtues of a great chieftain. 'To him the political philosophy alike of Mr Morley and Mr Chamberlain was repulsive – therefore, as a politician, he was an impossibility.'[20] His was the last generation capable of accumulating great wealth and confident of its transmission by means of the dynastic process. His also, perhaps, was the last generation to equate riches with responsibility. Duty, after all, lay at the heart of the feudal ideal – and at the heart of its chivalric revival. Ironically, in the very year of Bute's death, socialist Keir Hardy – born on the Bute estate in Ayrshire, not far from Dumfries House – was elected M.P. for Merthyr, the Welsh heartland of the Bute empire. Hardy's elected colleague was D. A. Thomas, later Lord Rhondda, industrial tycoon, champion of *laissez faire*. The stage was set for new combatants – ironmaster and collier – in secular, Marxist clothes. The age of paternalism was nearly over – squeezed out by the battle between Capital and Labour – and the 3rd Marquess posthumously reaped the odium of being almost its last protagonist. Henceforward the State would take over many of the functions of the great magnate: economic initiative, employment, education, security, patronage, conspicuous spending. The State would have different priorities. But the priorities of the 3rd Marquess were not ignoble: to build, and to build beautifully, and to see in beauty the image of the Almighty.

For in the last analysis it is as a patron of architecture that Lord Bute should be remembered. He can almost be compared to another great builder of a different age, William of Wykeham. The comparison would certainly have pleased him. Palaces, castles, monasteries, hospitals, schools; chapels, 'tin tabernacles' and churches: sixty buildings in thirty-two years. ... As well as innumerable small acts of artistic patronage, many involving Burges: jewelled ivory hair brushes for the Duke of Norfolk (1877);[21] gloves for Cardinal Manning (1872)[22][222]; mitres for the Bishop of Dunkeld (1878)[23][220]; a superb silver desert service for his schoolfriend and secretary, G. E. Sneyd (1880)[24][260–261]; a jewelled statue of St Margaret, Queen of Scotland (1876) for St Charles College, Bayswater;[25] and elaborate crucifixes (1871[247] and 1875),[26] reliquary (1870),[27][249] prayer book (1870)[28] and Madonna (1877)[29] for his own use. He owned so many seats that his progress must have seemed like a stately game of musical chairs. Building for him was a romantic passion. Yet most of his buildings were never finished. At the time of his death work was still in progress at Cardiff, at Caerphilly, at Castell Coch, at Falkland, at St Andrews, at Dumfries House, at Mochrum, at Mount Stuart, at St John's Lodge – and at many other places. 'Why should I hurry', he once remarked, 'over what is my chief pleasure?'[30] 'Perhaps [my] favourite pursuit', he wrote, 'is antiquarianism, as History is [my] favourite reading', but 'my luxury is art.'[31] And then, with a nice piece of understatement, 'I have ... a considerable taste for art and archaeology, and happily the means to indulge them'.[32] His supervision of the architects and artists he employed was often so close as to amount to complete direction. In particular, the iconographical similarity of so many decorative schemes betrays the existence of one controlling hand. He was indeed 'the best unprofessional architect of his generation'.[33] But his disparate talents, his vast potential as an architectural patron, required the stimulus of a creative mind of very different stamp. He found it in 'the soul-inspiring Burges'.

Billy Burges and 'the Bute': a strange partnership, but extraordinarily productive. Cardiff Castle and Castell Coch were, above all, their joint creations, professions of faith in the feudal ideal, dreams of 'pure art' in an alien world. Together they slew the dragon of philistinism in the very citadel of profit. Then both retreated symbolically, Bute to his island fastness, Burges to Tower House, Kensington.

Chapter Seven

FANTASTIC

'Massive, learned, glittering, amazing.'   W. R. LETHABY, 1935

Now from the macrocosm to the microcosm, from Bute's Wagnerian vision to a Tennysonian miniature: Burges's private Palace of Art. At Tower House, Melbury Road, Kensington, Billy Burges played out the last act in the High Victorian Dream. Enjoying Burges – like enjoying Tennyson or Rossetti – involves a willing suspension of disbelief, a readiness to share the Pre-Raphaelite vision. Peace then, sceptical reader, as we prepare to enter the Palace of Art.

First, Burges's ideal medieval interior:

We should find the ceiling boarded, with paintings on it, generally stars on a green ground; sometimes painted subjects, introduced either in circles or as heads in a border: the walls, if the apartment is a simple one, are simply white, with a pattern in red lines, after the fashion of masonry ..., a floriated border running immediately below the ceiling; if ... the apartment is a rich one, the walls have an imitation curtain up to a certain height, and then picture-subjects above. There were two distinct sorts of these; one, where the work was done 'decently', without gold and azure, in fact, in lampblack, red and yellow ochre ...; and the other, in full and brilliant colours, with burnished gold ornaments. ... But the great feature of our medieval chamber is the furniture; this, in a rich apartment, would be covered with paintings, both ornaments and subjects; it not only did its duty as furniture, but spoke and told a story. ... The floor would be paved with small tiles ... and in summer it appears to have been the fashion to strew sweet-scented heaths on it. ... Most probably our apartment would have a bed in it. ... There would be a great chair, and sundry divans, or benches, against the walls; the windows would be glazed and furnished with shutters; and ... the woodwork would probably be painted. At the end of the fourteenth century, and during the fifteenth century, this painted furniture was gradually supplanted by carved oak, and the walls were hung with tapestry, or sometimes panelled; the divans still continued, and in France and Belgium the glass, instead of being placed in a groove in the stone, was fixed in a wooden casement, placed at the back of the mullion; the lower part of this casement having no glass, but simply a lattice to keep out the birds; in bad weather it was closed by means of shutters. As the walls were very thick, seats were got in the window-jambs; and very pleasant places they must have been.[1]

The simpler type of chamber presented few problems. Burges was able to restore several rooms in the Vicars' Close at Wells to the satisfaction of J. H. Parker and other antiquaries. The richer apartment was more difficult to recreate. One of the few well-documented examples was Henry III's Painted Chamber in the Old Palace at Westminster. This was Burges's beau ideal of thirteenth-century secular painted decoration. He never saw it himself, for it vanished in the great fire of 1834. Instead he was dependant on careful drawings prepared by Stothard for *Vetusta Monumenta*, and by Edward Crocker for Sir G. Page Turner.[2] Here were none of the 'wretched' wallpaper 'abominations' of his own day, but richly historiated bands of Old Testament tales, stretching upwards from the painted curtains at floor level to the boarded ceiling with its powdering of medallion quatrefoils.[3]

By the mid-nineteenth century medieval furniture was rare, and medieval painted furniture very rare indeed. There were painted armoires at Bayeux and Noyon, and several painted items in the Uffizi.[4] There were descriptions of the Louvre of Charles V;[5] the residence of Jacques Duchié in Paris;[6] and houses decorated by Dello Delli in Florence.[7] But 'it is almost impossible for us', Burges admitted in 1867, 'to conceive the effect of a first-class piece of medieval sacred furniture covered with burnished gilding engraved and punched into patterns enriched with paintings by an artist like Giotto, and glittering with mosaics of gilt and coloured glass'.[8] He knew of a medieval painted chest at Newport, Essex.[9] He helped to restore the late medieval round table in the Chapter House at Salisbury.[10] And at Westminster Abbey he was able to study a few famous fragments at close quarters. Early English chests in the Triforium[11] and in the Chapel of the Pyx[12] – crude cast iron boxes like that in the sacristy at Salisbury[13] – were interesting and instructive. But three of the Abbey's greatest treasures electrified his imagination: the thirteenth-century Retable rediscovered by Blore in 1840;[14] the thirteenth-century Sedilia recorded by Sir Joseph Ayloffe in the 1770s;[15] and of course Edward I's Coronation Chair.[16] Burges stoutly defended the Retable against Viollet-le-Duc's attempts to appropriate its manufacture to France.[17] So fond of it was he that he copied its lateral elements as wall-cupboards in the Drawing Room at Tower House. But there was no way of reproducing the Coronation Chair without descending into cliché. 'When in all the freshness of its glass mosaics and its historiated gilding, it must indeed have been an artistic piece of furniture. . . . When are [we] going to [have] Retabula, Chairs, and Sedilia such as we see at Westminster?'[18]

Early Painted Furniture

It was in March 1859 that Burges first exhibited his answer to the 'dark ages' of

Georgian joinery: six pieces of painted furniture made during the previous year.[19] Two were for his own use: a wardrobe and a nest of pigeon holes.[20] Of the remaining four – buffet, sideboard, cabinet and escritoire – one seems to have been commissioned by James Nicholson (d. 1894);[21] three by Herbert George Yatman (d. 1911).[22] Yatman of Haslemere is not exactly a name to conjure with. But 'H. G. Yatman' deserves to be written up in letters of gold in any history of furniture. Before 1858 the only furniture Burges designed seems to have been 'in the Jacobean style'.[23] As early as 1851–6 he had designed furniture and fittings, made up by W. Caldecott, for Ruthin Castle, Denbighshire.[24] In 1858–62 he also designed a table, made up by J. D. Crace, for C. L. S. Cocks of Treverbyn Vean, Cornwall: circular, marquetried and inlaid with a coloured allegory of the 'Wheel of Fortune'.[25] But the furniture of 1858 was very different. That was also the year when Yatman's brother, the Rev. John Augustus Yatman of Winscombe, married: Burges's wedding present was a painted bedroom filled with furniture.[26] Now the furniture for Yatman of Winscombe was identifiably Burgesian, but not yet painted. The furniture for Yatman of Haslemere placed Burges in the *avant-garde* of furniture designers. From 1858 onwards – the year of the double Yatman commission – Burges's furniture is medieval in a way no other designer ever approached: in the language of the day, it is not only 'real' and 'true'; it is 'painted' as well as 'pointed'.[27] In structure it is architect's furniture, largely unmoulded, boxy and aedicular. Its background colours are heraldic; its painted panels Pre-Raphaelite.

One example is the 'Wines and Beers' sideboard (1859)[28][184], made up by Harland and Fisher. Painted by Poynter, its decoration illustrates 'the combat of Sir Bacchus and the redoubtable Sir John Barleycorn'. Bacchus is supported by the warlike figures of Burgundy, Hock and Champagne. Barleycorn has at his elbow reinforcements in the guise of Porter, Pale Ale and Scotch Ale. Inside – as though hiding their heads in shame – are four anaemic Neo-Classical cameos: Ginger Beer, Lemonade, Seltzer Water and Soda Water. Finally, there are six portraits: one faintly resembles Morris, another Rossetti; another may perhaps be identifiable by his favourite tipple – 'Gin Sling'. Bold, almost starkly simple in design, this piece clearly appealed to Morris: his 'St George' cabinet of the following year (1860) is suspiciously similar in conception.[29]

Nicholson seems to have been the patron who commissioned the 'Wines and Beers' sideboard.[30] It was bought, however, by the South Kensington Museum at the close of the 1862 Exhibition. Perhaps Nicholson changed his mind. Yatman was made of sterner stuff. The first item Burges designed for him had been halfway between furniture and jewellery, the Yatman Casket (1856).[31][246] Its model was the fifteenth-century shrine at Bruges, painted by Memling. Its style recalled Perugino. Its ironwork was by Potter; its painting by Poynter. But its bizarre range of decorative themes – illuminated on inset leather panels – was peculiar to Burges. Cleopatra and Prester John are there; so are the Aramaspii and the Jackdaw of Rheims. Burges has rifled the works of Marco Polo, Pliny and Herodotus; he has dipped into the *Ortus Sanitatis* of 1502 and the *Cento Novella Antichi* of Giovanni Fioretino as well as the

Ingoldsby Legends. And to very good effect. The decoration of the Yatman Casket is a miniature celebration of the power and legendary origin of gold and precious stones. 'Benvenuto Cellini', enthused the *Building News*, 'would here have found his touch and taste . . . at all events some praise is due to whoever had the moral courage to have such a thing painted.'[32]

Quite so. H. G. Yatman may well have been the first person to commission a piece of painted furniture since the Middle Ages. The exact chronology is difficult to document. But between 1855 and 1859 he commissioned at least three major and two minor pieces from Burges.

The Sun Cabinet (1858–9)[33][183], or buffet, was one of Yatman's most curious commissions. On a central bracket stood a sculptured figure of the Sun, and below were panels painted with humanised allegories of the metals anciently believed to be the product of the sun's rays: lead, brass, gold, silver, copper and iron. Inside, nails are hammered home by Tubal Cain, and Cyclops forges jagged thunderbolts. Perhaps Poynter was the artist. The 'Bacchus' wine cooler (1858) was another Yatman piece. Also by Harland and Fisher, and costing £120, it formed a focal point of the 1859 Exhibition.[34] This time the artists were Westlake and Morten.[35] Painted panels illustrated scenes from the thirteenth-century French poem *Le Martyre de S. Bacchus*; medallion heads symbolised various wines – 'sherry, for example, as a fair, and port as a dark beauty; champagne perhaps too coquettish, if the idea did not accord with the nature of that over-praised wine'.[36]

Yatman's escritoire – or the Yatman cabinet (1858)[37][VII; 179–80], as it is usually called – was more elaborate than either of these. It was made by Harland and Fisher, and cost £80. Its components were pine and mahogany. But its materials are quite secondary to its decoration. The general form is aedicular: a Gothic shrine, with gables, finials and simulated arcades. Calendars peep through its miniature dormer windows. And oil-painted panels retell a fable appropriate to its purpose: the story of Cadmus. Now Cadmus was the legendary hero who introduced the alphabet into ancient Greece. Hence his suitability as a patron of writing. His career is represented in six paintings by Poynter: Europa, sister of Cadmus; Cadmus himself fighting the dragon; the Sparti, grown up from dragon's teeth, engaged in combat; the nuptials of Cadmus and Hermione; Cadmus as governor of the Thebans; and Cadmus and Hermione partly changed into serpents. Gable images of History and Poetry; medallions of Pericles and Anaxagoras; and allegories of inscription (Assyrian cuneiform), composition (Dante) and publication (Caxton) complete the didactic sequence. Inside are portraits of Burges and Poynter themselves, mentor and pupil side by side. A justifiable conceit. For the Yatman cabinet has become almost a textbook cliché: the first major piece of Pre-Raphaelite furniture. Medieval fantasy had been paganised and domesticated for the drawing room. By integrating joinery, architecture and painting in miniature form, Burges had broken new ground in furniture design. As the *Art Journal* put it, tongue in cheek, Yatman could now boast 'a group of furniture such as Piers Gaveston might have ordered, had his London residence been in St James's Square'.[38]

With the International Exhibition of 1862 – for which Burges and Slater arranged the Ecclesiological Society's Medieval Court[39] – painted furniture went public. Morris, Marshall & Co. exhibited six articles; Prichard and Seddon five; Forsyth (i.e. Norman Shaw) and Fisher one each; and Burges five: Cocks's table, Yatman's cabinet, Nicholson's sideboard, a mirrored buffet (1859),[40] and his own Great Bookcase. Eighteen items in all. Painted furniture was no longer the preserve of a Pre-Raphaelite coterie, as in the 1859 show; it was now competing for the fashionable market. It wasn't even too expensive: a Morris cabinet with two figures by Burne-Jones was priced at 30 guineas; a run-of-the-mill lectern with 'commonplace little figures of apostles burnt in' by a process called pyrography, cost 40 guineas.[41] Classicists were horrified; upholsterers appalled. Burges rejoiced: 'The Pagan school' had 'just made up their minds to tolerate "Gothic" in churches, or occasionally in the exterior of a country house, provided the interior was finished in the usual rococo work.' But now 'the new school' had invaded 'this last citadel of so-called classicism ... not with the usual "old English carved oak", as it is called by auctioneers, but with furniture, full of pictorial art, of colour and gold, combined with simple forms, and often made of common materials. It is ceasing to be mere mechanic's work, and has become art and speaks all sorts of things and subjects. Here [is] an overturn of [all] general ideas upon the dignity of painting in general, and of easel pictures in particular'. Back, then, to the heroic days of Giotto and Fra Angelico.[42]

One result of 1862, as far as Burges was concerned, seems to have been a commission to design a particularly elaborate bookcase[206]. When the firm of Morris, Marshall, Faulkner and Co. had been founded in 1861, it was C. J. Faulkner who kept the books. Eventually, in 1865–9, Faulkner was replaced by a musical enthusiast from the west country named Warington Taylor (d. 1870). Taylor had been at Eton with Swinburne; had become a Catholic and been disinherited; and had been reduced to working as a book-keeper at the opera.[43] Late in 1862 he makes a brief appearance in Burges's diary. And then, in January 1863, appears the crucial clue: 'Taylor bookcase'.[44] At exactly the same time, 1862–3, Burges included in his notebooks a sketch for a processional frieze, based on the German legend of a tailor riding a goat.[45] This may have been a preliminary draft for Taylor's bookcase: massive double-doors with countercharged borders, fringed with iron, painted with a procession on a gold ground allegorising the Signs of the Zodiac, and mounted on a turned, ebonised stand. Early in 1863, the name 'Leighton' also appears among Burges's visitors.[46] 'Cimabue' had been a prominent exhibit in 1862. Could Leighton have been the artist responsible? The attitudes of the figures belong to Burges's standard repertoire, but their level of execution is unusually fluent.[47] And there is another, more intriguing possibility. Taylor was himself in close contact with Red Lion Square: he already preferred Webb's furniture to that designed by Burges, and in 1862 he persuaded

Rossetti to supply him with some 'superb' painted panels.[48] Could these be the panels for Taylor's bookcase? Whatever the attribution – Stacy Marks is a likely contender – one of the figures bears a resemblance to Rossetti himself. And the bookcase combines elements associated with Morris and Webb, as well as with Burges and Godwin.

Burges's painted furniture took him to the heart of the Pre-Raphaelite circle. But outside that circle, the pundits' praise was grudging. Dr Dresser – the Fergusson of applied art – condemned Burges's 'anachronistic' designs and 'doll's house' tricks.[49] The *Civil Engineer and Architect's Journal* had to admit that Burges had shown 'exuberant fancy'. But the results were 'curious' and 'not altogether pleasing'.[50] Benjamin Webb thought the 1859 pieces 'ingenious and clever', but 'too much of an archaeological *concetto*'; the *Ecclesiologist* conceded that the whole idea of Burges's furniture was 'piquant', 'sui generis', and an expression of his 'happy versatility' – but wasn't it all unnecessarily expensive and 'needlessly eccentric'? At least Burges's furniture was preferable to that of Morris & Co. Theirs was 'crude' in colour, 'grotesque' in design and 'preposterous' in conception – 'enough to bring the very word "medieval" into deserved contempt'.[51] Burges himself drew a distinction between his own furniture and that of Morris & Co. Theirs had as its 'general characteristic . . . an Eastern system of diaper combined with rather dark-toned pictures . . . [of] the Venetian school of colour'. It resembled a type supposedly 'used by the middle classes in the times of our forefathers'. Whereas his own 'would have been found in the houses of the nobility'. Like Morris's work, his furniture was 'painted all over' – unlike that of Prichard and Seddon, which consisted of marquetried oak with painted figure-panels – 'but the tone of colouring [was] much brighter . . . [with] the literature of Pagandom and the Middle Ages . . . side by side in the same bookcase or buffet'.[52] The *Builder* certainly noticed a difference. Burges's furniture displayed a mixture of 'perverseness' and 'real skill'; Morris's was merely 'rude and ugly'. Even so, was Burges heading in the right direction? Were his translations from masonry and manuscript into painting and joinery 'consistent with the best principles of Gothic'? 'Mr Burges's skill is so considerable that we cannot . . . allow him to get into . . . a wrong course.'[53] Certainly these early pieces by Burges, like those by Morris and Webb, are heavy. Purposely so: 'such as Barbarossa might have sat in'.[54] E. W. Godwin thought them unreasonably dogmatic: 'he did not wish to eat his dinner in a chair suited to Edward the Confessor.'[55] Even so, Burges's first Pre-Raphaelite furniture is far less gawky and angular than Philip Webb's. And in his later painted pieces he manages to modify the archaeological elements without abandoning their essentially Gothic form. Compared with Burges, Webb's work lacks integration and flair. Morris & Co. produced furniture which was painted; Burges designed painted furniture. And the design of every detail – mouldings, paintings, fittings – is directly due to Burges himself. The documentation is conclusive.

Well, where did Burges get the idea? It was recognised at the time, and has since become academically accepted, that 'the two armoires at Bayeux and Noyon had been at the bottom of it all'.[56] The painted panels, the folding doors, the gabled roof, the bulbous finials, the 'doll's house' scale – all stem from those two prototypes. The armoire at Bayeux was illustrated by César Daly in 1852;[57] by Viollet-le-Duc in 1858[58][181]; by W. E. Nesfield in 1862;[59] and yet again by E. W. Godwin, in 1873.[60] Godwin produced the most elaborate drawings and description, and came to the conclusion that its date was part late twelfth century and part early thirteenth century. In 1858 Burges had not yet seen it. It is hard to resist the conclusion that he worked from Viollet-le-Duc's engraving, published that very year. In 1853, however, he had himself examined the very similar armoire (*c.* 1300) at Noyon.[61] Publication of his Noyon drawings was delayed until 1870.[62] And by that date he had been anticipated by Vitet (1845),[63] by Didron (1846),[64] by Lenoir (1856),[65] and by Viollet-le-Duc (1858)[66][182]. Both armoires, therefore, were fairly well known in architectural circles before 1858. But no doubt it required Viollet-le-Duc's polychrome publication to trigger off the new trend. 1858 was the year Burges noted in his diary: 'Began my first piece of painted furniture.'[67] And as he later admitted, 'we all cribbed from Viollet-le-Duc'.[68]

The explanation, however, cannot be quite as simple as that. In 1856–8 Morris, Webb, Rossetti and Burne-Jones also began to produce painted furniture: in Red Lion Square, London, and at Red House, Bexley.[69] Holman Hunt and Millais had apparently painted a cupboard door 'for a lark' back in 1851.[70] Hunt had begun painting furniture in the Egyptian style in 1855–7.[71] And in 1857 Crace quoted Theophilus on painted furniture at the R.I.B.A.[72] But there is a difference between painted furniture and pictorial furniture. After all, Pugin had painted his organ lofts, notably that at Jesus College, Cambridge (1849). The progress of the Morris group in the field of secular pictorial furniture culminated in the St George cabinet of 1861,[73] and the Backgammon Players cabinet of 1862.[74] Burges was himself involved with the group in the decoration of another celebrated piece: King René's Honeymoon Cabinet (1861).[75] But somehow all these pieces fail to integrate furniture and painting in quite the Burgesian way. Maybe the whole Pre-Raphaelite generation was moving towards the same goal. And maybe Viollet-le-Duc crystallised the tentative approaches of his less systematic contemporaries. But it required Burges's special genius to translate a couple of medieval curiosities into a range of Pre-Raphaelite furniture. And even in terms of strict chronology, Burges takes the lead. His earliest ideas for the Yatman cabinet date from 1855.[76] Yatman's painted casket dates from 1856. That is also the year of Burges's designs for Lille: his confessionals have all the essential ingredients of High Victorian furniture, including painted panels.[77][176] Certainly, the Morris group were toying with painted furniture at the same time. But between 1855 and 1859 it was Burges, above all, who opened up a new dimension in English furniture design. It was a fashion easy to copy, but hard to equal. By 1862 one critic noted that 'the mania has spread far and wide'.[78] Painted panels certainly crept like a rash across the 'art furniture' of the 1860s and 1870s. But in popular, diluted form they were but pale imitations of Burges's vintage pieces. Stacy Marks may or may not have been right in thinking that Burges was first with his painted panels.[79] But it was Burges, more than anyone, who created the furniture appropriate to High Victorian Gothic.

TREVERBYN VEAN AND BINGLEY

Furniture, however, was only one ingredient in recreating the medieval interior. Domestic architecture, Burges complained in 1868, had lagged behind church work. The triumphs of the Gothic Revival had been largely ecclesiastical.

> We can all form a fairly correct idea of the interior of a Medieval church, but we find it much more difficult to realize the interior of a Medieval house, with its painted walls, its illuminated ceilings, its partially stained glass windows, its embroideries and its furniture, historiated in colours and gold. We have done one or two splendid churches; but none of the houses built in the Medieval style give us the faintest idea of the glories of a thirteenth-century domestic interior. I wish I could praise the Houses of Parliament on this head, but I cannot. In fact, the Medieval interior, or, rather, the interior founded on Medieval Art has yet to be done.[80]

Tower House, therefore – like the various essays which preceded it, and to which we must now turn – was Burges's attempt to do single-handed what the entire Gothic Revival had failed to do: to conjure up, in Victorian terms, the artistic spirit of a medieval house.

Many contemporaries regarded these attempts as the pinnacle of Burges's success.[81] But judging them today is far from easy. So often his interiors were never finished. No furniture was executed for Knightshayes. It is doubtful whether much was made for Bingley. None survives from Gayhurst, although two pieces at least were specially made: Lady Carrington's wardrobe and bookcase.[82] The fittings for McConnochie's house at Cardiff must always have been meagre. And often enough, when an interior by Burges was completed, it failed to survive the twentieth-century reaction against High Victorian excess. The Yatman interiors at Winscombe and Haslemere have very largely gone. The interiors which Burges may have executed in 1865–6 for W. J. Potts Chatto (1824–82) at The Daison, near Torquay, have gone completely.[83] Knightshayes suffered cruelly in the 1930s, like ill-fated Hetton in Evelyn Waugh's *Handful of Dust* (1934). Gone too are Burges's interiors for Spurrell at Faulkbourne, Essex (1868),[84] and for Rate at Milton Court, Dorking (1869–80).[85] Largely gone are Bingley and Treverbyn Vean. Nevertheless, all these fragments are valuable evidence of Burges's maturing style, stepping-stones towards his final achievement at Tower House.

Treverbyn Vean, Cornwall, was built *c.* 1858–62 by Col. Charles Lygon Somers Cocks (1821–85).[86] He was largely his own architect. While commanding a battalion of Coldstreamers in the Crimea, Col. Cocks had found time to study the flora of the Bosphorus. He was certainly interested in the arts, and commissioned Burges – whom he must have known through Cocks-Biddulph's bank and his relatives the Yorkes of Forthampton – to design a chimneypiece for his new manor house. Now Treverbyn Vean is situated in the Glyn Valley, near Liskeard, high above St Neot's stream. The legend of St Neot, therefore – obscurest of Cornish saints – was the theme chosen by Burges. His sculptor was J. B. Philip. Together they produced a chimneypiece bulging with symbols of the chase[118]. It must surely have astonished the gentry of eastern Cornwall. It certainly delighted the judges at the 1862 Exhibition.[87] Surrounded by Flemish tapestries, Turkish hangings, 'Jacobean' chairs and sub-Puginian tables, it formed the centrepiece of one of the earliest interiors which we can confidently label Burgesian.[88]

Alas, the effect can now only be judged from photographs. So also the interiors at Bingley. It was in 1865 that a Yorkshire cloth merchant named Garnett commissioned Burges and Morris to decorate the interior of his new house on the outskirts of Bingley, Oakwood Court.[89] Thomas Garnett (died 1916) was a cousin of Beanlands of Brighton. Hence the employment of Burges and Morris. For the stained glass – the Four Seasons, St George, and five Chaucerian heroines – Morris employed Burne-Jones.[90] For the sculptural decorations Burges employed Thomas Nicholls. Happily, Burges's book of designs[91] survives, a document crucial to our understanding of the evolving Burgesian dream – from Gayhurst and Treverbyn, through Bingley and Knightshayes to Cardiff and Tower House. Garnett owned a celebrated ceramic collection. Dutch china and Japanese vases perch daintily in ebonised cabinets and cling to every available protuberance. Painted panels with echoes of Gayhurst; floral friezes which anticipate Knightshayes and Tower House; an octagonal loo-table with peacock inlay; cabinets, divans and buffets which rival some of the carved fittings at Cardiff; even an upright piano with painted panels.

All this furniture has long since been dispersed, assuming that it was in fact executed. But two formidable chimneypieces survive, one *in situ*, the other in fragments. The Dining Room chimney[117] was originally to have boasted a monkey, as at Gayhurst and Tower House.[92] In the end Burges settled for a grotesque bracket of the Lincoln Imp school flanked by battlements and tourelles. The result is characteristically bulky. But the Drawing Room chimneypiece[116], as originally designed, would have been monstrous, even by Burgesian standards:

Its heavy sarcophagus-shaped mantel ... painted pink with red-and-yellow medallions ... stood on short thick columns (red) with foliated capitals (blue) ... [and lions couchant gasping beneath their superincumbent burden]. .... The iron grate, with encaustic tiles on the hearth ... was silhouetted against a diaper of red and yellow bricks in vertical chevrons. On the corners of the shelf were written DILIGENTIA / ET HONESTAS in Gothic capital letters. The overmantel, completing the impression of an elevated tomb was enclosed within a vast red-and-yellow, cusped and crocketted ogee arch, with a central panel showing a noble lady, dressed in yellow and seated amongst green foliage in rich relief. She held a red shield with a rampant lion in her left hand and a helmet on a post in her right. To her right stood two hounds, to her left three hares. . . . The real Burgesian *tours de force*, however, were the two battlemented castle towers on each side of the arch, each surmounted by a ring of heads and pairs of lions. The spandrels were filled entirely with flamboyant tracery. In the book [of designs Burges notes] 'Mem. Mr Nicholls to do the little heads in the castles, the lady, the dogs, the Hares, the two animals on capitals of columns, and the lion'.[93]

Not all the colouring was carried out. Even so, the millocracy of Bingley must surely have been amazed.

KNIGHTSHAYES, DEVON

Suspending disbelief – meeting the dreamer half-way – is particularly necessary at Knightshayes. For there the dream is entrancing, but sadly incomplete. Knightshayes was the work of Sir John Heathcoat-Amory Bt. (1829–1914), a lace-making magnate, a Liberal M.P., and an indefatigable Master of the Tiverton staghounds.[94] He built it *de novo*, at the very peak of Victorian country-house building: the early 1870s, when the profits of industrial expansion were at their height, and the agricultural slump of 1879–94 had not yet begun.[95] In fact the dramatic transition – from boom to near bankruptcy – that occurred on many estates during the 1870s is perfectly represented at Knightshayes. The paradox is painful. Heathcoat-Amory built a house he could not afford to decorate, by an architect whose speciality was interior design.

Burges began work in 1867; the foundation stone was laid on 16 April 1869.[96] In 1870 the design was published in a striking lithograph by Haig[97][67], and Burges presented the lady of the house with an Indian bracelet.[98] By 1873 it was Heathcoat-Amory's turn to be presented with a full-scale volume of drawings illustrating the future decoration of the house: a technicolour synopsis of the High Victorian Dream.[99] Now Burges's usual timetable for decoration ran as follows: first stone-carving, then wood-carving; then stained glass, then painting, then furniture, and lastly carpets and curtains. At Knightshayes it is unlikely that he was able to proceed beyond the second stage. By 1874 he seems to have completed the decorative stonework of the house, and to have moved on to the design of the woodwork.[1] That was as far as he got. Nicholls had moved in, but not Lonsdale. For in 1874 Burges was supplanted – on grounds of economy – by a cheaper, less fastidious designer, J. D. Crace (1838–1919).[2]

The planning of Knightshayes is practical and undogmatic. The house faces south, towards a sweeping view across the valley. The entrance front on the north side – in practice the rear elevation – is necessarily dark. But all the rooms on that side – the Great Hall and Staircase, the Gentleman's Room and Billiard Room – are precisely those in which direct sunshine is least necessary. The sunny apartments on the garden side constitute the house's principal living space: on the first floor, the Boudoir and main bedrooms; on the ground floor the four major reception rooms: Dining Room and Drawing Room as wings, each with a bay window; Morning Room and Library – 'a sort of Morning Room for gentlemen'³ – on each side of the central corridor axis. Each room makes its own contribution to the exterior silhouette. The carriage entrance at the north front sweeps round to face the bell turret and Billiard Room wing, idiosyncratically decorated with grotesque animal heads and a bulbous billiard-ball frieze. The garden front is balanced but not dogmatically symmetrical. In fact Burges's handling of gables, mullioned bays and chimney stacks adds up to a text-book example of the High Victorian principle of compensating asymmetry. Knightshayes looks best when viewed obliquely from the terrace, a fairy-tale series of mullions, gables and finials, culminating in a bulbous re-entrant bay. But even head-on, from the terraced gardens below, there is no monotony.

Eastlake's judgement on the exterior of Knightshayes is measured and just. The Ruskinian polychromy of Ettington in Warwickshire – by Prichard and Seddon – might display greater variety of texture. The Old English tile and timber of Leyes Wood in Surrey – by young Norman Shaw – might be handled with greater panache. But the virtues of Knightshayes were of a less meretricious kind:

> Knightshayes is eminently picturesque, executed with great vigour and a thorough knowledge of detail. ... Massive walls, bold gables, stout mullions nearly half the width of the lights which they divide, large and solid looking chimney shafts, corbelled from the walls or riding on the high-pitched roofs, are the principal incidents which give this building dignity and effect. Such gentler graces as are imparted into the design by the aid of mouldings or decorative sculpture (as in the central dormer) indicate a French origin. ... The class of art to which Knightshayes belongs is of a severer type than that adopted at Ettington, and less emphatically national than that which characterises Leyes Wood. The reddish local stone employed ... is extremely hard, and there is a kind of sympathy between its stern unyielding nature and the robust rather than refined character of [Burges's] design.⁴

'Knightshayes', commented the *Building News*, 'is stately and bold, and its medievalism is not obtrusive.'⁵ Certainly by comparison with Cardiff Castle or Castell Coch, Knightshayes is a model of restraint. Its elevations, in the language of the day, are severe, muscular and manly. Several of Burges's characteristic domestic motifs are there: the bold, fisted finials, for example, which appear elsewhere on furniture as well as on roof gables; or the smooth, stern grid of mullion and transom, handled to good effect not only in the main house but also in the gate lodge, in the vicarage at Chevithorne, and in the powerfully asymmetrical stable quadrangle. The local reddish sandstone is gritty and hard. Even the softer facings of brownish Ham Hill stone avoid any suggestion of flaccidity. The style is stripped and spare, and practical. It is muscular, but it is still domestic. It is, in fact, a secular version of Burges's favourite Early French. It was a language he used again – albeit vicariously and in garbled form – far away in America, at Trinity College, Connecticut.

Outside, Knightshayes is restrained. Inside, its decoration was to have been fantastic. Not one of its rooms was completed according to Burges's designs. But in several the decorations were actually begun. The Drawing Room, in design at least, must have been one of Burges's most amazing feats. Being a feminine citadel, its decorative theme was Love. The walls glowed with legendary love stories, such as that of Pyramus and Thisbe. The windows glimmered with portraits of lovers – Jason, Medea, Paris, etc. The ceiling panels were filled with images of love and spangled with stars of mirrored lead. Murrey-coloured curtains; carpets of 'Turkish, Persian, Indian or other Eastern production', copied perhaps from a carpet in a picture by Van Eyck;[6] panelling painted green – 'like a carriage panel' – with birds and flowers, and gilded mouldings, and a panelled cornice enriched with mother of pearl; and finally not one but two chimneypieces. The first would have been impressive: a frame for heraldry and for statuary representing celebrated writers on the theme of Love. The second would have been sensational: a mass of sculptured stone carved and gabled, representing the Assault on the Castle of Love[IX]. This was a theme Burges borrowed from a strange source: a fourteenth-century German ivory mirror-case which he exhibited at the Royal Archaeological Institute in 1857.[7] At Knightshayes, in 1870,[8] the scale is inflated to almost megalomaniac proportions. From the battlements wimpled ladies look down on the knights below. And guests at Knightshayes could even participate in the charade: a secret passage at the rear allowed them to stand upon the castle's ramparts and beckon to the Drawing Room below. Carving in this passage showed 'the various conditions of life offering their hearts to Cupid'.[9] Happily, something of this extraordinary vision survives, in the form of a stained glass window at Tower House.

For Burges's elaborate schemes were by no means wasted. The decorative programme at Knightshayes proved to be a trial run for several visual motifs employed by the architect later in his career. Nicholls's carved corbels in the Billiard Room – the triumph of Virtue over Vice through Wisdom – embody a theme repeated in different medium and scale on the door of Lord Bute's study at Cardiff. The mirrored ceiling of the Billiard Room was repeated with variations at both Cardiff and Tower House. The Four Seasons corbels in the staircase have their counterparts in other media in nearly every Burges design. The zodiac ceiling of the

Gentleman's Room, a theme borrowed from Buckingham St, reappears in Tower House and again in Bute's London house, St John's Lodge, Regent's Park. A variant of the stag chimneypiece in the same room had already appeared at Treverbyn Vean. A variation of the Library chimneypiece had already appeared at Bingley. The mermaid chimneypiece in the Boudoir, first used at Gayhurst, reappeared – famously – in Burges's own bedroom at Tower House. The fairy-tale frieze in the Morning Room was repeated in the Dining Room at Tower House and in the Nursery at Cardiff. The Morning Room dado, with flowers apparently climbing through the panelled sections – an idea also developed by Viollet-le-Duc – reappears at Gayhurst, at Cardiff and at Castell Coch. The Tennysonian and Chaucerian images in Drawing Room and Boudoir reappear in Cardiff Castle and in Tower House, and indeed in Burges's own illuminated copy of Tennyson's poems. The tulip vases in Morning Room and Library are almost a Burgesian signature tune, reappearing most memorably in the Summer Smoking Room at Cardiff. So are the Library's jelly-mould domelets – that motif he discovered at Messina – which reappear in almost every major Burges design. One of the Drawing Room chimneypieces, with full-sized figures in Gothic niches, was echoed in the Dining Room at Cardiff, and again in the Drawing Room at Castell Coch, and it might even have graced Trinity College, Connecticut. And so it goes on, Burges's habit of auto-plagiarism, a pardonable vice he shared with Tennyson. The Knightshayes Album is an epitome of Burges's stylistic vocabulary in the field of interior domestic design.

Among High Victorian country houses, Knightshayes is a collector's item. It makes Teulon's Elvetham look fussy, and Clutton's Minley anarchic. It makes T. H. Wyatt's Orchardleigh look tedious, and Scott's Walton repetitive. By comparison, Waterhouse's Eaton Hall seems overblown, and E. W. Pugin's Carlton Towers seems positively manic. At Knightshayes Burges was in top form. But those magical interiors remained a half-formed dream.

Mc.Connochie's House, Cardiff

Less ambitious than Knightshayes, but rather more in the public eye, was a house Burges designed for James Mc.Connochie (d. 1889).[10] Mc.Connochie was a Scots engineer employed by Messrs. Burges and Walker on Cardiff's Bute East Dock. He stayed on as Chief Engineer to the Bute Docks, and eventually became first a town councillor and then Lord Mayor. As a Scotsman and a Catholic he was a natural confidant for the Marquess of Bute. In 1871 he commissioned Burges to design him a house in Park Place, not far from Cardiff Castle. In 1872 Haig's seductive perspective[11][66] was shown at the Royal Academy. Building progressed throughout the following year.[12] By 1874 it was already being described as 'the best house in the town',[13] even though its interior decorations remained incomplete until Mc.Connochie's Mayoral year of 1880.[14]

Mc.Connochie's house has always had a good press. In 1872 the *Building News* called it 'free yet sober'.[15] And the *Builder* admitted grudgingly that it was 'very solid and satisfactory looking'.[16] Its materials were certainly sturdy: Caerphilly stone with Boxground facings; granite columns; iron casements; deal ceilings, mahogany panelling and teak stairs. And its solidity was guaranteed by the employment of Mc.Connochie's own workmen from the Bute Docks. Viollet-le-Duc chose to illustrate it in 1875.[17] Henry-Russell Hitchcock called it 'one of the best medium-sized stone dwellings of the High Victorian Gothic'.[18] Handley-Read admired its economy, integration and textural contrasts.[19] The compensating asymmetry of the elevations is certainly very skilful. And Burges's use of simplified Early French motifs – triple arched loggias, punchy plate tracery and broad-banded voussoirs – is masterly. Mc.Connochie's house has only one real weakness: its interior planning is sacrificed to a cumbersome and grandiloquent staircase. That was an error Burges avoided when he came to design Tower House.

Now Burges had already experimented with Mc.Connochie's mullion-and-transom, grid-pattern windows at Ightham Place, Kent. There, in 1869, he had enlarged an earlier house by adding a wing, entrance and staircase for the Rev. James Sandford Bailey (1824–1909).[20] Plain-featured, diminutive in scale, Ightham Place reveals the identity of its architect only by its fenestration, its spreading wrought-iron hinges, its massive drawing-room chimneypiece and its tie-beamed timber ceilings. As for the dormers of Mc.Connochie's house – their gables curved and hooded *à la Français* – Burges also used them again elsewhere: in the schoolhouse at Winchfield (1860–61); in the parsonage at Bewholme (1859);[21] and in the paired cottages (1873) which flank the vista at Studley Royal.[22] But these were all obscure and minor commissions. Mc.Connochie's house was an object of critical interest and comment, a well-publicised trial-run for Tower House, Kensington.

TOWER HOUSE, MELBURY RD, KENSINGTON

So much for the prolegomena. Now for Tower House itself. Burges retained his office in Buckingham St right to the end of his life. But by the early 1870s it must have been excessively crowded. From it, after 1878, he gradually decanted all his most treasured possessions. They went to fill a grander, more elaborate Palace of Art.

The second floor of 15 Buckingham St had six rooms, four overlooking the Thames. Over the years all these were crammed with Burgesian trophies. They must, in fact, have been crowded to the point of suffocation. Three rooms have been recorded: Burges's office[166], bedroom[167], and the clerk's study. The walls of the office (1861)[23] were divided into dado and frieze. The dado was enriched with conventional drapery similar to that in the Painted Chamber at Westminster; the frieze was alive with trees and branches festooned with birds ranging from the sparrow to the dodo – 'birds such as were never seen by mortal eye'.[24] The ceiling was divided into ornamental compartments and from its centre hung an ostrich egg.[25] Above the chimneypiece's brass overmantel[26] sat the Virgin and Child listening to angels playing musical instruments.[27] Over the doorway St Cecilia played her organ, blown by a ministering angel. Decoration was a gradual process, extending over at least thirteen years, from 1858 to 1871.[28] Here Burges had his 'own drawing table', a plain, workmanlike affair, with a rising top.[29] Burges's bedroom[30] was famous for its monstrous frieze (1863–4): mermaids and sea-monsters writhed and grimaced in and out of a Gothic arcade.[31] On the ceiling was painted the combat of Theseus and the Minotaur in the Labyrinth at Crete (1862).[32] Even the bedside chairs were decorated with monsters.[33] The clerk's study[34] was less terrific. Here the limited space was crammed with built-in, mirrored cupboards, and the painted frieze consisted of panels in imitation of stained glass, with figures perched between stout columns. On the ceiling (?1871) were six of the Signs of the Zodiac, arranged in a circle around a central figure of the sun.[35]

All these rooms have long since vanished. Their furnishings, indeed, were largely removed to Tower House in 1878. But many of their decorative features survive, adapted and transmogrified by Burges, in Melbury Rd. Buckingham St was an experimental accumulation. Tower House was conceived as a Palace of Art, planned, coherent, thought out over many years, the anthology of a lifetime.

By the 1870s Holland Park was beginning to rival St John's Wood and Chelsea as an 'artistic' area. Val Prinsep, Frederick Leighton, Luke Fildes, Hamo Thorneycroft, Mrs Russell Barrington, Colin Hunter, G. F. Watts, Marcus Stone – they all lived within strolling distance of each other.[36] Here Burges planned his new house, a pledge to the spirit of Gothic in an area given over to Queen Anne. Having rejected sites in Victoria Rd and Bayswater, he hit upon a plot of land near Holland House in the summer of 1875.[37] He began the drawings on 13th July; accepted estimates on 20th Dec.; and signed contracts on 31st Dec.[38] Structural work progressed during the next two years, and a lease from the Ilchester Estate was signed on 2nd Feb. 1877.[39] On 1st Jan. 1878 servants and furniture were moved in. On 16th Jan. Mrs Seddon chose the china.[40] On 5th March 1878 Burges 'first slept at Melbury Rd'; and on 28th May he first 'slept in [his] own Bedroom'. On June 5th he was 'At Home' in his dream house, and the FABS were his first guests.[41]

By 1875 Burges had designed – if not completed – all his major works. His personal style had been maturing over twenty years. His team of craftsmen had been tried and tested. In Tower House he was able to recapitulate many of his previous triumphs. The result is an extraordinary distillation of his own artistic career. It is more exotic than Pugin's home at Ramsgate; more personal even than Soane's strange house in Lincoln's Inn Fields. The exterior was designed carefully; not quickly but at the third attempt.[42] The interior became the labour of half a lifetime compressed into six frenetic years. Ironically, its creator barely lived to enjoy it: Burges died within three years of moving in.[43]

Tower House is not a mansion. It measures little more than 50 ft square. The fact that its exterior bulks large, and its interior creates an illusion of space, says much for its creator's architectural talents. The materials are plain: London gauge red bricks, with Bath stone dressings and Cumberland green slates. Its exterior – in the language of the day – is simple and massive, making bold use of geometrical forms, triangle, cube and cone. The entrance front[68] is striking only in its circular staircase turret, a focus and hinge for the axis of Melbury Rd. Was Burges thinking of the angle tower at Noyon?[44] It was a theme he had played with already at Cardiff, and in his Law Courts design. Conical angle towers are by no means peculiar to him: examples are fairly frequent in secular and domestic designs of the later 1870s.[45] But at Tower House this feature is used with deceptive ease. Its sturdy simplicity sets the keynote for the whole composition. There are few mouldings and fewer sculptures: only the carved capitals of the double porch (which recalls a *fortalice* by 'Greek' Thomson),[46] and the lintels over the library windows (which remind us of his enthusiasm for the winged beasts of Nineveh). The stern grid of mullion and transom is characteristically Burgesian. From the roof fly two weather vanes, the mermaid and the menaced heart: symbols which Burges adopted as his own. Two lead gargoyles echo those at Cardiff.[47] And in the garden gable is set a convex mirror, designed to catch and reflect the rays of the setting sun.

The plan is lucid and logical[68]. In essence, Burges has taken his plan for Mc.Connochie, reversed it, and turned the staircase into a central hall. By tucking the staircase inside the turret – a decision made not at the start but after initial designs had been prepared – he avoided the mistaken grandeur of Mc.Connochie's house. The double-decker central hall is left free as an access area for every major room: on the ground floor, dining room, drawing room and library; on the first floor, guest's bedroom, master bedroom and study.

The garden[69] was planned for summer tea-parties, but tea-parties of a rather exotic kind. In fact its layout recalls Alma-Tadema's *Sappho*. A paved terrace, or 'open lesche', took the form of a double *exhedra* approached by a low flight of steps. Jura marble seats swept round its semicircular ends, and a marble statue – a boy with a hawk by Nicholls[48] – crowned a flower-fountain in the centre of its mosaic floor. Here too were raised flower beds for appropriately medieval blooms, a Pre-Raphaelite garden in the heart of London.

> Heavily hangs the broad sun flower
> Over its grave i' the earth so chilly.
> Heavily hangs the hollyhock,
> Heavily hangs the tiger-lily.[49]

'Here on a summer's afternoon, Burges would give tea to a few friends, who lounged on the marble seats or sat on Persian rugs and embroidered cushions round the pearl-inlaid table, brilliant with tea service composed of things precious, rare and quaint.'[50] One teapot took the form of a pomegranate[232]; another (1868) was shaped like a fish.[51][229] Even the sugar basin, slop basin and the butter dish were made of gilded enamel.[52][228] The coffee pot had once graced the Summer Palace in Pekin.[53]

When students from the Architectural Association visited Tower House in 1877 they were 'astonished' not only at its 'ultra-medievalism', but at its 'archaic and massive' construction. The floors were 'of the amazing depth of 1 ft 9 ins clear – large and strong enough for a room of four or five times the size'. The ceiling beams, of 'short barbaric proportions' – each about one foot square – were reinforced with iron flitches and supported on stone corbels. Above these ceiling beams – of Danzig fir cased in deal – were Memel joists, felt sheeting and planed boarding. The gallery balustrade seemed robust enough 'for a bridge across the Thames'. Surrounded by so much marble, stone and bronze, the students imagined that they were in 'some twelfth- or thirteenth-century feudal castle'.[54] The walls themselves are immensely solid, up to two feet thick in places. And beneath the house are foundations fit for a fortress. The subsoil was clay, some of it soft and slushy, the remainder hard and treacherous. Burges took no chances. 'He is . . . putting in beds of concrete that are too astonishing', Norman Shaw told Luke Fildes in 1876; 'but then I suppose he is going in for a fortress.'[55]

In the art world, Tower House was an instant hit. And it remained so. When in 1893 the *Builder* published a giant panorama of the architecture of the previous half-century, Tower House was the only private town house to be included.[56] Mary Elizabeth Haweis – high-priestess of 'the religion of beauty' – thought it a veritable shrine of 'brightness, joyousness and strength'.[57] She was the wife of one of Burges's more dynamic clients, the Rev H. R. Haweis (1838–1901), a sensational preacher with an ear for music and an eye for publicity.[58] Mrs Haweis had an equally popular touch. She wrote art criticism in the gushing vocabulary of a ladies' magazine.[59] Still, her description of Tower House in its heyday is an intriguing document. Colour and allegory were her obsessions. She found Burges's home 'a treat to the eye and a lesson to the mind'; the product of 'genius', 'poetic feeling' and 'fun'; in truth, an 'Aladdin's palace'.[60] Since Mrs Haweis wrote, much has changed. The furnishings have been scattered, the treasures dispersed. But the structural decorations are nearly all intact. Collectors have tracked down items of furniture one by one. And the survival of hundreds of drawings and scores of early photographs makes it possible to reconstruct Tower House, room by room. So – in retrospect at least – let us enter Burges's Palace of Art.

Each room has its own iconography:
Entrance Hall: Time
Dining Room: Chaucer's *House of Fame*
Library: Literature and the Liberal Arts
Drawing Room: Love, its Fortunes and Misfortunes

Guest's Chamber: The Earth and its Productions
Burges's Bedroom: The Sea and its Inhabitants

Five doors open off the hall, and each is marked with its appropriate symbol. For the front door a latch-key; for the garden door a rose; for the library an open book; for the drawing (or music) room a pair of musical instruments; for the dining room a bowl and flask of wine. Front door (1876)[224] and garden door (?1880)[225] are covered with bronze, stamped with familiar Burgesian motifs: the Madonna and Child and the Ages of Man.[61] And between these doors stood a bronze table (1880), trefoil-shaped with cloven feet.[62] As Godwin noticed, the moulded details are already elephantine,[63] scaled up to maximise their visual impact. Billy Burges is at home. Even his dog Pinkie is immortalised as a Pompeian Cerberus in the mosaic pavement of the porch. In the hall itself the theme of the mosaic is the Cretan Labyrinth, with 'Theseus ... Ariadne ... Bacchus, and the dreaded Minotaur, all found within its mazes'[64][141]. But the porch remained unfinished. Its bronze panels were never cast; its bronze figure of Diogenes – bearing a lantern, 'looking for the honest man' – was never installed.[65]

But look up. The windows glimmer with stained glass. On the staircase, the 'Storming of the Castle of Love', from Chaucer's *Roman de la Rose*:

> In the central light at the top is Cupid seated with his bow and a sheaf of arrows. On the battlements on either side there are [trumpeting] damsels emblematical of Variety and Change. Below Cupid is the porter Danger on the look-out [with curved scimitar]. The [wimpled] damsels Fear and Shame, Distrust and Jealousy defend the castle by showering down roses; while the warriors below [emblematic of Hope] assail it with hearts thrown from catapults, and endeavour to [prize] open the portcullis, over which is written 'Welcome' [and behind which stands a maiden, waiting ...].[66]

A little lower down, the stained glass of the lower hall, also by Saunders from cartoons by Lonsdale, represents the Four Quarters of the Day:

> Four vast bells, wherefrom issue the spirits of the bells, toss and ring in the sky. Morning, noon, twilight, and gloomy night succeed each other; the stars and the planets, ruled by the great law of progression, are depicted with medieval *naïveté*, as caught in the hands of the spirits of time.[67]

The upper decorations of the hall (1878)[172] pursue the same theme: Time, Light and the Solar System.[68] At first floor level, the sun and moon, the morning and evening stars, are embodied in painted form. The Guests' Chamber door bears a special reminder: the Early Bird and the Worm. On the ceiling are the emblems of the constellations in the positions in which they were placed when the house was first occupied – a conceit familiar in several of Lord Bute's houses. And the upper flight of stairs is lit by windows recording the sad conclusion of the whole operation: parrots – his favourite birds – support the legend 'W. Burges, 1881'.[69]

Now for the principal apartments. Fame is the theme chosen for the dining room:[70] after all, reputations are made and unmade around the dinner table. The room's surfaces are all impermeable: cooking smells must be excluded from the Palace of Art. The ceiling panels (1881)[170] are enamelled iron, blazoned with symbols of the universe: Sol in the centre, surrounded concentrically by the Planets, the Signs of the Zodiac, the Winds and the Seasons.[71] On the floor, a Turkey carpet. The walls are lined with polished Devonshire marble to a height of six feet.[72] Burges intended to punctuate this formidable dado with four bronze panels sculptured in the likenesses of frogs.[73] These were cast but never installed. Only the focal figure, the Goddess of Fame (1880–81), was inserted above the marble chimneypiece[127]. This figure, supported by a trumpeting angel, was of bronze; its head and hands of ivory; its eyes of sapphire; and in its hand a globe of rock crystal.[74]

> The figure of Fame was in the House of Fame,
> Had al so fele up stondyng eres
> And tonges, as on bestes heres,
> And on hir fete wexen I saugh
> Partiches winges redely.

Such materials – chryselephantine in technique – anticipate the later *art nouveau* sculpture of Alfred Gilbert, William Reynolds-Stevens and George Frampton. Once again, Burges looks ahead of his time. Above the dado runs a tiled frieze of fairy figures[169]: Jack the Giant-Killer, Jack and the Beanstalk, the Yellow Dwarf, the Beast without Beauty and Reynard the Fox; Little Red Riding Hood riding on the Wolf, which in turn draws a chariot containing the Sleeping Beauty; the Dames from the story of Pearls and Toads; Blue Beard and Fatima; Peter Wilkins and his Winged Wife; Robinson Crusoe and Friday, and Robin Hood, Maid Marian and Friar Tuck; St George and the Dragon, Lady Godiva, St Genevieve and the Babes in the Wood; Aladdin followed by the Genie with stained glass windows under his arm; Ali Baba and the Forty Thieves; and Cinderella and her sisters.[75] Tall stories are part of the dining room rite: never were Pantomime figures employed more appropriately.

The windows are filled with figures equally appropriate to a dining room: men and women bearing soup, meat, fish and vegetables.[76] But in one corner stood an escritoire (1867–8)[198] – a relic of Buckingham St, painted by Rossiter – which took up the theme of Fame in a new guise: writing, its processes and purpose.

> On one side an urchin is learning to write; while the monk, his instructor, is punishing him for his slow progress by pulling his ear. In front, a young man who

has written a letter to his lady-love is represented as kissing it before depositing it in the trunk of a tree; a merchant is seen in his counting house writing up his ledger; and on the other side an old man is in the act of making his will. . . . Below are . . . figures illustrative of the estates of life – King, Priest, Warrior, Merchant and Labourer. At the sides there are emblematical figures of History and Poetry, and the portraits of two dogs . . . [Inside] the drawers have pictures [of] various modes of conveying intelligence – an Assyrian carving a cuneiform inscription [A.M. 3267], Sappho with her lyre, [Caxton] working at his press, and a young woman at the telegraph [A.D. 1868].[77]

On the other side of the room, in a gilt and painted sideboard[78] (1875–6) – its oaken drawers lined with marble – Burges kept his cutlery: silver knives and forks (1871), their ivory handles carved with anthropomorphic symbols of food;[79] gem-set, silver spoons (1879 etc.), engraved with grotesques, combining fourteenth-century and Pompeian forms.[80] On either side of the chimney, in a display cabinet[81] and two buffets[82] (1877) of walnut inlaid with box, nestled flagons, decanters, cups and goblets, a veritable treasure trove.

> . . . . cups
> Where nymph and god ran ever round in gold –
> Others of glass as costly – some with gems
> Movable and resettable at will.[83]

Mrs Haweis waxed ecstatic:

Cups of jade, knife-handles, goblets of silver and rock crystal set with gems . . . cameos, pearls, turquoise – cups such as that which Glaucus gave to the gambler Clodius, antique mother-o'-pearl flagons with a long pedigree . . . precious drinking vessels which those who have had the privilege of dining with Mr Burges know the pleasure (and pain) of handling . . .[84]

No wonder Burges supplied a copper cistern in his dining room so that these treasures could be washed after dinner without being removed downstairs.[85]

Burges's ecclesiastical metalwork was outstanding. But his secular silver and jewellery was in some ways more remarkable still. And it merits at least a brief digression. Burges regarded the early Victorian period as the nadir of the jeweller's art.[86] This decline was partly due to the triple division of labour between artist, craftsman and tradesman, and partly to the dearth of satisfactory models. In that respect, the state of jewellery design mirrored the state of the arts in general. Historically speaking, Burges divided jewellery into three kinds: the 'jewels of silver and jewels of gold' – Etruscan, Greek and Roman – in which enamels and precious stones were largely subordinate to their metallic setting; medieval jewellery made up in a fragile or 'frailly' way, almost entirely of precious stones, with just enough metal to hold them together; and Renaissance jewellery, composed chiefly of enamels and precious stones, but with metal appearing at intervals. First Sarno of Naples and then the Castellani family of Rome had revived the production of antique jewellery, copying Pompeian precedents and relics from the Regulini Galassi tomb near Rome, and using workmen from the Apennine village of St Angelo in Vardo.[87] In 1853 Burges had himself studied antique exhibits in the Museo Bourbonico at Naples, and had dicussed with Castellani Jnr the ancient techniques of soldering, setting and frosting. But with regard to medieval work, Burges was almost unique in the 1850s in looking to manuscript sources for inspiration. In particular, he looked to the British Museum. The third historical category, that of Renaissance jewellery, had in Burges's early days scarcely been revived. The Hope Vase[88] or Lord Stamford's Christ at the Column were beyond the skill of mid-Victorian craftsmen. The technique, Burges complained, was just not there: 'it is very galling, in these days of steam-engines and oxy-hydrogen blow-pipes, to be told that the Etruscans had a solder that we cannot obtain – a matter of chemistry, and not of art.'[89] The conjunction in 1862 of the International Exhibition and the Loan Exhibition of historic treasures made painful comparisons inevitable.[90] Even so, by that date, some progress had been made: 'it was [by then even] possible to gaze at a jeweller's window with some feeling of pleasure.'[91] And much of the credit was due to Burges.

As in architecture, so in metalwork, Burges aimed at boldness in every detail. He liked his engraved lines firm and blunt-ended, and his hatching crossed. He preferred figurative or naturalistic details, suitably conventionalised, to any form of geometric patterning. He loved *repoussé* work – bas reliefs bossed-up in silver or gold – as in the great dossal at Florence or the reliquary at Pistoia.[92] Best of all, he loved *cloisonné*: ribbonned filagree with enamelled interstices – Alfred's Jewel, for example;[93] or *champlevé*, where the metal cavities were scooped out and filled with enamels, opaque in the manner of Limoges, or translucent as in the famous Lynn cup.[94] Such techniques were only gradually revived in England in the mid-nineteenth century. The Gothic Revival had almost become a national style. We led the field in ecclesiology. But in the 1850s no English silversmith could match Poussielgue Rusand; no English manufacturer of *champlevé* could rival Barbedienne of Paris. Models for improvement were available: Burges had examined in the Bazaar at Constantinople specimens of nearly every sort of enamelling, imported from Persia – that 'last refuge of the arts of the middle ages'.[95] But enamelling in England lagged behind even the sluggish revival of stained glass. 'I am afraid we shall have no improvement', Burges noted in 1862, 'until such firms as Hardman and Skidmore and Hart take the matter into their own hands, [stop employing jewellery enamellers] and beginning entirely *de novo*, make their own enamels in their own workshops.'[96] That was the remedy eventually adopted, under Burges's own direction, by Barkentin and Krall. In the 1850s, too, much the same was true of *niello* work: decorative insets formed from a composition of sulphate of silver. When Burges tried to commission some, he was told to go to Russia. In this field Skidmore was better than Hardman. But medieval *niello* – as on the Duke of Hamilton's fifteenth-century book covers – remained an impossible model. Of course even enamel and filagree were nothing for Burges without jewels. And jewels set in strips, in the medieval way, *en cabochon*: not cut into facets, but held in a miniature claw or chaton box. 'These strips of jewels, and enamels, and filagree', Burges explained in 1858, 'are the great key to the decorations of jewellery of the Middle Ages . . . around the covers of books, or the edges of the divisions of altars or dossals, or around certain parts of chalices or ewers.'[97]

These jewelled strips are indeed the key to some of the finest treasures in Tower House, in particular to one pair of dining room decanters fit for Aladdin himself. Of 'barbarous opulence, jewel-thick',[98] they formed part of a set of three sketched out by Burges in 1858, designed in 1863–4, and made up in 1865–6.[99][238–239; 240] The first,[1] made by George Angell and Josiah Mendelson, commemorated the publication of *Art Applied to Industry*. It took the form of a pear-shaped bottle of tinted glass with a necking of porphyry, mounted in silver with rich *repoussé* work. Its silver spout is the head of a horned beast; its handle, carved from mother-of-pearl, consists of a weird winged creature with a lion's head, bat's ears and opal eyes, modelled on the ivory pommel of an Assyrian dagger in Burges's own collection.[2] Its cover is a Chinese jade carving of two horses and a monkey. Its mounting is studded with lapis lazuli, Persian seals, mother-of-pearl, Greek silver coins, intaglio gems and semi-precious stones. The second decanter,[3] also by Mendelson and Angell, commemorated the Crimea Memorial Church competition. Similar in design, it was even richer in effect: the bottle is of dark green glass, the necking of malachite, the mounting parcel-gilt; malachite is substituted for lapis lazuli; a rock crystal Chinese lion replaces the jade; the lion's head handle is carved in ivory; the Persian seals are replaced by carved coral; and some of the coins are gilt. The third decanter,[4] made by R. A. Green, was commissioned by James Nicholson[237; VI]. Apart from having its topmost crystal perched on a Gothic turret, the design is very similar to the first two decanters, equally rich and equally eclectic. Finally, to complete the set, Burges had designed two jewelled goblets – one (1862)[5] for his own use, made by Charles Hart[240–241]; another (1863)[6][237] for Nicholson – as gorgeous as the decanters themselves. Around their rims run bands of foliated silver studded with cameos and gems, amethyst, topaz and garnet. Silver and enamel, shaped to touch, and

> Myriads of topaz-lights and jacinth-work
> Of subtlest jewellery.[7]

Nicholson's goblet is slightly taller, more a chalice than a cup.[8] But inside Burges's cup are the creatures of the air, the earth and the sea; and lurking amongst them

Tennyson's Kraken – the menacing monster at the heart of the dream.

All five pieces epitomize Burges's approach to metalwork design. Motifs and materials are widely disparate, skimming the centuries in search of style. Medieval – English, French and Italian – Byzantine, Romanesque, Chinese, Japanese, even Assyrian; bronze, jade and glass, antique coins, crystal, ivory, silver, gold and a bewildering variety of jewels and gems. The *Builder* called them 'some of the best pieces of modern grotesque to be seen'.[9] Here is eclecticism in fantastic vein.

Still more so the claret jug and the cup which Lord and Lady Bute chose as mementoes from Burges's collection. The claret jug (1870)[10][244] celebrated the publication of Burges's *Architectural Drawings*. It consisted of an eighteenth-century Chinese sang-de-boeuf vase mounted in silver-gilt with filigree, enamel and semi-precious stones. Its body is caged with silver straps in a geometrical pattern, studded at each intersection with lumps of Chinese jade and amethyst. Around the neck runs a band of openwork tracery, filagree and coral. And the hinged cover, enamelled inside, is topped with a coral carving in the form of a sphinx and a female face. That was the item chosen by Lord Bute. He suggested to Lady Bute that she chose the Mermaid Bowl (1875).[11][234–235] Nothing could have been more evocative of its owner: gilt brass, decorated with silver and niello; its rim undulating with the sea-monster frieze of his Buckingham St bedroom; its centre engraved with a silver mermaid combing her golden tresses.

> Who would be a mermaid fair
> Singing alone, combing her hair
> Under the sea, in a golden curl
> With a comb of pearl.[12]

But Lady Bute chose the Cat Cup instead. Understandably. The Cat Cup (1867)[13][243] was made by Barkentin in commemoration of the Law Courts competition. Burges turned an architectural set-back into a triumph of decorative design. It takes the form of a Chinese beaker of carved rock crystal, scored with hieroglyphics, gem-set in silver gilt with elaborate enamelling. Its theme is the story of Puss in Boots. The base is set with pearls and opals. Gem-set silver foliage entwines the body of the cup. Six silver mice with blood-red eyes scamper round the rim. Atop the lid, on a nest of crystals, sits a cat of silver and pearl: from its emerald-studded collar drops a sapphire pendant; its eyes glisten with emeralds; beneath its paw a coral ball. And inside the lid Puss in Boots himself, encountering in exquisite enamels a swarm of flies, a rabbit, a giant and a long-haired maiden. The style owes something to twelfth-century France, something to seventeenth-century Nuremberg.[14] Its technical virtuosity sets standards for the finest metalwork of the Arts and Crafts phase. But the overall conception, the range of materials, the ingenuity, the inventiveness, the sheer gusto of design, is peculiarly, triumphantly Burgesian.

All these items were among the treasures regularly in use at Tower House. On special occasions they were displayed *en masse* on tables in the dining room or hall. Three tables in particular were used for this purpose, made of pine and walnut topped with panels of seventeenth-century pietra-dura set in borders of coloured marble. One features a pattern of birds and flowers (1872)[15][199]; another (*c.* 1867) a fountain and butterflies;[16] another (*c.* 1867) a parrot and other exotic birds.[17] Smothered with treasures, they must have glittered like Excalibur[228],

> . . . . rich
> With jewels, elfin Urin on the hilt,
> Bewildering heart and eye.[18]

Here were some extraordinary *bibelots*: an antique crystal salt-cellar, mounted in silver (1875);[19] a rose bowl (1863)[20] and water bottle[21][245]; a 'moss agate bottle', set in a jewelled mount;[22] a set of silver beakers engraved with symbols of the planets;[23] a mazer bowl (1878)[24][236] of burred maple rimmed with silver: one of a set designed by Burges for his friends;[25] a two-handled fruit bowl (1859)[26][230]; a green jade vase (mounted 1862–3)[27] and a white jade tazza (mounted 1875)[28][232]; one or more elaborate epergnes (1867);[29] a shell mounted in silver (1879);[30] a gilded orange on an enamelled stalk (1877);[31] and a battery of tiny crystal bottles encased in silver mounts.[32][231] Many of these treasures have vanished. Where is Burges's enamelled pocket watch?[33] Where is his Early French watch-stand?[34] As prices soar in the auction room, no doubt more pieces will come to light. Meanwhile detailed drawings survive. Burges controlled his silversmiths rigidly. One office drawing for a set of tea-spoons is endorsed by him with a curt note: 'more energy'.[35] that could almost stand as his motto. In their vigour, range and freedom of invention, these pieces of domestic metalwork are surely unique.

Stacy Marks remembered that Burges's talent as a designer of metalwork was 'extraordinary': 'he could design a chalice as well as a cathedral, and draw with his own hand all the necessary details. . . . His decanters, cups, jugs, forks, and spoons were designed with an equal ability to that with which he would design a castle.'[36] Indeed it was this mastery of the subsidiary arts which made Muthesius compare his genius with Pugin's.[37] In the breadth of his scholarship and in his precise knowledge of manufacturing techniques, he was unique among High Victorian designers of metalwork. The early Victorians had begun to master the historicist process. The late Victorians followed Burges still further in breaking down the barriers between artist and craftsman. The High Victorians – and Burges was outstanding in his generation – multiplied the range of available precedents and transformed the quality of available techniques. In the history of nineteenth-century metalwork, therefore, Burges is the link between the 1840s and the 1890s; between the limited medievalism of the age of Pugin and the febrile experiments of the *art nouveau*.

Occasionally Burges designed secular jewellery for presentation to friends and patrons.[38] Occasionally he received a specific secular commission: the ceremonial chain (1874) for the Mayor of Exeter, for instance.[39] But on the whole, apart from his work for Lord Bute, nearly all Burges's secular metalwork was made for Burges himself. Tower House became a veritable jewel chest. And every item was designed for use. Sometimes for very hard use. One day, Emerson called for a drink. Emerson's nephew takes up the story:

> Burges was a man of violent temper and asking Emerson to have a drink, completely failed to open the wine cupboard. Losing his temper, he smashed it to pieces and got the drinks. On being asked if he was going to have it repaired, he said he would throw it away for firewood. Emerson then said 'not the Rossetti panels', and being told 'yes', he asked to keep them and took them home.[40]

'What is the use of having pretty things', Burges used to say, 'unless one makes use of them.'[41]

So much, at last, for the dining room and its treasures. Now we can move into the drawing room[168]. Drawing rooms are traditionally ladies' territory. In Burges's drawing room,[42] therefore, Love is the obvious theme. In three ceiling compartments a medieval Cupid figures as King, Conqueror and Pilgrim.[43] Around the walls, Weekes's mythical lovers (1876–80) pose and pray like figures from a thirteenth-century manuscript:[44] Hero and Leander, Ariadne and Theseus, Pyramis and Thisbe, Cupid and Psyche, Venus and Adonis, Francesca da Rimini, Circe and Ulysses, Lancelot and Guinevere. The windows glimmer – between columns of green serpentine – with birds of splendid plumage and portraits of legendary heroines: Ninon, Rosamond, Aspasia, Cleopatra, Eve, Helen, Galiana, Joan of Arc and Beatrice.[45] This room was unfinished at Burges's death, and has since been altered.[46] But the magic is still potent.

The chimneypiece (1875–6)[125], portraying Chaucer's *Roman de la Rose*, is one of the most glorious that Burges and Nicholls ever produced. Carved out of Caen stone, painted and gilded, it dominates the room, bulging and shimmering like some elephant chameleon. Above, a gorgeous medieval Cupid, below the garden of love.

Gillaume de Lorris dreams that he sees a beautiful garden,

> With high walles embattailed,
> Portrayed without and well entayled
> With many rich portraytures.

These 'portraytures' represent the enemies of Love ... [along] the frieze of the chimneypiece: Poverty, with rents in his dress and a spoon in his cap. Envy, 'that never laugh'. 'Sorrow [that] was painted next Envy on the wall of masonry.'

> Full sad, pale megre also,
> Was never wight so full of woe.

> *Papaladrie* that seemed like a hypocrite. *Viellesse* . . . 'dire and dwined all for elde'
> . . . *Haine*, 'grinning for despitous rage'. Gillaume enters the garden [avoiding
> Danger] through a gate opened by Ideleness (*Oyseuse*), and finds the friends of
> Love dancing beneath the trees . . . handsome men and women in diapered robes,
> with their names written beneath in Provençale. Here are *Largesse, Richesse,
> Joliveté, Liesce, Deduit, Beauté, Dous regars*, and *Franchise*. On the opposite side of
> the chimneypiece to that in which [the Dreamer] is seen entering the garden, he is
> represented as plucking the rose, Jealousy meanwhile looking on.[47]

Nicholls's figures are carved with delicacy and grace. Lethaby, for one, recognised
their expression of the gentler side of medieval art.[48] 'Working together', Handley-
Read concluded, 'Burges and Nicholls had transposed a poem into sculpture with a
delicacy that is very nearly musical. The *Roman de la Rose* has come to life.'[49]

On either side of this chimneypiece, and in one of the side walls, Burges inserted
aumbries or wall cabinets[191–192]. Their doors consisted of painted panels, set in
pairs, taken from a strange upright cabinet (1869) which once stood in Buckingham
St.[50][195] They were probably placed in their new position about 1877. On the left of
the chimney, the Winds; on the right the Oceans, both probably by Weekes.[51] And on
an adjoining wall, Flowers and Fairies in a setting of stars, perhaps by Westlake.[52] The
inspiration of this third pair stems directly from the Westminster retable. But here the
medieval illumination has been transposed into stars of painted lead.[53] Almost as
exotic, and certainly as idiosyncratic, was the adjacent Burgesian armchair. Turned
and bobbined like Lady Bute's bedroom chair at Castell Coch, it managed to combine
Moorish and medieval English sources in an oddly easy alliance.[54][198]

Opposite the drawing room windows stood another Buckingham St piece, the
Medieval or Zodiac Settle (1869–71)[55][196], painted by Stacy Marks against a
background of Turkish embroidery.

> Sol is represented as seated on a throne; while on both sides of him are the signs of
> the Zodiac, engaged in dancing a breakdown. To his right may be seen Leo
> making love to Virgo; Cancer dancing vigorously, supported by the graceful
> Gemini; Taurus and Aries completing the figure. On his left Libra and Scorpio are
> footing it, followed by Sagittarius and Capricorn; then comes the most amusing
> group of Aquarius in the guise of a pump, administering the pledge to two flabby
> Pisces. Outside are the planets playing the dance music. St Cecilia and another
> female figure stand below under graceful foliage.[56]

Burges intended to eliminate chairs almost entirely from this room. In the centre he intended a circular ottoman, gilt, upholstered and decorated in thirteenth-century style. At its centre was to have stood a pedestal bearing a helmet supported by bronze figures.[57] This seems never to have been executed. Even so, Burges's drawing room must be counted one of his more successful creations. The colours and images of a joust or tourney have been compressed into a domestic setting.

In a way, the drawing room, like other rooms in Tower House, is really a jewel-box or receptacle for Burges's bizarre collection of *objects d'art*. Here 'rare and beautiful objects . . .[were assembled] chiefly from Eastern lands – costly jades and crystals from China and Japan, rich embroideries, interesting ivories, exquisite enamels, precious inlays, marvellous metal-work in bronze and silver and gold'.[58] Some of these treasures crowded the shelves of the drawing room's Peacock Cabinet (1873)[59][194], another Buckingham St piece in which jumbled porcelain, ivory and jade rivalled the background polychromy of a peacock's tail. No wonder Tower House seemed to Lethaby 'strange and barbarously splendid'; saturated with Burges's 'passion for colour, sheen and mystery. Here were silver and jade, onyx and malachite, bronze and ivory, jewelled casements, rock crystal orbs, marble inlaid with precious metals; lustre, iridescence and colour everywhere; vermilion and black, gold and emerald; everywhere device and symbolism, and a fusion of Eastern feeling with his [own Early French] style'.[60] Appropriately, here stood the elephant inkstand[227].

Sliding doors lead us from the drawing room into Burges's library. The mood of this room is set at once by its soft furnishings: braided velvet curtains, Anatolian rugs, deep colours and bold patterns. Here the chimneypiece (1875)[124] allegorises 'The Dispersion of the Parts of Speech at the Time of the Tower of Babel':

> The figure of the Assyrian King seated on a lion throne is that of Nimrod [in thirteenth-century garb]. Below, Queen Grammar, issuing from a gate with a portcullis, is seen sending forth the Parts of Speech on their journey. Her robe is embroidered with Hebrew, Greek and Latin alphabets. First in the procession come the Pronouns blowing trumpets, then Queen Verb, accompanied by a little dog and followed by two pages – the Articles, who precede a porter with a bale on his shoulders – the Noun, bearing the burden of the sentence. On the left side of Grammar there are two figures, symbolising Adjective and Adverb; two lovers arm-in-arm, signifying Conjunction and Preposition; and then Interjection, a man who seems shocked at their proceedings; while the note of Interrogation is represented in the curl of the dog's tail.[61]

And there is one final witticism. Around this chimneypiece run the letters of the alphabet, punctuated by a famous Burgesian joke: one letter has fallen below cornice level – the sculptor has dropped his 'H'.

These chimneypieces at Tower House – veritable altars to art – are some of the most amazing pieces of decoration Burges ever designed. 'Built out of cartloads of stone, butting their way out into space, or projecting top-heavily beyond their supports . . . they dominate the room in which they appear.'[62] On the Keatsian principle, here is an art which sets out to 'surprise by a fine excess'. In the library at Tower House the excess is very fine indeed. Haig's R.A. perspective was one of the hits of 1880.[63]

From the circular panels in the pitch-pine ceiling, six lawyers or theologians gaze down: Moses, St Paul, Luther, Mahomet, Aristotle and Justinian. The six windows overlooking the garden – from cartoons by Weekes – glow with allegories of Art and Science: Architecture (with Burges himself brandishing a plan of Tower House) and Sculpture; Poetry and Music; Astronomy and Chemistry (with the chemist's bottle labelled 'Aperient'); Literature and Manufacture; Science and Navigation; Painting and Agriculture.[64] There are no hanging lights, indeed there are very few hanging lamps – and no gas lights – anywhere in Tower House. Short-sighted Burges preferred to work at close range with a colza lamp perched by his papers. Comfort and space are guaranteed by generous divans, under the library windows and on either side of the fire. The walls are covered with fitted bookcases – the Alphabet Bookcases – or rather book cabinets, studded with marble and glazed foil, glowing with countercharged colours, and painted with a symbolic alphabet by Weekes (1876)[175]. 'A', for example, is an Architect (Burges himself, directing the building of Tower House); 'G' a glazier (the ubiquitous Saunders); 'K' a knave (anon.); 'P' a painter (Weekes himself); 'S' a sculptor (Nicholls, presumably), and so on.[65] Inside, the bookcase doors are painted with birds by Stacy Marks.[66] Between these cases the walls appear, covered with rough hessian painted with gilded patterns. And above the bookcase battlements glitters a frieze, embossed and gilded. Even the window blinds were decorated with appliqué work by Fisher. And the colza-oil table lamps were equal to their ambience: the oil containers were covered, not with china or glass cases, but with a series of two-inch rims from Japanese *cloisonné* enamel boxes, joined together by bronze rings.[67]

It was probably in the library that there stood a vital Buckingham St trophy, the Architecture Cabinet (?1858)[68][178]: 10 ft high, on stilt-like legs, and bristling with bulbous finials, as idiosyncratic as any piece of furniture Burges ever designed.

> Four massive square-cut pieces of timber form its supports; the lower part open, with rails on which to rest his portfolios; the upper storey – it is more like a house than a modern cabinet – is enclosed with folding doors, and above this is a machicolated parapet and a gabled roof of high pitch crowned with massive finials. The two armoires at Bayeux and Noyon had been at the bottom of it all.[69]

Indeed they had. The Architecture Cabinet rivals the Yatman Cabinet as Burges's earliest piece of painted furniture. It was exhibited in 1859.[70] But perhaps because it was not published until 1870–73,[71] its chronological significance has been overlooked. Godwin's testimony is clear: 'designed more than twenty years before [his death] . . . it stood at his elbow all the best years of his life, and though designed to contain only a few pigeon-holes for letters, it is both in contrivance and decoration full of quaint conceits ... [and is essentially] representative of the man.'[72] These conceits included painted allegories of 'the disagreeables of architecture, viz. Contract, represented as a hideous monster cut to pieces, because contracts are often broken; Measuring and Valuing, a monster with a rule; Arbitration, a monster showing an empty oystershell; Specification, a monster writing; Extras, a mermaid playing on a shell [temptation!]; Law, a monster, his tail interlaced with pieces of money ...'.[73]

Appropriately, the library at Tower House was dominated by Burges's most celebrated Buckingham St trophy: the Great Bookcase (1859–62; 1878)[74][VIII]. This remarkable piece of furniture was designed to contain Burges's collection of books on art. It was designed in 1859; it was perhaps made up by the firm of Thomas Seddon; and it was finished in time for the International Exhibition of 1862.[75] The theme of its decoration is Pagan and Christian Art, expressed in allegories of poetry, architecture, sculpture, painting and music. On the right or Pagan side: Rhodopis ordering the building of a pyramid (by E. J. Poynter); Sappho serenading Phaon (by Henry Holiday[76]); Apelles painting the first portrait (by Frederick Smallfield); and Pygmalion and Galatea (by Simeon Solomon). On the left or Christian side: St John and the New Jerusalem (by Solomon); the apparition of Beatrice to Dante (Dante by Poynter; Beatrice by D. G. Rossetti); Edward I and Torrel (by Albert Moore); and Fra Angelico painting the Virgin (by Thomas Morten). On the sides are St Augustine (by Solomon) and Plato (by Charles Rossiter); St Cecilia (by Morten) and Orpheus (by W. F. Yeames); the Sirens (by J. A. Fitzgerald); and the Harpies (by Fred Weekes). On the base appear four Metamorphosic figures: Arachne, the Pierides and Syrinx (all by Stacy Marks[77]). And running horizontally between each major section are bands of decoration by Poynter, symbolising Sea, Earth and Air: the shells and fishes of the ocean; the flowers and beasts of the field; the birds of the air; the stars of the firmament – as well as Aesop's Fables and the Story of Cock Robin (executed, like the eight spandrels of the arches across the centre, by Burges himself). Crowning the whole composition are the Muses (all by Poynter) inset along the cornice; and three painted gables: Religion and Love (both by N. J. N. Westlake) flanking Art, the centrepiece of the whole scheme (appropriately by E. Burne-Jones). Inside the doors are birds (by Stacy Marks). Finally, as if such a Pre-Raphaelite galaxy were insufficient, when the overladen bookcase fell in 1878,[78] Burges seems to have commissioned Weekes to add an extra band of decoration – allegories of eight Metals, replacing damaged images by Fitzgerald – above the Indian marble shelf.

Fourteen different artists in all. No wonder Handley-Read concluded that this Great Bookcase occupied 'a unique position in the history of Victorian painted furniture'.[79] Ten feet high and five feet wide, it was the bulkiest piece Burges ever designed. Its overall design is architectural: podium, entablature, cornice and gable. But these vestigially tectonic elements are almost lost in a swirling mass of pictorial form. Almost, but not quite. The painted furniture of Morris and Webb is little more than an easel or framework for paintings. Burges manages to incorporate pictorial elements without destroying the apparent structure of the design.

And now upstairs. Up the spiral steps to the Golden Chamber: guest's bedroom ·or nuptial bower. Mrs Haweis was overwhelmed:

> Up a narrow winding stair of stone, lighted with coloured windows and protected by soft curtains, we reach the bedrooms. What bedrooms! The guest chamber is made of fire and flowers . . . the bed, toilet-table, washstand, cabinets, are all plain gold. The shutters are plain gold. The windows[80] glow with [the] colours . . . [of] the *Alhambra*. . . . Through Moorish trellis work[81] these colours shine, the subjects being only visible by scrutiny. What is not pure gold is crystal; the knobs on the bedposts, the shelves of the tables, scintillate with facets. The whole room is like an ancient shrine or reliquary.[82]

Butterflies flutter across the ceiling (1879)[83][171]; frogs and mice wage war along the beams; the shutters glitter with painted figures ringing in the dawn;[84] flowers and plants festoon the frieze.[85] In the centre of the ceiling Burges placed one of those small convex mirrors he first used at Gayhurst. And from the centre of the four panels hang four emu's eggs – symbols of generation.[86] Above the red marble chimneypiece – graven with monsters grotesque and chained – a gilt china case (1878)[87] groaned beneath its burden of Eastern ceramics. Close by stood a dressing table topped with onyx and bluejohn (1879),[88] two tall gabled mirrors,[89] and a pier table (1880)[90] topped with mosaic from Sta Maria in Trastevere – its stones taken from the spot where St Paul preached to the Romans. Sleeping in this great room must have been an aesthetic feast. At least one visitor remembered creeping, 'somewhat abashed, . . . into the gorgeous bed, to awake in the early morning with just enough light streaming through the Oriental-like shutters to enable us to study . . . the brilliant decoration'; and the thought arose, 'was even the great Edward ever sheltered so well?'[91]

The guests' bed (1879)[202–203][92] glistens with gold leaf. Crystal bed knobs;[93] animal carvings by Nicholls;[94] bevelled silver plate glass; sunken panels filled with lapis lazuli or porphyry, glazed tinsel foil, or miniature 'missal' paintings on vellum. . . . And on the bedhead, Weekes's 'Judgement of Paris' (1872).[95] The three rival goddesses are clothed in thirteenth-century garb; Mercury stands on one side; Paris on the other, bowing towards Venus, whose robes are embroidered with hearts and doves.

The guests' (or 'Vita Nuova') washstand (1879–80)[201] is no less splendid than the bed. Mrs Haweis:

> Up to now a washstand has seemed an impertinent sort of affair, to be kept out of sight; but here we have a gem fit to splash at all day in poetic enjoyment. It is of gold, with fragments of bright stones and shells inlaid; those called *Venus's ears*

have been largely used. Every blank space is carved minutely in flowers, beautifully tinted, and we discern a lizard or two and some butterflies among them. Thick crystals inclose small shells, where a scent bottle, some hundreds of years old, and a toothpowder receptacle, some thousands, nestle and shine. Marble plates receive the soap. A fine bronze, which most of us would place on some table for ornament, here makes itself useful – a bull, from whose throat ajar the water pours into a *Brescia* basin, inlaid with silver fishes. How do you get the water in? See you that other bronze, a tortoise, which seems to creep beyond the bull's fell reach – it is a plug; twist him round and the bull fills the basin. Such is the use which *Aladdin* makes of bronzes, and I beg to add that the lapis and amber and crystal and marble are not *papier-maché* and glazed chalk – they are the real thing.[96]

Indeed they are. The Brescia marble basin is set on jewelled bearings; the horned-beast water tap is cast in bronze and damascened in gold; the gilded mahogany sides are inset with mother-of-pearl; even the soap trays were to be of Siena or Brocatella marble.[97] And the table-shelf is formed of very fine mosaic, in which are inserted plaques of porphyry, lapis lazuli, verde-antiche, giallo-antico and other semi-precious marbles.[98]

Guests hung their clothes in the Philosophy Cabinet (1878–9)[200][99] – so called, because it was painted with 'the troubles of philosophers and literary men'. First we see Socrates instructing a youth, whilst Xantippe pours water on his head. Next appears Martin Luther, disturbed in his studies by the devil-sent woman – but all is not lost: in his right hand he conceals an inkstand ready to hurl at the head of his tormentor. Next comes Aristotle: he bears the burden of a wife who simultaneously flirts with Alexander. The fourth figure is that of Diogenes, lecturing youth from a barrel while Lais eggs on a mischievous urchin to distract him. On the sides appear two figures fleeing the torments of matriarchy: Virgil and St Paul, escaping with ropes from open windows. To complete the allegory domestic animals gambol merrily, while below lurks the crocodile of lust.

Close to the guests' bedroom, Burges placed the armoury, sometimes called the study or Venus room. In its chimneypiece (1877),[129] carved by Nicholls, there are three medallions: Juno spinning, Minerva studying and Venus preening herself in a mirror.

> Juno nocte la vie active
> Et Pallas la contemplative
> Venus vie volupteuse.[1]

Stained glass roundels – Sapphire, Emerald, Diamond, Pearl, Ruby, Topaz – filter the outside light, as in the Clock Tower at Cardiff. Here Burges hung his collection of armour.[2] The armoury or Dante bookcase (between 1862 and 1869)[187] was another treasured piece from his Buckingham St study. Its lower doors – the Inferno – boasted figures of Cerberus, the Centaur Nessus, the Minotaur and Geryon. Each monster had a human head: portraits of four of Burges's friends. On one side were medallion heads of St Thomas of Canterbury; Etnizza and Justinian; a full-length figure of Leah; and, below, Dante and Vergil. On the other side were medallions of St Benedict, Constanza and Trajan; a full-length figure of Rachel; and, below, Charon.[3]

On the top floor, two attic rooms did duty – or prepared to do duty – as day nursery and night nursery. The day nursery chimneypiece (1877)[130] is one of Burges's most bizarre creations: through its entablature and hood grow the roots and tendrils of a beanstalk; below its corbel Jack climbs boldly upwards; and at its summit lurks the dreadful Giant, fanged and bearded, his taloned fingers bursting through the surface of the masonry.[4] The night nursery chimneypiece (1877)[128] is understandably less terrifying. Here three monkeys play at ball, skipping impishly about the chimney.[5] Both pieces, of course, were carved by Nicholls.

Inside the day nursery were at least two interesting pieces of furniture: the wardrobe and the 'Dog Cabinet'. The wardrobe (1875) was painted with comic sartorial symbolism: Adam, expelled from Paradise, is presented with a shirt, drawers, stockings, boots, vest and cloak; while below runs a comic procession of brushes, razors, combs, etc.[6] The 'Dog Cabinet' (1869)[193] was more ambitious: a Burgesian parody on a theme by Eastlake, panelled with portraits of his pet dogs painted by Rossiter.[7]

> His friends well remember Dandie, who was at times a terror to them; Bogie, the mother of numerous progeny; and the accomplished Pinkie, who died of old age not many years before his master. These dogs and their descendants were all portrayed on this remarkable piece of furniture. Dandie, on account of his quarrelsome disposition, has a copy of Dr Watts' Hymns before him; Bogie has a rat; Tiger a pen; the puppies Snob, Yokel, Swell and Curate occupy the angles, and Mrs Pullan's Pet and Peter the sides of the cabinet.[8]

Alas, like a number of other items from Tower House, this happy piece of canine nonsense has disappeared.

These attic rooms seem never to have been completely finished. But the nursery in particular contains four stained glass windows of familiar Burgesian pattern: Salamander, Sylph, Gnome and Undine.[9] They need not detain us long. It is time to descend the stairs again, and enter the Scarlet Chamber, the holy of holies: Burges's own Mermaid Bedroom.

Deep scarlet is the primary colour here, opaque and shiny, growing rich and dark, like dried blood; a background foil to the gold and silver of its subsidiary decorations (1878).[10] Against a backcloth like that even the darkest hues glow brightly. The carpet is Persian. The ceiling is studded with tiny convex mirrors set in stars of gilded lead, and designed to reflect the candlelight like stars in a midnight sky.[11][173] It is a ceiling which is fantastically eclectic, even by Burgesian standards, combining hints of Palermo, Florence, Cairo and medieval Suffolk. And – visually speaking – it sets out the room's bizarre terms of reference: the sky at night overlaps the sleeper as he drifts far out to sea. Fishes and eels weave their way through the mazy undulations of the frieze.[12] The famous mermaid chimneypiece (1877)[13][126] is irridescent with silver and gold. This is the definitive Burgesian mermaid. Her pedigree goes back via the Mermaid Bowl, Knightshayes and Gayhurst, to Viollet-le-Duc and the Cluny Museum, and ultimately back to early Christian symbolism.[14] Here she presides, coy and stately, over Burges's inner sanctum. Gazing into a looking-glass, combing her hair in the breeze, she rides above a foaming sea, through carved, tentacular waves of Japanese delicacy, painted on silver foil and tipped with real silver. Around her head are scattered sprigs of coral and seaweed. Above, an infant mermaid rises from a bed of shells. Burges's collection of Japanese prints seems to have provided him with inspiration here. But the spirit, even the forms, of *art nouveau* are already present. Comparisons have been made with Hokusai, Mackintosh and Gaudi.[15] And Burges's protean genius makes such comparisons perfectly feasible. By stretching the eclectic process to its limit he underlines the infinite flexibility of historicist modes. By shrugging off functionalist inhibitions, he not only anticipates the inventiveness and freedom of *art nouveau*; he holds out a beacon of inspiration in a world of sub-modernist mediocrity.

And yet this is a very private room, introverted and precious. The symbols scattered on beam and bedpost – the Rosicrucian alembic; the heart menaced by spears – seem curiously appropriate. Menaced by reality – threatened in particular by the conundrum of a New Style – Burges fled into a dream world of his own creation, a veritable Palace of Art.

Happily, humour will keep breaking in. Here stood a chest of drawers painted by Rossiter with comic allegories of its contents: an old woman mending stockings; a man with a towel; a girl mending a pocket handkerchief; a man at dinner with a napkin; a man trying on a shirt; and a sandwich man advertising a perfect fit. On either side it was painted with 'Clean Clothes' (an Oxford man in fresh flannels) and 'Dirty Clothes' (a navvy in a clay-stained smock).[16] Above it Burges placed a 'Stand for Cabinets' (c.1876), lighter than usual, its slender gilt columns standing out against a background of Eastern embroideries.[17]

Burges's dressing table – the 'Crocker Dressing Table' (1867)[18][188] – must have been one of his favourite pieces. He certainly added decoration to it as the years went on. It is an extraordinary design. The form of the finials comes from an armoire at Beauvais, via Viollet-le-Duc.[19] In the centre of, and surrounding, the circular mirror are portraits of the Crocker sisters by Smallfield.[20] Now the idea of a circular mirror surrounded by circular mirrors had already been used by Burges in the sideboard shown at the 1862 Exhibition. Burne-Jones used the same trick in 'Rosamund's

Bower'.[21] And both men were perhaps thinking of a looking glass in a picture by Van Eyck.[22] But the materials in Burges's dressing table are the product of his own brain:

> Lunettes of transparent glass with arabesques traced in gold, insertions of tin and mother of pearl, a slab of marble mosaic, steel hinges a quarter of an inch thick, drawer handles of tinned iron, finger rings of nickel-plated brass laid on fragments of velvet, Arabian trellis work framing portraits in oil . . . . and a cluster of bevelled mirrors set within revolving hoops. Flashing colours and unexpected reflections are allied in this splendid piece of Burges-Gothic to a fine overall silhouette. Few designers at this date would have used nickel on brass; none, perhaps, would have put in the cluster of bevelled mirrors, a device that later became commonplace.[23]

Here, as so often elsewhere, Burges is part of a fashion and yet outside it.

Burges's bed (1865–7)[24][185] encapsulates his elaborate dream-world. It is built of mahogany, painted blood red, carved with lions and bulbous finials, stencilled and gilded, and inset with paintings on glass and inlays of shell and tinsel. The bedstead itself glows with Holiday's Sleeping Beauty panel (1866).[25][186] Now Holiday's composition follows closely a marginal illustration in Burges's own illuminated copy of Tennyson's *Poems*.[26] The poem in question is 'The Day Dream': here Burges himself has become the Dreamer, asleep in his Palace of Art. As he lies dreaming, the sleeper is shrouded in a Chinese mandarin's robe, richly embroidered on a purple ground.[27] From the same bed, in Buckingham St, Burges had gazed upwards into the swirling monsters of the deep. In the Mermaid Chamber at Tower House, waking or sleeping, Aladdin is enveloped in the mazy waters of the sea, his reflection multiplied a thousand-fold in the star-shaped mirrors of the ceiling.

Next to the chimneypiece stood the Narcissus Washstand (1865–7),[28][189–90] an object long familiar in Buckingham St. Its red and gold decoration picks up a theme from Chaucer's *Romaunt of the Rose*:

> This is the Mirrour Perrilus in which the Proude Narcissus sey al his fair face bright.

The panels[29] were apparently first painted by Fitzgerald in 1866, and then apparently repainted by Weekes in 1872, when the lettering was renewed and border decorations added. Grotesque bronze creatures take on the duty of taps. The bronze shaving bowl boasts a silver frog. And Jennings's patent tip-up basin is cut out of solid marble and inlaid with five gold and silver fish.[30] These fishes may have been inspired by Carolingian prototypes from the Treasury of St Denis.[31] But they are treated with typically Burgesian wit.

It was this Narcissus Washstand which achieved a kind of posthumous immortality by haunting Evelyn Waugh's *alter ego*, Gilbert Pinfold.

A friend in London, James Lance [*sc.* Sir John Betjeman] who shared his taste in furniture, found, and offered him as a present a most remarkable piece; a wash-hand stand of the greatest elaboration designed by an English architect in the 1860s, a man not universally honoured but of magisterial status to Mr Pinfold and his friends. This massive freak was decorated with metal work and mosaic, and with a series of panels painted in his hot youth by a rather preposterous artist who later became President of the Royal Academy.

Alas! 'an essential part was missing . . . . a prominent, highly ornamental, copper tap'. Visions of this 'missing member' disturbed and baffled Pinfold's chloralised brain.[32]

Waugh's tragi-comedy was more appropriate than he knew. Next to Burges's bed stood a wardrobe (1859, 1870 and 1878–9),[33][174] painted by Smallfield with symbolic devices: a girl with distaff, signifying flax; a piping shepherd, signifying wool; shears, bobbins and other tailor's tools signifying clothing. Inside are Tennyson and Chaucer, twin founts of Burgesian inspiration, surrounded by a bevy of legendary heroines: Eve, Lucrezia, Fair Rosamund, Margaret Roper, Helen of Troy, Queen Elizabeth, Jephthah's daughter, Joan of Arc, Cleopatra, Iphigenia, Eleanor of Castile, Dido of Carthage and Medea. Truly a strange assembly. And on the side immediately next to the bed – within reach even – a stranger set of paintings: stylised poppies. Was this the cupboard of an opium smoker? As Burges slept beneath the mirrored waves, did narcotics blur the limits of reality? Surely, here in the Mermaid Bedroom, the boundaries limiting life and art, time and place, have been dissolved; the barriers blown. Did he know the eighteenth-century Chinese novel, the *Dream of the Red Chamber*?[34] Here in Burges's own red chamber, the Oriental overtones of the High Victorian Dream are at their most seductive.

Burges designed Tower House as 'a model residence of the thirteenth century'.[35] It was the most complete example of a medieval secular interior produced by the Gothic revival, and the last. Like Street's Law Courts in the sphere of public building, Tower House represents the *ne plus ultra* of domestic Gothic. As Rossetti and Morris said of Red House, it is 'a Palace of Art', 'more a poem than a house'.[36] But the interior of Tower House makes Red House look anaemic and jejune. No other architect produced such a bizarre expression of his own ego. Godwin called it 'one of the most remarkable houses that the Gothic Revival has given to the world'. 'A red-hot medievalist', he explained, might simply have produced a pastiche, a replica of Little Wenham Hall for instance. But Burges 'could distinguish between Archaeology and Art . . . . [he] was . . . . an evolutionist or developist rather than a revivalist'. At Tower House 'the art of the thirteenth century' reaches us 'through Burges'; 'and [it] is just as original in its way as Turneresque landscape or Macaulayan history'.[37] Lethaby too recognised this magical, alchemical process which converted archaeology into art. Tower House left him gasping: 'massive, learned, glittering, amazing'.[38]

Shortly before his death, Burges showed the future Sir William Richmond round his near-completed dream. As they entered the Mermaid Chamber, Richmond started back in terror: in a pre-vision of uncanny clarity, he saw Burges lying dead upon the bed.[39] Was he wearing his opal ring, his 'Rosicrucian' cross?[40] [248] Burges had certainly prepared himself for that moment. His health had never been robust. And only a few months before the end he took the precaution of dictating an abbreviated version of his diary, thus ensuring an accurate record of his life and work.[41] On his last visit to Cardiff, 28 March 1881, he 'had a long ride in a dog cart and got very cold'.[42] Somehow he struggled back to Tower House. There he lingered, half paralysed, for three weeks. He died on 20th April, and was buried at Norwood Cemetery, in the tomb he designed for his mother.[43] Oscar Wilde and Whistler were almost his last visitors. As he lay dying, the dreamer amidst his dreams, his shaky fingers sketched out one last fantastic chimneypiece.[44]

PART THREE

*Photographic Survey of the Work
of William Burges*

[The figures in square brackets in the text refer to the illustrations.]

LIST OF ILLUSTRATIONS

ARCHITECTURE: ECCLESIASTICAL

ARCHITECTURE: SECULAR

70 St Anne's Court, Soho (1864–5). *Building News* xiv (1867), 24/6.
71 Skilbeck's Warehouse, Upper Thames St, London (1865–6). *Building News* xiii (1866), 780.
72 St Anne's Court, Soho: exterior; since demolished. Photo: G.L.C.
73 Gayhurst, Bucks.: the privy (1859–60). Photo: A.F. Kersting.
74 Trinity College, Hartford, Connecticut, U.S.A.: prospective scheme (1873–4). *Building News* xvi (1874), 418.
75 Trinity College: Northam Towers (1882).
76 Speech Room, Harrow School: Burges's original scheme (1871). *Architect* xxvii (1882), 221.
77 Harrow Speech Room: modified design (1874). Harrow School Archives.
78 Castell Coch, Glamorgan: Burges's original scheme (1871–2). *Architect* xi (1874), 212.
79 Cardiff Castle, Clock Tower : plans and sections. *Architect* xxvii (1882), 203.
80 Cardiff Castle: a late eighteenth-century view from the North East. Mount Stuart Archives.
81 Cardiff Castle: the same view, showing Burges's additions. N.M.R.
82 Cardiff Castle: a late eighteenth-century view from the North West. Mount Stuart Archives.
83 Cardiff Castle: the same view, showing Burges's additions. N.M.R.
84 Castell Coch: view from the East. N.M.R.
85 Castell Coch: inner courtyard, looking South East. N.M.R.
86 Castell Coch: view from the North. N.M.R.
87 Rothesay Castle, Isle of Bute: visionary reconstruction (1871–2). J.K. Harrison, *The Isle of Bute in the Olden Time* ii (1895), frontispiece.
88 Castell Coch, during construction, in 1878. Photo: F. Bedford.
89 Cardiff Castle: the rustic bridge (1875), in 1878. Photo: F. Bedford.
90 Cardiff Castle, during construction, in 1878. Photo: F. Bedford.
91 Cardiff Castle: the Clock Tower from the courtyard, in 1879. Photo: F. Bedford.

SCULPTURE

92 Florence Cathedral: Burges's design for the West front (1863). Archivio Opera di S Maria del Fiore de Firenze.
93 Knightshayes, Devon: figure over entrance (*c.* 1869), carved by Thomas Nicholls. Photo: Robert Chapman.
94 St Augustine's Canterbury: missionary monument (1858–9), carved by Theodore Phyffers. Pullan, *Designs of W. Burges*, 4.
95 Lille Cathedral: Burges's design for the baldacchino (1856). Diocesan Archives, Lille.
96 Dossal, All Saints Episcopal Church, Edinburgh (1870): preliminary sketches by Burges. R.I.B.A.
97 Dossal, All Saints Episcopal Church, Edinburgh (1870): model by Nicholls. R.I.B.A.
98 All Saints, Fleet, Hants.: Lefroy monument (1861), carved by Nicholls. Photo: John Rawson.
99 Ricketts Monument (1867–8), Kensal Green Cemetery. Photo: the Author.
100 Gayhurst, Bucks.: the Caliban Staircase (1859–61). Photo: A. F. Kersting.
101 Gayhurst: Dining-Room chimneypieces (1861), carved by Nicholls. Photo: A. F. Kersting.

102 Worcester College, Oxford: Chapel. Finial (1864) modelled by Nicholls, carved by Robinson. Photo: A. F. Kersting.

103 Worcester College, Oxford: Hall. Chimneypiece (1877), carved by Fucigna. Photo: A. F. Kersting.

104 Worcester College Chapel: lectern and candelabrum (1865), modelled by Nicholls and carved by Jacquet. *Building News* xv (1868), 162.

105 Skelton: organ loft (1873), carved by Nicholls. Photo: A. F. Kersting.

106 Studley Royal: font (1874–5), modelled by Nicholls. Photo: A. F. Kersting.

107 Skelton: font (1874–5),carved byNicholls. Photo: A. F. Kersting.

108 Cork Cathedral: pulpit (1873–4). Photo: T. F. Shepherd.

109 Cork Cathedral: font (1869). Photo T. F. Shepherd.

110 Cork Cathedral: gargoyle (1868) on the West front – the Triumph of Virtue over Vice – carved by McLeod. Photo: T. F. Shepherd.

111 Cork Cathedral: gargoyle (1868) on the West front – the Triumph of Virtue over Vice – carved by McLeod. Photo: T. F. Shepherd.

112 Cork Cathedral: West front. Evangelistic beasts (1869–70), modelled by Nicholls, carved by Harrison; Resurrection tympanum (1878–9), carved by Nicholls; Portal bridegroom and virgins (1879–83), carved by Nicholls. Photo: T. F. Shepherd.

113 Cork Cathedral: plaster models in the North West tower. Photo: T. F. Shepherd.

114 Cork Cathedral: the David Door (1879; 1889), carved by McLeod and Nicholls. Photo: T. F. Shepherd.

115 Cork Cathedral: sedilia (1879–80), modelled by Nicholls, carved by Walden. Photo: T. F. Shepherd.

116 Oakwood Court, Bingley, Yorks: Drawing-Room chimneypiece (1865), in *c.* 1870; carved by Nicholls. Photo: Garnett colln.

117 Oakwood Court: Dining-Room chimneypiece (1865), in *c.* 1870; carved by Nicholls. Photo: Garnett colln.

118 Treverbyn Vean, Cornwall: the St Neot chimneypiece (*c.* 1860) in *c.* 1870; carved by Philip. Photo: Cocks colln.

119 Cardiff Castle: sea-lion on the 'animal wall' (1887–8), carved by Nicholls. N.M.R.

120 Cardiff Castle: doorways (*c.* 1876) at the foot of the Octagon Staircase, in 1878, carved by Nicholls. Photo: F. Bedford.

121 Cardiff Castle: Dining-Room chimneypiece (1873), carved by Nicholls. N.M.R.

122 Cardiff Castle: Library chimneypiece (1874), carved by Nicholls. Four figures represent the Greek, Assyrian, Hebrew and Egyptian alphabets; the fifth supposedly represents Lord Bute. N.M.R.

123 Cardiff Castle: Summer Smoking Room, Burges's final designs for the corbels. *Architect* viii (1872), 142.

124 Tower House: the Babel chimneypiece (1875) in the Library, carved by Nicholls. N.M.R.

125 Tower House: the *Roman de la Rose* chimneypiece (1875–6) in the Drawing-Room, carved by Nicholls. N.M.R.

126 Tower House: the Mermaid chimneypiece (1877) in Burges's Bedroom, carved by Nicholls. Photo: G.L.C.

127 Tower House: the Fame chimneypiece (1880–1) in the Dining-Room, modelled by Nicholls, cast by Moore. Photo: A. F. Kersting.

128 Tower House: the Monkey chimneypiece (1877) in the Night Nursery, carved by Nicholls. Pullan, *House of W. Burges*, 35.

129 Tower House: the Venus chimneypiece (1877) in the Armoury, carved by Nicholls. Pullan, *House of W. Burges*, 34.

130 Tower House: the Jack and the Giant chimneypiece (1877) in the Day Nursery, carved by Nicholls. Photo: A. F. Kersting.

PAINTED DECORATION, STAINED GLASS, MOSAIC, ETC.

131 Worcester College, Oxford: Burges's scheme for the Hall (1873). Worc. Coll. Archive.

132 Worcester College, Oxford: the Chapel (1864–70). Photo: A. F. Kersting.

133 Gayhurst, Bucks.: the Abbess's Room (1861; 1872). Painted by F. Smallfield. Photo: A. F. Kersting.

134 Harrow School: Burges's scheme for the Speech Room (1871). *Architect* xxvii (1882), 221.

135 St Paul's Cathedral: Burges's model showing proposed decoration (1874). Pullan, *Designs of W. Burges*, 1.

136 St Paul's Cathedral: Burges's model, as adapted by Sir William Richmond. Cathedral Archives.

137 Skelton: reredos (1873). Photo: A. F. Kersting.

138 Salisbury Cathedral: Chapter House. Burges's polychromatic decoration (*c.* 1857). Sculptor: J. B. Philip; artist: Octavius Hudson; manufacturer: H. Minton. N.M.R.

139 Cork Cathedral: chancel mosaic (1877), from cartoons by H. W. Lonsdale. *Building News* xxxviii (1880), 130.

140 Cork Cathedral: details of choir wall (*c.* 1876). Photo: T. F. Shepherd.

141 Tower House: Minotaur mosaic (*c.* 1877). Photo: G.L.C.

142 Studley Royal: chancel Te Deum (*c.* 1874); painted by H. W. Lonsdale (?). Photo: A. F. Kersting.

143 Skelton: Parable window in the South aisle (*c.* 1872); manufactured by Saunders, from sketches by Lonsdale and cartoons by Weekes. Photo: A. F. Kersting.

144 Studley Royal: sanctuary dome (*c.* 1874); painted by H. W. Lonsdale (?). Photo: A. F. Kersting.

145 Studley Royal: Revelation windows in the chancel (*c.* 1873); manufactured by Saunders, from sketches by Lonsdale and cartoons by Weekes. Photo: Gordon Barnes.

146 Cardiff Castle: Winter Smoking Room (1870–3), Clock Tower. Painted by F. Weekes and H. W. Lonsdale. A perspective by Axel Haig (1870).

147 Cardiff Castle: Peristyle (1873–6), Bute Tower, in 1878. Elijah tiles manufactured by Simpson, from cartoons by Lonsdale; bronze Madonna modelled by Fucigna, cast by Hatfield. Photo: F. Bedford.

148 Cardiff Castle: Lord Bute's Sitting Room (*c.* 1874), Bute Tower, in 1878; door painted with the Seven Deadly Sins by Sir William Douglas. Photo: F. Bedford.

149 Cardiff Castle: Lord Bute's Bedroom (1874–5), Bute Tower, in 1878. Sculpture: Fucigna; painting: Campbell. Photo: F. Bedford.

150 Cardiff Castle: Winter Smoking Room, in 1878. Photo: F. Bedford.

151 Cardiff Castle: Summer Smoking Room (1871–4), Clock Tower, in 1878. Painting: F.

Weekes and H. W. Lonsdale; sculpture: T. Nicholls. Tiles manufactured by Simpson. Photo: F. Bedford.

152 Cardiff Castle: Summer Smoking Room (1871–4), Clock Tower, in 1878. Painting: F. Weekes and H. W. Lonsdale; sculpture: T. Nicholls. Tiles manufactured by Simpson. Photo: F. Bedford.

153 Cardiff Castle: Lord Bute's Bedroom, Clock Tower, in 1878. Painted by F. Weekes and H. W. Lonsdale. Photo: F. Bedford.

154 Summer Smoking Room, painted vault, in 1878. Photo: F. Bedford.

155 Summer Smoking Room: tulip vases (1874).

156 Cardiff Castle: the Oratory (*c.* 1869–76). Painting: N.J.N. Westlake; sculpture: Fucigna.

157 Cardiff Castle: the Octagon Staircase (*c.* 1874–81). Painted by Campbell.

158 Cardiff Castle: Chaucer Room (*c.* 1877–90). Sculpture: Nicholls; Painting: Lonsdale. Photo: B.B.C.

159 Cardiff Castle: Banqueting Hall (*c.* 1875–93). Sculpture: Nicholls; Painting: Lonsdale.

160 Cardiff Castle: Arab Room (*c.* 1878–81). Painting by Campbell; stained glass by Saunders. N.M.R.

161 Cardiff Castle: Arab Room (*c.* 1878–81). Painting by Campbell; stained glass by Saunders. N.M.R.

162 Cardiff Castle: Burges's scheme for the Great Staircase; from a perspective by Axel Haig (1874). *Architect* xii (1874), 6.

163 Castell Coch: Drawing-Room (1879–87). Sculpture: T. Nicholls; furniture: J. S. Chapple; painting: C. and T. Campbell. N.M.R.

164 Castell Coch: Banqueting Hall (*c.* 1878–9). Sculpture: Nicholls; furniture: Chapple; mural painting: Campbell and Smith, from cartoons by Lonsdale. N.M.R.

165 Castell Coch: Drawing-Room, painted vault. N.M.R.

166 15, Buckingham St, Strand, London: Burges's Office, in *c.* 1876. Murals (1861), painted by Westlake (?); stained glass (1860) by Edward Burne-Jones. Burges, 'Own Furniture'.

167 15, Buckingham St, Strand, London: Burges's Bedroom in *c.* 1876. Sea-monster frieze (1863–4). Burges, 'Own Furniture'.

168 Tower House, Melbury Rd, Kensington: Drawing-Room. Murals (1876–80) by Weekes. Pullan, *House of W. Burges*, 15.

169 Tower House: Dining-Room. Tiled frieze (1879) by Campbell and Smith. Pullan, *House of W. Burges*, 8.

170 Tower House: Dining-Room. Ceiling panels (1881) from cartoons by Lonsdale. Photo: A. F. Kersting.

171 Tower House: Golden Bedroom. Ceiling panels (1879) painted by Campbell and Smith. Photo: A. F. Kersting.

172 Tower House: Staircase. Ceiling panels (1878) painted by Campbell and Smith. Photo: A. F. Kersting.

173 Tower House: Mermaid Bedroom. Mirrored ceiling (1878) painted by Campbell and Smith. Photo: A. F. Kersting.

174 Tower House: Mermaid Bedroom, in *c.* 1880. [Wardrobe panels (1859) painted by Smallfield.] Pullan, *House of W. Burges*, 26.

175 Tower House: Library, in *c.* 1880. [Alphabet Bookcase panels (1876) painted by Weekes.] Pullan, *House of W. Burges*, 6.

FURNITURE

176 Lille Cathedral: design for a painted confessional (1855). Diocesan Archives, Lille.

177 Lille Cathedral: design for a painted organ-case (1855). *Annales Archéologiques* xvi (1856), 205.

178 The Architecture Cabinet (?1858), in Burges's Office, in *c.* 1876. Burges, 'Own Furniture'.

179 The Yatman Cabinet (1858): in the Medieval Court, 1862 Exhibition. Photo: London Stereoscopic Co.

180 Yatman Cabinet: a preliminary sketch by Burges. R.I.B.A., Arc. iv.

181 Armoire at Bayeux. Viollet-le-Duc, *Mobilier*, i (1858), 6–11.

182 Armoire at Noyon. Viollet-le-Duc, *Mobilier*, i (1858), 6–11.

183 The Sun Cabinet (1858–9). Painted by E. J. Poynter (?). Photo: Sotheby's Belgravia.

184 The Wines and Beers Sideboard (1859). Painted by E. J. Poynter.

185 Burges's Bed (1865–7), at 15, Buckingham St, Strand, in *c.* 1876. Burges, 'Own Furniture'.

186 Burges's Bed: Sleeping Beauty panel. Painted by H. Holiday. Photo: A. F. Kersting.

187 The Dante Bookcase (after 1862), in Burges's Buckingham St. Study, *c.* 1876. Burges, 'Own Furniture'.

188 The Crocker Dressing Table (1867). Painted by F. Smallfield.

189 Gothic Overmantel above the Narcissus Washstand (1865–7; 1872), at 15, Buckingham St, Strand in 1877. Painted by F. Smallfield and F. Weekes. Pullan, *House of W. Burges*, 31.

190 The Narcissus Washstand at Combe Florey, Somerset, the home of Evelyn Waugh, to whom it was presented by Sir John Betjeman. Photo: A. F. Kersting.

191 Armoire (reassembled *c.* 1877) in the Drawing-Room, Tower House: the Winds. Painted by F. Weekes. Photo: A. F. Kersting.

192 Armoire (reassembled *c.* 1877) in the Drawing-Room, Tower House: the Oceans. Painted by F. Weekes. Photo: A. F. Kersting.

193 The Dog Cabinet (1869): with painted panels of Burges's pet dogs by C. Rossiter. Pullan, *House of W. Burges*, 38.

194 The Peacock Cabinet (1873), in Burges's Bedroom at Buckingham St, in *c.* 1876. Pullan, *House of W. Burges*, 18.

195 Upright cabinet (1869), at 15, Buckingham St, in *c.* 1876. Painted by F. Weekes and N. J. N. Westlake (?). Pullan, *House of W. Burges*, 19.

196 The Zodiac Settle (1869–71) at 15, Buckingham St, in *c.* 1876. Painted by Stacy Marks.

197 A stand for cabinets (*c.* 1876) above a chest of drawers, at 15, Buckingham St. Pullan, *House of W. Burges*, 33.

198 Chair and escritoire (1867–8). Painted by C. Rossiter. Burges, 'Own Furniture'.

199 Marble-topped table (*c.* 1867). Photo: Christie's.

200 The Philosophy Cabinet (1878–9). Later presented by Sir John Betjeman to Evelyn Waugh. Pullan, *House of W. Burges*, 23.

201 The Vita Nuova Washstand (1879–80). Photo: A. F. Kersting.

202 The Golden Bed (1879), with 'Judgement of Paris' panel. Painted by F. Weekes. Photo: A. F. Kersting.

203 The Golden Bed (1879). Photo: A. F. Kersting.

204 Castell Coch: Lady Bute's Bedroom. Bed, chairs and dressing table designed by J. S. Chapple (*c.* 1890) in the style of William Burges. N.M.R.

205 Castell Coch: Lady Bute's washstand (1891). Designed by Chapple in the style of Burges. N.M.R.

206 Painted bookcase (1863). Probably designed by Burges, with modifications by Warington Taylor or Philip Webb. Photo: Fine Art Society.

207 Painted escritoire (1865–7). Probably designed by Burges, with modifications by W. G. Saunders. Painted by C. Rossiter and H. Holiday (?). Photo: Fine Art Society.

METALWORK AND JEWELLERY

208 Chalice, alms-dish and paten (?1873): St Mary, Elvetham, Hants. Maker: J. Barkentin.

209 Chalice, paten, ciborium, etc. (?1861); in travelling case, for Rev. E. F. Russell of St Alban's, Holborn. Photo: F. Bedford.

210 Dossal (specimen design): St Michael and All Angels, Brighton. Maker: J. Barkentin.

211 Flagon (1862): St Michael and All Angels, Brighton. Maker: C. Hart.

212 Alms dish (?1862): St Michael and All Angels, Brighton. Maker (?) C. Hart.

213 Chalice (1862): St Michael and All Angels, Brighton. Maker: J. Hardman.

214 Chalice (1864): St Michael and All Angels, Brighton: Maker: J. Hardman.

215 Crozier (1866–7): Dunedin, New Zealand. Maker: J. Barkentin.

216 Burges's Dunedin Crozier published as a thirteenth-century original. *L'Art Pour Tous*, 31 Aug. 1875.

217 Lectern (1877): Cork Cathedral. Makers: Jones and Willis. Photo: Courtauld Institute.

218 Lectern (1877): Cork Cathedral. Makers: Jones and Willis. Photo: T. F. Shepherd.

219 Testament binding (1869): Worcester College, Oxford, chapel. Incorporating seventeenth-century Flemish panel. Maker: J. Barkentin.

220 Jewelled mitre (1878) for ? Bishop of Dunkeld. Photo: Studio Swain.

221 Gas bracket: Cork Cathedral. Photo: T. F. Shepherd.

222 Jewelled glove (1872) for Cardinal Manning. Photo: Studio Swain.

223 Bronze annulet (1874): Great Staircase, Cardiff Castle. Modelled by Nicholls. *Architect* xvii (1877), 322.

224 Bronze front door (1876): Tower House, Kensington. Photo: A. F. Kersting.

225 Bronze garden door (?1880): Tower House, Kensington. Photo: G.L.C.

226 Elephant Inkstand, Burges's diagrammatic drawing. R.I.B.A. 'Orf. Dom.', 26.

227 Elephant Inkstand (1862–3). Pullan, *Designs of W. Burges*, 20.

228 'A Table with Articles of Domestic Use', including decanters, cat-cup, sugar-basin and pomegranate tea-pot, *c.* 1876. Pullan, *House of W. Burges*, 40.

229 Fish tea-pot (1868). Photo: F. Bedford.

230 Two-handled fruit bowl (1859), etc. Photo: F. Bedford.

231 Ink-pot (1869); crystal bottles in silver mounts (1875–6), etc. Photo: F. Bedford.

232 Pomegranate tea-pot, white jade tazza (1875), cutlery, seals, etc. Photo: F. Bedford.

233 Jade bowl, dog-collar, etc. Photo: F. Bedford.

234 Mermaid Bowl (1875). Maker: (?) C. Hart.

235 Mermaid Bowl, Burges's diagrammatic drawing. R.I.B.A. 'Orf. Dom.', 2.

236 Mazer bowl (1878). Makers: J. Barkentin and C. Krall.

237 Nicholson's decanter (1866) and cup (1863). Makers: R. A. Green (decanter) and J. Hart (cup).

238 Burges's diagrammatic drawing (1858–64) for his own decanter. R.I.B.A. 'Orf. Dom.', 11.

239 Burges's diagrammatic drawings (1858–64) for his own decanters. R.I.B.A. 'Orf. Dom.', 12.

240 Burges's cup (1862) and decanters (1865). Makers: G. Angell and J. Mendelson (decanters); C. Hart (cup). Pullan, *Designs of W. Burges*, 17.

241 Burges's cup (1862). Maker: C. Hart.

242 Burges's cup (1862). Maker: C. Hart.

243 Cat Cup (1867). Maker: J. Barkentin. Photo: Studio Swain.

244 Claret jug (1870).

245 Water bottle. Photo: F. Bedford.

246 Yatman Casket (1856). Maker: Potter. Painting: E. J. Poynter. *Building News* v (1859), 885.

247 Burges's design for Lord Bute's crucifix (1871). Photo: Studio Swain.

248 Burges's jewelled cross.

249 Lord Bute's reliquary (1870). Pullan, *Designs of W. Burges*, 13.

250 Bronze door (1876): Cardiff Castle peristyle, Bute Tower. Maker: Hatfield. Photo: F. Bedford.

251 Doors (1872): Cardiff Castle, Clock Tower (Bachelor Bedroom and Winter Smoking Room). Metalwork: W. Shaville. Photo: F. Bedford.

252 Lord Bute's cameo-stand (?1872). Photo: Studio Swain.

253 Lady Bute's brooch (1873). Photo: Studio Swain.

254 Lord Bute's cruet (1877). Photo: Studio Swain.

255 Soup plate (1868). Maker: J. Hardman. Photo: Studio Swain.

256 Burges's drawings for Bute's soup plate. Photo: Studio Swain.

257 Burges's drawings for Bute's cruet. Photo: Studio Swain.

258 Lord Bute's claret jug (1869–70). Maker: J. Barkentin. Photo: Studio Swain.

259 Lord Bute's cup and cover (1875). Maker: J. Barkentin. Photo: Studio Swain.

260 Dessert service (1880), presented by Bute to G. E. Sneyd. Makers: Barkentin and Krall.

261 Dessert service (1880), presented by Bute to G. E. Sneyd. Makers: Barkentin and Krall.

N.M.R.: National Monuments Record, London.

U.S.P.G. Archive: United Society for the Propagation of the Gospel Archives.

Architecture : Ecclesiastical

Burges was not a religious man. His religion was the art of the Middle Ages, not its theology. The bulk of his church work was Anglican, but two of his greatest patrons – Lord Ripon and Lord Bute – were Roman Catholics. His dream was the church candescent, an aesthete's version of the church militant: Faith made manifest in Art. For Victorian High Churchmen the Georgian years were a time of spiritual torpor. For Burges they were 'the Dark Ages of Art'. He hated architectural 'prettiness' and 'chaste' effects. His designs – at Waltham Abbey, at Cork Cathedral, at the churches of Studley Royal and Skelton – bludgeon the spectator into applause. He loved powerful geometrical shapes, symbolic decoration, bright heraldic colours and menacing sculpture. He combined an unerring sense of mass with an insatiable relish for ornament. Above all, he understood scale. He could make small things look large, and large things look enormous. Even among his own generation of 'muscular' Goths – Street, Teulon and Butterfield for instance – he stands out as a master of architectural shock-tactics. But Burges could never be described as a 'Rogue': he had too sharp a sense of humour, too keen an eye for detail. Somehow he manages to balance the precision and delicacy of the Puginian era with a severity and exaggeration which is characteristically High Victorian.

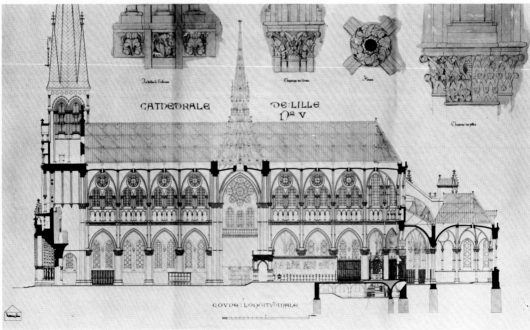

18 & 19 Lille Cathedral: winning competition design (1856).

20 Crimea Memorial Church, Constantinople: winning competition design (1856–7).

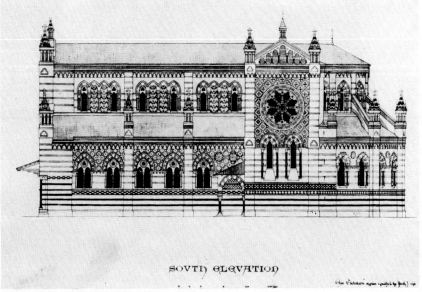

SOVTH ELEVATION

21 Crimea Memorial Church: interior design (1857).

22 Crimea Memorial Church: original South elevation (1857).

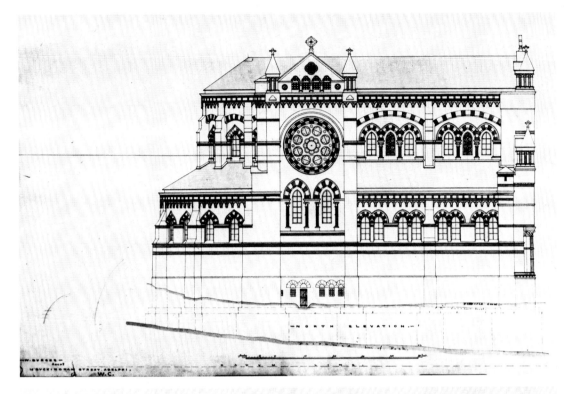

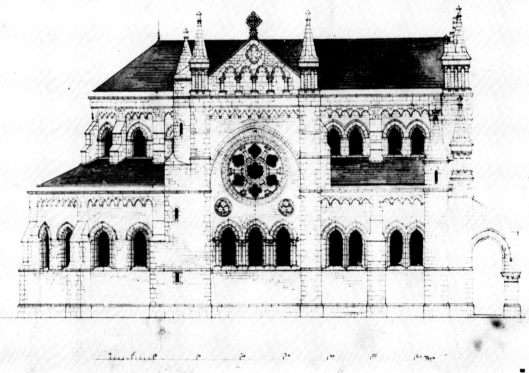

23 Crimea Memorial Church: modified North elevation (1859).

24 Crimea Memorial Church: final North elevation (1861).

26 St Mary's Episcopal Cathedral, Edinburgh: competition design (1873).

25 Brisbane Cathedral: prospective design (1859).

28 St Finbar's Cathedral, Cork (1863 onwards).

27 Edinburgh Cathedral: competition design (1873). Perspective by Axel Haig.

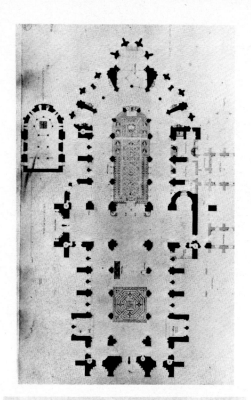

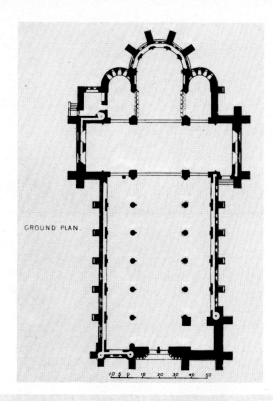

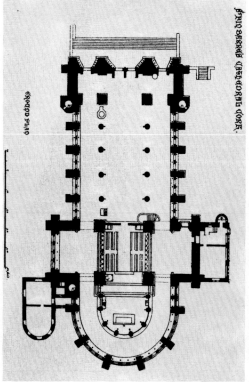

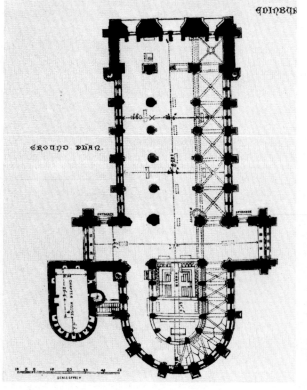

29 Plans: (a) Lille Cathedral (1856)   (b) Brisbane Cathedral (1859)

(c) Cork Cathedral (1863)   (d) Edinburgh Cathedral (1873)

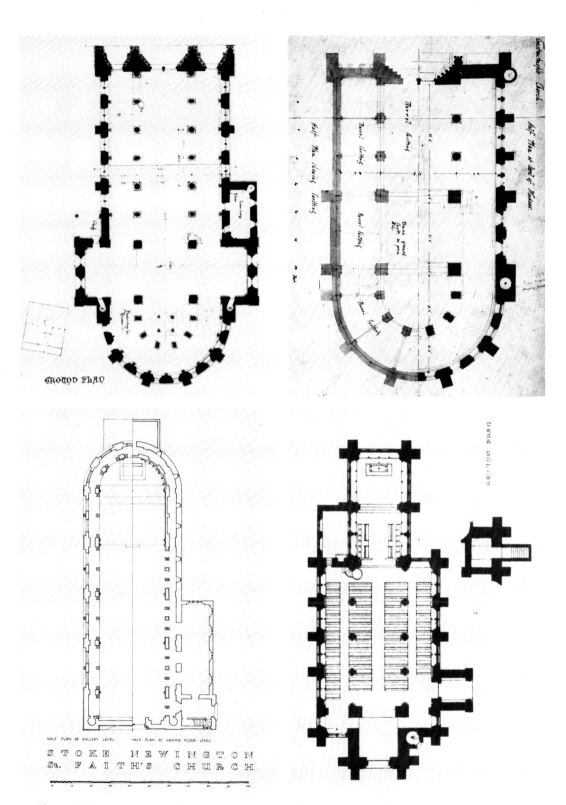

30 Plans: (a) Crimea Memorial Church, Constantinople: *left*, winning design (1856);
right, modified design (1859)

(b) St Faith, Stoke Newington (1871); a plan for a town church.

(c) Studley Royal (1870): a plan for a country church.

31 Cork Cathedral: interior.

32 Cork Cathedral: West front.

33 Waltham Abbey, Herts.: exterior East end (1861).

34 Waltham Abbey: interior East end; reredos (1861–76) carved by T. Nicholls; stained glass
(1860–1) manufactured by Powell, from cartoons by Burne-Jones.

36 St Faith, Stoke Newington: interior.

35 St Faith, Stoke Newington (1871–3; 1881–2; bombed 1944).

38 St Michael and All Angels, Brighton: nave (1892–5).

37 St Michael and All Angels, Brighton (1861–2; 1868; 1892–1914).

39 All Saints, Fleet, Hants. (1860–2). Before alteration in 1934.

40 St Mary, Moulsoe, Bucks: chancel (1861).

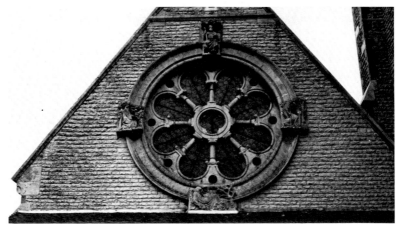

41 Holy Trinity, Templebrady, Crosshaven, Co. Cork (1866–8).

42 All Saints, Murston, Kent (1872–3).

43 St Michael, Lowfield Heath, Surrey (1867–8).

44 Christ the Consoler, Skelton-on-Ure (Skelton) Yorkshire (1870–6).

45 Skelton: nave, looking East.

47 Skelton: North aisle.

46 Skelton: nave, looking West.

49 Skelton: sanctuary.

48 Skelton: chancel, North arcade.

50 Skelton: South porch.

51 St Mary, Aldford-cum-Studley (Studley Royal) Yorkshire (1870–2).

53 Studley Royal: West porch.

52 Studley Royal: East front.

55 Studley Royal: view from the South East.

54 Studley Royal: avenue approach.

56 Studley Royal: sanctuary.

57 Studley Royal: sanctuary, South arcade.

59 Studley Royal: chancel, North arcade.

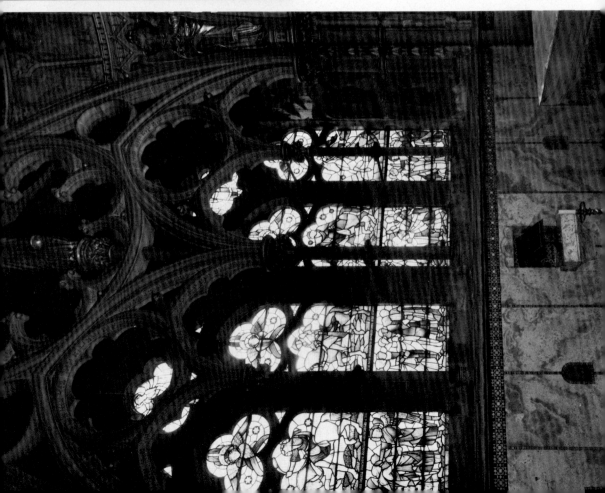

58 Studley Royal: sanctuary, North arcade.

Architecture: Secular

Church building was a challenge for any Victorian Goth. But the challenge of secular commissions was greater still. Here the problem of style was crucial. In an age of evolutionary thinking and technological change mid-Victorian architects became obsessed by the dream of a New Style, a style which would unite the beauties of the past with the necessities of the present: an architectural Holy Grail. Burges belonged to this generation, a generation of architects tortured by doubt. And these doubts were at their most acute not in church-building, nor in domestic architecture, but in the field of secular, urban design. Now civic and commercial buildings never formed a large part of Burges's practice. But each commission was important. Each posed, in varying form, the eternal conundrum of style. A city of London warehouse; a set of Soho lodgings; a home counties' town hall; an Indian art school; a public school theatre; an American college; and a monumental scheme for London's new Law Courts. Here, certainly, Burges was faced with stylistic challenge: a multiple test for the viability of Gothic in the mid-Victorian age. Despite torments of doubt, he succeeded in creating an eclectic, personal style based on the architectural language of the Middle Ages, the Renaissance and Islam. Contemporaries christened it Burgesian Gothic.

60 Law Courts, London: Burges's defeated competition design (1866). From a perspective by
Axel Haig.

61 Law Courts: Burges's Strand front (1866). From an elevation by R. Phéné Spiers.

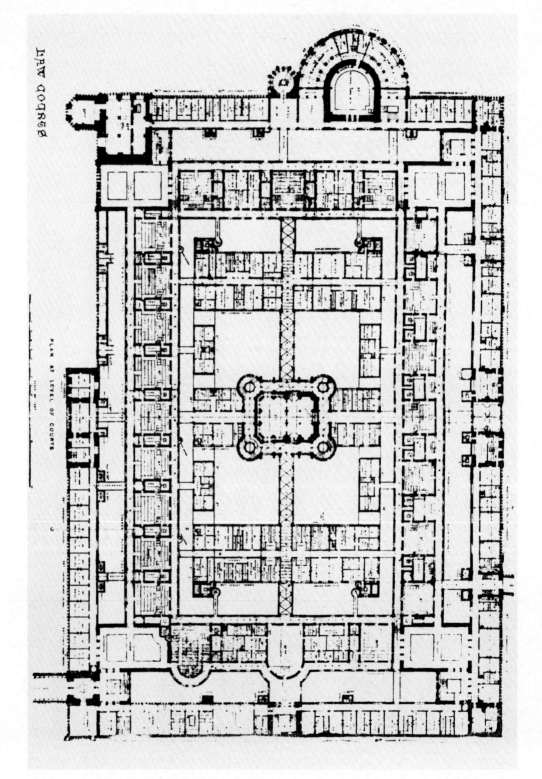

62 Burges's plan for new Law Courts (1866).

63 Dover Town Hall (1859-63; 1880-3; 1894).

64 Bombay School of Art: prospective design (1866).

65 Benedictine kitchen, Marmoutier.

66 House for James Mc. Connochie, Park Place, Cardiff (1871–80). From a perspective by Axel Haig.

67 Knightshayes, Devon (1867–74). From a perspective by Axel Haig.

68 Tower House, Melbury Road, Kensington (1875–81): with ground plan and first floor plan.

69 Tower House: garden front.

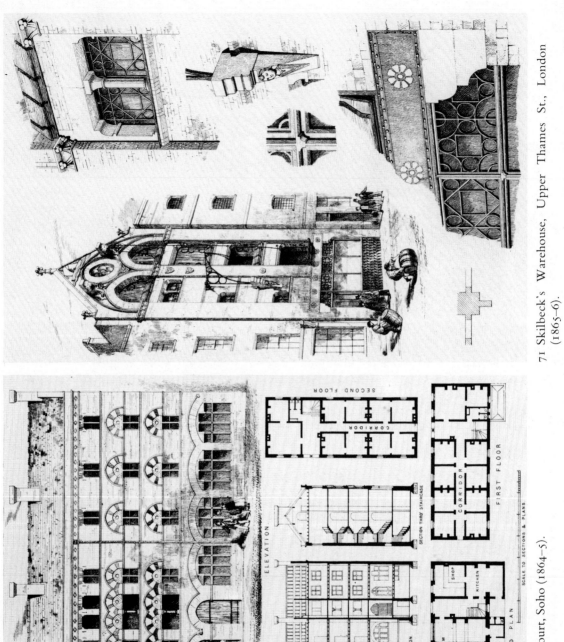

71 Skilbeck's Warehouse, Upper Thames St., London (1865–6).

70 St Anne's Court, Soho (1864–5).

ELEVATION.

SECOND FLOOR

CORRIDOR

FIRST FLOOR

CORRIDOR

SECTION THRO' STAIRCASE

LONGITUDINAL SECTION

SCHOOL ROOM

SHOP

KITCHEN

GROUND PLAN

SCALE TO SECTIONS & PLANS

73 Gayhurst, Bucks.: the privy (1859-60).

72 St Anne's Court, Soho: exterior; since demolished.

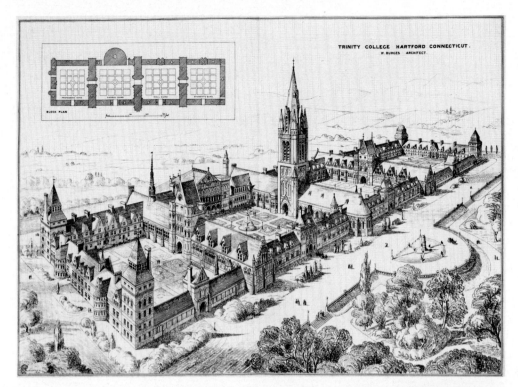

74 Trinity College, Hartford, Connecticut, U.S.A.: prospective scheme (1873–4).

75 Trinity College: Northam Towers (1882).

76 Speech Room, Harrow School: Burges's original scheme (1871).

77 Harrow Speech Room: modified design (1874).

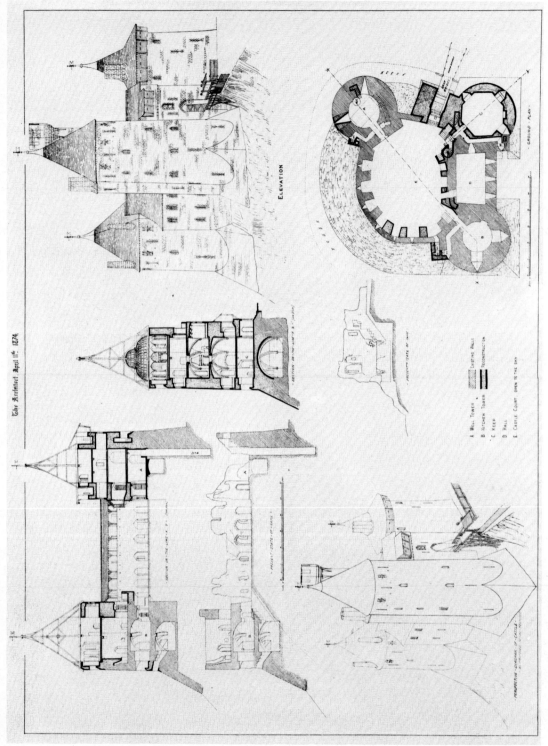

78 Castell Coch, Glamorgan: Burges's original scheme (1871–2).

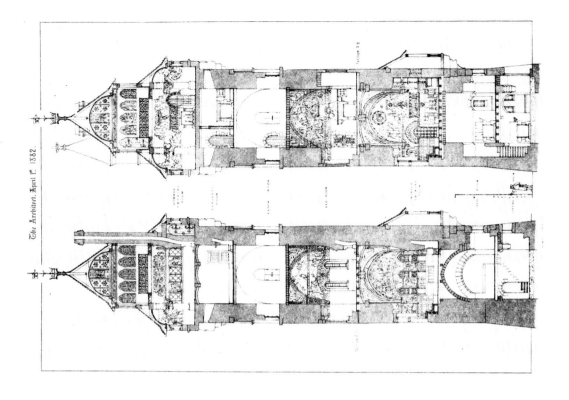

The Architect. April 1st. 1882.

The Architect. April 1st. 1882.

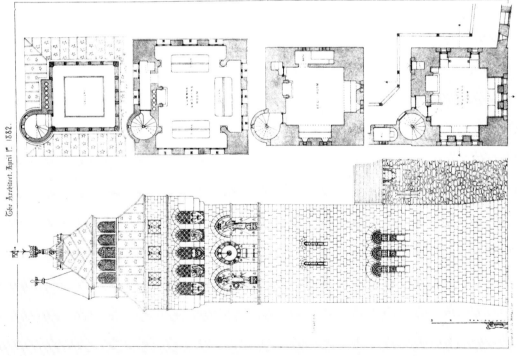

The Architect. April 1st. 1882.

79 Cardiff Castle, Clock Tower: plans and sections.

80 Cardiff Castle: a late eighteenth-century view from the North East.

81 Cardiff Castle: the same view, showing Burges's additions.

82 Cardiff Castle: a late eighteenth-century view from the North West.

83 Cardiff Castle: the same view, showing Burges's additions.

84 Castell Coch: view from the East.

85 Castell Coch: inner courtyard, looking South East.

86 Castell Coch: view from the North.

87 Rothesay Castle, Isle of Bute: visionary reconstruction (1871–2).

88 Castell Coch, during construction, in 1878. Photo: F. Bedford.

89 Cardiff Castle: the rustic bridge (1875) in 1878. Photo: F. Bedford

90 Cardiff Castle, during construction, in 1878. Photo: F. Bedford.

91 Cardiff Castle: the Clock Tower from the courtyard, in 1879. Photo: F. Bedford.

Sculpture

Sculpture for Burges was the voice of architecture. He regarded figure-drawing as an indispensable part of any architect's equipment. And he considered the study of antique and medieval sculpture crucial to any architect's training. In his commitment to the integration of architecture and sculpture, Burges was an out-and-out Ruskinian. But he was well aware of the difficulty inherent in reviving what was virtually a lost art. Happily, his talent for sculptural design was given full rein in a series of extraordinary monuments and memorials. From Cardiff to Kensal Green, from Fleet and Canterbury to Skelton and Studley Royal, from Waltham Abbey to Tower House, Kensington – Burges's instinct for sculptural form is unmistakeable. And the 1,260 pieces of sculpure built into the fabric of Cork Cathedral – each one personally designed by Burges, each one modelled under his superintendence and carved under his direction – add up to a formidable justification of his artistic theory and practice.

92 Florence Cathedral: Burges's design for the West Front (1863).

93 Knightshayes, Devon: figure over entrance (*c.* 1869), carved by Thomas Nicholls.

94 St Augustine's Canterbury: missionary monument (1858–9), carved by Theodore Phyffers.

96 & 97 Dossal, All Saints Episcopal Church, Edinburgh (1870): preliminary sketches by Burges and model by Nicholls.

95 Lille Cathedral: Burges's design for the baldacchino (1856).

99 Ricketts Monument (1867–8), Kensal Green Cemetery.

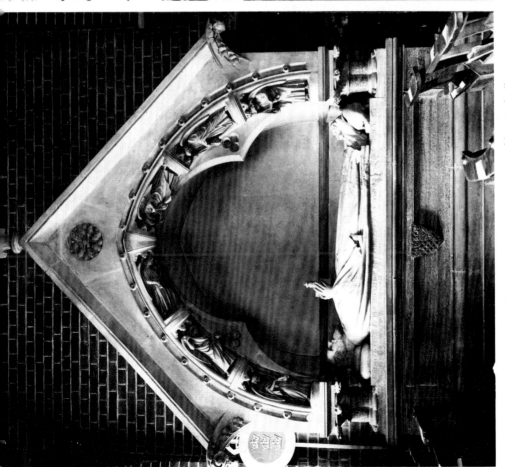

98 All Saints, Fleet, Hants.: Lefroy monument (1861), carved by Nicholls.

100 Gayhurst, Bucks.: the Caliban Staircase (1859–61).

101 Gayhurst: Dining-Room chimneypieces (1861), carved by Nicholls.

102 Worcester College, Oxford: Chapel. Finial (1864) modelled by Nicholls,
     carved by Robinson.
103 Worcester College, Oxford: Hall. Chimneypiece (1877), carved by Fucigna.

105 Skelton: organ loft (1873), carved by Nicholls.

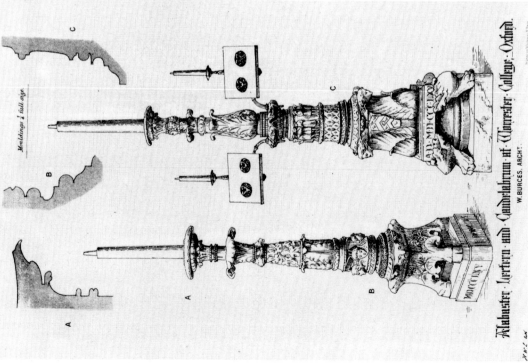

Alabaster Lectern and Candelabrum of Worcester College Oxford

W. BURGES. ARCHT.

104 Worcester College Chapel: lectern and candelabrum (1865), modelled by Nicholls and carved by Jacquet.

107 Skelton: font (1874–5), carved by Nicholls.

106 Studley Royal: font (1874–5), modelled by Nicholls.

109 Cork Cathedral: font (1869).

108 Cork Cathedral: pulpit (1873–4).

110 & 111 Cork Cathedral: gargoyles (1868) on the West front – the Triumph of Virtue over Vice – carved by McLeod.

112 Cork Cathedral: West front. Evangelistic beasts (1869–70), modelled by Nicholls, carved by Harrison; Resurrection tympanum (1878–9), carved by Nicholls; Portal bridegroom and virgins (1879–83), carved by Nicholls.

113 Cork Cathedral: plaster models in the
North West tower.

114 Cork Cathedral: the David Door (1879;
1889), carved by McLeod and Nicholls.

115 Cork Cathedral: sedilia (1879–80), modelled by Nicholls, carved by Walden.

117 Oakwood Court: Dining-Room chimneypiece (1865), in c. 1870; carved by Nicholls.

116 Oakwood Court, Bingley, Yorks: Drawing-Room chimneypiece (1865), in c. 1870; carved by Nicholls.

118 Treverbyn Vean, Cornwall: the St Neot chimneypiece (c. 1860) in c. 1870; carved by Philip.

120 Cardiff Castle: doorways (c. 1876) at the foot of the Octagon Staircase, in 1878, carved by Nicholls. Photo: F. Bedford.

119 Cardiff Castle: sea-lion on the 'animal wall' (1887–8), carved by Nicholls.

122 Cardiff Castle: Library chimneypiece (1874), carved by Nicholls. Four figures represent the Greek, Assyrian, Hebrew and Egyptian alphabets; the fifth supposedly represents Lord Bute.

121 Cardiff Castle: Dining-Room chimneypiece (1873), carved by Nicholls.

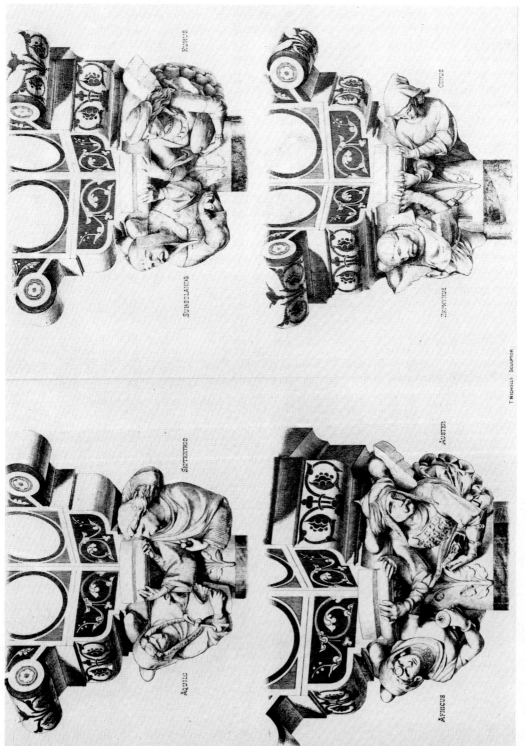

123 Cardiff Castle: Summer Smoking Room, Burges's final designs for the corbels.

125 Tower House: the *Roman de la Rose* chimneypiece (1875–6) in the Drawing-Room, carved by Nicholls.

124 Tower House: the Babel chimneypiece (1875) in the Library, carved by Nicholls.

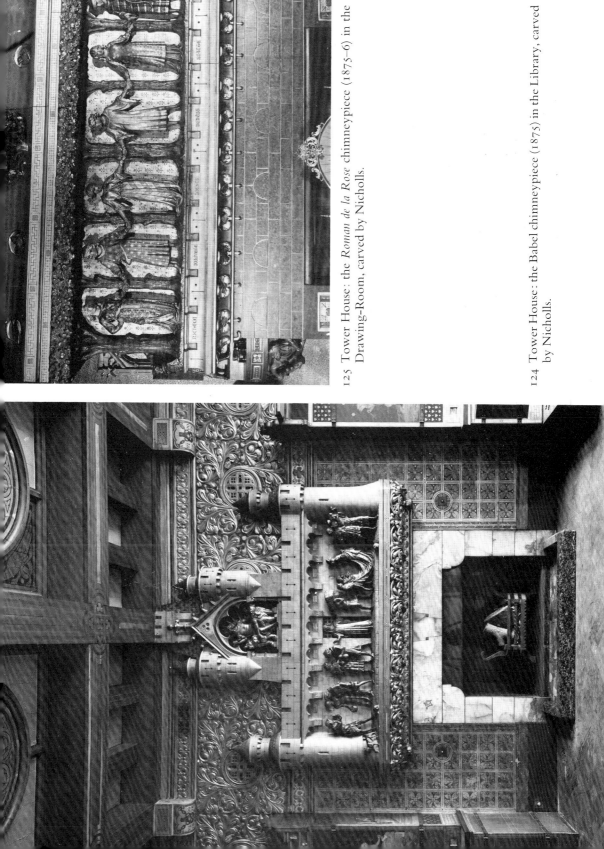

127 Tower House: the Fame chimneypiece (1880–1) in the Dining-Room, modelled by Nicholls, cast by Moore.

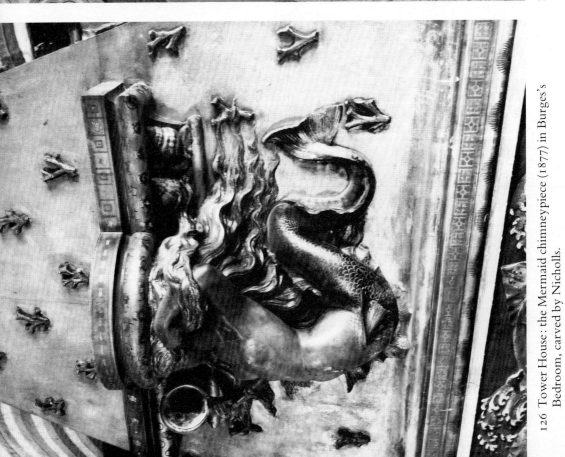

126 Tower House: the Mermaid chimneypiece (1877) in Burges's Bedroom, carved by Nicholls.

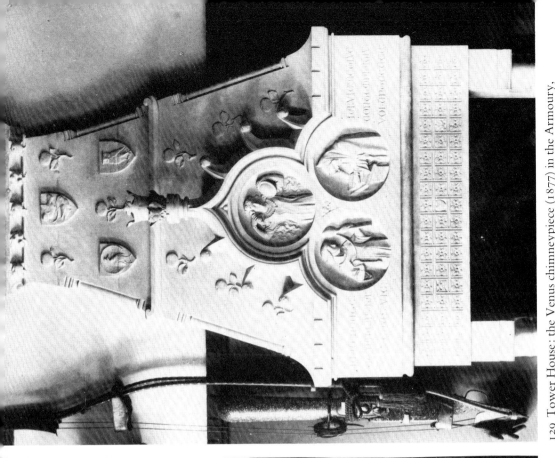

129 Tower House: the Venus chimneypiece (1877) in the Armoury, carved by Nicholls.

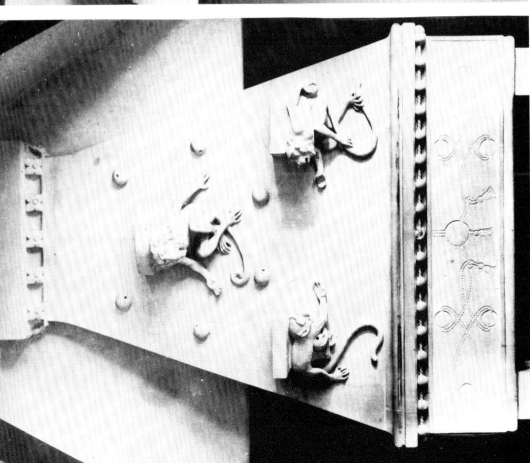

128 Tower House: the Monkey chimneypiece (1877) in the Night Nursery, carved by Nicholls.

130 Tower House: the Jack and the Giant chimneypiece (1877) in the Day Nursery, carved by Nicholls.

Painted Decoration, Stained Glass, Mosaic, etc.

Burges revelled in the minutiae of decoration. His use of mosaic was based on a knowledge of medieval techniques unequalled in his generation. In the field of stained glass, as designer, patron and pundit, he was involved in the production of some of the finest windows of modern times. As a master of the totality of interior design, he was – quite literally – unique. Burges assimilated the thirteenth century, mingled its features with Renaissance, Pompeian, Japanese, Assyrian and Islamic work, added a touch of personal fantasy – and ended up, almost despite himself, with a New Style. Only Burges managed to combine the surface abstraction of Islamic art with the robust three-dimensionality of thirteenth-century Gothic. In his work the calligraphic and sculptural elements of both traditions are fused in a new synthesis. The rooms of Cardiff Castle are not machines for living in. They are fantasy capsules, three-dimensional passports to fairy kingdoms and realms of gold. And at home in London – at Tower House, Melbury Rd., Kensington – Burges created his own dream-world: a multi-coloured fantasy, shimmering with stained glass, painted furniture and exotic metalwork, 'massive, learned, glittering, amazing'.

131 Worcester College, Oxford: Burges's scheme for the Hall (1873).

132 Worcester College, Oxford: the Chapel (1864–70).

133 Gayhurst, Bucks.: the Abbess's Room (1861; 1872). Painted by F. Smallfield.

134 Harrow School: Burges's scheme for the Speech Room (1871).

135 St Paul's Cathedral: Burges's model showing proposed decoration (1874).

136 St Paul's Cathedral: Burges's model, as adapted by Sir William Richmond.

137 Skelton: reredos (1873).

138 Salisbury Cathedral: Chapter House. Burges's polychromatic decoration (c. 1857).
Sculptor: J.B. Philip; artist: Octavius Hudson; Manufacturer: H. Minton.

139 Cork Cathedral: chancel mosaic (1877), from cartoons by H. W. Lonsdale.

140 Cork Cathedral: details of choir wall (*c.* 1876).

141 Tower House: Minotaur mosaic (*c.* 1877).

142 Studley Royal: chancel Te Deum (*c.* 1874); painted by H. W. Lonsdale (?).

143 Skelton: Parable window in the South aisle (*c.* 1872); manufactured by Saunders, from sketches by Lonsdale and cartoons by Weekes.

144 Studley Royal: sanctuary dome (*c.* 1874): painted by H. W. Lonsdale (?).

145 Studley Royal: Revelation windows in the chancel (*c.* 1873): manufactured by Saunders, from sketches by Lonsdale and cartoons by Weekes.

146 Cardiff Castle: Winter Smoking Room (1870–3), Clock Tower. Painted by F. Weekes and H. W. Lonsdale. A perspective by Axel Haig (1870).

147 Cardiff Castle: Peristyle (1873–6). Bute Tower, in 1878. Elijah tiles manufactured by
Simpson, from cartoons by Lonsdale; bronze Madonna modelled by Fucigna, cast by
Hatfield. Photo: F. Bedford.

148 Cardiff Castle: Lord Bute's Sitting Room (c. 1874), Bute Tower, in 1878; door painted
with the Seven Deadly Sins by Sir William Douglas. Photo: F. Bedford.

149 Cardiff Castle: Lord Bute's Bedroom (1874–5), Bute Tower, in 1878. Sculpture: Fucigna; painting: Campbell. Photo: F. Bedford.

150 Cardiff Castle: Winter Smoking Room, in 1878. Photo: F. Bedford.

151 Cardiff Castle: Summer Smoking Room (1871–4), Clock Tower, in 1878. Painting: F. Weekes and H. W. Lonsdale; sculpture: T. Nicholls. Tiles manufactured by Simpson. Photo: F. Bedford.

152 Cardiff Castle: Summer Smoking Room (1871–4), Clock Tower, in 1878. Painting: F. Weekes and H. W. Lonsdale; sculpture: T. Nicholls. Tiles manufactured by Simpson. Photo: F. Bedford.

153 Cardiff Castle: Lord Bute's Bedroom, Clock Tower, in 1878. Painted by F. Weekes and
H. W. Lonsdale. Photo: F. Bedford.

154 Summer Smoking Room, painted vault, in 1878. Photo: F. Bedford.

155 Summer Smoking Room: tulip vases (1874).

157 Cardiff Castle: the Octagon Staircase (c. 1874–81). Painted by Campbell.

156 Cardiff Castle: the Oratory (c. 1869–76). Painting: N. J. N. Westlake; sculpture: Fucigna.

159 Cardiff Castle: Banqueting Hall (*c.* 1875–93). Sculpture: Nicholls; painting: Lonsdale.

158 Cardiff Castle: Chaucer Room (*c.* 1877–90). Sculpture: Nicholls; painting: Lonsdale.

160 & 161 Cardiff Castle: Arab Room (*c.* 1878–81). Painting by Campbell; stained glass by Saunders.

162 Cardiff Castle: Burges's scheme for the Great Staircase; from a perspective by Axel Haig (1874).

164 Castell Coch: Banqueting Hall (c. 1878–9). Sculpture: Nicholls; furniture Chapple; mural painting: Campbell and Smith, from cartoons by Lonsdale.

163 Castell Coch: Drawing-Room (1879–87). Sculpture: T. Nicholls; furniture: J. S. Chapple; painting: C. and T. Campbell.

165 Castell Coch: Drawing-Room, painted vault.

166 15, Buckingham St, Strand, London: Burges's Office, in 1876. Murals (1861), painted by
 Westlake (?); stained glass (1860) by Edward Burne-Jones.

167 15, Buckingham St, Strand, London: Burges's Bedroom in *c.* 1876. Sea-monster frieze
 (1863–4).

168 Tower House, Melbury Rd, Kensington: Drawing-Room. Murals (1876–80) by Weekes.

169 Tower House: Dining-Room. Tiled frieze (1879) by Campbell and Smith.

170 Tower House: Dining-Room. Ceiling panels (1881) from cartoons by Lonsdale.

171 Tower House: Golden Bedroom. Ceiling panels (1879) painted by Campbell and Smith.

172 Tower House: Staircase. Ceiling panels (1878) painted by Campbell and Smith.

173 Tower House: Mermaid Bedroom. Mirrored ceiling (1878) painted by Campbell and Smith.

174 Tower House: Mermaid Bedroom, in *c.* 1880. [Wardrobe panels (1859) painted by Smallfield.]

175 Tower House: Library, in *c.* 1880. [Alphabet Bookcase panels (1876) painted by Weekes.]

Furniture

More than most of his generation, Burges despised Georgian and
Regency furniture. Veneering he regarded with suspicion;
upholstery he hated. His furniture therefore – boxy and aedicular;
painted with heraldic colours and Pre-Raphaelite panels – was
conceived as the ultimate answer to the 'dark ages' of Georgian
joinery. Drawing upon the talents of a veritable galaxy of artistic
friends, Burges in effect created the perfect medium for his talents:
the art of Pre-Raphaelite furniture. By integrating joinery,
painting and architecture in miniature form, he revolutionised
furniture design. Bookcases and cabinets; cupboards and chairs;
bedsteads and escritoires; washstands fit for Narcissus or Piers
Gaveston – Burges's furniture bespeaks an artist of dazzling
virtuosity. More than anyone, it was Burges, with his eye for detail
and his lust for colour, who created the furniture appropriate to
High Victorian Gothic.

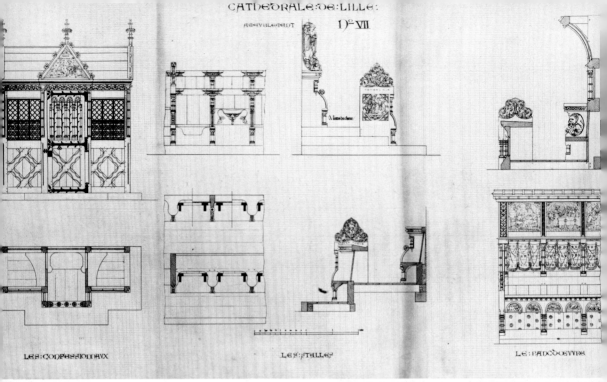

LES CONFESSIONNAUX   LES STALLES   LE BADCOEVVRE

176 Lille Cathedral: design for a painted confessional (1855).

177 Lille Cathedral: design for a painted organ-case (1855).

178 The Architecture Cabinet (?1858), in Burges's Office, in c. 1876.

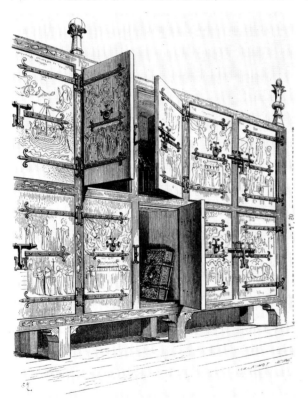

179 The Yatman Cabinet (1858): in the
Medieval Court, 1862 Exhibition.
Photo: London Stereoscopic Co.

180 Yatman Cabinet: a preliminary sketch
by Burges.

181 Armoire at Bayeux.

182 Armoire at Noyon.

184 The Wines and Beers Sideboard (1859). Painted by E. J. Poynter.

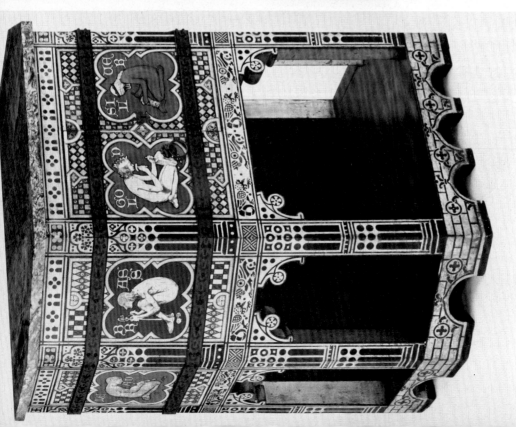

183 The Sun Cabinet (1858–59). Painted by E. J. Poynter (?).

186 Burges's Bed: Sleeping Beauty panel. Painted by H. Holiday.

185 Burges's Bed (1865–7), at 15, Buckingham St, Strand, in c. 1876.

188 The Crocker Dressing Table (1867). Painted by
F. Smallfield.

187 The Dante Bookcase (after 1862), in Burges's
Buckingham St Study, c. 1876.

190 The Narcissus Washstand at Combe Florey, Somerset, the home of Evelyn Waugh, to whom it was presented by Sir John Betjeman.

189 Gothic Overmantal above the Narcissus Washstand (1867; 1872), at 15, Buckingham St, Strand in 1877. Painted by F. Smallfield and F. Weekes.

191 & 192 Armoires (reassembled *c.* 1877) in the Drawing-Room, Tower House: the Winds and the Oceans. Painted by F. Weekes.

193 The Dog Cabinet (1869): with painted panels of Burges's pet dogs by C. Rossiter.

194 The Peacock Cabinet (1873), in Burges's Bedroom at Buckingham St, in *c.* 1876.

196 The Zodiac Settle (1869–71) at 15, Buckingham St, in
c. 1876. Painted by Stacy Marks.

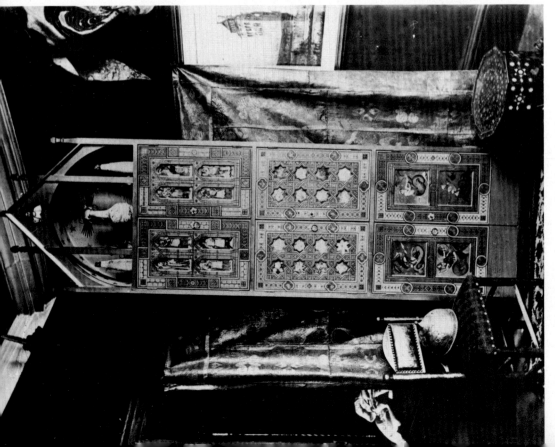

195 Upright cabinet (1869), at 15, Buckingham St, in *c.* 1876.
Painted by F. Weekes and N. J. N. Westlake (?).

198 Chair and escritoire (1867–8). Painted by C. Rossiter.

197 A stand for cabinets (c. 1876), above a chest of drawers, at 15, Buckingham St.

199 Marble-topped table (c. 1867).

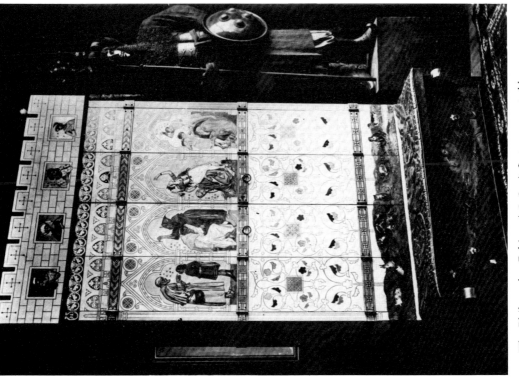

200 The Philosophy Cabinet (1878–9). Later presented by
Sir John Betjeman to Evelyn Waugh.

201 The Vita Nuova Washstand (1879–80).

202 & 203 The Golden Bed (1879), with 'Judgement of Paris' panel. Painted
by F. Weekes.

204 Castell Coch: Lady Bute's Bedroom. Bed, chairs and dressing-table designed by J. S. Chapple (*c.* 1890) in the style of William Burges.

205 Castell Coch: Lady Bute's washstand (1891). Designed by Chapple in the style of Burges.

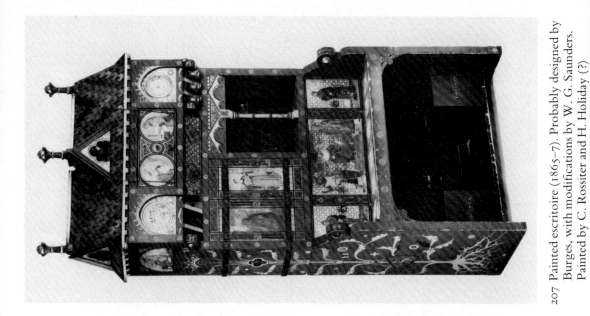

207 Painted escritoire (1865–7). Probably designed by Burges, with modifications by W. G. Saunders. Painted by C. Rossiter and H. Holiday (?)

206 Painted bookcase (1863). Probably designed by Burges, with modifications by Warington Taylor or Philip Webb.

Metalwork and Jewellery

Burges's genius as a designer is expressed to perfection in his jewellery and metalwork; the crystal Cat Cup; the Elephant Inkstand; jewelled decanters, gem-studded chalices, reliquaries, crosses, flagons and patens; soup-plates, knives and forks, bracelets, brooches, tea-pots, dog-collars, scent-bottles and pins. Such range, variety and originality is unique among nineteenth-century designers. Motifs and materials are widely disparate, skimming the centuries in search of style. Byzantine, Romanesque, Chinese, Japanese, Assyrian; medieval Gothic – English, French and Italian; bronze, jade and glass, antique coins, crystal, ivory, silver, gold and a bewildering variety of jewels and gems. Here is eclecticism in fantastic vein, and scholarship too. In the history of nineteenth-century metalwork, Burges is the link between the early and late Victorian periods; between the precise medievalism of Pugin and the febrile experiments of *art nouveau*. The result is unforgettable.

208 Chalice, alms-dish and paten (? 1873): St Mary, Elvetham, Hants. Maker: J. Barkentin.

209 Chalice, paten, ciborium, etc. (? 1861); in travelling case, for Rev. E. F. Russell of St Alban's, Holborn.

210 Dossal (specimen design): St Michael and
   All Angels, Brighton. Maker: J. Barkentin.

211 Flagon (1862): St Michael and All
   Angels, Brighton. Maker: C. Hart.

212 Alms dish (? 1862): St Michael and All Angels, Brighton. Maker: (?) C. Hart.

214 Chalice (1864): St Michael and All Angels, Brighton.
Maker: J. Hardman.

213 Chalice (1862): St Michael and All Angels, Brighton.
Maker: J. Hardman.

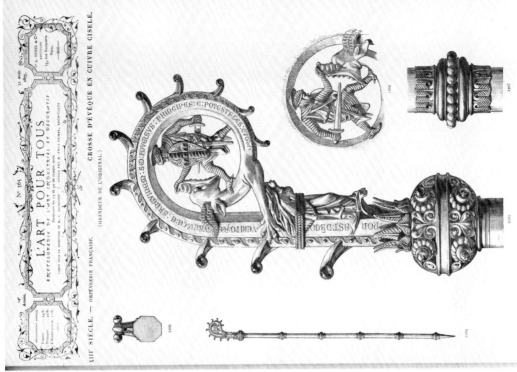

216 Burges's Dunedin Crozier published as a thirteenth-century original. *L'Art Pour Tous*, 31 Aug. 1875.

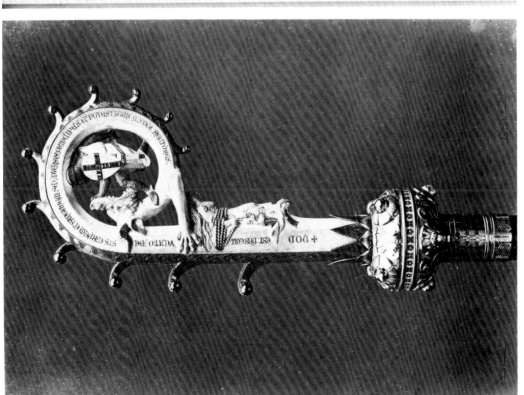

215 Crozier (1866–7): Dunedin, New Zealand. Maker: J. Barkentin.

217 & 218 Lectern (1877): Cork Cathedral. Makers: Jones and Willis.

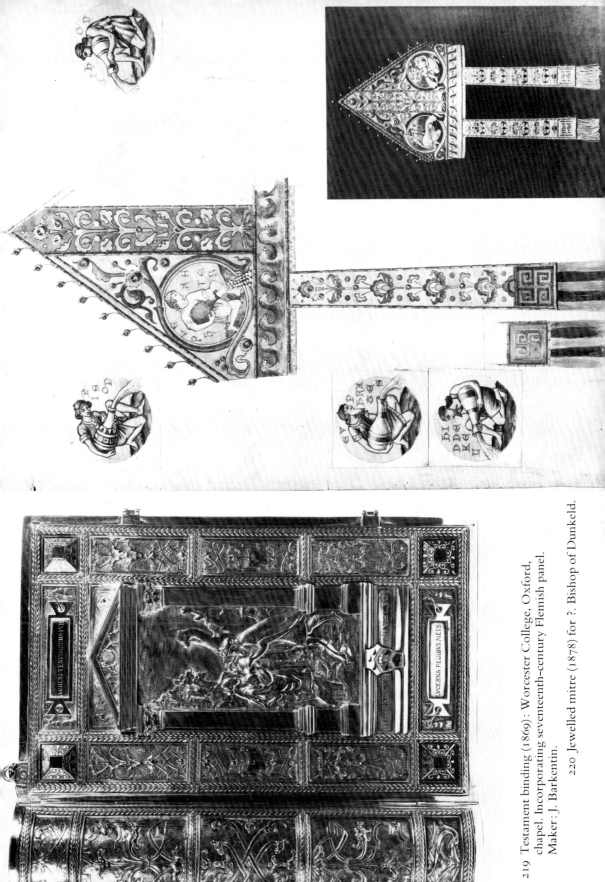

219 Testament binding (1869): Worcester College, Oxford, chapel. Incorporating seventeenth-century Flemish panel. Maker: J. Barkentin.

220 Jewelled mitre (1878) for ?. Bishop of Dunkeld.

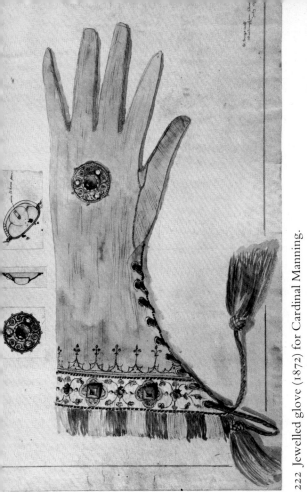

222 Jewelled glove (1872) for Cardinal Manning.

221 Gas bracket: Cork Cathedral.

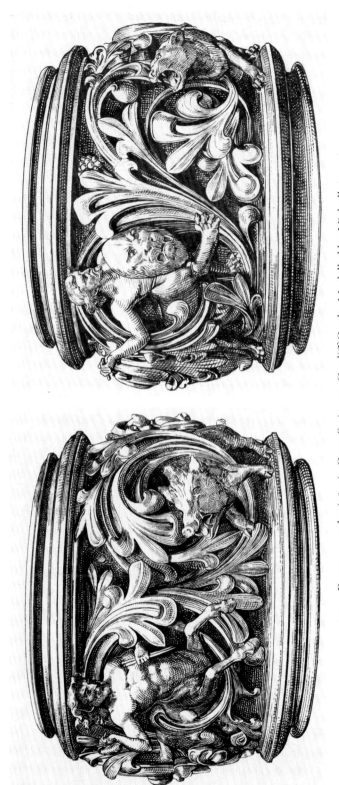

223 Bronze annulet (1874): Great Staircase, Cardiff Castle. Modelled by Nicholls.

225 Bronze garden door (? 1880): Tower House, Kensington.

224 Bronze front door (1876): Tower House, Kensington.

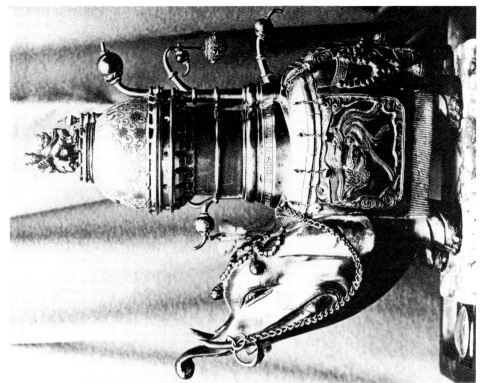

227 Elephant Inkstand (1862–3).

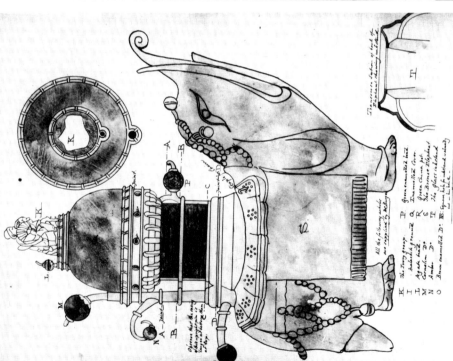

226 Elephant Inkstand, Burges's diagrammatic drawing.

228 'A Table with Articles of Domestic Use', including decanters, cat-cup, sugar-basin and pomegranate tea-pot, c. 1876.

229 Fish tea-pot (1868). Photo: F. Bedford.

230 Two-handled fruit bowl (1859), etc. Photo: F. Bedford.

231 Ink-pot (1869); crystal bottles in silver mounts (1875–6), etc. Photo: F. Bedford.

232 Pomegranate tea-pot, white jade tazza (1875), cutlery, seals, etc. Photo: F. Bedford.

233 Jade bowl, dog-collar, etc. Photo: F. Bedford.

234 Mermaid Bowl (1875). Maker: (?) C. Hart.

235 Mermaid Bowl, Burges's diagrammatic drawing.

236 Mazer bowl (1878). Makers: J. Barkentin and C. Krall.

237 Nicholson's decanter (1866) and cup (1863). Makers: R. A. Green (decanter) and J. Hart (cup).

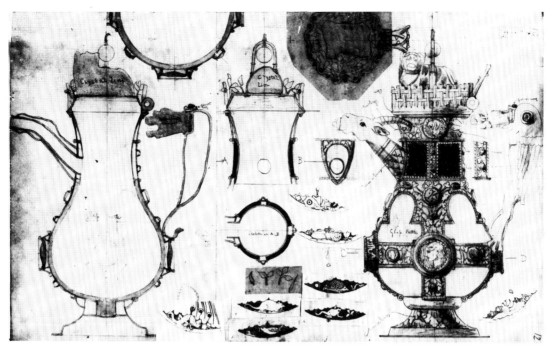

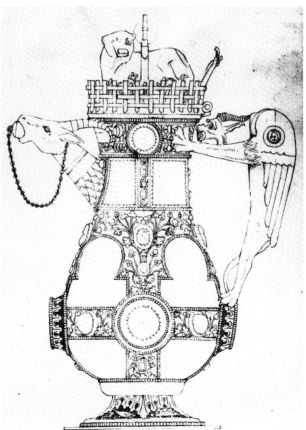

238 & 239 Burges's diagrammatic drawings (1858–64) for his own decanters.

240 Burges's cup (1862) and decanters (1865). Makers: G. Angell and J. Mendelson (decanters); C. Hart (cup).

241 & 242 Burges's cup (1862). Maker: C. Hart.

243 Cat Cup (1867). Maker: J. Barkentin.

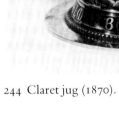

244 Claret jug (1870).

245 Water bottle. Photo: F. Bedford.

246 Yatman Casket (1856). Maker: Potter. Painting: E.J. Poynter.

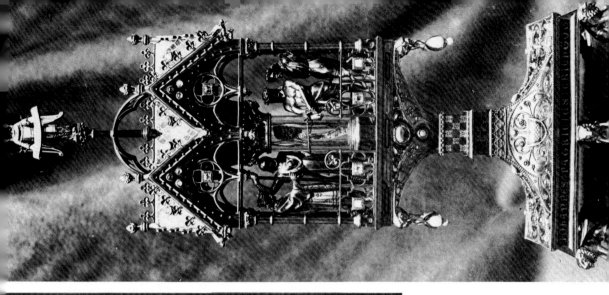

247 Burges's design for Lord Bute's crucifix (1871).

248 Burges's jewelled cross.

249 Lord Bute's Reliquary (1870).

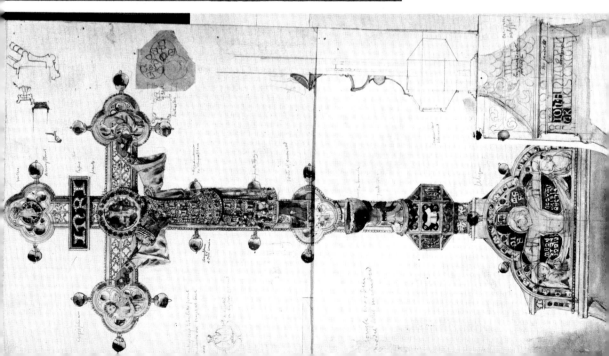

250 Bronze door (1876): Cardiff Castle peristyle, Bute Tower. Maker: Hatfield. Photo: F. Bedford.

251 Doors (1872): Cardiff Castle, Clock Tower (Bachelor Bedroom and Winter Smoking Room). Metalwork: W. Shaville. Photo: F. Bedford.

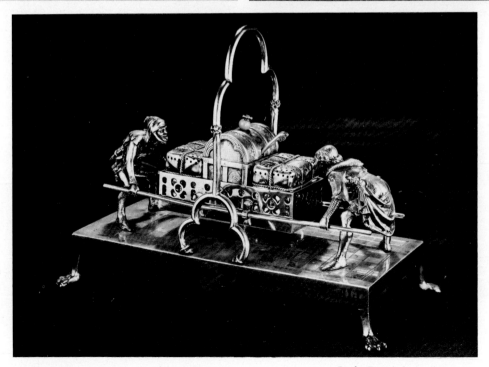

252 Lord Bute's cameo-stand (?1872).   253 Lady Bute's brooch (1873).

254 Lord Bute's cruet (1877).

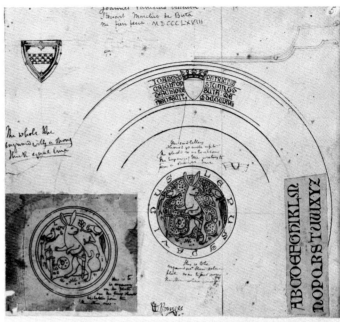

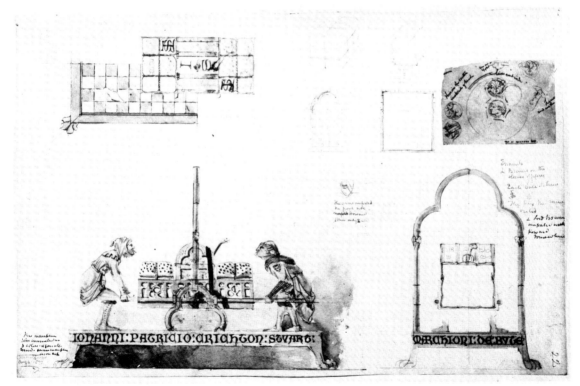

255 Soup plate (1868). Maker: J. Hardman.

256 Burges's drawings for Bute's soup plate.

257 Burges's drawings for Bute's cruet.

258 Lord Bute's claret jug (1869–70). Maker: J. Barkentin.

259 Lord Bute's cup and cover (1875). Maker: J. Barkentin.

260 & 261 Dessert service (1880), presented by Bute to G.E. Sneyd. Makers: Barkentin and Krall.

Notes and References

There are four chief deposits of Burges documents: in the Royal Institute of British Architects, Drawings Collection; in the Victoria and Albert Museum, Prints and Drawings Department; at Cardiff Castle; and in the Bute Archive at Mount Stuart. All four – amounting in total to many thousands of items – are still in process of being catalogued. Some of the references to these collections must therefore be regarded as provisional. There are further collections of manuscript material in the archives of St Paul's Cathedral, London, and St Finbar's Cathedral, Cork; at Lambeth Palace; at Trinity College, Hartford, Conn.; at Newby Hall, at Harrow School, at Worcester College, Oxford and at King's and Trinity Colleges, Cambridge; in the collection of Mr R. B. Weller; and in the hands of the architect's family. Apart from Burges's own published works (listed in Appendix A), and his Abstract of Diaries (in the author's collection), the other major source of information has been the mass of architectural, artistic and literary periodicals – hundreds of illustrated volumes – published during Burges's lifetime. For a full-scale bibliography of primary and secondary works relating to the Gothic Revival, readers are referred to the author's edition of C. L. Eastlake's *History of the Gothic Revival* (Leicester U.P. revised edition, 1978).

PRINCIPAL ABBREVIATIONS

A.: *The Architect* (1868–1926); thereafter united with the *Building News*.

A.A.: *Annales Archéologiques* (1844–70).

Abstract: W. Burges, 'Abstract of Diaries'.

A.A. Papers/Notes/Sketchbook/Jnl./Qtly.: *Architectural Association Papers/Notes/Sketchbook/Journal/Quarterly*.

A.P.S.D.: W. Papworth, ed., *Dictionary of Architecture* (Architectural Publications Society, 1852–92).

A.R.: *Architectural Review* (1896–).

Archaeol. Jnl.: *Archaeological Journal* (1844–).

B.: *The Builder* (1843–1966); thereafter known as *Building*.

B.M. Add. Mss.: British Museum Additional Manuscripts.

B.M., P. & D.: British Museum Prints & Drawings.

B.N.: *Building News* (1855–1926); thereafter united with *The Architect*.

Boase: F. Boase, *Modern English Biography* (1892–1921).

Burl. Mag.: *Burlington Magazine* (1903–).

C.E.A. Jnl.: *Civil Engineer and Architect's Journal* (1837–67).

C.L.: *Country Life* (1897–).

D.N.B.: *Dictionary of National Biography* (1885–).

E.: *The Ecclesiologist* (Cambridge Camden Society, 1842–68).

G.M.: *Gentleman's Magazine* (1731–1868).

I.L.N.: *Illustrated London News* (1843–).

Mt. St. MSS.: Bute Archives, Mount Stuart, Isle of Bute.

N.M.R.: National Monuments Record.

P.L.U.: Present Location Unknown.

Qtly. Rev.: *Quarterly Review* (1809–1967).

R.A.I.: Royal Archaeological Institute.

R.I.B.A. 'Orf. Dom.'/'Eccles.': W. Burges, 'Orfèvrerie Domestique'/'Ecclésiastique', Royal Institute of British Architects, Drawings Collection.

R.I.B.A., S.N.B.: W. Burges, 'Small Note Books', Royal Institute of British Architects, Drawings Collection.

R.I.B.A. Trans./Papers/Jnl.: *Royal Institute of British Architects Transactions/Papers/Journal* (1842–).

R.S.A. Jnl.: *Royal Society of Arts Journal* (1852–).

Sat. Rev.: *Saturday Review* (1855–1938).

V.&A., Estim. Bk.: W. Burges, 'Estimate Book', Victoria and Albert Museum, Library.

V.&A., P.&D.: W. Burges, 'Drawings', Victoria and Albert Museum, Prints and Drawings Department.

[The figures in square brackets refer to the illustrations.]

NOTES AND REFERENCES

EXPLANATION
between pp. 1–3

1 Evelyn Waugh, *Men at Arms* (1952).
2 See the discussions in *A.A.Qtly.* vii, no. 4 (1975), *passim*; *A.R.* clviii (1975), 264 *et seq.*; cxl (1976), 76 *et seq.*, 136 *et seq.* See also C. Brent Brolin, *The Failure of Modern Architecture* (1976). For the developing intellectual reaction against the Modern Movement and its aesthetic imperatives, see a symposium on D. Watkin, *Morality and Architecture* (Oxford, 1977), in *A.R.* clxiii (1978), 64–8.
3 I have explored this idea at some length in *The Greek Revival: Neo-Classical Attitudes in British Architecture, 1760–1870* (1972).
4 *A.* xxv (1881), 315.

PRELUDE
between pp. 5–10

1 *A.* iv (1870), 1. For Donaldson's career see Sandra Millikin, *R.I.B.A. Jnl.* lxxiv (1967), 542–4.
2 K. Clark, *The Gothic Revival* (1928; revised 1950).
3 H. S. Goodhart-Rendel, *Vitruvian Nights* (1932); *English Architecture Since the Regency* (1953).
4 D. Harbron, *Amphion, or the Nineteenth Century* (1930).
5 J. Betjeman, *First and Last Loves* (1952).
6 Evelyn Waugh, *Brideshead Revisited* (1945).
7 J. Summerson, *Victorian Architecture: four studies in evaluation* (1970), 17.
8 N. Pevsner, *Pioneers of the Modern Movement from William Morris to Walter Gropius* (1936); *Matthew Digby Wyatt* (1950); *High Victorian Design* (1951). See also C. McInnes, 'The Englishness of Dr. Pevsner', in *England, Half-English* (1961), 119–29.
9 H.-R. Hitchcock, *Early Victorian Architecture*, 2 vols. (1954); *Architecture: 19th and 20th Centuries* (1958).
10 He was born in 1870 and died on 6 Dec. 1935, leaving £3,369 5s. 1d. (*Who Was Who, 1929–40*, 588; Probate Office Records; E. Bénezit, *Dictionnaire ... des Peintres, Sculpteurs, etc.* iv, 1956, 579). See also Hilaire Belloc, Foreword to *The British Firing Line* (1917).
11 Matriculation 1935; B.A. 1938; M.A. 1942.
12 Ian Mackenzie-Kerr, a pupil.
13 Evelyn Waugh, *Put Out More Flags* (1942).
14 John Harper; Ian Mackenzie-Kerr.
15 Eric Newton contributed a critical evaluation. Handley-Read received £50 for his work. For a very different interpretation, see D. G. Bridson, *The Filibuster ... Political Ideas of Wyndham Lewis* (1972).

16 With John Harthan he had travelled extensively, visiting the Baroque churches of South Germany and Switzerland.
17 We used to joke that all writing on Victorian decorative arts before Floud was antediluvian.
18 Lavinia Handley-Read, 'A Lutyens Client in a Golden Age', *C.L.* cl (1971), 816–20.
19 Dr. Eva Mary Handley-Read died on 12 Feb. 1965, leaving £61,062. Mrs. Violet ['Lylie'] Grace Handley-Ham died on 25 April 1964, leaving £34,321. Mr. Osborne Wotton Handley died on 14 Oct. 1965, leaving £7,965 (Probate Office Records).
20 Letter to the Bloxham Gallery, 28 Oct. 1965. His regular haunts were the Portobello Road and Westbourne Grove (Friday afternoons, 1.30–3.00), Camden Passage, King's Road, Fulham Road, Camden Town and (occasionally) Brighton Lanes.
21 *The Times*, 4 March 1972.
22 C.H.-R. MSS., 3 July 1965.
23 'Children's Painting and Epilepsy', *The Studio*, cxxvii (1944), 152–7; (with Eric Newton), *The Art of Wyndham Lewis* (1951); 'Aspects of Victorian Architecture', in *From Dickens to Hardy*, ed. B. Ford (1958); 'Tinworth's Work for Doulton: i Sermons in Terra-cotta, ii Salt Cellars and Public Statues'. *C.L.*, cxxviii (1960), 430–31, 560–61; 'Sculpture and Modelling in Victorian Architecture', *Royal Soc. of British Sculptors 1960 Annual Report* (1961), 36–7. 'Prince Albert's Model Dairy', *C.L.*, cxxix (1961), 1524–6; 'The Albert Memorial Re-Assessed', *C.L.*, cxxx (1961), 1514–6; 'William Burges', in *Victorian Architecture*, ed. P. Ferriday (1963), 187–220; 'Notes on William Burges's Painted Furniture', *Burl. Mag.*, cv (1963), 496–509; 'England, 1830–1901', in *World Furniture*, ed. Helena Hayward (1965), 207–29; 'Jubilee Pyramid', *A.R.*, cxxxvii (1965), 234–6; 'Aladdin's Palace in Kensington: William Burges's Tower House', *C.L.* cxxxix (1966), 600–604; 'St. Fin Barre's Cathedral', *A.R.* cxli (1967), 422–30; 'High Victorian Design: an illustrated commentary', in *Design, 1860–1960*, ed. P. Thompson (Victorian Society, 1963), 23–7; *Victorian Church Art* (V. & A., 1971), 38–9, 41–3.
24 Frederick Cayley Robinson, A.R.A., R.W.S., R.B.A. (1862–1927).
25 Forrest Reid, *Apostate* (1947 ed.), last paragraphs. See B. Taylor, 'Forrest Reid and the Literature of Nostalgia', *Studies* lxv (1976), 291–6.
26 B.N. xv (1868), 57.
27 Written in the margin of his copy of Reynolds's *Discourses* (D. G. Rossetti, R.A. 1973; introduction,

between pp. 10–14

J. Gere, 10). 'Examples endure, interpretations fade; observe accurately, the rest may follow ... We find what we are looking for, so a flush of quotations does not necessarily reflect the truth ... Surveys ... are suspect' (C.H.-R., MSS.).

28 Lytton Strachey, *Eminent Victorians* (1918), preface.

29 'Aspects of Victorian Architecture', in *From Dickens to Hardy*, ed. B. Ford (1958), 441, n.10. 'Our knowledge of documents and theories is beginning to outweigh our knowledge of the visual facts' (C.H.-R., MSS.).

30 J. Mordaunt Crook, 'Patron Extraordinary: John, 3rd Marquess of Bute', in *Victorian South Wales: architecture, industry, society*, ed. P. Howell (Victorian Society, 1970), 3–22.

31 J. Mordaunt Crook, *The Greek Revival: Neo-Classical Attitudes in British Architecture* (1972); 'Architecture', in *The Age of Neo-Classicism* (Arts Council, 1972), *passim*.

32 *The History of the King's Works*, ed. H. M. Colvin: vol. V, 1660–1782, by H. M. Colvin, J. Mordaunt Crook, K. Downes and J. Newman (1976); vol. VI, 1782–1851, by J. Mordaunt Crook and M. H. Port (1973).

33 J. Mordaunt Crook, 'The Villas in Regent's Park', *C.L.* cxliii (1966), 22–5, 84–7.

34 C. L. Eastlake, *A History of the Gothic Revival*, ed. J. Mordaunt Crook (Leicester 1970; revised 1978).

35 J. Mordaunt Crook, *The British Museum* (1972).

36 Suddenly, near Tiverton, Devon. As early as 1964 Handley-Read admitted that Burges was proving 'unpackageable' and 'irreducible' (letter to J. M. Richards, 18 June 1964).

37 'Notes on William Burges's Painted Furniture', *Burl. Mag.* cv (1963), 496–529.

38 Tennyson, *Idylls of the King. Geraint and Enid*.

39 Letter of 17 August 1965, to Françoise Chiarini.

40 Letter of 20 Nov. 1966, to Mr. Webb.

41 Tennyson, *Idylls of the King. Merlin and Vivien*.

42 Sadly the reference was incomplete.

43 *B.N.* xxxiii (1877), 369.

44 W. G. Howell, 'Castell Coch', *A.R.* cix (1951), 39–46.

45 Charles Harry Ralph Handley-Read died 15 Oct. 1971, leaving £161,768. Joan Lavinia Handley-Read died 9 Dec. 1971, leaving £270,899 (Probate Office Records).

46 *The Times* 4 March 1972, 11 March 1972; *The Guardian* 4 March 1972.

47 Brian Reade, memorial address, V. & A. Library typescript, Box II, 196F.

48 Caroline Tisdall, *The Guardian* 4 March 1972. See also M. Girouard, 'Two Collectors Extraordinary', *C.L.* cli (1972), 614–5; T. Stainton, Introduction to *Paintings, Water-colours and Drawings from the Handley-Read Collection* (Fine Art Society, 1974).

1. THE DREAM

between pp. 15–18

1 For a relevant discussion, including Freud's theories of art and dreams, see P. G. Kuntz, 'Art as Public Dream: the practice and theory of Anaïs Nin', *Jnl. of Aesthetics and Art Criticism*, xxxii (1974), 525–37.

2 'The idea of comparing one's own age with former ages ... is an idea essentially belonging to an age of change ... the present times are pregnant with change' (J. S. Mill, 'The Spirit of the Age', *The Examiner*, 9 Jan. 1831).

3 Anonymous contemporary critic, quoted in G. M. Young, *Portrait of an Age* (Oxford, 1960 ed.), 68, n.2. See also W. E. Houghton, *The Victorian Frame of Mind, 1830–70* (New Haven, 1957).

4 Letter to Charles Eliot Norton, 17.6.1870, quoted in K. Clark (ed.), *Ruskin Today* (1964), 63.

5 Quoted in M. Harrison and B. Waters, *Burne-Jones* (1973), 6.

6 Quoted in J. H. Buckley, *The Victorian Temper* (Camb., Mass., 1951), 164. Frederick Harrison summed up the opposite viewpoint: 'The Vatican with its syllabus, the Medievalists-at-all-costs, Mr. Carlyle, Mr. Ruskin, the Aesthetes, are all wrong about the 19th c. It is *not* the age of money-bags and cant, soot, hubbub, and ugliness. It is the age of great expectation and unwearied striving after better things.' (*Fortnightly Rev.* xxxi, 1882, 411).

7 E. Burke, *Complete Works*, V, 149.

8 Alice Chandler, *A Dream of Order: The Medieval Ideal in Nineteenth-Century English Literature* (1970), 65. I am much indebted to Dr. Chandler's analysis.

9 W. Cobbett, *A History of the Protestant Reformation in England and Ireland*, i (1829), VIII, 192.

10 See also Ruskin: 'The worship of the Immaculate Virginity of Money, mother of the Omnipotence of Money, is the Protestant form of Madonna Worship' (*Val D'Arno*, lect. X).

11 W. Cobbett, *Rural Rides*, ed. G. D. H. Cole and Margaret Cole, i (1930), 167–8.

12 W. Cobbett, *Selections*, ed. A. M. D. Hughes (Oxford, 1923), 159.

13 J. M. Cobbett and J. P. Cobbett (eds.), *Selections from Cobbett's Political Works*, i (n.d.), 469.

14 *ibid.*, i, 295.

15 W. Cobbett, *A History of the Protestant Reformation in England and Ireland* i (1829), V, 149.

16 S. T. Coleridge, *Complete Works* iv, 288. For general discussions of Coleridge's sources of inspiration, see N. Fruman, *Coleridge: the Damned Archangel* (1972) and J. Beer, *Coleridge's Poetic Intelligence* (1977).

17 R. Southey: *Sir Thomas More; or Colloquies on the Progress and Prospects of Society*, 2 vols. (1829). For Macaulay's belligerent review, see *Edinburgh Rev.* xxxi (1830).

18 Georgiana Burne-Jones, *Memorials of Edward Burne-Jones* i (1904), 117. Horace Walpole 'lived in a horrid set of years and people; all the century

between pp. 18–21

through is like a wet Saturday afternoon to me, and the word eighteenth century sinks me down into despair. When Blake comes I begin to revive, and when Coleridge comes I am wide awake, and have been happily staring and seeing ever since' (*ibid.* ii, 1904, 319: 1897).

19 He saw the future of Europe as a battle 'between the feudal system of society, as variously modified ... and the levelling principle of democracy ... Bad as the feudal times were, they were far less injurious than these commercial ones to the kindly and generous feelings of human nature, and far, far more favourable to the principles of honour and integrity' (*Colloquies* I, 79; II, 414, 246–7, 250).

20 C. Whibley, *Lord John Manners and His Friends*, 2 vols. (1925). For Manners' retreat in Scotland, St. Mary's Tower near Birnam (1860–63), see *ibid.* ii, 141; *Blackwood's Mag.*, Sept. 1882.

21 C. Kent, *Dreamland* (1862), 238–41; T. H. Escott, *A Young England Novel* (n.d.). Smythe was the last person in England to fight a public duel, in 1852 (*D.N.B.*).

22 A. Baillie-Cochrane, 'In the Days of the Dandies, iii: The Young England Party', *Blackwood's Mag.* cxlvi (1890), 312–30.

23 E. J. Boyce, *A Memorial of the Cambridge Camden Society* (1888); J. F. White, *The Cambridge Movement* (1962).

24 'Romanism is taught *Analytically* at Oxford [and] ... *Artistically* at Cambridge' (Rev. F. Close, *The 'Restoration of Churches is the Restoration of Popery*, Cheltenham, 1844).

25 Whibley, *op. cit.*, i (1925), 66. To Manners Faber had written in 1839: 'you shall be my Pope in politics' (*ibid.*, 69). But after Faber became a Catholic in 1845 the two friends never met again.

26 *ibid.*, 68, n.1.

27 *ibid.*, 72, n.1: 'Styrian Lake' (1842).

28 Another Cambridge High Tory, he was later editor of the *Morning Post* (*D.N.B.*).

29 Disraeli portrayed Smythe as Coningsby, Manners as Sydney, Baillie-Cochrane as Buckhurst and Ambrose Phillipps as Eustace Lyle. The book was dedicated to Thomas Hope of Deepdene, brother of Beresford-Hope.

30 Whibley, *op. cit.*, i, 84.

31 *ibid.*, i, 75; Sir R. Filmer, *Patriarcha* (1680).

32 Whibley, *op. cit.*, 109. See also S. Prickett, *Romanticism and Religion: the Tradition of Coleridge and Wordsworth in the Victorian Church* (1976).

33 Whibley, *op. cit.*, 133.

34 G. B.-J., *Memorials, op. cit.*, ii (1904), 56. For Digby as littérateur, see *D.N.B.*

35 Phillipps became a convert in 1824, at the age of fifteen. He hoped to go to Oxford, to Newman's Oriel College. His later friends among the Oxford Movement included J. R. Bloxam and Forbes, Bishop of Brechin. He was a founder member of the Cambridge Camden Society. His tutor was Archdeacon Thorp. See [C. Tandini and Mrs. Phillipps de Lisle], *Two Sermons preached on the death of Ambrose Lisle March Phillipps de Lisle* (1878). For the bizarre consequences of Phillipps's attempts to promote Christian unity, see P. Anson, 'Ambrose Phillipps de Lisle and the Order of Corporate Reunion', in *Bishops at Large* (1964), 57–90.

36 They were followed in 1830 by the Hon. and Rev. George Spencer, later known as Fr. Ignatius of St. Paul, the Passionist. These three made up 'a trinity of Trinity', a Catholic Revival in miniature at Cambridge, years before the Oxford Movement (B. Holland, *Memoirs of Kenelm Henry Digby*, 1900, 47). In the years 1850–1910 there were 586 Oxford converts and 346 from Cambridge (W. G. Gordon-Gorman, *Converts to Rome*, 1910). Of these 346 Cambridge men, 102 were from Trinity.

37 B. Champneys, *Coventry Patmore* 2 vols. (1900).

38 *Modern Painters*, iii, 252.

39 M. Paraclita Reilly, *Aubrey de Vere (1814–1902): Victorian Observer* (Lincoln, Neb. 1958), 129: letter to C. E. Newton, 21 Dec. 1881.

40 J. Anstruther, *The Knight and the Umbrella* (1963); M. Trappes-Lomax, 'The Eglinton Tournament', *C.L.* lxxix (1936), 322–4.

41 N. Dillon (ed.), *Maxims of Christian Chivalry from The Broadstone of Honour* (1924), 3–4.

42 *ibid.*, 134–5.

43 *ibid.*, 18.

44 *ibid.*, 82.

45 *Modern Painters* v, ch. ix.

46 *St. Mark's Rest*, para. 88; *Modern Painters* v, 209. 'The Reformation succeeded in proclaiming that existing Christianity was a lie; but substituted no theory of it which could be more rationally or credibly sustained; and ever since, the religion of educated persons throughout Europe has been dishonest or ineffectual' (*Val d'Arno*, lect. iii, para. 75).

47 E. S. Purcell, *Life and Letters of Ambrose Phillipps de Lisle* (1900), 119: 11 Jan. 1835.

48 *ibid.*, 193–4. Digby himself lies in St. Mary's cemetery, Kensal Green. Digby had a substantial private income. 'When Socialism has been fully established, and we are all Government employées, no one will have time to write a book like *Mores Catholici*' (B. Holland, *Memoir of Kenelm Henry Digby*, 1919, 6).

49 letter to Shrewsbury, 1840 (Purcell, *op. cit.*, ii, 209–12).

50 letter to Phillipps, 17 July 1853 (*ibid.*, 248).

51 Kenelm Digby, *Ouranogaia*, canto ix.

52 Purcell, *op. cit.* ii, 289, 312.

53 *D.N.B.*; *Two Sermons, loc. cit.*

54 Phoebe Stanton, 'Sources of Pugin's *Contrasts*', in J. Summerson (ed.), *Concerning Architecture* (1968), 120–39.

55 B. Ferrey, *Pugin* (1861), 88–9.

between pp. 22–27

56 See also Ruskin: 'Renaissance architecture is the school which has conducted men's inventive and constructive faculties from the Grand Canal to Gower St.; from the marble shaft, and the lancet arch, and the wreathed leafage, and the flowing and melting harmony of gold and azure, to the square cavity in the brick wall' (*Stones of Venice*, iii, ch. i, para. 1–2). Disraeli writes of 'your Gloucester Places, and Baker Streets, and Harley Streets, and Wimpole Streets, and all those flat, dull, spiritless streets' (*Tancred*, 1845, i, ch. 10).

57 'Remarks on Articles in the *Rambler*', quoted in Ferrey, *op. cit.*, 163–4.

58 Wordsworth, in Purcell, *op. cit.*, i (1900), 62; ii (1900), 289–93, 334, 341. Its chapel was later enlarged by Pugin (1848–53). Pugin's dream of Gothicising Garendon Park was never fulfilled. His drawings survive (Purcell, *op. cit.*, ii, 286). E. W. Pugin later made some alterations (*ibid.*, 287).

59 Foundation 1835; temporary chapel 1837; monastery 1839–44. Pugin gave his services *gratis* (Pugin, *Dublin Rev.* XII, 121; A. Cruikshank, *Guide to the Abbey of Mount St. Bernard*, n.d.; Purcell, *op. cit.*, i, 108–10). For Pugin visiting Overbeck's studio in 1847, see Purcell, *op. cit.*, i, 343.

60 quoted in Phoebe Stanton, *Pugin* (1971), 108, 189.

61 in Shipley (ed.), *The Church and the World* iii (1868), 581.

62 *B.* i (1843), 69.

63 G. G. Scott, *Personal and Professional Recollections* (1879), 86, 241, 373.

64 *ibid.*, 372.

65 D. Gwynn, *The Second Spring, 1818–52* (1942); J. Bossy, *The English Catholic Community, 1870–1950* (1975).

66 letter to Phillipps, 1.12.1839 (Purcell, *op. cit.*, ii, 223).

67 letter to Phillipps, 18.12.1840 (*ibid.*, ii, 213–5).

68 letter to Phillipps (*ibid.*, ii, 218).

69 Ferrey, *Pugin, op. cit.*, 127.

70 letter to Shrewsbury, 1839 (Purcell, *op. cit.*, ii, 219).

71 letter to Phillipps, 7.2.1841 (*ibid.*, ii, 226).

72 Newman did, however, admit to Phillipps in 1857, 'If England is converted to Christ, it will be as much due (under God) to you as to any one' (Purcell, *op. cit.*, i, 372).

73 G. B.-J., *Memorials, op. cit.*, ii (1904), 285.

74 D. Knowles, *Bare Ruined Choirs: the Dissolution of the English Monasteries* (1976), 320.

75 A. L. Phillipps de Lisle and J. Talbot, Earl of Shrewsbury, *An Appeal to the Catholics of England on behalf of the Abbey Church of St. Bernard* (1842). Plates by Pugin, 'that great restorer of Christian art . . . that great man whom God has raised amongst us to rebuild the walls of our ruined Zion.'

76 D. Gwynn, *Lord Shrewsbury, Pugin and the Gothic Revival* (1946), xiii–xiv, 73, correcting exaggerated lists in M. Trappes-Lomax, *Pugin* (1932), deriving

from the *Catholic Directory* (1854) and Gillow, *Biographical Dictionary of English Catholics* (1885–1902). See also, R. Furneaux Jordan, 'Pugin's Clients', *Cornhill Mag.*, Autumn 1962.

77 Purcell, *op. cit.*, ii, 333 : 18 Jan. 1848.

78 Phoebe Stanton, 'Welby Pugin and the Gothic Revival' (Ph.D., London, 1950).

79 H. de Saint-Simon, *Le Nouveau Christianisme* (1825). For the German context, see W. D. Robson-Scott, *The Literary Background of the Gothic Revival in Germany* (1964). See also P. Rosenberg, *The Seventh Hero : Thomas Carlyle and the Theory of Radical Activism* (1974); J. Clubbe, ed., *Carlyle and his Contemporaries* (Durham, N. Carolina, 1976).

80 J. Carlyle, *Past and Present* (1842), X, 211–2.

81 *ibid.*, X, 36.

82 *ibid.*, X, 263–4.

83 *Works*, ed. Cook and Wedderburn, xxxvii (1909), 189.

84 *Modern Painters*, iii (1856); *Works*, ed. Cook and Wedderburn, V (1904), 321–2.

85 G. B.-J., *Memorials, op. cit.*, i (1904), 92.

86 *ibid.*, 147.

87 *ibid.*, 153.

88 Canon Dixon, quoted in E. P. Thompson, *William Morris : Romantic to Revolutionary* (1955), 63.

89 'The Relation of National Ethics to National Arts', Rede Lecture, 1867. *Works*, xix, 163–94.

90 'The Deteriorative Power of Conventional Art', 1868. *Works*, xvi, 259–92.

91 *Modern Painters*, II, *Works*, iv, 49.

92 *Stones of Venice*, VI, ii.

93 See also Carlyle: 'while civil Liberty is more and more secured to us, our moral Liberty is all but lost' ('Signs of the Times', *Edinburgh Rev.* xlix, 1829).

94 The Nature of Gothic, paras. 13–16, 21, in *Stones of Venice* (1851–3).

95 *Time and Tide*, 25th letter: 'Hyssop'.

96 see Joan Evans and J. H. Whitehouse (eds.), *Diaries of John Ruskin*, 3 vols. (1956–9), index.

97 Guild of St. George, Reports, in *Works*, ed. Cook and Wedderburn, XXX. See also M. E. Spence, 'The Guild of St. George', *Bulletin of the John Rylands Library* xl (1957–8).

98 *Unto This Last* (1860), 'Ad Valorem'.

99 *ibid.*, Essay iii, para. 54.

1 Chandler, *op. cit.*, 206.

2 *Fors Clavigera*, xxii, 270–71. Elsewhere he calls this viewpoint Toryism 'of the old school, Sir Walter Scott's and Homer's' (*Praeterita* i, 1).

3 quoted in P. Henderson, *William Morris* (1973 ed.), 40.

4 P. Faulkner (ed.), *William Morris: Early Romances in Prose and Verse* (1973).

5 W. Morris, *How I Became a Socialist* (1894).

6 quoted in E. P. Thompson, *op. cit.*, 74.

7 W. Morris, *The Earthly Paradise* (1868–70), 'The Apology'.

8 E. P. Thompson's final judgement in *William*

between pp. 27–34

Morris, Romantic to Revolutionary (1977 ed.), 792.

9 quoted in Henderson, *op. cit.*, 288.

10 E. P. Thompson (1977), *op. cit.*, 801.

11 *Stones of Venice*, Kelmscott Edition (1892), i.

12 J. W. Mackail, *Life of William Morris*, i (1901 ed.), 78.

13 R. Macleod, *Style and Society: architectural ideology in Britain, 1835–1914* (1971), 62.

14 quoted in Henderson, *op. cit.*, 283. 'All these uglinesses are but the outward expression of the innate moral baseness into which we are forced by our present mode of society' ('How I became a Socialist', *Collected Works*, xxiii, 2).

15 *Communist Manifesto* (1888 ed.), in L. S. Fever (ed.), *Marx and Engels: Basic Writings on Politics and Philosophy* (1969), 51.

16 B. Glasier, *William Morris and the Early Days of the Socialist Movement* (1931), 31–2.

17 Morris's writings 'provide the material for a critique of 20th c. Socialism (and Communism) as much as for a critique of 19th c. capitalism' (Asa Briggs, ed., *William Morris: Selected Writings*, 1962, 17).

18 For a summary by Morris of Marx's historical view, as developed in *Capital*, see 'The Hopes of Civilisation', in A. L. Morton (ed.), *Political Writings of William Morris* (1973), 159– 181. For a recent discussion of the transition from feudalism to capitalism, see W. Letwin, 'The Contradictions of Serfdom', *Times Literary Supplement* 25 March 1977, 373.

19 quoted in Henderson, *op. cit.*, 375.

20 See A. L. Morton (ed.), *Three Works by William Morris* (1968).

21 'The Hopes of Civilisation', in A. L. Morton (ed.), *Political Writings of William Morris* (1973), 162–3.

22 W. R. Lethaby, *Philip Webb* (1935), 94. Norman Shaw had little sympathy with 'that rampant (but defunct) Socialist ... Being an advanced Socialist he cannot do with much less than from 100% to 250% clear profit' (quoted in A. Saint, *R. N. Shaw*, 1976, 258).

23 quoted in Henderson, *op. cit.*, 296, 308. Morris was unrepentant: 'I *am* a sentimentalist in all the affairs of life, and I am proud of the title' (E. P. Thompson, 1977, *op. cit.*, 718).

24 W. B. Yeats, *Autobiographies* (1955 ed.), 175.

25 G. B.-J., *Memorials, op. cit.*, i (1904), 164.

26 *ibid.*, i, 167; ii, 332.

27 Rosalie G. Grylls, *Portrait of Rossetti* (1964), 66.

28 quoted in Harrison and Waters, *op. cit.*, 14.

29 quoted in Grylls, *op. cit.*, 67.

30 letter to Sir Sydney Cockerell, in *Friends of a Lifetime*, ed. V. Meynell (1940), 30.

31 G. B.-J., *Memorials, op. cit.*, i, 182.

32 *ibid.*, i, 169.

33 J. Dixon Hunt, *The Pre-Raphaelite Imagination, 1848–1900* (1968), 75–6; R. E. Vincent, *Gabriele Rossetti in England* (Oxford, 1936), 109.

34 quoted in Evelyn Waugh, *Rossetti* (1928; new ed. 1975), 68, n.1.

35 W. Pater, *Appreciations* (1889), 223.

36 originally 'Vanna Primavera' (*Dante Gabriel Rossetti, R.A.*, 1973, no. 360).

37 W. Morris, 'The Story of the Unknown Church', in P. Faulkner (ed.), *William Morris: Early Romances in Prose and Verse* (1973), 146–7.

38 G. B.-J., *Memorials, op. cit.*, i, 97–8.

39 *ibid.*, i, 112.

40 *ibid.*, i, 113–14.

41 *ibid.*, i, 96.

42 *ibid.*, ii, 110.

43 Rossetti, *Letters*, ed. O. Doughty and J. R. Wahl, i (1965), 293: 6 Mar. 1856.

44 Hunt, *op. cit.*, 44.

45 G. B.-J., *Memorials, op. cit.*, i, 143.

46 Hunt, *op. cit.*, 28, 34, 53. Oscar Wilde described him as 'a dreamer in the land of mythology ... a seer of fairy visions, a symbolic painter' (*Dublin Univ. Mag.*, xc, 1877, 118).

47 G. B.-J., *Memorials, op. cit.* ii, 97–8.

48 quoted in *Apollo* cii (1975) 314 *et seq.*

49 G. B.-J., *Memorials, op. cit.* ii, 318

50 Harrison and Waters, *op. cit.* 153, 155. He described Avalon as 'a magical land that I dream about' (G. B.-J., *Memorials, op. cit.* ii, 168: 1886).

51 eg. J. Morris, *The Age of Arthur* (1973), 116–23; Elizabeth Jenkins, *The Mystery of King Arthur* (1975).

52 A. E. Baker, *Tennyson Concordance* (1914), 158–60.

53 Tennyson, 'The Higher Pantheism'.

54 G. B.-J., *Memorials, op. cit.*, i, 76.

55 quoted in Hunt, *op. cit.*, 23.

56 quoted in C. Ricks, *Tennyson* (1972), 92.

57 *ibid.*, 90–91.

58 *ibid.*, 92.

59 quoted in Henderson, *op. cit.*, 305.

60 G. B. Shaw, *The Perfect Wagnerite* (1818).

61 quoted in Henderson, *op. cit.*, 205. For Ruskin's hostile dismissal of The Meistersingers, in a letter to Georgiana Burne-Jones, 30 June 1882, see K. Clark (ed.) *Ruskin Today* (1964), 77.

62 G. B.-J., *Memorials, op. cit.*, ii, 43.

63 W. Morris, *The English Pre-Raphaelites* (1891).

64 J. S. Mill, *The Spirit of the Age* (1831).

65 quoted in Macleod, *op. cit.*, 114.

66 Oscar Wilde, intro. to R. Rodd, *Rose Leaf and Apple Leaf* (1882). It was in a review of William Morris's poems that Walter Pater first stated the amorality of art: 'Not the fruit of experience but experience itself is the end. ... To burn always with this hard gem-like flame, to maintain this ecstasy, is success in life ... wisdom [is] ... the love of art for art's sake ... for art comes to you professing frankly to give nothing but the highest quality to your moments as they pass, and simply for those moments' sake' (*Westminster Rev.* lxvii, 1868, 309–12).

between pp. 34–35

67 quoted in Harrison and Waters, *op. cit.*, 110.
68 G. B.-J., *Memorials, op. cit.*, ii, 18–19, 29.
69 quoted in Harrison and Waters, *op. cit.*, 159.
70 *R.I.B.A. Jnl.* xxiv (1917), 255.

2. THE DREAMER
between pp. 36–40

1 *B.N.* xxxvii (1879), 353–4.
2 Within weeks of the book's appearance, it was almost certainly Burges who – as 'Georgius Oldhousen' – wrote a letter to the *Building News* complaining about architects who let the professional side down by advertising (*B.N.* xxxvii, 1879, 478).
3 R. Kerr, *The Ambassador Extraordinary*, i (1879), 206–7, 341; ii, 122.
4 *ibid.*, i, 216.
5 *ibid.*, ii, 101, 126.
6 *ibid.*, i, 330–31.
7 *ibid.*, ii, 99.
8 *ibid.*, i, 213, 319.
9 *ibid.*, 289.
10. *ibid.*, i, 313–9.
11 'Alfred this year in my office' (Abstract, 1859); 'Family councils about Alfred Feb. 5' (*ibid.*, 1860); 'Alfred to Mc. Connochie's' (*ibid.*, 1866).
12 Mary was christened Mary Leschallas Burges. Alfred's godfather was John Leschallas's brother William (d. 12 Dec. 1852), a London wholesale stationer and paper-maker on whose warehouse Burges worked in 1858 (Abstract, 1858). John Leschallas left £500,000, including £1000 each to William Burges and his brother Alfred, £3000 to Alfred Burges Snr. and £2000 to Mary (Probate records, Somerset House). William also inherited a screen (Abstract, 1878). See also obits. *Times*, 7 Dec. 1877, 9 and Boase, ii, 393. The bulk of the fortune went to his cousin Henry Pigé, who married in 1872 and became Henry Pigé Leschallas in 1874.
13 *C.E.A.Jnl.*, viii (1845), 194.
14 *ibid.*, vi (1843), 249–50, 281–2.
15 *B.* x (1852), 439.
16 *ibid.*, xii (1854), 461.
17 *C.E.A.Jnl.* ii (1839), 38.
18 *ibid.*, xv (1852), 385–6.
19 *ibid.*, xiii (1850), 366.
20 *ibid.*, xviii (1855), 186–8; xx (1857), 256–7.
21 *ibid.*, xx (1857), 256–7.
22 *B.* x (1852), 253.
23 *C.E.A.Jnl.* xviii (1855), 186–8; xx (1857), 256–7.
24 A great mass of concrete along the Thames, 30 ft. wide, 673 ft. 6 ins. long, 27 ft. high (*ibid.*, i, 1837–8, 12, 32).
25 Copy with date, inscription and bookplate, in the Fowler Colln., John's Hopkins Univ., U.S.A.
26 Probate records, Somerset House.
27 The second and third portions of the Bute East Docks were finished in 1860. Chief engineers:

Messrs. Walker, Burges and Cooper; resident engineer: John Mc. Connochie (*B.N.* vi, 1860, 942).
28 In 1839 he was in 'Cockayne's class', in 1840 'Carr's class', in 1841 in 'Fearnley's and J. Edward's classes', in 1842 'in Hayes Snr. Class and in Dr. Major's class for one quarter' (Abstract, *passim.*). School Calendars for the Junior Dept. show him in the Upper First Class in 1839–40 (King's College archives). Burges had previously attended several junior schools: Renfield's School, Manor House, Enfield (Abstract, 1834); Miss Atkinson's, Cannon St., Westminster (*ibid.*, 1835), Whitehead's School, Ramsgate (*ibid.*, 1837); and Dr. Wallace's, Edmonton (*ibid.*, 1838).
29 W. M. Rossetti, *Reminiscences* (1910), 155.
30 F. J. C. Hearnshaw, *Centenary History of King's College* (1929); 'Entered the Applied Science dept . . . 20 April' (Abstract, 1843).
31 *ibid.*, 1837.
32 'Left at the end of Michaelmas term' (*ibid.*, 1843). He had spent the previous long vacation with a Mr. Hawkins of Granton, near Edinburgh, perhaps learning to draw.
33 Burges's letter of acceptance, 18 May 1857 (King's College archives).
34 For Burges's 1859 design, see *B.* xl (1881), 581. The job went to Gilbert Scott (Abstract, 1860). Burges was responsible for minor alterations in 1852 (*ibid.*, 1852).
35 *A.*, xxv (1881), 315.
36 H. M. Colvin, *Biographical Dictionary of British Architects, 1600–1840* (1978), 115–20.
37 *E.* v (1846), 19n. His first recorded design had been the 'title page for [a] Survey of [the] Estates of St. Bartholomew's Hospital' (Abstract, 1844).
38 Flying Barn Cottage and New Lodge, Cumberland Gate (V. & A., P. & D., A. 182K, 8739 A.94; J. Mordaunt Crook and M. H. Port, *The History of the King's Works*, vi, 1973, 398, n.4).
39 Library chimneypiece (V. & A., P. & D., A.182B).
40 Thorganby with West Cottingwith, East Riding (V. & A., P. & D., A.182, M; BM. Add. MS. 47610).
41 Door and ironwork (V. & A., P. & D., A.182.O; *King's Works, op. cit.*, vi, 254).
42 Abstract, 1848; *King's Works, op. cit.*, vi, 291.
43 B.M., Add. MS. 47610; *King's Works, op. cit.*, vi, 177, n.3. In 1845 Burges was living close by at 2, Lambeth Terrace. Between 1834 and 1848 his family lived in York Rd., Lambeth.
44 Georgiana Burne-Jones, *Memorials of Edward Burne-Jones*, ii, 203.
45 G. G. Scott, ed., *Gleanings from Westminster Abbey* (1861), 105. For Burges's drawings, see V. & A., P. & D., 93 ES, 8827, 35.
46 'He used to jeer at Blore for declining to give his opinion on the age of a wall because there were no mouldings on it, saying he should have known by the size, working and bonding of the stones, and by

between pp. 40–44

the mortar joints' (Aitchison's memoir, *R.I.B.A. Trans.*, 1883–4, 206).

47 J. Carter, *Specimens of Ancient Sculpture and Painting*, 2 vols. (1780–94).

48 *Catalogue of . . . the library of W. Burges* (Puttick and Simpson, 1882), no. 55. This volume was bought by Sir William Emerson. In 1850 Burges sketched the Convent of the Assumption at Bruges from an angle identical to that chosen by Pugin (compare Ayling, *Photographs from Sketches by A. W. Pugin*, ii, 438 with R.I.B.A., 'Domestic Art', 42, iii).

49 *R.I.B.A. Papers*, 1867–8, appendix.

50 Abstract, 1849.

51 'On the Art of Mosaic, Ancient and Modern', *Trans. Soc. of Arts* (1847); 'Mosaic as Applied to Architectural Decoration', *R.I.B.A. Papers* (1847); *Specimens of the Geometrical Mosaic of the Middle Ages* (1848).

52 See N. Pevsner, *M. D. Wyatt* (1950). Wyatt contributed the section on Renaissance ornament to Owen Jones' *Grammar of Ornament* (1868 ed.), 109–27.

53 *A Report on the Eleventh French Exposition of the Products of Industry* (1849). See also his *Paris Universal Exhibition; Report on Furniture and Decorations* (1856) and *Report on the Art of Decoration at the International Exhibition, Paris, 1867* (1868).

54 *Enquiries into the Willingness of Manufacturers . . . to support Periodical Exhibitions of the Works of Industry of All Nations* (1849).

55 The saga of the Crystal Palace is best followed in G. F. Chadwick, *The Works of Sir Joseph Paxton* (1961). For details of its design, see *B.* viii (1850), 10, 20, 45, 81, 92, 178, 241, 265, 277, 298, 308, 313, 337.

56 *B.* xxvii (1869), 906; xxxv (1877), 541, 545, 550; xxxvi (1878), 49, 391; *A.* xvii (1877), 331, 339.

57 'Window for D. Wyatt now in Chichester Cathedral' (Abstract, 1851). Probably the window by Charles Gibbs Snr. referred to in *E.* xviii, N.S. xv (1857), 341 and xix, N.S. xvi (1858), 138. A pencil sketch in the Mellon Collection, and a newspaper cutting from the collection of Capt. John Wyatt, suggest however that Clayton was responsible for the cartoon (J. M. Robinson, *The Wyatts*, 1979, 215).

58 'With Digby Wyatt preparing Exhibition buildings' (Abstract, 1851). Wyatt's own scheme was officially produced in conjunction with Owen Jones and C. H. Wild (*Art Jnl.*, catalogue 1851, xvii). Wyatt wrote the section on 'The Construction of the Building' in vol. i of the *Official Description and Catalogue*, 49–81. Burges visited the Exhibition with his father on 15 May (Abstract, 1851). He may similarly have helped Wyatt with a 'Competition for an Institute in the North' (Abstract, 1851).

59 'Wrote letterpress for metalwork' (*ibid.*, 1851).

60 'Papers for Wyatt's book on Exhibition' (*ibid.*, 1852). For a review, see *B.* xi (1853), 246. Many of

the plates were drawn by Frederick Smallfield and lithographed by Francis Bedford.

61 J. B. Waring, *Masterpieces of the Industrial Art and Sculpture at the International Exhibition, 1862*, 3 vols. (1862).

62 *Jnl. of Design* ii (1849), *passim.*

63 M. D. Wyatt and J. B. Waring, *The Fine Arts Courts in the Crystal Palace* (1854): i, Italian; ii, Renaissance; iii, Medieval; iv, Byzantine; v, Medieval Sculpture. Pullan assisted Wyatt in designing the Medieval and Byzantine sections.

64 *Jnl. of Design* ii (1849–50), 72; iv (1850), 78. N. Pevsner, *Some Architectural Writers of the Nineteenth Century* (Oxford, 1972), 155–6, 160.

65 R.I.B.A., Arc. IV, 34; 'Designed St. Edward's Shrine, March 22' (Abstract, 1852). The drawing was exhibited at the Institute of British Architects (*A.* xxv, 1881, 300).

66 Aitchison's memoir, *R.I.B.A. Trans.* 1883–4, 207.

67 *ibid.*

68 *ibid.*, 206. Wyatt grew up at Troy House. Mon., a romantic seventeenth-century seat. (Robinson, *The Wyatts*, 202.)

69 For a transcription of Du Sommerard's vision of Troy Town, see H. Shaw, *Dresses and Decorations* (1843), n.p.

70 'Work for Clutton'; 'Regularly in Clutton's office' (Abstract, 1851).

71 *ibid.*

72 *ibid.*, 1852–3.

73 'Worked on Hardy's Church for Clutton' (Abstract, 1851); *B.* x (1852), 358 and xi (1853), 665; Pevsner, *Staffs.*, 123–4. The church was erected by John Hardy Snr. and Jnr. of Dunstall Hall, through a bequest by Charles Arkwright. The gravestone of Hardy Snr. (d.1854) may be by Burges.

74 'Hatherop Church for Clutton' (Abstract, 1855); Verey, *Glos. Cotswolds*, 270–2. Hatherop Castle dates from 1850 to 1856, and Burges may also have been involved ('Lord de Mauley's work', Abstract, 1853). Chapel stained glass by O'Connor, 1855.

75 'To Bremmar [sic] House with Clutton (Sir J. Hulse)'; 'Sir Charles and Lady Hulse' (Abstract, 1855); 'Lady Hulse' (*ibid.*, 1856). Dean Hulse of Salisbury may be the link here.

76 'Clutton joined me at Lille' (*ibid.*, 1855); 'With Clutton to Lille' (*ibid.*, 1856).

77 Abstract, 1856. The row seems to have been patched up in the 1860s. 'With Nicholson saw Clutton and went to Yatton' (*ibid.*, 1864). 'To Wallingford with Clutton' (Abstract, 1866).

78 *ex inf.* Dr. Penelope Hunting.

79 25 June 1856 (Abstract).

80 'Had stock from my father . . . Opened Banking Account at Cocks Biddulph and Co.' (Abstract, 1861); 'Price's bank failed' (*ibid.*, 1866); 'Bought Great Eastern press shares' (*ibid.*, 1880). Burges's account with Cocks Biddulph does not appear to

between pp. 44–50
have survived.

81 *B.* xxxiii (1875), 1146.

82 *E.* xxvii, N.S. xxv (1860), 385.

83 Abstract, 1845–7.

84 *B.* xxxiv (1876), 31–2; *R.I.B.A. Papers* 1875–6, 79. For Burges's 1848 drawings, see V. & A., P. & D., 93 E3, 14, 44.

85 Abstract, 1848, 1852. For Burges's drawing of the screen in Bishop Alcock's chapel, see his *Architectural Drawings* (1870), pl. xviii; for Prior Crauden's chapel, see V. & A., P. & D., 93 E1, 8823, 26–7 and 93 E5, 8827, 22–4.

86 Abstract, 1849.

87 *ibid.*, 1850; *B.N.* XL (1881), 473. His companions were Salter and Warren.

88 Abstract, 1851.

89 'Took T. Mackerness to school at Paris' (*ibid.*, 1852).

90 *ibid.*, 1853.

91 *ibid.*, 1853–4 (route); R.I.B.A., S.N.B., iv–xiii.

92 Abstract, 1853.

93 Beauvais: 1853, 1855, 1856, 1862, 1863, 1864, 1865, 1867, 1869, 1875, 1879; Rouen: 1853, 1855, 1858, 1860; Amiens: 1853, 1856, 1860, 1862; Châlons: 1853, 1854; Chartres: 1855, 1862; Tours: 1851, 1863.

94 'Nowhere is there to be found more boldness of construction, or purity and loveliness of detail than here' (*B.N.* v, 1859, 650).

95 R.I.B.A., S.N.B. vii (1854), 1.

96 Abstract, 1873, 1877, 1879; R.I.B.A., S.N.B., xv, xlv, lvi, lx.

97 *Studio* vii (1896), 3.

98 'Saw Over Beck's [sic] studio' (Abstract, 1854).

99 *ibid.*

1 *R.I.B.A. Trans.* 1883–4, 204–6. Burges designed the candlesticks and draped fabrics. See *Art Jnl.* 1897, 58 and V. & A., P. & D., 52c: E. 1847–1910; 737 and 741–1896.

2 *R.I.B.A. Trans.* 1883–4, 204–6.

3 'Made clasps for Dante' (Abstract, 1854).

4 'Deane did Tennyson illustrations' (Abstract, 1875). Colln. J. Mordaunt Crook.

5 *R.I.B.A. Trans.* 1883–4, 204–6.

6 Abstract, 1855.

7 *ibid.*

8 Abstract, 1860–61; R.I.B.A., S.N.B., xxix– xxx.

9 Abstract, 1873; R.I.B.A., S.N.B., xv. In Florence he stayed with Lonsdale.

10 Abstract, 1879.

11 *E.* xxiii, N.S. xx (1862), 26; R.I.B.A., S.N.B., xxix (1860).

12 Burges advised on the layout of a new street near the Chiaga River, between the Toledo and the Corso Victor Emmanuel: the world of King Bomba was to give way to a Neapolitan vision of Haussmann's Paris (Report, wmk. 1864, Weller MSS.; Abstract, 1865). Alas, little was done: when

Ruskin went there in 1874 he still found it 'the most disgusting place in Europe' (*Works*, XXIII, xxxii).

13 'Journey to Italy to study for Constantinople' (Abstract, 1856); R.I.B.A., S.N.B., xxii.

14 *E.* xix, N.S. xvi (1858), 24.

15 G. J. Grelot, *A Late Voyage to Constantinople*, trans. J. Phillips (1683).

16 A. Vercellio, *Habiti Antichi*.

17 *R.I.B.A. Jnl.* 1868–9, 221. Cf. G. Goodwin, 'Turkish Architecture, 1840–1940', *Art and Archaeology Research Papers* ii (1977), 1–14.

18 *B.N.* iv (1858), 167. See also Burges's chapter in W. G. Thornbury, *Turkish Life and Character* ii (1860), 282, 284, 292. This volume was optimistically dedicated by Thornbury 'To my dear friend, William Burges, the erection of whose memorial church in Constantinople will not only form an epoch in the History of Oriental Christianity but will add another interest to that wonderful city'. Thornbury's book has a double theme: the danger of Russian domination, *and* the decadence and corruption of the Turkish Empire. Burges used the 'profits of literary labour' in 1858 to pay for a goblet, made for his own use, to his own design.

19 G. Fossati and L. Haghe, *Aya Sofia, Constantinople, as recently restored* (1852). The brothers Fossati, originally from Switzerland, were employed by the Tsar in Moscow before moving to Constantinople in 1837 to build his new embassy there. They restored Sta. Sophia in 1847–9.

20 W. Saltzenberg, *Alt-christliche Baudenkmale von Constantinopel* (Berlin, 1854). Both Fossati and Saltzenberg contain inaccuracies, but they were the only scholarly works available until Texier and Pullan's *Byzantine Architecture* (1864) and Lethaby and Swainson's *Sancta Sophia* (1894).

21 *B.N.* iv (1858), 163–7. For a general guide, see Murray's *Handbook* (1892).

22 *ibid.*, 163–5, pl. 5. Lavers of Southampton St. reproduced the pattern on Burges's instructions. For the original glass, see M. Levey, *The World of Ottoman Art* (1976), ill.

23 *B.N.* iv (1858), 164, 166, ills. by Burges.

24 Hilary Sumner-Boyd and J. Freely, *Strolling Through Istanbul* (Istanbul, 1973), 31.

25 Abstract, 1857.

26 *B.* xxxiv (1876), 18.

27 *B.* xx (1862), 368.

28 *B.* xxxiii (1875), 1146.

29 *R.I.B.A. Trans.* 1881–2, 24–7.

30 *R.I.B.A. Papers*, 1876–7, 207.

31 'The more perfect development of thirteenth-century art, viz. the French school, is very like what the Greeks might have produced if they had to work in a different material and different climate, with the advantage of the knowledge of the pointed arch' (*R.I.B.A. Papers*, 1875–6, 156). 'The best work of the thirteenth century ... approximates in feeling to Greek art; earnest studies of the best

between pp. 50–55

Gothic work of the thirteenth century, will lead us, step by step, back to Greek work' (E. W. Godwin, 'Studies and Mouldings', *B.N.* xxxvi, 1879, 261, citing a 'favourite' Greek moulding of Burges).

32 *B.* xx (1862), 368; 'Lecture on Pagan Architecture at Kensington' (Abstract, 1862).

33 'Basle, Berne, Interlaken, Lucerne, St. Gothard' (*ibid.*, 1861).

34 Chillon, L'Aigle, Lausanne, Neuchatel (R.I.B.A., S.N.B., xxxvii, 1869).

35 For Anglo-Swiss Gothic, see *Zeitschrift für Schweizerische Archäologie und Kunstgeschichte* xxix (1972). *Ex inf.* Mr. Andrew Saint.

36 'Majorca, Bendinat ... La Palma, Alaro, Belsor, Barcelona' (Abstract, 1874). 'Bought Spanish photos' (*ibid.*).

37 G. E. Street, *Some Account of Gothic Architecture in Spain* (revised ed. 1869).

38 W. R. Lethaby, 'Medieval Architecture', in G. C. Crump and E. F. Jacob, *The Legacy of the Middle Ages* (Oxford, 1926), 63.

39 *G M* ccxiii (1862), 243.

40 *Archaeological Jnl.* xiii (1856), 138–44. 'Drew Beauvais mitre' (Abstract, 1855). The drawings are now in the Soc. of Antiquaries' Library, B.P., Misc., i, 6, and V. & A., P. & D., 93 E5, 8827 : 60. See also W. C. J. d'Ebner, *Geschichte der Kaiserlichen etc.* (Nuremberg, 1787); N.-X. Willemin, *Monuments Inédits* (1839), pl. 21; G. Knight, *Normans in Sicily* ii (1838), 242; *Regali Sepolchri del Duomo di Palermo* (Naples, 1784).

41 *Archaeol. Jnl.* xviii (1861), 174–5; Soc. of Antiquaries, Misc. Portfolio, iv, 7.

42 *Mémoires de la Société Académique du Dep. de l'Oise*, iii (Beauvais, 1857), 266.

43 W. C. J. d'Ebner, *op. cit.*; M. D. Wyatt, 'Textile Manufactures and Embroideries', *Archaeol. Jnl.* xviii (1861), 173 n.6. For medieval vestments see also, F. Bock, *Geschichte der Liturgischen Gewänder des Mittelalters* (Bonn, 1856–71); C. Cahier and A. Martin, *Mélanges Archéologiques* 6 vols. (1847–68); C. H. Hartshorne, *English Medieval Embroideries* (1848).

44 *G.M.* N.S. xiv (1863), 553–63.

45 G. Williams, *The Holy City: or historical and topographical notices of Jerusalem*, 2 vols. (1849) and *Dr. Pierotti and his Assailants, or a defence of Jerusalem Explored* (1864). See also Sir C. W. Wilson, *The Recovery of Jerusalem*, ed. W. Morrison (Palestine Exploration Fund, 1871). Burges designed Williams's memorial tablet in King's College Chapel, Cambridge (V. & A., Estim. Bk. 8 July 1878; R.I.B.A., S.N.B. lviii, 1878, 43 and lix, 1878–9, 76).

46 *B.* xxi (1863), 386.

47 *G.M.* ccxiii (1862), 10–11.

48 For a complete list of exhibits, cf. R. Alcock, *Catalogue of Works of Industry and Art Sent from Japan* (1862).

49 Eg. ill. of Japanese screen, *B.N.* xviii (1870), 151, 155; lectures on Japanese art, *B.N.* xxii (1872), 221–3.

50 *G.M.* ccxiii (1862), 244–54.

51 *E.* xxiii, N.S. xx (1862), 339.

52 Eg. V. & A., P. & D., 93 E.5, 8827: 48–58 (list of prints, c.1840–50).

53 The intermediary was Reichensperger (*E.* xviii, N.S. xv, 1857, 18–22, 367 and xxiv, N.S. xxi, 1863, 335).

54 *E.* xlii (1882), 482.

55 'In his little pocket-books ... the cunning fingers were ever busy noting down the art longings and thoughts of the yet busier brain; and of the many lovely works he has left behind him, I know of none to compete in interest with those tiny memorandum books, containing as they do his first ideas of nearly everything he subsequently carried out, and of many a dream beside' (E. W. Godwin, *B.A.* xv, 1881, 213).

56 *B.N.* xiv (1867), 771n.

57 *B.N.* xv (1868), 31.

58 *B.A.* xv (1881), 214.

59 in O. Shipley, ed., *The Church and the World* iii (1868), 588.

60 *B.N.* xxvi (1874), 79.

61 *E.* xxi, N.S. xviii (1860), 246–51.

62 *B.* xiv (1856), 420. Millais's picture 'The Huguenot' (1852) secured his election as A.R.A. For a contemporary critique of 'The Huguenot refusing to wear the Catholic badge', see *Fraser's Mag.* xlvi (1852), 234–5.

63 *G.M.* ccxiv (1863), 268. Browning's poem 'The Bishop orders his tomb at St. Praxed's church' satirises the vanity and decadence of the Renaissance church.

64 'What was meant by originality? It was going back to nature. Pre-Raphaelitism had done that. It had gone back to a pure system of colouring and to nature. Study was the basis of all art. And in working out the principles of painting as well as of architecture, he did not see why they should not work out a new style by going back to true principles' (*E.* xxi, N.S. xviii, 1860, 246–51).

65 *E.* xix, N.S. xvi (1858), 234.

66 *E.* xxi, N.S. xviii (1860), 246–51. Two years later when Digby Wyatt supported Hope by pleading for 'a national style' through 'a system of enlightened eclecticism', Street revealed the instincts of a true Goth with a nicely circular argument: He was glad to hear Mr. Digby Wyatt's re-echo of [Hope's] aspirations after that catholicity which was to involve the unity of their art. No doubt when true principles were properly developed, unity would follow, and Mr. Digby Wyatt would then find himself and all other architects working in Gothic' (*ibid.*, 235–6).

67 *Art Applied to Industry* (1865), 95–108.

between pp. 56–60

68 *ibid.*, 106.

69 *ibid.*, 107.

70 *B.* xxxiii (1875), 1146.

71 *B.* xviii (1860), 359.

72 See statistics cited in J. D. Rosenberg, *The Darkening Glass: a portrait of Ruskin's Genius* (1961), 214, n.7.

73 *B.* xviii (1860), 395.

74 *ibid.*

75 Published in Vienna in 1796, from woodblocks sponsored by the Emperor Maximilian *c.*1590.

76 *B.N.* xxxvii (1879), 143–5.

77 For examples of Burges's drawings from B.M. MSS., see V. & A., P. & D., 93 E3, 28, 30, 32, 49, 52–5.

78 J. Hewitt, *Ancient Armour*, 3 vols. (Oxford, 1855–60).

79 A. F. Demmin, *Weapons of War*, trans. C. C. Black (1870).

80 S. R. Meyrick, *Critical Inquiry into Ancient Armour*, 3 vols. (1824); *Illustrations of Ancient Arms and Armour* (1830), plates by J. Skelton.

81 Anna Stothard, *Monumental Effigies* (1817), text by J. A. Kempe.

82 T. and G. Hollis, *Monumental Effigies* (1843).

83 J. G. and L. A. Waller, *Monumental Brasses* (1842–64).

84 C. Boutell, *Monumental Brasses and Slabs* (1847).

85 H. Haines, *A Manual of Monumental Brasses* (Oxford, 1861).

86 J. H. Hefner-Alteneck, *Trachten des christlichen Mittelalters*, 3 vols. (Mannheim, 1840–54).

87 H. Shaw, *Dresses and Decorations* (1843).

88 C. Bonnard, *Costumes des 13–15 cs*, 2 vols. (Paris, 1829), plates by P. Mercuri.

89 N.-X. Willemin, *Monuments Inédits* (1839), text by M. Potier.

90 F. W. Fairholt, *Costume in England* (2nd ed., 1860).

91 J. E. J. Quicherat, *Costume en France* (Paris, 1875), originally published in the *Magasin Pittoresque*. Burges also recommended illustrated works by J. S. Cotman and N. Humphreys. See *A.* xvi (1876), 224.

92 *B.N.* xxvi (1874), 127.

93 Planché also wrote a *History of British Costume* (1834), and chapters on costume in Knight's *Pictorial History of England* (1837). Burges described his *Pursuivant at Arms; or Heraldry founded upon Truth* (1852) as 'perhaps the only sensible book on what many consider as the vain science of heraldry'. He also credited Planché with proving that Cockerell's study of the West front at Wells cathedral was no more than an 'iconographical romance'. For an obituary of Planché, see *B.N.* xxxviii (1880), 669.

94 'The jambieres look like Jack boots ... worn by innumerable Amazons in ... burlesques' (*A.* xvi, 1876, 188). Burges approved of the heraldry in

'Richard III' at Drury Lane, devised by his friend Stephen Tucker (*A.* xvi, 1876, 239). For illustrations of Godwin's costumes for 'Othello', see *B.A.* xiv (1880), 179; for 'The Merchant of Venice', see *B.A.* xiii (1880), 78; for 'Hamlet', see *B.A.* xv (1881), 192.

95 'All of us naturally like to see beautiful objects and beautiful dresses, and since pageants have become things of the past, and since our religious ceremonies have been destroyed by the Reformation, the theatre is the only resource for the sight-loving public' (*A.* xvi, 1876), 224).

96 *R.I.B.A. Jnl.* ii (1860–61), 23; *C.E.A. Jnl.* xxiv (1861), 18–20.

97 *Church and the World, op. cit.*, iii, 589.

98 *ibid.*, 591.

99 *E.* xxiii, N.S. xx (1862), 336. At the Paris Exhibition of 1867, however, he was less optimistic (*B.N.* xiv, 1867, 869).

1 *G.M.* ccxxiii (1862), 186–7.

2 *A.* ix (1873), 13.

3 *B.* xxix (1871), 231.

4 *B.N.* xxvi (1874), 682.

5 *B.N.* xxiv (1873), 261.

6 *B.N.* xxxv (1878), 627, 683–4.

7 *B.N.* xxxviii (1880), 530.

8 *American Architect and Building News* xii (1882), 88. Cf. also R.I.B.A., S.N.B., xli (1871), 15–20.

9 *G.M.* ccxv (1863), 677.

10 *B.* xx (1862), 426.

11 *B.N.* v (1859), 898.

12 R.I.B.A., S.N.B., xiii (1856), 89.

13 *Art Applied to Industry*, 7, 11, 12, 108, 112, 117, 119, 120. Burges suggested that the R.I.B.A. should sponsor life classes (*C.E.A. Jnl.* xxiv, 1861, 18; *R.I.B.A.* Papers 1860–61, appendix, 6); and he was largely responsible for the holding of Saturday evening life-classes at the A.A. (*B.N.* xi, 1864, 303, 327–8, 347–8 and xiii, 1866, 175). He may have had some connection with the Bedford School of Art in Store St. (*C.E.A. Jnl.* xvi, 1853, 116): 'Designed Bedford's Almanack' (Abstract, 1851–2).

14 *Art Applied to Industry*, 5. For Dyce, see obit. *B.N.* xi (1864), 139. For Burges's drawings of live models, and anatomical exercises, see R.I.B.A. misc. 4. He once 'spent a whole year in drawing from a skeleton' (*B.N.* xi, 1864, 303). Burges rescued the young Goscombe John from the drudgery of copying Faux's *Anatomy*: 'Send him into the fields and let him draw horses and sheep' (Fiona Pearson, *Goscombe John*, 1979, 9).

15 R.I.B.A., S.N.B., xxi (1856), 30.

16 *B.* xvii (1859), 9.

17 *Art Applied to Industry*, 119. 'No one could be an architect without the power of drawing the figure. To obtain this power there was no royal road; they must fag for it; it could be obtained only by work. They should take as models Greek sculpture and the human figure, and even here the most careful

between pp. 61–64

selection was necessary. There were very few perfect models, he had ... met with but three in his life. The perfect figure could only be drawn by a sort of eclecticism; the enlightened artist, after studying the *genus*, would then depict the perfect individual' (*B.* xxix, 1871, 231). Curiously, Burges supplied the figures in J. R. Cole's drawing of Butterfield's All Saints, Margaret St. (Abstract, 1855; *I.L.N.* 24 March 1855).

18 *ibid.*, 111.

19 *B.* xiv (1856), 409.

20 *Art Applied to Industry*, 112.

21 *B.* xxxiii (1875), 1146.

22 *B.N.* xiv (1867), 752. He thought 'a very wonderful lithograph' by Kell and E. J. Tarver, of the Westminster Abbey cloisters, would have been better published alongside Gustave Doré than by the Architectural Association. He even criticised Lonsdale for publishing a perspective of St. Mary Overie, Southwark, instead of a measured drawing (*ibid.*).

23 *B.N.* iv (1858), 162.

24 *Art Applied to Industry*, 112.

25 *B.* xix (1861), 190.

26 *R.I.B.A. Trans.* 1860–61, 15; *C.E.A. Jnl.* xxiii (1860), 374. For preliminary notes, see R.I.B.A., S.N.B., Sept. 1860.

27 Architectural drawings by Italian architects exhibited at Florence in 1861 were 'nearly all elevations ... coloured up in the manner our fathers delighted in ... either shaded up with Indian ink until they look as if they had been put up the chimney, or else tinted over with yellow ochre or burnt umber until they appear to have undergone a lengthened process of baking; either of which styles has the advantage of making good architecture look bad, and bad architecture look passable, so that the designer never knows what he is about ... The Italian architects appear also to have a great disinclination to put scales to their drawings, or to write on the plans ... It is much to be hoped that when the next exhibition of Italian art takes place, the countrymen of Dante will give some indication of having studied the noble domestic architecture of his time. Already a beginning has been made by the restoration of the Bargello' (*B.* xix, 1861, 710–11).

28 *B.N.* xiv (1867), 770.

29 *Jnl. of Design* i (1849), 125–6. The standard textbook was C. Boutell, *Monumental Brasses and Slabs* (1847). For a list by Burges of notable brasses, see R.I.B.A., S.N.B., xvix, (1856). For his drawings from brasses, see V. & A., P. & D., 93 E3, 38–41.

30 *B.N.* xii (1865), 557–8.

31 *R.I.B.A. Trans.* 1883–4, 206. Allen published a book on *Cottage Building* in 1849–50. He was Curator of the Architectural Museum until dismissed in 1861 (Abstract, 1861).

32 *R.I.B.A. Trans.* 1883–4, 207.

33 *B.N.* xii (1865), 557–8.

34 B.M. Cott. Aug. I, vol. i, 2.

35 B.M. Cott. Aug. II, vol. i.

36 B.M. Cott. Aug. I, vol. i, 4.

37 B.M. Cott. Aug. I, vol. ii, 76; Cott. Aug. III.

38 *Vetusta Monumenta* iv (1815).

39 Musée Wicar, Lille.

40 'They were neither drawings with the finished *abandon* of penmanship with which Mr. Street has revolutionised pen-and-ink architectural sketching, nor yet mnemonic scratches as Mr. Petit rejoiced in before he took to his colour-box' (*E.* xxvi, N.S., xxiii, 1865, 352–3).

41 *R.I.B.A. Jnl.* ii (1860–61), 23; *C.E.A. Jnl.* xxiv (1861), 18–20.

42 *Church and the World, op. cit.*, 587.

43 R.I.B.A., S.N.B., xvii (1850). For Burges's drawings from the Berri Bible, B.M., see V. & A., P. & D., 93 E3, 24; from the 'Poems of Christine de Pisan' (B.M. Harl. 4431), see *ibid.*, 48.

44 *G.M.* ccxix (1865), 145–54. For reproductions by Westlake and Purdue, see *B.N.* xii (1865), 298, 302–3 and xxiv (1873), 531. See also *E.* xxvi, N.S. xxiii (1865), 296–7.

45 For Burges's drawings of B.M. 4425, see V. & A., P. & D., 93 E3, 53.

46 N. H. J. Westlake, *The Litany sketched from a Psalter executed in England about 1320* (1858) and *Old Testament History illustrated by a series of Designs by an English Artist about 1310* (1858); N. H. J. Westlake and W. Purdue, *Illustrations of Old Testament History in Queen Mary's Psalter* (1865).

47 'The ... MS. was found of the most essential service ... one of the stories – Joseph riding behind the seneschal of the King of Egypt – [being] precisely identical both in the stone and on the vellum' (*G.M.* ccxix, 1865, 145–54).

48 M. J. B. A. Lassus, [A. Darcel], M. J. Quicherat and R. Willis (eds.), *Facsimile of the Sketch-Book of Wilars de Honecort* (1859); H. Omont (ed.), *Album de Villard de Honnecourt* (Paris, 1906).

49 *B.N.* v (1859), 897–8. For recent discussions, see F. Bucher, 'Medieval Architectural Design Methods', *Gesta* xi, no. 3 (1973), *Gazette des Beaux Arts* lxi (1963), 132; *Art Bulletin* lix (1977), 315–9 and lx (1978), 393–4.

50 *B.* xvi (1858), 758. Compare Burges's own drawings of Beauvais, Dijon, Troyes and Châlons-sur-Marne (V. & A., P. & D., 93 E1, 8823, 1–18, 38–9) and Amiens (*ibid.*, 93 E4, 55–16).

51 *R.I.B.A. Trans.* 1860–61, 19; *C.E.A. Jnl.* xxiii (1860), 376. See also R.I.B.A., S.N.B., xxiv (1857), 65–6.

52 *B.* xvi (1858), 771–2; R. Blomfield, *Architectural Drawing and Draughtsmanship* (1912), 16.

53 *B.* xlii (1882), 374. Lot 281. It was bought by Sir William Emerson. By comparison, twenty-five volumes of Burges's measured drawings and

between pp. 65–69

sketches went for £286. Emerson bought Burges's copy of Willis's *Wilars* (lot. 50) for £4.5.0 (R.I.B.A. priced copy of Puttick and Simpson's catalogue, 1882).

54 *R.I.B.A. Trans.* 1860–61, 24–8.

55 The fashion seems to have been set by John Dobson (1787–1865), a pupil of Sir Robert Smirke, who had trained with John Varley (*Burlington Fine Arts Club ... Drawings by Deceased British Architects*, 1884, 46).

56 eg. East end, Waltham Abbey, R.A. 1861, no. 673; Conduit St. Gallery, 1870: Architectural Exhibition, no. 155 (Now at the R.I.B.A. See *B.* xxviii (1870), 382); or Chapel Interior, Worcester College, Oxford (1865): Worc. Coll. Archives.

57 *R.I.B.A. Trans.* 1860–61, 23; *C.E.A. Jnl.* xxiv (1861), 18–20.

58 *B.N.* v (1859), 898.

59 'Heroes and Hero-Worship: the Hero as Architect', *B.* xvi (1858), 794–5.

60 *B.* xvi (1858), 775.

61 eg. drawings for Congleton Town Hall, *B.N.* xii (1865), 10, 13.

62 R. W. Lethaby, *Philip Webb* (1935), 137.

63 P. Waterhouse, 'The Ethics of the Sketch-Book', *R.I.B.A. Jnl.*, 3rd series, iii, 1896, 489.

64 *A.* iv (1870), 44–5.

65 *B.N.* xxvi (1874), 443. Spiers's *Orders of Architecture* appeared in 1890.

66 *B.N.* xxvi (1874), 470 and xxxii (1877), 85–6.

67 *B.N.* xiv (1867), 752.

68 B. xix (1861), 190. Burges was himself a member of the committee of the Architectural Photographic Association.

69 *B.N.* xii (1865), 557.

70 A detailed advertisement and prospectus was issued early in 1865, and by the summer several proof plates were ready (*E.* xxvi, N.S. xxiii, 1865, 60, 184).

71 *B.N.* xix (1870), 264.

72 *Architectural Drawings* (1870), 1.

73 The *Dictionnaire* appeared between 1854 and 1868.

74 Burges was no theorist. The prospectus managed to include the major *non-sequitur* at the heart of the Gothic Revival: 'The selection consists principally of details ... the object ... being to show parts of the construction on a working scale: for although our present construction may sometimes differ from that obtaining in ancient times, still it is necessary to know the latter, as it materially influences the forms' (*E.* xxvi, N.S. xxiii, 1865, 60).

75 R.I.B.A., S.N.B., v (1853–4), 133.

76 *B.* xl (1881), 532.

77 *A.* v (1871), 9–10. For Burges's preliminary drawings see V. & A., P. & D., 93 E1 and 93 E4.

78 There seem to have been several variants, at least one of which was drawn on vellum. Compare V. & A., P. & D., A.182, E.4667–1910 (given by Mr. Sydney Vacher who bought it in Nov. 1910 at the

Puttick and Simpson sale of Aitchison's collection); *B.* xvi (1858), 374–5; Pullan, *Designs of William Burges*, 5–6 and frontispiece. The drawing was exhibited at the Architectural Exhibition, no.41 (Abstract, 1858). For details, see *B.* xiv (1856), 603 and xvi (1858), 460, 595, quoting *Gloucester Mercury*. The V. & A. version was exhibited at the R. A. Winter Exhibn., 1937, no. 1491.

79 'Design for Gloucester Fount' (Abstract, 1856); R.I.B.A., S.N.B., 1857, Jan.-June.

80 R.I.B.A. 'Stonework', 27r. and v. See also Vellum S. B. for the fountain at Prato. For other fountain designs, see S.N.B., xxii (1857), 73.

81 *B.* xvi (1858), 374.

82 *E.* xix, N.S. xvi (1858), 43. See also *ibid.*, xx, N.S. xvii (1859), 194. At the Architectural Exhibition of 1860 (no. 239) Burges revealed several 'fanciful drinking fountains' (*E.* xxi, N.S. xviii, 1860, 175).

83 *B.* xix (1861), 555.

84 *B.A.* xv (1881), 213.

85 Group I, class iv, no.60, 3 and 4 (*R.I.B.A. Papers*, 1866–7, appendix).

86 Abstract, 1860–61. It was no. 233 in the Architectural Exhibition, 1861 as 'Bird's Eye View of a Medieval Town' (*B.* xix, 1861, 244). Compare V. & A., P. & D., I 52 A, E.445–1965 (given by Miss Eleanor M. Hollyer) with Pullan, *Designs of William Burges*, pl.23, and *B.N.* xxvi (1874), 419.

87 *E.* xxiii, N.S. xx (1862), 163.

88 *Once A Week* vi (1862), 84.

89 A. Service, 'A. Beresford Pite', in *Edwardian Architecture and its Origins*, ed. A. Service (1975), 394–404.

90 Burges possessed the following Dürer prints: 'The Arch of Maximilian'; 'The Nuremberg Chronicle'; 'Four Naked Women'; 'Coat of Arms with Skull'; 'St. Jerome in the Cell'; 'Coat of Arms with Cock on Helmet'; 'Idleness'; 'Melancolia'; 'Knight and Death'; 'The Great Fortune'; 'St. Hubert and the Stag'; 'The Rape of Amymone'; 'Lady and Gentleman walking with Death'; 'The Little Courier'; 'Lady on Horseback with Squire'; 'The Bargain'; 'The Assemblage of Warriors'; 'The Sow with Eight Legs'; 'The Standard Bearer'; 'The Witch'; 'The Three Cherubs'; 'The Crucifixion'; as well as six volumes of photographs (Sale Catalogue, Glendinning, lots 50, 70, 120, 237, 11 Nov. 1918). Burges's print of 'The Woman and the Dragon' – lent 'with characteristic generosity' – was borrowed for reproduction by the *Building News* (*B.N.* xxv, 1873, 506, 516–17).

91 G. G. Zerffi, *B.N.* xxxi (1876), 279–80.

92 *B.N.* xxxi (1876), 100.

93 *B.N.* xxxi (1876), 622.

94 *B.N.* xxxi (1876), 312.

95 *B.N.* xxx (1876), 680.

96 'The Virgin and the Butterfly'; 'Christ Taking Leave of his Mother' (*B.N.* xx, 1871, 41, 49, 56, 198–9, 235–6, 252).

between pp. 69–76

97 'The Nativity', *B.N.* xxix (1880), 732, 773. In their precision and facility they were said to rank, for architects, with engravings by Wenceslaus Hollar and John Carter (C. B[ruce] A[llen], 'Albert Dürer, and how to work in his way': 'The Apocalypse', *B.N.* xx, 1871, 424–6). In 'perfection of truth and exactitude of representation', they were models 'for the student of architectural art' (H. W. Lonsdale), 'Notes on Albert Dürer', *B.N.* xxiv, 1873, 504).

98 *B.N.* xxxvii (1879), 473–4; *Qtly. Rev.* cxlviii (1879), 376–407.

99 G. G. Zerffi, *B.N.* xxv (1873), 505. For related studies of Dürer, see *A.* ii (1869), 284–5; xvii (1877), 363–4; xxii (1879), 264–5.

1 *B.N.* xxiv (1873), 689.

2 *B.N.* xxiv (1873), 718–19. See also E. Gibbon, *Decline and Fall of the Roman Empire* (1828 ed.), iv, 411 and C. Kingsley, *Hermits* 2 vols (1868).

3 Tennyson, 'St. Simeon Stylites'.

4 Tennyson, *Idylls*: 'Gareth and Lynette'.

5 *ibid*. 'The Coming of Arthur'.

6 R.I.B.A., S.N.B., xxix (1860), 26.

7 R.I.B.A., S.N.B., xxviii (1860), 37.

8 R.I.B.A., S.N.B., xxii (1857), 74.

9 R.I.B.A., S.N.B., xxxii (1865), 8.

10 Tennyson, *Idylls*: 'Gareth and Lynette'.

11 *ibid*. 'The Holy Grail'.

12 Kerr, *Ambassador Extraordinary* ii, 155.

13 *R.I.B.A. Jnl.*, 3rd ser., xix (1912), 643.

14 'Received in Institute' (Abstract, 1860).

15 'Row about Gold Medal, Institute, May 2' (*ibid.*, 1864).

16 'Hope P.R.I.B.A.' (*ibid.*, 1865).

17 *B.N.* xl (1881), 515.

18 *B.* xxxiii (1875), 1145–6.

19 *ibid.*

20 *B.* xxxiv (1876), 17.

21 *B.* xx (1862), 335.

22 *B.* xxx (1872), 458; *R.I.B.A. Papers*, 1871–2. He was also a member of the Conference Management Committee.

23 *A.* xix (1878), 329 and xx (1878), 333–4, 344; *B.A.* ix (1878), 259–60. This was the subject of an earlier debate in 1867: 'Institute resolution about returning drawings' (Abstract, 1867).

24 *A.* xxii (1879), 270.

25 *B.N.* xxxix (1880), 78–9.

26 *B.N.* xl (1881), 374.

27 See *B.N.* xl (1881), 343, 403–4, 436, 467–8, 499–500, 531–2, 561; A. E. Street, *Memoir of G. E. Street* (1888), 264–6.

28 W. G. Newton, *F.A.B.S. An Outline of its Early History* (1930), a privately printed edition of about fifteen copies. The B.M. purchased Sir Aston Webb's copy in 1965 for £8 (press mark 2736a 4).

29 The idea may have originated from the Architectural Lending Library, operating from Bromp-

ton Square (*Almanack of the Fine Arts*, 1850, 154).

30 But he noted its foundation meeting in his diary for 1859: 'FABS. at Hayward's', and he attended a meeting in 1862: 'Dec. 3 to FABS.' 'My first FABS, 1864' appears twice, as an important event. In 1863 he notes: 'FABS. Hadfield elected', but there is no record of this in the list of members.

31 Burges came to know Hayward's sanatorium, gymnasium, masters' houses and laboratories at Harrow at close quarters (*R.I.B.A. Jnl.* 3rd. series xiii, 1904–5, 582).

32 Burges would also have known him as Secretary of the Arundel Society.

33 R.I.B.A. MSS., 'FABS File'.

34 W. E. Nesfield, R.I.B.A. Sketchbook, 133.

35 'My FABS at Windsor' (Abstract, 1869).

36 'FABS. June 5 at house' (*ibid.*, 1878).

37 Other meetings noted are 1864 'June FABS. at West. Club'; 1867 'FABS at [Joseph] James's'; 1875 'FABS Audley End and Ely'; 1876 'FABS Banbury and [W] Roxton'; 1877 'FABS Coombe Abbey, Warwick Castle'; 1878 'FABS Salisbury and Wilton'; 1880 'FABS Bury St. Edmunds, Hengrave Barton Hall'.

38 *B.* lxxvii (1899), 407, 418–19.

39 Later reduced to £2 2s. 10d. (R.I.B.A. MSS., 'FABS File').

40 *ibid.*, 1 Mar. 1859.

41 *ibid.*, 10 Feb. 1859.

42 'Joined the Verulam' (Abstract, 1875). E. W. Godwin was also a member (V. & A., Estimate Book, address list).

43 Annual exhibitions began in 1855 and ended in 1870, when the R.A. acquired more space for architectural exhibits by moving from Trafalgar Square to Burlington House (*A.* iv, 1870, 286–7). For annual catalogues, see V. & A. Library.

44 *R.I.B.A. Trans.* 1883–4, 207.

45 *B.N.* xv (1868), 88.

46 *B.N.* xxxviii (1880), 784; A. Quiney, *J. L. Pearson* (1979) 128. In 1871 Burges was put up for A.R.A. with Pearson and M. Digby Wyatt: all three failed.

47 *B.N.* xl (1881), 141; Abstract 1881.

48 *B.N.* iv (1858), 1122.

49 Abstract, 1859–61.

50 Diaries of G. P. Boyce, *Old Water Colour Society*, 4 May 1858.

51 *Rules of the Hogarth Club, and List of Membership* (privately printed, 1860); 'The Modern Pre-Raphaelite Painters', *Art Jnl.* xx (1858), 374; W. M. Rossetti, *Ruskin, Rossetti, Pre-Raphaelitism* (1899), 216–17, 284, 289–90; T. S. R. Boase, *Victorian Art* (Oxford, 1959), 292.

52 *C.E.A. Jnl.* xx (1857), 283. Fuller Russell collected Italian Primitives, wrote *The Ancient Knight, or Chapters in Chivalry* (1849), and edited *Hierugia Anglicana* (1843).

53 Boyce, *op. cit.*, 29: 7 May 1858.

54 *E.* xxv, N.S., xxii (1864), 243. First Clutton, then

between pp. 76–80

Joseph Clarke, became its Secretary; Scott its Treasurer. Its Curator was Burges's early mentor, C. Bruce Allen. Its bankers were Burges's bankers, Cocks, Biddulph & Co. of 43, Charing Cross. Its photographer was Bedford Lemere, its moulders Farmer and Brindley.

55 *London Topographical Record* ii (1903), 39; *B.* xii (1854), 335. In 1857–69 the casts were temporarily housed at South Kensington.

56 *B.* xxvii (1869), 587. Demolished c. 1935.

57 *R.I.B.A. Papers* 1869–70, appendix.

58 *Architectural Museum Catalogue* (1855), 9, 22–3, 37–8, 44; G. G. Scott, *Guide to the Royal Architectural Museum* (1877) and *Recollections* (1879); *B.* viii (1850), 500 and xi (1853), 20.

59 Foundation, *B.* xv (1857), 249; annual reports, *B.N.*, *passim*.

60 A. Hamilton Thompson, Centenary Address, *Archaeol. Jnl.* c (1943), 1–15; Joan Evans, 'The R.A.I.: a retrospect', *ibid.*, cvi (1949), 1–11. For Burges's involvement, see *ibid.* xxxviii (1881), 318, 449.

61 Sir William Cunliffe Brooks, Bt., M.P. (1819–1900), of Brooks' Bank, Manchester, was a member of the Ecclesiological Society (*E.* xviii, N.S. xv, 1857, 374). If Burges designed him a church ('Cunliffe Brooks' Church', Abstract, 1860) it seems to have remained unbuilt.

62 *G.M.* N.S. xix (1865), 528. 'Wollaston's Font' (Abstract, 1862). P.L.U.

63 Abstract, 1880.

64 *Archaeol. Jnl.* ix (1852), 297.

65 *ibid.*, xiii (1856), 297.

66 *ibid.*, 416.

67 *ibid.*, 181.

68 *ibid.*, xiv (1857), 75. Burges also lent items to the R.A.I. exhibition of 'Sculpture in Ivory' in 1863 (*ibid.*, xx, 1863, 368).

69 *ibid.*, xiv (1857), 280.

70 *ibid.*, 96. Cf. Tower House and Knightshayes, Devon, pp. 304, 310.

71 *ibid.*, xv (1858), 88.

72 *ibid.*, xvi (1859), 178.

73 *ibid.*, 182.

74 *ibid.*, 89.

75 *ibid.*, xviii (1861), 71. 'Through the kindness of Mr. Thornbury'.

76 *ibid.*, xix (1862), 173.

77 From Yarde House, Kingsbridge, Devon; given to a friend of Burges by Robert Swansborough (*G.M.*, N.S. i, 1863, 327).

78 *Archaeol. Jnl.* xx (1863), 185.

79 *ibid.*, 198; *G.M.* N.S. i (1863), 598.

80 *Archaeol. Jnl.* xx (1863), 377.

81 *ibid.*, xxi (1864), 102, 274.

82 *ibid.*, xxiv (1867), 76.

83 Besides sponsoring chromolithographs of Italian primitives and early Renaissance artists, it published several works of interest to Burges: *Designs for Goldsmiths, Jewellers etc. by Hans Holbein*, ed. G. W. Reid (1869); *Catalogue of Ivory Carvings*, ed. E. Oldfield (1855); *Sculptured Ornament of the Monastery of Batalha*, with photographs by Thurston Thompson (1868); *The Treasure of Petrossa* [found in Rumania, 1837; exhibited Paris, 1867], ed. R. H. Soden Smith (1869); *Ecclesiastical Metal Work of the Middle Ages* [mostly at South Kensington], ed. A.C. King (1868); *Decorative Furniture: French, English, Italian, German, Flemish*, 2 vols. (1871); *Decorative Plate, chiefly Portuguese, German and Italian* (1869); *Sepulchral Monuments in Italy*, ed. G. E. Street (1878). See *B.N.* xiv (1867), 414 and xvii (1869) 145–6; F. W. Maynard, *Twenty Years of the Arundel Society*, 1849–68 (1869) and *Five Years of the Arundel Society, 1869–73* (1873); A. Bird, 'The Arundel Society', *C.L.* clix (1976), 1513–15. Didron was the Arundel Society's agent in France.

84 'To Arundel with Lonsdale' (Abstract, 1875); 'To Arundel with Chapple' (*ibid.*, 1877).

85 *Rules of the Arundel Club and List of Members* (1863); T. H. S. Escott, *Club Makers and Club Members* (1914), 264–8.

86 Escott, *op. cit.*, 257–64; G. A. F. Rogers, *The Arts Club* (1920).

87 'Elected at Arts Club' (Abstract, 1863).

88 'Row at Arts Club about Builders' (*ibid.*, 1863).

89 'Cups for Art Club' (*ibid.*, 1878). See 36 n. 25.

90 *Swinburne Letters*, ed. C. Y. Lang i (1959), 155 n., 162 n.; ii (1959), 21 n.; vi (1962), 242.

91 D. Harbron, *The Conscious Stone* (1949), 101.

92 Athenaeum MSS; Abstract, 1874.

93 H. C. Nicoll, *Story of Christ Church, St. Leonard's-on-Sea* (1909). The foundation stone was laid by Hope in 1873 (Boase, supp. iii; *Guardian* 14 Aug. 1895, 1194).

94 Boase, iii; *Masonic Portraits* (1876), 81–7.

95 Of Horton Old Hall, Bradford; later M.P. for the West Riding and for Wigan; author of *Our Church and her accusers* (1872). See biography by H. L. P. Hulbert (1914), and *Who Was Who*.

96 Boase, iii, 773.

97 *D.N.B.*; *Guardian* 26 April 1876 (obituary by Gladstone); *The Times* 21, 22, 24, 27, 28 April 1876.

98 *D.N.B.*

99 Boase, i, 1390

1 *D.N.B.*

2 Boase, ii; *The Times* 10 March 1899, 1.

3 His poems were illustrated by Richard [Dickie] Doyle, Kate Greenaway and Randolph Caldecott, all well known to Burges (*D.N.B.*; *My Confidences*, ed. A. Birrell, 1876).

4 Boase, ii.

5 *D.N.B.*; Boase, ii; *The Times* 12 Feb. 1891; *Good Words* April 1891, 233–7. Burges altered Queen's College, Harley St., in 1852 for Rev. C. G. Nicolay, Prof. of Geography at K.C.L. (Abstract, 1852; *CEA Jnl.* xv, 1852, 192).

between pp. 80–83

6 *D.N.B.*; *Reminiscences*, ed. A. Brodie (1881).

7 *Who Was Who*.

8 Boase, supp. iii, 75; *The Times* 27 Dec. 1894, 4.

9 *D.N.B.*; Boase, iii.

10 Boase, supp. ii; *The Times* 11 Jan. 1898, 4.

11 Boase, supp. ii; *The Times* 6 Dec. 1890, 5. He published *Notes on Venetian Ceramics* (1868).

12 Boase, i; *D.N.B.*; *Graphic* xxi (1880), 252. He published *Grotesque Animals, invented, drawn and described* (1872) and sat on the committee of the Architectural Museum (*Men of the Time*, 1899, 262). For items of medieval metalwork in his collection, see B. Talbot, *Ancient and Modern Furniture, Metalwork, Tapestries etc.* (1876), pl.41.

13 *D.N.B.*; Boase, i; *The Times* 12 Feb. 1884, 6.

14 *D.N.B.*; Boase, ii; *The Times* 22 Aug. 1868, 7.

15 Abstract, 1851. A writing clerk, W. J. Carter.

16 *ibid.*, 1855.

17 *ibid.*, 1869–70. Another draughtsman, working on King's College Chapel, Cambridge, in 1874 was J. A. Reeve (*A.* xiii, 1875, 304). He succeeded Burges at Waltham Abbey.

18 'Pupils Lee, Holmes [? C. E. M. Holmes] and Tatsuno' (*ibid.*, 1880).

19 *R.I.B.A. Jnl.* 3rd ser. xx (1913), 256.

20 *ibid.*, xxvii (1919–20), 474.

21 *ibid.*, xliv (1936–7), 194, 247.

22 He moved on to Waterhouse, and edited the A.A. Sketch Book before setting up practice in 1886.

23 *A.* xxxi (1884), 339.

24 *B.N.* lix, ii (1890), 94, portrait.

25 *B.N.* xlvii (1884), 14.

26 *B.* xxxiv (1876), 928 and xlix, ii (1885), 321; *B.N.* xlviii (1885), 1006.

27 *R.I.B.A. Jnl.* 3rd ser. xxvii (1919–20), 459, 474; *B.* cxix (1920), 274. Conder wrote several articles on Japanese buildings, costumes and gardens, see H. Suzuki, 'Josiah Conder and England', *Kenchikushi Kenyu* xl (1976–9), 1–15; H. Laski, 'Josiah Conder's Bank of Japan, Tokyo', *Jnl. Soc. Arch. Hist.* xxxviii (1979).

28 *B.N.* xxx (1876), 400–4.

29 'The style is early Gothic, but the details have, where possible, without incongruity been infused with a Japanese spirit, more especially in the internal architecture and fittings' (*B.* xlvii. ii, 1884, 790).

30 *B.* xxxvii (1879), 368–71.

31 'Conder's china came, Sept. 29' (Abstract, 1878).

32 'Tatsuno came, Sep. 27' (*ibid.*, 1880).

33 *R.I.B.A. Jnl.* 3rd ser. xxvii (1919–20), 459.

34 'Emerson came to me' (Abstract, 1865).

35 He returned in 1869 (*ibid.*, 1869) and read a paper to the R.I.B.A. on the Taj Mahal (*R.I.B.A. Trans.* 1869–70, 195–203; *B.* xxviii 1870, 660–62).

36 *R.I.B.A. Trans.* 1883–4, 152.

37 St. Mary's (1876–9): *B.N.* xxxviii (1880), 10; *A.* xvii (1877), 400.

38 Filey Mausoleum (1885); sculpture by Nicholls: *B.N.* xlix (1885), 206.

39 No. 178–9 (1890–91): *B.* lx (1891), 508.

40 Sutton Court, Little Sutton (1879): *B.N.* xl (1881), 264, 294. An interior view by Bedford Lemere (N.M.R.) shows a rather Burgesian staircase.

41 *A.* viii (1872), 36: perspective by A. H. Haig.

42 *B.* l (1886), 78, 198; *B.N.* l (1886), 88, 176, 496.

43 *A.R.* xvii (1905), 186–7.

44 *B.N.* xxiv (1873), 212.

45 *B.N.* xxvii (1874), 641; Murray's *Handbook to Bombay* (1881), where he is also credited with the design of Treacher's Buildings.

46 *B.N.* xxvii (1874), 637.

47 *B.N.* xxxii (1877), 338; liii (1887), 790, 860; xviii (1870), 387; *A.* iii (1870), 104; *B.* xxviii (1870), 358; lxv (1893), 282; B. F. L. Clarke, *Anglican Cathedrals Outside the British Isles* (1958), 19.

48 *A.* ix (1873), 304 and xiii (1875), 276; *B.N.* xxxiii (1877) 614; Murray's *Handbook to Bengal* (1882), 362 *et seq.*

49 *A.* xxi (1879), 235 and 355.

50 *B.* lxviii (1895), 354; *Academy Architecture* ii (1895), 55.

51 Such stylistic loyalty was criticised as excessive: *B.N.* xviii (1870), 370 and xxvii (1874), 634, 643, 664; *A.* iii (1870), 263.

52 Burges's Law Courts design seemed a little too close for most critics: *B.N.* xxxiii (1877), 614, 648–9; *A.* ix (1873), 304 and xiii (1875), 276.

53 *R.I.B.A. Trans.* 1883–4, 152.

54 *B.N.* lviii (1890), i, 503, 536.

55 *B.N.* xviii (1870), 446.

56 *A.* xviii (1877), 58, 328; *B.* xxxvi (1878), 266; *B.N.* xxxi (1876), 230. Lonsdale's glass was executed by Saunders. Sculpture was by Earp and mosaic by Burke and Co. Lonsdale and Lee also designed metalwork in the Burges manner, eg. candelabra by Barkentin and Krall presented to the Bishop of Southwell (*B.* xlix, 1855, ii, 10).

57 eg. his paper on Italian polychromy (*B.* xii, 1873, 520). He founded the Colour Decoration Class and was one of the originators of the *A.A. Sketchbook*.

58 *B.N.* xviii (1870), 427.

59 *B.N.* lviii (1890), i, 720. 'T. Deane at Cardiff. I made a long stay there' (Abstract, 1872). He was responsible for illustrating Burges's copy of Tennyson (*ibid.*, 1875), and worked on drawings of Welsh castles for Castell Coch and Cardiff (1872–3). See V. & A., P. & D., 93 E2.

60 *B.N.* xxxii (1877), 386: Library.

61 The Deane family's design of a Market House and Town Hall for Lord Brabazon at Bray, Co. Wicklow, does however include a rather Burgesian fountain (*A.* xxvii, 1882, 117).

62 Gower's Walk, Free Schools, Rupert St., Whitechapel (*B.* xlix, 1885, 54); New Church, Collier Row, Essex (*B.N.* xlvii, 1884, 1034); St. Thomas's, Brentwood, Essex (*ibid.*, 52).

between pp. 83–85

63 In 1887 he changed his name to E. C. Ayton-Lee (*B.N.* lviii, 1890, i, 720: portrait).

64 *B.N.* xxiv (1873), 719; *A.* ix (1873), 346. He was a pupil of Prichard of Llandaff (*B.* xc, 1906, 442).

65 *B.N.* xxiv (1873), 411–18, 422–7.

66 *B.N.* xxiv (1873), 476, 482–3.

67 'Chapple came, Jan. 9' (Abstract, 1859).

68 In 1883 he moved to 7 John St., Adelphi (Caulfield letter book, Chapter House Archives, Cork: 1 Oct. 1883).

69 Abstract, 1869 and 1874, July 30th.

70 'Chapple left [Albert] Saunders' (Abstract, 1877).

71 Caulfield letter book, 2: 2 May 1881.

72 *ibid.* Chapple was also an executor to the will not only of Burges but of Burges's father.

73 eg. 'The Decoration of Basilicas and Byzantine Churches', *R.I.B.A. Papers* 1875–6, 15–27 and *B.* xxxiii (1875), 1033–4, 1057–8; *Eastern Cities and Italian Towns* (1879); *Elementary Lectures on Christian Architecture* (1879); 'The Iconography of Angels', *Archaeological Jnl.* xliii (1886), 317.

74 Pullan, *Studies in Architectural Style* (1883), pl. 96.

75 *B.* xiii (1855), 364, 384.

76 He exhibited a 'Design for a Cathedral Altar Screen' in the Paris Exhibition of 1855 (*B.* xiii, 1855, 148).

77 *Studies in Architectural Style*, pls. 12–32.

78 *R.I.B.A. Trans.* 1882–3, 33–4.

79 *Studies in Architectural Style*, pls. 3–8.

80 *B.N.* xxxviii (1880), 368. See also Pullan's 'Design for a 13th c. Cathedral', *ibid.*, 782. Pullan's designs for Truro are in V. & A., P. & D.

81 *Studies in Architectural Style*, pls. 56–70; (V. & A., P. & D., E.10; Q.5c).

82 *ibid.*, pls. 71–2.

83 *ibid.*, pls. 73–5.

84 *A.* xxviii (1882), 398–9.

85 Pullan's church was for a site at the Porta del Popolo.

86 *Studies in Architectural Style*, pls. 90–92.

87 *ibid.*, pl. 93.

88 *Architectural Designs of William Burges* i (1883), ii (1887); *The House of William Burges* (1886); 'Works of the late William Burges', *R.I.B.A. Trans.* (1881–2), 183–200.

89 *A History of the Discoveries at Halicarnassus, Cnidus, and Branchidae* (1862–3).

90 *Byzantine Architecture* (1864); *Principal Ruins of Asia Minor* (1865).

91 *Antiquities of Ionia* iv (1881); *A.* xviii (1877), 344.

92 *Studies in Architectural Style*, pls. 9–10.

93 *A.* x (1873), 242; *B.* xxxi (1873), 366; *B.N.* xxix (1875), 84. A Lombardic octagonal structure in the grounds of Mr. Henfrey's villa on Lake Maggiore, opposite the Isola Bella.

94 At the Villa Cimella, Nice (*A.* xxvii, 1882, 327).

95 Castel Oleggio, near Arana, for the Marquis Del Pozzo (*A.* xxvi, 1881, 239; *R.I.B.A. Trans.* N.S. vi, 1890, 249–54).

96 For his drawings of sculpture at Compostela, Bourges, Santiago, Chartres and Amiens, see *A.* i (1869), 246, 259, 294–6; ii (1869), 128; iii (1870), 21, 225; iv (1870), 348.

97 For his design for a National Mausoleum, see *A.* v (1871), 158, 172.

98 *Villa and Cottage Architecture* (Blackie, 1868), 42.

99 *A.* i (1869), 247; ii (1869), 128.

1 *R.I.B.A. Papers*, 1870–71, appendix.

2 *Art Jnl.* (1871), 171; *B.* xxix (1871), 346 (International Exhibition).

3 Candelebra, Southwell Minster, with E. C. Lee (*B.* xlix, 1885, 10); advertisement for Richardson, Ellson & Co., Art Metal Workers (*Art Jnl.* 1897, 52).

4 Panels for Shakespeare Memorial Theatre, Stratford-on-Avon (*B.N.* xlvii, 1884, 14).

5 Lord Bute's book on *Arms of the Royal and Parliamentary Burghs of Scotland* (1897).

6 eg. Shakespeare windows for J. G. R. Rogerson, Esq., Beech Cottage, Allerton: Aldridge and Deacon architects (*B.N.* xli, 1881, 861; xlii, 1882, 12); screen for S. Bennet Esq., Leicester: Goddard and Paget architects (*B.N.* xlii, 1882, 12); and windows for a house at Birkenhead; G. Aldridge architect (*B.N.* xlix, 1885, 966).

7 *R.I.B.A. Papers*, 1869–70, appendix tipped in, V. & A., PP.23c.

8 eg. 1864 (no. 129) and 1863 (no. 3).

9 eg. 'Morning', 'Noon' and 'Night' for Percy G. Stone, architect (*B.N.* xlviii, 1885, 448, 528, 606).

10 Lee and Lonsdale, in particular, were keen members of a drinking club known as the Picts and Goths (for comic invitations, see V. & A. GG. 68B).

11 *B.N.* lviii (1890), i, 405, portrait; *R.I.B.A. Jnl.*, 3rd ser. xxiii (1916), 334–6. Like Burges, Spiers was educated at King's College School, and like Burges he worked briefly as an assistant to M. D. Wyatt. Among Spiers's minor works were alterations to Louise Jopling's studio, either at 8 Clareville Grove or at 28 Beaufort St. (Louise Jopling, *Twenty Years of My Life, 1867–87*, 1925, 51, 154).

12 M. D. Wyatt, *Industrial Arts of the Nineteenth Century* (1851), x, pls. 125, 150.

13 Abstract, 1860, 1861, 1867.

14 *Art Jnl.* 1883, 336.

15 E. A. Armstrong, *Axel Herman Haig* (1905), 11–14, 16, 20; *Art Jnl.* 1892, 1. It was Burges who sent Haig to Italy and Sicily, in particular to Palermo, Monreale and Cephalu. For Haig's topographical views, see eg. Bruges (*A.* xxv, 1881, 11); Genoa (*A.* xix, 1878, 208); Palermo (*ibid.*, 112).

16 *D.N.B. Supp.*; H. S. Marks, *Pen and Pencil Sketches*, 2 vols. (1894). For examples of his work see *B.N.* xvi (1869), 255–6; *A.* xxvi (1881), 9, 39, 57, 73, 89, 107, 125, 143.

17 Clement and Hutton, *Artists of the Nineteenth Century* (1893).

between pp. 86–90

18 *D.N.B.*; A. L. Baldry, *Albert Moore* (1894).

19 *D.N.B.*; A. R. Life, 'That Unfortunate Young Man Morten', *Bull. John Rylands Library* lv (1973), 369–402.

20 M. H. S. Smith, *Art and Anecdotes: recollections of W. F. Yeames, his life and friends* (1927).

21 Graves, *R.A. Exhibitors*, ii, 122.

22 *Who Was Who, 1916–28*, 1111–12. For examples of his glass, see *B.* xliv (1883), 174 (Ledbury); xlviii (1885), 83 (St. John's Wood); lv (1888), 470 (New York). For his work with Bentley at St. Francis, Notting Hill, see *C.E.A. Jnl.* xxv (1862), 249.

23 *D.N.B.*; H. Holiday, *Reminiscences of My Life* (1914); A. L. Baldry, *Henry Holiday* (1930). For examples of his work, see *B.N.* xliv (1883), 830 (St. Margaret's, Westminster); *B.* liii (1887), 328 (Philadelphia); *B.* lvii (1889), 192 (New Jersey).

24 *D.N.B.*; *Who Was Who*.

25 Abstract, 1853–4; V. & A., P. & D., 93 E6, 8825, 45–6 (Monreale mosaic, endorsed 'this is a drawing of Poynter's').

26 Abstract, 1865.

27 *R.I.B.A. Trans.* 1884, 232.

28 The house was rebuilt in 1905–7 by Paul Waterhouse, and has since been rebuilt again (*London Topographical Record* ix, 1914, 32; *Survey of London* xviii, 1937, 65, 75, pl. 46a; H. B. Wheatley and P. Cunningham, *London Past and Present* i, 1891, 296–7; G. G. Williams, *Guide to Literary London*, 1973, 78–9).

29 *London Street Directory*, 1857 and 1879.

30 Another friend was Augustus Mordan, Boyce's brother-in-law, a painter who exhibited two pictures by Boyce at the Old Water Colour Soc. in 1898–9 (Boyce, diary, ed. A. E. Street and R. Davies, *Old Water Soc. Club* ix, 1941, 23 Jan. 1852 and 19 Nov. 1857). Burges designed him a card case (Abstract, 1858).

31 Planned 1868; by 1870 Boyce was able to show Gilbert Scott round (Boyce, diary, 20 April 1868 and 23 Feb. 1870). 'Jock' Stevenson used Boyce's drawing 'Back of an Old House, Dorchester' as an advertisement for Queen Anne: to persuade 'people who would otherwise prefer purple slates on drab stocks and cement and thin window bars and plate glass, [to] swallow red tiles and red brick and thick window bars' (*ibid.*, 20 June, 1872).

32 *ibid.*, 30 Dec. 1852.

33 *ibid.*, 29 June 1857.

34 *ibid.*, 2 July 1857.

35 *ibid.*, 17 Jan. 1859.

36 *ibid.*, 19 Feb. 1858.

37 *ibid.*, 13 Nov. 1862.

38 *ibid.*, 13 March 1860; 5 Feb. 1864.

39 *ibid.*, 1 June 1868.

40 Doughty and Wahl, *Letters of D. G. Rossetti* i (1965), 161. Rossetti to Ford Madox Brown, 2 Nov. 1853.

41 *Abstract, 5 Oct. 1862*.

42 *ibid.*, 1869.

43 *ibid.*, 1861.

44 *ibid.*, 1860.

45 *ibid.*, 1861.

46 *Old Water Colour Soc. Club* ix (1941) and *A.R.* v (1898–9).

47 For accounts of London's underworld, with particular reference to the Judge and Jury Club, see S. M. Ellis, ed., *A Mid-Victorian Pepys: the letters and memoirs of Sir William Hardman* (1923), 156–7, 210–16 and *The Hardman Papers: a further selection, 1865–8* (1930), 300; R. Fulford, ed., *The Greville Memoirs* (1963 ed.), 193–4; S. Fiske, *English Photographs* (1869), 174; B. Harrison, 'Pubs', in H. J. Dyos and M. Wolff, eds., *The Victorian City: Images and Realities* i (1973), 172–3, 187–8, pl. 32.

48 Boase, ii, 1143; J. Bradley, *Rogue's Progress* (1965).

49 Obit., Caulfield letter bk., *op cit*, 5. In fact he left £40,000 (Probate Records, Somerset House).

50 'Ratting at the Westminster Pit' (1825), ill. in Christina Hole, *English Sports and Pastimes* (1949), pl. 52.

51 *Cornhill Mag.* xi (1865), 228, *The Adventures of Mr. Verdant Green*, ch. ix, ill.

52 Augustus Hare, *Story of My Life* ii (1896), 28: 1.856.

53 'Went to a ratting with F. Aitchison at Jemmy Shaw's' (Abstract, 1855); 'Ratting Nov. 6' (*ibid.*, 1866); 'Rats' (*ibid.*, 1869); 'Great Rat Hunt' (*ibid.*, 1870).

54 D. O. Hunter Blair, *3rd. Marquess of Bute* (1921), 218.

55 Abstract, *passim*.

56 R.I.B.A., S.N.B. liii, 23 (Barkentin). Burges designed several ('Designs by W. Burges', photos by F. Bedford, presented to C. L. Cocks, 1869; Sotheby's Belgravia, 18 Nov. 1977, lot 254).

57 Abstract, *passim*.

58 *ibid.* Dandie's collar, designed by Burges, was made of blue leather studded with coral (Benson album).

59 *ibid.*, 21 Feb. 1881.

60 R.I.B.A. Nesfield sketchbook, 56.

61 R.I.B.A., 'Stonework', 10 *verso*.

62 Hunter Blair, *Bute*, 218.

63 *A.* xv (1881), 213.

64 D. Harbron, *The Conscious Stone* (1949), 63.

65 However he remained in partnership with Henry Crisp of Bristol from 1864 to 1871.

66 'Conway with Godwin' (Abstract, 1865); 'With Godwin at Ross Bay, Ireland' (*ibid.*, 1867).

67 'With Mrs. S. and Miss Charlton and Godwin to Theatre' (*ibid.*, 1866); 'Godwin and Mrs. Taylor' (*ibid.*, 1868); 'Godwin and Mrs. W.' (*ibid.*).

68 'Godwin at Blackheath' (*ibid.*, 1866); *B.A.* xv (1881), 214. Burges seems to have paid him £100 for this work (Harbron, *op. cit.*, 84).

69 Harbron, *op. cit.*, 72.

70 Abstract, 1874. For Ellen Terry, see her *Memoirs* (1933) and W. G. Robertson, *Time Was* (1931).

between pp. 90–96

71 Beerbohm's essay '1880'.

72 *B.A.* xv (1881), 213. He thought it, however, a fault in the right direction (*B.N.* xxiii, 1872, 35).

73 Harbron, *op. cit.*, 154.

74 see p. 44.

75 Abstract, 1871.

76 *ibid.*, 1860.

77 *ibid.*, 1862.

78 *ibid.*, 1869.

79 *ibid.*, 1866.

80 *B.A.* xv (1881), 213.

81 'B.V. at Surrey' (Abstract, 1872); 'Bought breastplate with B.V.' (*ibid.*, 1873). For Thomson's sad career, see J. Salt, *Life of James Thomson* (1889); B. Dobell, *The Laureate of Pessimism* (1910).

82 Walford was sub-editor of *Once A Week*, and had been misled into employing Hogg. See *The Times* 20, 22, 23, 24 Aug. 1861 and 10 Sept. 1861.

83 *Rossetti Letters*, *op. cit.*, ii (1965), 417–9. 'Saw Hogg brought up' (Abstract, 1861); 'Hogg died' (*ibid.*, 1865).

84 Abstract, Nov. 1865.

85 Hayward seems to have been a particularly close friend – see his caricature of 'Burges with his 'air cut' (R.I.B.A., S.N.B., xxix, 1860, 88). 'Asked Institute about Hayward' (Abstract, 1873).

86 eg. shopping list, R.I.B.A., S.N.B., xxxiv (1867), 93.

87 *Reader* no. 91 (1864), 392/1; *Knowledge* 27 July 1883, 49/2.

88 Abstract, 1864.

89 eg. R.I.B.A., S.N.B., xxi (1856), 2, 95.

90 No. 4 of Rossetti's Nonsense Verses, quoted in W. M. Rossetti, *Rossetti Papers* (1903), 494. Burges copied Blake's poem, 'Little Boy Lost', in R.I.B.A., S.N.B., xxvii (1859), 66. His appearance seems to have remained youthful: F. G. Stephens thought he was Street's pupil (Bodleian MS. DON. e 77 f.79).

91 E. Charteris, *Life and Letters of Edmund Gosse* (1931), 149: 23 April 1881.

92 Mt. St. MSS., Lady Bute letters, Sept. 1873, to her sister Angela, later Lady Herries. The painter J. B. Burgess was known as 'pretty Burgess', to distinguish him from Billy (*B.N.* lxxiii, 1897, 745).

93 *B.A.* xv (1881), 214.

94 Harbron, *op. cit.*, 37.

95 Abstract, 1866.

96 Louise Jopling, *op. cit.*, 94, 96: 1876.

97 Abstract, 1881.

98 Abstract, 1873–80.

99 *A.* xvi (1876), 224.

1 *G.M.* ccxii (1862), 3–14.

2 *G.M.* ccxiii (1862), 32–41.

3 *ibid.*, 1–12, 241–54.

4 *ibid.*, 513–25.

5 *G.M.* ccxv (1863), 4–12, 671–80.

6 *G.M.* ccxix (1865), 686–96.

7 *Art Applied to Industry*, 13.

8 *R.I.B.A. Papers*, 1875–6, 80.

9 To Sir F. Madden, B.M. Eg. MS. 2845, f.s. 199, 202, 205: 1852.

10 G. G. Scott (ed.), *Gleanings from Westminster Abbey* (1863), 82n.

11 M. B. Adams, *R.I.B.A. Jnl.*, 3rd ser. xix (1912), 643.

12 eg. the authors are taken to task for omitting all reference to 'M. de la Vogué's excellent book on Les Eglises de la Terre Sainte (1863),' as well as for deficient references: 'why quote second-hand?' (*B.N.* xii, 1865, 115).

13 *B.N.* xii (1865), 558. Tarver's frontispiece appeared in L. W. Ridge, *The Priory Church of S.S. Mary B.V. and Blaise, at Boxgrove, Sussex* (1864).

14 *B.* xxxiv (1876), 17.

15 *B.A.* vi (1881), 214.

16 *R.I.B.A. Trans.* 1883–4, 206.

17 *A.* iii (1870), 34.

18 *B.N.* xiv (1867), 771.

19 *Dublin Builder* viii (1860), 96.

20 *B.N.* xxx (1876), 490. Street himself admitted Burges's ease and generosity in lectures (*R.I.B.A. Trans.* 1881–2, 7–8).

21 *B.* xxxiv (1876), 18.

22 *B.N.* xxix (1875), 684. For a comparison of the Hotel Ecoville at Caen (1538) and Wichcord's mixed Re-Renaissance St. Stephen's Club (1874), see *B.N.* xxiv (1875), 280–81, 318–9.

23 *B.N.* xv (1868), 122–3, 139–40.

24 *B.N.* xi (1864), 118.

25 *B.* xix (1861), 190.

26 *A.* v (1871), 285. *Oratio recta*; report in *oratio obliqua*.

27 obit., *B.N.* xxxvii (1879), 363–4, 422.

28 *B.N.* xii (1865), 605.

29 Abstract, 1848.

30 *B.* xx (1862), 491. Lord Dundreary was a leading character in Tom Taylor's play *Our American Friend* (1858). Ellen Terry played the part of Mary Meredith during its run at the Haymarket.

31 'Voted. Liberals got majority ... General Election. Gladstone premier' (Abstract, 1880).

32 *Art Applied to Industry*, 6–7.

33 *Church and the World*, *op. cit.*, 578, 597.

34 *G.M.* ccxv (1863), 7.

35 Abstract, 1865, 1869.

36 *ibid.*, 1878.

37 *ibid.*, 1870.

38 *ibid.*, 1879. See V. & A., P. & D., 93 E9, 17 for a petal-shaped bowl bearing Burges's device of a heart menaced by spears, endorsed: 'This was given to J. Davidson in exchange for a Salade of the 15thc. in May 1879'. The item in question is B.M. [Dept. of British and Medieval Antiquities, Register] 1881: 8.2, no.26. Davidson died 3 Dec. 1880 (Abstract, 1880).

39 Abstract, 1873; B.M. Register, *op. cit.*, 1881: 8.2, no.49/51.

40 Abstract, 1876; B.M. Register, *op. cit.*, 1881: 8.2, no.24/25.

between pp. 96–98

41 Abstract, 1878.

42 *ibid.*, 1880; B.M. Register, *op. cit.*, 1881: 8.2, no. 154. See also Burges and de Cosson, *Ancient Helmets and Examples of Mail* (1881), 131, no.36, pl.205.

43 Abstract, 1874.

44 *ibid.*, 1875.

45 *ibid.*, 1876.

46 *B.A.* xvi (1881), 407, 438, 467. It is perhaps worth noting that when several items in Weekes's possession found their way into Burges's collection, their attributions had to be reversed or modified (*Ancient Helmets, op. cit.*, 89, 107, 124).

47 B.M. Register, *op. cit.*, 1881: 8.2, nos.24–176.

48 'Meyrick Collection on Sale' (Abstract, 1872). Dealers from whom Burges obtained pieces included Wareham of Castle St.; Rollin and Feuardent of Great Russell St.; Valentine; and the Gothic Hall near Bond St. Jess Barkentin of 291, Regent St., assisted in conservation work.

49 This late 15th/early 16thc. Flemish piece had been used as the parish alms-box. It was discovered in fragments by Burges, displayed in London, repaired and replaced. It was sold at Sotheby's in 1974 for £22,000 and is now in H.M. Tower of London Armouries.

50 *Archaeol. Jnl.* xxxvi (1879), 78–87, 103.

51 *Ancient Helmets, op. cit.*; 'Exhibition of armour ... armour catalogue' (Abstract, 1880).

52 V. & A., Estimate Book, May and July, 1880.

53 *Ancient Helmets, op. cit.*, 92n.1.

54 *ibid.*, 140.

55 B.M. Register, *op. cit.*, 1874: 7.25, no.1; O. M. Dalton, *Catalogue of Ivory Carvings* (1919), 91, no. 249, pl. xciii; M.H. Longhurst, *English Ivories* (1926), no. li. An attempt has recently been made to show that this item is a forgery. See J. Leewenberg, 'Early 19thc. Gothic Ivories', *Aachener Kunstblätter*, Band 39 (1969), 137, fig. 41 (*Ex. Inf.* Neil Stratford).

56 B.M. Register, *op. cit.*, 1877: 2.9, no. 1. From the collection of S. Benique.

57 *ibid.*, 1879: 2.3, nos. 1 and 2.

58 *ibid.*, 1880: 7.24; Dalton, *Catalogue of Engraved Gems* (1915), 19, no. 113, pl. xi; Abstract, 1880.

59 B.M. Register, *op. cit.*, 1881: 8.2, nos. 1–23.

60 *ibid.*, nos. 13–17.

61 *ibid.*, no. 4; Dalton, *Catalogue of Finger Rings* (1912), 272: no. 1938, pl. xxvi.

62 Register, *op. cit.*, 1881: 8.2, nos. 2–3.

63 *ibid.*, nos. 7–12.

64 *ibid.*, no. 21.

65 *ibid.*, nos. 19–20.

66 Sale Catalogues: Puttick and Simpson (20 March 1882); Glendinning (11 Nov. 1918).

67 Add. MS. 31843. Previously in the collections of Dr. Hawtrey, Provost of Eton, and Sir William Tite. Bought by Quaritch in 1874 for £23.

68 Add. MS. 31834. Previously in the collections of Francis Duroveray and Sir William Tite. Bought by Quaritch in 1874 for £56.10s.

69 Add. MS. 31873. Previously in the collections of T. Windus and Sir William Tite. Bought by Ellis and White in 1874 for £9.

70 Add. MS. 31830. Burges's bookplate is dated 1853.

71 Add. MS. 31831.

72 Add. MS. 31832. Previously owned by Willett Lawrence Adye and William Bragge.

73 Add. MS. 31845. Signed by Burges, 1873.

74 Add. MS. 31844.

75 Add. MS. 31838. Sold, from the library of William Bragge, in 1876.

76 Add. MS. 31842.

77 Add. MS. 31835–6 and 31839. Burges's bookplate is dated 1853.

78 Add. MS. 31841.

79 Add. MS. 31840. Bought by Burges from Quaritch in 1874 for £40 (Abstract, 1874).

80 Add. MS. 31833. The binding is dated 1873, the flyleaf 1872.

81 Abstract, 1879.

82 Cf. Burne-Jones: 'A painter ought not to be married; children and pictures are too important to be produced by one man' (G.B.-J., *Memorials of E. Burne-Jones*, i, 230).

83 Didron's chief works were: *Iconographie Chrétienne, L'Histoire de Dieu* (Paris, 1843; trans. E. J. Millington, 1851); a sumptuous but unfinished monograph on Chartres, with J. B. Lassus and A. Darcel (Paris, 1842); *Manuel d'Iconographie Chrétienne* (Paris, 1845), an edition of the work of Dionysius, monk of Fourna d'Agrapha, dedicated to Victor Hugo, which Burges described as 'the key to the whole science of Christian iconography'; and the *Annales Archéologiques* (1844 onwards). Didron told Burges shortly before his death: 'I have done something in this life; when I die the five-and-twenty volumes of the *Annales* will be my monument' (*B.N.* xv, 1868, 31–2). Like Burges, Didron personally sponsored the manufacture of stained glass and metalwork. Like Burges, he argued forcibly against arbitrary and wholesale restoration. But unlike Burges, he was able to campaign from a governmental base: he was Secretary to Guizot's Comité des Arts et Monuments.

84 H. Holiday, *Reminiscences of My Life* (1914), 88, 109. In 1862 Emma Crocker sat as 'the Bride' for Holiday's 'The Bride and the Daughters of Jerusalem'. She appears in one of Rossetti's limericks:

'There is a young maiden called Emma,
Who puts me in quite a dilemma ...'

Holiday married Emma's close friend Kate Raven.

85 Jopling, *op. cit.*, 154, 262. At 28, Beaufort St., Chelsea. The studio was converted into a chapel in

between pp. 98–101
1886 and later demolished (*ibid.*, 261, 292–5).

86 *ibid.*, 185. Her first husband was a gambler named Romer, her third was George Rowe. Her son, Lindsay Millais Jopling (d.1967) had two god-fathers: Sir John Millais and Sir Coutts Lindsay.

87 *ibid.*, 94.

88 *G.M.* ccxix (1865), 154.

89 Abstract, 15 Jan. 1841. Unless this is a mistake for 'confirmed'.

90 Grand Lodge Archives, London.

91 J. W. Sleigh Godding, *A History of the Westminster and Keystone Lodge* (Plymouth, 1907). Typical members were the Tory politician Sir Michael Hicks Beach ('Black Michael') and his cousin, William Mount of Wasing Place, Berks. Visiting members from Jerusalem Lodge included Octavius Hansard and Matthew [?Digby] Wyatt.

92 Abstract, 1866.

93 *ibid.*, 1868.

94 *ibid.*, 1868.

95 *ibid.*, 1874.

96 R. F. Gould, *History of Freemasonry*, ed. H. Poole, iii (1951), 115–16.

97 V. & A., Estimate Book, 4 Aug. 1878.

98 Abstract, 1868.

99 R.I.B.A., S.N.B. viii (1854), flyleaf. He seems to have been in Sicily at the time. He used this symbol as his monogram in the 1856 Crimea Memorial Church competition (R.I.B.A., S.N.B., xliv, 191). The device is formally identified in R. P. Pullan, *The Designs of William Burges* (1885/6), 9.

1 B.M. Bibl. Reg., 17A1.

2 ed. Halliwell-Phillipps (1840; 1844).

3 B.M. Add. MS. 23, 198; ed. M. Cooke (1861). Bought by the B.M., 1850.

4 See D. Knoop and G. P. Jones, *A Short History of Freemasonry to 1730* (1940); *The Genesis of Freemasonry* (1947).

5 G. Oliver, *The Origin of the Royal Arch Order of Masonry* (1867), 2, citing *London Mag.* 1824.

6 eg. stained glass, Winscombe Hall, Somerset. For Rosicrucian symbolism, see F. Hartmann, *The Secret Symbols of the Rosicrucians* (Boston, 1887); Magnus Incognito, *The Secret Doctrine of the Rosicrucians, illustrated with the Secret Rosicrucian Symbols* (Chicago, 1918).

7 H. Jennings, *The Rosicrucians, their Rites and Mysteries* (1840; 4th ed. 1907); A. E. White, *The Real History of the Rosicrucians* (1887); J. Yarker, *The Arcane Schools* (1909); C. Mc. Intosh, *The Rosy Cross Unveiled* (1980).

8 Frances Yates, *The Rosicrucian Enlightenment* (1972), 217.

9 R. F. Gould, *History of Freemasonry*, ed. R. Poole, iii (1951), 267; A. E. Waite, *The Brotherhood of the Rosy Cross*, ed. J. C. Wilson (New York, 1961), 425–6.

10 Mrs. Blake [Edith Osborne], *The Realities of Freemasonry* (1879), 40.

11 Grand Lodge Archives, London.

12 Waite, *op. cit.*, 563. An editor of the *Manchester Guardian*, John Harland, was a Brother. In 1859 the society published an edition of E. Dudley's *Tree of Commonwealth* (1509).

13 J. Croxton, *A History of the Ancient Hall of Samlesbury in Lancashire* (1871); *A True Relation of what passed between Dr. Dee and some spirits* (1659); C. W. Heckethorn, *Secret Societies* 2 vols. (1875); G. Oliver, *Origin of the Royal Arch* (1867); Parkinson, *Shakespeare, a Freemason*; Edith Osborne, *Realities of Freemasonry* (1879). Lord Bute possessed a copy of E. Philalettes, *The Fame and Confession of the Fraternity of the Rosie Cross* (1652).

14 Waite, *op. cit.*, 564–5; Gould, *op. cit.*, iv (1951), 270.

15 W. W. Westcott, *History of the Societas Rosicruciana in Anglia* (1900), 6. For discussion by John Dove of the interrelationship of Freemasonry and Rosicrucianism through ancient symbols, see *B.* xvii (1859), 38–40; xxi (1863), 245–7, 273–4, 402–5, 492–5.

16 A. E. Waite, *The Real History of the Rosicrucians* (1887), 422–6.

17 'Lord Lytton died' (Abstract, 1873). Lytton's novel *Zanoni* (1842) pursues a Rosicrucian theme. He claimed to have been received into Adeptship in the ancient Rosicrucian Lodge at Frankfort-on-the-Main (W. W. Westcott, *Data of the History of the Rosicrucians*, 1916).

18 Mackenzie claimed secret knowledge of Rosicrucian practices deriving from 17th c. Germany (Waite, *op. cit.*, 564) and wrote *The Royal Masonic Cyclopaedia* (1877).

19 Following Payne Knight's investigation of Priapic worship, Jennings derived all religion, and Rosicrucianism in particular, from phallic cults (H. Jennings, *Phallicism Celestial and Terrestrial, Heathen and Christian*, 1884–5; *The Rosicrucians*, 4th ed. 1909).

20 Westcott, *op. cit.*, 10.

21 Tucker was a founder-member of the S.P.A.B. He wrote several works on genealogy and edited Planché's *Extravaganzas* (1879). Planché (1796–1880), a friend of Burges, was Rouge Croix Pursuivant from 1854 to 1866, being succeeded by 'General' de Haviland, a giant soldier of fortune born in America of Guernsey stock, educated in Russia, trained in Spain, and an eccentric antiquary after Burges's own heart (*Survey of London Monographs* xvi, College of Arms, 1963, 164, 191).

22 Its 3rd Magus, Dr. W. W. Westcott, died in Natal in 1925 (*Who Was Who. 1916–28*, 1111). But the society still exists, and Rosicrucians flourish in America.

23 Sar Merodach Joseph Péladan, *L'Art idealiste et mystique doctrine de l'Ordre et du Salon annuel des Roses-Croix (du Temple et du Grael)*, (Paris, 1894). Mainstream Rosicrucian thinking dismissed this as

page 101

an aberration: 'more ... voluptuous aestheticism than philosophical study' (F. Leigh Gardner and W. W. Westcott, *Rosicrucian Books*, 1903, 58).

24 B. Waters and M. Harrison, *Burne-Jones* (1973), 174–5.

3. IN SEARCH OF STYLE
between pp. 102–10

1 G. G. Scott, *Secular and Domestic Architecture, present and future* (1858), 263.

2 E. Viollet-le-Duc, *Entretiens sur l'architecture* i (1863), 179.

3 T. L. Donaldson, 'On a New Style in Architecture', *A. A. Papers* (1847).

4 *B.* xix (1861), 190.

5 *B.N.* xii (1865), 557.

6 *B.N.* xv (1868), 44, 83–4 (Royal Society of Arts).

7 *G.M.* ccxiii (1862), 253.

8 *R.I.B.A. Trans.* 1860–61, 15; *C.E.A. Jnl.* xxiii (1860), 374.

9 *G.M.* ccxv (1863), 6.

10 *B.* xx (1862), 428, R.I.B.A. discussion. Kerr noted: 'he repudiated all philosophy in the matter'.

11 G. H. Guillaume, *B.N.* xi (1864), 871. Scott called these the 'retrospective' and the 'prospective' elements (*Secular and Domestic, op. cit.*, 272).

12 *Qtly. Rev.* cxiv (1863), 289–331. Review of Samuel Smiles, *Lives of British Engineers*, 3 vols (1862).

13 J. Fergusson, *History of the Modern Styles of Architecture* (1862), preface, 318, 406–8.

14 *ibid.* 129.

15 *Macmillan's Mag.* xxv (1871–2), 250–56.

16 *Qtly. Rev.* cxiv (1863), 289–331.

17 *E.* xxiii, n.s. xx (1862), 229.

18 *The Condition and Prospects of Architectural Art* (1863), 13.

19 *E.* xxiii, n.s. xx (1862), 229.

20 *Qtly. Rev.* cxiii (1863), 176–207: review of *South Kensington Museum: Italian Sculpture* (1862) and *Loan Exhibition Catalogue*, ed. J.C. Robinson (1862).

21 *The Common Sense of Art* (Architectural Museum, 1858), 10, 13, 14, 19, 21; *Public Offices and Metropolitan Improvements* (1857), 24.

22 *The English Cathedral of the Nineteenth Century* (1861), 31–2. J. Sulman similarly defined eclecticism as 'not ... the haphazard jumbling of incongruous fragments but a judicious combination and modification of forms' (*B.* xxxiv, 1876, 18).

23 His motto in the Lille competition.

24 Lassus was a dogmatic anti-latitudinarian: 'The situation is grave. In these days no one believes, everyone enquires; the artist has no longer faith except in his reason, no other rule than his personal taste; he analyses everything, and ... [hopes] to create ... a completely new art ... I am perfectly convinced, in the state of anarchy into which art is now reduced, that there remains to us only one anchor of safety, unity of style; and, as we have no art belonging to our own time – everyone is convinced of it and deplores it – there is only one thing for us to do: that is, to choose one from among the anterior epochs, not in order to copy it, but in order to compose [as in music or poetry], while conforming to the spirit of that art' (*E.* xvii, N.S. xiv, 1856, 284–7, 322–4, 414–21; xviii, N.S. xv, 1857, 46–9, 89–91).

25 *B.N.* iv (1858), 617.

26 T. Hope, *An Historical Essay on Architecture* (1835), 561.

27 *Macmillan's Mag.* xxv (1871–72), 250–56. Hope was speaking of Fowke's defeated design, in similar style, for the Natural History Museum.

28 *Qtly. Rev.* cxiii (1863), 176–207.

29 *Qtly. Rev.* cxii (1862), 179–219: review of *Official Catalogues* (1862), and J. Hollingshead, *History of the International Exhibition* (1862). As for the first arrangement of exhibits: 'The groves of Blarney were order and good taste in comparison with the conglomeration of telescopes, organs, lighthouses, fountains, obelisks, pickles, furs, stuffs, porcelain, dolls, rocking-horses, alabasters, stearine, and Lady Godiva, which reduced the nave to a striking similitude of a traveller's description of Hog Lane, Canton.'

30 *Qtly Rev.* cxiii (1863), 176–207.

31 eg. Gilbert Scott: 'Our architecture must embrace within its pale, the semi-circular, the semi-ellipse, the segmental and the pointed arches, but would reserve a strong preference for the pointed' (*Secular and Domestic Architecture*, 1858, 267–8).

32 *E.* i (1842), 134.

33 *Qtly. Rev.* cxii (1862), 179–219.

34 Tennyson, *In Memoriam*.

35 'We need a master mind which can grasp the great principles which pervade all good art, and which, out of the immense fund of material left us by the Greek, the Roman, the Byzantine, the Medieval and Oriental decorators, can sift out all that is good, and out of it generate a perfect style worthy of the highest efforts of which our art is capable.' (*Secular and Domestic Architecture*, 270).

36 *Qtly. Rev.* cxiii (1863), 176–207.

37 'Imagination in Architecture', *Works*, ed. Cook and Wedderburn, xvi, 348–9.

38 *Architectural Mag.* iv (1837), 277–87.

39 Phoebe Stanton, 'Welby Pugin and the Gothic Revival' (Ph.D., London, 1950), 348.

40 B. Ferrey, *Pugin*, 258.

41 to Hardman, quoted in N. Pevsner, *Some Architectural Writers of the Nineteenth Century* (1972), 115.

42 G. B.-J., *Memorials of Edward Burne-Jones* i (1904), 101.

43 quoted in P. Thompson, 'Paxton and the dilemma of 19th c. Architecture', *The Listener* 7 July 1966, 15.

44 quoted in Pevsner, *Architectural Writers*, 192.

between pp. 110–15

45 *E.* xii (1851), 269 *et seq.*

46 *Seven Lamps, Works,* ed. Cook and Wedderburn, viii, 66.

47 'Answer to Mr Garbett', *Works* ed. Cook and Wedderburn, ix, 455–6.

48 Fergusson, *True Principles of Beauty in Art* (1849), 119–21.

49 Fergusson, *History of the Modern Styles of Architecture* (1862), 491.

50 *ibid.* 476, 478, 480, 483.

51 C. H. Driver, *B.N.* xxxvi (1879), 141.

52 *R.I.B.A. Trans.* (1865–66), 15–30. For the fragmentation of 'the architectural professions', see J. Mordaunt Crook, 'The Pre-Victorian Architect: Professionalism and Patronage', *Arch. Hist.* xii (1969), 62–78.

53 'Church restoration – the seduction of antiquity – have robbed our rising generation of architects of what should have been their inalienable property in art, and another fast-rising profession have appropriated it. We mean the use of iron, artificial stone, new modes of construction, and the thousand appliances and inventions science has thrown in our way' (G.H. Guillaume, in *B.N.* xxvi, 1874, 412; xxvii, 1874, 45).

54 for Pickett's *Metallurgic Architecture* (1844), see P. Collins, *Arch. Rev.* cxxx (1961), 267.

55 *E.* xiii, N.S. x (1852), 248.

56 see G. German, *The Gothic Revival. in Europe and Britain* (1972), 116, 148. 'C'est de l'architecture antediluvienne, plus monstrueuse et plus bossue que le mastodontes les plus rebarbatifs' (*A.A.* xii, 1853, 229).

57 *Secular and Domestic Architecture,* 109–11.

58 S. Muthesius, 'The Iron Problem in the 1850s', *Arch. Hist.* xiii (1970), 58–63.

59 Dr. Ackland, *E.* xvi, N.S. xiii (1855), 249.

60 *E.* xxii, N.S. xix (1861), 25–6.

61 Muthesius, 'The Iron Problem in the 1850s', *Arch. Hist.* xiii (1970), 58–63.

62 *The English Cathedral of the Nineteenth Century* (1861), 66–7.

63 quoted in German, *Gothic Revival,* 164.

64 *Art Applied to Industry* (1865), 49.

65 *E.* xxviii, N.S. xxv (1867), 155–6.

66 *Recollections of Sir T. G. Jackson,* ed. B. H. Jackson (Oxford, 1950), 56.

67 *Art Applied to Industry,* 51.

68 *ibid.,* 51–2.

69 R.I.B.A., S.N.B., 1858, Oct.

70 'Like all the world, I am waiting for the new style which is to come ... the NEW STYLE about which so much has been said ... and so little has been done' ('Iron as a Building Material', *R.I.B.A. Papers,* 1864, 97–107).

71 Street seems to have been thinking of an iron *urinoir* which still survives in an alley between Chancery Lane and the Law Courts, probably designed by M. D. Wyatt.

72 discussion following J. A. Picton, 'Iron and Mild Steel as Building Materials', *R.I.B.A. Trans.* (1879–80), 149–161; *B.N.* xxxviii (1880), 624–5.

73 'Ironwork: its Legitimate Uses and Proper Treatment', *R.I.B.A. Trans.* 1865–6, 15–30.

74 *B.N.* xxxviii (1880), 624–5.

75 *R.I.B.A. Trans.* 1865–6, 15–30.

76 *Seven Lamps*: Lamp of Obedience, *Works,* ed. Cook and Wedderburn, viii, 252.

77 *ibid.,* 258.

78 Street's caution with regard to 'the luxury of Venetian architecture' won Ruskin's especial praise: his 'designs were pure beyond anything he had ever seen in modern architecture, in exquisite propriety of colour and in fineness of line' (*Works,* ed. Cook and Wedderburn, xvi, 462: 15 Feb. 1859). Ruskin particularly praised Street's rebuilding of St. Paul's, Herne Hill (1858–9).

79 *Works,* ed. Cook and Wedderburn, x, 458–9: 16 Mar. 1872, letter to *Pall Mall Gazette,* prompted by (?) Coventry Patmore's review of Eastlake's *Gothic Revival.*

80 *Works,* ed. Cook and Wedderburn, viii, 13.

81 Street admitted that Northern Gothic was 'more vigorous, grand and perfect', particularly as regards sculpture (*Works,* ed. Cook and Wedderburn, xvi, 469: 15 Feb. 1859).

82 *E.* xxi, N.S. xviii (1860), 43.

83 *B.* xviii (1860), 251.

84 eg. John Ball, 'The Four Primary Sensations of the Mind: the Sublime, the Beautiful, the Low or Ridiculous, and the Painful', *Jnl. of Design,* v (1851), 124–7, 169–73; vi (1851), 37–48, 102–6. Ball includes a percentage-based 'Table of Sensations'.

85 *E.* xxviii, n.s. xxv (1860), 291: Ashwell, Rutland.

86 *E.* xx, N.S. xvii (1859), 185: All Saints, Margaret St.

87 Beresford-Hope, *The Common Sense of Art* (1858), 19.

88 P. Thompson, *Butterfield* (1871), 507–8.

89 eg. G. E. Street, 'The Study of Foreign Gothic Architecture, and its Influence on English Art', in O. Shipley (ed.), *The Church and the World,* i (1866), 397–41 (a plea for the cautious use of French, German and occasionally Italian forms); *Brick and Marble in the Middle Ages: notes on a tour in North Italy* (1855); reviewed *E.* xvi, N.S. xiii (1855), 299–305. Street considered that Venetian palazzi offered excellent models 'on which to build our nineteenth-century style of domestic architecture ... The windows are large, wide and numerous. The fronts are regular ... [or] irregular ... and ... sash windows ... need be in no way un-English, as those who have seen the new museum at Oxford will at once allow'. After all, sash windows could always be supplied *behind* shafted mullions, in the Venetian manner. (*B.* xvii, 1859, 146–8, 170–71 to Architectural Photographic Society).

between pp. 115–20

90 G. G. Scott, 'On the Pointed Architecture of Italy', *E.* xvi, N.S. xiii (1855), 142–8; *Recollections*, 228.

91 G. E. Street, 'On German Pointed Architecture', *E.* xviii, n.s. xv (1857), 162.

92 eg. St. George's Fields, Lambeth.

93 *E.* i (1842), 209; vi (1846), 98–101; viii (1847), 90–92, 141–7. B. Webb, 'On Pointed Architecture as adapted to tropical climates', *Trans. Eccles. Soc.* (1845), 199–218; *Sketches of Continental Ecclesiology* (1848).

94 P. Thompson, *Butterfield* (1971), 147.

95 *E.* xviii, N.S. xv (1857), 246.

96 *B.* xxv (1867), 386.

97 *B.* xix (1861), 403.

98 Scott, *Recollections*, 159.

99 ibid., 204.

1 ibid., 163.

2 *E.* xxii, N.S. xix (1861), 354; xxiii, N.S. xx (1862), 16.

3 *Works*, ed. Cook and Wedderburn, viii, 15.

4 ibid., xxiii, 269.

5 *B.N.* xii (1865), 605–6.

6 *B.N.* xxxv (1878), 313–4.

7 *B.N.* xii (1865), 605–6. Probably a bank – now the National Westminster – in Wells.

8 W. Burges, *Art Applied to Industry* (1865), 111.

9 *B.N.* xii (1865), 606.

10 *B.* xiii (1855), 306.

11 *B.* xix (1861), 192.

12 *B.* xix (1861), 408: R.I.B.A. discussion.

13 *B.N.* xii (1865), 557.

14 ibid., 605.

15 *E.* xviii, N.S. xiv (1857), 20.

16 *B.* xxv (1867), 386. As an example of the superiority of Early French over Early English, Burges cited some work in Oxford (Early French) and the same architect's work in Bishopsgate, London (Early English). See *B.N.* xii (1865), 606.

17 *B.* xix (1861), 403. In 1884 Kerr described England as 'the very home of rough and ready muscularity' (*R.I.B.A. Trans.* 1883–4, 218–30). For another view, see E. Sharpe's lectures on Early French, *B.N.* xxvii (1874), 745, 790–94.

18 Obit. *A.A.* xxv (1865), 124, 377–95. He edited the first 25 vols.

19 Burges on Didron, *B.N.* xv (1868), 31. Romanesque was merely 'embryonic', late Gothic 'moribund'; only thirteenth-century Gothic was 'pure and powerful' (*A.A.* xiv, 1854, 385).

20 'Avis', *A.A.* xxvii (1870), 409.

21 Obit. *A.A.* xvii (1857), 307–13.

22 Obit. *A.A.* xix (1859), 314–27.

23 Obit. *A.A.* xxiv (1864), 324–9.

24 *A.A.* i (1844), 120, pl. i, drawn by Viollet-le-Duc.

25 Eglise de Chablis (Yonne), North portal, *A.A.* xv (1855), 270, ill.: this horseshoe shape was used by Burges, *inter alia*, at Chiswick church.

26 *A.A.* ii (1845), 362, pl. vi, drawn by H. Gerente.

27 *A.A.* ii (1845), 19, pl. i (restoration); xiii (1853), 357–8.

28 eg. 'La Sainte-Chandelle d'Arras', x (1850), 321–5 and xi (1851), 174–6, where the decorative borders provide a likely source for Burges's characteristic border of flowing tendrils and grotesque, humanised beasts (cf. inkstand, author's colln.). Similarly, the boldly modelled annulet in gilded bronze, from candelabra at Milan, was embodied in idea, though not in detail, in Burges's central column for the unfinished Great Stairs at Cardiff (*A.A.* xiv, 1854, 341, ill.). Didron's article on 'Bronzes et Orfèvrerie du Moyen Age' in 1859 included details of many pieces of interest to Burges. In particular two tiny reliquaries: the thirteenth-century 'Chasse' in the church of St. Thibault, Côte-d'or, heavily hinged and finialled, anticipates the basic shape of Burges's painted furniture; and the Chasse d'un Abbé' (13th–14th c.) in the Cluny Museum, with its four supporting angels, anticipates the idea of Lord Bute's Cruet (*A.A.*xix, 1859, 18–19).

29 *A.A.* iv (1846), 325–53, by Viollet-le-Duc.

30 *A.A.* iv (1846), 369–75, by Didron, E. Boesilvald and L. Vitet.

31 *A.A.* vii (1847), 169; viii (1848), 61, by Viollet-le-Duc; xi (1851), 363.

32 *A.A.* ix (1849), 73: St. Denis; x (1850), 18–25: Breteuil, 60–68: Merles, Breteuil, 233–41, 305–11: St. Omer; xi (1851), 16–23, 65–71: St. Omer; xii (1852), 137–53: St. Omer, 281–93: St. Pierre-sur-Dives.

33 *A.A.* xii (1852), 300–19, 392–5, by Didron.

34 eg. Daniel Rock, 'L'Archéologie Catholique en Angleterre', *A.A.* xi (1851), 137–47; Great Exhibition publications, xi (1851), 292–316; Beresford-Hope, 'L'Art Religieuse En Angleterre', xiii (1853), 332–7 and his obituary of R. C. Carpenter, xv (1855), 207–8.

35 In 1850 Didron correctly predicted that English architects would abandon the fourteenth century and go back to thirteenth-century models (*A.A.* x, 1850, 283–4). In 1851 he noticed that even Pugin was 'moving towards the thirteenth century, although too slowly for our liking' (*A.A.* xi, 1851, 292–4).

36 eg. *E.* xx, N.S. xvii (1859), 79. In this he differed from J. M. Neale and Benjamin Webb who always preferred English Decorated.

37 in Shipley (ed.), *Church and World* iii (1868), 582.

38 'When we consider not only how much he writes, but the knowledge, and, above all, the research involved in what he writes, his productions become simply wonderful. Had he only lived some five centuries back, the German critics would most certainly have discovered that there were at least three distinct Viollet-le-Ducs … if he had not got three heads and three pairs of hands, at least he ought to have them' (*G.M.* ccxv, 1863, 675).

between pp. 120–22

39 eg. the upper part of the pediment of the central portal at Rheims, or the hourds applied to the upper part of the Donjon at Courcy.

40 *G.M.* ccxv (1863), 6. Perhaps Burges was thinking of his old master Blore: 'one of the most minute and beautiful architectural draughtsmen that the world has ever beheld', but an architect whose works often disappoint in plan, silhouette and detail (*Art Applied to Industry*, 1865, 110).

41 *G.M.* ccxv (1863), 677.

42 *B.N.* xii (1865), 115, 225; T. G. Jackson, *Recollections*, 55.

43 B. xxxi (1873), 1001, following a paper on Pierrefonds by Phéné Spiers. Burges's criticisms were supported by Horace Jones, Benjamin Bucknall and C. F. Hayward.

44 *The English Cathedral of the Nineteenth Century*, 45. For contemporary French examples of Early French, see *Gazette des Architectures et du Batiments* N.S. iii (1865), 69 and iv (1866), 310–14.

45 *B.N.* xii (1865), 605.

46 The Sainte Chapelle at Riom; the courtyard of the Hotel de la Chaussée, Bourges; an apartment and a group of carved enrichments in the old Hotel de Ville, Bourges; and sculptured tympana in both the latter buildings. There are no obvious sources of inspiration for Burges, though he must have enjoyed the snail nibbling away at foliage on a crocket from Bourges (pl. 16), and the clutch of 'Epis or Girouettes' – chimneys, weather-vanes, lead finials, etc. – from the rooftops of Bourges and Beaune (pl. 14). The book was dedicated to Baron de Mauley, for whom both Clutton and Burges had worked at Hatherop, Glos.

47 *Archeological Jnl.* x (1853), 264. Clutton specifically disclaimed any absolute excellence in the domestic architecture of fifteenth-century France: 'I by no means consider it either as the very best development of the domestic art of the Middle Ages, [nor do] I wish to recommend it as a perfect model for imitation'. (Clutton, *Domestic Architecture of France*, 63).

48 *A.A.* xiii (1853), 280.

49 Eg. Amiens, Auxerre, Beauvais, Bourges, Chartres, Le Mons, Notre Dame and the Sainte Chapelle in Paris, Rouen, Sees, Sens, Strasbourg, Semur, Toul, Assisi (Lower Chapel), Florence, Lucca, Pistoia, Milan, Naples (Sta. Chiara, San Giovanni a Carbonara, San Domenico Maggiore, San Giovanni de Pappacoda), Padau, Pisa (Capella della Spina).

50 Eg. the trefoil leaves and berried fruit in the capitals at Amiens, Auxerre and Le Mans; the wheel window in the West gable at Bourges; or the bulbous finials from the Ste. Chapelle (pls. 12, 28).

51 Eg. Jacques Coeur's house at Bourges: the doorway casing (pl. 13) is reminiscent of Burges's doorways in the Great Hall at Cardiff, and parts of the roofline

recall the later sections of the same castle; a timber house at Beauvais: the timber colonnettes (pl. 11) recall Burges's aisle at Carrigrohane and his window jambs at Dover.

52 Eg. Amiens, Bayeux (Armoire), Bourges, Châlons, Chartres, Coutances, Laon, Montreale in Burgundy, Noyon, Rouen, Sens, Vézelay. Nesfield also offered a few Italian models, eg. Orvieto, Padua, Pisa, Viterbo (fountain).

53 *B.N.* xxxiii (1877), 610–11.

54 Although dedicated to Butterfield, it was really Burgesian in inspiration, with detailed studies of carvings and mouldings drawn from the usual thirteenth-century French prototypes. The Bayeux *armoire* also appears (pls. 8–9). There was a copy in Burges's library.

55 T. H. King and G. J. Hill, *The Study Book of Medieval Architecture and Art* (1858–65), iii, pls. 33–42.

56 *ibid.* iii, pls. 49–60.

57 *ibid.* iii, pls. 75–83 (Cathedral); iii, pls. 84–8 (St. Remi).

58 *ibid.* i, pls. 1–6 (St. Ived), drawn by Norman Shaw.

59 *ibid.* i, pls. 7–8 (Notre Dame).

60 *ibid.* i, pl. 99 (Sarcophagi).

61 *ibid.* i, pls. 57–64 (Notre Dame).

62 *ibid.* i, pls. 50–56 (restored by Viollet-le-Duc).

63 *ibid.* i, pls. 27–43 (St. Etienne).

64 *B.N.* xii (1865), 605–6.

65 *E.* xix, N.S. xvi (1858), 362–72; xx. N.S. xvii (1859), 18–26, 91–100, 178–84, 332–40. He also adds: Rouen, Meaux, Troyes, Montes, St. Leu, St. Germer (which he especially admired), Senlis, St. Etienne at Beauvais, Fécamp, St. George de Boscherville, Limay, Gassiecourt, Champagne, Bourges, Sees and Coutances.

66 *E.* xix, N.S. xvi (1858), 240.

67 *B.* xix (1861), 190. In 1872–74 Burges produced a design for a new altar and reredos: 'I have endeavoured to steer a middle course between the pure Perpendicular of the architecture of the Chapel and the equally pure Renaissance of the rood screen. Happily we are not without examples of this *via media*', e.g. Bishop West's Chapel, Ely (*A.* xiii, 1875, 304–5). For details, see Pullan, *Designs of William Burges*, 18–20, 63–4; R.I.B.A., S.N.B. xli (1871), 24 and xliii (1872), 62; V. & A., Estim. Bk. Aug. 1875; Abstract 1872, 1873, 1874; A. Doig, *Architectural Drawings . . . King's College, Cambridge* (1979), 60–61. E. W. Godwin called this design 'one of the most beautiful combinations of architecture and sculpture of this or any age' (*B.A.* vi, 1881, 214).

68 *B.* xix (1861), 237. In 1867 – through Beresford Hope – Burges produced a design for the entire rebuilding of Trinity College Chapel in Early French (Trinity Coll. Archives, Bursar's minutes 16 Feb. 1867; Report and plans, Weller MSS.; R.I.B.A., S.N.B., xxxiii, 1867, 77; Abstract, 1867).

between pp. 122–26

69　*Seven Lamps*, in *Works*, ed. Cook and Wedderburn, viii, 63.

70　*B.N.* xii (1865), 638. See also a Puginian call for English vernacular building methods rather than 'third-rate' French sculpture and unnecessary string-courses (*B.* xvii, 1864, 500); and a violent anonymous criticism of thirteenth-century painting and decoration as merely 'rude and barbarous' (*B.N.* xiii, 1866, 617).

71　'O.O.O' in *B.* xxi (1863), 447. 'Our modern sculpture has no *life* in it: it wants "go" ...' See also *ibid.* 813–4, where both Italian and French Gothic are rejected, and Renaissance too: 'it only expresses the epicurean filth of the "Hermaphrodite" of Becatelli'.

72　*E.* xxiv (1863), 127–8. Designed initially in 1861, revised in 1863 and c.1868, All Saints became progressively more English and less Continental in style (*E.* xxii, 1861, 124; *B.* xxviii, 1870, 891).

73　*Land and Building News* ii (1856), 57.

74　*Secular and Domestic Architecture*, 192.

75　*Preliminary Discourse* [at University College], (1842), 28–30.

76　R. A. lectures, 1857 onwards, quoted in J. Mordaunt Crook, 'Sydney Smirke: the architecture of compromise', in *Seven Victorian Architects*, ed. J. Fawcett and N. Pevsner (1976), 64–5.

77　*B.N.* xxii (1872), 321. For a vigorous reply in defence of Gothic see *B.N.* xxii (1872), 343–4.

78　Alternatively he proposed a neo-Fergussonian view: the New Style would not be Greek or Gothic; it must therefore be some hybrid combination of Romanesque and Renaissance (*B.N.* xxvi, 1874, 412).

79　*B.N.* xxii, 1872, 321.

80　H. S. Goodhart-Rendel, 'Rogue Architects of the Victorian Era', *R.I.B.A. Jnl.* lvi (1949), 251–9. With rather less justification, Goodhart-Rendel also included 'Greek' Thomson, John Shaw, James Wild, James Maclaren, E. S. Prior and Beresford Pite.

81　Scott, *Recollections*, 228.

82　Burgesian Early French 'called forth a legion of imitators, who easily caught up some of the tricks of the style, but lacked altogether the skill needful to turn it to any good use, and who covered the land with buildings which for downright ugliness surpass all others even in this age of ugly buildings. No one was stronger in his condemnation of these things than Mr. Burges himself, but they did not shake his faith in his favourite style' (J. T. Micklethwaite, *The Academy*, xix, 1881, 325–6).

83　*Art Applied to Industry*, 113–8.

84　Precedents for 'eccentric incisions' could be found, in the font at Old Stantonbury, for example. But modern architects who pursue the fashion indiscriminately merely 'confound ingenuity with art' (*B.N.* xiv, 1867, 753).

85　'Great balls of marble or fluor-spar, reminding us of the eyes of the monsters that Schiller's Diver beheld when he plunged into the whirlpool' (*Church and World*, 584).

86　*B.* xxv (1867), 386. 'That acmé of ugliness and bad taste' (*Church and World*, 596).

87　*B.* xxv (1867), 386.

88　*Church and World*, 582. Burges on originality: 'Their proceedings are about as reasonable as ... those of a man who, failing to write a poem, should claim originality by trying to alter the orthography of a language'. For ugliness, cf. W. M. Mitchell: 'There is much truth in the accusation of Professor Kerr, that there is an incredible worship of ugliness amongst us' (*B.N.* xxiv, 1873, 584–5). In 1858 Gilbert Scott was already objecting to 'that intentional queerness and artistic ugliness which some of our young architects labour to produce' (*Secular and Domestic Architecture*, 275).

89　*The Sacristy* iii (1873), 28.

90　'Beauty no more depends on crockets, pinnacles, foliage and encaustic tiles, than it does upon violently coloured bricks, the straight-sided arch, or drain pipes instead of marble ... Art consists neither in prettiness nor ugliness ... but in beauty and feeling' (*Church and World*, 597–8).

91　J. Stevens Curl and J. Sambrook, 'E. Basset Keeling' *Arch. Hist.* xvi (1973), 60–69.

92　He was much praised by the *Land and Building News*, but consistently condemned by the *Ecclesiologist* for 'all those eccentricities which render Mr. Lamb the most affected and *outré*, and at the same time ineffective, of our ecclesiastical architects' (*E.* xvi, n.s. xiii, 1855, 38–9).

93　'The so-called Victorian architecture may be described as a violation of all canons of good taste, combined with a total disregard to the just principles of construction' (*Church and World*, 576).

94　T. Harris, *A Few Words to show that a National Architecture, adapted to the Wants of the Nineteenth Century, is attainable* (1860). We need 'an indigenous style of our own ... [for this] age of new creations ... Steam power and electric communications [are] entirely new revolutionizing influences. So must it be in Architecture' (*Victorian Architecture*, 1860). 'Iron and glass ... have succeeded in giving a distinct and marked character to the future of architecture ... The architecture of the nineteenth century ... cannot be expected to reach its full development in our time, but the future of that style, the Victorian style ... is assured' (*Examples of the Architecture of the Victorian Age*, 1862, 57–8). See also D. Harbron, 'Thomas Harris', *A.R.* xcii (1942), 63–6; P. F. R. Donner [N. Pevsner], 'A Thomas Harris Florilegium', *A.R.* xciii (1943), 51–2.

95　*E.* xxii, N.S. xx (1861), 13.

96　J.P.S., 'Spurious Eclecticism', *B.N.* xxiii (1872), 35. One house he had in mind was Holdenby House, Northants, by W. Slater and R. H. Carpenter, ill.

between pp. 126–33

B.N. xxiii (1872), 11. Other offenders, in domestic work, were David Brandon and T. Roach Smith. One infectious source of error was Eastbury Manor House, Essex.

97 *E.* xxiii, N.S. xx (1862), 337.

98 *B.* xix (1861), 404.

99 *E.* xxiii, N.S. xx (1862), 337.

1 *B.* xix (1861), 192.

2 *Art Applied to Industry*, 7–8.

3 'At present we all seem to agree that the thirteenth century is the best to start from, but we shall never get on until we work solely in this style, and introduce sculpture wherever we possibly can. But I do not very clearly see how this is to be attained when one man builds an Egyptian villa, and another something in the Arabian style, while another has a predilection for late German Gothic and its stump tracery, and a fourth goes in for Sir Christopher Wren and what is called the City style' (*B.* xix, 1861, 191).

4 *Art Applied to Industry*, 7–8.

5 *B.N.* xii (1865), 605.

6 *Art Applied to Industry*, 8.

7 *E.* xxviii, N.S. xxv (1867), 155–6.

8 *B.* xxv (1867), 385–6. In the discussion that followed, J. P. Seddon dissented from Burges's 'desponding view' (*B.* xxv, 1867, 394).

9 *C.E.A. Jnl.* xxx (1867), 176.

10 *Church and World*, 575.

11 *A.* xv (1876), 16.

12 Handley-Read seems to have been unaware of the evidence quoted here. As late as 1967 he wrote: 'In Burges there is no guilt, no tension, nothing to explain ... I can discover no shred of evidence for a feeling of guilt, no friction between his aims, ideals and actual achievements. In short, there is no "problem" ...' (C.H.-R. MSS.).

13 *B.N.* xix (1870), 271.

14 *International Exhibition, 1862, Catalogue of Fine Art Dept.* (1862), 81.

15 *B.N.* xv (1868), 440.

16 See A. Saint, *Richard Norman Shaw* (1976), 24 *et seq.*

17 *ibid.* 130 *et seq.* 'The sketchbook has borne its cargoes back from the brick miracles of Bruges and Nuremberg, and from the placid wharves of Holland' (P. Waterhouse, *R.I.B.A. Jnl.* 1876, 489).

18 In a paper read to the St. Albans Architectural and Archeological Society (*B.N.* xxviii, 1875, 285).

19 'It has been said, with great truth, that the real restorer of Medieval art was Sir Walter Scott ... In the same way, Thackeray ... has made Queen Anne's style popular' (*B.* xxxiii, 1875, 1145). 'Byron made the world Philhellenists' (*B.N.* xxxi, 1876, 120). Thackeray's house on Palace Green Kensington, dates from 1868.

20 *B.N.* xix (1870), 271.

21 *A.* iii (1870), 314–5, signed 'John Smith'; iv (1870), 10–11, 24–5.

22 *A.* x (1873), 327.

23 *A.* x (1873), 156–8, 169–70.

24 *A.* x (1873), 3, 27–8, 237–8.

25 *A.* xi (1874), 1–2, 32, 55–6, 69–71, 109–10, 145–6, 159–60.

26 *A.* xi (1874), 63–6, 96–7, 139–40.

27 *A.* xi (1874), 121, 157.

28 *B.N.* xx (1871), 337.

29 *B.N.* xxvi (1874), 82, 125, 307.

30 'Queen Anne is Dead', *B.N.* xxviii (1875), 333, 457; 'Consistency and Refinement in Architecture', *B.N.* xxx (1876), 33.

31 *B.N.* xxviii (1875), 587.

32 *B.N.* xxx (1876), 35, 55–6.

33 *B.N.* xxviii (1875), 285.

34 *B.N.* xxviii (1875), 249. For a middle-of-the-road acceptance of Queen Anne, by E. F. C. Clarke, see *B.N.* xxviii (1875), 277.

35 *B.N.* xxviii (1875), 313 (ill.), 387, 415.

36 'The Seventeenth and Nineteenth-Century Revivals', *B.N.* xxxi (1876), 171.

37 Children's Hospital, Cardiff (*B.N.* xxxii, 1877, 486); Elizabethan House (*B.N.* xxxviii, 1880, 600–61).

38 *B.N.* xxxv (1878), 687.

39 *B.N.* xxxix (1880), 614, 620–21.

40 See J. T. Emmett, *Six Essays*, ed. J. Mordaunt Crook (1972).

41 Fred. C. Deshon, 'Free (and Easy) Classic', *B.N.* xxviii (1875), 304, 332, 363.

42 *B.N.* xxviii (1875), 396.

43 *B.N.* xxviii (1875), 651. This is a remarkably early use of the term: the building to which it was (rather improbably) applied was Bodley and Garner's School Board Offices on the Embankment, London (*B.N.* xxix, 1875, 10–13, ills.).

44 *B.N.* xxviii (1875), 709.

45 *B.N.* xxxii (1877), 2.

46 *A.* ix (1873), 271.

47 *B.N.* xxxii (1877), 205–6. For a vigorous reply on behalf of Gothic 'honesty', see *ibid.*, 211.

48 eg. *B.N.* xxxiii (1877), 101, ills.; xxxv (1878), 585, ills.; xxxvi (1879), 201, ills.; xxxvii (1879), 299–300.

49 *B.N.* xxxvi (1879), 289. For an amusing squib by E. J. Tarver, see *A.* xv (1876), 56.

50 E. W. Godwin, 'Modern Dress', *A.* xv (1876), 368.

51 *A.* xv (1876), 16.

52 *A.* ix (1873), 271.

53 'The Style of the Future', *B.N.* xxviii (1875), 425. Kerr called Queen Anne 'the bric-a-brac style' (*R.I.B.A. Trans.* 1883–4, 218–30).

54 Stables (1881).

55 At Marlborough, Street also used tile-hanging in the Norman Shaw manner to cover his experimental use of concrete (*B.N.* xxviii, 1875, 715; xxix, 1875, 78).

56 eg. Thorne's commentary on the architecture of 1874 in *The British Almanac and Companion*,

between pp. 133–39

reviewed in *A.* xii (1874), 311; or A. Payne, 'Periods of Transition in Architectural Style, and is the Present Day one?', *ibid.* 321–2.

57 *B.N.* xxxi (1876), 414, 420–21, ills.

58 *B.N.* xxvi (1874), 269.

59 'The Ex-Classic Style called Queen Anne', *B.N.* xxviii (1875), 441.

60 *B.N.* xxvii (1874), 8, 58.

61 *B.A.* ix (1878), 8.

62 *B.N.* xxvi (1874), 256, 262–5.

63 *B.N.* xxxi (1876), 492, 497, ill.

64 *B.N.* vii (1861), 893; *B.* xix (1861), 282.

65 *B.N.* xii (1865), 8–11; *B.* xxii (1864), 528–30.

66 *B.N.* xiv (1867), 702.

67 *B.N.* xxxiv (1878), 268–9, ill.

68 *B.N.* xxxii (1877), 36; xxxviii (1880), 124.

69 M. Girouard, 'The Victorian Artist at Home': *C.L.* clii (1972), 1370–74.

70 *B.N.* xxviii (1875), 441; *A.* xiv (1875), 70.

71 *B.* xxxiii (1875), 1145.

72 *B.* xxxiv (1876), 18.

73 'On the Recent Reaction of Taste in English Architecture', Architectural Conference, R.I.B.A., *B.N.* xxvi (1874), 689.

74 See J. Mordaunt Crook, *The Greek Revival: Neo-Classical Attitudes in British Architecture, 1760–1870* (1972), 143. Professor T. Roger Smith agreed: 'We have no modern European style; but ... modern European taste ... is more nearly in harmony with [the Renaissance] than with Gothic' (*B.N.* xxvi, 1874, 269).

75 'The Gothic Secessionists and "Queen Anne"', *B.N.* xxxiii (1877), 504–5.

76 'It was not the differentia of the Queen Anne style that was its attraction; all that is a mere bundle of preposterous whims; it was the fact that in the style there was yet left some feeling of the Gothic' ('The Revival of Architecture', *Fortnightly Rev.* May 1888, reprinted in *Architecture, Industry and Wealth*).

77 *B.* xx (1862), 426.

78 'The sash window has been registered with Magna Carta, Habeas Corpus and Trial by Jury, as the Englishman's birthright, and it seems hopeless to dream of his relinquishing his privilege ... [and] plate-glass is one of the most useful and beautiful inventions of our day (*Secular and Domestic Architecture*, 35–6).

79 *B.N.* xxix (1875), 747.

80 *B.N.* xxvi (1874), 690. Stevenson later admitted the weakness of any architectural theory based solely on Truth: 'The principle of absolute Truth in architecture has to bend to many modifications in actual practice ... There is no more necessity for showing the grain of wood and forbidding paint, or for brick and stone walls without plaster, than there is for nature exposing to view our viscera'. Still, 'in what is loosely called the "Queen Anne" style, we find that natural mode of simple honest London

building worked out in an artistic form ... it displays more perfectly than modern Gothic the principle of Truth on which the Gothic revival insisted' (*B.N.* xxviii, 1875, 248).

81 Queen Anne was a hybrid, belonging neither to the style of modern Europe (Classic), nor to the style of medieval Europe (Gothic); it was a 'popular and local mode, which ... differs from both, but takes after both, essentially a minor art style, and obviously transitional' (*R.I.B.A. Trans.* 1883–4, 218–30).

82 eg. J. D. Sedding, *B.N.* xxx (1876), 267.

83 'Late Gothic – Shall it be Revived?', *B.N.* xxxiii (1877), 609–10.

84 He called for a 'hearty revival' of its latest and flattest forms ('The Revival of the Later Styles of English Gothic', *B.N.* xxxiii, 1877, 680–82). See also 'Perpendicular Architecture', *B.N.* xxxviii (1880), 650–53.

85 'The Claims of Late Gothic and Renaissance considered', *B.N.* xxxiv (1878), 49–50.

86 *B.N.* xxxviii (1880), 178, 237.

87 *B.N.* xxxviii (1880), 297.

88 Scott, *Secular and Domestic Architecture*, 204.

89 *E.* xix, N.S., xvi (1858), 238.

90 *Art Applied to Industry*, 91–2. Beresford-Hope agreed: he regarded metalwork and ceramics as the most probable engines of architectural progression (*Qtly. Rev.* cxiii, 1863, 176–207). Kerr traced the High Victorian renaissance of the minor arts – the South Kensington school in fact – to the influence of public exhibitions, notably 1851 and 1862 in England, 1855 and 1867 in France (*R.I.B.A. Trans.* 1883–4, 218–30).

91 *American Architect and B.N.* i (1876), 17.

92 *A.* xxi (1879), 80.

93 *American Architect and B.N.* iii (1878), 117.

94 G. Aitchison, *R.I.B.A. Trans.* 1883–4, 207.

95 Scott, *Recollections*, 372.

96 *B.* xxxiii (1875), 1145.

97 *B.N.* xxii (1872), 321.

98 *Art Jnl.* 1886, 180; Pullan, *Designs of William Burges*, 20; R.I.B.A. 'Orf. Dom.', 25–8; 'Elephant Inkstand ... Elephant made up' (Abstract, 1862–3). P.L.U. It commemorated literary labours of 1862, and was originally one of two inkstands at Buckingham St. The other (1869) – itself as craggy as an elephant's foot – was of carved teak, encrusted with crystal and gems (Burges, 'Own Furniture', R.I.B.A. Album, 37–8; Pullan, *Designs*, 21; R.I.B.A. 'Orf. Dom.', 28v. Bought 1964 by Handley-Read for £17.10s.0d.; colln. J. Mordaunt Crook). Burges designed another elephant inkstand for Garnett of Bingley (Bingley Album, 1867). Compare the elephant door panels at Sens (Nesfield, *Sketches from France and Italy*, pl. 84).

4. RENAISSANCE
between pp. 140–43

1 *E.* xxii, N.S. xix (1861), 155–61. Burges believed the artist responsible to be Francesco di Domenico da Gambossi, and the date 1434 (*E.* xxiii, N.S. xx, 1862, 30). Modern scholars suggest designs by Ghiberti, executed by the German glass-painter Niccolo di Piero (G. Kauffmann, *Florence*, 1971, 42).

2 *E.* xxii, N.S. xix (1861), 155–61 and xxiii, N.S. xx (1862), 29–30; *B.* xxiv (1866), 213; *A.* ix (1873), 302–3. For recent accounts of the chequered career of the West front, see *Il Museo Dell'Opera del Duomo*, ed. L. Becherucci and G. Brunetti, i (Firenze, 1971), intro; F. K. B. Toker, 'Florence Cathedral: the design stage', *Art Bulletin* lx (1978), 214–31.

3 Abstract, 1862.

4 *E.* xxiv, N.S. xxi (1863), 60, 119.

5 *ibid.*, 235.

6 The first three consolation prizes were given to Carlo del Conte Lorenzo Cappi of Turin (no. 42), Mariano Falcini of Florence (no. 25), and Wilhelm Peterson of Copenhagen (no. 38). See *B.* xxi (1863), 174.

7 Winners were chosen in each of four different classes, according to the disposition of the facade: Peterson, Majorfi, Falcini and De Fabris.

8 Second was Cipolla of Rome; third Alvino of Naples. For correspondence relating to Burges's entry, see Archivio Opera di S. Maria del Fiore de Firenze, Serie xi-2-27, 31; xiii-1-48, 58, 63, 70. A two-volume photographic record of competition entries also survives. Burges directed that his design ('Flos Florum', no. 21) should remain among the cathedral archives. For Burges's sculptural sketches, see R.I.B.A., 'Stonework', 5r. For Viollet-le-Duc's role, see *Le Voyage d'Italie d'Eugène Violet-le-Duc, 1836–7* (Paris, 1980), 192.

9 For an illustration of the original, unfinished facade, see G. Kauffmann, *Florence* (1971), 64.

10 Compare *B.* xxiv (1866), 215; *A.* ix (1873), 302; *B.* xlv (1883), 132; *A.* xliv (1890), 53.

11 T. Wright, *The Town of Cowper* [Olney, Bucks.], (1893); J. J. Sheahan, *History and Topography of Bucks.* (1862), 537. In 1857 J. Reynolds Rowe prepared a set of measured drawings of the property which were later handed over to Burges (*R.I.B.A. Trans.* xxxii, 1881, 195). For exterior views, see *C.L.* xiii (1903), 87.

12 The family had also owned Cressing, Essex.

13 'Gayhurst, Tickford' (Abstract, 1859). Burges's work probably consisted of brick additions (Sheahan, *op. cit.*, 460).

14 'Roman pavement, Wycombe' (Abstract, 1863); 'Wycombe Conservatory' (*ibid.*, 1866); 'Dined with Eyre and Dashwood' (*ibid.*, 1866); *ex inf.* Lady Carlile, 1962. About 1911 the Carrington family sold Wycombe Abbey and bought Gwydyr Castle, Llanrwst, North Wales.

15 'Lord Carrington's town house' (Abstract, 1863). The house, now dem., was held on a yearly tenancy from the Crown at £800 p.a. (Bucks. R.O., D/CN., Box 25/7).

16 'Moulsoe Church' (Abstract, 1861); 'Moulsoe public' (*ibid.*, 1863).

17 R.I.B.A. Purple album, 'Stonework', 14; R.I.B.A., S.N.B. xxvi (1859), 98 and xxxv (1868–9), 41. Besides her tomb, Burges also designed an alabaster tablet, sculptured with the Three Marys at the Sepulchre, to Charlotte Lady Suffield (1810–59), Carrington's much loved niece (Architectural Exhibn., 1861, no. 213, 8; 'Lady Suffield's Monument', Abstract, 1859; 'Row about Lady Suffield's Monument', *ibid.*, 1860; R.I.B.A., S.N.B. xxvi, 1859; Bucks. R.O., D/CN, C1, c, 2 July 1859). This 'row' possibly refers to a rejected design for an effigy-tomb: in 1862 Burges exhibited an 'ideal figure of a young lady', with alto relievo figures of the Four Ages of Man, all by Nicholls (*E.* xx, N.S. xxiii, 1862, 74, 226; *G.M.* cxxxii, 1862, 669). Burges re-used the tablet motif when he designed a 'brass' for Abp. Longley (1794–1868), at St. Mary, Addington, Surrey ('Longley's brass', Abstract, 1871). Lady Suffield, Lady in Waiting - to the Duchess of Cambridge, was the widow of Edward, 4th Baron Suffield (1813–53), a celebrated horseman and gambler (Charles, 5th Baron Suffield, *My Memories*, 1913, 40, 81–3, 127). Both the 4th and 5th Barons Suffield were Freemasons. Was Carrington?

18 Bucks. R.O., D/CN, C5, 25 Jan. 1860.

19 His son, Sir Walter Carlile Bt., M.P. (1862–1950), sold the property in 1931, but lived on as life tenant until his death. The house was bought in 1931 by Lord Hesketh (d.1950), and sold in 1951 by his third son, Maj. J. Fermor Hesketh, to the Swiss Bank Corporation. In 1963 it became Rodbourne College (*C.L.* cxxiii 1963, 667) and in 1971–9 it was converted into flats.

20 eg. Tudoresque work in the attic, d.1882; outbuildings, d.1883.

21 *Complete Peerage*; *G.M.* N.S. v (1868), 677; Boase, i, 546.

22 G. Murray, *Side Lights on English Society* (1883 ed.), 253–9.

23 *Queen's Messenger* 17 June 1869, 237–8.

24 *ibid.*, 274–9. For Murray's earlier diplomatic career and later journalism – Labouchere called him the most brilliant journalist of the century – see Boase, ii, 1843; *Parliamentary Papers* 1868–9, lxiv, 353–658; E. Yates, *Recollections* ii (1884), 309–30; J. Hatton, *Journalistic London* (1882), 106–10; H. R. Fox Bourne, *English Newspapers* ii (1887), 301–11.

25 eg. 'Pater Ventosus made a bad shot yesterday and left his mark behind him – I believe the carpenter had to plane the seat. How nasty' (Bucks. R.O., D/CN, C1, 30 Nov. 1859, Carrington to his son).

between pp. 143–48

26 Bucks. R.O., D/CN, Ci, b., 6 Oct. 1858.

27 Abstract, 1859.

28 Bucks. R.O., D/CN., Ci, c, 2 Oct. 1859.

29 Graves, *R. A. Exhibitors* i, 344, no. 643. The draughtsman Burges employed was E. S. Cole (*C.E.A. Jnl.* xxiii, 1860, 159).

30 'A quiet tongue makes a wise head'; 'Prosper thou the works of our hands'; 'Une douce response a-doucit la colère'; 'More speed less haste'; 'Gang warily'; 'Chi va piano va sano'. See also R.I.B.A. S.N.B. xxx (1861), 42; 'Backstairs, Gayhurst', 'Girder, Gayhurst' (Abstract, 1861).

31 'Dining Room Chimneys, Gayhurst' (Abstract, 1861); R.I.B.A. Vellum S.B., 9.

32 R.I.B.A., S.N.B. xxxii (1865), 14.

33 R.I.B.A. 'Stonework', 31 July 1865; S.N.B. xxxii (1865), 20. This chimneypiece has been removed.

34 'Smallfield did room, Gayhurst' (Abstract, 1861); Bucks. R.O., D/CN, C.5, 18 July 1861 and C.15, 30 July 1872. Fisher's estimate for gilding was £51. For preliminary sketches, see R.I.B.A., vii, Renaissance, 91. Compare the painted panels in the Abbey of St. Amand, Rouen (*Architectural Drawings*, 1870, 56).

35 R. Reynolds Rowe, *R.I.B.A. Trans.* xxxii (1881–2), 195. The plumbing was removed by Sir Walter Carlile, who used the building as a battery house for the electric light plant (*ex inf.* Lady Carlile, 1962).

36 'Gayhurst W.C.' (Abstract, 1860–61); R.I.B.A., S.N.B. xxvii (1859), 60 and xxviii (1860), 31, 40, 51–2, 63–4.

37 No. 238, at the Architectural Exhibition Soc. Gallery in Conduit St. (*E.* xxii, N.S. xix, 1861, 162; *B.* xix, 1861, 244; Arch. Ex. Soc. cat., 1861 April-June).

38 *R.I.B.A. Papers* 1866–7, Appendix, Paris Exhibition, Group I, cl. iv, no. 7, ii.

39 Boase, iii, 1038. His poems were edited by W. M. Rossetti (1897). He exhibited several portrait medallions at the R.A., including one of William Holman Hunt (Graves, *R.A. Exhibitors*, viii, 1906, 27).

40 Tupper MSS., sold Sotheby's, 6 July 1971, lot 755.

41 *R.I.B.A. Trans.* xxxii (1881–2), 194.

42 See Burges's sketches, R.I.B.A., vi, Polychromy, 22–3 (Blois); vii, Renaissance, 11–17, 22–3, 32–3, 64–5, 77 (Blois), 30 (Langeais). For other examples which Burges would have known, see C. Daly, *Motifs Historiques d'Architecture et de Sculpture D'Ornement* i (1869) and *Decorations Intérieures* i (1880); N.-X. Willemin and A. A. Pottier, *Monuments Francais*, 2 vols. (Paris, 1839), esp. ii, 226–7.

43 In 1860 Burges records a visit to the formal garden in the Palais Royale, Paris (R.I.B.A., S.N.B. xxix, 1860, 40).

44 R.I.B.A., S.N.B. xxix (1860), 42. The source has yet to be identified.

45 R.I.B.A. i, Details, 58. Burges visited Tours in 1851 and 1863. Ropework motifs also occur at Blois (R.I.B.A. vii, Renaissance, 13). For a variant design for the Guard Room tympanum, see R.I.B.A., S.N.B., lxiv, 273.

46 No. 2 at the Architectural Exhibition, 1862 (*C.E.A. Jnl.* xxv, 1862, 95; Arch. Ex. Soc. cat., March–June 1862).

47 *E.* xxi, N.S. xviii (1860), 195.

48 'Gallery Castle Ashby'; 'Lord Northampton' (Abstract, 1875). Burges produced four alternative estimates, all involving panelling by Walden, stained glass by Saunders and chimneypieces by Nicholls (V. & A., Estimate Book, August 1875). The scheme was presumably forestalled by the death of the 3rd Marquess of Northampton – who had previously employed M. D. Wyatt and E. W. Godwin – in 1877. The Long Gallery was eventually re-fitted by T. G. Jackson in 1884 (H. Avray Tipping, *English Homes* III, ii (1927), 153–78; N. Pevsner and Bridget Cherry, *Northamptonshire*, 1973, 144–5).

49 R.I.B.A., VII, Renaissance, 76, 91.

50 V. & A., P. & D., 93 E9. P.L.U.

51 Carrington ordered three copies.

52 Lithograph by J. D. Wyatt, and description, *C.E.A. Jnl.* xxxvi (1863), 371.

53 *B.* xx (1862), 250. Scott signs himself pseudonymously 'A Goth'.

54 Chapel Ctee. Minutes, Worc. Coll. Archives, 1 June 1863; 'Drawing etc., Worcester College' (Abstract, 1863).

55 *G.M.* ccxvii (1864), 561; C. H. Daniel and W. R. Barker, *Worcester College* (1900), 213.

56 'Oxford, stopp'd with Parker' (Abstract, 1864).

57 *Annual Register* 1919, 202–7; *Who Was Who, 1916–28*, 262. For a friendly letter from Burges to Daniel, inviting him to Christmas dinner, see Worc. Coll. Archives, 23 Dec. 1868.

58 Boase, i, 683. Collis became Past Master and Grand Chaplain in the Middlesex Province (H. E. M. Icely, *Bromsgrove School*, Oxford, 1953, 62). Burges also worked at Stratford and Bromsgrove, where he may have reported on the chapel at Bromsgrove School (?1869). For Stratford see Weller MSS., 27 June 1870; R.I.B.A., SNB xl (1871), 28–40; Abstract, 1870, 1872.

59 *Who Was Who, 1916–28*, 262.

60 Daniel and Barker, *op. cit.*, 223. The beaker is marked C.K[rall].

61 Haydenreich and Lotz, *Architecture in Italy, 1400–1600* (1974), pls. 67–9, 181.

62 eg. drawings, Worc. Coll. Archives, Burges portfolio, 44.

63 *Building World* v (1881), 81.

64 See *Oxford: A Handbook for Visitors* (J. Parker & Co., 1875), 252–3.

65 SS. Gregory, Augustine, Boniface, Aldelm, Oswald, Edward, Etheldreda, Ambrose, Jerome,

between pp. 148–53

Alban, Wilfrid, Albinus, Edmund, Frideswide, King Alfred and the Venerable Bede.

66 *A.* xxxvi (1886), 325. For Burges's description of the flooring, see *E.* xxvi, N.S. xxii, 336–7.

67 *E.* xxvi, N.S. xxiii (1865), 336–7, ill.; 'Worcester College pavement' (Abstract, 1865). A specimen of this technique was first exhibited in the S.C.R. The cost was estimated at £145.15s.0d., plus £5 for cartoons, and £50 for marble steps (Chapel Ctee. Minutes).

68 Before hitting upon the final design, Burges toyed with schemes for the Signs of the Zodiac, the Labours of the Year, the Good Shepherd, the Rose of Sharon and the Agnus Dei.

69 A dispute over workmanship held up Fisher's payment until 1871 (Worc. Coll. Archives, TD 4, MS. 290). For Burke as 'the parent of modern mosaic in England', see *A.* xxii (1879), 82.

70 'Architectural Mosaic', *B.N.* xxxvi (1879), 294–5, 347–9, 407–8, 437–9.

71 *B.N.* xxxv (1878), 174, 259–60.

72 'Mosaic Pavements', in Scott, *Gleanings from Westminster Abbey*, 97–103.

73 'Incontestably the most perfect specimens existing anywhere'. Glass mosaic was not normally suitable for flooring: La Zisa at Palermo was an exception (Scott, *op. cit.*, 101, n.).

74 H. Holiday, *Reminiscences* (1914), 105–6. Burges and Holiday called on Millais and 'showed great tact' in persuading him to withdraw.

75 Chapel Ctee. Minutes, 28 May 1864; 'Worc. Coll. decoration and windows' (Abstract, 1864).

76 Millais's window was exhibited in the West gallery at the South Kensington Museum. For the whole episode, see *E.* xxv, N.S. xxi (1864), 107–8, 117, 222, 247, 249 and xxvi, N.S. xxiii (1865), 42; *B.N.* xi (1864), 605.

77 This sccheme was fixed on 5 Dec. 1864 (Chapel Ctee. Minutes, *op. cit.*). Several alternatives were rejected: Micah for Zachariah; Reuben for Hosea; Elisha for Daniel; and the Resurrection (David) for the Baptism (Joel).

78 Holiday, *op. cit.*, 162.

79 Chapel Ctee. Minutes, *op. cit.*

80 Worc. Coll. Archives, TD 4, MS. 290, 8 and 13 Sept. 1870.

81 *R.I.B.A. Jnl.* 3rd series, xix (1912), 643.

82 Correspondence, 1865–75, Worc. Coll. Archives. A motion at a college meeting of 1874 – 'that the four images . . . be taken down and destroyed' – was defeated.

83 Chapel Ctee. Minutes, 1 Dec. 1864.

84 Worc. Coll. Archives, letter of 7 Nov. 1865.

85 Sketch, n.d., Worc. Coll. Archives, TD 4., MS. 290; 'Organ seat Worc. Coll.' (Abstract, 1865). The organ itself was by Nicholson of Worcester (estimate £250).

86 *E.* xxvi, N.S. xxiii (1865), 336; 'Candelabra and lectern for Worc. Coll.' (Abstract, 1865).

87 Chapel Ctee. Minutes, 25 Nov. 1869. Daniel acquired the larger panels in Rome, Burges the smaller panels in Flanders (Daniel to Mrs Lott: 4 March 1884, colln. N. Ramsay).

88 Jacquet of Stanford St., Vauxhall Bridge Rd. (*B.N.* xv, 1868, 162, 165). Lectern, 7 ft. high; candelabra, 5 ft. 6 in. high. Working from Burges's sketches, Nicholls supplied models, eg. for the dolphins (Worc. Coll. Archives, Burges portfolio, 18–20).

89 R.I.B.A., vii, Renaissance, 55–62; Metalwork, 27. There is a cast in the V. & A.

90 F. Hamilton Jackson, *Intarsia and Marquetry* (1903), pls. 1, 2 12, 13, 18.

91 *R.I.B.A. Jnl.* 3rd series, ix (1902), 296.

92 *Contemporary Rev.* xxiv (1874), 750–51.

93 *The Times* 20 May 1872, 7d.

94 *The Guardian* June, 1872; *A.* vii (1872), 319. He also wrote a Latin poem to Burges.

95 Daniel and Barker, *op. cit.*, 214.

96 For the design of this piece, see Worc. Coll. Archives, Burges portfolio, 28 (wmk. 1875), 31 (d.1877), 33, 70–72 (d.1876), 80 (wmk. 1873; d.1873).

97 Worc. Coll. Archives, MS. 294; [J. Campbell], 'The Hall', *Worcester College, 1964–66*, 10–20; Daniel and Barker, *op. cit.*, 220.

98 Worc. Coll. Archives; H. M. Colvin, *Catalogue of Architectural Drawings in the Worcester College Library* (1964), 64, nos. 513–6.

99 Campbell, *loc. cit.* Crace's treatment was even more summary: he received a fee of 20 gns. (Worc. Coll. Archives, MS. 294, 30 Nov. 1876).

1 Preliminary drawings (wmk. 1873–5, d.1875–9), Worc. Coll. Archives; details in Estimate Book, V. & A., 1876–9. 'Began Worc. Coll. Hall' (Abstract, 1876); 'Worc. Coll. heraldry . . . chimney piece . . . Hall finished' (*ibid.*, 1877). Panelling: Walden of Maiden Lane, London; chimneypiece: Fucigna of Newman St., Oxford St., London; heating: Phipson of Salisbury St., London.

2 eg. compare Burges's chimneypiece decoration with motifs in the Palazzo del Consiglio, Verona (*A.A. Sketchbook*, VII) and the Torre Monument, S. Fermo Maggiore, Verona (*ibid.*, VIII).

3 'We have more need for a few good lecture rooms furnished with a lecture-desk, black-board, maps etc. . . . This matter of the shields [is just] a dodge to 'screw' money out of people . . . Won't it make the college contemptible to have its Hall labelled with the names of obscure commoners?' (protest by E. Wallace, quoted by Campbell, *loc. cit.*).

4 The sideboard (inscr. 'D. D. Ricardus Cresswell, S.T.B., Olim Socius') is now at Knightshayes, Devon. The panelling has been partly redistributed near the entrance to the S.C.R. The glass is in store at the V. & A.; the chimneypiece in store at Worcester College. For controversy over 'restoration', see *The Times* 20 May 1966 and *C.L.* cxxix

between pp. 153–58

(1966), 1407.

5   Boase, iii, 691.

6   *V.C.H., Beds.* iii (1912), 92.

7   'To see Magniac at Sharnbrook' (Abstract, 1869); 'Magniac Mausoleum' (*ibid.*, 1870).

8   Pevsner, *Beds.* (1968), 141–2.

9   Ills., Christie's Sale Cat. of Hollingworth Magniac's collection, 2 April 1892. The collection had been catalogued by Sir Charles Robinson in 1862. For catalogues of Charles Magniac's effects, see Phillips cat. 8 Nov. 1892 (V. & A.) and 8–9 June 1893 (Fitzwilliam Museum).

10   *Archaeol. Jnl.* xxxviii (1881), 410–17.

11   *Letters of T. B. Macaulay*, ed. T. Pinney, iii (1976), 276, 278.

12   *A.* xv (1876), 240.

13   *A* . iv (1870), 31. 'A reproach to this great nation' (*The Times* 9 June 1870, 9). 'Disgracefully dirty . . . oppressive . . . dull' (*B.N.* xv, 1868, 168). Gladstone made much of the taunts of Cardinal Wiseman as to the pagan nature of its decorations (*B.N.* xix, 1870, 48). 'We have outlived the age of religious lethargy' (*The Times* 14 July 1870, 8).

14   *B.N.* xv (1868), 540.

15   *B.N.* xix (1870), 22.

16   Canon Liddon, *A.* v (1871), 81. Let us have 'mosaics, marbles, gilding, paintings, statuary, pavements, stained glass, and colour decoration of the richest order' (*A.* iv, 1870, 15).

17   *A.* xxi (1879), 89–90, 105–6.

18   'It is a matter for rejoicing that St. Paul's yet remains to be completed. Had its internal adornment been undertaken by Wren, we should doubtless have only had more scrolls, more acanthus-leaves, and more pudding-faced cherubs with a structural incapacity for sitting down. No architect of equal genius ever turned out such poverty-stricken and unmeaning detail as he; and it is a matter for exceeding thankfulness that the hints of his intentions which remain are few and vague. He had a gift for making striking compositions out of hackneyed details, but the details *were* hackneyed, nevertheless' (*B.N.* xxiii, 1872, 317).

19   *R.I.B.A. Trans.* 1871, 52; *B.N.* xxii (1872), 448.

20   H. H. Milman, *Annals of St. Paul's Cathedral* (1868), 471–2.

21   *B.N.* xxi (1871), 245–6.

22   G. L. Prentice, *St. Paul's in its Glory . . . 1831–1911* (1955), 2–3.

23   *ibid.*, 29.

24   W. R. Matthews, ed., *History of St. Paul's* (1957), 268.

25   *B.N.* xix (1870), 22.

26   quoted in *The Times* 1 April 1899.

27   *D.N.B.*; *R.I.B.A. Jnl.*, 3rd ser. x (1903), 213–4, 337.

28   *A.* iii (1870), 128.

29   W. Longman, *The Three Cathedrals dedicated to St. Paul* (1873), 166.

30   *E.* xxi, N.S. xviii (1860), 327.

31   A 'huge and frightful apparatus . . . making the church look like a veritable toy and doll's house' (*B.N.* xv, 1868, 707).

32   Barry would have preferred an organ at the West end (A. Barry, *Life and Works of Sir Charles Barry*, 1870, 320–22; *E.* xxi, N.S. xviii, 1860, 177–8).

33   Like that at St. John Lateran, Rome (*E.* xxii, N.S. xix, 1861, 103–8).

34   *B.N.* xx (1871), 219, 244. See also, J. T. Micklethwaite, *What shall be done with St. Paul's?* (1874) and *Notes and Queries* 5th ser., iii (1874), 1–4.

35   *B.N.* xx (1871), 267. Burges was supported by C. B. A[llen], *B.N.* xxi (1871), 245–6. See also Burges's 'Memoranda on the Ritual Arrangements of St. Paul's Cathedral', 27 June 1873 (R.I.B.A. S.R. 726.6, 42. 12, 729).

36   *Remarks and Suggestions on the . . . Completion of St. Paul's* (1871); *B.N.* xx (1871), 486–7; *A.* v (1871), 287–8, 320; A. E. Street, *Memoir of G. E. Street* (1888), 234–6. Replying to Fergusson, Street suggested as one alternative the commissioning of Burges to design a baldacchino under the dome.

37   In the *Pall Mall Gazette*, summarised in *B.N* xxvii (1874), 62–3.

38   W. C. Fynes Webber, June 1874 (R.I.B.A. S.R. 726.6, 42.12, 729).

39   *B.N.* xxi (1871), 54; *A.* v (1871), 151, 163.

40   *E.* xix, N.S. xvi (1858), 320. Penrose's pulpit is now in the Crypt; its predecessor, a Grecian design by Robert Mylne (1803), is now in the North Triforium Aisle.

41   *B.N.* xv (1868), 802–3.

42   They were removed in 1974.

43   *B.N.* xxvi (1874), 629, 686; xxvii (1874), 652.

44   *Victorian Church Art* (V. & A. catalogue, 197), H. 86–9.

45   Given by the Drapers' Co.

46   Given by Thomas Brown of Longman's, publishers; made by Strahüber and Ainmiller; unveiled 14 March 1867; destroyed in World War II (*Victorian Church Art*, H2, ill.).

47   Eg. *B.N.* xxi (1871), 60 and xxiii (1872), 271. 'More a macadamised road than a sunbeam' (*Art Jnl.* 1872, 76). The *Ecclesiologist* proposed the following models: Sta. Maria del Popolo, Rome, and several churches in Arezzo (glass by Claude and Guillaume de Marseilles); Sta. Maria Novella, Florence; Florence Cathedral (though the glass was earlier); Siena Cathedral (glass by Perino del Vaga); Bruges Cathedral; St. Gudule, Brussels; the chapels of Lincoln, Wadham and Queen's College, Oxford; the East window of Peterhouse, Cambridge (Flemish glass); the West window at Ely; the apse at Lichfield; King's College Chapel, Cambridge; St. George, Hanover Square; St. Andrew, Holborn; and Lincoln's Inn Chapel (*E.* xxii, N.S. xix, 1861, 103–8). For an attack on foreign artists, see *B.N.* xi (1864), 243. For later suggestions, see F. H.

between pp. 158–61

Sutton, *Painted Glass for St. Paul's Cathedral* (1870).

48 *E.* xxi, N.S. xviii (1860), 177–8; Graves, *R.A. Exhibitors*, vi (1906), 102: 1860, no. 670. This proposal by Penrose – showing a baldacchino and ambones – is preserved in the Trophy Room at St..Paul's (no. 123; *Victorian Church Art*, V. & A., 1971, H1). Another, no. 113, shows a rather different baldacchino.

49 *B.N.* xxiii (1872), 432.

50 *B.N.* xxiii (1872), 107–8; Graves, *op. cit.*, 1866, no. 801; 1873, no. 1155; Penrose's scheme for choir and East end, drawn by Richard Groom, 1872 (R.A. 1875 no. 939).

51 *E.* xxii, N.S. xix (1861), 158. Ruskin's view was similar: 'the mosaics … are a barbarism; a great pity. They are fine as mosaics, but all mosaics of this square kind [ie. flat tesserae] are abominable' (*Diaries*, ed. Joan Evans and J. H. Whitehouse, i, 1956, 117: 29 Nov. 1840).

52 *B.N.* xix (1870), 360. It was placed beneath the Cotton memorial window in the S.E. aisle. In c.1860 Burges may also have been instrumental in presenting a mosaic head, removed from Torcello and sold in Venice, to the Dean and Chapter (*E.* xxii, N.S. xix, 1861, 155–7).

53 *The Times* 13 May 1872, 8.

54 *B.N.* xix (1870), 109, 127.

55 *A.* viii (1872), 114.

56 *St. Paul's Cathedral Fund: Speeches … 8th Feb. 1861* (1861).

57 'High Church contributed for the sake of the anticipated glories of mosaic and picture, colour and gold, embroidery and incense. Low Church contributed in the hope that grandeur might spring out of severity and simplicity, or at least that cleanliness might come in aid of godliness. Broad Church contributed upon the patriotic principle that come what might there must be some good done. Even Nonconformity could contribute with a clear conscience when the object in view was to beautify one of the great popular temples of England' (*A.* xii, 1874, 297).

58 *The Times* 12 March 1872, 11.

59 *The Times* 15 May 1872, 8.

60 See their letter of protest, *The Times* 6 June 1872, 7.

61 In particular, Tite and Bentinck worked closely together (*B.* xxxviii, 1880, 803). The sale of Sir William Tite's library (Sotheby's, 1874) included Dugdale's *St. Paul's* (1658), with a MS. insertion: 'Private and Confidential Proposal for the Completion of St. Paul's Cathedral' (lot. 980, bought by Quaritch). Bentinck published a pamphlet on *The Completion of St. Paul's* in 1874.

62 *B.N.* xxii (1872), 448.

63 As a Goth, Burges had 'out-Heroded Herod'; 'the anomaly was so unique and complete that many wondered and more laughed' (*B.N.* xxvii, 1874, 603).

64 *B.* xxix (1871), 299.

65 *B.* xix (1861), 192. A 'debased mass of absurdities' (*B* xx, 1862, 426). See also *G.M.* ccxiv (1963), 282.

66 Letter, Sept. 1870.

67 Appeal, 13 July 1870.

68 *A.* vi (1871), 39.

69 'Iconography of St. Paul's' (Abstract, 1871). The invitation arrived, via Hope, on 26 July 1870. Burges asked £250; he was offered £150 (R.I.B.A. MS. 'St. Paul's Cathedral', 726.6, 42.12; SP. 729). I owe the identification of this MS to Miss Dorothy Bosomworth.

70 *A.* vi (1871), 73.

71 Including the Munich School's 'Conversion of St. Paul', removed from the West window to the Eastern window of the North chancel aisle.

72 For Burges's original scheme and sketches, see 'Reports' I, no. 7 (Weller MSS.); transcript, 27 Feb. 1871, R.I.B.A. S.R. 726.6, 42.12, 729.1).

73 Mrs. Jameson, *Sacred and Legendary Art* (1866); Lady Eastlake, *The Life of Our Lord* (1864); Didron, *Manuel d'Iconographie Chrétienne* (Paris, 1845); J. H. Parker, *The Calendar of the Anglican Church* (1851).

74 *A.* vi (1871), 87.

75 Chapter Minutes, Sub-Committee for Decoration, 22 April 1872. 'Elected architect to St..Paul's Cathedral' (Abstract, 1872). The Articles of Agreement were dated 8 Aug. 1872 (E. J. Harding album of cuttings, St. Paul's Cathedral Library).

76 Lord Mayor Gibbons, Tite, Bentinck, Fergusson and Murray (*The Times* 13 May 1872, 10). See also *A.* vii (1872), 256; *B.* xxx (1872), 379.

77 Abstract, 1873. Burges had arranged to meet Lonsdale in Florence. His trip to Italy cost him £100 (R.I.B.A. MS., *op. cit.*).

78 27 March 1874. For Burges: Hope, Longman, Church; against: Bentinck, Fergusson, Oldfield, Parry. The making of the nave model cost £10.18s.8d., the choir model £30.18s.8d. (R.I.B.A., S.N.B., 1874–5). 'Model of St. Paul's' (Abstract, 1873); 'St. Paul's Model going on' (*ibid.*, 1874). But Burges's final estimate of the cost of the two models, including travel, hire of exhibition rooms, Lonsdale's painted work etc., was £321 (R.I.B.A. St. Paul's MS., *op. cit.*, 8 March 1875). Burges's model, later adapted by Richmond, and still later by Godfrey Allen, survives in the North Triforium Aisle, outside the Trophy Room.

79 Protest, 4 June 1874.

80 Eg. *B.* xxxii (1874), 633; *B.N.* xxviii (1875), 81, quoting *British Quarterly Rev.* (1874).

81 General meeting, 3 Nov. 1874 (*B.* xxxii, 1874, 1001–2). The Dean wrote Burges a personal letter, expressing his 'deep disappointment', and praising Burges's 'zeal and labour' (R.I.B.A. St. Paul's MS., *op. cit.*, 5 Nov. 1874).

82 Abstract, 6 Nov. 1874.

83 1874, nos. 1327–8, with figures by H. W. Lonsdale; 1875, nos. 952, 995, 1005, drawn and coloured by

between pp. 161–64

A. H. Haig (A. Graves, *R.A. Exhibitors* i, 1905, 344). 'Haig did St. Paul's views' (Abstract, 1875). For adverse criticism, see *B.N.* xxviii (1875), 510, 594; *B.* xxxviii (1875), 381. Two proposals drawn by Haig (995 and 1005) survive in the Trophy Room at St. Paul's: nos. 120 (*Victorian Church Art*, H10) and 150.

84 R.I.B.A. St. Paul's MS. *op. cit.*, 3 Feb. 1875. This sum represented 2½% on the hypothetical cost of executing the two model schemes. Penrose received £200 more, as Burges put it, 'for doing nothing' (*ibid.*, 4 Feb. 1875). After further negotiation, Burges received an extra £321 for making the model, and an *ex gratia* payment of £250, making £1746 in all (*ibid.*, 17 March 1875).

85 Abstract, 1875, 1877.

86 Executive Committee minutes, 10 June, 1871; Article of Agreement, 8 Aug. 1872.

87 *Parentalia*, 292, n.a.

88 Wren lost control of the decoration of St. Paul's in 1712, and was dismissed in 1718. The dome was painted between 1715 and 1719. Thanks to the influence of Lord Halifax, Thornhill was preferred to Sebastiano Ricci; he had previously defeated Pellegrini. Some surviving sketches by Thornhill – presumably those now in the Trophy Room – were bought by Burges in Brompton Rd. for 10/6d, and presented to the Dean and Chapter (R.I.B.A. St. Paul's MS., *op. cit.*). Eight of Thornhill's preliminary sketches survive (V. & A., D.1086/93–1886), as does Pellegrini's model (V. & A., P.24 – 1953, Room 58).

89 *A. and B.N.* cxlv (1936), 395–60. See also a model in the Trophy Room.

90 Published by William Emmett; ill. W. Longman, *Three Cathedrals*, *op. cit.*, 149.

91 Engraved by Rooker from a drawing by John Gwynn, R.A. (an architect friend of Wren's grandson, Stephen Wren, who published *Parentalia*), with figures by Samuel Wale, R.A.

92 Newton, *Works*, i (1782), 106.

93 *Parentalia*, 262.

94 *A.* xii (1874), 59. Similarly, G. E. Street: 'If [Wren's] mosaics were to be at all like all others of the same period, we may perhaps be grateful that he never carried his idea into execution' (open letter to George Richmond, R.A., 29 Feb. 1871).

95 *A.* x (1873), 121. 'Wren's taste bears the same relationship to pure and refined architecture as the paintings of Rubens do to the quaint simplicity of Van Eyck – as the witty but licentious dramas of the Restoration do to the works of Shakespeare and Ben Jonson' (*Fraser's Mag.* N.S. viii, 1873, 284–97).

96 'Wren, in an unfortunate age, drew his inspiration through the muddy intercepting strata of Roman and Renaissance work'. Contemporary architects: were 'adrift in a rudderless boat'. Bernini was 'but a blind leader of the blind, a flounderer in a hopeless slough of despond' (J. P. Seddon, *A.* vii, 1872, 247–8, 319).

97 *A.* xii (1874), 57–9.

98 Burges to Church, 23 Nov. 1874; *A.* xii (1874), 309.

99 Letter by E. C. Robins, *B.N.* xxv (1873), 353.

1 Pullan, *R.I.B.A. Trans.* xxxii (1881–2), 194.

2 R.I.B.A., S.N.B., xv (1873). Burges also visited Santa Maria Aracaeli in 1873.

3 *A.* xi (1874), 292.

4 For a detailed description of Burges's design by William Longman, first published as a pamphlet in 1874, see *A.* xxii (1879), 271–2. For Burges's explanatory proposals, see R.I.B.A., 726.6, 42.12, 729. For Burges's preliminary sketches, see a composite volume entitled 'Decoration of St. Paul's', formerly in the Surveyor's Office in the Chapter House, St. Paul's, and now in the Library. For assistance in identifying this document, I am grateful to Dorothy Bosomworth.

5 *R.I.B.A. Papers* (1870–71), 157–74. For Penrose defending later proposals – Leighton and Poynter developing Stevens – see *ibid.*, 1878–9, 93–104.

6 R.I.B.A., 726.6, 42.12, 729. It was in December 1873 that Penrose, previously placid, turned against Burges's scheme – 'cutting up and objecting to everything' (R.I.B.A. St. Paul's MS., *op. cit.*).

7 *Art Jnl.* 1873, 253, 293.

8 *Athenaeum* 1881, i, 599.

9 'Clearly Mr. Burges has strong Medieval tendencies, but he is far from an exclusively one-sided man ... Though pronounced in his architectural bias and tastes, he is legitimately impressionable and teachable' (*B.N.* xxii, 1872, 401).

10 Burges's scheme 'would make our great Protestant temple ... more like a magnificent music-salon or gin palace than a cathedral' (*B.N.* xxvii, 1874, 1–2).

11 Eg. a Thunderous leader on popular taste (*The Times* 29 June 1874, 11); or a leader against Burges's 'Jesuit' style which threatened to plunge art 'into ... barbarism' (*The Times* 15 June 1874, 11).

12 *B.N.* xxvii (1874), 1780.

13 *Church Builder* 1872, 235–7. At present, St. Paul's is '... a magnificent, unfinished skeleton. The crude light streaming through its commonplace windows, falling on the dense London atmosphere, forms strong cross lights, which break up the interior, so as to destroy its aesthetic unity. Under this cold, dull light the dust-coloured walls and furniture look bare and cold. The judgement with a sort of reluctance admits that the dimensions of the building are imposing, and its proportions grand, and its architectural features fine; but the instinctive taste declares that the effect is dull and bare and uninteresting and unlovely' (*ibid.*, 1874, 86–8). See also, *ibid.*, 1874, 143–6; 1875, 86–8; 1878, 209–11.

14 *B.* xxxii (1874), 407–8.

15 *A.* vii (1872), 266; *B.N.* xxii (1872), 469: a defence of Burges by A. P. Goodman.

between pp. 164–67

16 Burges's proposals 'would make St. Paul's a churchman's bauble, a display of the mean follies that half-educated clerics and a clique of semi-sanctimonious draughtsmen presume to call religious art.' Angels, martyrs etc. were 'but an "artistic" form of profane swearing – a mere expletive substitute for fancy and invention' (*Quarterly Rev.* cxxxiii, 1872, 342–86).

17 Sandra Blutman, *R.I.B.A. Jnl.* 3rd series, lxxiv (1967), 542–4.

18 *B.N.* xxvi (1874), 630.

19 Wren's St. Paul's was 'marvellously pure, considering the period in which he lived: for he reverted to the school of Vignola and Palladio of the beginning of the sixteenth century, instead of adopting the perversions of the French and Italian schools of his own period, represented by Blondel and Bernini; men of genius, but instances of artificial aberration in the former, and of extravagant puerility in the latter.'

20 *The Times* 15 June 1874, 10. Donaldson preferred Hittorf's St. Vincent de Paul, Paris.

21 *B.N.* xxvii (1874), 536; *The Times* 18 June 1874, 11 and 28 Oct. 1874, 10.

22 *A.* xii (1874), 297. Burges called Fergusson's article in the *Contemporary Rev.* 'personal and scurrilous' (R.I.B.A. MS. *op. cit.*, 1 Oct. 1874).

23 An attempt 'to wash the Paganism out of this too classic temple', and introduce instead 'gloom ... mysticism, and crude art'. See *Contemporary Rev.* xxiv (1874), 750–71; summarised, *A.* xii (1874), 175–6 and *B.N.* xxvii (1874), 413–4.

24 J. Fergusson, *Proposal for the Completion of St. Paul's Cathedral* (1874).

25 *B.N.* xxvii (1874), 546; *B.* xxxii (1874), 940–41. Scott had been called in to arbitrate between Burges and Penrose in 1870–71 (R.I.B.A. MS. *op. cit.*).

26 *A.* vii (1872), 247–8, 266.

27 *A.* xii (1874), 36.

28 *Fraser's Mag.*, Aug. 1874; reprinted in *A.* xii (1874), 58. He had previously been more critical (*A.* vi, 1871, 40). For a less enthusiastic critique by G. H. G[uillaume], see *B.N.* xxvi (1874), 625. He considered Burges's colour-scheme too dark. So did Basil Champneys in the *Pall Mall Gazette* (*ibid.*, 630). Godwin later claimed that Burges admitted the validity of some of his subsidiary criticisms (*B.A.* xv, 1881, 214).

29 *Saturday Rev.* 1872. pt.i, 335–6 and 1874, pt.i, 586–7. Donaldson's 'dithyrambic' complaints were dismissed as 'Tupperian' *non-sequiturs*. His preferred examples – St. Peter's, Rome and St. Vincent de Paul, Paris – were 'Popish mass-houses both'. As for the *Daily Telegraph* and the *Guardian*, they failed to approve Burges's scheme largely because they failed to take the trouble to understand it (*ibid.*, 776–7).

30 R. P. Pullan, *The Designs of William Burges* (1885),

no. 2.

31 R.I.B.A. St. Paul's MS., *op. cit.*

32 *The Times* 13 May 1872, 8.

33 Burges to Church, 23 Nov. 1874: *A.* xii (1874), 309.

34 *E.* xix, N.S. xvi (1858), 262–3.

35 *A.* xii (1874), 176.

36 W. H. Hutton, ed., *Autobiography of Robert Gregory*, 1912, 207–8.

37 One exception was 'J.C.J.' in *E.* xxv, N.S. xxii (1864), 12–15.

38 *The Times* 27 May 1872, 7.

39 *B.* xxxii (1874), 584, 634.

40 Report on Burges's nave model (R.I.B.A., 726.6, 42.12, 729). Another critic, 'C.B.', supplied Wren with an alibi: 'there was no sufficient art education ... to enable him to form a just and definite conception' (*B.* xxxi, 1873, 81–2).

41 *Punch* lxvi (1874), 269.

42 *B.N.* xxvi (1874), 690 and xxvii (1875), 2.

43 *B.N.* xxvi (1874), 710; *A.* viii (1872), 351–2.

44 *The Times* 15 Dec. 1874; *B.* xxxii (1874), 631.

45 R.I.B.A. St. Paul's MS., *op. cit.*, 3 July 1874.

46 *A.* v (1871), 287–8.

47 *B.* xxxii (1874), 543.

48 Later he wrote to his wife: 'While I worked this morning I thought of your Sunday expedition to St. Paul's, and wondered if the church crushed and depressed you, as it does me, and if you could pray in it, and to whom, and if you had any hope that a prayer could get past the cornice, and if in your heart you said "O Lord, how great is thy pomp, how crushing thy judgements; mercifully forgive thy servant if she seeks consolation elsewhere than in thy architectural presence, and confesses with thy servant David that one day in thy house is better than a thousand".' (G. B.-J., *Memorials of Edward Burne-Jones* II, 219–20).

49 *A.* xii (1874), 297.

50 Eg. the mosaics at Sta. Maria Maggiore, Rome; or those in Galla Placida's chapel at Ravenna. 'There is a Classical-Christian style, Greek in origin, Roman by adoption; and the more Classical it is, the more Primitive Christian it is; and it may be employed in St. Paul's with the help of modern study, science and art-power ... Very much has been learnt about the subjects and character of Classical Christian decoration since the time of Brunelleschi or Bramante; and to ignore all that knowledge in restoring St. Paul's would be a public act of indifference to Christianity ... [Besides] the Anglo-Puritan suspicion of church art has been already to some extent disarmed by Mr. Butterfield's mosaics [at Keble]' (*Church Quarterly Rev.* ii, 1876, 447–64; *A.* xvi, 1876, 49).

51 *Trans. St. Paul's Ecclesiological Soc.* i (1879–80).

52 G. L. Prestige, *St. Paul's in its Glory ... 1831–1911* (1955), 207–8.

53 *A.* xvi (1876), 364–5; E. Oldfield, *St. Peter's and St. Paul's* (1878).

between pp. 167–69

54 R.I.B.A. St. Paul's MS., *op. cit.*, 24 April 1877.

55 *B.N.* xxxv (1878), 50–51, 72–3; *A.* xx (1878), 37–8, 49–50.

56 *B.* xlvii (1884), 11–13, ill.

57 *A.* xx (1878), 207; *B.N.* xxxv (1878), 412.

58 *B.* xlvii (1884), 313–4.

59 *B.* xliii (1882), 740–42.

60 *B.N.* xxxvii (1879), 55–6, 167; *The Times* 31 May 1879, 8. The scheme was exhibited at the Egyptian Hall. See Pullan, *Studies in Architectural Style* (1883), 13. Wilson (1809–82) published studies of Michaelangelo, frescoes and stained glass. He was a friend of Charles Winston. For illustrations of these later schemes, see J. Mordaunt Crook, 'William Burges and the Completion of St Paul's', *Antiquaries Jnl.* lxxx (1980), pt. ii.

61 *A.* xxii (1879), 32–5.

62 *B.* xlviii (1885), 164, ill.

63 *A.* xxii (1879), 271–2, ills.

64 W. R. Matthews, ed., *History of St. Paul's Cathedral* (1957), 280–81. See also T. Garner, 'The new altar screen in St. Paul's Cathedral', *St. Paul's Ecclesiological Soc.* ii (1880–81), 167–8.

65 Dean and Chapter Minutes, 8 Nov. 1888.

66 Prestige, *op. cit.*, 211–2.

67 M. C. Church, *Life and Letters of Dean Church* (1895), 235.

68 Somers Clarke album, V. & A., 72.D.15: *The Times* 24 Feb. 1899, MS. endorsement.

69 'A.R.J.', *Builders' Jnl.* 31 May 1899.

70 Somers Clarke album, *op. cit.*, 4.

71 Matthews, *op. cit.*, 281.

72 Matthew and John: Watts; Four Prophets: Stevens; Mark and Luke: Stevens and Britten.

73 For details see Somers Clarke, *The Recent Decoration of St. Paul's* (1894); A. L. Baldry, 'The New Decoration of St. Paul's', *Mag. of Art* xxii (1897), 12–18; W. B. Richmond, 'The Decoration of St. Paul's', *Jnl. R.S.A.* xliii (1894–5), 715–24.

74 *The Times* 4 March 1899. See also Samuel Howe, 'The Spoiling of St. Paul's', *Fortnightly Rev.* April 1899, 634–46. In the House of Lords, Kimberley and Salisbury silenced the 'hysterical diatribe of the omnipotent Earl': Dean Gregory was uncontrollable in law; and anyway there was no such absolute as 'Taste' (*The Times* 22 April 1899).

75 *Spectator* 25 March 1899.

76 *The Times* 6 May 1899.

77 *The Times* 22 May 1899.

78 *I.L.N.* 8 June 1895, 100.

79 *The Times* 1 April, 1899.

5. GOTHIC
between pp. 170–72

1 *B.N.* xiv (1867), 421.

2 'Many a worshipper of Mammon would turn aside to breath his hopes or to demand pardon in a place which his conscience must tell him is more sacred than his own home; and not only would it be more sacred, but it would inevitably in course of time become more splendid' (*E.* xxviii, N.S. xxv, 1867, 151; *B.* xxii, 1864, 789).

3 *R.I.B.A. Trans.* 1884, 232. Beresford-Hope thought this judgement a smart caricature: 'historical portraiture of the Du Maurier school ... not that of Livy or Tacitus' (*ibid.*, 233).

4 'Lille has certainly escaped hitherto the ecclesiological movement. [This competition] is just the thing to kindle it. The gorgeous array of possible spires, and at least conceivable gables and crosses, breaking up the sordid monotony of the ugly swamps and fens which surround this most unpicturesque of towns will, we are convinced, animate the local sluggishness' (*E.* xxii, N.S. xiv, 1856, 83).

5 *E.* xvi, N.S. xiii (1855), 217.

6 *B.* xiii (1855), 382; *Kölner Domblatt* 3 Feb. 1856.

7 *B.* xiv (1856), 218, 240. For fuller details, see *Compte-Rendue du Concours* (Lille, 1856).

8 Abstract, 1855.

9 *ibid.*, 1856.

10 'Heard about Lille, April 14' (*ibid.* 1856).

11 *Land and Building News* ii (1856), 481.

12 *Sat. Rev.* ii (1856), 152.

13 *E.* xvii, N.S. xiv (1856), 288.

14 L. Detrez, *Notre Dame de la Treille* (Lille, 1944).

15 *E.* xvi, N.S. xiii (1955), 1–5; *B.* xiii (1855), 58; *A.A.* xiv (1855), 386–8.

16 *E.* xvii, N.S. xiv (1856), 292.

17 G. C. Evans and R. P. Pullan, *Photographs of Designs for Lille Cathedral* (Wimborne Minster, 1860); *E.* xvii, N.S. xiv (1856), 291.

18 Prizes: Clutton and Burges, Street; Medals: Isaac Holden and Son of Manchester, Cuthbert Broderick of Leeds, Evans and Pullan; Credits: Goldie of Sheffield, J. L. Pedley of Birmingham, Robinson of London. T. H. King planned to compete, and young Norman Shaw helped him with designs (A. Saint, *R. N. Shaw*, 1976, 9). Philip Webb helped Street with his entry, and William Morris accompanied Street when he took the drawings to Lille (W. R. Lethaby, *Philip Webb*, 20). According to Hope, death prevented R. C. Carpenter from competing (letter 4 April 1856, Lille Diocesan Archives). For Pullan's design, see Pullan and Evans, *Lille*, dedicated to Hope. See also *C.E.A.Jnl.* xix (1856), 147.

19 *E.* xvii, N.S. xiv (1856), 161.

20 B. F. L. Clarke, *Church Builders of the Nineteenth Century* (1969 ed.), 153.

21 'Mr. Lassus has many and powerful friends ... It may be "de rigueur" that the work ... be entrusted to a "compatriote", and one professing the national faith' (*E.* xvii, N.S. xiv, 1856, 288). For Verdier's protest, see the R.I.B.A. Lille Album. Verdier had collaborated with one of the defeated contestants, de Corte of Ghent.

22 For criticism of Leroy's defeated design – 'weak ...

between pp. 173–75

mediocre ... inadequate' – see *E*. xvii, N.S. xiv (1856), 95, 166. 'Saw Abbé Martin's Lille' (Abstract, 1857).

23 *B*. xiv (1856), 420.

24 *E*. xvii, N.S. xiv (1856), 288.

25 *B.N.* iv (1858), 391.

26 *A.A.* xvi (1856), 260; *E*. xvii, N.S. xiv (1856), 288.

27 Street's cloister, Clutton's North door and some of Burges's mouldings (*B*. xvi, 1858, 90–91). For criticism of the Martin-Leroy design, see *E*. xvi, N.S. xiii (1856), 223–4.

28 *A.A.* xv (1855), 204.

29 W. Eden Nesfield, *Specimens of Medieval Architecture* (1862), pl.55.

30 A. E. Street, *Memoir of G. E. Street* (1888), 25; *C.E.A.J.* xxvii (1864), 38; R.J. Johnson, *Specimens of Early French Architecture* (1864), pl.52; G. Truefitt, *Architectural Sketches on the Continent* (1847), pl.21.

31 T. H. King, *Study Book of Medieval Architecture*, i (1858), pl.5.

32 Burges, *Architectural Drawings*, pls.xxxv–vi.

33 *Annales Archéologiques* xvi (1856), 205 *et seq.*, 264.

34 eg. Viollet-le-Duc, *Dictionnaire*, iv, 76; v, 376.

35 *Annales Archéologiques* xvi (1856), 206. Didron gives an elaborate analysis of the iconography of the design, based on Burges's own description ('Iconography of Lille for *Annales*', Abstract, 1856).

36 Clutton's recent excavation of a fourteenth-century Tree of Jesse at Merevale Abbey (*E*. x, N.S. vii, 1850, 304) may have supplied the idea.

37 R.I.B.A., S.N.B. xxi (1856), 22.

38 Bibliotheque Municipale, cited by Didron, *A.A.* xvi (1856), 206. Burges seems to have borrowed from drawings published in *A.A.* i (1844), 54–62. For Burges's sketches and drawings, see R.I.B.A., S.N.B. xx (1856), 37, 39; Lille Album, x; V. & A., P. & D., E. 503, 1963 [probably the drawing which Burges sent to Didron, *A.A.* xvi, 1856, 223], 523, 525, 530. For Handley-Read's discussion of these drawings, see *Victorian Church Art*, D 11.

39 Didron points to the candlestick at Rheims Cathedral, brought from St. Remi (*A.A.* xvi, 1856, 220).

40 The *Ecclesiologist* answered Lassus as follows: 'the object sought for is not a mere dead representation of the French style of 1200–1250, but a church in which the needs and experiences of the middle of the nineteenth century are embodied according to the architectural principles of the style. The successful competitor ought to be the man who has with a true eclecticism laid hold of every real advance made in construction or in taste during the last six centuries, and has assimilated it ... into his design, congruously with the principles of the prescribed period' (*E*. xvii, N.S. xiv, 1856, 284–7).

41 *Recollections* (1879), 167, 205–6.

42 *E*. xvii, N.S. xiv (1856), 209; *B*. xvi (1858), 13, 33; Abstract, 1858; Architectural Ex. 1857–8, no. 371–82.

43 *E*. xvii, N.S. xiv (1856), 89.

44 *ibid.*, 164.

45 Lille Album, ix. In part, it seems to have been modelled on a design by Viollet-le-Duc (*A.A.* viii, 1852, end insert).

46 *E*. xvii, N.S. xiv (1856), 80, 89.

47 *Journal de Lille* 18 April, 1856; *Revue Générale de l'Architecture* xiv (1856), 33–46, 72–86.

48 *A.A.* xvi (1856), 228.

49 See B. Foucart, 'Un débat exemplaire: la reconstruction des Jubés au XIXᵉ siècle', *Revue de l'Art* no.24 (1974), 59–71, 97.

50 Shaw's drawings, R.A. 1858 (A. Saint, *R. N. Shaw*, 1976, 14). Emerson's organ at Brighton was inspired by Lille.

51 There are two deposits of drawings: in the Lille Diocesan Archives, and in the R.I.B.A. The latter's Lille Album was given by Sir John Betjeman to Charles Handley-Read, who bequeathed it to the R.I.B.A.

52 Lille Album, vii.

53 *B.N.* iii (1857), 332.

54 'Journey to N. Italy to study for Constantinople', 'Began Constantinople' (Abstract, 1856); 'Constantinople sent in Jan. 1', 'Got Constantinople Feb. 3' (*ibid.*, 1857).

55 Bodley was placed third, Slater 'fourth'; Pullan, Truefitt and White were among those 'specially mentioned'; Aitchison and Pullan (again) were among the also rans. For a full list, with critical comments, see *E*. xviii, N.S. xv (1857), 100; *B.N.* iii (1857), 345–7; *C.E.A. Jnl.* xx (1857), 124–5. For Pullan's designs see R. P. Pullan, *Photographs of a Design for the Memorial Church, Constantinople* (Wimborne Minster, 1860) and *Studies in Architectural Style* (1883), 9, 12–15, 22.

56 *E*. xviii, N.S. xv (1857), 177; *C.E.A.Jnl.* xx (1857), 173. Burges's exterior perspective (R.I.B.A. Arc. IV/v/1) was coloured by Cole, who also worked for Street, Butterfield, Conybeaᵣe and others.

57 *E*. xix, N.S. xvi (1858), 42, 244; *Art Jnl.* xxi, N.S. iv (1858), 54.

58 *The Times* 1 Nov. 1858, 8.

59 Pullan, *Architectural Designs of W.B.* (1883), 7.

60 The architectural press noticed this with 'astonishment' and 'indignation' (*B*. xvi, 1858, 743; *B.N.* iv, 1858, 1107, 1122).

61 *B.N.* xv (1868), 573; *E*. xxix, N.S. xxvi (1868), 180. The final cost was £23,000. But within twenty years an appeal had to be launched for maintenance funds, and for repairs by R. H. Carpenter (*Crimea Memorial Church Appeal*, 1890).

62 *B.N.* iii (1857), 304–5; *E*. xvii, N.S. xiv (1856), 294–6, 360–62. The contest was also published in the *New York Church Jnl.*; by Didron in *Annales Archéologiques* xvi (1856), 260–63; by Reichensperger in the *Organ für Christliche Künst*; and in

between pp. 176–83
Holland by Alberdingh Thijm in the *Dietsche Worande*.

63 *B.N.* iii (1857), 240.

64 Grüner, *Specimens of Ornamental Art* ii (1853), pls. 44–5. Burges possessed a copy.

65 R.I.B.A., S.N.B. xi (1856), 43–4.

66 See Willis, *B.N.* iii (1857), 240.

67 Memoir accompanying drawings, *B.N.* iii (1857), 335.

68 *B.* xv (1857), 115.

69 *Annales Archéologiques* xvii (1857), 54.

70 *E.* xviii, N.S. xv (1857), 103.

71 *Clerical Jnl.* 16 April 1863, 426 (*ex inf.* Stephen Wildman).

72 *B.N.* iii (1857), 335, 358–9. For detailed drawings, see Pullan, *Architectural Designs of W.B. ... Stonework* (1887), 1–7. For notes on local materials, see R.I.B.A., S.N.B. xxii–xxiv (1857).

73 *E.* xviii, N.S. xv (1857), 103.

74 *B.N.* iii (1857), 145.

75 *E.* xviii, N.S. xv (1857), 102.

76 *B.* xv (1857), 151; *B.N.* iii (1857), 333; R.I.B.A. Arc. IV.

77 [Beresford-Hope in] *Sat. Rev.* iii (1857), 217–20, 330–31.

78 *B.N.* iv (1858), 1122.

79 *E.* xviii, N.S. xv (1857), 374 and xix, N.S. xvi (1858), 170, 244, 258, 267. Negotiations for the site were conducted by Lord Clarendon and Lord Stratford de Redcliffe.

80 *B.* xvi (1858), 743. The estimate was thus reduced to £18,000.

81 *E.* xx, N.S. xvii (1859), 265.

82 *E.* xxi, N.S. xviii (1860), 41, 180–81.

83 *ibid.*, 162.

84 *B.* xxii (1864), 511. The contractors were Messrs. Rogers and Booth of Gosport.

85 Pullan mentions three modifications (*R.I.B.A. Trans.* xxxii, 1882, 185) and a total of four sets of designs survive. However, the U.S.P.G. archives indicate that a fifth set ('No. 2') may also have been prepared.

86 *E.* xxi, N.S. xix (1861), 235. This progessive truncation can be traced in Burges's plans and correspondence, now in the U.S.P.G. Achives, and in V. & A., P. & D., Q.4b.

87 *E.* xxiv, N.S. xxi (1863), 164.

88 *B.* xxvi (1868), 119.

89 For Burges's three-bay plan, see Hope, *English Cathedral of the Nineteenth Century*, 91, reprod. *E.* xxii, N.S. xix (1861), 169. [30a]

90 *E.* xviii, N.S. xv (1857), 258.

91 *R.I.B.A. Trans.* xxxii (1882), 185.

92 Awarded 'on the decision of Mr. Cockerell' (U.S.P.G. Archives).

93 For a similarly polychrome church, erected in Syria to designs by Duthoit, see *Gazette des Architectures et des Batiments*, iii (1865), 56–7.

94 'Brisbane begun' (Abstract, 1859).

95 B. F. L. Clarke, *Anglican Cathedrals Outside the British Isles* (1958), 103. Burges had hopefully prepared a design 'to be built gradually' (*E.* xxi, N.S. xviii, 1860, 41).

96 Details in Pullan, *Architectural Designs of W.B.: stonework*, 8–15. The altar (pl. 15) is related to sketches in R.I.B.A., S.N.B. xxx (1861), 51.

97 *E.* xxii, N.S. xix (1861), 21.

98 *ibid.*, 19–21, 242 (plans and sections); *B.N.* vi (1860), 791 (interior).

99 *C.E.A.Jnl.* xiii (1860), 162.

1 *R.I.B.A. Trans.* xxxii (1882), 186.

2 *B.* xviii (1860), 251.

3 *B.N.* xxiv (1873), 64; *A.* viii (1872), 197.

4 *B.N.* xxiv (1873), 33–4; *B.N.* xxiv (1873), 37–8.

5 *A.* viii (1872), 197.

6 *A.* viii (1872), 198; *B.N.* xxiv (1873); 34.

7 *B.N.* xxiv (1873), 34; *B.* xxxi (1873), 97–8, 165; xxxii (1874), 1030; *B.N.* xxiv (1873), 122.

8 Plans, elevations, sections: R.I.B.A., Arc. IV, vii, 1–9. Ills.: *B.* xxxi (1873), 227; *B.N.* xxiv (1873), 34–5, 300; *A.* ix (1873), 86, 122 and xxvii (1882), 251. Haig's perspectives of Burges's designs were exhibited at the R.A. in 1873, nos. 1133 (exterior) and 1148 (interior): the former is in the author's collection.

9 *R.I.B.A. Trans.* xxxii (1882), 199; Pullan, *Architectural Designs of W.B.*, 17–18.

10 eg. M. B. Adams, *R.I.B.A. Jnl.*, 3rd series xix (1912), 643.

11 *R.I.B.A. Trans.* xxxii (1882), 196.

12 Pullan, *Studies in Architectural Style* (1883), 34–7; *B.N.* xxxviii (1880), 368.

13 V. & A., P. & D., Q.3c.

14 ill., *Victorian Church Art*, D.15.

15 *Christian Remembrancer* v (1843), 591.

16 'On the Origins and Uses of Chapter Houses', *B.* xii (1854), 498.

17 Brown's *Strangers' Handbook to Salisbury Cathedral* (1889), 55.

18 *Iconography of the Chapter House, Salisbury* (1859), 6.

19 *ibid.*, 10.

20 Salisbury Cathedral Archives, Bundle 7.

21 *ibid.*, Bundle 10.

22 'Looking after Salisbury Chapter House ... stopped with G. Lapworth' (Abstract, 1855–6).

23 R.I.B.A., 'Stonework', i; *B.* xiv (1856), 436. The contractor was to be J. White. The vestibule now has a tiled pavement.

24 P. Hunting, 'The Life and Work of Henry Clutton' (Ph.D., London, 1979).

25 *E.* xviii, N.S. xv (1857), 207 and xx, N.S. xvii (1859), 159.

26 *E.* xvi, N.S. xiii (1855), 85–97.

27 *B.* xiii (1855), 108 and xiv (1856), 198.

28 *B.* xiii (1855), 302; *E.* xvii, N.S. xiv (1856), 375.

29 *E.* xvii, N.S. xiv (1856), 375.

30 *G.M.* ccvii (1859), 136–40.

between pp. 183–89

31 *The Guardian* 6 Aug. 1856.

32 *The Iconography of the Chapter House, Salisbury* (1859), reprinted from *E.* xx, N.S. xvii (1859), 109–14, 147–62. For Burges's notes and sketches, see also R.I.B.A., S.N.B. xxi (1856), 45–7; xxvi (1859), 63, 109; xxx (1861), 68. For a recent study of the iconography see Pamela Z. Blum, 'A Study of the Thirteenth-Century Sculptures in the Spandrels of the Blind Arcade of the Salisbury Cathedral Chapter House' (M.A., Yale, 1968).

33 Boase, ii, 1493.

34 Brown's *Handbook, op. cit.*, 55–6; Cathedral Archives, Chapter Minutes, 6 May 1860.

35 For this debate see *Architect's Jnl.* 1 and 22 Feb. 1967; *Church Times* 10, 17 and 24 Feb. 1967; *Sunday Times* 12 Feb. 1967; *The Times* 25, 27–8, Jan. 1967; *Daily Telegraph* 27 Jan. 1967.

36 T. F. Bumpus, *Cathedrals of England and Wales* (1927), 57.

37 Abstract, 1853.

38 *E.* xx, N.S. xvii (1859), 431; 'Waltham begun' (Abstract, 1859).

39 *B.* xi (1853), 168; xiii (1855), 414; xviii (1860), 71. Carving by Samuel Honchet.

40 W. Beattie, *Castles and Abbeys of England* i (1844), 261–80; *History of the King's Works*, ed. H. M. Colvin, i (1963), 88–9.

41 *Report ... on Waltham Abbey Church* (Oxford, 1860), 9–10; preliminary MS. draft, with sketches (Weller MSS); drawings prior to restoration, R.I.B.A., Arc. IV, 38–45.

42 R.I.B.A., S.N.B. xxviii (1859), 31–2. 'To Shaw, Christ's Hospital, about Waltham Pillar'; 'Waltham ceiling, gallery and pillar' (Abstract, 1859–60). The pier in question was presumably the second from the East on the South side, against which the pulpit stood. The pews were broken up and used for building cottages; plain oak benches were supplied by Burrell of Norwich (*Morning Post*, 4 May 1860).

43 'To Peterborough to see ceiling' (Abstract, 1860). Burges believed that most Norman churches had flat roofs (*R.I.B.A. Papers* 1862–3, 124). He also admired the boarded ceilings of Norwegian churches (*ibid.*, 1864–5, 107). A lithograph of the Peterborough ceiling had been published by W. Strickland in 1850.

44 V. & A., P. & D., E.5240–61, Box 27a; *A.R.* ii (1897), 6–7; S. Wildman, 'The Decorative Work of E. J. Poynter' (B.A. Cantab. 1974), 11–12.

45 K. Campbell, *Campbell, Smith & Co.* (1973), 4, 54.

46 *E.* xxi, N.S. xviii (1860), 242. Some critics would have preferred a border (*B.N.* xviii, 1870, 387).

47 *E.* xxi, N.S. xviii (1860), 220–26.

48 Watercolour, V. & A., P. & D., A.114, E.3234–1932.

49 *Report, op. cit.*, 10–11, 13.

50 G. G. Scott, *Kirkstall Abbey and its Restoration (1873)*.

51 *B.A.* xv (1881), 214.

52 R.I.B.A., S.N.B. xxvii (1859), 65; xxviii (1860), 19; xxx (1861), 54.

53 *E.* xxi, N.S. xviii (1860), 174.

54 *B.* xix (1861), 313: no. 673, 'Sketch in Waltham Abbey'.

55 *I.L.N.* xxxix (1861), 402; Pullan, *Architectural Designs of W.B.* (1883), 3.

56 *Cassell's Illustrated Exhibitor* (1862), 44; *Art Jnl. Catalogue* (1862), 124; *Official Cat.*, Brit. Divn., pt. ii, class xxx, no. 5702.

57 *E.* xxiii, N.S. xx (1862), 169; *B.* xx (1862), 499.

58 Group I, cl. iv, no. 7, i (*R.I.B.A. Papers*, 1866–7, appendix).

59 No. 155 (*A.* iii, 1870, 224; *B.* xxviii, 1870, 382; *B.N.* xviii, 1870, 387). Figures by Burges?

60 The gift of Mrs. Margaret Edenborough in memory of her husband, Lt. Col. S. B. Edenborough, J.P. See inscription lettering account, V. & A., Estim. Bk., 8 April 1876. For variant sketches see R.I.B.A., 'Stonework', 5 v. Nicholls was paid £599 (R.I.B.A., S.N.B. xli, 1875, 11 Feb. 1875).

61 *A.* iv (1870), 63; R.I.B.A. 'Stonework', 3.

62 *E.* xxiii, N.S. xx (1862), 237, 338.

63 *B.* xxii (1864), 788.

64 *E.* xxviii, N.S. xxv (1867), 150, 152; R.I.B.A., S.N.B. vii (1854), 81.

65 *B.* xix (1861), 529.

66 Architectural Exhibition Soc. Cat. (1857–8), no. 245. Executed by Lavers and Barraud.

67 *E.* xxv, N.S. xxii (1864), 377.

68 *G.M.* cxxxiii (1862), 8.

69 For details see J. Gordon-Christian, *Artifex* i (1968), 30–46; *Jnl. Brit. Soc. of Master Glass Painters* xiii (1859–63), 321–5; *Apollo*, Nov. 1930; H. J. Powell, *Glass-Making in England* (Cambridge, 1923).

70 *B.N.* xiii (1866), 19.

71 C. Winston, *An Inquiry into the Difference of Style observable in Ancient Glass Paintings ... with Hints on Glass Painting*, 2 vols. (1847, revised 1867).

72 *B.N.* xiii (1866), 17.

73 For details of this firm's work, see M. Harrison, *Connoisseur* clxxxiii (1973), 194–9.

74 For both these firms, see M. Harrison, *Connoisseur* clxxxii (1973), 251–4.

75 *B.* xxii (1864), 901.

76 For Poynter's early glass, see Wildman, *op. cit.*, 7–8.

77 Westlake recorded Burges's help in his *Who's Who* entry.

78 John Hardman Powell (1827–95) was the son of William Powell (d.1861) of Birmingham. In 1850 he married Pugin's daughter Anne (Boase, ii, 1607; *The Times* 4 March 1895; *The Tablet* 9 March 1895).

79 See A. C. Sewter, *The Stained Glass of William Morris and His Circle*, 2 vols. (1974–6), reviewed by M. Harrison, *Connoisseur* clxxxvii (1974), 144. For discursive notes on several different firms, see also forty-five articles by T. F. Bumpus, 'Stained Glass

between pp. 189–91

in England Since the Gothic Revival', *A.* lxii–vi (1899–1901), *passim*. The best modern study is M. Harrison, *Victorian Stained Glass* (1980).

80 Winston preferred fifteenth- and sixteenth-century glass to thirteenth-century work (J. B. Waring, *Catalogue of Drawings from Ancient Glass Paintings by the late Charles Winston*, Arundel Soc. Exhib. 1865, annotated copy, B.M. R.A. c.5602/6).

81 'Saunders came to me ... Saunders called Nov. 6' (Abstract, 1865).

82 'Saunders ill and left ... Saunders returned May 29 (*ibid.*, 1866); 'Saunders went abroad' (*ibid.*, 1870). In 1870 he appears in the subscription list to *Architectural Drawings* as resident in Poitiers.

83 'Holiday and Saunders dissolved' (*ibid.*, 1867).

84 'Chapple left Saunders, July 2' (*ibid.*, 1877).

85 Lonsdale never set up independently, but stayed within Burges's office.

86 'Saunders left England' (*ibid.*, 1860). However, from 1883 to 1902, glass continued to be produced by Worrall under the name of Saunders & Co.: ie. Saunders in partnership with Edwin de Lisle (Saunders ledger, *passim*). Ill health may not have been the only cause of Saunders' spasmodic career. According to Knowles, 'he had married a wife who was well to do, which caused him to neglect his work' (*ex inf.* Martin Harrison).

87 *G.M.* cxxxiii (1862), 7.

88 *B.* xix (1861), 529.

89 *E.* xxi, N.S. xviii (1860), 181.

90 Harrison and Waters, *Burne-Jones, op. cit.*, 31.

91 M. Harrison, *Jnl. Brit. Soc. of Master Glass Painters*, xv (1972–3), 63. Burne-Jones's cartoons for Christ in Majesty and the Third Day of Creation are now in the U.S.A. Preliminary sketches are in the Birmingham City Art Gallery. Grieve later worked for Saunders & Co. (*ex inf.* Martin Harrison).

92 Powell, *History of Painted Glass*, (1923).

93 Abstract, 1859.

94 One other window: a lancet made by Morris & Co. in 1896 for Rottingdean church, Sussex (Harrison, *Jnl. Brit. Soc. Master Glass Painters, op. cit.*, 64).

95 'He invited me to ... sketch ... at his offices where he had books on stained glass, and gave me much valuable assistance with regard to technical points of which I then had no experience' (H. Holiday, *Reminiscences*, 1914, 95: 1863; A. L. Baldry, *Henry Holiday*, 1930, 13). In 1863 Burges commissioned Holiday to design two windows, one with a portrayal of Noah's ark, P.L.U. (Holiday, *op. cit.*, 97).

96 H. Stacy Marks, *Pen and Pencil Sketches*, i, 221. Eg. the Powell window by Stacy Marks at St. Andrew, S. Shoebury, Essex (1858).

97 *G.M.* cxxxiii (1862), 9.

98 *B.N.* xiii (1866), 18.

99 Harrison, *Jnl. Brit. Soc. Master Glass Painters, op.*

cit., 64.

1 H.-R. Hitchcock, *Architecture: Nineteenth and Twentieth Centuries* (1963 ed.), 178.

2 In mem. Beal Colvin of Mangham's Hill, d. 19 Sept. 1864: Baptism of Our Lord, Last Supper and Christ in Glory. Still *in situ*.

3 The gift of Col. Edenborough, in mem. Mrs. Edenborough: Six Old Testament Women. Only the figure of Eve survives. 'It owes its peculiar brilliancy to the employment of enamelled colours for the shades, instead of the usual brown smear' (*Morning Post*, 4 May 1860). This two-light Decorated window was re-discovered by Burges.

4 In mem. Charles Carr, of Waltham, butcher, d. 20 Aug. 1850. Destroyed.

5 In mem. William Kent Thomas, of Sewardstone, Destroyed.

6 Presented by Rev. J. Francis: The Four Evangelists. Destroyed.

7 In Mem. Rosabel, wife of H. Domain Saunders, of Honey Lands, Waltham, d. 16 Aug. 1867. Three-light window: the Martyrdom of St. Stephen. Destroyed. Burges notes: 'Saunders (Waltham)' in Abstract, 1868.

8 In mem. Mrs. Margaret Banbury, of Warlies Park, d. 2 Dec. 1876. Four-light Decorated window: Angel Gabriel and Five New Testament Women. The spandrel figures of angels playing musical instruments survive. The cost was £161 17s. 0d. (V. & A., Estim. Bk., 26 March 1877).

9 Destroyed. But see G. H. Johnson, *Waltham Abbey* (1913), and R.I.B.A., S.N.B., xxviii (1860), 35 and Vellum, S.B., 33. The design reappeared at Tower House.

10 Johnson, *op. cit.* This design reappears at Studley Royal.

11 *E.* xxi, N.S. xviii (1860), 181.

12 R.I.B.A., S.N.B. vii (1854), 82. Burges recommended similar false windows for Cologne: 'subjects painted on a ground of burnished silver or tin foil, like the blank windows of Florence Cathedral' (*E.* xviii, N.S. xv, 1857, 22). Holiday's false windows were 'painted in oil colours, with copal varnish as a vehicle, the ground being silver foil on wood' (*E.* xxii, N.S. xix, 1861, 160). See also Theophilus [Rogers], *Encyclopaedia of Christian Art*, trans. R. Hendrie (1847).

13 The clearest contemporary description of the whole process is C. Winston, 'A Lecture on Glass Painting', 1859, in [J. L. Petit, ed.], *Memoirs Illustrative of the Art of Glass Painting by the Late Charles Winston* (1865), 231–55. See also A. N. Didron, *Manufacture de Vitraux* (1850). For more general observations, see G. A. Poole, 'Painted Glass in Connection with Architecture', *E.* xxv, N.S. xxii (1864), 251–61.

14 By W. J. Walker of London (*Morning Post* 4 May 1860).

15 'Roof of aisle, Waltham' (Abstract, 1867).

between pp. 191–95

16 By Hart, Son and Peard (V. & A., Estim. Bk., 15 Sept. 1875).

17 Johnson, *op. cit.*; W. Winters, *Visitors Handbook* (1870, 1877). Now removed to St. John's, South Hackney.

18 'Waltham Lady Chapel being restored' (Abstract, 1874); W. Winters, *History of the Lady Chapel, Waltham Abbey* (1875).

19 *A.* xiii (1872), 10–11; Weller MSS; *A.* xv (1876), 46, 66, 82; *A.* xxvii (1882), 251. J. A. Reeve was Clerk of Works; in 1886 he designed the wooden screen, carved by Forsyth, separating the chapel from the abbey proper. Further restoration took place in the 1930s, when the present stained glass was inserted.

20 Of Warlies Park, Waltham. In 1859–60 Burges had produced designs for his father, Charles Buxton, M.P. (1823–71): 'Fountains [?at Spitalfields] for Buxton' (Abstract, 1858–60); and visited him at Foxwarren Park, Surrey (Abstract, 1859). See sketches, R.I.B.A., S.N.B. xxvii (1859), 35, 67 and Vellum S.B. These designs – powerfully geometrical – were exhibited in 1860 (Archital. Exn. Soc. 1860, No. 239). The Buxton Memorial Fountain, Westminster – to the slave-reforming first Baronet – was however designed by S. S. Teulon, 1865 (Pevsner, *London*, i, 19, 546). For Charles Buxton's amateur practice in architecture, see J. Llewellyn Davies, *Notes of Thought by ... Charles Buxton M.P.* (1873). The only public fountain erected to Burges's designs is that commemorating Sir Maxwell Steele Graves Bt. at Mickleton, Glos. (1875). Its Gothic form echoes Viollet-le-Duc (*Dictionnaire*, v, 1861, 528); its portrait medallions were carved by F. Scarlett Potter (*B.* xxxiii, 1875, 1155).

21 *Trans. St. Paul's Eccles. Soc.* i (1877–80), iv–vii. For measured drawings by A. B. Plummer, see *B.* xxxii (1879), 1152–3; *B.N.* xxxvii (1879), 120–21, 170, 201.

22 V. & A., Estim. Bk., 3 July 1876.

23 *Report* (1860), title page.

24 *Morning Post* 4 May 1860.

25 Quoted in [R. G. Gilbert and F. H. Maycock], *St. Augustine's College, Canterbury* (Canterbury, 1971). See also G. F. Maclear, *St. Augustine's Canterbury* (1888) and R. J. E. Boggis, *A History of St. Augustine's College, Canterbury* (1907).

26 *English Churchman* 13 Sept. 1843.

27 H. W. and I. Law, *The Book of the Beresford Hopes* (1925), 159.

28 *ibid.*

29 *E.* ix, N.S. vi (1848), 7.

30 *E.* xx, N.S. xvii (1859), 263.

31 *ibid.*, 52.

32 Gilbert and Maycock, *op. cit.* One of the young missionaries commemorated was Jeremiah Lebopena Moshueshue, son of the King of the Basutos, who d. 26 Aug. 1863, aged 23. He is also commemorated by a striking gravestone and stained glass window at Gilbert Scott's St. Michael, Welshampton, Salop. (*C.E.A.Jnl.* xxvi, 1863, 257; *Daily Telegraph* 9 Jan. 1967).

33 'Did monument, St. Augustine's Canterbury' (Abstract, 1858); R.I.B.A., S.N.B., xiv (1858), 31.

34 R. Gunnis, *Dictionary of British Sculptors* (1951), 301–2; Boase, vi, 133, 395; *Art Jnl.* 1858, 48. Phyffers supplied the brass altar frontal for Clutton's Blessed Sacrament chapel in the church of the Immaculate Conception, Farm St., London. Among other works, Phyffers seems also to have been employed on the restoration of St. Augustine's, Harleston, Suffolk in 1860 (Gunnis, *op. cit.*; Pevsner, *Suffolk*, 250). According to Gunnis, he also worked on Salisbury Chapter House.

35 *E.* xxi, N.S. xviii (1860), 33; *I.L.N.* 14 Jan. 1860, 29.

36 Pullan called the memorial 'perhaps the most beautiful' of all Burges's designs for sculpture (*The Designs of W.B.*, no. 4).

37 *Victorian Church Art*, G.24.

38 'Began Lefroy's church ... To Lefroy's place and Rickman's' (Abstract, 1860). Lefroy had previously employed Ferrey to restore Crondall church (1847), and Harding to design Church Cobham (1841).

39 'To Winchfield, Seymour's' (Abstract, 1860); 'Seymour's School' (*ibid.*, 1861); C. F. Seymour, *Winchfield* (1898). The school was extended later in the nineteenth century, and has since been converted into a private house.

40 'Lefroy died' (Abstract, 1861); 'Consecration of Fleet Church' (*ibid.*, 1862).

41 Gen. Sir H. Lefroy, *Notes and Documents of the Lefroy Family* (1868). A. W. Lefroy of Cork was one of the chief subscribers to Cork Cathedral.

42 R.I.B.A., 'Stonework', 4. For general sketches, see V. & A., P. & D., Q.5C, D565 – 85 – 1897.

43 *E.* xxi, N.S. xviii (1860), 310, 322 and xxii, N.S. xix (1861), 242.

44 'Lefroy's Church and Effigy' (Abstract, 1861).

45 Architect, A. J. Stedman. The rose window dates from 1906, the apse windows from 1900.

46 *A. and B.N.* cxxxviii (1934), 331–2. Goodhart-Rendel noted: 'this beautiful church is indescribable in words' (G.-R. Index, N.M.R.).

47 Also 'Ireland at Lifeslan (Burne-Jones). Cork. Queenstown' (Abstract, 1863).

48 'Cork Cathedral competition ... Jones and Bainbridge called about Cork May 9 ... To Cork, stopped with Bainbridge' (*ibid.*, 1862); A. C. Robinson, *St. Finbarre's Cathedral* (Cork, 1897), 17.

49 Burges's motto was 'Non Mortuus sed Virescit'. Other entrants included: W. J. Barre, Fr. Wallen, Messrs. Vaughan and George, W. M. Fawcett, W. A. Carter, Mileham, J. P. Jones, Clifton J. West, C. H. Driver, W. Lightly, C. N. Beazley (*B.* xx,

between pp. 195–99

1862, 753 and xxi, 1863, 218; *D.B.* iv, 1862, 261; *C.E.A.J.* xxvi, 1863, 192; *E.* xxiv, N.S. xx, 1863, 164–5). Godwin's design was published in *B.N.* xxi, 1871, 9. A design by Thomas Worthington survives in the office of Thomas Worthington and Sons, Manchester. Competition drawings were exhibited at the Polytechnic Hall, Cork Athenaeum, on 11 Oct. 1862; admission 6d.

50 Second prize went to T. N. Deane (*B.N.* x, 1863, 100; *B.* xxi, 1863, 97). Many expected the Deane family to win on their home ground. One local competitor signed his entry: 'Timeo Danaos' ['I fear the Danes']. See *R.I.B.A. Jnl.* 3rd ser, vii, 1899, 49n.

51 J. S. Donnelly, *The Land and People of Nineteenth-Century Cork* (1977); D. H. Akenson, *The Church of Ireland: Ecclesiastical Reform and Revolution, 1800–85* (1971). See also an account of building in Cork, *Dublin Builder* vi (1864), 136.

52 eg. *Blackwood's Mag.* Aug. 1865.

53 *Southern Reporter* 6 May 1868. This was also the theme of sermons preached at the cathedral's consecration in 1870.

54 See local newspaper cuttings, 1862–75, collected by R. Caulfield (Cork Cathedral Chapter House Archives). These include extracts from the following papers: *Cork Advertiser, Cork Herald, Southern Reporter, Cork Examiner, The Constitution, Irish Times, The Independent, Irish Churchman* and *Northern Whig*. The argument is summarised in *B.N.* x (1863), 118, 157–8, 205.

55 *B.* xxiii (1865), 70. For an illustration, see *Mag. of Art* xviii (1894–5), 300.

56 *D.B.* vii (1865), 9. He called it 'an ugly church in a painfully overcrowded churchyard, surrounded by sad and squalid dwellings' (*A.* v. 1869, 37). Burges promised that any valuable fragments would be built into the new structure (*B.* xxii, 1864, 956). But he made little attempt to do so. The old choir stalls were purchased for use in the local masonic lodge (Minutes, No. 1 Lodge, Ireland). A photograph of March 1865 survives, showing Walker, Caulfield, Dobbin and Hewett posing in the old Western doorway, just before its demolition.

57 Book of Furniture Designs (1876 onwards), 41 (Cork Archives).

58 R. B. McDowell, *The Church of Ireland, 1869–1969* (1975), 3.

59 R. S. Gregg, *Memorials of the Life of John Gregg* (Dublin, 1879), 67, 121, 209–10. Gregg's style was characterised by 'a very rapid elocution, great gesticulation and repeating the same thing over and over again in slightly varied language' (quoted by McDowell, *op. cit.*, 138).

60 Her memorial brass was re-set into the pavement next to Burges's pulpit at Cork. See J. Day, *Elizabeth Aldworth* (Cork, 1941).

61 *Cork Advertiser* 13 Jan. 1865; 'Cork 1st stone laid' (Abstract, 1865); T. W. MacDonnell, *Life and Correspondence of W. C. Maggee, Archbishop of York* (1896).

62 *B.N.* x (1863), 551 (exterior) and xi (1864), 424 (interior); exhib. R.A., 1863, no. 925.

63 'Limestone for Cork decided' (Abstract, 1865).

64 Burges exhibited a view of these portals at the R.A., 1868, no. 892 (*B.N.* xv, 1868, 308).

65 Rough estimates for the vestry were proposed in 1880 (V. & A., Estim. Bk., 28 Nov. 1880).

66 See *B.* xxi (1863), 351, ill.; *B.N.* x (1863), 345.

67 R. Caulfield, *Handbook of the Cathedral Church of St. Fin Barre* (Cork, 1881), 7. Caulfield was Secretary to the Building Committee. Burges encouraged him to write up the cathedral's progress: 'What a thing it is to have the pen of a ready writer. What a book you will be able to make when the Cathedral is complete. I hope you are making notes for it. Cork Cathedral ought to have a Guidebook better than any other church' (Caulfield letter book, 19 Aug. 1878).

68 *Cork Advertiser* 9 March 1864.

69 *ibid.*, 12 Jan. 1865.

70 Cork Archives. Burges designed a Benefactors' Book in 1879, brass-bound and inlaid with silver and enamel (R.I.B.A., S.N.B., lxi, 1879–80, 54; 'Orf. Eccles.', 8–9; V. & A., Estim. Bk., 28 Nov. 1879, 31 Dec. 1879, 5 Jan. 1880). Barkentin and Hart supplied alternative estimates.

71 Crawford, of Beamish and Crawford, brewers, lived at Lakelands, Cork.

72 Caulfield cuttings, *op. cit.*; *B.N.* xxix (1875), 657.

73 Robinson, *op. cit.*, 19; *B.N.* xxv (1878), 103.

74 eg. Walker 'grumbled' over payment, 1865 (R.I.B.A., S.N.B., 1865).

75 Advertisements for fresh tenders were put out on 8 Feb. 1867 (Caulfield cuttings, *op. cit.*).

76 *E.* xxix, N.S. xxvi (1868), 312.

77 *B.* xxviii (1870), 995. Robinson, *op. cit.*, says £40,000.

78 Hill's diary survives in the possession of D. E. Parkinson Hill, 25 Catherine St., Waterford; see also R.I.B.A., S.N.B. xxxviii (1869–70).

79 'Delany's tender for Cork spires, May 21' (Abstract, 1876). For progress, see *B.N.* xxxii (1877), 76.

80 *B.N.* xxxiv (1878), 383.

81 Burges would have known Balthasar's account in *Revue Archéologique* xv (1858–9), 200–215.

82 *B.N.* xxvi (1874), 282; Viollet-le-Duc, *Dictionnaire* iii (1859–61), 346. Burges called it 'exquisite' (*G.M.* ccxv, 1863, 678). This church, near the Somme, was largely destroyed in the First World War, and has since been rebuilt.

83 T. H. King, *Study Book* i (1858, pls. 7–8. Drawings of Notre Dame, Etampes, 'measured by Tanner', survive in Cork Archives.

84 Presented by Burges himself.

85 See Burges's drawing in M. D. Wyatt, *Metalwork*

between pp. 199–204

(1852), pl. 34 and H. Shaw, *Ornamental Metalwork*
(1836), pl. 43.

86 In the churches of San Francesco and San Nicolo in
    Treviso, the trilobe section appears in double form
    (*C.I.T. Guides: Veneto*, 203–4).

87 Handley-Read, *A.R.* cxli (1967), 430.

88 *E.* xxix, N.S. xxvi (1868), 180.

89 D. S. Richardson, 'Gothic Revival Architecture in
    Ireland' (Ph.D., Yale, 1970, 598).

90 *E.* xxiv, N.S. xxi (1863), 119, 130, 164, 213–4, 227,
    231, 255 (plan); *G.M.* ccxv (1863), 48, 313.

91 *B.N.* xiv (1867), 334, reviewing Haig's 1867, R.A.
    exterior perspective, no. 912.

92 to E. R. Robson, 1863 (Burne-Jones MSS., Fitz-
    william Museum, Cambridge). For J. P. Seddon
    on the dangers of Early French: the risk of aiming
    at 'sturdiness' and producing 'stumpiness', see
    C.E.A. Jnl. xxvii (1864), 38.

93 *B.A.* xv (1881), 213.

94 Caulfield press cuttings, *op. cit.* The actual measure-
    ments are: external 176 ft. 6 in. × 71 ft. 6 in. (across
    nave), 98 ft. 4 in. (across transepts); internal 162 ft.
    6 in × 56 ft 6 in. (across nave), 81 ft. 4 in. (across
    transepts). See *Cork Herald* 25 Sept. 1866.

95 *B.* xxi (1863), 350; *B.N.* x (1863), 550.

96 R.I.B.A., S.N.B. xxxi (1862–3), 47. Perhaps he was
    thinking of Wimborne Minster.

97 *E.* xxiv, N.S. xxi (1863), 214.

98 G. H. Kinahan, 'Marbles and Limestones', *Jnl. Roy.
    Geol. Soc. Ireland* viii (1886), 124–204. Ex inf. Dr.
    W. E. Nevill.

99 *A.* v (1869), 37.

 1 Nicholls to Burges, 30 Sept. 1879 (Caulfield letter
    book, *op. cit.*).

 2 Eastlake, *Gothic Revival*, ed. J. Mordaunt Crook,
    354.

 3 to the Bishop of Ossory, 17 May 1878 (Caulfield
    letter book, 124).

 4 *ibid.*, 120: 4 May 1878.

 5 Robinson, *op. cit.*, 23; Caulfield, *op. cit.*, 51; sketch,
    R.I.B.A., S.N.B., xxxv (1868–9), 2.

 6 Working drawings in Cork Cathedral archives.

 7 Caulfield letter book, 30: 16 April 1877, and 19 July
    1879.

 8 *ibid.*, 8 Feb. 1879.

 9 ills: *A.* v (1869), 179; *A.* xxvii (1882), 221; *B.N.*
    xliv (1883), 868. 'Drew Cork beasts' (Abstract,
    1868).

10 *A.R.* cxli (1967), 427.

11 Eastlake, *loc. cit.* Another critic praised their
    'unusual force and noble vigour' (*Archaeol. Jnl.* xl,
    1883, 474).

12 Caulfield letter book, 45: 16 Jan. 1877; 109: Feb.
    1878.

13 *ibid.*, 47–8: 18 June 1877.

14 *ibid.*, 133: 29 March 1878.

15 *ibid.*, 96: Dec. 1877.

16 *ibid.*, 112: 25 March 1878.

17 *ibid.*, 120: 4 May 1878.

18 *ibid.*, 12 March 1879. The original gable design was
    cheaper (V. & A., Estim. Bk., 3 June 1876).

19 Chastity subduing Lust; Faith blinding Idolatry;
    Pride and Humility; Avarice wounded by Libe-
    rality – all themes borrowed by Burges from the
    Psychomachia of Prudentius (Caulfield, *op. cit.*, 49).
    For details of other gargoyles, see *ibid.*, 50.

20 *A.R.* cxli (1967), 428.

21 Caulfield letter book, 124: 17 May 1878.

22 *ibid.*, 129: 23 May 1878.

23 *ibid.*, 124: 17 May 1878.

24 Several of Nicholls' plaster models survive in the
    North West tower. For sketches and details of cost,
    see Caulfield letter book, 119: 1 May 1878, and
    Book of Sculpture (1878), Cork Archives; also V.
    & A., Estim. Bk. 13 Oct. 1875 and 25 Jan. 1876.
    North (or Crawford) Portal: SS. Philip, Barthol-
    omew, Simon, John the Baptist, Andrew, James,
    Thomas and Matthias; tympanum: Expulsion
    from Paradise, Adam and Eve, Cain and Abel.
    South (or Bishop's) Portal: SS. Mark, Matthew,
    Jude, Peter, Paul, James the Less, John the
    Apostle, Luke; tympanum: Solomon's Temple,
    Noah, Abraham and Isaac. Central Portal: Five
    Wise Virgins and Five Foolish Virgins, flanking
    central figure of Bridegroom; tympanum: The
    Resurrection. For iconographical details, see Caul-
    field, *op. cit.*, 44–8. The Wise and Foolish Virgins
    theme is also to be found at Strasbourg. Burges
    originally intended the central trumeau figure to
    represent Christ the King. Presumably because of
    Protestant objections, this was replaced by the
    Bridegroom – just as the figures of Christ and
    censing angels in the gable had to be replaced by the
    Angel with the Book. In the Resurrection tym-
    panum he had also to clothe both the Blessed and
    the Damned. For this he consulted Orcagna's
    paintings in the Campo Santo, Pisa, via G. P.
    Lasinio's folio of 1832 (Richardson, *op. cit.*, 593–4;
    A. iii, 1870, 147–8; *B.A.* xv, 1881, 214).

25 Furniture Designs, *op. cit.*, intro.

26 Caulfield letter book, 14: 16 Oct. 1876. For a list of
    work in hand, see R.I.B.A., S.N.B., 1875–6.

27 *B.N.* x (1863), 345, reviewing Haig's interior
    perspective at the R.A., no. 925.

28 Report, Oct. 1868 (inserted in Subscription List, no.
    2, Cork Archives; R.I.B.A., S.N.B., xxxvi (1869),
    14–15. Burges outfaced Protestant opposition: 'the
    archdeacon and Dr. Webster are ... bitter against
    me. ... They have rejected two windows ... mine
    is one ... I am utterly disgusted and the sooner
    Gladstone makes short work [of the Irish Church]
    the better ... I am sorry to see Puritanism so
    rampant in Cork ... I wish we could transport this
    building to England ... [Still] I dare say ten years
    will make a great change' (Burges to Caulfield,
    1869–71, Bodleian MS. TOP. ENG. Misc.e.108).

29 'Drew Cork clerestory figures' (Abstract, 1868).

between pp. 204–208

West window approved 13 Jan. 1876; clerestory windows approved at various dates, 1874–8 (Stained Glass Designs, Cork Archives).

30 Strong Room, Cork Archives; Caulfield, *op. cit.*, 8.

31 'Lonsdale doing Cork glass' (Abstract, 1869). Cartoons approved at various dates, 1874–81 (Stained Glass Designs, Cork Archives).

32 Caulfield, *op. cit.*, 8.

33 For full details of iconography and dedication, see *ibid.*, 9–25.

34 Perhaps the lighter surrounds distract the eye from the central figures, but Burges could point to precedents at Salisbury, Lincoln, Exeter and Gloucester (C. Winston, *Memoirs Illustrative of the Art of Glass-Painting*, ed. J. L. Petit, 1868, 56).

35 *A.R.* clxi (1967), 429.

36 Caulfield letter book, 85: 17 Nov. 1877.

37 Caulfield, *op. cit.*, 39–40; Robinson, *op. cit.*, 30, 40.

38 Compare examples in Italy: the Palazzo Aiutamicristo, 1490–95 (L. H. Heydenreich and W. Lotz, *Architecture in Italy, 1400–1600*, 1974, pl. 128); in Spain: entrance gate, Cordova mosque (*A.R.* xv, 1904, 251) and Casa Consistorial, Barcelona (G. E. Street, *Gothic Architecture in Spain*, ed. G. G. King, 1914, 82–3); and Sicily: palazzo Trapani, first half sixteenth century (A. Blunt, *Sicilian Baroque*, 1968, pl. 3).

39 Caulfield, *op. cit.*, 38, pl. 4; *A.* xxiii (1880), 425.

40 *B.N.* xxxiv (1878), 287; *Victorian Church Art*, D 11 (d.); Caulfield letter book, 53–4, 2, 4 July 1877. Higher tenders were submitted by Hatfield and Hart (Furniture Designs, Cork Archives). See also *A.* xxiii, 1881, 425.

41 Compare examples at Rouen and Chartres (F. Rogers, *Drawings and Sketches … in England and France*, 1867, pls. 23, 28). See also Burges, *Architectural Drawings*, 33; *B.N.* xxxvi (1879), 51.

42 By his son, the Rev. J. R. Gregg, who also presented the embroidered altar cloth (Caulfield, *op. cit.*, 29). A new altar frontal designed by Prof. Tristram was made in 1937.

43 Pullan, *Architectural Designs of W.B.*, pl. 18.

44 *ibid.*, 30.

45 Modelled by Nicholls (V. & A., Estim. Bk., 19 May 1879); executed by Burke and Co., £325 (*ibid.*, 8 May 1879).

46 Caulfield, *op. cit.*, 31. Presented by J. H. Bainbridge and Elinor Gregg in memory of Jane Bainbridge (d. 1859) and A. C. Bainbridge (d. 1876).

47 At 8, Rue Perignon. Their London address was Newman St., off Oxford St. Lonsdale's cartoons (£51): Furniture Designs, 4–5, Cork Archives. See also Caulfield letter book, 64, 70, 81: 31 Aug., 14 Sept., 13 Nov. 1877. For Burke's work elsewhere, see *A.* xxii (1879), 82–3.

48 Mogiat Firmo, Fabeiain Ugo, Martino Guisepe, Sabena Agelo and Conti Onorato (Caulfield, *op. cit.*, 36, pl. 3).

49 V. & A., Estim. Bk., 2 March 1876. For cartoons etc. see V. & A., P. & D., R.11 b; *B.N.* xxxvii (1879), 742–3 and xxxviii (1880), 130, 132–3, 220, 222–3.

50 Burges's working drawings, xv (Cork Archives). Burges was never happy about the organ at the West end: it partially blocked the rose window. It was later sunk in a pit in the North transept (Caulfield letter bk., 26 Nov. 1886).

51 R.I.B.A., 'Stonework', 9 v. Presented 1870 by the Rev. W. K. W. Chafy Chafy (1841–1916) – Dr. Collis's curate at Stratford – in memory of his grandfather the Rev. S. Kyle, Bishop of Cork (1770–1848): 'did font for Chafy Chafy' (Abstract, 1869). The metal-bound font-cover was cast by Fagan and Sons, Dublin.

52 W. H. Hill, MS. Diary; drawings, 21 Feb. 1873, Cork Archives. It formed a memorial to the Rev. H. T. Newman, Dean of Cork 1842–64. The reading stand of lacquered brass – a winged dragon, emblematic of sin, taking flight at the sound of the Gospel – was made by W. T. Harris of Cork (Caulfield, *op. cit.*, 39, 44n.).

53 eg. *B.* xliv (1883), 837.

54 Cutting, Caulfield letter book, 138.

55 Handley-Read, *A.R.* cxli (1967), 430.

56 P. Collins, *Changing Ideals in Modern Architecture* (1965).

57 R.I.B.A., Arc. IV, vi, 1; *Paris Universal International Exhibition, 1878: Cat. of British Section*, pt. i, class 4, no. 33; Caulfield, *op. cit.*, 25–9, pl. 2; *B.* xxxv (1877), 442; *A.* xvii (1877), 306 and xxvii (1882), 251; drawings: Furniture Designs, 16, Cork Archives. Gregg's portrait by Nicholls was carved from a photograph (Caulfield letter book, 99–100, 122, 129: 21 Dec. 1877, 3 Jan. 1878, 8 May 1878, 23 May 1878).

58 Caulfield, *op. cit.*, 31, pl. 2. Presented by Gregg's son. Drawings: Furniture Designs, 12–13, Cork Archives.

59 Caulfield letter book, 27: 26 March 1877. For the stall plates, see V. & A., Estim. Bk., 7 Feb. 1881.

60 Cutting from *Limerick Chronicle*, Caulfield letter book, 138.

61 *A.R.* cxli (1967). 428.

62 *A.* v (1869), 37.

63 W. E. Nevill, 'Cork Red Marble', *Geological Mag.* xcix (1962), 481–91.

64 V. & A., Estim. Bk., 2 March 1876 (Burke & Co.); 21 Aug. 1876 (Sebthorpe & Co.). Some of the green columns owe their colour to the paintbrush.

65 Hitchcock, *Architecture, 19th and 20th Centuries* (1963 ed.), 181.

66 quoted by Sir John Betjeman, *Listener*, 2 Jan. 1975, 15. Comper seems to have borrowed this dictum from J. L. Pearson.

67 Rev. A. C. Robinson, *Mag. of Art* xviii (1894–5), 304. For more factual descriptions, see J. G. F. Day and H. E. Patton, *The Cathedrals of the Church of*

between pp. 208–11

Ireland (Dublin, 1932); T. M. Fallow, *The Cathedral Churches of Ireland* (1894).

68 *Archaeol. Jnl.* xl (1883), 474.

69 *Irish Builder* xiii (1871), 15.

70 *A.* xxv (1881), 307.

71 Boase, supp. ii, 499–500.

72 Drawings, 1 Aug. 1865 (Representative Church Body MSS., Dublin). The main body of the church was designed by Joseph Welland in 1854 (*ex inf.* Dr. D. S. Richardson).

73 East window in mem. Arthur Lionel Tobin, Royal Welsh Fusiliers, d. 12 Oct. 1858; three lights: Temperance, Fortitude and Justice. Sir Thomas Tobin was a member of the Cork Cathedral Building Committee.

74 Burges correspondence, Caulfield letter book, 51: 20 June 1877, 57–8; 10 July 1877. Bainbridge, of Frankfield, Co. Cork, also has a memorial window in Cork Cathedral, where the credence table was presented by his family.

75 V. & A., Estim. Bk., 14 Nov. 1877 (£47 3s. 6d.). The windows illustrate two texts: 'Consider the lilies of the field' and 'Peace, be still'. The Cathedral had been previously restored in the 1750s by Bishop Pococke, and in the 1860s by Sir T. N. Deane. For details, see R. Langrishe, *Handbook to St. Canice's Cathedral, Kilkenny* (Kilkenny, 1879); J. Graves and J. G. A. Prin, *History ... of ... St. Canice, Kilkenny* (Dublin, 1857); T. N. Deane, in *R.I.B.A. Jnl.*, 1865–6, 79–87; M. McCarthy in *Studies* (1976–7).

76 R. Kerr, *Ambassador Extraordinary*. For a view of Kilkenny, see *B.* xxx (1872), 707.

77 'Crosshaven Church begun' (Abstract, 1866); 'Crosshaven Glass' (*ibid.*, 1868); *Cork Advertiser* 1 Nov. 1866. The builder was Robert Walker of Cork; the estimate £1,700 plus £600 for the tower.

78 *B.N.* xxviii (1875), 195. The idea was adopted by T. Honey at Dunleavy, Co. Donegal (*A.* xvii, 1877, 246).

79 D. S. Richardson, *op. cit.*, 638; *Irish Builder* xv (1873), 106; Representative Church Body MSS.

80 Chapple produced amended designs in 1884–5 (Caulfield letter book, 12 Sept. 1884, 25 Nov. 1884, 31 March 1885, 10 April 1886; drawings at Templebrady Rectory). The Chancel marbling is dated 1886. Campbell executed painted work in 1887 (K. Campbell, *Campbell, Smith & Co.*, 1973, 76).

81 cf. Forthampton, p. 225.

82 *Burke's Landed Gentry of Ireland*.

83 V. & A. Estim. Bk., Dec. 1887: rose window £105 3s. od.; lancets £22 19s. 5d. Rose window: 'The Good Samaritan'; lancets: 'God be merciful to me a sinner', 'A sower went forth to sow his seed', and 'I have found the piece which I had lost', 'I have found my sheep which was lost'. Inscription: 'These stones shall be for a memorial'.

84 Sir A. Wagner, 'The Wagners of Brighton', *Sussex Archeol. Collns.* xcvii (1959), 35–57.

85 *Brighton Guardian* 12 Oct. 1870; Mrs. W. Pitt Burne, *Gossip of the Century* iv (1899), 187–200.

86 F. Arnold, *Robertson of Brighton* (1886), 116–23. Robertson (1816–53) was appointed to Trinity Chapel, Brighton in 1847. There is a bust of him at Brasenose College, Oxford.

87 Augustus Hare, *Story of My Life* i (1896), 79. A bronchitic missionary to the fallen women of Brighton, he died at an early age in Malta (J. N. Simpkinson, *Memoir of the Rev. G. Wagner*, 1862).

88 For Fr. Wagner's architectural career, see *Sussex Daily News* 15 Jan. 1902; N. Taylor, 'Wagnerian High Church', *A.R.* cxxxvii (1965), 213–7; H. Hamilton Maughan, *Some Churches of Brighton* (1922), *Wagner of Brighton* (Loughlinstown, 1949) and *Seven Churches* (1950). Among the more sensational events of his career was the Constance Kent murder case, when Wagner refused to break the confessional seal. After a lifetime of philanthropy, he left nearly £50,000 to his favourite churches (Probate Records, Somerset House).

89 Drawings, V. & A., P. & D., Q.5 c., D. 563, 97.

90 '... the chancel being taken out of the East end ... the [surrounding] space, which in the unreformed communion would be occupied by chapels, is here made available for vestry, sacristy etc. ... The chancel is entirely lighted from the West end, while the small windows of the vestries define its extent in the side elevations' (*E.* xxiv, N.S. xxi, 1863, 119).

91 Crawford (1783–1869) was also 7th Earl of Belcarres and 1st Baron Wigan. As Lord Lindsay, his eldest son Alexander – the future 25th Earl (1812–80) – was the author of *The History of Christian Art* (1847 and 1885). Both Earls died at Dun Echt, Aberdeenshire – the great house by G. E. Street – but were buried at All Saints, Wigan. There in 1872, as part of the Hon. Colin Lindsay's restoration, Burges may have been responsible for alterations (R.I.B.A., S.N.B., xl, 1871–2, 72; 'To Wigan about church', Abstract, 1872; Pevsner, *South Lancs.*, 424). W. A. Lindsay, the 24th Earl's grandson, was Beanlands' executor. At his death in 1926, Burges's designs for St. Michael's seem to have been destroyed by Lindsay's assistant at the College of Arms, Gerald Cobb. James, 26th Earl of Crawford (1847–1913) was a leading Fremason (H. T. Falkard, ed., *Wigan Public Library: works relating to Freemasonry*, 1892).

92 A. Beanlands to W. W. Begley, 15 Oct. 1913 (C. H.-R. typescript).

93 *C.E.A. Jnl.* xxii (1859), 213; *E.* x, N.S. xvii (1859), 67–8.

94 Bodley to F. M. Simpson, 1896 (C. H.-R. typescript, Simpson to Begley, 25 July 1913).

95 Still *in situ*.

96 These vestments have been attributed to Kempe and dated 1868 (H. Hamilton Maughan, *Some*

between pp. 211–16

Brighton Churches, 1922, 73–78).

97 T. H. King, *Orfèvrerie et ouvrages en métal du moyen-age . . . d'après les anciens modèles* (Bruges, 1852).

98 *E.* xix, N.S. xvi (1858), 290. Notes for this important lecture are to be found in R.I.B.A., S.N.B. xxv (1858), 39 *et seq.* Burges charged 10% commission on metalwork, as against 5% for buildings (Pullan, *Studies in Architectural Style*, 1883, 6).

99 *Art Jnl.* 1880, 171–2; *Ecclesiastical Art Rev.* i (1878), 73–4; *Victorian Church Art*, 82, citing *B.* xxxviii (1880), 128 and *B.N.* lviii (1870), 640.

1 *Art Jnl.* 1863, 231, 253 and 1864, 77. Mark entered at Goldsmiths' Hall, 1862 (Mark Bk. vi, 116). His daughter m. Sir George Wemyss; their son carried on the firm in New York.

2 The Keith firm was taken over by Cox and Sons, c. 1869, and John Keith himself died in poverty (Bute letters, Mt. St., MSS.; *E.* xxviii, N.S. xxv, 1867, 183). Barkentin worked from 291, Regent St.; Frank Theodore was in this office 1906–14, working on metalwork for Khartoum and Liverpool Cathedrals.

3 Quoted in A. Saint, *R. N. Shaw*, 298.

4 *Ex inf.* Lt. Cmdr. Frank Theodore. Mark entered at Goldsmiths' Hall, 1883 (Mark Bk. viii, 77). The firm survived until 1932. See H. J. L. J. Massé, *Art Workers' Guild, 1884–1934* (1935), 91, 136.

5 R.I.B.A. 'Orf. Eccles.', 20. Engraving: David, Malachi, Abel, Noah; 'ego sum vitis vera et pater agricola est; ego sum vitis vos palmites'. Still *in situ.* Similar to Burges's flagon at Selsley, Glos. Exhib.: *Copy or Creation* (1967), C. 15.

6 Still *in situ*; a plainer version of the Mermaid Bowl.

7 Begley, *loc. cit.* These have since disappeared. A surviving cross, of ebony mounted in brass, might possibly be by Burges.

8 *E.* xxviii, N.S. xxv (1867), 54; R.I.B.A., 'Orf. Eccles.', 2. Rediscovered, with Burges's original sketch, by the Rev. Anthony Symondson in 1964, and now in the V. & A. Mr. Symondson's discoveries, generously communicated, have been of particular value in unravelling the story of St. Michael's.

9 A paten by Hardman, 1863, makes up the set. For a detailed description, citing Burges's sketches and instructions in R.I.B.A., 'Orf. Eccles.', 17, 26, and an article by Didron on 'Iconographie des Anges' in *Annales Archéologiques* xviii (1858), 33, see *Victorian Church Art* (1971), D.3. This chalice was also exhib. in *Copy or Creation* (1967), C.14.

10 Engraved: 'Hic Calix in [?] ecclesiae sancti michaelis in civitate Brighton fabricatus est MDC-CCLXIV'. R.I.B.A., 'Orf. Eccles.', 15–16.

11 Bodley 'bought [it] over his head for another church, my uncle having found it and told him about it' (A. Beanlands to W. W. Begley, 12 Aug. 1913, 15 Oct. 1913, C. H.-R. typescript). Whatever the quarrel, the triptych found its way to St. Michael's, and is still *in situ.* When the commission went to Burges, Bodley 'felt it very much' (M. B. Adams to Begley, 28 July 1913, C. H.-R. typescript).

12 *B.N.* xv (1868), 70. For Burges's sketches, see R.I.B.A., S.N.B. xxxiv (1867), 30.

13 *D.N.B.*; P. F. Anson, *Fashions in Church Furnishings, 1840–1940* (1963), 208–9. One of Purchas's colleagues at St. James's Chapel, Brighton, was Charles Walker, author of *The Ritual Reason Why* (1866).

14 Now in the V. & A.

15 'Rev. Purchas' (Abstract, 1865); 'Sketch for Purchas' (ibid., 1866).

16 P. Lacroix, and F. Seré, *Le Moyen Age et la Renaissance* iii (Paris, 1850). For full documentation, see *Victorian Church Art*, D.9.

17 R.I.B.A., 'Orf. Eccles.', 14. 'The paten habitually used with the Purchas Chalice is also by Hardman, decorated with an Agnus Dei against a floriated cross and dated 1877 (*Victorian Church Art*, D.10).

18 H. Hamilton Maughan, *Some Brighton Churches* (1922), 83.

19 W. W. Begley, 'St. Michael and All Angels', *Brighton and Hove Parochial Gazetteer*, i, no. 11, Oct. 1915.

20 See J. S. Chapple's version of Burges's designs, R.I.B.A., P4/1, 1–6.

21 E. G. L. Mowbray to Begley, 20 July 1914 (C. H.-R. typescript). In 1889 Saunders executed two clerestory windows – angels – for Beanlands (Saunders ledger, 53: 17 Oct. 1889).

22 The Eastern Jesse window cost £254 12s. 6d. (ibid., 92: 27 April 1895).

23 *A.R.* xliv (1918), 61–2.

24 Pullan, *Architectural Designs of W.B.*, pls. 5–8. Compare a similar minor work by Burges: the East end (1861) of Decimus Burton's Holy Trinity, Eastbourne ('Chapel, Eastbourne', Abstract, 1861); altered by A. R. G. Fenning, 1909–10 (J. Nairn and N. Pevsner, *Sussex*, 1965, 487).

25 Sketches, R.I.B.A., S.N.B. xxix (1860), 84, 87.

26 Abstract, 1867; inscriptions 1867 and 1868. The parish was orignally part of Charlwood.

27 R.I.B.A. 'Stonework', 7.

28 R.I.B.A. 'Stonework', 9 r., 11.

29 *E.* xx, N.S. xvii (1859), 123; xxi, N.S. xviii (1860), 40, 180, 189–90.

30 G.R. index, N.M.R. For Burges's sketches of the Ages of Man, see R.I.B.A., S.N.B. xxix (1860), 79–80. The glass is probably by Hardman, but Burges worked on a window design while on holiday in Ireland with E. W. Godwin (R.I.B.A., S.N.B. xxxiv, 1867, 7–8). Lowfield Heath church is now dangerously close to Gatwick Airport.

31 Foundation stone, 24 May 1869; consecration 23 Dec. 1869.

32 Nairn, Pevsner and Cherry, *Surrey* (1971), 400.

between pp. 216–22

33 'Murston Church begun' (Abstract, 1872). Drawings in the vestry have been transferred to Kent Co. Archives, Maidstone.

34 *B.* xxxi (1873), 253. The site and flints were presented by Mr. Sneed. The builders were Adcock and Rees of Dover. The tiles are by Godwin of Lugwardine. See also *B.N.* xxiv (1873), 631 and *B.A.* ii (1874), 124.

35 *E.* xxv, N.S. xxii (1864), 226.

36 *E.* xxviii, N.S. xxv (1867), 155.

37 T. F. Bumpus, *London Churches Ancient and Modern* ii (c. 1903), 98–9; *A.* lxv (1901), 162. Narthex estimates, V. & A., Estim. Bk. 16 July 1878. Compare a contemporary basilcan scheme by E. A. Heffer for St. Bridget, Wavertree, Liverpool (*B.* xxix, 1871, 546–7).

38 *E.* xxii, N.S. xix (1861), 187; 'Hoddesdon church designed' (Abstract, 1861). The job went to Joseph Clarke (*ex inf.* Rev. P. Gordon).

39 A few of Burges's drawings, and a fragment of mosaic, survive at the church. The altar plate, stamped Keith, may be by Butterfield. See also H. S. Kingsford, *A Short Account of St. Thomas's Church, Stamford Hill, Clapton Common* (privately printed, 1913); photos, Council for Places of Worship, London.

40 Abstract, 1868, 1871, 1872. For seating and cost calculations, see R.I.B.A., S.N.B. xlii (1871), 60–63. Foundation stone 25 March 1872; consecration 17 May 1873. Contractor: Messrs. Ashplant and Son, Bishopsgate St.

41 *B.N.* xxiv (1873), 349. Estimates for the vestry approved in 1879 (V. & A. Estim. Bk. 25 June 1879).

42 A. Quiney, *J. L. Pearson* (1979), 105–12.

43 *B.N.* xlv (1883), 89; *B.* l (1886), 240–41.

44 *Ex inf.* Gordon Barnes.

45 *B.N.* xxx (1876), 165. See also *B.N.* xxiv (1873), 349.

46 T. F. Bumpus, *London Churches Ancient and Modern* ii (c. 1903), 315.

47 For the contemporary use of cast iron columns in churches, see eg. St. Jude, S. Kensington (G. and H. Godwin, *B.* xxix, 1871, 366–7); Durban R.C. church, Natal (Goldie and Child, *B.* xxxvi, 1878, 991); and Boileau's iron and concrete church at Vésinet, near Paris (*B.* xxiii, 1865, 800, 805).

48 *ibid.*; *A.* lxv (1901), 161.

49 J. Summerson, *Heavenly Mansions* (1963 ed.), 238.

50 P. F. Anson, *Fashions in Church Furnishing* (1965 ed.), 203–4. Burges remained friendly with Webb, and at the behest of the Ecclesiological Society designed funeral cards for Vigers (*E.* xxiv, N.S. xxi, 1863, 121, 235) and a 'Tablet of Benefactions' for Rev. A. P. Forbes, Bishop of Brechin (Abstract, 1857; *E.* xix, N.S. xvi, 1858, 68).

51 'Tomb and Window, Wells St.' (Abstract, 1862); R.I.B.A., 'Stonework', 12; Benjamin Webb,

'Diary', 1862, *passim*. Murray was buried at Kilndown.

52 R.I.B.A., S.N.B. ix (1856), 75 and xxi (1862–3), 26; *A.* lxvi (1901), 10; sketch by J. Atwood Slater, *B.* xlvii (1884), 12, 30.

53 Bumpus, *London Churches*, ii, 159–61. 'Perhaps a more perfect adaptation of the mural canopied Italian Gothic tomb does not exist.'

54 Exhib. 1862 (*A.* lxiv, 1900, 11–12; *G.M.* ccxiii, 1862, 6).

55 *E.* xxiii, N.S. xx (1862), 179, 219, 227 and xxv, N.S. xxii (1864), 117; *B.* xx (1862), 499. Destroyed.

56 Anson, *op. cit.*, 214.

57 *E.* xxix, N.S. xxvi (1868), 63–4, 179, 218: *B.N.* xv (1868), 103, 162, 164 (drawing by Lonsdale); *Victorian Church Art*, D.4; 'Webb's Litany Desk' (Abstract, 1867); V. & A., copy at Highclere, Hants.

58 An elaborately bound altar-book (now in the V. & A.), made by Barkentin in 1870, and presented by John Naegli Sharp in memory of his father, was designed by G. H. Birch, very much in Burges's style. The candlesticks are credited to Lonsdale in *B.N.* xxviii (1875), 615.

59 He was a loyal member of Webb's congregation (Webb, 'Diary', *passim*).

60 V. & A., Estim. Bk., 28 Dec. 1875.

61 R.I.B.A., 'Orf. Eccles.', 12, 13, 17; *E.* xxix, N.S. xxvi (1868), 372; *Victorian and Edwardian Decorative Arts* (1952), O 8; *Victorian Church Art*, D.5; 'Webb's Chalice' (Abstract, 1867); Webb, 'Diary', 1867–70, *passim*.

62 *B.N.* xxviii (1875), 615.

63 *Trans. St. Paul's Eccles. Soc.* i (1880–81), xxi.

64 For Burges's detailed sketches and instructions, see 'Orf. Eccles.', 15.

65 'Webb's tomb' (R.I.B.A., S.N.B. lxii, 1880, 88; lxiii, 1880–81, 6); 'Watson' (Abstract, 1881); B. Webb, *In Memoriam ... Sermons preached in ... St. Andrew's Wells St. ... after the death and funeral of Emma Jane Knight Watson* (privately printed, 1881). Burges's design for an elaborate canopied tomb was not executed. The Watson tomb in Brompton Cemetery (South terrace) consists of a Gothic headstone carved with a crucifixion. Webb also commissioned Burges to design a brass, in the chapel of Trinity College, Cambridge, to Hope's tutor, Archdeacon Thomas Thorp (1797–1877): V. & A., Estim. Bk., 6, 29 Oct. 1880. Thorp is commemorated by an elaborate monument at Kemerton, Glos. See Boase, iii, 964.

66 Boase, ii, 741–2; *I.L.N.* lxxxiii (1883), 428, portrait. Marling lived at Stanley Park, and later at Sedbury Park, Glos., a bleak Neo-Classical house by Smirke.

67 Gibson died at Hove, Sussex.

68 D. Verey, *Gloucestershire: the Cotswolds* (1970), 389, 435; *C.L.* cxlix (1971), 1249.

69 *Victorian Church Art*, D.1. See R.I.B.A. 'Orf. Eccles.', 10, 48 and plate for Rev. E. F. Russell [209].

between pp. 222–25

70 *ex inf.* Charles Oman. P. R. B. Braithwaite, *Church Plate of Hampshire* (1909), 8–9: chalice, paten and two flagons.

71 *Victorian Church Art*, D.2. For Burges's designs, see R.I.B.A. 'Orf. Eccles.', 34.

72 V. & A., P. & D. 93 E 9 (10–11); 'Wakeman did Gibson's jewellery' (Abstract, 1863); 'To Gibson at Stonehouse' (*ibid.*, 1865); 'Gibson' (*ibid.*, 1872).

73 Verey, *op. cit.*, 288. The church was restored by Bodley in 1876.

74 *Gloucester Jnl.* 20 March 1909. The carving was also by a local man, Joshua Wall. Some of Webb's drawings, ex. J. R. Holiday colln., are now in the colln. of the Hon. C. Lennox-Boyd.

75 *E.* xxvi, N.S. xxiii (1865), 366; 'Jenner's crozier' (Abstract, 1865).

76 *E.* xxvii, N.S. xxiv (1866), 63.

77 *E.* xxviii, N.S. xxv (1867), 54.

78 'Crozier for Dunedin' (Abstract, 1866); 'Dunedin Crozier' (*ibid.*, 1867); *E.* xxviii, N.S. xxv (1867), 124, 252; *B.* xxv (1867), 467 and xxvi (1868), 333: no. 401. Similarly, in 1862, Burges designed a cope for Rev. T. N. Staley, first Bishop of Honolulu (Abstract, 1862). For Jenner and Staley see Boase, supp. ii, 768–9 and iii, 701.

79 Pullan, *Designs of W.B.*, pl. 14. 'A good example of the characteristic vigour with which Burges reproduced a Medieval idea; the crockets and the position of the sculpture in the curve of the staff are derived from Medieval work [cf. R.I.B.A., V, 'Metalwork', 37: Cluny Museum]; but the design of St. George and the dragon, and the bound woman below, is completely original ... and the dragon growing out of the staff-end is Medieval in the best sense; it has the Medieval spirit, quite apart from anything like copyism' (*B.* liii (1887), 693). Compare the captive princess and armed knight with Burges's drawing for Bute's bedroom chimneypiece, Cardiff (Cardiff Drawgs. xvii, 67, 67a b.).

80 Vellum S.B., 32; 'Orf. Eccles.', 19; P. Howell, *Victorian Churches* (1968), 33.

81 *L'Art Pour Tous: Encyclopaedia de l'Art Industriel et Decoratif*, ed. E. Reiber and C. Savageot, xiv (1875), 1457, figs. 303–7.

82 F. S. Meyer, *Ornamentale Formenlehre*, revised and translated as a *Handbook of Ornament*, ed. H. Stannus (1894), pl. 225 (4). Alas, Handley-Read failed to see the joke.

83 For all these quotations, see S. T. Madsen, *Restoration and Anti-Restoration* (1977).

84 *E.* xxii, N.S. xix (1861), 112.

85 'In Louis Philippe's time a terrible restoration took place in the sculpture, and Blessed Virgins were metamorphosed into apostles, and apostles into Blessed Virgins' (*R.I.B.A. Papers* 1860–61, 214; *B.* xix, 1861, 163).

86 'Could not the Society forward a remonstrance to Mr. Guinness, and tell him publicly that he is doing wrong?' (*E.* xxv, N.S. xxii, 1864, 221).

87 *ibid.*

88 *R.I.B.A. Papers* 1865–6, 147–8; *B.* xxxi (1873) 1001. 'M. Viollet-le-Duc, as an archaeologist, as a painter, as an artist, is well worth study and deference, but as an architect in the true sense of the word I am sorry to say I cannot regard him. I regret to say this, but I have seen M. Viollet-le-Duc's works, and they have bitterly disappointed me. I do not think that the impression ought to go abroad that we regard him as a great architect. The most hideous thing I ever saw was a sort of lodge of his at Coucy – which was something frightful, something awful. His *Dictionnaire* has to be looked at a long time to enable us to understand what he is about. Luckily very few people could read his French, and therefore it did very little harm. He is very logical, but his premises are wrong. I think we ought to be very careful how we study him. If you study his writings carefully and thoroughly for years, you might learn a very great deal from them, but to the statement that he is a great architect, I entirely demur. I have been over Pierrefonds, and think it very good on the whole, but I think some of it very ugly' (*A.* x, 1873, 323). For a recent scholarly assessment, see *Viollet-le-Duc* (Paris, 1980).

89 *A.* x (1873), 341.

90 Burges to Pearson, 12 March 1879 (colln. Mrs. R. C. Mogan; *ex inf.* Dr. A. Quiney). Burges produced reports on the Market Cross at Cheddar, Somerset (Abstract, 1858–9); All Saints, Waldeshare, Kent (*ibid.*, 1874–5); Cressingham Priory, Norfolk (*ibid.*, 1856).

91 C. Wilson, 'The Original Design of the City of London Guildhall', *Jnl. Brit. Archaeol. Assocn.* cxxix (1976), 1–14.

92 J. B. Hilling, *Cardiff and the Valleys* (1973), 116.

93 *B.* xxii (1865), 788. Burges's restoration of St. Margaret, Darenth, Kent (1866–68) is a good example of his cautious approach. For details, see *E.* xxviii, N.S. xxv (1867), 85–9; Abstract, 1866–68. He recommended tiles by Godwin of Lugwardine. Saunders produced the glass (*Eccles. Art Rev.* 1878, 29). J. H. Parker had led a visit of the R.A.I. to Darenth in 1863 (*G.M.* ccxv, 1863, 587).

94 'Yatman's brother's memorial ... To Winscombe and Wells' (Abstract, 1858). Fragments of a garden memorial survive at Winscombe Hall, as do Railton's designs for interior decoration. The house is dated 1855, 1859, 1862 and 1871; the lodge, containing medieval fragments, is 1875. Burges seems to have cooperated with the owner, an amateur architect.

95 Pevsner, *N. Somerset and Bristol* (1958), 341.

96 'Joseph York. Reginald York' (Abstract, 1863).

97 Burges also designed the rustic altar rail (G. J. Yorke, *St. Mary the Virgin, Forthampton*, privately printed, 1975). About the same time Burges designed a rectory (since altered) at Aspley Guise,

between pp. 225–30

Beds., for an ex-curate of Forthampton, the Rev. Hay Macdowell Erskine ('Erskine's parsonage', Abstract, 1864).

98 R.I.B.A., 'Stonework', 2; 'Forthampton dossal' (*ibid.*, 1866). The colouring is modern.

99 'York's work at Forthampton'; 'Barraud'; 'Saunders came to me' (*ibid.*, 1865). D. Verey, *Glos.: the Vale and Forest of Dean* (1977 ed.), 460 credits the East window to Saunders and the pulpit window to Holiday and Saunders. (*ex inf.* Martin Harrison).

1 *E.* xxviii, N.S. xxv (1867), 153, 155.

2 *B.* xxii (1864), 788.

3 *Archaeol. Jnl.* xxi (1864), 209.

4 *Archaeologia* xxxviii (1860), 431–8. Tracings were made by Parker, and reduced by C. A. Buckler, in 1859. See also *G.M.* cxxx (1860), 547–56.

5 *Archaeol. Jnl.* xvi (1859), 89 and xxi (1864), 209–15; *B.N.* vii (1862), 330–32; 'Burningham' (Abstract, 1865, 1867); R. Sewill, *Free Men of Charlwood* (1951), 38–53. The paintings illustrate 'The Legend of St. Margaret' and 'Les Trois Vifs et les Trois Morts'. In 1864–7, Burges seems to have been responsible for internal refurbishment, including the painting of the screen (I. Nairn and N. Pevsner, *Surrey*, ed. B. Cherry, 1971, 141–2, pl. 26).

6 *Archaeol. Jnl.* xvi (1859), 89.

7 *G.M.* cxxxii (1862), 513–25.

8 Lambeth MS. 1726, fs. 31–63: 9 Nov. 1876; R.I.B.A., S.N.B., liii (1876), 70–71. A previous report had been prepared by J. P. Seddon.

9 V. & A., Estim. Bk., 9 Nov. 1876. The altar frontal was later added to designs by J. A. Reeve (*B.* xlix, 1885, 641).

10 The structure was restored in the early 1950s by Seely and Paget.

11 1846: Member of the Incorporated Law Society; 1852–7: partner, Thomas Brook Bridges Stevens and Bonnor, 49 Pall Mall; 1858–93: in independent practice, same address (Law List). George Bonnor exhibited Renaissance jewellery at South Kensington (*Cat. Loan Exhibn., Ancient and Modern Jewellery*, 1872) and was elected F.S.A., 1871. Webb was a close friend ('Diary', *passim*.).

12 *Survey of London* xxxviii (1976), 269, 363.

13 W. R. O'Byrne, *Naval Biographical Dictionary* (1849), 977; *G.M.* ccxxi (1867), 406.

14 In 1832. For Dorton, see *C,L.* xv (1904), 522–5.

15 [Capt. Ricketts], *The Popularity of the Royal Naval Services* (privately printed, 1826).

16 She died in 1873: there is a brass (Hart, Son, Peard & Co.) bearing emblems of the four evangelists at St. James, Boarstall, Bucks.

17 Declared at £18,000; resworn 1875 at £30,000 (Probate Records, Somerset House).

18 R.I.B.A., 'Stonework', 16; W. Lake, *History of Cornwall* (1870), 233. For Cook, see *D.N.B.* and J. Grant, *The Saturday Review* (1873).

19 Carving by Jacquet and Nicholls (R.I.B.A.,

'Stonework', 25; *G.M.* 1866, ii, Nov.; *B.* xix, 1861, 12–13). 'Visit to Lord Redesdale' (Abstract, 1863); 'Lord Redesdale's work' (*ibid.*, 1869). Redesdale (1805–86) was a High Tory Protestant bachelor who left £195,000 (*D.N.B.*).

20 R.I.B.A., 'Stonework', 21–4.

21 Pevsner, *London*, ii, 303.

22 [G.B.-J.], *Memorials of E. B.-J.*, ii (1904), 264–5.

23 He owned 21,770 acres in Yorkshire and Lincolnshire, gross annual rental value £29,126 (J. Bateman, *Great Landowners of Great Britain*, 1883, 381). He left £127,292 15s. 8d. (Probate records, Somerset House).

24 *D.N.B.*

25 'No other Governor-General, from Dalhousie to Curzon, accomplished so much' in breaking down the old 'evil "Nigger" tradition' of government (L. Wolf, *Life of 1st Marquess of Ripon* ii, 1921, 157, 160, quoting Sir Auckland Colvin). 'Lord Ripon's viceroyalty ... was in truth the awakening hour of the new movement towards liberty in India' (W. S. Blunt, *India Under Ripon*, 1909, 1). For a hostile view, see his *Times* obituary, 10 July, 1909: 'Lord Ripon's Viceroyalty lingers as a disturbing nightmare and a cruel chasm in the path of natural evolution ... "The Oriental ... expects to be ruled" ...'; and a reply from Cardinal Bourne, 12 July 1909. See also, F. H. Pellew, 'Lord Ripon', *National Rev.* ii (1883), 588–95.

26 Wolf, *op. cit.*, ii, 68, 170.

27 He contributed to *Politics for the People*, but his essay on *The Duty of the Age* (1852) was deemed too subversive for publication (Wolf, *op. cit.*, i, 22–42).

28 Ripon Papers cliv, B.M. Add. MS. 43644, fs. 16–38.

29 Wolf, *op. cit.*, i, 57. Burges notes in his diary 'Fountains restoration' (Abstract, 1873). The extent of his involvement is unclear.

30 Wolf, *op. cit.*, i, 354–5. Seven windows (?by J. Hungerford Pollen) from this chapel are now in St. Wilfrid's, Ripon.

31 A. Hare, *The Story of My Life* vi (1900), 293.

32 Anne Pollen, *J. Hungerford Pollen* (1912), 356.

33 Wolf, *op. cit.*, i, 157–9.

34 *ibid.*, i, 46.

35 *ibid.*, i, 293–4. For a defence, see J. Gornall, *Secession to Rome* (1874). The key figures in his conversion seem to have bee Fr. Dalgairns – a disciple of Newman – and his cousin Lady Amabel Kerr (Ripon Papers cxxxv, B.M. Add. MS. 43625, fs. 99, 124 etc.).

36 *Swinburne Letters*, ed. C. Y. Long, ii (1959), 339–40: 8 Sept. 1874.

37 Ripon Papers cxxxv, B.M. Add. MS. 43625, fs. 86–9: 7 Aug. 1873.

38 Diaries, Ripon Papers cli–iii, B.M. Add. MSS. 43641–3: 8 Dec. 1878.

39 Wolf, *op. cit.*, i, 323.

40 Edward Lloyd, E. C. H. Herbert and Count Alberto de Boyl. Those who escaped were Lord

between pp. 230–35

and Lady Muncaster and Lloyd's wife and daughter (*The Times* 14 April 1870, 5 and 7 May 1870; *I.L.N.* lvi, 1870, 491, 557; *Parliamentary Papers* 1870–71).

41 There is also a stained glass window in Ripon Minster (1870); a brass in York Minster (1871); the Vyner Memorial Window (1872) by Burne Jones and J. Fairfax Murray at Christ Church Cathedral, Oxford; a monument at Gautby, Lincs.; and a memorial window (1872) by Holiday in the English Church at Athens (A. C. Baldry, 'Henry Holiday', *Walker's Qtly*. xxxi–ii, 1930, 47–69). Lady Mary Vyner embroidered the altar frontal designed by Burges – with birds and butterflies in a geometrical pattern – for Skelton (*C.L.* clxviii, 1980, 2409). For family history, see [C. Vyner] *The Vyner Family* [*c*. 1876].

42 'Saw Lord Ripon and Lady Vyner about Studley church Oct. 18 (Abstract, 1870); 'Began Skelton' (*ibid.*); R.I.B.A., S.N.B., xxxix (1870–71), 33.

43 R.I.B.A., S.N.B., xli (1871), 3 and liv (1876), 82. 'First stone Studley, March 25' (Abstract, 1871); 'First stone Skelton, May 17' (*ibid.*). The Skelton stone was laid 'very quietly'. But for Studley, a silver trowel was supplied. 'We had the union jack', Burges told Ripon, 'and it was a question whether two Chinese flags found at Studley could not have also done duty, but they were rejected. Mr. Holy, at Mr. Thompson's suggestion, appeared in a surplice, which was an improvement on his ordinary attire in which he contemplated performing the ceremony in the first instance' (Ripon Papers cxxxiii, B.M. Add. MS. 43623, f.110: 28 March 1871).

44 *B.* xxix (1871), 470; Pevsner, *Yorks, West Riding*, 504. One preliminary estimate for Studley is £9,600 (R.I.B.A., S.N.B., xxxix, 1870–71, 76). At Studley Burges ran into legal difficulties with the contractor, C. Barry Jnr. acting as arbitrator: 'Arbitration about Studley, 1st meeting, Jan. 30' (Abstract, 1877).

45 Full details, *B.* xxxvi (1878), 65–6; *Guide* (1890). A volume of detailed drawings, prepared by Lonsdale under Burges's direction, survives among the Vyner archives, at Newby, as do Burges's designs for cottages.

46 *Victorian Church Art*, D.8; Pullan, *Designs of W.B.* (1885), pl. 12; R.I.B.A., 'Stonework', 8. Compare R.I.B.A., S.N.B. xli (1871), 49–50 and xlvi (1874), 63. Walden charged £318 for the cover (R.I.B.A., S.N.B. li, 1875, 11 Feb. 1875).

47 R.I.B.A., S.N.B., xlvi (1873), 52, 54.

48 Redfern charged £110 (R.I.B.A., S.N.B., li, 1875, 2 Oct. 1874).

49 'A double-set of tracery, forming a sort of screen ... which gives a very fine effect of light and shade' (Pullan, *Architectural Designs of W.B.*, pl. 55). In 1869–71 Burges also inserted 'double plane tracery' in the East window of Holy Trinity, Minchinhampton, Glos. For details, see Weller MSS., 28

April 1869; Abstract 1871). 1869; Abstract 1871).

50 *B.* xxix (1871), 470.

51 Cf. the West window of York Minster before restoration (E. S. Prior, *Gothic Architecture*, 198).

52 Vellum S.B., 29; R. Barber, *Companion Guide to S.W. France* (1977), pl. 2. For the decoration of the organ case, see V. & A., Estim. Bk., 14, 19 June and 8, 12 Oct. 1875.

53 Pevsner, *Yorkshire W. Riding*, 59, 477.

54 G-R. Index, N.M.R.

55 'Book furniture', V. & A., Estim. Bk., 19 June 1876. Barkentin was also responsible for repairing a chalice, and supplying a paten and flagon (*ibid.*, 2 Feb. 1877).

56 Vases, garden seats, gates, statues and 'two Alcibiades dogs', still *in situ* (V. & A., Estim. Bk., 31 Oct. and 13 Dec. 1876; 22 Jan, 26 Feb., 28 Aug. and 12 Nov. 1877).

57 P. Leach, *Guide* (1981). Burges even thought of converting the obelisk into a crucifix (R.I.B.A., S.N.B., xlvi 1873, 32).

58 *B.N.* xl (1881), 473–4.

59 'Gold cross Lord Ripon' (Abstract, 1871). Presumably for Studley Royal. Also 'Clasps and bosses Ld. Ripon' (*ibid.*, 1872).

60 'Reliquary for Ld. Ripon' (*ibid.*, 1876); V. & A., Estim. Bk., 10 July 1876; R.I.B.A., S.N.B. liii (1876), 23 and liv (1876–7), 33: Barkentin. Presumably for his private chapel.

61 V. & A., Estim. Bk., 16 May 1876.

62 V. & A., Estim. Bk., 16 May 1876: 'cross reliquary'.

63 Ripon Papers cxxxiii, B.M. Add. MS. 43623, f.110: 28 March 1871; *B.* xxix (1871), 470.

64 Burges, *Architectural Drawings*, 50.

65 Viollet-le-Duc, *Dictionnaire*, ix (1868), 305: triforium and clerestory at Lincoln.

66 Vellum S.B., 29.

67 Pevsner, *Some Architectural Writers of the Nineteenth Century*, 67, n.19.

68 *B.N.* xvii (1869), 460.

69 *B.N.* xvi (1869), 204.

70 *B.N.* xxix (1875), 198–9, 206–7. And his design for Worcester College chapel. See also *A.* viii (1872), 19 and ix (1873), 150–52, 173–4, 180–82.

71 Pevsner, *Yorkshire, W. Riding*, 218, 625.

72 Banister Fletcher, *History of Architecture* (1975 ed.), 494.

73 *Ex inf.* H. Lotz, W. Langson and D. S. Richardson. The Paduan dome has fictive handkerchief vaults; Brunelleschi's use of dome and pendentives in Florence is structural. The domes of Padua and Studley are both covered with figures of the Heavenly Host arranged in tiers. Burges visited Padua in 1856 and (crucially) in 1873.

74 P. Morey, *Charpente de la Cathedrale de Messine* (Paris, 1841).

75 See Haig's perspective, R.I.B.A., Arc. IV, i; *A.* xi (1874), 346 and xxvii (1882), 235. For a variant

between pp. 235–40

dossal design, see R.I.B.A., S.N.B., lii (1875), 47–8.

76 Each slab cost 200 guineas (*Guide*).

77 *R.I.B.A. Trans* xxxii (1882), 188.

78 'Onyx eyes for Lion' (R.I.B.A., S.N.B., xlviii, 1874, 24).

79 The painted work was executed in 1877 by Campbell and Smith; the larger figures were painted by Weekes (28 angels, 12 children, 20 seraphs), the smaller ornaments by Fisher (V. & A., Estim. Bk., 6 Sept. 1876; 17 Feb., 28 June, 31 Aug. 1877). 'Studley decoration' (Abstract, 1877).

80 Ripon Papers, cxxxiii, B.M. Add. MS. 43623, f.110: 28 March 1871. 'Got the windows up' (R.I.B.A., S.N.B., xliii, 1872, 59: 21 Oct. 1872).

81 The figure with dividers – representing Architecture – before the temple, echos the titlepage of Viollet-le-Duc's *Dictionnaire* i (1854).

82 Cf. Burges's print of Dürer's 'The Woman and the Dragon' (*B.N.* xxv, 1873, 506, 516–7).

83 H. Read, *English Stained Glass* (1926), 224.

84 R.I.B.A., S.N.B., l (1874), 7–8.

85 eg. R.I.B.A., S.N.B., xl (1871), 76 and xlvii (1874), 61–2; R.I.B.A., 'Stonework', 8; Vellum S.B., 9. See also S.N.B., 1875 Sept. and 1876 May: '... went to Studley ... at the church all day painting the font'. White was paid £120 for marble work (R.I.B.A., S.N.B., li, 1875, 2 Feb. 1875). The figures recur in the bronze door at Tower House.

86 Pevsner, *Yorkshire, W. Riding*, 504.

87 Pullan, *Architectural Designs of W.B.*, 16.

88 Pevsner, *loc. cit.*

89 The crucifixion group is flanked by statues of St. George (Ripon's patron saint), St. Bernard (of Fountains Abbey), St. Gabriel and St. Wilfrid (of York).

90 Pevsner, *loc. cit.*

91 *20th Annual Report of the Ecclesiological Soc.* (1859), 9.

92 'Skilbeck warehouse' (Abstract, 1865–6); R.I.B.A., S.N.B., xxxii (1865), 64. Messrs. Skilbeck: Joseph Skilbeck (d.1860), drysalter and freemason (G. W. Wollaston and J. Tindal-Robertson, *A Short History of the Old Union Lodge, no. 46*, 1935, 155); John Skilbeck of Springfield, Upper Clapton (V. & A., Estim. Bk., addresses). Burges had already worked on a City warehouse in 1858, at 32 Bridge Row, for Messrs. Millington and Hatton, stationers ('Worked at Millington's warehouse for Mr. Leschallas', Abstract, 1858). John Leschallas took over this business after the death of his brother William in 1852. One of their products was Moinier's linen writing paper; Moinier was related to Leschallas.

93 Nicholls was the sculptor; J. and C. I'Anson the contractors. The cost was £1,413.11.0d. (*B.* xxiv, 1866, 850–51).

94 *C.E.A. Jnl.* xxx, 1867, 88.

95 *B.N.* xiv (1867), 337.

96 Warehouses in Southwark St. (*B.N.* xxiv, 1873, 220).

97 J. Summerson, 'London: the Artifact', in H. J. Dyos and M. Wolff, eds., *The Victorian City: Images and Realities* i (1973), 316.

98 Eastlake, *Gothic Revival*, ed. J. Mordaunt Crook, Appendix no. 280.

99 T. Harris, *Three Periods of English Architecture* (1894), 149.

1 *E.* xxvii, N.S. xxv (1866), 310–11.

2 *B.N.* xxvi (1874), 30.

3 *The Echo* 23 April 1881.

4 *B.N.* xiii (1866), 800. Burges's only other commercial building remains obscure: 'Alterations in Strand for friends of F. Michel' (Abstract, 1871).

5 St. Elizabeth's Almshouses (1860), for six spinsters; endowed by Alfred Burges Snr. and Jnr., William Burges, Pullan, A.S. [?] and William Foord Tribe, in memory of Elizabeth Burges. ('Workhouse Chapel', Abstract, 1860). In 1866 Burges also designed additions to the Harry Humphrey Almshouses (1858). See Kelly's *Directory of Sussex* (1867) and *B.* xxiv (1866), 258.

6 The accounts are dated 1863–4 (Yorke MSS., Forthampton, *ex inf.* Mr. Gerald Yorke).

7 Previously called Joldwyns, and once the dower house of John Evelyn, Milton Court was later the scene of many soirées given by Rate's wife Mary Mackintosh (Augustus Hare, *Story of My Life*, vi, 1900, 227). Burges seems to have been responsible for redecorating the hall, billiard room and boudoir (V. & A., Estim. Bk., 5, 9 Dec. 1875; R.I.B.A., S.N.B. xli, 1871, 85, 87; 'Rate's boudoir ... Derby races with Rate', Abstract, 1872), as well as other works ('Joldwyns for Rate', *ibid.*, 1869; 'Additions for Rate, Dorking', *ibid.*, 1880). See also I. Nairn, N. Pevsner and B. Cherry, *Surrey* (1971 edn.), 368. Rate subscribed to Burges's *Architectural Drawings*.

8 N. Pevsner, 'Early Working Class Housing', in *Studies in Art, Architecture and Design* ii (1968), 18–37; J.N. Tarn, *5% Philanthropy ... Houses in Urban Areas, 1840–1914* (Cambridge, 1975); E. Gauldie, *Cruel Habitations, A History of Working Class Housing, 1780–1918* (1974).

9 *R.I.B.A. Papers* 1866–7, 52; *B.N.* xiv (1867), 24, 26.

10 *E.* xxv, N.S. xxii (1864), 208, 248.

11 Eastlake, *op. cit.*, Appendix, no. 249.

12 Dover Public Library MSS.: Dover Corporation Minutes, and Scrap Book; J. Barrington Jones, *Annals of Dover* (Dover, 1916); J. Newman, *N.E. and E. Kent* (1969) 287–8. Chapple's extension dates from 1894, and the bell turret from 1914.

13 'Maison Dieu, Dover' (Abstract, 1859); 'Coats of Arms for Dover ... To Dover, Maison Dieu ... Dover for a week ... [John] Clayton at Dover' (*ibid.*, 1860).

14 *C.E.A.Jnl.* xxvi, 1863, 256; *B.* xix (1861), 596–7; *E.* xxi, N.S. xviii (1860), 310.

15 *G.M.* ccxii (1862), 556–8; *B.N.* xxiv (1873), 60;

between pp. 240–45

Fine Arts Qtly. Rev. Jan. 1865, 419. The West windows had previously been filled with glass by Wailes.

16 *B.* xl (1881), 517, 570.

17 See *The Dover and County Chronicle*, 1883.

18 'Additions Maison Dieu, Dover' (Abstract, 1880); 'Dover' (*ibid.*, 1881). This men's prison had been built in 1867; Burges adapted the nearby women's prison as a Police Station and lock-up in 1880 (V. & A., Estim. Bk., 9 Aug. 1880).

19 Hall and Parlour ceiling have jelly-mould dome-lets; the hall has columns of cast iron, and originally had floral and geometrical decorations painted by Campbell and Smith, as well as a stone *pulpitum* within the proscenium arch (J. Barrington Jones, *Dover Year Book, Almanack and Directory*, 1883, 10–16; *B.* xlv, 1883, 57). The windows – Wardens of the Cinque Ports – are from cartoons by Lonsdale.

20 J. Lockwood Kipling (1837–1911) moved there from South Kensington in 1865, the year after marrying Alice Macdonald, Burne-Jones's future sister-in-law. Some of Lockwood Kipling's sculpture is still to be seen in Emerson's Burges-style Crawford Market (C. Carrington, *Rudyard Kipling*, 1955, 47; A. Wilson, *Rudyard Kipling*, 1977, 5, 15, pl. 2).

21 'Began Bombay' (Abstract, 1865); 'Sent off Bombay, April 4' (*ibid.*, 1866); Report, May 1866 (Weller MSS.); *R.I.B.A. Papers* 1867–8, 77–85 and *Special Papers* ix (1867), 43; Pullan, *Architectural Designs of W.B.* i (1883), 28–9 and ii (1887) 23–8.

22 *The Chromolithograph* i (1863), 99. Burges concluded his report to the R.I.B.A. with the melancholy news that his design had been superseded by an engineer's scheme modelled on Capt. Fowke's South Kensington.

23 *E.* xxvii, N.S. xxiv (1866), 119, 244.

24 *B.N.* xv (1868), 480.

25 V.-le-Duc, *Dictionnaire* iv (n.d.), 462. The kitchen had, however, already appeared in A. Lenoir, *Architecture Monastique* ii (1856), 350, pl. 495, of which Burges had a copy.

26 *A.* xxv (1881), 369.

27 See J. Mordaunt Crook, 'Italian Influence on Victorian Gothic', *Accademia Nazionale dei Lincei*, Q.N. 241 (1977–8), 39–65.

28 Burges had been made an hon. member of the American Institute of Architects in 1870, but in that he was not unusual among British architects (*B.* xxix, 1871, 192).

29 'Memorandum of a Tour in England, Scotland and Wales', quoted in G. Weaver, *History of Trinity College* i (Hartford Conn., 1967), 178. For Glenalmond, see G. St. Quinton, *History of Glenalmond* (Edinburgh, 1956).

30 *B.N.* xxvi (1874), 418; Pullan, *Architectural Designs of W.B.* i (1883), 68–71 and ii (1887), 30–34.

31 The theatre was estimated at £20,000 and the chapel at £11,625 (Trinity Coll. Archives).

32 Burges's report, 29 Sept. 1874 (*ibid.*).

33 His plans were presented to Trinity College in 1929 by the Avery Library, Colombia Univ., New York. See also the Minutes of the College's Board of Trustees, 1874–80. For Kimball, see M. Schuyler *American Architecture*, ed. W. H. Jordy and R. Coe (Camb. Mass., 1961), ii, 121 *et seq.*

34 'Beginning of Hartford Coll., U.S. America' (Abstract, 1872); 'Hartford Coll. begun . . . Mr. and Mrs. Jackson, America . . . Kimball' (*ibid.*, 1873); 'Hartford Coll. going on . . . Took Kimball to Cardiff . . . Kimball left Oct. 2' (*ibid.*, 1874).

35 Burges's Report, 16.

36 H.-R. Hitchcock, *Architecture: Nineteenth and Twentieth Centuries*, 187–8. For Keller's nearby High School, see *B.N.* xlv (1883), 11.

37 Weaver, *op. cit.*, 183–4.

38 *New England Mag.* iv (1886), 405.

39 Hattie Howard, *Poems* (Hartford, 1886), 25–7, quoted in Weaver, *op. cit.*, 185.

40 21 Aug. 1875.

41 *B.N.* xiii (1886), 871.

42 *B.* xl (1881), 728.

43 *American Architect and Building News* ii (1877), 225–6.

44 V. & A., Estim. Bk., 19 Feb. 1877.

45 eg. elevations endorsed 'Sent by Kimball from America 20 Feb. 1876' (Trinity College archives).

46 ill. *Scribner's Monthly* xi (1876), 612; R.I.B.A., S.N.B., xlvi (1873), 13–14.

47 In 1877–78 Burges designed a new block of college buildings – in Tudor, Perpendicular and French Gothic – along the line of Wilkins's screen in King's Parade (King's Coll. Archives: Portfolio of Designs (Oct. 1877), Box 141 (corresp.), Congregation Book 1876–78; Cambridge Univ. Archives: Add. 5083, fs. 153, 163 (corresp.); R.I.B.A., S.N.B., lvi (1877), 55–6. See also *A. and B.N.* cxxxiv (1933), 340–45; A. Doig, ed., *Architectural Drawings . . . King's College, Cambridge* (1979), 63–5.

48 'Ripon Grammar School' (Abstract, 1873). Burges received £250 for these designs, P.L.U. (Ripon Grammar School archives, Governors' Muniments, *ex inf.* Dr. W. J. Petchey).

49 Compare Richardson's Austin Hall at Harvard Law School (*B.* xlix, 1885, 858). For Richardson and Burges, see Hitchcock, *op. cit.*, 166, 168, 170, 193, 222, 264, 267. Richardson's only house in England, for Sir H. Herkomer ('Lululaund', Bushey, Herts., 1886–7), seems almost a tribute to Burges (J. F. O'Gorman, *H. H. Richardson and His Circle*, Harvard, 1974, no. 15). Burges seems also to have designed one other school abroad: in Trinidad, 1861, for R. W. Keate. See Abstract, 1861.

50 H. Montagu Butler, 'Harrow Benefactors and Benefactions', in *Harrow School*, ed. E. W. Howson and G. Townsend Warner (1898), 145. For general

between pp. 245–51

accounts of the Harrow School buildings, see J. Summerson, in *C.L.* 14, 21 July (1934), 36–42, 64–9; E. D. Laborde, *Harrow School, Yesterday and Today* (1948).

51 Report, 23 Dec. 1871 (Weller MSS.); *A.* viii (1872), 8.

52 'Masters will enter from the centre of the portico ... visitors from the side stairs, and ... pupils from the various rooms on the high level' (Report, *op. cit.*).

53 For these, see *Gazette des Architectes et du Batiment* xii (1876), 29, 45, 113.

54 *R.I.B.A. Papers*, 1866–7, 9.

55 *ibid.*, 1864–5, 49; R.I.B.A., Vellum S.B., 12.

56 *Archaeol. Jnl.* xl (1883), 474.

57 'Harrow begun' (Abstract, 1871); 'Harrow going on fitfully' (*ibid.*, 1874); 'Harrow begun Feb. 23 ... Harrow agreement drawn up' (*ibid.*, 1875); 'Harrow going on' (*ibid.*, 1876); 'Harrow opened July 5' (*ibid.*, 1877). Sketches, sections and working drawings in the Vaughan Library, Harrow School – including designs for a gymnasium and rectangular theatre topped by a trilobe roof – indicate the development of Burges's designs.

58 V. & A., Estim. Bk., 10, 23 Nov. 1876.

59 B. P. Lascelles, 'Speech-Day', in Howson and Warner, *op. cit.*, 203–4.

60 For these competitions, see J. Mordaunt Crook and M. H. Port, *The History of the King's Works*, vi (1973); M. H. Port, 'The New Law Courts Competition, 1866–7', *Architectural History* xi (1968), 75–93; J. Summerson, *Victorian Architecture: Four Studies in Evaluation* (1970), 77–117.

61 G. Somers Clarke, P. C. Hardwick, T. H. Wyatt and John Gibson declined.

62 *Parliamentary Debates* 3rd ser. clxxxv (1867), 814–23.

63 *R.I.B.A. Trans.* xxxii (1882), 23. 'Put on Law competition ... Began Law Courts June 24 ... Godwin at Blackheath Law Courts June 29' (Abstract, 1866); 'Finished Law Courts' (*ibid.*, 1867); 'Law Courts settled' (*ibid.*, 1868). Godwin was unable to compete (Port, *op. cit.*); so Burges paid him £100 for his assistance (Harbron, *Conscious Stone*, 84).

64 Quoted in *R.I.B.A. Trans.* 1882, 199–200. For plans and sections, see Pullan, *Architectural Designs of W.B.* i (1883), 39–43.

65 *E.* xxviii, N.S. xxv (1867), 113.

66 J. Summerson, *op. cit.*, 104.

67 *E.* xxviii, N.S. xxv (1867), 113–20.

68 *ibid.*, 292.

69 *B.* xlvi (1884), 713.

70 A. Rotch, in *American A. and B.N.* ix (1881), 237. Goodhart-Rendel would seem to have endorsed this view: 'It is a tempting antithesis to suggest that Street was greater than his works, but that Burges's works were greater than Burges' (*English Architecture Since the Regency*, 147).

71 According to E. W. Pugin (*The Times*, 13 Sept. 1871, 10).

72 Fergusson and Emmett were hostile to all the competitors. E. W. Pugin attacked Burges and Street in *The Times*, 15, 19 Aug. 1867, and in the *Westminster Gazette*. The *Athenaeum* and *Standard* rallied to Burges's defence. For a temperate discussion, see *C.E.A.Jnl.* xxx (1867), 97–8. The *Saturday Review* also plumped for Burges (*Sat. Rev.*, xxiii, 1867, 561–3).

73 *B.N.* xiv (1867), 147.

74 *B.N.* xiv (1867), 202–3, 270.

75 *B.N.* xiv (1867), 202–3.

76 *American A. and B.N.* ix (1881), 237.

77 Pullan, in *R.I.B.A. Trans.* 1882, 185.

78 Scott, *Recollections* (1879), 275.

79 *R.I.B.A. Trans.* 1883–4, 209.

80 *B.* xlvi (1884), 713. See also Street to F. G. Stephens, 27 Jan. 1867, Bodleian MS., Don., e.77, f.18.

81 *B.* xxv (1867), 593.

82 Summerson, *op. cit.*, 116.

83 *B.* xxv (1867), 885.

84 *B.* xxv (1867), 89–91, 309–11.

85 *B.* xlvi (1884), 713; *R.I.B.A. Trans.* xxxiv (1884), 232.

86 *B.* xlvi (1884), 729.

87 *B.* xxv (1867), 144.

88 *A.* vi (1871), 126.

89 *ibid.*, 127; *The Times* 23 June 1868, 11; 30 Nov. 1871, 5; 2 Dec. 1871, 5; 22 Jan. 1872, 10; 26 Mar. 1872, 9.

90 For a defence of Street's design, see A. E. Street, *Memoir of G. E. Street* (1888), 143–75.

91 Summerson, *op. cit.*, 115.

92 *B.N.* xxii (1872), 362.

93 *B.A.* viii (1877), 17: comparative ills.

94 *B.N.* xvii (1869), 393, 435; xviii (1870), 132 and xxv (1873), 252; *B.* xxvii (1869), 840 and xxx (1872), 907.

95 In 1863–64 Burges entered a competition for Bradford Exchange. He was defeated by the local firm of Lockwood and Mawson. For details, see *B.* xxiii (1865), 332; A. Saint, *R. N. Shaw*, 54–7, 444.

96 *B.N.* xxii (1872), 468–9 and xxv (1873), 254–7, 257; *A.* ii (1869), 206, 279, 302.

97 *B.N.* xvii (1869), 265, 435, 468.

98 *A.* ii (1869), 290.

99 Colln. Sir John Summerson.

1 *B.N.* xviii (1870), 132.

2 *B.* xlii (1882), 481.

3 *A.* xxv (1881), 369.

4 eg. Lockwood and Mawson's Bradford Town Hall.

5 *A.* v (1872), 39.

6 *B.* xliv (1883), 837.

7 *B.N.* xl (1881), 473.

8 eg. Edward Horner (*B.N.* xxviii, 1880, 456); Glover and Salter (*B.N.* xlvii, 1884, 233; *A.* xxxii,

page 252

1884, 71, 87); G. S. Doughty (*B.N.* xlvi, 1884, 366); Percy Stone (*B.N.* xlvi, 1884, 1023 and xlvii, 1884, 904).

9 *R.I.B.A. Jnl.* 3rd ser. xxiii (1916), 334–6. For Haig's views of the interior and Strand frontage, see *B.N.* xiv (1867), 202–3, 273, 294, 302, 309; V. & A., P. & D., A.182, E 382 – 1923.

10 Burges to Reichensperger, 1 Feb. 1868 (Sotheby's 15 Oct. 1976, lot 507).

11 *The Echo* 23 April 1881.

12 *B.A.* xv (1881), 214.

13 *B.* xl (1881), 531–2.

14 Mt. St. MSS., to Lord Bute, 3 Jan. 1884.

15 Hence Goodhart-Rendel's dictum: Burges's 'few executed designs reach a degree of absolute merit superior to that in any works of Street' (*English Architecture Since the Regency*, 147).

16 *A.* xxv (1881), 315. 'Burges put his whole being into anything he undertook' (D. Harbron, *Amphion*, 1930, 136).

17 *B.* xxxiii (1875), 1145.

6. FEUDAL

between pp. 253–56

1 Abstract, 1865.

2 This may well have been so. Certainly as a young man he was the richest in Britain. In the 1890s he was probably overtaken by the 1st Duke of Westminster (1825–99), who was said to be worth £14,000,000 in 1894; and perhaps by Charles Morrison (1817–1909), a financier who left nearly £11,000,000 (W. D. Rubinstein, 'British Millionaires, 1809–1949', *Bull. Inst. Hist. Res.* xlvii, 1974, 202–23). At his death Bute's estates were valued at £5,026,000; his personal property at £1,864,310 (*Complete Peerage* ii, 1912, 445). Recent research suggests £1,142,000 for personalty and unsettled realty (Rubinstein, *op. cit.*, 211), plus c.£8,000,000 for settled estates (based on a thirty-three years' multiple of the annual return given in J. Bateman, *Great Landowners of Great Britain*, 1883, 69. Bateman, however, doubted the accuracy of this entry). Bute's spending and philanthropy have yet to be computed. The Bute family's finances have been admirably analysed in J. Davies, 'Glamorgan and the Bute Estate, 1766–1947' (Ph.D., Swansea, 1969), and *Cardiff and the Marquesses of Bute* (Cardiff, 1980).

3 He lived at Bute House, Brompton, an Adam property, c. 1795–c. 1805; the house was demolished 1845–6 in laying out Bute Street, S. Kensington.

4 Horace Walpole, *Letters*, Nov.–Dec. 1766.

5 *John, 2nd Marquess of Bute*, reprinted from *Cardiff and Merthyr Guardian*, March, April 1848.

6 Bute Papers, Cardiff Central Lib., cited by Davies, *op. cit.*, 32.

7 For the Butes versus the Guests, the Crawshays etc., see J. Davies, 'The Dowlais Lease, 1748–1900', *Morgannwg* xii (1968), 37–66; J. P. Addis, *The Crawshay Dynasty, 1765–1867* (Cardiff, 1957); J. H. Morris and L. J. Williams, *The South Wales Coal Industry, 1841–75* (Cardiff, 1958); M. J. Daunton, 'Dowlais Iron Co.', *Welsh Hist. Rev.* vi (1972), 16–45; A. H. John, *The Industrial Revolution in South Wales, 1750–1850* (Cardiff, 1951); I. Bulmer Thomas, *Top Sawyer* [David Davies of Barry] (1938); M. S. Taylor, *The Crawshays of Cyfarthfa Castle* (1967).

8 Bute MSS., Nat. Lib. Wales, 26 Dec. 1844, cited by Davies, *op. cit.*, 141.

9 In 1878 Bute owed £550,000 to the Equitable Insurance Co. (D. Cannadine, 'Aristocratic Indebtedness in the Nineteenth Century: the Case Re-Opened', *Econ. Hist. Rev.*, 2nd ser., xxx (1977), 624–50).

10 For details, see Davies, op. cit., M. J. Daunton, 'Aristocrat and Traders: the Bute Docks, 1839–1914', *Jnl. Transport Hist.* N.S. iii (1975), 65–85; *Glamorgan Historian* viii (1972).

11 Executant engineers: James Green and George Turnbull; builders: Messrs. Dalton and Turnbull; advisory engineers: Telford, Cubitt and Smeaton.

12 Engineer: Robert Stephenson.

13 Advisory engineers: John Rennie and John Plows; construction engineers: Walker, Burges and Cooper; resident engineer: John Mc. Connochie; builders: Messrs. Hemingway and Pearson.

14 For a detailed plan of the docks, plus statistics of trade, see the *Supplement to the Pictorial World* 27 May 1886.

15 Daunton, *Jnl. Transport Hist.*, op. cit., 73. The dominant figure in the management of the Bute estates was Sir W. T. Lewis (1837–1914). See *D.N.B.*

16 W. Rees, *Cardiff* (1962); W. E. Minchinton, ed., *Industrial South Wales, 1750–1914* (1969); M. J. Daunton, *Coal Metropolis, 1870–1914* (Leicester, 1977). For the growth of building in Cardiff, 1870–78, see *A.* xxiii (1880), 60. For Bute's attitude to development, see *B.* xxxii (1874), 912 and *B.N.* xxxiii (1877), 321.

17 'The docks were more a parasite [on the Bute estates] than an asset. The demands of the dock for capital dominated the estate ... The Bute estate would have been in a better position financially if it had not itself provided the docks at Cardiff' (Daunton, *Jnl. Transport Hist.*, op. cit., 76–7).

18 Cardinal Newman to Catherine Anne Bathurst, 3 Jan. 1869 (C. S. Dessain and T. Gornall, eds., *Letters and Diaries of J. H. Newman*, xxiv, 1973, 197, 300).

19 *The Times* 4 Jan. 1869, 6.

20 Mt. St. MSS., Jnl. 'written by Miss Boyle at my dictation', 4 Sept. 1855. In later years Bute presented a copy of Digby's *Broad Stone of Honour* to Harrow School Library (Blair, *Bute*, 26).

21 For the whole process, see Hunter Blair, *Bute*, 39 *et seq.*

between pp. 256–58

22 Dom Bede Camm, *Forgotten Shrines* (1910), 343–50. Restored 1862 by C. A. Buckler.

23 Evelyn Waugh, *Unconditional Surrender* (1961).

24 *Complete Peerage* iii (1913), 539–41, Appendix G. For fuller lists, see W. G. Gorman, *Converts to Rome* (1910).

25 See Capel's own account of Bute's conversion in *San Francisco Examiner* 25 Nov. 1900. Capel (1836–1911) was a noted preacher, confessor and polemicist in the 1860s and 1870s, but left England under a cloud following a scandal in connection with the abortive Catholic university in Kensington (*D.N.B.*; Augustus Hare, *Story of My Life*, ii, 1896, 486–7; Newman's *Letters*, *op. cit.*, 1868–9, index; *Men of Mark* i (1876), 32; *Men of the Time* (1879), 197–8; C. M. Davies, *Unorthodox London* (1873), appendix).

26 *The Times* 4 Jan. 1869; 13, 14, 16 June 1870.

27 Ed. V. Bogdanor (Oxford, 1975). See also D. E. Painting, 'Disraeli and the Roman Catholic Church', *Qtly. Rev.* ccciv (1966), 17–25; R. W. Stewart, *Benjamin Disraeli* (New Jersey, 1972) and *Disraeli's Novels Reviewed, 1826–1968* (1974); J. Holloway, *The Victorian Sage* (1953); D. Hudson, ed., *Munby : Man of Two Worlds* (1972), 284 : 5 May 1868; *The Times* 26 April 1921, 13.

28 Earl of Ilchester, *Chronicles of Holland House, 1820–1900* (1927), 434. She eventually married a German prince, and died young (R. Neville and C. E. Jerningham, *Piccadilly to Pall Mall*, 1908, 47–8).

29 G. W. E. Russell, *Portraits of the Seventies* (1916), 259. She married the 8th Duke of Marlborough in 1869 and was divorced in 1883.

30 At the old Brompton Oratory. Disraeli signed the register; Manning and Capel officiated. The Pope sent a blessing and a cameo brooch (later mounted in gold by Burges: Mt. St. drawings[252]). The eight bridesmaids received lockets studded with rubies and diamonds (by ? Crichton of Edinburgh). Bute presented Manning with cloth of gold *chirotheca* ceremonial gloves, designed by Burges (Blair, *op. cit.*, 107; 'Cardinal Manning's gloves', Abstract 1872; Mt. St. drawings [222]). Bute presented two seven-branched candlesticks, designed by Burges, to Brompton Oratory in 1879 (V. & A., Estim. Bk. 23 Jan. and 6 Sept. 1878; 'Candelabra placed in Brompton Oratory', Abstract, 1879; R.I.B.A., S.N.B. liv, 1876–7, 19). For the marriage ceremony, of which Ruskin heartily disapproved, see Ruskin, *Works*, xxvii, 1907, 304, 334, 337; *The Times* 17 April 1872; *The Standard* 17 April 1872; *The Graphic* 27 April 1872.

31 'He read, and thought, and prayed himself into communion with the Universal Church' (*The Tablet* xcvi, 1900, 577). For discussions and intrigues, see Bute Guardianship Papers, Sandon, Harrowby MSS. xlii (1850–68).

32 Augustus Hare, *op. cit.*, v (1900), 169–71.

33 e.g. 'The Roman Catholic who is not a revolutionary is in a state of mortal sin' (Fr. Camillo Torres, *The Times* 18 June 1973, 16).

34 quoted in *Innes Rev.* xv (1964), 47–55.

35 Or 'Proper' (J. H. Matthews, in *The Tablet* xcvi, 1900, 577; Blair, *op. cit.*, 51n). Hunter Blair had joined the Papal Zouaves at the barricades in 1870, and was received into the church in Rome in 1875, formally renouncing his masonic honours. He was ordained in 1886, became Master of Hunter Blair Hall, Oxford (later St. Benet's) in 1899 and Abbot of Fort Augustus in 1913 (*The Tablet* clxxiv, 1939, 369; *The Times* 13 Sept. 1939, 8). He had been at Oxford with Oscar Wilde, and arranged a papal audience for him in 1877. Mgr. Ronald Knox found him 'a jolly old bird' (Evelyn Waugh, *Ronald Knox*, 1959, 158).

36 W. H. Salter and R. Haynes, *The Society for Psychical Research* (1970 edn.); R. Pearsall, *The Table Rappers* (1972).

37 J. L. Campbell and T. H. Hall, *Strange Things* (1968). After Bute's death she was shipped abroad as agent for the Bute property in Jerusalem.

38 Mt. St. MSS., 27 Aug. 1894; 5, 19 Sept. 1895.

39 For MSS. at Mt. St., see *3rd Rep. Hist. MSS. Commn.* (1872); Catalogue by Henry Gough, Neilson Colln., Nat. Lib. Scotland, MS. 2767; *MSS. Belonging to the Italy Office of the Inquisition in the Canary Islands*, ed. Bute and W. de G. Birch, 2 Vols. (1903).

40 Augustus Hare, *op. cit.*, iv (1900), 270.

41 Mt. St., Diary, 31 Jan. 1886.

42 *ibid.*, 3 Nov. 1889.

43 'With E[velyn] K[irwan]', *ibid.*, 23 Aug. 1891.

44 *ibid.*, Oct.–Nov. 1894.

45 *ibid.*, Nov. 1895 and 24 June 1896.

46 *ibid.*, 1895.

47 'Went to meeting wearing hood; students assembled to see me pass, cheered, and didn't laugh – so suppose it was impressive and not grotesque' (*ibid.*, 24 Nov. 1893). He was photographed in this garb (*ibid.*, 29 Nov. 1893) [11]. See Blair, *Bute*, 202, and *Medley of Memories* (1919), 214.

48 Diary, *op. cit.*, 29 June 1886; 7, 9 Oct. 1886.

49 R. Macdonald, 'The "Tin Cathedral" at Oban, 1886–1934', *Innes Rev.* xv (1964), 47–55; D. Weeks, *Corvo* (1971). Bute also appears as 'Edward Lancaster' in a novel by Rolfe.

50 A. Calder-Marshall, *The Enthusiast* (1962), 189, 193; P. F. Anson, *Building Up The Waste Places* (1973), 96; Blair, *Bute*, 101. Llantony monastery was begun in 1870, to designs by Buckeridge, but never completed. In 1924 it was acquired by Eric Gill.

51 *Notable American Women*, ed. E. T. James (Camb. Mass., 1971); *Nineteenth-Century American Women Neo-Classical Sculptors* (Vassar, 1972). *Ex inf.*, Richard Dorment.

between pp. 258–64

52 Blair, *Bute*, 126. Reviewed, *Blackwoods Mag.* cxxvii (1880), 80–99. See also J. Baudet, *The Roman Breviary: its sources and history* (1909).

53 *The Scotsman* 19 Nov. 1900; Blair, *Bute*, 144.

54 Mt. St. MSS., letters to Lady Bute.

55 *ex. inf.* Sir John Betjeman, 22 Jan. 1975.

56 *Western Mail* 15 Oct. 1900, 6.

57 *ibid.*, 10 Oct. 1900, 7. For Bute as a lecturer, see *The Buteman* 6 Feb. 1875, 3.

58 MS. account, Mt. St. MSS., F.31.

59 Augustus Hare, *op. cit.*, iv (1900), 269.

60 *Western Mail* 10 Oct. 1900, 4.

61 *The Tablet* xcvi (1900), 577.

62 Mt. St. MSS., Bute letters, 29 Jan. 1873.

63 *South Wales Daily News* 21 April 1881.

64 Abstract, 1870.

65 Mt. St. MSS., Bute letters, 28 Feb. 1875.

66 Abstract, 1874. On this trip Burges visited Barcelona, Majorca, La Palma, Alaro and Belsor.

67 Abstract, 1877.

68 *ibid.*, 1873, 1880.

69 Mt. St. MSS., Bute Letters, Sept. 1879.

70 Mt. St. MSS., Lady Bute letters, Sept. 1873. 'Gave jewel to Lady Bute' (Abstract, 1873). Brooch designs: V. & A., P. & D., 93E.9, 11 i; R.I.B.A., S.N.B. xl (1871), 12: 'Lady B. brooch' (Abstract, 1871). In 1875 he designed for a crystal cup mounted in gold (Abstract, 1875; Burges drawgs., Mt. St., f.11; account £32, James Spilling, Mt. St. MSS.). P.L.U. And in 1873–5 a 'circlet', 'coronet' or 'tiara' (R.I.B.A., S.N.B., xlvii, 1874, 82 and xlix, 1874, 13–14; Burges to Bute, 28 Nov. 1873, Mt. St. MSS.; A. Hare, *Two Noble Lives*, iii, 365). P.L.U.

71 *ibid.*, 23 Aug. 1874.

72 Abstract, 1881; V. & A. Estim. Bk. 20 March 1881.

73 Mt. St. MSS., Bute letters [Sept. 1879].

74 Mt. St. MSS., Lady Bute letters, 22 April 1881.

75 *ibid.*, Bute letters, 24 July 1881.

76 Mt. St. MSS., 16 Oct. 1873.

77 'Began Cardiff' (Abstract, 1865).

78 *Who's Who in Architecture* (1926). Grant was responsible for the West gate (1921), North gate (1919–23) and Keep (1923). The site of the Roman North Gate was uncovered in 1899 (Mt. St. MSS., Grant letters, 16 Oct. 1899).

79 Compare Burges's drawings of the 'Byzantine Wall', Constantinople, and the 'Wall of Aurelius', Rome (V. & A., P. & D., 93E.2, 129–30).

80 *Merthyr Guardian* 19 Dec. 1868.

81 Soane Museum, xxxvii, 47–50 (1777).

82 *Jnl. and Correspondence of Miss Berry*, ed. Lady T. Lewis ii (1865), 98: 20 Sept. 1799.

83 Smirke drawings, R.I.B.A. H12/19/1–3 (wmk. 1817). A further plan of 1830, possibly by Smirke, shows the layout of rooms prior to Burges (*Plans and Prospects*, Welsh Arts Council, 1975, no. 6).

84 Details, G. T. Clark, 'Cardiff Castle', *Archaeologia Cambrensis*, 3rd ser. viii (1862), 249–71; 5th ser. vii

(1890), 283–92.

85 'Reports, no. 2, Cardiff', Feb. 1866 (Weller MSS.). Drawings were prepared in 1865–6 by John Mc. Connochie (Cardiff Drawgs., xxi, 48). I have been grateful, at different times, to Mr. E. H. Jones of Cardiff City Library, and Mr. J. T. Ineson, F.R.I.B.A., and Mrs. P. Sargent, of the South Glamorgan Architect's Dept., for making the collection of Burges drawings at Cardiff available to me.

86 V. & A., P. & D., 93E.2, 91.

87 L. H. Heydenreich and W. Lotz, *Architecture in Italy, 1400–1600* (1974), pl. 99. 88 eg. beamed galleries along the battlements (V. & A., B. & D., 93 E.2, 67), and towers (*ibid.*, 104).

89 Viollet-le-Duc, *Dictionnaire*, vii (1864), 34.

90 'To Chillon, worked there all day' (R.I.B.A., S.N.B., xxxvii, 1869, 23–4, 156; V. & A., P. & D., 93E.2, 68 and 93E.4, 16; Burges, *Architectural Drawings*, pl. 22; *C.L.* cxv (1954), 260–63).

91 R.I.B.A., S.N.B. xxxvii (1869), 33.

92 *ibid.*, 63.

93 With W. S. Barber (R.I.B.A., S.N.B., xxxviii, 1869–70, 29, 33).

94 A. Beanlands to W. Begley, 15 Oct. 1913 (C. H-R. typescript).

95 Weller MSS., 14 April 1868.

96 *ibid.*, 'Report', *op. cit.*

97 *ibid.*, newspaper cutting.

98 *A.* v (1871), 185, 276. The bell itself was a half-scale model of that in the Victoria Tower, Westminster (*A.* vi, 1871, 124).

99 Cardiff Drawgs., xxi, 25–6.

1 R.I.B.A., S.N.B., xli (1871), 27; Cardiff Drawgs. xxi, 24b, 27; *A.* x (1873), 200. For Burges consulting Bute as to design, see Mt. St. MSS., 26 May 1868.

2 *A.* xi (1874), 146. Burges based his allegories on J. J. A. Worsaae, *Nordiske Oldsager* (Kjöbenhaun, 1859); C. de Linas, *Les Casques de Falaise* (Arras and Paris, 1869); P. H. Mallet, *Northern Antiquities* 2v. (1847).

3 R.I.B.A., S.N.B., xli (1871), 26; *A.* xii (1874), 6 and xxvii (1882), 203.

4 Cardiff Drawgs. xxvii.

5 *A.* ix (1873), 114 and xxvii (1882), 203.

6 R.I.B.A., S.N.B., xl (1871), 48, 82; Cardiff Drawgs., xxi, 37b, 40b.

7 Cardiff Drawgs., xxi, 22, 22b. Versions of these 'Jewels' were made by Saunders & Co. as late as 1885–88 for export – via George Keller – to Hartford, Connecticut, and Cleveland, Ohio (Garfield National Monument). See Saunders ledger, 13 April 1885, 15 March 1887, 30 Aug. 1888.

8 'Si lector posita prudenter cuncta revolvat
Hic finem primi mobilis inveniet
Sepes trina canes et equos homines superaddis
Cervos et corvos aquilas immania cete'.
'Mundi quoque sequens pereuntis triplicat annos

between pp. 264–68

Sphericus archetypum anno domini, MDCCLXXI'. 'Smoking Room pavement Cardiff' (Abstract, 1871). 'The tower is all done except the tiles in the top room' (Mt. St. MSS., 25 Jan. 1873). The gallery door is dated 1873, a cartoon for the tiles 1874.

9 *A.* viii (1872), 316 and ix (1873), 114. The foliage is by E. Clarke and Son of Llandaff.

10 Based on C.J. Hygenus, *Astronomi de Mundi et Sphere* (Venice, 1512). For Burges's preliminary schemes, see Cardiff Drawgs. xxi, 33; R.I.B.A., S.N.B., xxxix (1870–71), 73, xli (1871), 25, xliii (1872), 67 and xlv (1873), 65–6. Final scheme, Cardiff Drawgs. xxvii, 33.

11 R.I.B.A., S.N.B., xli (1871), 60; *A.* viii (1872), 142. For mermaid variations, see *A.* xxvii (1882), 203.

12 *A.* xii (1874), 56; 'Weekes did metals' (Abstract, 1872).

13 Cast by Redfern (Burges to Bute, Mt. St. MSS., 28 Nov. 1873). See R.I.B.A., S.N.B., xlv (1873), 57; *A.* v (1871), 276.

14 Cardiff Drawgs. xxi, 32 (wmk. 1865).

15 Mt. St. MSS., Sept. 1873.

16 *ibid.*, 24 Feb. 1872.

17 Kerr, *Ambassador Extraordinary* ii, 111; iii, 101.

18 Cardiff Drawgs. xxi, 66. P.L.U.

19 Viollet-le-Duc, *Mobilier* i (1858), 50; A.H. Haig's exhibition view (1870).

20 Matching side-tables, P.L.U. Liberty's were selling Indian furniture, of ebony inlaid with ivory, in the 1890s (*Liberty Exhibition*, V. & A., 1975).

21 Cardiff Drawgs. xxi, 49b, 50, 51, 67 a–h.

22 *B.* xvi (1858), 502–4.

23 Godwin operated at Lugwardine from 1851, and at Withington from 1861.

24 In 1850 Maw & Co. bought up the accumulated stock of Chamberlain & Co. and Fleming St. John and Barr. In 1852 they moved from Worcester to Benthall, near Broseley. In 1883 they moved again, to nearby Jackfield. Maw was elected F.S.A. at the second attempt (Candidates Certificates, 8 Dec. 1859, 15 Nov. 1860).

25 J.G. Nicholls, *Examples of Inlaid Gothic Tiles* (1841) and *Examples of Decorative Tiles Sometimes Termed Encaustic* (1845); A.W.N. Pugin, *Floriated Ornament* (1848); H. Shaw, *Specimens of Tile Pavements* (1858).

26 *Minton, 1798–1910* (V. & A., 1976); M. Messenger, 'Encaustic Tiles in the Nineteenth Century', *C.L.* clxiii (1970), 214–5; H. Minton, *Old English Tile Design* (1842). In the 1860s G.G. Scott worked with Minton; in the 1870s so did J. Moyr Smith.

27 'Tiles for Maw' (Abstract, 1865); *B.* xiv (1867), 128–32; *Jnl. of Decorative Art*, Sept. 1887; J.F. Blacker, *The ABC of Nineteenth-Century English Ceramic Art* (1924), 345; M. Messenger, 'Tile Designs of Maw & Co.', *C.L.* clxiv (1928), 28–9. In the 1880s and 1890s their chief designers were Walter Crane and C.H. Temple. In 1862 Burges

had felt obliged to exclude printed tiles by Morris & Co. from the Medieval Court (A. Vallence, *William Morris*, 1897, 80).

28 Of 456 West Strand. Founded 1833 as a decorating firm; in the 1870s they commissioned wall paper, tiles and mosaic work for exhibition at their St. Martin's Lane showrooms. They were 'London agents for the sale and laying of Maw & Cos' pavements' (Cardiff Drawgs., xxi, 29).

29 [Rosamund Allwood], *Victorian Tiles* (Wolverhampton, 1978); J. Barnard, 'Decorated Victorian Tiles', *Antique Dealer and Collector's Guide* (1972), 82–8, and *Victorian Ceramic Tiles* (1980).

30 R.A. no. 744 (Winter Smoking Room), 752 (Summer Smoking Room).

31 *B.N.* xix (1870), 428, 431.

32 *A.* v (1871), 276.

33 *A.P.S.D.*, supp. vol., ills.

34 H. Gally Knight, *Saracenic and Norman Remains* (1840), pl. xx.

35 *A.* v. (1871), 276.

36 Vellum S.B., 20–21; Viollet-le-Duc, *Dictionnaire*, iv, 462; *Victorian and Edwardian Decorative Art*, B. 30.

37 Cardiff Drawgs., xxi, 56; *A.* ix (1873), 8.

38 Cardiff Drawgs., xxi, 19, 20.

39 Official Cat., Brit. Section, pt. i, class 4, no. 32.

40 *B.* xxviii (1870), 359.

41 *A.* xi (1874), 146.

42 *Archaeol. Jnl.* xl (1883), 475.

43 *B.N.* xviii (1870), 351. Later on the same journal settled for 'thought and feeling' (*B.N.* xxvi, 1874, 2).

44 *B.* xxviii (1870), 359.

45 D. Harbron, *The Conscious Stone* (1949), 72.

46 *A.* xi (1874), 147; *R.I.B.A. Trans.* 1881–2, 21–3.

47 Mt. St. MSS., Bute letters, 28 Feb. 1872.

48 *ibid.*, 29 Jan. 1873.

49 *ibid.*, 24 Jan. 1873.

50 *ibid.*, 2, 3, 5, 6, 11, 13 March 1875.

51 See D. Cannadine, 'Aristocratic Indebtedness in the Nineteenth Century: The Case Re-Opened', *Econ. Hist. Rev.*, 2nd ser. xxx (1977), 624–50.

52 Abstract, 1874. In the interval, Burges showed round at least two colleagues: William White, and F.H. Kimball from U.S.A. (*ibid.*).

53 Mt. St. MSS., Bute letters, 25 Feb. 1875.

54 *ibid.*, 2, 3, 5, 6, 7, 10, 13 March 1875.

55 *ibid.*, 11 March 1875.

56 R.I.B.A., S.N.B., liii (1875), 47.

57 Mt. St. MSS., Bute letters, 7 Feb. 1872.

58 *B.N.* xviii (1870), 387; 'Lord Bute's stables' (Abstract, 1869); R.I.B.A., S.N.B. xxxv (1868–9), 38–9, 57–9.

59 'Cardiff stables' (Abstract, 1872); *A.* xi (1874), 150–51; R.I.B.A. Arc IV, i, 1–9. Builder: Estcourt of Gloucester (*Plans and Prospects, op. cit.*, no. 23).

60 Cardiff Drawgs., roll 7; Blair, *Bute*, 78.

61 R.I.B.A., S.N.B., xxxv (1868), 36, 55; *Victorian Church Art*, D 6: misattributed to Burges's Convent

between pp. 268–71
of the Good Shepherd, Cardiff.

62 'Temporary Chapel, Cardiff' (Abstract, 1878); 'Heating of temporary chapel from main boiler' (V. & A. Estim. Bk., 22 Oct. 1878); R.I.B.A., S.N.B., lviii (1878), 61.

63 Cardiff Drawgs., xxvii.

64 'The Altar at present in the Domestic Chapel here at Falkland, together with the bronze cross and candlesticks [P.L.U.] belonging to it . . . part of the fittings of the Domestic Chapel formerly at Cardiff, designed by the late Mr. Burges, which I have had the intention of re-erecting on the upper part of the keep of Cardiff Castle as a Domestic Oratory for the set of family rooms I have had the intention of building there' (Mt. St. MSS., codicil, 2 Dec. 1895). The Archbishop's Chapel, Edinburgh (1906–7) was designed by R. W. Schultz, in accordance with a further codicil (ibid., 3 Dec. 1895), to accommodate the unfinished fittings of the Falkland Domestic Chapel, including woodwork and sculpture (B. xcii 1907, 271). The Private Chapel at Falkland House, also by Schultz, remains *in situ*; as does the chapel at Falkland Palace, restored by John Kinross.

65 Mt. St., MSS., Bute letters, 24 Jan. 1873.

66 *ibid.*, 12 July 1874.

67 Monogrammed date.

68 V. & A. Estim. Bk., 6 Jan. 1876.

69 *ibid.*, 12 June 1876: £45. Possibly inspired by J. H. Hefner-Alteneck, *Trachten des Christlichen Mittelalters* I (Frankfurt, 1840–54), i, pl. 7: Burges possessed a copy.

70 *Art Jnl.* 1881, 192; 'Lord Bute's Oratory' (Abstract, 1872) . . . Shields for Oratory at Cardiff' (*ibid.*, 1876). Burke supplied the marble (V. & A. Estim. Bk., 26 Jan. 1876). Westlake received £150 in part payment (Mt. St. MSS., 5 Sept. 1876; R.I.B.A., S.N.B., li, 1875, 70, 75).

71 V. & A. Estim. Bk., 29 May and 7, 12 June 1876. Hart, Son and Peard's estimate (£91) was accepted in preference to Barkentin's (£120). The 'B.V. Panel' was cast by Hatfield from that at Studley (*ibid.*, 27 April 1876; R.I.B.A., S.N.B., lii, 1875, 90, 92).

72 *A.* xviii (1877), 158. By Hart, Son & Peard.

73 Vellum S.B., 19; *C.I.T. Guide, Toscana* i (Florence, 1934), 25, 41.

74 R.I.B.A., S.N.B., xliii (1872), 16; allegorical figures, *ibid.*, xlv (1873), 73.

75 *Jnl. of Decorative Art* xi (1891), 21.

76 K. Campbell, *Campbell, Smith & Co.* (1973), 3, citing *The Topical Times* 17 Nov. 1894; *Art Jnl.* 1887, 192.

77 R.I.B.A., S.N.B., xlvi (1873), 13–14; *Scribner's Monthly*, March 1876.

78 R.I.B.A., S.N.B., xlvi (1873), 15, 38, 40.

79 Cardiff Drawgs., xvii, 89; V. & A. Estim. Bk., 1 Feb. 1877. Fisher was responsible for the turquoise patterned hearth (*ibid.*, 14 Sept. 1875).

80 Cardiff Drawgs., xvii, 83 (wmk. 1872); V. & A. Estim. Bk. 31 Aug. 1877.

81 Cardiff Drawgs., xvii, 79.

82 *ibid.*, xvii, 80A, Roll 6; Mt. St. MSS., Burges to Bute, 16 Oct. 1873.

83 Cardiff Drawgs., xvii, 80–82, 84; R.I.B.A., S.N.B., xlviii (1874), 27.

84 Mt. St. MSS., Frame's memo, May 1890.

85 H. Gally Knight, *The Normans in Sicily* (1838), 244.

86 P. Morey, *Charpente de la Cathédrale de Messine* (Paris, 1841), pls. 3–4. Burges possessed a copy.

87 Lo Faso Pietransanta, Duca di Serradifalco, *Del Duomo di Monreale* (Palermo, 1838).

88 Burges possessed a copy of J. C. Murphy's *Arabian Antiquities of Spain* (1815), with plates showing combinations of classical columns, Arab domes and Gothic battlements. H. Gally Knight described Monreale as 'Latin in its shape, Roman in its colonnade, Byzantine in its mosaics, Greek in its sculpture, Saracenic and Norman in many of its mouldings, features and details . . . a most curious combination of styles' (*Normans in Sicily*, 280–90).

89 A.C.T.E. Prisse D'Avennes, *L'Art Arabe* (Paris, 1877), ii, pl. lxix.

90 Cardiff Drawgs., xvii, 75, 77.

91 Of Bute, see *A.* xxi (1879), 89; Haig's view.

92 *D.N.B.*, eg. 'The Alchemist' (1855), 'The Rosicrucians' (1856).

93 V. & A. Estim. Bk., 10 April, 21 July, 30 Aug. 1876; Cardiff Drawgs., xvii, 69, including Burges's instruction for enamelling and engraving; R.I.B.A., S.N.B., xlix (1874), 42–3 and liv (1876), 33. Bronze heraldry by Hatfield, 1875 (Cardiff Drawgs., xvii, 67–8).

94 V. & A. Estim. Bk., 10 April, 21 July 1876.

95 R.I.B.A., S.N.B., l (1875), 23–4.

96 R.I.B.A., S.N.B., li (1875), 15–16; Cardiff Drawgs., xvii, 59, 64 (wmk. 1876).

97 Cardiff Drawgs., xvii, 70–72. For the W.C., see *ibid.*, 5.

98 V. & A. Estim. Bk., 14 May 1879.

99 'Stone panes of glass, to use an Irishism' (E. xxii, N.S. xix, 1861, 157).

1 Burne-Jones, after visiting the marble yard of Farmer and Brindley, 1891 (G. B.-J., *Memorials of E. B.-J.*, ii, 223).

2 R.I.B.A., S.N.B., xliii (1872), 13; V. & A. Estim. Bk., 2 Nov. 1875; Cardiff Drawgs., xvii, 19. The bird glass in the lobby was made by Saunders, in 1876, from drawings by Richard Holmes (Cardiff Drawgs., xvii, 21, 61–2).

3 V. & A. Estim. Bk., 23 Nov. 1875.

4 Mt. St. MSS., 20 Oct. 1884.

5 Cardiff Drawgs., xvii, 8 (wmk. 1872) and 33 (tendril carvings by Nicholls).

6 *ibid.*, 16 (section, wmk. 1872). Preliminary sketches, R.I.B.A., S.N.B., xlv (1873), 65–6; xlix (1874), 54; li (1875), 78.

7 Black marble, Belgian granite and Sicilian mosaic

400 Notes and References

between pp. 271–73

were supplied by Burke & Co. (V. & A. Estim. Bk., 25 Aug. 1875). For tiles, see *ibid.*, 12, 18, 24 Aug. 1875; Cardiff Drawgs., xvii, 18 A–C. For cross sections, see *ibid.*, 4, 23, 26, 44–6. For a previous scheme, with pink marble columns, see *ibid.*, 25.

8 *A.* xviii (1877), 72 and xxvii (1882), 251; R.I.B.A., S.N.B., li (1875), 60. Designed by Burges, modelled by Nicholls (plaster model: £78 18s. od., V. & A. Estim. Bk., 28 Nov. 1876), cast by Hatfield (*ibid.*, 23 Aug. 1876). For alterations, see *ibid.*, 2 Jan. 1879.

9 For variants, see Cardiff Drawgs., xvii, 57 and 58 a–b. Hatfield, Barkentin and Fucigna were responsible, although Phyffers also sent in estimates (R.I.B.A., S.N.B., liv, 1876–7, 32 and lvii, 1877–8, 5; V. & A. Estim. Bk., 13, 18 Jan. 1876).

10 E. K. Guhl and W. Korner, *The Life of the Greeks and the Romans* (1875), 456, fig. 455; E. Trollope, *Illustrations of Ancient Art*, pl xiii (6). Burges possessed both books. Hart's estimate was £88 each, weight 196 lbs.; Hatfield's was £192 (V. & A. Estim. Bk., 12 June 1877). Burges notes: 'make handles sufficiently strong' (Cardiff Drawgs., xvii, 54).

11 Elijah's controversy with the prophets of Baal (Kings 1/18). Tiles by Simpson; cartoons by Lonsdale, 1874 (Cardiff Drawgs., xvii, 51–2, 53, 53a, and cartoon colln.).

12 V. & A. Estim. Bk., 10 April 1876.

13 Cardiff Drawgs., xvii, 55–6; R.I.B.A., S.N.B., liv (1876–7), 10–11, 87. Hatfield's estimate was £100 (V. & A. Estim. Bk., 28 June 1877).

14 *Art Jnl.* 1881, 192. Haig was commissioned to make a perspective view from Burges's own drawings (V. & A. Estim. Bk., 22 Jan. 1877).

15 Abstract, 1861; *A.* xxi (1879), 281.

16 *A.* xxi (1879), 281.

17 V. & A. Estim. Bk., 14 Oct. 1875. For finials etc., see *ibid.*, 30 Sept. 1875. 'Cardiff Bridge' (Abstract, 1875). The West gate, crossing the moat further South, was constructed in 1921.

18 R.I.B.A., S.N.B., xlviii (1874), 44, 46; Cardiff Drawgs., xxvii, 43 a–c; V. & A. Estim. Bk., 6 Feb., 21 March, 10 April 1877.

19 The St. David's Door.

20 Over the entrance porch.

21 Saunders & Co. were still producing versions of these in 1888–91 (Saunders Ledger, 1887–9).

22 'I want ... some rich and beautiful work, so please do your best' (Frame to Nicholls, 20 May 1884, Frame letter bk., Mt. St. MSS.).

23 Cardiff Drawgs., xxvii; *B.N.* xlii (1882), 268, 358, 572; 696.

24 R.I.B.A., S.N.B., xlii (1872), 9–10, 17, 44, 64; Cardiff Drawgs., xiv, 62: 30 Aug. 1877, 18 June 1877 and 19 Nov. 1879. These drawings suggest several preliminary investigations.

25 V. & A. Estim. Bk., 5 Sept. 1877.

26 *ibid.*, 7 Jan. 1881.

27 The fire dogs recall Viollet-le-Duc, *Dictionnaire*, vi (1863), 73

28 V. & A. Estim. Bk., 9 Jan. 1879, 20 May 1880; Cardiff Drawgs., Roll 1 and xxvii, 40 a–e.

29 Fiona Pearson, *Goscombe John* (1979), 25, 78.

30 Mt. St. MSS., Frame letter bk., 880: 3 July 1889; 887: 6 Aug. 1889; 897: 10 Aug. 1889.

31 Camb. Univ. Lib., Add. MS. 5083, f. 163.

32 For construction, see V. & A. Estim. Bk., 12 Aug. 1875. For chimneys by Nicholls, tiles by Simpson and painting by Campbell, see *ibid.*, 29 Jan., 30 Sept. and 19, 24 Nov. 1879. For sub-Burgesian furniture, see Cardiff Drawgs., xviii, 1–3.

33 V. & A., P. & D., 93 E.2, 27–8: drawn for Burges by T. M. Deane, 1872.

34 Under Sesom-Hiley's direction (eg. nursery, Cardiff Drawgs., xxvii, 14), in general accordance with Burges's designs. The Tank Tower has a rainwater head d.1914, but Burges's drawings – including nursery, skittle alley and kitchen, are d.1879–80 (Cardiff Drawgs., xviii, 4). For preliminary exterior designs by Burges, see *ibid.*, xxii, 75 a,b. For Burges's kitchen designs (1880), see Cardiff Drawgs., viii, 19. Lonsdale's drawings for the nursery frieze (repeated in Tower House) are now in the colln. of Mr. John A. Evans. During the mid-nineteenth century the nursery was situated above the Drawing Room, in the apartment which became Lady Bute's bedroom after 1872 (H. Sesom-Hiley, *Cardiff Castle*, reprinted from *Cardiff Times* and *S. Wales Daily News*, 1912, 21).

35 V. & A., P. & D., 93 E.2, 105–8.

36 e.g. 'I have seen Mr. Lonsdale and he will be very glad to go to Cardiff and make the sketches for the Hall, Chapel and [Guest] Tower decorations under your direction' (Burges to Bute, 9 June 1874, Mt. St. MSS.).

37 Mt. St. MSS., Bute letters, 29 Jan. 1873; 28 Feb. 1875.

38 Cardiff Drawgs., xxvi Lonsdale's cartoons for stained glass, 26 Nov. 1873), xvii (furnishing sketches, 26 Feb. 1880), xxvii, 25–6 (marquetry panels, with insects etc.) and 29–30 (walls and doors).

39 'Cardiff Library Decorations' (Abstract, 1880). 'There has been a great deal done down here, and some of the rooms, e.g. the library, look beautiful' (Mt. St. MSS., Bute letters, 1 June 1881). One door is inscribed 1880.

40 Cardiff Drawgs., Roll 4. Pullan worked on at least one of these cartoons.

41 Variants, R.I.B.A., S.N.B., xlvii (1874), 2, 15. Nicholls charged £270 (V. & A. Estim. Bk., 15 Nov. 1873).

42 *ibid.*, 6 March, 28 April, June 1880.

43 *ibid.*, Sept. 1879, June 1880.

44 *ibid.*, 23 Nov. 1880.

45 *ibid.*, 11 July, 15 Sept. 1878; 21 Aug. 1879; 16 Nov.

between pp. 273–76
1880. 'Gillow began Cardiff bookcases' (*Abstract, 1878*).

46 *A.P.S.D.*, ill. vol., drawn by Burges.

47 Cardiff Drawgs., xxii, xxiv.

48 Cardiff Drawgs., xii. Bute took particular interest in this part of the design, giving it 'very great consideration indeed' (Mt. St. MSS., Burges to Bute, 9 June 1874).

49 *A.* xxiii (1880), 81. 'Lonsdale did sketches for Cardiff Hall' (*Abstract*, 1875).

50 *A.* xxiii (1880), 81, 169, 251; plan: Cardiff Drawgs., xxvii.

51 For this macabre story, see W. Beattie, *Castles and Abbeys* ii (1844), 309–13.

52 The same source supplied the prototype for the doorway tympana (R. N. Shaw, *Architectural Sketches from the Continent* (1858), 13–14.

53 Cardiff Drawgs., xii, xiv, xxvii.

54 Inscription; V. & A. Estim. Bk., 21 Sept. 1880.

55 Cardiff Drawgs., S. William Frame. The sideboard was designed by Burges in 1874 and executed in 1878–9 (R.I.B.A., S.N.B., xlviii, 1874, 47, 49; Cardiff Drawgs., heraldry folder). For comic animal carving, see R.I.B.A., S.N.B., lii (1875–6), 93–4.

56 Cardiff Drawgs., xii; V. & A. Estim. Bk., 28 Dec. 1876 (fireplace), 30 March 1881 (bays).

57 *ibid.*, 1 Jan, 23 and 26 Feb., 8 March 1876; 30 Sept. 1879; 16 Jan. 1880.

58 *ibid.*, 30 Sept. 1879; 29 April 1880.

59 Burges consulted Rice Merrick's *Book of Glamorganshire Antiquities* (1578; ed. Sir I. Phillips Bt., 1825); Cardiff Drawgs., xxii; xxiv, 69; xxvii, 33, 33a; xxix, 32.

60 Cardiff Drawgs., xxix, 32.

61 W. Beattie, *Castles and Abbeys of England* i (1884), 32, ill.

62 Sections, d.1880 (Cardiff Drawgs., vi); Mt. St. MSS., Frame letter bk., 649: 24 Aug. 1888, Campbell's final bill for painting.

63 For other Pre-Raphaelite versions of this theme, by Burne-Jones and Spencer-Stanhope, see M. Harrison and B. Waters, *Burne-Jones*, pls. 17, 184, 265.

64 Mt. St. MSS., Frame letter bk., 8, 9, 28: 6 Feb. 1884. F. G. Smith was also working as cartoonist for the firm at this time. (*Ex inf.*, Martin Harrison).

65 A. Normand, *Architecture des nations étrangères* (Paris, 1870); *Linderhoff Palace* (Official Guide, Munich, 1976); and French periodicals cited in B. Bergdoll, 'The Architecture of A. M. Duthoit, 1837–89' (B.A. Cantab., 1979), 100. César Daly visited Cairo in 1869–70 (*Revue Generale de l'Arch.* 1883, 198–9); *B.* xxxvi (1878), 887.

66 Quoted in *Eastern Encounters* (Fine Art Soc., 1978), 40.

67 See general discussion, *Apollo* ciii (1976), 258; Sarah Searight, *The British in the Middle East* (1969).

68 *Eastern Encounters, op. cit.*, 46.

69 J. P. Seddon, *Memoirs . . . of Thomas Seddon* (1858); *R.S.A.Jnl.*, 8 May 1857, 360–62; *Athenaeum*, 7 June 1856, 719.

70 The poem first appeared in Bradlaugh's *National Reformer*. Thomson is otherwise known for 'The City of Dreadful Night' (*Diary of W. M. Rossetti*, 1870–73, ed. Odette Borand, Oxford, 1977, 157 n.2, 266–7).

71 'B.V. at Surrey' (*Abstract*, 1872); 'Bought breast-plate with B.V.' (*ibid.*, 1873).

72 *B.N.* xxvi (1874), 68 (Egyptian-Arabic architecture); V. & A., P. & D., 93 E4, p. 43 (Capella Palatina, Palermo). Axel Haig was specifically despatched to Palermo by Burges, and drew the honeycombed ceilings there in 1875. For background see A. Racinet, *L'Ornement Polychrome*, 2 v. (Paris, 1869–87); J. Bourgoin, *Les Arts Arabes* (Paris, 1867). In 1870 Burges designed a 'Kiosque' for Col. C. H. Luard (1837–1905). See Abstract 1869–70. P.L.U.

73 e.g. pls. xxviii–ix: 'La Mosquée El Moyed'; and *B.* xlviii (1885), 232. Burges also owned J. Bourgoin, *Les Arts Arabes* (1873) and C. E. Clerget, *Mélanges d'Ornements de tous les styles Persan, Mauresque, Arabe etc.* (Paris, ?1843). For 'Moucharabieh' screens see Bourgoin, pl. 23 and *B.N.* xliv (1883), 250.

74 Prisse D'Avennes, III, pls. cxxxiv–cxxxviii: 'Moucharabyeh et Grillages en Bois' (eighteenth century); pl. cxliv: 'Gama El-Seydeh Zeynab: chemsah ou vitrail en plâtre ajouré (fourteenth century); pl. cxl: 'Maison Sidi Youçouf Adami, chambre de la nourrice'. For a technical account of stalactitic construction, see *ibid.*, I, 176 *et seq.* For 'Arabian' lattice, see L. Parvillée, *Architecture et Decorations Turques* (Paris, 1874); *Revue Generale de l'Architecture* 1879; Texier and Pullan, *Architecture Byzantine* (Paris, 1864); 62; E. T. Rogers, 'Street scenes, Cairo', *Art Jnl.* 1880, 214: 'The upper projecting windows are made of lattice work . . . small pieces of turned wood resembling large beads, and ornamental reels, and rosettes . . . in which the apertures for light are very small. They are sometimes painted green or red. A window of this kind is called a 'meshrebîyeh' or a place for drink, because water coolers are placed within to be exposed to a current of air.'

75 V. & A. Estim Bk., 3 Dec. 1880.

76 Ceramic variations, Cardiff Drawgs. xxviii, 18–20.

77 R.I.B.A., S.N.B., lxii (1880), 86.

78 By S. J. Waring & Sons, dem.1926 (*C.L.* clvi, 1974, 1599).

79 Sir R. Sykes, *Sledmere Guide*, pl. 17, p. 24.

80 By Romaine-Walker, 1888–90.

81 J. Mordaunt Crook, *C.L.* cliii (1973), 1797.

82 Bergdoll, *op. cit., passim.*; *Revue Generale de l'Architecture* 1877, pls. 3–7.

83 By Somers Clarke, *B.N.* x (1863), 200.

between pp. 276–80

83a By Digby Wyatt, 1858, in Fife House, Whitehall Yard (ill., *I.L.N.* 6 March 1858, 228–30). Wyatt also designed a Moorish billiard-room (1864) at 12 Kensington Palace Gardens (*Survey of London* xxxvii, 1973, 168, pl. 95).

84 By T. Hayter Lewis, 1852–54; burnt 1882 (*Survey of London* xxxiv, 492–9). For a Moorish drawing room of c.1894, see E. Aslin, *19th c. Furniture* (1962), pl. 106.

85 'Arab room' (Abstract, 1881); Cardiff Drawgs., d.26 March 1881. Some drawings for glass are signed by Pullan after Burges's death (Cardiff Drawgs., xxi).

86 By J. P. Grant. The adjacent room, between the stairs and the Banqueting Hall, is dated '1785, 1874, 1928'. For the decision to abandon Burges's scheme, see Mt. St. MSS., 4th Marquess to 3rd Marchioness, 20 Oct. 1927).

87 R.I.B.A., S.N.B., lii (1875), 60, 62. 'Octagon staircase' (Abstract, 1876, 1881); 'Octagon staircase decoration' (*ibid.*, 1880). Painted by Campbell (1884).

88 R.I.B.A., S.N.B., xlix (1874), 72.

89 Cardiff Drawgs., xxvii, 24; *E.* xxii, N.S. xix (1861), 93–8; 'Lord Bute's lion' (Abstract, 1878). Nicholls charged £30 for modelling the lion (V. & A. Estim. Bk., 15 Feb. 1879). For rival estimates by Hart and Barkentin, see *ibid.*, 28 Nov. and 4, 9 Dec. 1878.

90 *B.* xxxii (1874), 409.

91 R.A. 1146: *Marble Halls, op. cit.*, 29; *A.* xii (1874), 6 and xxvii (1882), 203; R.I.B.A., S.N.B., xlv (1873), 63, xlvi (1873), 20 and lviii (1878), 61; Cardiff Drawgs., xxvii, 3–4; 'Cardiff staircase' (Abstract, 1874), 'Great staircase' (*ibid.*, 1880).

92 *A.* xvii (1877), 322 (modelled by Nicholls).

93 *B.* xxxii (1874), 409.

94 *A.* xi (1874), 147.

95 *A.* vii (1872), 39.

96 *B.N.* xxvi (1874), 539.

97 *Contemporary Rev.* xxiv (1874), 750–51; *A.* xii (1874), 175.

98 *D.N.B.*; *Studio* xvi (1899), 115. Goscombe John joined the Bute workshop in 1874, working on the dining room shutters; he trained under Nicholls, 1881–6, and executed a statue of St. John the Baptist (1894) for Bute's garden at St. John's Lodge, Regent's Park. His father Thomas John (1834–93) – Bute's foreman woodcarver and inlayer – executed an oak staircase (c.1875–6) for Mount Stuart, later transferred to St. John's Lodge. P.L.U. (Pearson, *Goscombe John*, 73–4, 78n.).

99 *A.* ix (1873), 8; Cardiff Drawgs., xxi, 55–6. Inlay by Thomas John; metalwork by William Shaville of Long Acre, London.

1 Cardiff Drawgs., xxix, 8, 8a, 9, 9a.

2 e.g. *ibid.*, xxi, 73–89.

3 *ibid.*, xxi, 20–21.

4 *ibid.*, xvii, 38.

5 *B.N.* lxii (1892), 8, 69; Mt. St. MSS., Frame letter bk., 303; 18 July 1887, 582; 14 June 1888, 659: 21 Sept. 1888, 667: 3 Oct. 1888; *Plans and Prospects* (Welsh Arts Council, 1975), no. 12: models; Wilars de Honecourt, *Sketchbook*, ed. Lassus, Quicherat and Willis (1859), pl. xiii. Until c.1930 they stood in front of the moat garden facing Castle St. On removal to their present site they were supplemented by additional figures carved by Carrick of Edinburgh. In general at Cardiff, Burges supplied sketches and Nicholls models for all the sculpture; executant carvers, sent down from Nicholls' workshops in London, included Charles Bursill, Henry Gunthorp and Nathaniel Hitch (Pearson, *Goscombe John*, 77).

6 The Bute family presented Cardiff Castle to the Corporation of Cardiff on 24 June 1948, following the death of the 4th Marquess in 1947 (for his architectural career, see obits. *Glasgow Herald* 28 April 1947; *Scotsman* 26 April 1947). Family interest in Cardiff Docks had already been relinquished in 1922, and most of their Cardiff property in 1938. The 4th Marquess was a doughty opponent of 'modernismus'. In one battle with the Cardiff Corporation, he announced: 'If that is modern architecture, then I thank God for my castle' (*Sunday Express* 22 May 1936, 9). On the eve of the General Strike in 1926, his factor asked for instructions. Back came the telegraphic reply: 'Raise the drawbridge!' (*ex inf.* Lord Boyd of Merton).

7 G. T. Clark, in *Archaeologia Cambrensis*, N.S. i (1850), 241–50.

8 Tennyson, *Idylls*: 'The Marriage of Geraint'.

9 Report, 27 Dec. 1872, 15 (D. of E. Lib.). For ills. from this report, see *A.* xi (1874), 212–4, 225–6. For preliminary notes, see R.I.B.A., S.N.B., xliii (1872), 33, 37–8, 56; xliv (1872–3), 7, 38.

10 Mt. St. MSS., Bute letters, 11 March 1875. Burges's diary contains few references to Castell Coch: there is a seven-year gap between 'Began Castell Coch' (Abstract, 1872) and 'Castell Coch great room' (*ibid.*, 1879).

11 *B.N.* xxi (1871), 158.

12 The architects were Kempson and Fowler of Llandaff (*Western Mail* 7 June 1892). Tiles, modelled on fifteenth-century specimens found on site, were made by Godwin of Lugwardine.

13 *King's Works* i (1963), 231–2; W. Rees, *Caerphilly Castle* (Cardiff, 1937); G. T. Clark, in *Archaeologia Cambrensis*, N.S. i (1850), 251–304. Burges drew the West gate, from measurements by T. M. Deane, 1872 (V. & A., P. & D., 93 E.2, 41–6).

14 Blair, *Bute*, 200.

15 Weller MSS.; V. & A., P. & D., 93 E.2, 34: June 1874; J. K. Hewinson, *The Isle of Bute in the Olden Time* ii (1895), frontispiece and 107 *et seq.*; 'Report on Rothesay Castle ... To Rothesay' (Abstract, 1871); 'Rothesay report' (*ibid.*, 1872); 'To

between pp. 280–84

Rothesay' (*ibid.*, 1874); R.I.B.A., S.N.B., xlii (1871), 6–52, 75–8. For the castle prior to restoration, see *I.L.N.* 1 Sept. 1888.

16 'In a year the Kitchen Tower will be finished – and will really have more room in it than Mochrum' (Mt. St. MSS., Bute letters, 1 Sept. 1875). 'I went yesterday morning to Castell Coch with Burges. I believe it will get on fast, and that the two halls, cellar, ground-floor room, kitchen, and great, lesser and least bedrooms with the wall-gallery will be done by the autumn (*ibid.*, 9 May 1876). For the Kitchen Tower, see Cardiff Drawgs., xxxiv, 1875–7.

17 'Castell Coch is very comfortable ... At the same time, it still wants a lot doing to it' (Mt. St. MSS., Bute letters, 1 June 1881).

18 Cardiff Drawgs., 1877, endorsed 'Hoard not to be done ... No hoard'. A similar 'Bretache' survived on the Castle St. front of Cardiff Castle until World War I.

19 Cardiff Drawgs., xxxii, 1877–9; plans and sections, R.I.B.A., Arc. IV, iii, 1–4 and IV, iv, 1 7.

20 *B.* xxii (1864), 448–50.

21 M. Girouard, *The Victorian Country House* (1971), 155 and *C.L.* cxxxi (1962), 1092. For other accounts, see W. G. Howell in *A.R.* cix (1951), 39–46; P. Floud, *Castell Coch* (1974); T. Measham, *Castell Coch and William Burges* (1978). The contractor was Albert Estcourt of Gloucester; the Clerk of Works, J. T. Wright; the master mason, William Blight. The great size of the limestone blocks resulted in the death of at least one labourer, George Maidment (*S. Wales Daily News*, 1 July 1879). Burges's red-brown roof tiles have recently been replaced with green. His glazed ridge-tiles – by Doulton of Lambeth – modelled on one original example, survive.

22 Viollet-le-Duc, *Dictionnaire*, s.v. 'Tour' (ix, 1868, 67 *et seq.*); *Architecture Militaire* (1854).

23 Report, *op. cit.*, 5–6, 11–14; V. & A., P. & D., 93 E.2, 99–102: from measurements by T. M. Deane, 1872.

24 *ibid.*, 7. He might also have found precedents for conical towers at Nunney Castle, Somerset, and Conisborough Castle, Yorkshire.

25 A. A. Pettigrew, 'Welsh Vineyards', *Trans. Cardiff Naturalists' Soc.* xvi (1884), 6 and lix (1926), 25; *Western Mail* 15 Nov. 1929.

26 According to legend, Castell Coch is haunted by the ghost of a man who buried treasure in its foundations (A. D. Hippesley Cox, *Haunted Britain*, 1973, 143, 145).

27 'Report', *op. cit.*, 16.

28 It cost £60 (V. & A. Estim. Bk., 2 May 1878).

29 The Kitchen furniture is even plainer, but well detailed – e.g. the cupboard, of oak studded with steel.

30 Painted by Campbell and Smith (V. & A. Estim. Bk., 12 March 1878).

31 Burges's drawings (Cardiff Drawgs.) showing chimneypiece and gallery as executed are d.Nov. 1879.

32 'Report', *op. cit.*, 11.

33 Whether Burges derived this motif from Viollet-le-Duc is not clear; it was certainly picked up from Burges by the Arts and Crafts Movement, e.g. Harrison Townshend's Whitechapel Art Gallery.

34 Tennyson, *Idylls*: 'The Marriage of Geraint'.

35 Girouard, *Victorian Country House*, 156; *C.L.* cxxxi (1962), 1095, cover pl., and 1175.

36 Cardiff Drawgs., xxxii, 1879.

37 V. & A. Estim. Bk., 28 Sept. 1880.

38 eg. Mt. St. MSS., Frame letter bk., 71: 6 Oct. 1886; 79: 16 Oct. 1886; 300: 14 July 1887 and 313: 29 July 1887.

39 Mt. St. MSS., Frame letter bk., 44: 16 Aug. 1886; 168: 3 Jan. 1887; 346: 13 Sept. 1887. Bute took particular exception to the peacock as 'badly done and unlike the bird'.

40 *ibid.*, 110: 11 Nov. 1886; 225: 4 March 1887.

41 The bed resembles M. B. Adams, *Examples of English Houses and Furniture* (1888), pl. 24. Dressing table and washstand are plainer versions of those at Tower House.

42 Drawgs., Nov. 1891, tipped into 'Report', *op. cit.*; E. Aslin, *Nineteenth-Century English Furniture* (1962), 63, pls. 75–6; R. W. Symonds and B. B. Whineray, *Victorian Furniture* (1962), 49, pl. 71.

43 Cardiff Drawgs., xxxii, 1879.

44 e.g. Mt. St. MSS., Frame letter bk., 274: 19 May 1887; 308: 20 July 1887; 630: 9 Aug. 1888.

45 *ibid.*, 342: 9 Sept. 1887; 346: 13 Sept. 1887.

46 *ibid.*, 303, 18 July 1887. Burges's painted model (*A.R.* cix 1951, 46), P.L.U.

47 Cf. Viollet-le-Duc, *Mobilier* i (1858), 178; *B.N.* xlv (1883), 258–9.

48 Tennyson, *Idylls*: 'The Coming of Arthur'. Eight of these windows, made by Saunders from cartoons by Lonsdale, are now in the colln. of Hon. C. Lennox-Boyd; others are at Cardiff Castle (Cardiff Drawgs., xxxiii, 1876–7; V. & A. Estim. Bk., 16 July 1878). Their iconography – saints and angels – was based on Mrs. Jameson, *Sacred and Legendary Art* (1848 etc.). Pullan seems to have helped with this section of the work. See also R.I.B.A., S.N.B., liv (1876–7), 52.

49 V. & A. Estim. Bk., 12 Aug. 1875, 12 March 1877, 24 Dec. 1878.

50 'Cardiff Chapel, Barn' (Abstract, 1870). This convent, for the sisters of the Good Shepherd, in Ty Gwyn Rd., was dem. c. 1967. The balacchino seems to have been at least partly Bute's own design (R.I.B.A., S.N.B., xxxix, 1870–71, 27). Bute also 'set up a great screen and rood in the Fathers of Charity's church', Cardiff – i.e. St. Peter's Roath (Blair, *Bute*, 93).

51 Completed to slightly different designs by J. F. Bentley and N. H. J. Westlake. 'To Dumfries

between pp. 284–87

House about church' (Abstract, 1878); 'Can glass be put in which is at Balmory and Chiswick ... yes' (R.I.B.A., S.N.B., lxii (1880), 26); W. de L'Hôpital, *Westminster Cathedral and its Architect* ii (1919), 608. Saunders supplied the glass, from cartoons by Lonsdale (V. & A. Estin. Bk., 16 July and 26 Sept. 1878; 10 Jan., 25 Sept. and 25 Nov. 1879; 10 Feb. 1880). Westlake told Bute that he had tried to keep Bentley to 'an earlier and more Burgesslike' style; 'Mr. Burges was so fond of the open broad character of work and so disliked the acute or *perfect decorated*' (Mt. St. MSS., 2 Dec. 1884). The interior decoration – apart from the painted roof of the apse – has been much altered.

52 H. S. Goodhart-Rendel, *English Architecture Since the Regency* (1953), 148.

53 At St. Margaret's Roath: *A.* vii (1872), 303, 319; *B.* xxviii (1870), 564. The North transept (1885) incorporates a Bute family mausoleum.

54 At Glasgow University: *B.N.* xxxviii (1880), 10, 23 and xlv (1883), 208. Obits.: *B.* civ (1913), 643; *B.N.* civ (1913), 773, 880; *R.I.B.A. Jnl.* xx (1912–13), 614, 648.

55 For details of these later works, see J. Mordaunt Crook, 'Patron Extraordinary: John, 3rd Marquess of Bute', in *Victorian South Wales: Architecture, Industry and Society*, ed. P. Howell (Victorian Soc., 1970), 3–22.

56 *C.L.* xxxi (1912), 130–38; cxxvi (1959), 118–21, 178–81; cliv (1973), 364–6. See also I. Moncreiffe, *The Royal Palace of Falkland* (Edinburgh, 1973 edn.). Bute had been impressed by Kinross's *Details from Italian Buildings, Chiefly Renaissance* (1882).

57 Obit.: *B.* clxxx (1951), 663; *Who's Who in Architecture* (1926); D. Ottewill, 'R. W. Schultz' (M. A., Courtauld, 1977 and *Architectural History* xxii, 1979, 88–115). It was presumably as a pupil of Rowand Anderson that Schultz first encountered Bute.

58 'I told Burges to put up the stained window' (Mt. St. MSS., Bute letters, 22 Sept. 1879); 'I think you had better leave the chapel as it is. The decorations are very pretty and not at all heathen in character ... The only thing I thought of doing to it was taking out the brown wooden bookcases ... [and replacing them with] sacred images or pictures' (*ibid.*, n.d.). After Burges's death Lonsdale was responsible for four windows of the Seasons in the great dome at Cardiff; these were later transferred to St. John's Lodge (Mt. St. MSS., Frame letter bk., 822: 17 May 1889; 838: 23 May 1889).

59 R.I.B.A., S.N.B., li (1875), 57; *C.L.* xxxii (1912), 162–7.

60 Mt. St. MSS., Bute letters, 26 Aug. 1875. Park seems to have been the executant architect.

61 Hunter Blair, *Medley of Memories* (1919), 126.

62 Cf. *Vitruvius Scoticus*, pl. 31. During the 1760s, James Craig produced designs for alterations which seem not to have been executed. See [Catherine Armet], *Mount Stuart* (Rothesay, 1966), 4; prints by W. Watts (1785) and W. Daniell (1817); watercolour by Hannah Tighe, wife of Lord James Stuart (colln. Hon. P. Crichton-Stuart).

63 *North British Daily Mail* 14 Sept. 1868, 3.

64 Abstract, 1876. A libel action against the *Hornet*, an ephemeral journal, involved several members of the Pre-Raphaelite circle. Some judged it wiser to leave London.

65 Blair, *Bute*, 218; Mt. St. MSS., Campbell and Smith, 14 June 1877.

66 Mt. St. MSS., Bute letters, 29 Jan. 1873.

67 *ibid.*, Bute's list of figures.

68 *ibid.*, Bute letters, 10 March 1875.

69 Mt. St. MSS., telegram: 3 Dec. 1877. After the fire Bute's family lived at Balmory House, where Burges undertook minor works (V. & A. Estim. Bk., 3 Sept. 1878).

70 Mt. St. MSS., Bute letters, 2 April 1872.

71 Contractor: Patterson; Clerk of Works: Stewart (Anderson's diary, 1879; colln. Sir William Kinninmonth).

72 *B.N.* xl (1881), 141, 789.

73 [Armet], *op. cit.*, 7.

74 Anderson's diary, 1913–14 (*ex inf.* Dr. Peter Savage).

75 *Western Mail* 10 Oct. 1900. Groome, *Ordnance Gazetteer of Scotland* ii (1885), 76 suggests £200,000.

76 Obit. *B.* cxxi (1921), 732.

77 *The Times* 3 June 1921, 13.

78 *B.* xxxvii (1879), 862; *A.* xxii (1879), 73; *B.N.* xxxvii (1879), 109.

79 Also, perhaps, the N.W. front of Blois (Banister Fletcher, *History of Architecture*, 1975 edn., 870).

80 To H. D. Grissell, 15 Sept. 1870 (Blair, *Bute*, 92).

81 Blair, *Bute*, 114.

82 *ibid.*, 243. Bute sent Anderson to Saragossa; he returned with photos of relics of Peter de Luna (Mt. St. MSS., Diary, 14 Nov. 1895).

83 Figures drawn by Ballantine, modelled by Hayes and cast by Fisher and Laidlaw of Edinburgh under Balfour Paull's direction (Anderson diary, *op. cit.*; Mt. St. MSS., 22 Jan. 1912).

84 The mosaic Madonna on the East front is also Russian, executed in 1898, also at the St. Petersburg Academy.

85 Mt. St. MSS., Bute letters to Anderson, re Galston church.

86 Description by T. L. Donaldson, *B.N.* xix (1870), 489–90.

87 Blair, *Bute*, 242–3.

88 *A.* ix (1873), 222.

89 K. Campbell, *Campbell, Smith & Co.* (1973), 51: 1890–91; Mt. St. MSS., Frame letter bk., 549–50: 5 May 1888.

90 *B.* liv (1888), 313. For details, see Mt. St. MSS., Frame letter bk., 404: 14 Dec. 1887; 548: 5 May

between pp. 287–91

1888.

91 e.g. Mt. St. MSS., Frame letter bk., 638: 13 Aug. 1888; Frame's memorandum, May 1890, 12–15.

92 Mt. St. MSS., Frame letter bk., Frame to Campbell 261: 5 May 1887; 392: 5 Nov. 1887; 406: 15 Dec. 1887.

93 ibid., 570: 25 May 1888; 815: 15 May 1889; 973: 18 Dec. 1889.

94 Mt. St. MSS., Bute letters, 7 March 1890.

95 Mt. St. MSS., Frame letter bk., 983: 31 Dec. 1889.

96 Diary, 30 Oct. 1890. His obit. (*B.* xc 1906, 442), however, describes him as 'architect to the Marquess of Bute'; and he received £1000 in Bute's will.

97 e.g. his Wrennish design for the Imperial Institute (*A.* xxxviii, 1887, 93; *B.N.* liii 1887, 115), or his Venetian Renaissance Edinburgh Medical School (1878).

98 *B.N.* xxiv (1873), 473; xxx (1876), 382.

99 Mt. St. MSS., Diary, Jan., March, 1889; Sept. 1890; May 1891. Bute letters, 23 Aug. 1890.

1 ibid., Frame letter bk., 838: 23 May 1889. The total cost was £636 6s. 6d. (Saunders ledger, 65: May 1889 – Dec. 1890). By comparison, Saunders's three windows over the front door cost £35 11s. 0d. (*ibid.*, 105: 1897).

2 *Jnl. Soc. Psychical Research*, Nov. 1900.

3 Hunter Blair, *Flying Leaves* (n.d.), 219.

4 By H. H. Hess of Gouda (1781); altered.

5 Mt. St. MSS., Diary, Aug.–Sept. 1886.

6 ibid., 1888; Bute letters, 2 Aug. 1891; Blair, *Bute*, 164–5.

7 Mt. St. MSS., Diary, 10 July 1894.

8 *A.* xxiii (1880), 105; *The Times* 25 May 1974.

9 Bute to H. D. Grissell, 15 Sept. 1870 (Blair, *Bute*, 94).

10 24 soup plates; 18 fish plates (catalogue, plate chest 1A; Burges drawings, fs. 19–26, Mt. St. MSS.). See also V. & A. Estim. Bk., 20 April 1878. One specimen plate (Hare soup) is now in a private collection. Burges also designed a set of cutlery, 'silver gilt, enamelled and engraved' (Barkentin £50: V. & A. Estim. Bk., July 1879; Mt. St. Burges drawgs. 12 b. (16); *Victorian and Edwardian Decorative Arts* (1952), J9). P.L.U.

11 'Lord Bute's cup done' (Abstract, 1875); Burges drawgs., f.10 (wmk. 1874); catalogue, plate chest no. 21, Mt. St. MSS. It is 7¼″ high.

12 V. & A. Estim. Bk., 22, 26 July 1880: £58; 'Water bottle, Lord Bute' (Abstract, 1880). The base forms a separable bowl. 'The engraver to look at these tracings when he is doing the work' (Burges drawgs., fs. 13, 14; catalogue, plate chest no. 21, Mt. St. MSS.). It is 10¼″ high.

13 'Lord Bute's decanter' (Abstract, 1870); Burges drawgs., fs. 2, 3, 12; catalogue, plate chest no. 21, Mt. St. MSS. It is 12¼″ high.

14 'Lord Bute's cruet' (Abstract, 1877); R.I.B.A., 'Orf. Dom.', 30 and S.N.B., 1876–7, 53–7; Burges drawgs., f.15; catalogue, plate chest no. 25, Mt. St. MSS.; V. & A. Estim. Bk., 7 Aug. 1877: £40.

15 *Jnl. Soc. Psychical Research*, Nov. 1900. One of Bute's last projects was to employ T. H. Mawson and Dan Gibson in designing a rock garden and Stations of the Cross (1893–9). See T. H. Mawson, *The Art and Craft of Garden Making* (1912), 197–8; *Life and Work of an English Landscape Architect* (1927), 46, 55–6.

16 Tennyson, *Idylls*: 'Lancelot and Elaine'.

17 *idem*. 'To the Queen'.

18 'In Paradisum' (Funeral rites, Mt. St. MSS.).

19 Bute had a horror of burial in the earth. His oaken coffin, decorated by H. W. Lonsdale, was therefore placed in an open sarcophagus of white marble made by Farmer and Brindley, designed by R. W. Schultz, and covered with a black satin pall (drawgs., Mt. St. MSS.).

20 *Sat. Rev.* Oct. 1900. He opposed 'the blighting disease of Liberalism' (Blair, *Bute*, 79: 5 Nov. 1869).

21 A wedding present for the 15th Duke, studded with 'sapphires, emeralds, rubies and one or two amethysts' (Barkentin, £42 the pair: V. & A. Estim. Bk., 16 Oct. 1877); Burges drawgs., Mt. St. MSS., f.35; 'Duke of Norfolk's brushes ... to Arundel with Chapple' (Abstract, 1877). P.L.U.

22 Blair, *Bute*, 105–7; Burges drawgs. f.9 (July 1872), Mt. St. MSS. P.L.U.

23 Bute gave £5,000 towards the erection of a cathedral in Dundee, to commemorate the re-establishment of the Catholic Bishopric of Dunkeld (*A.* xx, 1878, 92). Two mitres (P.L.U.) were probably designed by Burges for the same purpose: one embroidered with pearls (*A.* xxi, 1879, 327); the other studded with gems in Celtic pattern [220] ('Lord Bute's mitres', Abstract, 1878). See Burges drawgs., fs. 7–8, Mt. St. MSS.; V. & A. Estim. Bk., 26 June 1878, 4 July 1878, 24 Dec 1878. Cf. also Burges's article on the Beauvais mitre, *A.A.* xvii (1857), 227, and his related drawings, Soc. of Antiquaries, Misc. Portfolio, iv, 6–7 (drawn Aug. 1855), i, 6–7.

24 An epergne, four rose-water dishes, four flagons and twelve spoons: silver gilt, enamelled, studded with agate and lapis lazuli. A wedding present from Bute, designed by Burges ('Sneyd's wedding present', Abstract, 1880; R.I.B.A. 'Orf. Dom.', 31); made by Barkentin and Krall, 1880–81 (R.I.B.A., S.N.B., lxii, 1880 May–Sept.; V. & A. Estim. Bk., 26 July 1880: £359; Burges drawgs., Mt. St. MSS., fs. 31–4); bought by the V. & A. in 1964 for £900 (Circ. 184, 185, 189, 1964). For Sneyd – 'an awful Liberal' – see Blair, *Bute*, 23, 79).

25 F. J. Kirk, *Reminiscences of an Oblate* (1905), 76–7; R.I.B.A., S.N.B. lv (1877), 55–6. P.L.U.

26 Burges drawgs., Mt. St., f.5, 1875 but wmk. 1871. Along the lines of Cusack Smith's cross for Wells St. (V. & A., Estim. Bk., 28 Dec. 1875; 'Designed crucifix for Lord Bute', Abstract 1871). P.L.U.

page 291

27 'Lord Bute's reliquary' (Abstract 1870; R.I.B.A., S.N.B., xxxviii, 1869–70, 67); Burges drawgs., Mt. St. MSS., f.4; Pullan, *Designs of ... Burges*, pl. 13. P.L.U. Bute presented a reliquary to his friend Charles Philip Dawson (1849–92) of Barrow Hill, Derbyshire, about this time (Mt. St. MSS., letter to Bute, 8 Aug. ——).

28 'Lord Bute's prayer book' (R.I.B.A., S.N.B., xxxviii, 1869–70, 76). P.L.U.

29 Barkentin £238 (V. & A. Estim. Bk., 18 June 1877 and 11 Jan. 1878). P.L.U.

30 Blair, *Bute*, 241.

31 *ibid.*, 111.

32 *ibid.*, 105.

33 *ibid.*, 217.

7. FANTASTIC
between pp. 293–95

1 *Art Applied to Industry*, 70–73.

2 V. & A., P. & D., 93 E.3 (32, 34, 36–9); *King's Works*, i, 499; vi, 59, 115–6, 119.

3 *B.N.* viii (1862), 331. Burges much preferred wall paintings to wall paper. But he did occasionally admit to wallpaper design, eg. for Messrs. Jeffrey & Co. (*B.N.* xxiii, 1872, 291 and xxvi, 1874, 492–3, 507, 509. See also, *Art Jnl.* 1887, 201). For his work at Wells, see *E.* xxiv, N.S. xxi (1863), 309 and J. H. Parker, *Architectural Antiquities of Wells* (1866).

4 *G.M.* ccxiii (1862), 3.

5 H. Sauval, *Histoire et Rechèrches des Antiquités de la ville de Paris* ii (Paris, 1824), 11 *et seq.*

6 L. de Laborde, *Notice des Emaux, Bijoux et Objets Divers esposés dans les galeries du Musée du Louvre* (Paris, 1852–3).

7 G. Vasari, *Lives of the Painters*, trans. A. B. Hinds (1949 ed.), i, 218–21.

8 *E.* xxviii, N.S. xxv (1867), 153.

9 Cited by Burges in M. D. Wyatt, ed., *Industrial Arts of the Nineteenth Century* ii (1854), xc.

10 *ibid.* (Burges therefore knew of this in 1852); 'Drew at Salisbury various pieces of furniture' (Abstract, 1856).

11 Drawings by Burges in Scott, *Gleanings from Westminster Abbey* (1863), pl. xvii.

12 *ibid.*, pl. xviii, later transferred to the P.R.O.

13 *ibid.*, 95.

14 *ibid.*, pls. xxi–xxiii.

15 *ibid.*, pl. xxiv; *Vetusta Monumenta* ii (1789).

16 Scott, *Gleanings, op. cit.*, pls. xxv–xxvi. Burges employed S. W. Tracy to draw out the painted decorations 'by the help of a dark lantern and a strong lens'. (Soc. of Antiquaries, red portfolio, Westminster Abbey, 19 Jan. 1863).

17 *Mobilier*, i (1858), 000.

18 Burges, in Scott, *Gleanings, op. cit.*, 126; Burges drawgs., Soc. Antiqs. Lib.

19 Architectural Exhibn., 1859, no. 120. Both C. Handley-Read (*Burl. Mag.* cv, 1963, 496–509) and

N. Cromey-Hawke (*Connoisseur* cxci, 1976, 32–43) omit all mention of this important exhibiton.

20 see p. 320, 327.

21 James Nicholson, lead merchant of 20 Upper Thames St. and Salmon's Cross, Reigate, executor of J. J. Leschallas. He left £6,696 9s. 2d. (Probate Records, Somerset House). James Nicholson of Reigate and the Rev. J. Y. Nicholson of Aller, Som. (d.1904), both subscribed to Burges's *Architectural Drawings* (1870).

22 In 1860 he was living at 41, Welbeck St.; by 1870 he was living at Ferndene, Haslemere, and subscribing to Burges's *Architectural Drawings*. He left £79,023 17s. 3d. (Probate records, Somerset House). His mother (d. 1858) left £60,000.

23 *E.* xix, N.S. xvi (1858), 347–8. Presumably for Treverbyn Vean, see p. 300–301.

24 R.I.B.A., S.N.B., xx (1856), 35, 43–5. 'Furniture for Caldecott for Ruthven Castle' (Abstract, 1852); 'Drew and finished Caldecott's furniture for Ruthven' (*ibid.*, 1853); 'Lamps for Ruthven Castle' (*ibid.*, 1855); 'Sideboard for Caldecott' (*ibid.*, 1856). Henry Clutton was in charge of the rebuilding, for Hon. Frederick West, M.P. (*B.* xi 1853, 578–9). The sideboard in question was probably that carved by Phyffers and exhibited in 1862 (Waring, *Masterpieces of the Industrial Arts* iii, 1863, 258). Flanking lamps were originally intended, and carvings from Tennyson's *Idylls*. Burges may also have been involved with the chimneypiece in the Billiard Room, possibly that exhibited in 1851. See *1851 Exhibn. Official Cat.*, ii, 731: no. 19, Wynne and Lumsden, chimneypiece by Clutton for Ruthin Castle.

25 'Col. Cocks' table' (Abstract, 1858–62); V. & A., P. & D., 93 E 8, 19–23.

26 The bedroom's decoration has been overpainted, but the furniture (side-table, looking glass, bed and two wardrobes) survives. The Rev. Yatman married Anna (d.1922) daughter of Rev. William Hamilton Turner, vicar of St. Andrew, Banwell, Somerset; her brother died at Tien-Tsin in North China in 1860, and Burges designed a memorial to him in Banwell church ('Turner slab', Abstract, 1861; R.I.B.A., 'Stonework', 20).

27 'Yatman's furniture ... Yatman's painted furniture' (Abstract, 1858).

28 V. & A., P. & D., 93 E 8, 27; Architectural Exhibn., 1859, Great Gallery, no. 120 (iii); J. B. Waring, *Masterpieces of Industrial Art and Sculpture at the International Exhibn.*, iii (1862), 155; E. Aslin, *Nineteenth-Century English Furniture* (1962), 61–2; *C.L.* cxxxii (1962), 205: misattributed to Webb and Morris. Now at the William Morris Museum, Walthamstow (V. & A. loan, no. 8042: 1862). An upper section is shown in Burges's drawings (and in *The Artist*, July–Dec. 1879, 396–7). By 1874 its 'rabid Gothic style, painted in all the colours of the rainbow', was widely regarded as 'rather a foolish

between pp. 295–99

joke'. (*B.* xxxii, 1874, 841).

29 Now in the V. & A.

30 'Nicholson's buffet' (Abstract, 1859); 'Nicholson' (*ibid.*, 1856).

31 'Yatman's casket' (*ibid.*, 1856); Architectural Exhibn., 1857–8, no. 449, placed 'among the collection of Constantinopolitan marbles collected by Mr. Burges' (*E.* xix, N.S. xvi, 1858, 46). P.L.U.

32 *B.N.* iv (1858), 101; v (1859), 878, 885.

33 Architectural Exhibn., 1859, no. 120 (v); 'Sun Cabinet, Yatman' (Abstract, 1859); R.I.B.A., Arc. IV, misc., 5 and S.N.B. xxv (1858), 52–5; V. & A., P. & D., 93 E 8. The Sun Cabinet passed to Yatman's daughter Mrs. Laura D'Oyly (sale ticket *in situ*), and was eventually sold (Sotheby's Belgravia, 6 Dec. 1978, lot. 156: £6,900) to a private collector. The upper section, shown in Burges's drawings, does not survive.

34 Architectural Exhibn., 1859, North Gallery, no. 19. P.L.U.

35 'Morten did S. Bacchus for Yatman' (Abstract, 1858).

36 *E.* xx, N.S. xvii (1859), 194.

37 R.I.B.A., Arc. IV and S.N.B., xxv (1858), 52, 55; V. & A., P. & D., 93 E 8, 1 (inset stereoscopic photo of its 1862 Exhibition setting) [179]; Architectural Exhibn., 1859, no. 120 (ii); Waring, *Masterpieces, op. cit.*, ii (1862), 155; *Ill. Cat. of the International Exhibn.* ii (1862), class xxx, 15, U.K. no. 5736; [V. & A.], *The International Exhibition of 1862* (1962), pl. 25, n.25: Circ. 217–1961; [V. & A.], *English Cabinets* (1972), 35.

38 *Art Jnl.* v (1859), 125. Piers Gaveston, Edward II's favourite, died in 1312. Two slim vertical side-cabinets (V. & A.) form part of Yatman's set.

39 Medieval court with Slater' (Abstract, 1862); *E.* xx, N.S. xxiii (1862), 73–5, 126, 168–76, 204, 221, 226–7; *B.N.* viii (1862), 231–2 and ix (1862), 98–101. Burges won a medal for his general contribtion, prizes for his effigy (no. 5703) and tomb (no. 5679), and a specific commendation for his St. Neot chimneypiece (*E.* xx, N.S. xxiii, 1862, 204; *G.M.* ccxii, 1862, 664–5, 670–71).

40 No. 5736, made by Harland and Fisher: 'Fisher's sideboard' (Abstract, 1859); V. & A., P. & D., 93 E 8, 1, inset stereoscopic photo. This item may possibly have been painted by Rossetti: according to Waring, *Masterpieces, op. cit.*, Rossetti did paint a piece by Harland and Fisher for the 1862 Exhibition. P.L.U.

41 *G.M.* ccxiii (1862), 4.

42 *E.* xxiii, N.S. xx (1862), 337–8.

43 P. Henderson, *William Morris* (1973 ed.), 105.

44 Abstract, 1863.

45 R.I.B.A., S.N.B., xxxi (1862–3), 65; F. Nick, *Die Hof – und Volks – Narren*, 2 vols. (Stuttgart, 1861). *Ex inf.* Simon Jarvis and Lionel Lambourne.

46 Abstract, 1863.

47 The bookcase came to light in Brighton in 1978, was exhibited at the Fine Art Society in 1979 (*Morris and Co.*), and is now in the Cecil Higgins Art Gallery.

48 Fitzwilliam Museum, Burne-Jones MSS., xxiii, 7, n.d., but datable from internal evidence to 22 Oct. 1862.

49 C. Dresser, *Principles of Decorative Design* (1873), 64. J. Moyr Smith, however, thought the 'Wines and Beers' sideboard too plain (*Ornamental Interiors Ancient and Modern*, 1887, 52–3).

50 *C.E.A. Jnl.* xxii (1859), 142.

51 [Benjamin Webb in] *Bentley's Qtly. Rev.* i (1859), 626; *E.* xix, N.S. xvi (1858), 268, 347–8; xx, N.S. xvii (1859), 194; xxiii, N.S. xx (1862), 74, 170–71.

52 *G.M.* ccxiii (1862), 5.

53 *B.* xvii (1859), 197, 214–5; xx (1862), 421.

54 D. G. Rossetti, 1856, quoted in Harrison and Waters, *Burne-Jones, op. cit.*, 26.

55 D. Harbron, *The Conscious Stone* (149), 39.

56 E. W. Godwin, *Art Jnl.* 1886, 301.

57 *Revue Générale de l'Architecture* x (1852), 129–134, drawing by Ruprich Robert.

58 *Mobilier* i (1858), 6–8.

59 Nesfield, *Specimens of Medieval Architecture* (1862), 8–9. These drawings were made in 1859 (R.I.B.A. Sketch Book).

60 *B.N.* xxv (1873), 231, 235.

61 Visit on Long Journey (Abstract, 1853); V. & A., P. & D., 93 E 5, 32 (1858), 93 E 7, 41 and 93 E 4, 76. The Noyon armoire was destroyed in World War I.

62 *Architectural Drawings*, 61–2.

63 D. Ramée and M. Vitet, *L'Eglise de Noyon* (Paris, 1845), pl. xv.

64 *A.A.* iv (1846), 369–75. Didron published several items of Gothic furniture around this date.

65 A. Lenoir, *Architecture Monastique* ii (1856), 297, pl. 457. Also another painted armoire at Vernusse, used as a retable (*ibid.*, 295, pl. 458).

66 *Mobilier* i (1858), 9–11.

67 Abstract, 1858.

68 *B.N.* xii (1865), 115, 225; T. G. Jackson, *Recollections*, 55.

69 Chairs, settle (still at Red House), piano, wardrobe (1856–7; shown at the Hogarth Club, 1860; now in the Ashmolean) and dresser (1859–61; now in the V. & A.). Some at least of these were made up by the boys of the Euston Rd. Boys Home. See E. Aslin, *Nineteenth-Century English Furniture* (1962), 57; *Victorian and Edwardian Decorative Arts*, ed. P. Floud (1952), 41, i, 3; G. B.-J., *Memorials of E. B.-J.*, i, 147, 205–9; Harrison and Waters, *Burne-Jones*, 26–7, 178; R. W. Symonds and B. Whinneray, *Victorian Furniture* (1962), pl. 52.

70 At Worcester Park Farm (J. G. Millais, *Life and Letters of Sir J. E. Millais*, i, 1899, 127–8).

71 *C.L.* cxxxvii (1965), 720.

72 *R.I.B.A. Trans.*, vii (1856–7), 113.

between pp. 299–305

73 Painted by Morris, designed by Webb. See. Aslin, *op. cit.*, 57B; Symonds and Whinneray, *op. cit.*, pl. 53. Now in the V. & A. 341–1906.

74 Painted by Burne-Jones, designed by Webb. See P. Floud, in *Concise Encyclopaedia of Antiques*, ed. L. G. Ramsay (1957), 22, 3B. Now in the Metropolitan Museum, New York.

75 J. P. Seddon, *King Réné's Honeymoon Cabinet* (1898); Aslin, *op. cit.*, pl. 59. It was shown in 1862 (*Exhibn. Cat.*, class xxx, U.K. no. 5815). Now in the V. & A., W. 10–1927.

76 'Yatman cabinet' (Abstract. 1855); R.I.B.A., Arc IV. Whether these earliest designs also involve painted panels is by no means clear.

77 R.I.B.A., Lille Album, vii: 'Les frontons seront peints'; 'Furniture for Lille' (Abstract, 1856); *Victorian Church Art, op. cit.*, D 11 (c).

78 *C.E.A. Jnl.* xxv (1862), 356.

79 H. S. Marks, *Pen and Pencil Sketches* i (1894), 221.

80 Burges, in Shipley, ed., *The Church and the World* iii (1868), 586–7.

81 eg. *B.* xl (1881) 532.

82 Abstract, 1859.

83 'Chatto's house' (Abstract, 1865); 'To Wallingford with Chatto … Visit to Chatto at Taunton [*sc.* Torquay] … Mr. and Mrs. Chatto' (*ibid.*, 1866). Chatto, a Catholic and owner of a Terracotta Works at Watcombe, Devon, left over £122,000; he largely paid for Hansom's church of Our Lady and St. Denis, Torquay (Probate Records, Somerset House; obit. *Trans. Devonshire Assocn.*, xiv, 1882, 118; *Torquay Directory and South Devon Jnl.*, 8 Feb. 1882). The Daison at St. Marychurch was dem. 1936.

84 'Decorations for Spurrell' (Abstract, 1868): presumably Rev. F. Spurrell (d.1892), vicar of Faulkbourne, Essex.

85 See also Shirley Bury, in *Burl. Mag.* 1975.

86 The dining room was panelled with cedar wood brought from Bermuda by Admiral Boscawen; the timbered roofs of the galleried entrance hall, dining and drawing rooms were made of teak from the ship *Orinoco* which ferried Cocks's battalion to the East in 1854 (W. Lake, *History of Cornwall*, 1870, 410; G. C. Boase, *Collectinea Cornbiensis*, Truro, 1890, col. 151; Walford's *County Families*, 1897).

87 *E.* xxiii, N.S. xx (1862), 169; *Art Jnl. Catalogue* (1862), 205; *G.M.* cxxxii (1862), 669; Waring, *Masterpieces, op. cit.*, ii, 155.

88 Contemporary photographs: Yorke colln., Forthampton, Glos., and ex-colln. John Somers Cocks, now Nat. Trust, Saltram, Devon (*ex inf.* M. Trinick and G. Barnes). The chimneypiece was destroyed c.1950. 'To Liskeard' (Abstract, 1868) may possibly refer to later work.

89 Designed 1864 by George Knowles and William Wilcox.

90 A. C. Sewter, *The Stained Glass of William Morris and his Circle* ii (1975), 17.

91 R.I.B.A., Garnett left over £84,000. (Probate Rec.).

92 R.I.B.A., S.N.B. xiv (1865), 20.

93 N. Taylor and A. Symondson, 'Burges and Morris at Bingley', *A.R.* cxliv (1968), 35–8; Pullan, *Architectural Designs of W.B.*, pl. 74

94 Obit. *The Times* 28 May 1914, 12; *Who Was Who*, 1897–1916.

95 M. Girouard, *The Victorian Country House*, 6; F. M. L. Thompson, *English Landed Society in the Nineteenth Century* (1963).

96 'Amory's house' (Abstract, 1867); 'Knightshayes' (*ibid.*, 1868); 'First stone at Knightshayes … Knightshayes going on' (*ibid.*, 1869). Builder: Fletcher of Salisbury; contract: £14,080 for carcass alone, excluding facing stone, cast iron casements etc.

97 *A.* iv (1870), 7.

98 R.I.B.A., v. 59 (2); 'Gave bracelet to Mrs. Amory' (Abstract, 1870).

99 'Amory's book finished' (*ibid.*, 1873). The book survives at Knightshayes. For details, see J. Mordaunt Crook, 'Knightshayes, Devon: Burges versus Crace', *Nat. Trust Yearbook* i (1975–6), 44–55.

1 'Amory's woodwork' (Abstract, 1874).

2 Obits. *B.* cxvii (1919), 531, 534; *B.N.* cxvii (1919), 458; *R.S.A. Jnl.* lxviii (1919), 29–30. See also his *Art of Colour Decoration* (1913).

3 R. Kerr, *The Gentleman's House* (1864), ed. J. Mordaunt Crook (1972), 116.

4 Eastlake, *Gothic Revival*, ed. J. Mordaunt Crook (Leicester, 1978 ed.), 356–7, Appendix no. 327. 'Though the main front is uniform in its general masses, the entrance doorway is not precisely in the centre. This slight deviation from … symmetry … was no doubt adopted for convenience of internal arrangement, and is an instance of the ease with which a Gothic elevation may accommodate itself to exigencies of plan without sacrifice of artistic effect. In the case of an Italian villa such a licence would have been almost impossible'.

5 *B.N.* xviii (1870), 351.

6 Knightshayes Album, 1.

7 *Archaeol. Jnl.* xiv (1857), 96. Previously considered Italian or French, this carving – now thought to be from Cologne – was acquired by the V. & A. in 1872 from John Webb for £110. A Surrealist, erotic version of the same theme (1936) is to be found in a drawing by Man Ray (I.C.A. Exhibn., 1975; R. Penrose, ed., *Man Ray*, l.89).

8 'Drew Castle of Love' (Abstract, 1870); R.I.B.A., S.N.B. xxxiv (1870–71), 4, 6.

9 Knightshayes Album, 28 *et seq.*

10 Obit. *Western Mail* 29 March 1889. He designed, *inter alia*, a temporary roof over the great hall at Caerphilly (*B.N.* xxi, 1871, 83–6) and the graving dock linking the Bute East and West Docks (*B.N.* xxxviii, 1880, 29)

between pp. 305–307

11 R.A. no. 1210; R.I.B.A. Arc. IV, ii, 5; *A.* xxvii (1882), 221; Pullan, *Architectural Designs of W.B.*, pl. 38; *Plans and Prospects, op. cit.*, (1875), no. 22.

12 'Took plans . . . lunched with [Mc.Connochie] over his house' (R.I.B.A., S.N.B., xlvi, 1873, 3); *B.N.* xxii (1872), 401; *A.* vi (1871), 314.

13 *A.* xi (1874), 146.

14 Drawing Room decorations by Nicholls and by Campbell Smith (V. & A., Estim. Bk., 27–8 Jan. 1880); 'Mc.Connochie's decoration' (Abstract, 1880); 'Mrs. Mc.Connochie . . . died' (*ibid.*, 1879).

15 *B.N.* xxii (1872), 401.

16 *B.* xxx (1872), 358.

17 *Habitations Modernes* i (1875), 47–9. Burges disputed the accuracy of these drawings. Cf. working drawings, Glamorgan District Council.

18 *Architecture: Nineteenth and Twentieth Centuries* (1958), 188.

19 *Victorian Architecture*, ed. P. Ferriday, 217.

20 'To Bailey at Ightham' (Abstract, 1864); 'Bailey's House, Ightham' (*ibid.*, 1869); R.I.B.A., S.N.B. June–Sept. (1869), 56. In 1866–9, following the death of Bailey's father, Capt. James Alderson Bailey, in Brighton ('To Bailey, Brighton', Abstract, 1858), Burges completed an heraldic catafalque-tomb for the Bailey family in Ightham churchyard (R.I.B.A., S.N.B., xxxvi, 1869, 59), and an heraldic brass to Bailey's parents-in-law – Mary and Demetrius Grevis-James of Ightham Court – in Ightham church (*ibid.*, 60). The Grevis-James window, by Clayton and Bell above the Burges brass, was admired by Burges in Oct. 1868 for its 'imitation of the antique' (E. Bowra, *St. Peter's Ightham*, Ightham, 1970, and 'The Dutch James Family of Ightham Court', *Archaeologia Cantiana* lxxxiii (1968), 111–24; T. F. Charlton, *The Family of Charlton of Wrotham*, 1951). Bailey seems previously to have lived nearby at Nepicar House, Wrotham, following his marriage in 1857 to Lavinia Grevis-James; there Burges added a plain brick wing (1857?) in keeping with its Georgian character. Charles Villiers Bailey, F.S.A. (d.1877), of 6 Mount St., a clerk in the Privy Council Office, subscribed to Burges's *Architectural Drawings*.

21 Abstract 1859; *E.* xxi, N.S. xviii (1860), 41, 180, 189–90.

22 R.I.B.A., S.N.B., xlv (1873), 58.

23 Pullan, *Designs of W.B.*, 1; 'Decoration own Room' (Abstract, 1861); R.I.B.A., Arc. IV, xxxvi, 1–19.

24 H. S. Marks, *Pen and Pencil Sketches*, i (1894), 219.

25 'Rigged up ostrich egg' (Abstract, 1855).

26 R.I.B.A. photograph album, 'Own Furniture', 40.

27 'Picture over mantelpiece in own room' (Abstract, 1861). Westlake may possibly have been the artist, cf. his paintings – strong in outline, flat in colour – at J. F. Bentley's St. Francis, Pottery Lane, Notting Hill, London (*C.E.A.Jnl.* xxv, 1862, 249).

28 'Drew roundels for window in own room' (Abstract, 1858); 'Window blinds' (*ibid.*, 1871). These roundels of the seasons (R.I.B.A., Arc IV) reappear at Winscombe and at Tower House.

29 R.I.B.A., Arc. IV, xxvi, 1–2.

30 Pullan, *House of W.B.*; 'Own Furniture', 2–3. Beside the bed hung Dürer's 'Melancholia'; also Burges's 'Sabrina Fountain', 'St. Simeon Stylites' and 'Designs for Metalwork' (R.I.B.A., 'Orf. Dom.', frontispiece).

31 'Figures and fish own bedroom' (Abstract, 1863); 'Mermaids for bedroom' (Abstract, 1864); 'Own Furniture', 1.

32 'Own Furniture', 26; 'Theseus and Minotaur done' (Abstract, 1862).

33 Chairs now in the V. & A., and at William Morris Gallery, Walthamstow. See V. & A., P. & D., 93 E 8, 28–30.

34 'Own Furniture', 9.

35 *ibid.*, 27; 'Ceiling of little room done' (Abstract, 1871).

36 P. H. Ditchfield, *London's West End* (1925), 263.

37 'Looked at home Victoria Rd.' (Abstract, 1875); 'Looked at Bayswater site, March 29' (*ibid.*); 'Began with Driver Melbury Rd.' (*ibid.*). Burges produced rough plans for reconstructing both rejected properties: in Victoria Rd. (R.I.B.A., Arc IV, xxxix, 1) and Bayswater (*ibid.*, Arc IV).

38 Abstract, 1875.

39 'Own house building' (*ibid.*, 1876); 'House building' (*ibid.*, 1877); 'My lease signed Feb. 2' (*ibid.*). The contractors were Ashby Bros. of Kingsland Rd.; the carcass cost £6,000.

40 'Engaged the Faugembergues' (*ibid.*, 1877); 'Faugembergues and household things came, Jan. 1' (*ibid.*, 1878).

41 *ibid.*, 1878.

42 The first design (R.I.B.A., Arc IV, xl, 1–12) was plainer and duller, the second (*ibid.*, xli, 1–7) heavier and less free than the final scheme (*ibid.*, xlii, 1–31 and xliv).

43 Burges bequeathed Tower House to the Pullans. Thence it passed via his niece Elizabeth Ormiston (later Elizabeth Watson, d.1931), to Col. T. H. Minshall. When Col. Minshall sold the house and contents in 1933, its lease was bought by Col. E. R. B. Graham. On his death in 1962 Col. Graham bequeathed the tail-end of the lease to Sir John Betjeman. Between 1963 and 1965 the house was empty and subject to vandalism (*Kensington News* 21 Aug. 1964). In 1966—7 it was restored under a new lease by Lady Turnbull, with the aid of grants of £4,000 and £3,000 from the Historic Buildings Council and the Greater London Council (*C.L.* cxxxviii, 1965, 699; *The Times* 12 Oct., 30 Nov., 12 Dec., 1967). In 1969 she sold the property: Mr. Richard Harris paid £75,000 for the lease, outbidding Liberace (*The Times* 2 April 1969). In 1974 it was sold again: Mr. Jimmy Page paid

between pp. 308–12

£350,000 for the lease, outbidding Mr. David Bowie.

44 *B.N.* xxxii (1877), 6.

45 eg. J. Tarring, Paisley Town Hall (*A.* xiv, 1875, 348); E. Heffer, house for T. G. Ross (*B.N.* xxx, 1876, 648); C. H. Howell, house at Lydney (*B.N.* xxxii, 1877, 216); T. L. Watson, country house (*B.N.* xxi, 1871, 215).

46 Burges was interested in Thompson's work (*B.N.* xiv, 1867, 374).

47 V. & A., Estim. Bk., 30 Oct. 1876.

48 *ibid.*, 10 April 1878: £16. P.L.U. Seats and mosaic cost £150 (*ibid.*, Feb. 1878).

49 Tennyson, 'Song'.

50 *Art Jnl.* 1886, 172.

51 Pullan, *House of W.B.*, 40; Cocks Album. 'Fish teapot bought' (Abstract, 1868). See further designs for grotesque teapots, R.I.B.A., 'Orf. Dom.', 35.

52 V. & A., Estim. Bk., 5 Oct. 1876.

53 Photograph album presented by Burges to Sir John Benson, 29 Nov. 1870 (Welsh National Museum, Cardiff).

54 *B.N.* xxxii (1877), 375–6.

55 V. & A. MSS., 86, PP7, misc., ed. A. Saint, *Architectural History* xviii (1975), 65: 23 March 1876.

56 *B.* lxiv (1893), 12.

57 Mrs. Haweis, *Beautiful Homes* (1882; reprinted from *The Queen*, 1880–81), 14.

58 Haweis consulted Burges over the improvement of his church, St. James, Westmorland St., Marylebone ('Haweis about his church', Abstract, 1872; R. H. Robbins, 'St. Marylebone Church . . . [and] Chapels', *London Topographical Soc.* xxiii, 1972, 97–109). He lived at The Amber House, near Lord's Cricket Ground, before moving in 1882 to Rossetti's old house in Cheyne Walk. He was an ardent Wagnerian. See also Louise Jopling, *Twenty Years of My Life, 1867–87* (1925), 201–2; *Men of the Time* (1879), 495–6; Downey's *Cabinet Portrait Gallery*, 4th ser. (1893); *D.N.B.* The chapel was demolished c.1905.

59 'She was thought peculiar and so she was. But she was a unique woman, brilliant, fascinating, with the intellect of half a dozen men controlled by a bodily machinery that thundered away . . . and . . . at last tore her to pieces . . . She lived on her nerves' (Bea Howe, *Arbiter of Elegance*, 1967, 16). Her works include *The Art of Dress* (1879), *The Art of Beauty* (1878), *The Art of Decoration* (1881), *Chaucer for Schools* (1881), *Tales from Chaucer* (1887), *Chaucer's Beads* (1884) and *Chaucer for Children* (1877).

60 *Beautiful Homes*, 15, 22. For more prosaic recent accounts, see Handley-Read in *C.L.* cxxxix (1966), 600–604; *Survey of London* xxxvii (1973), 144–8.

61 Inscription: 'new doorway' (Abstract, 1880). For estimates by John Ayres Hatfield, Barkentin and

Hart, see V. & A., Estim. Bk., 10, 13 April and 10, 21 Oct. 1876; 24 April, 13 June 1877. See also R.I.B.A., Arc. IV, xlvi, 1–14 and sketch by W. Luker Jnr. (n.d.), Kensington Public Library. Compare the Studley font and the Cork, Studley and Cardiff doors.

62 R.I.B.A., Arc. IV, misc. 22; S.N.B. 1877–8, Oct.–Feb. and 1878, Feb.–Sept.; 'Bronze table for self' (Abstract, 1880). Colln. W. Wentworth Watson.

63 *Art Jnl.* 1886, 172.

64 *A.* xxii (1879), 83: general survey of Burke's mosaic practice. See also R.I.B.A., Arc. IV, xlvi, 1–14 and xlvii, 1. Burges noticed that the minotaurs in the paving of the choir at St. Omer resembled those of the *Ovid Moralisé* in the library at Rouen (*B.* xiii, 1855, 305).

65 *R.I.B.A. Jnl.* 3rd ser., xxiii (1916), 132; Arc. IV, xlvi, 1–14.

66 Pullan, *House*, xx; V. & A. Estim. Bk., 27 Nov. 1876.

67 Haweis, op. cit., 16; Pullan, *House*, 7. Compare Dickie Doyle's illustration for Dickens, *The Chimes* (*Mag. of Art*, 1882, 226). Since replaced by roundels of the Four Seasons.

68 'Hall decorations' (Abstract, 1878); R.I.B.A., Arc. IV, xlvii, 1–46 and li 1 *et seq.* Campbell and Smith's estimate: V. & A., Estim. Bk., 23, 29 March 1878. Since altered. The background colour was originally *not* plain white: the lower part was marbled; the upper section stencilled with red ashlar-markings.

69 See also Burges's sketches for staircase windows of the Four Elements (R.I.B.A., S.N.B., lv (1877), 77). Saunders & Co. were still producing versions of 'Weekes's Elements' in 1883–85 (Saunders Ledger, 1883–85).

70 R.I.B.A., Arc. IV, xlviii, 1–28.

71 'Own dining room ceiling' (Abstract, 1881): V. & A. Estim. Bk., 1 Dec. 1880 and 25 Jan. 1881: enamelling by Simpson, £126 and cartoons by Lonsdale, £35. For the materials, cf. the sheet metal decorations in the old dining room at the V. & A.; for the design, cf. a similar ceiling in Buckingham St..

72 V. & A. Estim. Bk., 25 Nov., 14 Dec. 1876.

73 *ibid.*, 24 Sept. 1880: J. Moore, £14; 'Bronze frogs cast' (Abstract, 1880).

74 'Bronze fame' (Abstract, 1880–81); V. & A. Estim. Bk., 3 March and 5, 7 April and 18 Oct. 1880: cast by James Moore of Thames Ditton (*Survey of London*, xxxvii, 1973, 148). Stolen 1963. P.L.U.

75 Pullan, *House*, 8. Tiles by Campbell and Smith: estimates, V. & A. Estim. Bk., 19, 24 Nov. 1879.

76 By Saunders (V. & A. Estim. Bk., 27 Nov. 1876). Since largely replaced.

77 Pullan, *House*, 10–11; V. & A., P. & D., 93 E8, 5; *B.N.* xxvi (1874), 425. Sold 1933, lot 116; £20. P.L.U. Inside was a profile portrait of Burges. The

between pp. 312–15

bookshelves contained Froissart's *Chronicles*, Sismondi's *Republiques Italienes*, Gould's *Curious Myths of the Middle Ages*, and Wightwick's *Hints to Young Architects*. A cabinet with very similar iconography, but with the additional features of a clock and bells, was designed by Saunders – presumably under Burges's direction – in 1865–7 (sold Sotheby's Belgravia, 6 Dec. 1978, lot 166: £21,000); now in the Manchester City Art Gallery.[207]

78 Pullan, *House*, 9; R.I.B.A., S.N.B. lii (1875–6), 38 and Arc. IV; V. & A. Estim. Bk., 8 Oct., 8 and 11 Dec. 1875, 20 Jan. and 13 June 1886. P.L.U.

79 R.I.B.A., 'Orf. Dom.', 29 and S.N.B. xxxvi (1869), 4–13. Six from the Handley-Read colln. (Christie's, 3 Nov. 1964, lot 90: £20) are now in the Cecil Higgins Art Gallery, Bedford.

80 See F. S. Meyer and H. Stannus, *Handbook of Ornament* (1894), pl. 231 (2–12). 'Own Tea spoons' (Abstract, 1879); R.I.B.A. 'Metalwork', 84a and 'Orf. Dom.', 31–2 ('given to Cox's foreman'); 12 Silver spoons and 2 enamelled spoons, Barkentin, £30 (V. & A., Estim. Bk., 6 Aug. 1880); 12 silver spoons, Cox, £9 (*ibid.*, 13 March 1879); gilt tea spoons, Barkentin, £18 (*ibid.*, 8 March 1879); 4 salt spoons, Barkentin, £5 (*ibid.*, 10 March 1879). Six dessert spoons are now in the colln. of Mrs. L. Sachs.

81 Pullan, *House*, 8. P.L.U.

82 Fitted with plate glass and carved with monkeys (V. & A., Estim. Bk., 26 Feb. 1877: £40 each). P.L.U.

83 Tennyson, *The Lover's Tale*, IV, 192 *et seq.*

84 Haweis, *op. cit.*, 17.

85 *B.N.* xxxvii (1880), 497.

86 *G.M.* ccxiv (1863), 403–11.

87 Castellani, *Archaeol. Jnl.* xviii (1861), 365–72 and xix (1862), 275–6; A. Castellani, *A.* xvi (1876), 255–6, 265–6. Discoveries from the Regulini Galassi tomb were placed in the Etruscan Museum of the Vatican. See also Shirley Bury, in *Burl. Mag.*, cxvii (1975) 664–8.

88 'A book might be written on this one vase alone . . . My friend M. Didron would call it a poem in Orfèvrerie' (*E.* xix, N.S. xvi, 1858, 226).

89 *B.* xx (1862), 491. 'A translation of Cellini's treatise would be . . . a very great boon . . . to the modern workman'.

90 *B.* xx (1862), 506–7. Burges also made comparisons at the Malines Loan Exhibition of 1864 (*B.N.* xi, 1864, 719–20).

91 *B.* xx (1862), 368.

92 *E.* xix, N.S. xvi (1858), 222–3.

93 H. Shaw, *Dresses and Decorations of the Middle Ages* (1843).

94 J. Carter, *Ancient Sculpture and Painting* (1780–94).

95 *E.* xix, N.S. xvi (1858), 224–5.

96 *E.* xxiii, N.S. xx (1862), 339. 'Hardman has a very tolerable light blue; Keith a good transparent red upon gold; Skidmore a good transparent green,

and Hart has also one or two fair colours; but by the side of these are often to be seen enamels whose colours positively shock the eyes, so violent and bright are they' (*B.* xx, 1862, 506–7; *G.M.* ccxii, 1862, 673–6 and ccxiii, 1862, 9, 12; *E.* xxiii, N.S. xx, 1863, 23–67, 339).

97 *E.* xix, N.S. xvi (1858), 226.

98 Tennyson, *Maud*, I, xiii, 12.

99 R.I.B.A., 'Orf. Dom.', frontispiece; 'Drew decanters' (Abstract, 1863; 'designed decanter' (*ibid.*, 1864). 'Mr. Burges showed the committee an exquisite wine-flagon (secular) and two jewelled chalices executed under his superintendance' (*E.* xxvi, N.S. xxiii, 1865, 227).

1 R.I.B.A., 'Orf. Dom.', 10–11; *B.N.* xxvi (1874), 418; *B.* liii (1887), 700; Pullan, *Designs of W.B.*, 17; *Victorian and Edwardian Decorative Art* (1972), B. 87, ill. back cover. Bought by Handley-Read (Phillips, Son & Neale, 8 Nov. 1968, lot 215: £1,800 the pair); now in the Cecil Higgins Art Gallery. Compare the woven palisading – a favourite motif – with that of the sixteenth-century Glynne cup in the V. & A. Angell, of the Strand, exhibited in 1862 (*Jewellers, Goldsmiths and Watchmakers Mag.*, i, 1862, 74–5, 78).

2 Bequeathed to B.M. See R. S. Barnett, *Cat. of Nimrod Ivories* (1857), 228, pl. cxxvi, v, ii.

3 R.I.B.A., 'Orf. Dom.', 12; *B.N.* xxvi (1874), 430; *B.* liii (1887), 100; Pullan, *Designs of W.B.*, 17; *Victorian and Edwardian Decorative Art* (1972), B. 88, ill. front cover. Bought by Handley-Read (see n. 1 above); now in the Fitzwilliam Museum, Cambridge (M.16 – 1972).

4 *Victorian and Edwardian Decorative Arts* (1952), 54, J.6; Patricia Wardle, *Victorian Silver* (1963), pl. 49. It cost £48 15s. 2d. (accounts, R. A. Green, 14 Feb. 1866). Green, of the Strand, also exhibited in 1862 (*Jewellers, Goldsmiths and Watchmakers Mag.*, ii, 1862, 157). Now in the V. & A. There may be a link here with Thomas Green ('merchant', d.1876, leaving £5,000), for whom Burges repaired Eastlands, Dulwich, Surrey (Abstract, 1859).

5 R.I.B.A., 'Orf. Dom.', 13–14; *E.* xxiv, N.S. xxi (1863), 119; Pullan, *Designs of W.B.*, 17; 'My own cup' (Abstract, 1862). Now in the colln. of Mr. Jimmy Page.

6 Early sketch, R.I.B.A., S.N.B. xxxi (1862–3), 87. *Victorian and Edwardian Decorative Arts* (1952), J.7. It cost £31 (accounts, 29 Sept. 1863, Joseph Hart & Son). Now in the V. & A.

7 Tennyson, *Idylls*: 'The Passing of Arthur'.

8 Cf. R.I.B.A. 'Orf. Eccles.', 7.

9 *B.* liii (1887), 693.

10 *Victorian and Edwardian Decorative Arts* (1952), J.8; *Victorian and Edwardian Decorative Art* (1972), B.89; Pullan, *Designs of W.B.*, 18; R.I.B.A., 'Orf. Dom.', 12, d. 2 July 1867. It passed by descent through Lord Colum Crichton-Stuart to the Hon. Richard Bigham. It was bought by Handley-Read

between pp. 315–17

(Christie's, 18 July 1968, lot 249a: 1,500 gns.) and is now in the V. & A.

11 *Victorian and Edwardian Decorative Art* (1972), B. 102; Pullan, *Designs of W.B.*, 22; R.I.B.A., 'Orf. Dom.', 2. Probably by Hart, Son, Peard & Co. of Wyck St., Strand. They exhibited an apparently similar bowl in the Paris Universal Exhibn., 1867 (*Cat. British Section*, 1867, Appendix 122). Now in the V. & A. For Viollet-le-Duc's mermaid, see *Dictionnaire* i (1858), 492, fig. 109.

12 Tennyson, 'The Mermaid', from *Poems, Chiefly Lyrical* (1830); in Burges's illuminated edn. (1858), 58.

13 'Cat cup made' (Abstract, 1867); 'Broke cat cup' (*ibid.*, 1869); V. & A., P. & D., 93 E9, 13; Pullan, *Designs of W.B.*, 18.

14 For a rock crystal vase, mounted à la Burges, given by Suger to the Treasury of St. Denis, see J. Labarte, *Histoire des Arts Industriels au Moyen Age* i (1872), 410, pl. xxxii.

15 Sold 1933, lot 118; £15. Colln. Cmdr. M. Minshall?

16 Sold 1933, lot 119: £9 10s. 0d. Sold 1971 as one of a pair (Christie's, 8 July 1971, lot 100: 2,000 gns.; *Review of the Year*, 1970–71, 336–7; *C.L.* cl, 1971, 609). Now in Birmingham City Art Gall., M.134.7.

17 Unsold 1933, lot 120. Sold 1971, see above; bought with the aid of the N.A.C.F. for Lotherton Hall, Yorks (Leeds City Art Gall., 32/71). See Pullan, *House*, 40; V. & A., P. & D., 93 E8, 9; R.I.B.A., Arc. IV, xvii, 101 and iv, xxv, 1.

18 Tennyson, *Idylls*: 'The Coming of Arthur'.

19 Barkentin: £13 (V. & A., Estim. Bk., 15 Sept. 1875). P.L.U.

20 R.I.B.A., 'Orf. Dom.', 3. P.L.U.

21 *ibid.*, 4; Pullan, *House*, 40; 'Designs by W.B.' (photographs by F. Bedford, presented to Col. Cocks, 1869; sold Sotheby's Belgravia, 18 Nov. 1977, lot 254: £655). P.L.U.

22 R.I.B.A., 'Orf. Dom.', 9. P.L.U.

23 *ibid.*, 18. P.L.U.

24 *ibid.*, 16; R.I.B.A., S.N.B. lvi (1877), 49; Barkentin: £9 (V. & A., Estim. Bk., 7 March 1878). Private collection.

25 'Cups for Art Club' (Abstract, 1878). Commissioned first by Butterworth, then by Schultz and Wilson (V. & A., Estim. Bk., 8, 28 Feb. 1878). The others, of silver instead of wood (Hart: £45 12s. 6d. *ibid.*), were for A. Rivington, A. C. Bell, H. Curzon, B. Frere and R. W. Edis (R.I.B.A., 'Orf. Dom.', 16). P.L.U.

26 Cocks album.

27 'Foot of jade vase' (Abstract, 1862); 'Jade vase made up' (*ibid.*, 1863); R.I.B.A., 'Orf. Dom.', 19; Pullan, *House*, 40; *G.M.* ccxv (1863), 48; *E.* xxiv, N.S. xxi (1863), 181. P.L.U.

28 R.I.B.A., 'Orf. Dom.', 20; Pullan, *House*, 40; 'bought jade vase' (Abstract, 1866); 'Jade cup mounted', Barkentin: £15 5s. 0d. (V. & A., Estim. Bk., 4 Nov. 1875); 'Mounting jade vase ... like great green jade vase', Barkentin: £34 (*ibid.*, 20 Dec. 1878). P.L.U.

29 R.I.B.A., 'Orf. Dom.', 21, 34; R.I.B.A., S.N.B. xiv (1865), 56. P.L.U.

30 Cox & Sons: £5 5s. 0d. (V. & A., Estim. Bk., 13 Aug. 1879). P.L.U.

31 Barkentin: £11 (*ibid.*, 18 Sept. 1877). P.L.U.

32 *ibid.*, 10 Feb. 1875, 17 Jan. 1876, 7 April 1876; Cocks album. P.L.U.

33 V. & A., P. & D., 93 E9, 19.

34 R.I.B.A., 'Orf. Dom.', 39–40. 'Bought niello watch' (Abstract, 1871); 'Bought watches, self and Chapple, July 30' (*ibid.*, 1874).

35 R.I.B.A., 'Orf. Dom.', 32.

36 H. S. Marks, *Pen and Pencil Sketches* i (1894), 221.

37 H. Muthesius, *Das Englische Haus* iii (1911), 75.

38 Burges exhibited 'Designs for secular jewellery' in 1863 (Archital. Ex., 202). Several items remain to be identified, eg.: pendant badges for Gambier Parry (Abstract, 1865) and brooches for '– Seddon' and 'Miss Tribe' (V. & A., P. & D., 93 E9, 10–11). For the Ven. W. H. Tribe, Burges reported on St. Peter, Stockbridge, Hants. ('Tribe's church failed', Abstract, 1866), and designed a set of agate-handled knives (V. & A., Estim. Bk., 3 Jan., 1879). Tribe became father-in-law to Herbrand, 11th Duke of Bedford, and Archdeacon of Lahore. Hence two more abortive commissions: 'Tribe's Library' and Lahore Cathedral (Abstract, 1879–80). W. F. Tribe was a family friend in Worthing.

39 'Exeter chain' (Abstract, 1873); 'Gold chain for Exeter' (*ibid.*, 1874); R.I.B.A., S.N.B. xlix (1874), 9, 10, 69, 77; *B.N.* xliv (1885), 490. Presented by the R.A.I. (*Archaeol. Jnl.* xxx, 1873, 447–8 and xxxi, 1874, 414–7). Made by W. Page of 31–3, Great Portland St. (*Jnl. Générale des Beaux Arts*, 24 Oct. 1874, 185). The collar weighs 22 oz., the badge 7 oz. The decoration embodies the symbolism of the city's arms.

40 The two panels show the Seven Ages of Man. They are now in the V. & A. (Circ. 168–9, 1952, purchase price: £9 19s. 6d.). The story is told by Sir W. L. Bousfield, Emerson's nephew (MS. note on panels). The identity of the wine cupboard is uncertain: perhaps it was the sideboard with mirrors shown in 1862. The incident probably took place in Buckingham St.

41 Pullan, *House*, 40.

42 R.I.B.A., Arc. IV, 6, 1 *et seq.*

43 Since removed.

44 'Weekes made sketches, Drawing Room' (Abstract, 1876); 'Settled prices of paintings with Weekes' (*ibid.*, 1879); 'Weekes did Drawing Room pictures' (*ibid.*, 1880); V. & A. Estim. Bk., 24 Nov. 1879.

45 Figures by Saunders (V. & A., Estim. Bk., 27 Nov. 1876) from Lonsdale's cartoons; parrots by

between pp. 317–22

Campbell and Smith (*ibid.*, 15 Dec. 1880).

46 The green panelling intended by Burges was never installed. The lovers' frieze remained incomplete, and has recently been restored by Campbell and Smith. For a sketch of one of the corbels, see R.I.B.A., S.N.B. lv (1877), 91–2.

47 Pullan, *House*, 16; *British Architect and Northern Engineer* ix (1878), 6–8; R.I.B.A., S.N.B. lii (1875–6), 73–4 and Arc. IV; V. & A. Estim. Bk., 15 May 1876, 23 Sept. 1878: £170 plus £74 3s. od. for painting by Campbell and Smith.

48 *B.* lxvi (1894), 310. Compare Lethaby's drawing with Burges's (R.I.B.A., Arc. IV).

49 *C.L.* cxxxix (1966), 602.

50 Pullan, *House*, 19. Unsold in 1933, lots 139–41. The upper section of the tall cabinet became a display cabinet in the guests' bedroom at Tower House. See also Burges's designs for a sideboard (V. & A., P. & D., 93 E8, 11), P.L.U.

51 R.I.B.A., Arc. IV, xix, 1; *R.I.B.A. Jnl.* 3rd ser. xxiii (1916), 135.

52 *Victorian and Edwardian Decorative Arts* (1952), 54, J.11; *Victorian and Edwardian Decorative Art* (1972), B. 14–15. Bought by Handley-Read, 1965; now in the Cecil Higgins Art Gallery.

53 Scott, *Gleanings from Westminster Abbey* (1863), 105–12, pl. xxiii; R.I.B.A., Arc. IV., xix, 1.

54 Pullan, *House*, 11. One source is perhaps the so-called Bishop's chair (c.1400) at Hereford (*B.N.* xxxiii, 1877, 333).

55 'Marks did zodiac panel' (Abstract, 1871); H. S. Marks, *Pen and Pencil Sketches* i (1894), 220. It is inscribed 1869 and 1870.

56 Pullan, *House*, 17; R.I.B.A., Arc. IV, xxi, 1–2. Unsold in 1933, lot 113; presented by Sir John Betjeman to Evelyn Waugh; now in the collectn. of Mr. Auberon Waugh.

57 *R.I.B.A. Jnl.* 3rd ser. xxiii (1916), 135.

58 Godwin, *Art Jnl.* 1886, 301.

59 Pullan, *House*, 18; 'Peacock Cabinet in hand' (Abstract, 1873); R.I.B.A., S.N.B., 1872–3, Dec.–March, and Arc. IV xxii, 2v., 69–72. This was four years before Burges noted 'Saw [Whistler's] Peacock Room' (Abstract, 1877). Now in the colln. of Mrs. Elizabeth Bonython.

60 W. R. Lethaby, *Architecture, Mysticism and Myth*, ed. G. Reuben (1974), 254.

61 Pullan, *House*, xiii; R.I.B.A., S.N.B. lii (1875–6), 75; V. & A., Estim. Bk., 9 Nov. 1876, 7 Jan. 1878: £100 plus £54 for painting by Campbell and Smith; *B.N.* xlix (1885), 77–8. For a sketch by Burges on Athenaeum writing paper, see R.I.B.A., Arc. IV. The fireplace tiles are by Simpson (V. & A., Estim. Bk., 7 Feb. 1877). For the use of Mexican onyx, see *B.* xxiv (1876), 414.

62 Handley-Read, *C.L.* cxxxix (1966), 601.

63 *A.* xxiii (1880), 314; *B.* xxxviii (1880), 554; *B.N.* xxxviii (1880), 507 and xlix (1885), 568. 'Haig drew

Library for R.A.' (Abstract 1880); V. & A., Estim. Bk., 28 Oct. 1879: £30. Now in the colln. of Mrs. Eleanor Mallock. One critic thought that the chimneypiece was inspired by the choir screen at Amiens (*The Times* 5 July 1880, p.5).

64 By Saunders (V. & A., Estim. Bk., 27 Nov. 1876). The Arachne window repeats that at Cardiff.

65 *B.* ix (1878), 98, 110, 146, 170, 195, 218, 222, 266 (engravings by T. Raffles Davison from drawings by Weekes); 'Weekes began bookcases' (Abstract, 1876). Burke supplied the marble; Walden made up the cabinets; Campbell and Smith supplied background painting; Weekes charged £2 15s. od. per panel, Marks £1. os. od. per bird's head (V. & A., Estim. Bk., 27 April, 12 June, 25 Sept., 9 Nov. 1876; 23 April, 13 June, 17 Sept. 1877); R.I.B.A., Arc. IV, drawings by Weekes.

66 The Duke of Westminster was so impressed that he commissioned him to paint some bird panels in the small drawing room at Eaton Hall (*Mag. of Art* iv, 1881, 138; H. S. Marks, *Pen and Pencil Sketches*, i, 1894, 217).

67 *R.I.B.A. Jnl.*, 3rd ser. xxiii (1916), 137.

68 'Own Furniture', 11–12; V. & A., P. & D., 93 E8, 5. P.L.U.

69 Godwin, *Art Jnl.* 1886, 301.

70 Architectural Exhibn., 1859, 120 (i).

71 *B.N.* xix (1870), 352, 354; *Furniture Gazette* 6 Sept. 1873, 345.

72 Godwin, *loc. cit.* It is painted with the Seven Lamps, one of Burges's very few directly Ruskinian references. The porcupine frieze reappears in the Wines and Beers sideboard.

73 *B.N.* xix (1870), 352, 354, 376.

74 Pullan, *House*, 14; R.I.B.A., Arc. IV, xiv, 1–21; and S.N.B. xxxi (1862–3), 64; Handley-Read in *Burl. Mag.* cv (1963) 502–3 and *World Furniture*, ed. Helena Hayward (1968), 207, 224. Bought in 1933 (lot 117: £50) by Kenneth Clark on behalf of the Ashmolean Museum; now on loan to the V. & A.

75 'Own large Bookcase' (Abstract, 1859); 'Great Bookcase in progress' (*ibid.*, 1860); 'My Bookcase to Seddon's' (*ibid.*, 1862).

76 A. L. Baldry, *Holiday* (1930), 75: 1861.

77 Marks, *Pen and Pencil Sketches*, i, 220: 'under Burges's superintendence and from his suggestion'.

78 'Bookcase at Melbury Rd. fell, Aug. 18' (Abstract, 1878).

79 *Burl. Mag.* cv (1963), 504. Additional attributions of panels to Fred Walker and Holman Hunt have yet to be substantiated.

80 By Saunders (V. & A., Estim. Bk., 27 Nov. 1876). Since replaced.

81 'Four Eastern blinds using up old turned work ... all mahogany', Walden: £27 16s. od. (*ibid.*, 14 Oct. 1878). For various alternative designs, see R.I.B.A., Arc. IV, viii, 1–8.

82 Haweis, *op. cit.*, 19; *American Architect and B.N.* viii (1880), 20; R.I.B.A., Arc. IV, lii, 1 *et seq.*

between pp. 322–25

83 'Ceiling of Guest's room' (Abstract, 1879). Estims: V. & A., Estim. Bk., 3, 10 Jan. 1879.

84 Pullan, *House*, 24; perhaps by Weekes (R.I.B.A., Arc. IV, 69–72, no. 70).

85 V. & A., Estim. Bk., 26 April 1879. Since altered, but recently restored by Campbell and Smith. Fisher painted the canvassed walls (*ibid.*, 1 March 1879).

86 W. F. Lethaby, *Architecture, Mysticism and Myth*, ed. G. Reuben (1974), 255.

87 Pullan, *House*, 25. Now in the colln. of Mr. Auberon Waugh.

88 Made up by Poole and Walden (V. & A., Estim. Bk., 16 June and 24, 30 Sept. 1879). Sold 1933 (lot. 111: £10). P.L.U.

89 Sold 1933 (lot 108: £5 10s. 0d. and lot 110: £1 10s. 0d.). P.L.U.

90 V. & A., Estim. Bk., 1879: mosaic set by Burke for £5. Unsold 1933. Now in the colln. of Lord Poole. In later years, at least, this seems to have served as an altar.

91 *Archaeol. Jnl.* xliii (1886), 472.

92 V. & A., Estim. Bk. 11, 14 July 1879: gold leaf. 'Bedstand for guest's room' (Abstract, 1879). Sold 1933 (lot 107: £40). Now in the V. & A.

93 Set by Barkentin (V. & A., Estim Bk., 9 June 1879).

94 V. & A., Estim Bk., 25 June 1879. The rest of the bed was made up by Walden (*ibid.*, 12 March, 1879).

95 'Judgment of Paris, Weekes' (Abstract, 1872). This originally formed part of a glazed panel at Buckingham St. (Pullan, *House*, 22; 'Own Furniture', 19, 30). For Burges's preliminary sketches, see R.I.B.A., S.N.B., xxx (1861), 53 and Arc. IV, 66–8.

96 Haweis, *op. cit.*, 20–21; *American Architect and B.N.* viii (1880), 20; Symonds and Whinery, *op. cit.*, 49, pl. 72; *Victorian and Edwardian Decorative Arts* (1952), J.3. Sold 1933 (lot 109: £17). Now in the V. & A.; float stolen, P.L.U.

97 V. & A., Estim. Bk., 27–8 Jan. 1880.

98 *R.I.B.A. Jnl.*, 3rd ser. xxiii (1916), 138; Barkentin cast the water tank 'float in copper gilt' for £1 18s. 0d. (V. & A., Estim. Bk., 5 March 1880); and damascened the animal-top in gold (*ibid.*, Oct. 1879: £5). Hatfield proposed to charge £10 for 'casting and chasing a beast and a cork' (*ibid.*, 23 Aug. 1879). Hart and Barkentin both tendered for the silver fish (*ibid.*, Sept. 1879). Poole supplied the marble (*ibid.*, 25 June 1879). The washstand itself was made up by Walden for £55 (*ibid.*, 30 Sept., 2 Oct. 1879).

99 Pullan, *House*, 23; V. & A., Estim. Bk., 6 Jan. 1879 ('Own wardrobe'); R.I.B.A., Arc. IV, xxvii, 1–6. Sold 1933 (lot 112: £10 10s. 0d.). Presented by Sir John Betjeman to Evelyn Waugh, and now in the colln. of Mr. Auberon Waugh. The base has been removed.

1 Pullan, *House*, 34; V. & A., Estim. Bk., 29 July 1877: £40 14s. 0d.; R.I.B.A., S.N.B. xlvi (1873), 33.

2 Cases by Walden (V. & A., Estim. Bk., 15 April 1878 and 7, 28 March 1881).

3 Pullan, *House*, 35; 'Own Furniture', 24; Benson Album. P.L.U.

4 Pullan, *House*, 36; V. & A., Estim. Bk., 28 July 1877: £21 10s 0d.; RIBA., Arc IV, lvi, 1 *et seq*

5 V. & A., Estim. Bk., 28 July 1877: £26; R.I.B.A, Arc. IV, lviii, 1 *et seq*. Cf. similar chimneypieces at Gayhurst and Bingley.

6 Pullan, *House*, 37; R.I.B.A., S.N.B. li (1875), 15–16 and Arc. IV, xxv, 1–7. Perhaps painted by Weekes. P.L.U. This room may also have contained a linen-press (Walden: £6, V. & A., Estim. Bk., 10 Sept. 1878) which may or may not be related to one surviving cupboard, overpainted c.1890 (Sotheby's Belgravia, 6 Dec. 1978, lot 167: £850).

7 'Rossiter painted puppies' (Abstract, 1869).

8 Pullan, *House*, 38; V. & A., P. & D., 93 E8, 5; R.I.B.A., S.N.B. xxxv (1868–9), 68 and Arc. IV, xxii, 1–3; 'Own Furniture', 22. Cf. Knightshayes billiard room chimneypiece.

9 As at Buckingham St. and Winscombe. The Four Seasons windows in the Mermaid Bedroom belong to the same series: Saunders was still using their designs in 1889 (Saunders Ledger, 23 Jan. 1889).

10 R.I.B.A., Arc. IV, liv–vi. 'Own bedroom decorations' (Abstract, 1878).

11 V. & A., P. & D., 93 E7, 37v.; Lethaby, *Architecture, Mysticism and Myth*, 254. Burges seems to have derived this idea from the church of St. Mary, Bury St. Edmunds, Suffolk (J. K. Colling, *Gothic Ornaments*, i, 1848, viii).

12 By Campbell and Smith: £45 (V. & A., Estim. Bk., 28 Feb. 1878).

13 By Nicholls: £35 (*ibid.*, 2 Feb., 30 June 1877).

14 It also appears in the family crest of one of Burges's patrons, Cusack Smith. For the whole subject see L. Jewitt, 'The Mermaid of Legend and of Art', *Art Jnl.* 1880, 141–4, 193–6.

15 N. Pevsner, *Pioneers of Modern Design* (1960 ed.), 90, 93, 97, 112; R. Schmutzler, *Art Nouveau* (1964), 271, pl. 52; I. Cremona, *Il Tempo Dell' Art Nouveau* (1964), 64, pls. 60–62.

16 'Own Furniture', 5; R.I.B.A., Arc. IV, 110; Marks, *Pen and Pencil Sketches*, i, 221. P.L.U.

17 Pullan, *House*, 33; Godwin, *Art Jnl.* 1886, 303. P.L.U.

18 Pullan, *House*, 30; R.I.B.A., S.N.B. xxxiii (1867), 38 and xxxiv (1867), 38; Arc. IV, xvii, 1–4; V. & A., P. & D., 93 E8, 38 (70); 'Own dressing table' (Abstract, 1867); *Victorian and Edwardian Decorative Art* (1972), B.13. Unsold 1965 (Philip, Son & Neal, sale 16886, lot 4); bought by Handley-Read from the Lacquer Chest, Kensington, for £45. Restored 1966 by Herbert Lank and C. Geoffrey-Dechaume (Viollet-le-Duc's sculptor's grandson). Now in the

between pp. 325–28
Cecil Higgins Art Gallery.

19 *Mobilier*, i, 8, fig. 8.

20 'Smallfield did the Crocker portraits for dressing table' (Abstract, 1867).

21 Burne-Jones persuaded his father to make a mirror of the same design (G. B.-J., *Memorials of E. B.-J.*, i, 215: 1860).

22 *B.N.* xxxvii (1879), 473: National Gallery no. 186.

23 Handley-Read, in *C.L.* cxxxix (1966), 603.

24 Pullan, *House*, 26, 28; R.I.B.A., S.N.B. xxxiii (1867), 45 and Arc. IV, xv, 1–4; V. & A., P. & D., 93 E8, 3, 4, 37; 'Red bedstead' (Abstract, 1865); *Victorian and Edwardian Decorative Arts* (1952), J.2; *Victorian and Edwardian Decorative Art* (1972), B.12. Bought by Handley-Read, 1967. Now in the Cecil Higgins Art Gallery.

25 'Sleeping Beauty for bed done' (Abstract, 1866).

26 5th ed. (1848), 309. Colln. J. Mordaunt Crook.

27 'Quilt made' (Abstract, 1864).

28 'Red ... washstand' (Abstract, 1865); 'Washstand going on' (*ibid.*, 1866).

29 R.I.B.A., Arc. IV, xvi, 1–8; 'Washstand pictures, Weekes' (Abstract, 1872); Benson album.

30 *B.N.* xxxviii (1880), 497.

31 Louvre, Paris, Orf. 12 (Gall. d'Apollon).

32 Evelyn Waugh, *The Ordeal of Gilbert Pinfold* (1957). Waugh wrongly assumed that the painted panels were by Poynter. The washstand had been bought by Sir John Betjeman in Lincoln and presented to Evelyn Waugh, who christened it 'the Betjeman benefaction' (M. Davie, ed., *Diaries of Evelyn Waugh*, 1976, 722; M. Amory, ed., *Letters of Evelyn Waugh*, 1980, 417). It is now in the colln. of Mr. Auberon Waugh.

33 Pullan, *House*, 32; 'Own Furniture', 20–21; Godwin, *Art Jnl.*, 1886, 305; V. & A., P. & D., 93 E8, 7; Architectural Exhibn., 1859, 120 (iv): £17. This wardrobe seems to belong to at least three phases of design. The exterior panels were shown in 1859; the interior paintings, with quotations from (?) Tennyson and Chaucer, are dated 1870; the fittings were altered in 1878–9 (V. & A., Estim. Bk., 21 Jan. 1878), when some repainting occurred (*ibid.*, 6 Jan. 1879).

34 Tsao Hsueh-Chin and Kao Ngoh, *Dream of the Red Chamber*, trans. Chi-Chen Wang, ed. A. Waley: 'the greatest Chinese novel ever written'. See also *New York Review of Books* xxvii (1980), no. 10: 10–16.

35 Pullan, *House*, intro.

36 G. B.-J., *Memorials of E. B.-J.*, i, 196: 1859, 284; 1864.

37 *British Architect and Northern Engineer* ix (1878), 6; *Art Jnl.* 1886, 172.

38 Lethaby, *Architecture, Mysticism and Myth* (1974 ed.), 254–6; *Philip Webb and his work* (1935), 72–3.

39 Mrs. A. M. W. Sterling, ed., *The W. B. Richmond Papers* (1926), 304–5.

40 Designed by Burges, probably for his own use, the ring is now in the V. & A.; the gold cross, set with ruby, sapphire and emerald, and inscribed 'Per Crucem ad Lucem', is now in the B.M. (Sotheby's 28 Sept. 1978, lot 378).

41 'This treasury of reference ... a biographer's dream' (C. H.-R. to Mrs. B. Mallock, 1963).

42 Abstract, 1881.

43 R.I.B.A. 'Stonework', 17. The floral knot motif may derive from a slab at Elstow, Beds. (E. L. Cutts, *Sepulchral Slabs and Crosses*, 1849, pl. xlix). The funeral on 26 April, was attended by J. L. Pearson, Street, Waterhouse, Seddon, Somers Clarke, Aitchison, Horace Jones, Stacy Marks, Marcus Stone, R. P. Pullan, J. Chapple and J. H. Christian (Bodleian MS., DON, e81, f.115; B. xl, 1881, 532). Burges's death certificate (Somerset House) specifies 'spinal myelitis'.

44 R.I.B.A., S.N.B., lxiii (1881), 81.

William Burges: List of Publications

(printed books, essays, articles, letters, reviews, drawings, designs
and reports published by William Burges)

(a list of abbreviations used in this appendix appears
at the beginning of Notes and References, page 342).

1850

'Practical Illustrations of Damascening', *Jnl. of Design*, iii (1850), 161–5. Reprinted in M. D.
Wyatt, *Metalwork* (1852), l–li.

1851

[contrib.], M. D. Wyatt, *The Industrial Arts of the Nineteenth Century*, 2 vols. (1851–3), 14
articles (Attrib.): Furniture, I, lxxv; II, xc, cxxv, cxliii, cl. Glass, II, lxxxvi, cxix. Enamel, I,
li; II, cvii, cxlv. Damascening, II, cli. Metalwork, I, xli; II, cxiii, cliii.

1852

[contrib.], M. D. Wyatt, *Metalwork and its Artistic Design* (1852), plates vi, x, xiv, xxxiv,
xxxviii, xlvii, xlviii, xlix, l. Reprinted as *Specimens of Ornamental Art Workmanship in Gold,
Silver, Iron, Brass and Bronze* (1852).

1853

[contrib.], H. Clutton, *Domestic Architecture of France from the Accession of Charles VI to the
Demise of Louis XII* (1853), plates v, ix, xiii, xiv, xv, xvi, 8, 78(1).

1855

'Incised Slabs and Pavements', *B.* xiii (1855), 304–7; *E.* xvi, n.s. xiii (1855), 199–203 (ills.)
[Architectural Museum]. Reprinted in H. Shaw, *Specimens of Tile Pavements* (1858).

1856

'Notice of an Ancient Mitre Preserved in the Museum at Beauvais', *Archaeol. Jnl.* xiii (1856), 94,
139–44 (ills.) [R.A.I.].

'Ornamental Leadwork', *B.* xiv (1856), 409–10, 418–20; *E.* xvii, n.s. xiv (1856), 384–7 (ills.).

[contrib.], V. Didron, 'Remporte le premier prix au concours de Notre-Dame de la Treille à
Lille', *A.A.* xvi (1856), 204–30 (ills.).

[discussion], 'Christian Sculpture', *E.* xvii, n.s. xiv (1856), 221.

[report], 'Cressingham Manor House'. [P.L.U.]

1857

'Iconography of Cologne Cathedral', *E.* xviii, n.s. xiv (1857), 18–22, 91–3 (ills.).

'Paganism in the Middle Ages', *E.* xviii, n.s. xiv (1857), 205–14 (ills.) [Ecclesiological Soc.].

'Memoir' accompanying competition design for Crimea Memorial Church, *B.N.* iii (1857), 335.

'Notices of the Precious Objects Presented by Queen Theodalinda to the Church of St. John the Baptist, at Monza', *Archaeol. Jnl.* xiv (1857), 8–24 (ills.) [R.A.I.].

'Note sur des Etoffes anciennes fabriquées en Sicile', *Mémoires de la Société Academique du Dep. de l'Oise*, iii (Beauvais, 1857), 266; *Revue de l'Art Chrétienne* ii (1858), 36–7.

[with V. Didron], 'Iconographie des Chapiteaux du Palais Ducal, à Venise', *A.A.* xvii (1857), 69–88, 193–216; xviii (1858), 81–90 [reprinted, Paris, 1857].

[discussion] 'Polychromatic Decoration', *B.* xv (1857), 730; *R.I.B.A. Papers* (1857–8), 55–6. [R.I.B.A.]

1858

[contrib. drawing, 1848], W. Papworth (ed.), *Dictionary of Architecture* (A.P.S.D.): s.v. 'Capital', Les Andelys. s.v. 'Ceiling', West's Chapel, Ely Cathedral [drawing, 1848]. s.v. 'Clerestory', St. Peter, Norwich. s.v. 'Corbel', St. Lawrence, Nuremberg; Town Hall, Damme. s.v. 'Font, Font Cover', Louvain; Leau. s.v. 'Lectern', Tirlement; Leau; Norwich. s.v. 'Metalwork', Evreaux; Beauvais.

'Architectural Experiences of Constantinople', *B* xvi (1858), 88–90, 104–8; *B.N.* iv (1858), 163–7 (ills.); *R.I.B.A. Trans.* 1881–2, 17–21. [Architectural Exhibition].

'Altar Plate', *E.* xix, n.s. xvi (1858), 221–32, 285–90 (ills.) [Ecclesiological Society].

'What we learn from the Chertsey Tiles', *B.* xvi (1858), 502–5 (ills.).

[with V. Didron and G. Aitchison], 'La Ragione de Padoue', *A.A.* xviii (1858), 331–43; xix (1859), 241–52 (ills.) [reprinted, Paris, 1860].

[discussion] 'Mosaic', *E.* xix, n.s. xvi (1858), 184 [Ecclesiological Soc.].

[discussion] 'St. Paul's Cathedral', *E.* xix, n.s. xvi (1858), 262 [Ecclesiological Soc.].

[discussion] 'Metalwork', *E.* xix, n.s. xvi (1858), 267 [Ecclesiological Soc.].

[discussion] 'An Architect's Sketchbook of the Thirteenth Century', *B.* xvi (1858), 758, 770–72, 775, 794–5.

'The Conventional Ornament of the Thirteenth Century', *B.N.* iv (1858), 1292, 1299; *B.* xvii (1859), 8–10 [Architectural Museum].

1859

[review], *Facsimile of the Sketchbook of Wilars d'Honnecourt*, ed. Darcel, Lassus, Quicherat and R. Willis, *B.N.* v (1859), 897–8.

[discussion], 'Wilars d'Honnecourt', *C.E.A. Jnl.* xxii (1859), 16.

[plans], 'Sketchbook, Wilars d'Honnecourt', *E.* xx, n.s. xvii (1859), 37.

'Iconography of Salisbury Cathedral Chapter House', *E.* xx, n.s. xvii (1859), 109–14, 147–62 [reprinted, 1859].

[drawings with F. Warren, 1853], 'The Upper Triforium of the Apse of Beauvais Cathedral', *B.N.* v (1859), 650, 653.

'Mural Paintings, Charlwood Church, Surrey, and St. Brelade, Jersey', *Archaeol. Jnl.* xvi (1859), 89 [R.A.I.].

1860

[letter] 'Brisbane Cathedral', *B.* xviii (1860), 271.

'Turkish Art and Architecture', in W. G. Thornbury, *Turkish Life and Character*, ii (1860), 263–93.

'The Legend of Waltham Abbey and the History of the Church', *E.* xxi, n.s. xviii (1860), 226–33 (ills.) [reprinted, 1860].

Waltham Abbey Church: a report on [its] present condition . . . together with a Sketch of its History and Present State (Oxford, 1860).

[discussion], 'Illuminated Manuscripts', *B.* xviii (1860), 395; *R.I.B.A. Papers* (1859–60), 171–2 [R.I.B.A.].

'Architectural Drawing', *R.I.B.A. Papers* (1860–61), 15–23; *C.E.A. Jnl.* xxiii (1860), 374–7 and xxiv (1861), 18–20; *B.* xviii (1860), 747–51; *B.N.* vi (1860), 897–9 [R.I.B.A.].

[discussion] 'Pre-Raphaelitism and the Gothic Revival', *E.* xxi, n.s. xviii (1860), 249 [Ecclesiological Soc.].

[discussion] 'Use of Pine in the Middle Ages', *E.* xxi, n.s. xviii (1860), 310–11; *B.* xviii (1860), 548 [Ecclesiological Soc.].

'French Portals', *The Universal Decorator*, ed. F. B. Thompson and J. W. Ross (1860), 148; *B.N.* vi (1860), 190–91 [Architectural Photographic Exhibition].

[discussion], 'Colour in Architecture', *B.* xviii (1860), 359 [Cambridge].

1861

'The Exhibition at Florence in an Art Point of View', *B.* xix (1861), 710–11.

'Florence', *E.* xxii, n.s. xix (1861), 93–8, 155–61.

[letter], 'King's College, Chapel, Cambridge', *B.* xix (1861), 255.

[discussion], 'French Restoration', *E.* xxii, n.s. xix (1861), 112 [Ecclesiological Soc.].

'On the Photographs in the Architectural Photographic Exhibition', *B.* xix (1861), 190–92, 237, 255; *B.N.* vii (1861), 251–3.

'Ancient and Modern Stained Glass', *B.* xix (1861), 529, 558.

[review], A. J. B. Beresford-Hope, *The English Cathedral of the Nineteenth Century*, *B.* xix (1861), 402–4.

[discussion], Pagan-Christian art; restoration, *B.* xix (1861), 163; *R.I.B.A. Papers* (1860–61), 212–14 [R.I.B.A.].

[discussion] Waltham Abbey, *B.* xix (1861), 335 [Architectural Exhibition Soc.].

[discussion] Ventilation; Vitruvius, *B.* xix (1861), 407–8; *R.I.B.A. Papers* (1860–61), 277 [R.I.B.A.].

'Ancient Tissues from Bayonne and Sicily', *Archaeol. Jnl.* xviii (1861), 174–5 (ills.). [R.A.I.].

[discussion], Figure-drawing in examination, *R.I.B.A. Papers* (1860–61), appendix, 6 [R.I.B.A.].

1862

'The Late Exhibition of Renaissance and Medieval Antiquities at Florence', *G.M.* ccxii (1862), 3–14.

'Short Memoir on Tomb of Bailly of Amerigo de Narbonne', *G.M.* ccxii (1862), 451–2; *Archaeol. Jnl.* xix (1862), 90–91 [R.A.I.].

'The Maison Dieu at Dover', *G.M.* ccxii (1862), 556–8.

'Supplemental Notes on Florence', *E.* xxiii, n.s. xx (1862), 26–32.

'The International Exhibition', *G.M.* ccxii (1862), 663–76; ccxii (1862), 3–12.

'The Loan Exhibition at South Kensington', *G.M.* ccxii (1862), 32–41.

'The Japanese Court', *G.M.* ccxiii (1862), 243–54.

'The Polychromy of Swedish Churches', *G.M.* ccxiii (1862), 515–25.

[summary]'Pagan Art', *B.* xx (1862), 368 [Architectural Exhibition Soc.].

[discussion] 'The 1862 Exhibition', *E.* xxiii, n.s. xx (1862), 236–7 [Ecclesiological Soc.].

[discussion] 'The 1862 Exhibition', *G.M.* ccxiii (1862), 186 [Ecclesiological Soc.].

'The Late Exhibition', *E.* xx (1862), 336–9.

'What was done by the Greeks and what is done by the present classic (?) school', *B.* xx (1862), 426–7.

[discussion] 'Colour', *B.* xx (1862), 428–9; *R.I.B.A. Papers* (1861–2), 190 [R.I.B.A.].

'Notes on the coloured marble statues in the Museo Bourbonico at Naples', *B.* xx (1862), 459.

'A Few Facts for the workman who visits the Loan Museum at South Kensington', *B.* xx (1862), 491–2, 506–7.

'The Various Systems of Coloured Decoration in the Middle Ages', *B.N.* viii (1862), 330–32.

1863

'Notes on Some Recent French Archaeological Publications', *G.M.* ccxiv (1863), 3–12.

[letters], Cork Cathedral, *Dublin Builder* v (1863), 28–9.

[discussion], Norman vaults and ceilings, *R.I.B.A. Papers* (1862–3), 123–4 [R.I.B.A.].

'Notes on Medieval Mosaic', *G.M.* ccxiv (1863), 267–82.

'Antique Jewelry and its Revival', *G.M.* ccxiv (1863), 403–11 (ills.).

[Anon. review] 'Comte de Vogué on the Holy Places at Jerusalem', *G.M.* ccxiv (1863), 553–63.

[review] N. M. Mandelgren, *Monuments Scandinaves du Moyen Age avec les Peintures et autres Ornements qui les décorent* (Paris, 1862), *E.* xxiv, n.s. xxi (1863), 87–90.

'Notice of Some French Periodical Works Published During the Present Year', *G.M.* ccxv (1863), 671–80.

'Church of the Holy Sepulchre, Jerusalem', *B.* xxi (1863), 328–9, 384–6 (ills.)

[contrib.] G. G. Scott, *Gleanings from Westminster Abbey* (2nd ed. 1863) 'Tomb of Henry VII', 80–84. 'Metal Work', 85–95. 'Mosaic Pavements', 97–103. 'Retabulum', 105–13. 'Sedilia', 115–20. 'Coronation Chair', 121–6. 'Shrine of Edward the Confessor', 127–41. 'Tombs', 142–89. 'Brasses', 189–93.

[report] 'Coronation Chair, Westminster', *G.M.* n.s. xiv (1863), 322 [Soc. of Antiquaries].

'Mural Paintings at Chalgrove Church, Oxon.', *Archaeologia*, xxxviii (1863), 432 [ills. by J. H. Parker and C. A. Buckler].

1864

'Mural paintings discovered in Charlwood Church, Surrey, with some remarks on the more ordinary polychromy of the thirteenth century', *Archaeol. Jnl.* xxi (1864), 209–15 (ills.) [Soc. of Antiquaries].

[discussion], E. J. Tarver, 'Figure Drawing Applied to Architecture', *B.N.* xi (1864), 303.

'The Modern Development of Medieval Art', *B.* xxii (1864), 448–50; *B.N.* xi (1864), 459–62, 467; *C.E.A. Jnl.* xxvii (1864), 195–8 (ills.). [Architectural Association] Reprinted in *Art Applied to Industry* (1865).

'The Fine Arts in Connection with the Church', *B.* xxii (1864), 788–9; *B.N.* xi (1864), 785, 802–3; *G.M.* n.s. xviii (1865), 64; *C.E.A. Jnl.* xxvii (1864), 321–2 [Church Congress, Bristol].

'The Loan Museum at Malines', *B.N.* xi (1864), 719–20.

'History of Our Lord by Lady Eastlake', *G.M.* ccvii (1864), 169–80; *B.N.* xi (1864), 591–2.

[discussion] 'Restoration: St. Patrick's, Dublin', *E.* xxv, n.s. xxii (1864), 220–21 [Ecclesiological Soc.].

[discussion] 'Restoration: Westminster Abbey', *E.* xxv, n.s. xxii (1864), 221 [Ecclesiological Soc.].

[discussion] 'Lyndhurst Church, Reredos', *E.* xxv, n.s. xxii (1864), 221–2 [Ecclesiological Soc.].

[discussion] 'Church Plate', *E.* xxv, n.s. xxii (1864), 222 [Ecclesiological Soc.].

[discussion] 'Town Churches', *E.* xxv, n.s. xxii (1864), 226 [Ecclesiological Soc.].

[discussion] 'Worcester College, Oxon., Chapel Glass', *E.* xxv, n.s. xxii (1864), 222 [Ecclesiological Soc.].

[report], 'Stained Glass', *E.* xxv, n.s. xxii (1864), 377 [Cambridge Architectural Soc.].

[letter] 'Cork Cathedral', *B.* xxii (1864), 956.

[discussion] Architectural Education, *R.I.B.A. Papers* (1864–5), 24 [R.I.B.A.].

[discussion] Theatres, *R.I.B.A. Papers* (1864–5), 49 [R.I.B.A.].

[discussion] Modern Gothic, *B.N.* xi (1864), 826 [Architectural Assocn.]

1865

'Worcester College Chapel Pavement', *E.* xxvi, n.s. xxiii (1865), 336–7 (ills.).

[letter] 'Competitions', *B.N.* xii (1865), 417–18, 436, 472.

[discussion] Timber Roofs, *R.I.B.A. Papers* (1864–5), 107 [R.I.B.A.].

'Measured Drawings *versus* Sketches', *B.N.* xii (1865), 557–8, 605–6, 638.

[drawings] 'Door at Châlons-sur-Marne; Girouette formerly at Tournai', *B.N.* xii (1865), 478, 482–3 (ills.). Reprinted in *Architectural Drawings* (1870).

'Art Applied to Industry, a series of lectures', *B.N.* xi (1864), 118–19, 134, 154, 168, 182, 203, 224 [Cantor Lectures, Royal Soc. of Arts]. Reprinted as *Art Applied to Industry* (Oxford and London, 1865).

[review] 'The Reproduction of the MS. Bib. Reg. 2 B. VII, by Messrs. Westlake and Purdue', *G.M.* n.s. xix (1865), 145–54.

'Verroterie Cloisonnée', *G.M.* ccxix (1865), 686–96.

[review] C. Texier and R. P. Pullan, *Byzantine Architecture* (1864), *B.N.* xii (1865), 114–16.

[discussion], Roof, Guildhall, London, *R.I.B.A. Papers* (1864–5), 184–5 [R.I.B.A.].

[letter] 'St. Fin Bar's Cathedral', *Dublin Builder*, vii (1865), 9.

[discussion], Art-Workmen, *R.I.B.A. Papers* (1865–6), 44 [R.I.B.A.].

1866

'Winston's Stray Papers on Stained Glass', *B.N.* xiii (1866), 17–19.

[discussion], Masonry jointing, *R.I.B.A. Papers* (1865–6), 97 [R.I.B.A.].

[letter] 'Glasgow Cathedral Windows', *B.N.* xiii (1866), 108–9.

[discussion], Carcassonne, *R.I.B.A. Papers* (1865–6), 147–8 [R.I.B.A.].

[letter] 'Figure Class of the Architectural Association', *B.N.* xiii (1866), 175.

[report] 'Darenth Church, Kent', *G.M.* ccxv (1863), 587 [R.A.I.].

1867

'Why we have so little Art in our Churches', *E.* xxviii, n.s. xxv (1867), 150–56; *B.N.* xiv (1867), 421–2 [Waynflete Soc.].

[discussion], Murals at Wallington, Northumberland, *R.I.B.A. Papers* (1867–8), 44 [R.I.B.A.].

[anon. letter] 'Medieval Fountains', *B.N.* xiv (1867), 83.

[letter] 'Mr. Burges and the *Ecclesiologist*', *B.N.* xiv (1867), 449.

'Our Future Architecture', *B* xxv (1867), 385–7, 394; *B.N.* xiv (1867), 373–4; *C.E.A.Jnl. xxx* (1867), 174–5, 175–7 [Architectural Assocn.].

Law Courts Commission: Report to the Courts of Justice Commission (1867).

[review] *Architectural Association Sketch Book*, *B.N.* xiv (1867), 752–3.

'The Art Student: Art Education', *B.N.* xiv (1867), 869.

1868

'The Late M. Didron', *B.N.* xv (1868), 31–2.

'Prizes for Art Workmen at the Society of Arts', *B.N.* xv (1868), 44, 83–4.

'Dean Stanley's *Memorials of Westminster Abbey*', *B.N.* xv (1868), 122–3, 139–40.

'Monsieur Lameire's Drawings at the Architectural Exhibition', *B.N.* xv (1868), 372–4, 391.

[contrib.] 'Art and Religion', in *The Church and the World*, ed. O. Shipley, iii (1868), 574–98.

'Proposed School of Art at Bombay', *R.I.B.A. Papers* (1867–8), 77–85.

1869

'The New Cathedral of St. Finbar at Cork', *A.* i (1969), 36–7.

'The Evangelistic Beasts' [Cork], *A.* i (1869), 179.

[discussion], Churches at Constantinople, *R.I.B.A. Papers* (1868–9), 221 [R.I.B.A.].

'South Kensington and M. Lameire's Drawings', *A.* i. (1869), 270–71.

[discussion], Ancient plan of Rome, *R.I.B.A. Papers* (1869–70), 18–19 [R.I.B.A.].

[letter] 'Bradford Town Hall', *A.* ii (1869), 279.

'La Ragione de Padoue: description des peintures de la grande salle', *A.A.* xxvi (1869), 188–203, 250–71.

1870

[review] *The Sacristy*, ed. Gould, *B.N.* xx (1871), 267–8.

[discussion], Arabic decoration, *R.I.B.A. Papers* (1869–70), 88 [R.I.B.A.].

[drawing] 'Window, Hôtel de Ville, Rouen', *B.N.* xix (1870), 312, 314. Reprinted in *Architectural Drawings* (1870).

[discussion], Cologne Cathedral, *R.I.B.A. Papers* (1869–70), 150 [R.I.B.A.].

Architectural Drawings (1870). Costume Plates reprinted in H. W. Lonsdale and E. J. Tarver, *Illustrations of Medieval Costume* (1874).

[letter] 'The Bexley Heath Competition', *A.* iii (1870), 34.

'Sculpture of the Western Gable of Cork Cathedral', *A.* iii (1870), 147–8.

[review] 'Dean Stanley's Westminster Abbey', *A.* iii (1870), 301–2.

'Dossal in All Saints Church, Edinburgh', *A.*iv (1870), 63 (ills.).

'The Decorations of St. Paul's', *A.* iv (1870), 128.

1871

'On a Monument in the Cloister of St. Maria Anunciata, at Florence', *Archaeol. Jnl.* xxxviii

(1871), 49–59 (ills.) [R.A.I.].

[after-dinner speech] 'Art', *A.* v (1871), 285.

[letter] 'The Holy Cross of Dunfermline', *A.* vi (1871), 122.

'The New Tower at Cardiff Castle', *A.* v (1871), 276 (ills.).

'On the Old Examples of Figure Carving', *B.* xxix (1871), 231 [Architectural Assocn. at Architectural Museum].

1872

[letter] 'Completion of St. Paul's', *A.* vii (1872), 256; *B.* xxx (1872), 379; *The Times*, 15 May 1872, 8a.

[letter] 'Completion of St. Paul's', *A.* vii (1872), 277; *The Times*, 27 May 1872, 7d.

'The Lady Chapel at Waltham Abbey', *A.* viii (1872), 90–91 (ills.).

1873

[letter] 'The Battle of the Styles', *A.* ix (1873), 13.

[letter] 'Edinburgh Cathedral Competition', *A.* ix (1873), 28.

[letter] 'A Trade Secret', *B.N.* xxiv (1873), 261.

[discussion], Viollet-le-Duc, *R.I.B.A. Papers* (1873–4), 63 [R.I.B.A.].

[speech and letter] 'Archaeology and Architecture; Viollet-le-Duc', *A.* x (1873), 323, 341; *B.* xxxi (1873), 1001.

1874

[with W. Longman] *A Description of Models for the Adornment of St. Paul's, now exhibiting at the Royal Academy* (1874).

'St. Simeon Stylites', *B.N.* xxvi (1874), 148.

Report on the Condition of the Eastern Part of King's College Chapel (1874).

Castell Coch, *A.* xi (1874), 213–4, 225-16.

[letter] 'Sir James Thornhill's Sketches', *A.* xi (1874), 187.

[letter] 'St. Paul's Cathedral', *A.* xi (1874), 309; *The Times*, 28 Nov. 1874, 10d.

1875

'On Things in General: (i) The Present State of our Art. (ii) The Institute. (iii) Prospects of Future Progress in Architectural Education', *B.* xxxiii (1875), 1145–6; *B.A.* iv (1875), 362–4; *B.N.* xxix (1875), 684, 762–4; *A.* xiv (1875), 367–70 [Architectural Association].

'Designs for a New Altar-Screen and Sedilia for King's College Chapel, Cambridge', *A.* xiii (1875), 304–5 (ills.).

1876

[letter] ' "Shop Expenses" among Organ Builders', *A.* xv (1876), 37.

[with J. A. Reeve] 'Notes on the Dates of Waltham Abbey', *A.* xv (1876), 46.

'The Importance of Greek Art and Literature to the Practice of Gothic Architecture', *A.* xv (1876), supp. 16–17, 18–20, 396–7; *B.A.* v (1876), 332–3; *B.* xxxiv (1876), 619–20; *R.I.B.A. Trans.* (1881–2) 25–7. [Conference of Architects, R.I.B.A.].

[discussion], 'Ely Cathedral', *B.* xxxi (1876), 31–2; *R.I.B.A. Papers* (1875–6), 79–83. [R.I.B.A.].

[letter]'*Henry V* at the Queen's Theatre', *A.* xvi (1876), 188.

[discussion], The Erechtheum, *R.I.B.A. Papers* (1875–6), 156–8 [R.I.B.A.].

'Archaeology on the Stage', *A.* xvi (1876), 221, 224–5, 238–40.

1878

[letter] 'Professional Practice and Etiquette', *B.N.* xxxv (1878), 627.

'The Institute Conference for 1878 and Tradesmen's Rights', *B.A.* ix (1878), 259–60; *A.* xix (1878), 329 and xx (1878), 330.

1879

'The Tomb and Helm of Thomas la Warre in the Church at Broadwater, Sussex', *Archaeol.Jnl.* xxxvi (1879), 78–87, 103 (ills.). [R.A.I.].

'Books on Medieval Costume', *B.N.* xxxvii (1879), 143–5.

[Georgius Oldhousen, pseud.], 'The Ethics of Advertising', *B.N.* xxxvii (1879), 478.

'Il Caporale at Orvieto', *Archaeol. Jnl.* xxxvi (1879), 353–7 [R.A.I.].

'Embroidered Mitre', *A.* xxi (1879), 327 (ills.).

1880

'Salade Belonging to the Baron de Cosson', *Archaeol. Jnl.* xxxvii (1880), 179–83 (ills.) [R.A.I.].

[with Baron de Cosson], 'Catalogue of the Exhibition of Ancient Helmets and Examples of Mail', *Archaeol. Jnl.* xxxvii (1880), 445–594 (ills.). Reprinted posthumously, 1881.

[letters] 'Architectural Charges', *B.N.* xxxviii (1880), 530.

[letters] 'The Funds of the R.I.B.A.', *B.N.* xxxix (1880), 78–9.

[letter] 'A Wonderful Stove', *B.N.* xxxix (1880), 546.

'On two pillars from the high altar in Henry VII's chapel at Westminster', *Proceedings Soc. Antiquaries*, 2nd ser. viii (1880), 262–4.

1881

[letter] 'The New President of the R.I.B.A.', *B.N.* xl (1881), 374.

[posthumous] 'Chapel, King's College, London', *B.* xl (1881), 581.

1882

[posthumous] 'Mr. Burges's Advice to a Young Architect', *American Architect and Building News*, xii (1882), 88.

1883

[posthumous] *The Architectural Designs of William Burges*, ed. R. Popplewell Pullan (1883).

1885

[posthumous] *The Designs of William Burges*, ed. R. Popplewell Pullan (1885).

[posthumous] *The House of William Burges*, ed. R. Popplewell Pullan (1885).

1887

[posthumous] *The Architectural Designs of William Burges: details of Stonework*, ed. R. Popplewell Pullan (1887).

William Burges: List of Works

William Burges: List of Works

ABBREVIATIONS

W.B.: William Burges
C.H.: Cecil Higgins Art Gallery, Bedford
Dem.: demolished
I.S.: in situ
P.C.: private collection
P.L.U.: present location unknown
S.A.: since altered
U.X.: unexecuted
V. & A.: Victoria & Albert Museum

DATE	LOCATION AND COMMISSION	PATRON	PRESENT STATE	PAGE
1844	St Batholomew's Hospital: title page, estate survey.	–	P.L.U.	40 n. 37
1845	[with E. Blore] Moreton Hall, Cheshire: fittings.	G. H. Ackers	S.A.	40 n. 39
	— New Lodge, Cumberland Gate, Windsor Great Park.	Crown	I.S.	40 n. 38
	— Flying Barn Cottage, Windsor Great Park.	Crown	I.S.	40 n. 38
1846	— Thicket Priory, Yorks.: fittings.	Rev. J. Dunnington-Jefferson	S.A.	40 n. 40
	— Westminster Abbey: restoration.	–	S.A.	40
	— Glasgow Cathedral: details.	–	–	40 n. 41
	— Lambeth Palace Chapel: alterations.	Abp. Canterbury	S.A.	40 n. 43
1848	— Buckingham Palace: decoration.	Crown	S.A.	40 n. 42
1851	[with M. D. Wyatt] 'Competition for an Institute in the North'.	–	–	41 n. 58
	— Chichester Cathedral: Huskisson memorial.	–	I.S.	41 n. 57
1851–2	(?) Bedford School of Art, Store St.: Almanack.	–	P.L.U.	60 n. 13

DATE	LOCATION AND COMMISSION	PATRON	PRESENT STATE	PAGE
	Temporary church, Brighton.	Rev. Arthur Wagner	Dem.	210–1
	8, Whitehall, London: alterations.	Lord Carrington	Dem.	142
(?) 1863	15, Buckingham St./Tower House: rose-bowl.	W.B.	P.L.U.	316
(?) 1863	— water-jug.	W.B.	P.L.U.	316
(?) 1863	— mounted crystal bottles.	W.B.	P.L.U.	316
(?) 1863	— moss agate bottle.	W.B.	P.L.U.	316
(?) 1863	— silver beakers.	W.B.	P.L.U.	316
1863–4	St Michael and All Angels, Brighton: chalice.	Rev. Charles Beanlands	I.S.	213
	St James, Winscombe, Som.: restoration.	Rev. J. A. Yatman	I.S.	224–5
	Forthampton, Glos.: almshouses.	Joseph and Reginald Yorke	I.S.	225
1863–6	Bradford Exchange, Yorks.: competition design.	–	U.X.	251 n. 95
	[with J. H. Parker] Vicars' Close, Wells, Som.: restoration, Vicars' Hall.	J. H. Parker	I.S.	294 n. 3
1863–1904	St Finbar's Cathedral, Cork, Ireland.	Bp. John Gregg	I.S.	195–208
1864	Aspley Guise, Beds.: rectory.	Rev. H. M. Erskine	S.A.	225 n. 97
	Wycombe Abbey, Bucks.: alterations.	Lord Carrington	S.A.	142
	Worcester College, Oxford: coin cup.	W.B.	I.S.	147
1864–5	Naples, Italy: town-planning scheme.	–	U.X.	47 n. 12
1864–6	St Anne's Court, Soho, London.	L. M. Rate	Dem.	240
1864–9	Worcester College, Oxford: chapel.	–	I.S.	146–52
1865	Pendant badges.	Gambier Parry	P.L.U.	317 n. 38
	St Peter, Carrigrohane, Co. Cork: extensions.	Rev. Robert Gregg	I.S.	208
	Worcester College, Oxford: chapel lectern and candelabra.	Rev. J. D. Collis; Rev. H. C. O. Daniel	I.S.	150–1
	— chapel organ seat.	–	I.S.	150
1865–6	Gayhurst, Bucks.: wardrobe.	Lady Carrington	P.L.U.	300
	Pendant.	Lady Carrington	P.L.U.	146
c.1865 (?)	Oakwood Court, Bingley, Yorks.: decorations.	Thomas Garnett	S.A.	301–2
	Salmon's Cross, Reigate, Surrey: claret jug.	James Nicholson	V. & A.	314
1865–6	15, Buckingham St./Tower House: chest of drawers.	W.B.	P.L.U.	325
	— pair of claret jugs.	W.B.	Fitzwilliam Mus.; C.H.	314

DATE	LOCATION AND COMMISSION	PATRON	PRESENT STATE	PAGE
	Cardiff Castle: soup and fish plates.	Lord Bute	Mount Stuart.	289
1867–74	Knightshayes, Devon.	Sir J. Heathcote-Amory Bt.	S.A.	302–5
	Chevithorne, Devon; Vicarage.	Sir J. Heathcote-Amory Bt.	I.S.	304
1868; 1892–9	St Michael and All Angels, Brighton: extensions.	Rev. Charles Beanlands	I.S.	211–5
1868	(?) Faulkbourne Hall, Essex: decorations.	Rev. F. Spurrell	S.A.	300 n. 84
	The Assumption, Moulsoe, Bucks.: Carrington memorial.	Carrington family	I.S.	143
	St Merteriana, Tintagel: memorial to J. D. Cook.	A. J. Beresford-Hope M.P.	I.S.	228
(?) 1868	15, Buckingham St./Tower House: ring and cross.	W.B.	V. & A.; B.M.	328
1868	St Mary, Freeland, Oxon.: altar plate.	R. A. R. Bennet	I.S.	222
1868–9	St Mary, Batsford, Glos.: memorial to Hon. Frances Mitford.	Lord Redesdale	I.S.	228
1868; 1871–3; 1881	St Faith, Stoke Newington.	Dr. Robert Brett	Dem.	217–9
1868–75	Cardiff Castle, stables.	Lord Bute	I.S.	267–8
1869; 1872; 1875; 1880	Milton Court (Joldwynds), Dorking, Surrey: alterations.	L. M. Rate	S.A.	240 n. 7
1869	Worcester Coll., Oxford, chapel: Testament bindings.	Rev. H. C. O. Daniel	I.S.	150–1
1869; 1877	15, Buckingham St./Tower House: cabinet/aumbries.	W.B.	I.S. and C.H.	318
1869	15, Buckingham St./Tower House: inkstand.	W.B.	P.C.	139 n. 98
	— dog cabinet.	W.B.	P.L.U.	324
	St John Baptist, Outwood, Surrey.	–	S.A.	216
(?) 1869	Bromsgrove School, Worcs.: chapel, report.	Rev. J. D. Collis	–	146 n. 58
1869	Ightham Place, Kent: extensions.	Rev. J. S. Bailey	I.S.	306 n. 20
	Holy Trinity, Minchinhampton, Glos.; restoration.	–	I.S.	232 n. 49
1869–70	Cardiff Castle: claret jug.	Lord Bute	Mount Stuart	289–90
1869–71	15, Buckingham St./Tower House: 'Zodiac' settle.	W.B.	P.C.	318
1860s–70s	— dog collars.	W.B.	P.L.U.	89 n. 56
c.1870	Waltham Abbey: altar and sedilia.	Col. Edenborough; Rev. J. Francis	I.S.	191
1870	Cardiff Castle: reliquary.	Lord Bute	P.L.U.	291 n. 27
	— prayer book.	Lord Bute	P.L.U.	291 n. 28
	15, Buckingham St./Tower House: claret jug.	W.B.	V. & A.	315
	St Peter, Sharnbrook, Beds.: Magniac memorials.	Magniac family	I.S.	153–4

Date	Work	Client		Page
1870–72	Cardiff, Ty Gwynn Rd.: Good Shepherd convent. 'Kiosque'.	Lord Bute	Dem.	284 n. 50
	All Saints Episcopal Church, Edinburgh; reredos	Col. C H. Luard	P.L.U.	275 n. 72
		–	I.S.	185
1870–77	Holy Trinity, Stratford-on-Avon, Warwicks.: report.	Rev. J. D. Collis	–	146 n. 58
	St Paul's Cathedral: scheme for decoration.	–	U.X.	154–69
1870–76	Christ the Consoler, Skelton-on-Ure, Yorks.	Lady Mary Vyner	I.S.	229–32
1870–78	St Mary, Aldford-cum-Studley, Yorks.	Lord Ripon	I.S.	229–37
1871	[with H. W. Lonsdale] St Andrew, Wells St.: vases and candlesticks.	Rev. Benjamin Webb	Kingsbury, Middx.	220
	St Mary, Addington, Surrey: memorial to Abp. Longley.	Longley family	I.S.	143 n. 17
	Strand, London: alterations.	'friends of F. Michel'	Dem.	239 n. 4
1871–2	Studley Royal, Yorks.: cross.	Lord Ripon	P.L.U.	233 n. 59
1871–4	Rothesay Castle: scheme for reconstruction.	Lord Bute	U.X.	280
1871; 1875	Wallpapers.	Jeffery & Co.	P.L.U.	294 n. 3
1871–7	(?) Cardiff Castle: crucifix.	Lord Bute	P.L.U.	291 n. 26
	Harrow School: speech room.	A. J. Beresford-Hope, M.P.	S.A.	245–6
	—laboratories, classrooms, gymnasium.	A. J. Beresford-Hope, M.P.	U.X.	245–6
1871–80	Cardiff, Park House.	James McConnochie	I.S.	305–6
c.1872	Cardiff Castle: furniture.	Lord Bute	I.S.; P.L.U.	264–5
1871; 1879 etc.	15, Buckingham St./Tower House: side table.	W.B.	P.C.	322
	— cutlery.	W.B.	P.C.; C.H.	312
1872	(?) Brompton Oratory, Sth Ken.: chirotheca.	Lord Bute	P.L.U.	256 n. 30
(?) 1872	Cardiff Castle: cameo stand.	Lord Bute	Mount Stuart	256 n. 30
	St James, Westmorland Place, Marylebone.	Rev. H. R. Haweis	U.X.	309 n. 58
	(?) All Saints, Wigan: report.	Hon. Colin Lindsay	–	211 n. 91
1872–3	All Saints, Murston, Kent.		Incomplete.	216
1872–4	King's College, Cambridge: chapel reredos.	–	U.X.	122 n. 67
1872–91	Castell Coch, Glam.: excavation, reconstruction, fittings, decoration.	Lord Bute	I.S.	279–84
1873	15, Buckingham St./Tower House: 'Peacock' cabinet.	W.B.	P.L.U.	314
	Cardiff Castle: brooch for Lady Bute.	W.B.	Mount Stuart.	259 n. 70
	Cuddesdon Coll., Oxon.: altar-plate.	–	I.S.	222

DATE	LOCATION AND COMMISSION	PATRON	PRESENT STATE	PAGE
(?) 1873	St Mary, Elvetham, Hants.: altar-plate.	—	I.S.	222
1873	Edinburgh: St Mary's Cathedral, competition design.		U.X.	180–1
1873–4	Studley Royal, Yorks.: cottages.	Lord Ripon	I.S.	231 n. 45
1873–5	Ripon, Yorks.: Grammar School.	Lord Ripon	U.X.	244 n. 48
1873–5	Mount Stuart, Isle of Bute: oratory.	Lord Bute	I.S.	285
	Cardiff Castle: tiara for Lady Bute.	Lord Bute	P.L.U.	259 n. 70
1873–8	St Thomas, Upper Clapton, London: alterations.		Dem.	216–7
1873–9	Worcester Coll., Oxford: hall alterations.		S.A.	152–3
1873–5	— hall sideboard	Richard Cresswell	Knightshayes, Devon.	153 n. 4
1873–82	Trinity Coll., Hartford, Conn., U.S.A.	Abner Jackson	Incomplete.	243–4
1874	St Paul, Brighton: 'Purchas' chalice (?)		V. & A.	213–4
(?) c.1874	15, Buckingham St./Tower House: watch and stand.	W.B.	P.L.U.	316
1874	Exeter Guildhall: mayoral chain.	Royal Archaeological Institute	I.S.	317 n. 39
1874–5	All Saints, Waldeshare, Kent: report.	—	—	224 n. 90
1874–6	Cardiff Castle: statue of St John the Evangelist.	Lord Bute	I.S.	270
1875	Bayswater, London: house scheme.	W.B.	U.X.	307
	Victoria Rd., London: house scheme.	W.B.	U.X.	307
1875–81	Tower House, Melbury Rd., Kensington.	W.B.	S.A.	306–28
1875	Tower House, Kens.: white jade tazza.	W.B.	P.L.U.	316
	— wardrobe.	W.B.	P.L.U.	324
	Cardiff Castle: cup and cover.	Lord Bute	Mount Stuart	289
	— crystal cup for Lady Bute	Lord Bute	P.L.U.	259 n. 70
	Tower House, Kens.: salt cellar.	W.B.	P.L.U.	316
	Castle Ashby, Northants.: Long Gallery.	Lord Northampton	U.X.	145 n. 48
	St Andrew, Wells St.: crucifix.	W. R. Cusack Smith	Kingsbury, Middx.	220
	Cardiff Castle: rustic bridge.	Lord Bute	Dem.	271
	Mickleton, Glos.: fountain.	family of Sir J. M. S. Graves Bt.	I.S.	192 n. 20
	Tower House, Kens.: mermaid bowl.	W.B.	V. & A.	315
1875–9	Cardiff Castle: bronze fountain.	Lord Bute	I.S.	271
1875–6	Tower House, Kens.: sideboard.	W.B.	P.L.U.	312

DATE	LOCATION AND COMMISSION	PATRON	PRESENT STATE	PAGE
	Truro Cathedral: design.	–	U.X.	181
	Tower House, Kens.: mazer bowls.	W.B.	P.C.; P.L.U.	316
	Mitres for Bp. of Dunkeld.	Lord Bute	P.L.U.	291 n. 23
c.1878	Lahore Cathedral: design.	Ven. W. H. Tribe	U.X.	317 n. 38
1878–9	Cardiff Castle: crucifix and candlesticks.	Lord Bute	P.L.U.	268 n. 64
	Brompton Oratory, Sth. Ken.: candelabra.	Lord Bute	I.S.	256 n. 30
	King's Coll. Chapel, Cambridge: memorial to Rev. G. Williams.	–	I.S.	51 n. 45
c.1878	Tower House, Kens.: 'Philosophy' cabinet.	W.B.	P.C.	323
1878–80	— pair of mirrors.	W.B.	P.L.U.	322
1879	St John, Cumnock, Ayrshire.	Lord Bute	Incomplete.	284
	Chiswick House, Middx.: chapel.	Lord Bute	Dem.	284
	28, Beaufort St., Chelsea: studio.	Louise Jopling	Dem.	98 n. 85
	Tower House, Kens.: mounted shell.	W.B.	P.L.U.	316
	Cardiff Castle: cutlery.	Lord Bute	P.C.	291
	Cork Cathedral: benefactors' book.	Bp. Robert Gregg	I.S.	198 n. 70
	Agate-handled knives.	Ven. W. H. Tribe.	P.L.U.	317 n. 38
	Tower House, Kens.: dressing table.	W.B.	P.L.U.	322
	— 'Golden' bed.	W.B.	V. & A.	322
1879–80	— 'Vita Nuova' washstand.	W.B.	V. & A.	322–3
1880	— pier table.	W.B.	P.C.	322
	Mount Stuart: water bottle for Lord Bute.	Lady Bute	Mount Stuart.	289
	Tower House, Kens.: bronze table.	W.B.	P.C.	310
	Library.	Ven. W. H. Tribe	P.L.U.	317 n. 38
(?) 1880	Tower House, Kens.: garden door.	W.B.	I.S.	310
1880	— bronze frogs.	W.B.	P.L.U.	311
	Dover, Kent: Police Station.	–	S.A.	241 n. 18
	Trinity Coll. Chapel, Cambridge: mem. to Archdeacon T. Thorp.	A. J. Beresford-Hope, M.P.	I.S.	221 n. 65
	Memorial to Rev. W. Scott.	A. J. Beresford-Hope, M.P.	P.L.U.	—
	Dessert service for G. E. Sneyd.	Lord Bute	V. & A.	291 n. 24

1880–81	Tower House, Kens.: bronze 'Fame'.	W.B.	P.L.U.	311
1881	Brompton Cemetery: mem. to Emma Jane Knight Watson.	Watson family	U.X.	221 n.65
	Mount Stuart: pearl shell bottle for Lady Bute.	W.B.	Mount Stuart	259
c.1887–91	Castell Coch: furniture, by J. S. Chapple.	Lord Bute	I.S.	283

Index

(bold figures refer to illustration numbers)